RICHARD GROSS

THEMES, ISSUES AND DEBATES IN PSYCHOLOGY

SECOND EDITION

Hodder & Stoughton
A MEMBER OF THE HODDER HEADLINE GROUP

Orders: please contact Bookpoint Ltd, 130 Milton Park, Abingdon, Oxon OX14 4SB. Telephone: (44) 01235 827720. Fax: (44) 01235 400454. Lines are open from 9.00–6.00, Monday to Saturday, with a 24 hour message answering service. You can also order through our website www.hodderheadline.co.uk.

British Library Cataloguing in Publication Data
A catalogue record for this title is available from the British Library

ISBN 0 340 857846

First Published 2003
Impression number 10 9 8 7 6 5 4 3 2 1
Year 2007 2006 2005 2004 2003
Copyright © 2003 Richard Gross

Typeset by Phoenix Photosetting, Chatham, Kent
Printed in Great Britain for Hodder & Stoughton Educational, a division of Hodder Headline Plc, 338 Euston Road, London NW1 3BH by Martins The Printers, Berwick upon Tweed

DEDICATION

To my mother, who died before I could add to her collection of my books of which she was so proud. In loving memory.

CONTENTS

Picture credits   X

Introduction   xi

Acknowledgements   xii

1 The person as psychologist   1
Introduction   1
The lay person as psychologist: people as scientists   2
Common-sense psychology: looking for hidden causes of behaviour   2
Man-the-scientist: Kelly's psychology of personal constructs   10
Homo psychologicus: human beings as natural psychologists   12
Conclusion   14
Summary   14

2 Attribution   17
Attribution and everyday psychology   17
Causes and perceived causes   17
Attribution theory and theories of attribution   18
Attribution and emotion   23
Attribution and attitude change   26
The self-serving bias (SSB) and depression   28
Attributional style, achievement motivation and gender   29
Attributional style and marital relationships   30
The self-serving bias as a cultural phenomenon   33
Attributional bias, prejudice and discrimination   34
Attribution and impression management   36
Attribution and helping behaviour   37
Summary   39

3 The idiographic and nomothetic approaches to the study of behaviour   43
Psychology: the study of individuals or the study of people?   43
Historical background   45
Reconciling the nomothetic/idiographic approaches   54
Idiographic methods, old and new   55
Conclusions: a different way of looking at the research process   56
Summary   58

4 Traits and situations as causes of behaviour — 61

Common-sense views of personality — 61

Consistency of behaviour and psychological abnormality — 62

Personality and social psychology — 62

Some key issues in the study of personality — 64

The meanings of 'interactionism' — 65

Conclusions — 71

Summary — 72

5 Heredity and environment — 75

Framing the questions — 75

Nativism, empiricism and interactionism — 76

The nature of 'nature' — 77

Heredity: chromosomes, genes and DNA — 78

The nature of nurture: what is the environment? — 80

Behaviour genetics: going beyond the nature–nurture debate — 86

Drawing some conclusions and raising some important issues — 90

Summary — 93

6 Psychology, women and feminism — 95

What is feminist psychology? — 95

Sexism within the psychology profession — 96

Heterosexism in the psychology profession — 99

The feminist critique of science — 99

The masculinist bias — 101

What's different about feminist research? — 108

So how *is* gender constructed? — 111

So are women and men different – and, if so, how? — 113

Concluding comments: what's better about feminist psychology? — 113

Summary — 114

7 Normality and abnormality — 117

Abnormality, deviance and difference — 117

Criteria for defining psychological abnormality — 119

An interim summing up: what have we learnt so far? — 123

The case of homosexuality: normal or abnormal? — 123

The objective nature of mental disorders: do they exist? — 129

The cross-cultural study of mental disorder 131
The culture-bound nature of psychiatry 135
Summary 137

8 Cross-cultural psychology 141
Culture as part of the nature–nurture debate 141
What is cross-cultural psychology? 142
What is this thing called culture? 146
Doing cross-cultural research: conceptual and methodological issues 153
Some concluding comments 160
Summary 162

9 Attachment and separation through the life cycle 165
What is attachment? 166
Attachments, affectional bonds and other relationships 167
Similarities between adult and childhood attachments 170
Romantic love conceptualized as an attachment process 171
Adult attachment research since 1987 175
Attachment, exploration and work 176
Religious behaviour: God as a secure base and safe haven 177
Attachment among older adults 179
Attachment, separation and loss 180
Summary 182

10 Psychology and ethics 185
Ethical questions: do psychologists need to ask them? 185
Psychologists as investigators and as practitioners 186
Research with human participants 188
The use of animals in psychological research 200
Psychologists as agents of change 203
Summary 208

11 Psychology as science 211
Science as a recurrent theme 211
A brief sketch of the history of science 212
Some (other) influences on the development of psychology 217
The development of psychology as a science: the early days 219

What should the subject matter of psychology be? 225
The social nature of scientific research 227
The uniqueness of psychology 232
A shift towards studying people as people 234
The changing face of science 236
Summary 238

12 Free will and determinism 241

Why are psychologists interested? 241
What do we mean by free will? 246
The views of William James: soft determinism 251
The views of Sigmund Freud: psychic determinism 253
The views of B.F. Skinner: free will as an illusion 256
The views of Carl Rogers: freedom and the fully functioning person 258
The views of Erich Fromm: the fear of freedom 259
The views of George Kelly: freedom and personal constructs 260
Sociobiology: extreme biological determinism 261
Drawing some conclusions: freedom as an evolutionary reality 263
Summary 264

13 Consciousness and the mind—brain relationship 267

Consciousness and the subject matter of psychology 267
Knowing where to start: does consciousness exist? 268
The nature of consciousness 273
Can a machine be conscious? Does having a brain matter? 280
Consciousness and the importance of having a body 282
What is consciousness *for*? Taking an evolutionary approach 283
The relationship between mind and brain 286
Summary 292

14 Parapsychology 295

Paranormal, unusual and anomalistic experiences 295
Belief in the paranormal 296
Experimental investigation of paranormal phenomena 299
Philosophical and methodological issues 302
The placebo effect: a case study in parapsychological research 306
Summary 310

15 Theoretical approaches to psychology   313

The behaviourist approach   313
The psychodynamic approach   319
The cognitive approach   327
The social constructionist approach   330
The evolutionary psychological approach   336
Conclusions   340
Summary   341

References   345

Index   373

PICTURE CREDITS

The author and publishers would like to thank the following for permission to reproduce material in this book:

Figure 1.3 Yann Arthus-Bertrand/CORBIS; Figure 2.1 Haydyn West/PA Photos; Figure 2.2 Bob Battersby; Figures 2.4, 4.1, 4.2a), 6.3 and 7.3 Ronald Grant Archive; Figure 2.8 Jose Luis Pelaez, Inc./CORBIS; Figure 2.10 Hekimian Julien/CORBIS SYGMA; Figure 2.11 Department for Transport; Figure 3.4a) Andrew Brookes/CORBIS; Figure 3.4b) Phil Schermeister/CORBIS; Figure 3.5 Oxford Scientific Films; Figure 4.2b) Ronnie Kaufman/CORBIS; Figures 5.1, 11.1, 12.3, 15.1 and 15.2 Bettman/CORBIS; Figures 5.7 and 11.4 Wellcome Photo Library; Figures 5.11, 11.6, 12.2 and 12.4 AKG Images; Figure 8.3 Geray Sweeney/CORBIS; Figure 8.4 Thomas Hartwell/CORBIS SABA; Figure 9.1 Larry Williams/CORBIS; Figure 9.2 Jennie Woodcock/Reflections Photolibrary/CORBIS; Figure 9.3 and 9.4 Burstein Collection/CORBIS; Figure 10.3 Mary Evans Picture Library; Figure 11.2 Science and Society Picture Library; Figure 11.5 CORBIS; Figure 13.2 Bridgeman Art Library; Figure 13.3 Laura Dwight/CORBIS

Every effort has been made to obtain necessary permission with reference to copyright material. The publishers apologise if inadvertently any sources remain unacknowledged and will be glad to make the necessary arrangements at the earliest opportunity.

INTRODUCTION

Themes, Issues and Debates in Psychology was originally published in 1995, so, by most standards, a second edition is well overdue. However, the basic themes, issues and debates covered in that first edition seem to have remained essentially the same. There are very few books that I am aware of that adopt a thematic approach, as opposed to a topic-based approach. The thematic approach allows one to draw from many areas of psychology — such as social, cognitive, individual differences, developmental and physiological — as well as the more philosophical, theoretical and critical aspects of the discipline. This is relevant both to the synoptic element of A2 specifications, and undergraduate students.

I have added two new chapters to the 13 of the first edition:

> **1** a chapter on the *major theoretical approaches*, namely behaviourist, psychodynamic, cognitive, humanistic, social constructionist and evolutionary; feminist psychology is covered in one of the existing chapters, and these approaches are already discussed in several other chapters
>
> **2** a chapter on *parapsychology*.

Other changes include the updating, rewording, and reorganizing of existing material. This is limited in some chapters, but quite extensive in others. The chapter summaries are more concise, there are more boxes, and web addresses have been added at the end of each chapter.

During my 30 years of teaching Psychology on a variety of courses, and giving talks at student conferences, I have come to regard the traditional carving-up of the discipline into distinct sections/topics/areas as artificial — almost a distortion of what Psychology 'really is'. This has led me to favour the *thematic* approach mentioned above: if we can find links and connections between topics and areas of research that are 'officially' separate and distinct, the mass of material students always complain about (with good reason) may seem less daunting. Just as importantly, thinking about how, say, ethical and methodological issues, culture and gender, are always relevant when 'evaluating' or 'critically discussing' any area of research, should help you to write better essays, seminar papers and practical reports.

In adopting a thematic approach, I am assuming at least some degree of familiarity with the concepts, ideas, theories and research studies used to illustrate a particular theme, issue or debate (although sometimes I have chosen to describe these in some detail). For this reason, *Themes, Issues and Debates* is meant to *complement* other textbooks, which you will need to provide the basic material in sufficient detail. The topic-based approach of most textbooks, and the thematic approach of this one, can sit side-by-side quite happily at various points in your course. *Themes, Issues and Debates* isn't designed to be used *after* you have absorbed all the information from the main textbooks, but rather as a way of synthesizing, integrating, as well as revising (some of) that information *as you go along*.

ACKNOWLEDGEMENTS

I would like to thank Lynn Brown for her highly efficient copy-editing of the manuscript. Any remaining errors are, as ever, mine. Thanks too to Emma Woolf at Hodder for her support, not just in this project but in everything I do. Also, thanks to Jon Berkeley for (another) great cover.

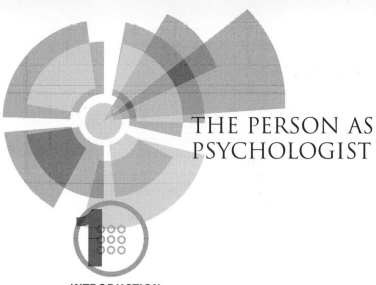

THE PERSON AS PSYCHOLOGIST

INTRODUCTION

As an alternative to the customary definition of psychology as the scientific study of behaviour and mental processes, I'd like to propose that a more useful way of thinking about the discipline of psychology is to see it as part of the sum total of what people do. Like other scientific disciplines, *psychology is a human activity*, albeit a rather special one, as we will see.

Similarly, psychologists (also like other scientists) are, first and foremost, *people* – they are people long before they become psychologists, and being a psychologist is only a part of their total activity as a person. It follows from this that if we are to properly understand what psychology is, and how it has changed during its history, as well as its achievements and limitations, we need to understand (among other things) *psychologists as people*.

However (you're probably saying to yourself), this is what psychologists do – how can we understand psychologists as people before we've looked at what psychologists say about people (as people)? We seem to be facing a conundrum: are psychologists in some sense studying themselves? Exactly! One of the things that makes psychology unique as a scientific activity is that the investigator and the subject matter are, in all essential details, the same. Instead of having physicists studying gravity or light (which are definitely not human), or astronomers studying the stars and solar system (which are also definitely not human), we have a small number of human beings (psychologists) studying a much larger number of human beings (people) – but apart from these labels, there's no difference (that is, they are all 'people').

If that's so, surely we could learn something about psychologists as people by turning things around and looking at *people as psychologists*. In other words, if we want to understand psychologists as people before we can properly appreciate what they do as scientists, why not begin by looking for ways in which we're *all* scientists, as part of our everyday social activity? This way of looking at 'ordinary' people (non-psychologists or lay people) is one that psychologists themselves have found useful. Two research areas in which this model of ordinary people is made quite explicit are (i) that part of social psychology concerned with how we form impressions of other people's personality and how we explain the causes of their (and our own) behaviour (*person/social perception*), and (ii) that part of individual differences concerned with personality – specifically, Kelly's *personal construct theory*.

THE LAY PERSON AS PSYCHOLOGIST: PEOPLE AS SCIENTISTS

According to Gahagan (1984):

It has at times been observed that had the physical sciences not been developed to their contemporary level the world would be a very different place, one in which we would have little control over communications, disease, food production, and so forth. If, however, psychology as a scientific activity had not emerged, less difference between the contemporary world and the past would be detectable.

This isn't meant as a criticism of psychology, but rather as a way of drawing attention to the fundamental point, that 'human beings have the capacity to reflect on their own behaviour and reflect on its causes; the human being is essentially a psychologist and always has been' (Gahagan, 1984).

To the extent that we, as ordinary people, can already do the kinds of things that psychologists, as scientists, are trying to do (that is, reflect on the causes of behaviour), we're bound to be less affected than we are by other sciences which, by definition, are the domain of people with special training and expertise. This isn't to say, however, that the science of Psychology (with a capital 'P') has no influence on human psychology (with a small 'p'). Indeed, Richards (2002) and others argue that Psychology can actually *change* its subject matter (psychology) unlike any other scientific discipline (see Chapter 11). These two claims – that people are already psychologists, and that Psychology changes people's psychology – are not, however, contradictory; rather, they're two sides of the same coin.

The examples Gahagan gives of how science has changed the world are all *applications* of scientific knowledge (technological aspects of science). Equivalent 'technologies' can be found within psychology. Clinical psychology, for example, is aimed at helping people to change their behaviour when this is considered to be 'abnormal' in some way (see Chapters 7 and 10). However, the kinds of changes that Richards is talking about aren't applications of psychological theory and research. Psychology has the potential for influencing how we 'do' psychology in our everyday lives – that is, the way we think about ourselves and others, the kinds of explanations we provide of behaviour, the theories we construct about 'what makes people tick'.

Gahagan claims that 'the infant science of psychology ... has as yet had little effect on the existing heritage of lay people's psychology'. This is because of what we've said about people already being psychologists. She is also implying, however, that, given time, lay people's psychology (or *common-sense psychology*) *will* change. Richards (and others) believe that this has already happened (see Chapter 11).

COMMON-SENSE PSYCHOLOGY: LOOKING FOR HIDDEN CAUSES OF BEHAVIOUR

Fritz Heider, a European who emigrated to the USA, was greatly influenced by Gestalt psychology (see Chapter 2). He wanted to apply this theory of object perception to the perception of people (*social* or *person perception*). The publication of his book *The Psychology of Interpersonal Relations* (1958) marked a new era in social psychology (Leyens and Codol, 1988).

For Heider, the starting point for studying how people understand their social world is 'ordinary' people. How do people usually think about and infer meaning from what goes on around them? How do they make sense of their own and other people's behaviour?

Figure 1.1 Fritz Heider (1896–1989) introduced the notion of commonsense psychology

These questions relate to what Heider called common-sense psychology. He saw the 'ordinary' person (the 'person in the street') as a *naïve scientist*, linking observable behaviour to unobservable causes (much as the professional scientist does):

The causal structure of the environment, both as the scientist describes it and as the naïve person apprehends it, is such that we are usually in contact only with what may be called the offshoots or manifestations of underlying core processes or core structures ... Man is usually not content simply to register the observables that surround him ... The underlying causes of events, especially the motives of other persons, are invariances of the environment that are relevant to him; they give meaning to what he experiences and it is these meanings that are recorded in his life space and are precipitated as the reality of the environment to which he then reacts.
(Heider, 1958)

So, a fundamental feature of common-sense psychology is the belief that underlying people's overt behaviour are causes, and it is these causes, rather than the observable behaviour itself, that provide the meaning of what people do. Such basic assumptions about behaviour need to be shared by members of a culture, for without them social interaction would be chaotic. Indeed, common-sense psychology can be thought of as part of the belief system that forms part of the culture as a whole, and that distinguishes one culture from another. According to Bennett (1993):

What interested him [Heider] was the fact that within our culture we all subscribe to essentially the same version of everyday psychology – for example, that human behaviour often reflects inner determinants such as abilities, wants, emotions, personalities, etc., rather than, say, witchcraft or the spirit forces of our ancestors ... Of course, it is important that we do subscribe to a common psychology, since doing this provides an orientating context in which we can understand, and be understood by, others. Imagine a world in which your version of everyday psychology was fundamentally at odds with that of your friends – without a shared 'code' for making sense of behaviour, social life would hardly be possible ...

Of course, common-sense psychology (at least that shared by members of western cultures) doesn't involve the belief that internal, unobservable causes are the *only* causes of behaviour. In fact, Heider identified two basic potential sources or causes of behaviour, namely *personal* or *dispositional* (internal), and *situational* or *environmental* (external). This distinction lies at the heart of *attribution theory*, which deals with the general principles that govern how the social perceiver selects and uses information to arrive at causal explanations (Fiske and Taylor, 1991). In other words, one of the major 'tasks' we all face in our daily interactions with others is deciding whether their behaviour can be explained in terms of internal causes (such as abilities, emotions, personality, motivation and attitudes) or external causes (such as the behaviour of other people, the demands of the situation, and aspects of the physical environment). This decision is the *attribution process*, and it's what theories of attribution try to explain.

Understanding which set of factors should be used to interpret another person's behaviour will make the perceiver's world more predictable and give him/her greater control over it. Heider's basic insights provided the blueprint for the theories of attribution that followed (Hewstone and Antaki, 1988); these are discussed in Chapter 2.

According to Antaki (1984), attribution theory promises to: 'uncover the way in which we, as ordinary men and women, act as scientists in tracking down the causes of behaviour; it promises to treat ordinary people, in fact, as if they were psychologists'. So, if we're all already psychologists, it's not surprising that the science of psychology should have had as little impact as Gahagan, for one, thinks it has. There already exists a body of 'knowledge' (a set of beliefs and assumptions) that we all use for interpreting and predicting people's behaviour (common-sense or *folk* psychology). This is part of our culture, and so is highly resistant to change, and is deeply ingrained in our everyday social interactions.

Are there, though, psychological theories that have proved so powerful that they have become absorbed by the culture and so have become part of common-sense psychology? By becoming absorbed into the culture, they may become detached from the identity of the psychologist(s) responsible for them, becoming part of what we take for granted about human beings. Popular beliefs such as 'male homosexuals had too close a relationship with their mothers as children', 'the child's first few years are critical', and 'boys need a father' can all be traced, more or less directly (and more or less accurately), to Freud's psychoanalytic theory. It's not the (objective) truth or otherwise of these claims that's relevant here, but the impact they've had on the thinking and experience of ordinary people (see Chapters 11 and 15).

There's no doubting the tremendous impact Freud has had, both on Psychology and psychology. According to Clift (1984):

He [Freud] has provided us with a set of ideas and concepts which, both in literature and everyday conversation have helped us to formulate questions about ourselves, our inner experience and our social conditioning. He helped to explode the myth of 'rational Man' and has brought us face to face with our irrational selves, a new image of ourselves at least as valid as any other major image-of-man that Social Science has offered and perhaps as challenging and disturbing as any it is ever likely to offer.

Similarly, Thomas (1990) argues that:

Sigmund Freud is probably the most famous of all psychologists . . . His ideas and development of them by other people have influenced our conception of morality, family life and childhood and thus perhaps the structure of our society.

And they have changed our attitudes to mental illness. Freudian assumptions are now part of the fabric of literature and the arts.

The conceptual tools of the everyday psychologist

In making sense of human action, the everyday ('amateur') psychologist draws upon a considerable range of constructs and conceptual 'tools', which fall into two broad categories:

1 *psychological* (or *mentalistic*) – these are properties of the individual (desires, emotions, personality and other *internal* sources)

2 *social* – these are properties of the group(s) and society we belong to (rules, norms, roles and other *external* sources).

EVERYDAY MENTALISTIC PSYCHOLOGY

According to Wellman (1990, in Bennett, 1993), two vital constructs lie at the heart of everyday thinking about action: desire and belief. What people do results from their *believing* that certain actions will bring about ends that they *desire*. Almost every time we ask someone why they did something, we'll be trying to find out about their desire or belief – or both.

In everyday psychology, these are accepted as the causes of what we do: 'Beliefs and desires provide ... the internal mental causes for overt actions' (Wellman, 1990, in Bennett, 1993). However, the everyday psychologist also has some idea ('theory') about what causes desires and beliefs. Specifically, beliefs arise from perception, while desires result from basic emotions and physiological causes. Also, action is seen as producing certain *reactions*, typically *emotional* ones. Other people's emotions provide important cues about how to behave towards them (for example, try to comfort them, or steer clear of them), as well as insights into the strengths of their desires and beliefs.

Although emotion is clearly a basic construct of everyday psychology, it's not all there is in the lay person's conceptual 'tool bag'. Other key 'tools' – and perhaps the most important of all – are *thinking* and *intention*.

○ *Thinking* is an active process, in which the mind is engaged in a variety of directive processes, such as attention, interpretation, and storing information and recalling it. This means that beliefs, for example, can arise in the absence of direct perception, and may result from inference (which *is* based on direct perception).

○ *Intentions* mediate between desire and action. They 'function to actualize (some but not all) desires', that is, they translate our wants into strategic courses of action that will help us to satisfy those wants. This translation involves planning and other cognitive activity and information processing.

However, everyday psychology also involves trying to understand *recurrent* patterns of behaviour (as opposed to one-off, specific, acts). For this purpose, we commonly identify *personality traits* to explain and predict people's behaviour, and once we have, we're in a better position to predict all kinds of desires and beliefs the person might have. Particular actions can now be seen in a broader, more coherent, psychological context.

EVERYDAY SOCIAL PSYCHOLOGY

This is usually more implicit than the mentalistic counterpart, and Wellman has much less to say about it. As most social psychologists would agree, action is to a considerable degree constrained by forces outside the individual, such as norms and conventions (see Chapter

4). According to Wegner and Vallacher (1977, in Bennett, 1993), people are 'implicit situation theorists' who subscribe to 'a set of expectations concerning the rules of behaviour in various settings'. Expectations also apply to the behaviours of people occupying particular social roles in particular situations. Everyday social psychology also includes our understanding of *event episodes*, which are *scripted* episodes – 'a predetermined stereotyped sequence of actions' (Schank and Abelson, 1977) – such as eating at a restaurant. Wellman's account of everyday psychology is summarized in Figure 1.2.

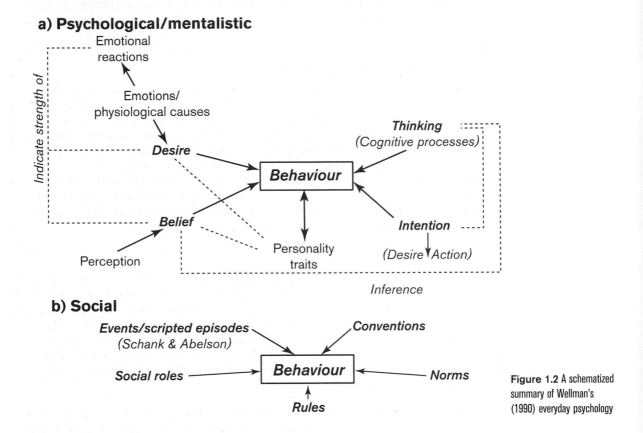

Figure 1.2 A schematized summary of Wellman's (1990) everyday psychology

Implicit and explicit theories: some similarities between formal and informal psychology

Ordinary peoples' assumption that behaviour is caused by either internal or external factors, combined with the attribution process, are part of the way in which we form impressions of others. Only if we attribute internal causes can we take the behaviour to indicate what the person is like; external causes, by definition, refer to influences on behaviour distinct from the actor him/herself. However, there's much more involved in forming impressions of others than simply attributing causes. As Gahagan (1984) says:

When we form impressions of others we are making guesses or inferences based both on whatever selection of data, derived from our observations of them, are at hand and the theories that we already have about them. The study of person perception is the study of how the lay person uses theory and data in understanding other people.

FORMING IMPRESSIONS

The kinds of theories the lay person uses when forming impressions of others are referred to as *intuitive theories* (see, for example, Nisbett and Ross, 1980) or *implicit personality theories*. The most extensively investigated (and, arguably, the most important) examples are *stereotypes* and the related process of *stereotyping*, which Oakes *et al.* (1994) define as 'the process of ascribing characteristics to people on the basis of their group memberships'.

Box 1.1 An example of stereotyping

We observe a man wearing a grey, pinstripe suit and carrying a copy of the *Financial Times* and a briefcase (the data), label him as a 'businessman', and then infer that, like other businessmen, he votes Conservative (the theory). We already have an implicit theory of businessman, a generalized belief about the characteristics shared by this particular group of human beings. So, when we observe a member of this group, without knowing anything at all about him as an individual, we immediately 'know' what he's like. The very limited data are supplemented by the theory, which then allows us to predict what this complete stranger is likely to think and believe, what his values are, and so on. (Here, 'voting Conservative' is shorthand for a long list of values, attitudes and beliefs, and so constitutes a stereotype in its own right.)

Being able to make such predictions based on such limited information gives us a sense of being in control, even if they're not actually put to the test (or even if they're not confirmed if they are). As a kind of *person schema*, stereotypes illustrate the general cognitive tendency to store knowledge and experience in the form of simplified, generalized representations. (Imagine what it would be like if we had to store details of each individual chair, cat or person we encounter!) As Atkinson *et al.* (1990) say, 'Without schemata and schematic processing, we would simply be overwhelmed by the information that inundates us. We would be very poor information processors.'

The importance of schemas (or schemata) and other implicit personality theories lies not in their accuracy, but in their capacity for making the world a more manageable place in which to live. If psychologists are to understand human behaviour, they must look not at *how good* people are at explaining and predicting the world (especially the world of human behaviour), but rather at *how they go about doing it*. According to Asch (1952):

We act and choose on the basis of what we see, feel, and believe . . . When we are mistaken about things, we act in terms of our erroneous notions, not in terms of things as they are. To understand human action it is therefore essential to understand the conscious mode in which things appear to us.

An early advocate of the view that it's essential to understand people's constructions of the world was Schutz (1932, in Bennett, 1993), a sociologist, according to whom:

All our knowledge . . . in common-sense as in scientific thinking, involves constructions . . . strictly speaking, there are no such things as facts, pure and simple. All facts are from the outset facts selected from a universal context by the activities of our minds . . . This does not mean that, in daily life or in science, we are unable to grasp the reality of the world. It just means that we grasp merely certain aspects of it, namely those which are relevant to us.

This highlights the 'conceptually driven' nature of our everyday understanding; it is guided not by the intrinsic properties of the world, but by our prior ideas and beliefs about it. The data provided by the external environment are still relevant (as the example of the businessman illustrates), but these are 'filtered' through our schemas and implicit theories, so that we're incapable of seeing things 'as they really are' (see Chapters 11 and 15).

WHAT DOES THIS MEAN FOR SCIENCE?

If we accept this constructionist argument, then it's not surprising that people disagree about 'the way the world is' in their everyday dealings with each other. When applied to science, the constructionist viewpoint raises some very important – and awkward – questions regarding the nature of scientific activity and the status of scientific knowledge.

The *positivist* view of science maintains that the distinguishing characteristic of science is its *objectivity*. The scientist, equipped with appropriate empirical methods, has access to the world 'as it really is', which assumes that the observations, measurements, experiments, and so on, s/he performs are unbiased, and that data can be collected without any kind of preconception or expectation influencing their collection.

However, by analogy with the lay person's use of theory and data to understand other people, the scientist (including the scientific psychologist) also collects data through the 'lens' of theory; there's simply no way of avoiding it. According to Popper (1972), observation is always pre-structured and directed, and this is as true of physics as it is of psychology. Similarly, Deese (1972) argues that, despite the reliance of science on observation, data play a more modest role than is usually believed. The function of empirical observation isn't to find out what causes what, or how things work in some ultimate sense, but simply to provide justification for some particular way of looking at the world. In other words, observation justifies (or not) a theory the scientist already holds (just as the everyday psychologist already has stereotypes of particular social groups), and theories determine what kinds of data are collected in the first place.

The interdependence between theory and data is shown in Deese's belief that (i) theory in the absence of data isn't science, and (ii) data alone don't make a science. Both theory *and* data are necessary for science, and so-called facts don't exist independently of a theoretical interpretation of the data:

$$\text{Fact} = \text{Data} + \text{Theory}$$

ARE INTUITIVE/IMPLICIT THEORIES REAL THEORIES?

Wellman (1990, in Bennett, 1993) identifies three essential features of a theory:

1 *coherence* – the different concepts that make up the theory should be interconnected, making it impossible to consider a single concept in isolation; in other words, the meaning of any given concept is determined by its role in the theory as a whole

2 *ontological distinctions* – it 'carves up' phenomena into different kinds of entities and processes, making fundamental distinctions between different classes of things

3 *causal explanatory framework* – it accounts for the phenomena it deals with by identifying their causes.

Wellman believes that in terms of these three criteria, everyday psychology can reasonably be considered to constitute a theory.

Implicit and explicit theories: some differences between formal and informal psychology

Even if we agree with Wellman that the everyday psychologist's implicit theories share certain features with scientific theories, it is difficult to deny that the scope of implicit theories is nothing like as broad as that of scientific/academic psychology (Bennett, 1993). There are other important differences as well.

THE MEANING OF 'IMPLICIT' AND 'EXPLICIT'

The lay person may be only dimly aware, or completely unaware, of the reasoning s/he has followed when making inferences about others, and this reasoning may change from situation to situation. They draw on their theories in an unselfconscious way ('theories as lived'; see below). This is part of what 'implicit' conveys.

By definition, the scientist must be able to show how his/her theory was developed and hypotheses derived. They use their theories *as theories*. So, while lay people might use constructs about what causes people to act as they do (the *attribution* process), a scientific psychologist produces *constructs about constructs* – that is, an explanation of everyday explanation (a 'second level' explanation, such as *theories of* attribution). This is what 'explicit' conveys.

APPLYING SCIENTIFIC METHOD

Scientists are obliged to follow scientific method, a set of rules governing the use of theory. These include *falsifiability* – being able to show that the theory is false, rather than merely finding data to support it (i.e. *verification*; see Popper, 1959). Everyday psychologists, of course, aren't obliged to follow the rules of scientific method, and tend to look for evidence that supports their position.

THE PURPOSE OF PSYCHOLOGICAL THEORIES

The psychologist as scientist is trying to construct scientific laws of human behaviour and cognitive processes (or, at least, establish general principles), often for their own sake. The lay person, however, is using theories as 'guidelines for their everyday transactions with others' (Gahagan, 1991).

For example, whereas you or I might avoid someone who looks very aggressive or whom we believe to be short-tempered, the psychologist studying aggression may be interested in finding out what cues people use to judge others as aggressive, or why some people are actually more aggressive than others. In other words, the lay person's intuitive/implicit theories serve a *practical/pragmatic* purpose. They 'guide his daily behaviour, and make the behaviour of others appear more intelligible and predictable than it would otherwise. We have to make sense of others' behaviour in order to act at all ourselves' (Gahagan, 1984).

Berger and Luckmann (1966) talk about 'recipe knowledge', knowledge that gets results, as the primary purpose of lay theories. Scientists, though, are interested in 'truth' (rather than usefulness); they want to construct as full an account as possible of the structures, processes and contents associated with a particular phenomenon.

The relationship between formal and informal psychology

Professionals and ordinary people have in common the task of trying to understand other people's motives and their personalities. The professional 'spies' on the lay person as s/he undertakes the task of 'being' a psychologist. Since *person perception* is the term given by professional psychologists to the study of the lay person as psychologist, this represents the convergence of professional and lay, formal and informal psychology (Gahagan, 1991).

According to Harré *et al.* (1985):

The task of scientific psychology consists of making the implicit psychologies of everyday life explicit, and then, in the light of that understanding, applying the techniques of theory-guided empirical research to develop, refine, and extend that body of knowledge and practices.

Harré *et al.* cite Freud's theory of dreams as an obvious extension of our common-sense or folk beliefs about the source of dream contents. Common sense forms 'part of the literature' – that is, a proper part of the body of knowledge available in the science of psychology. Agreeing with Heider, Harré *et al.* say that common sense is the platform from which the enterprise of psychology must start.

MAN-THE-SCIENTIST: KELLY'S PSYCHOLOGY OF PERSONAL CONSTRUCTS

Three years before the publication of Heider's book in which he proposed the notions of common-sense psychology and the naïve scientist, George Kelly published a book called *A Theory of Personality: The Psychology of Personal Constructs* (1955).

According to Kelly, not only are scientists human, but humans can also be thought of as scientists. Personal construct theory (PCT) is a theory about the personal theories of each one of us, and one of its distinctive features is that it applies as much to Kelly himself (as the originator of the theory) as to everyone else. If science is first and foremost a human activity, a form of behaviour, then any valid psychological theory must be able to account for that activity or behaviour; this, of course, includes the construction of psychological theories (in the case of scientific psychology). PCT can do this quite easily (not true of most psychological theories), and so is said to display *reflexivity*.

According to Weiner (1992): 'It is puzzling that while psychologists try to explain the behaviour of their clients, or people in general, the theories they have formulated cannot account for their own scientific activity.' However:

Kelly's theory . . . can explain scientific endeavours, for Kelly considered the average person an intuitive scientist, having the goal of predicting and understanding behaviour. To accomplish this aim, the naïve person formulates hypotheses about the world and the self, collects data that confirm or disconfirm these hypotheses, and then alters personal theories to account for the new data. Hence, the average person operates in the same manner as the professional scientist, although the professional scientist may be more accurate and more self-conscious in their attempts to achieve cognitive clarity and understanding.

Our hypotheses about the world take the form of *constructs*. These represent our attempt to interpret events (including the behaviour of ourselves and others), and they're put to the test every time we act.

Kelly was originally trained in physics and mathematics, and he worked for a time as an engineer. Not surprisingly, perhaps, he chose the model of *man-the-scientist*. He wondered why it was that only those with university degrees should be privileged to feel the excitement and reap the rewards of scientific activity (Fransella, 1980):

When we speak of *man-the-scientist* we are speaking of all mankind and not merely a particular class of men who have publicly attained the stature of 'scientists'. We are speaking of all mankind in its scientist-like aspects.
(Kelly, 1955)

This model of human beings not only seems intuitively valid (people really are as the model describes them), but it has quite fundamental implications for how we make sense of (construe) what is going on in psychological research, and how it needs to be conducted if anything meaningful is to come out of it. In Kelly's own words:

It is customary to say that *the scientist's ultimate aim is to predict and control*. This is a summary statement that psychologists frequently like to quote in characterizing their own aspirations. Yet, curiously enough, psychologists rarely credit the human subjects in their experiments with having similar aspirations. It is as though the psychologist were saying to himself, 'I, being a *psychologist*, and therefore a *scientist*, am performing this experiment in order to improve the prediction and control of certain human phenomena; but my subject, being merely a human organism, is obviously propelled by inexorable drives welling up within him, or else he is in gluttonous pursuit of sustenance and shelter.

In other words, in their role as scientists, psychologists perceive people as something less than whole persons, certainly as something very different form themselves. People are 'reduced' to the status of *subject*, implying that the psychologist is in control and dictates what will happen in the experimental situation, while the other merely responds to events in a passive and unthinking way. Not only is the term dehumanizing (Heather, 1976; see also Chapter 10), but there is a fundamental methodological issue involved. Another psychologist who (implicitly) regards people as intuitive scientists is Orne (1962), who introduced the term *demand characteristics* to refer to all the cues that convey to the 'subject' the experimental hypothesis (and, hence, represent important influences on his/her behaviour).

The mere fact that experimental psychologists do all they can to conceal from their subjects the true purpose of an experiment (and thus prevent them from, consciously or unconsciously, complying with it) suggests that the former believe that the latter, like themselves, 'search for meaning in their environment, formulate hypotheses, and act on the basis of these belief systems' (Weiner, 1992). If ordinary people didn't engage in essentially the same kind of intellectual activities as scientists, it wouldn't be necessary to use the often elaborate controls and deceptions that are an almost inevitable feature of traditional experimental research (see Chapter 11).

How, though, can people be both 'subjects' (very different from the psychologist) and, at the same time, capable of figuring out (or at least puzzling about) what is going on in the mind of the psychologist (much as the psychologist is doing in his/her role as scientist)? Using Kelly's concept of constructs, 'we might see the subject as one who is desperately trying to construe the construction processes of the psychologist' (Fransella, 1980). From this perspective, the term 'subject' is inappropriate; not only are ordinary people scientists, but psychologists can only hope to understand and predict others' behaviour to the extent they're aware of the constructs those others place upon events. Some behaviour might appear extraordinary to the observer, but be totally meaningful in the context of the actor's own worldview. As Fransella (1980) says, 'To understand the behaviour of others, we have to know what construct predictions are being put to the test.'

As a consequence of the 'human-as-scientist' model, the psychologist and the client ('subject') are now equal partners; the former is no longer of higher status and 'in charge' (Weiner, 1992). According to Bannister and Fransella (1980):

Construct theory sees each man as trying to make sense out of himself and his world. It sees psychology as a meta-discipline, an attempt to make sense out of the ways in which men make sense out of their worlds. This not only puts the psychologist in the same interpretive business as his so-called subject – it makes them partners in the business, for on no other basis can one man understand another.

If 'subject' reduces the person to something less than a whole person, for PCT the person is the irreducible unit: 'Traditional psychology is not, in the main, about persons. By making the person the central subject matter of psychology, construct theory changes the boundaries and the content of the existing science' (Bannister and Fransella, 1980).

Research within a PCT framework would look very different from its conventional, 'mainstream' form. It would be about 'the process whereby people come to make sense of things', and would involve working *with* and not *on* subjects. The researcher's constructions would be made explicit and the results obtained

... will be seen as less important, in the end, than the whole progress of the research itself – which, after all, represents one version of the process it is investigating. The crucial question, about any research project, would then be how far, as a process, it illuminated our understanding of the whole human endeavour to make sense of our lives, and how fruitful it proved in suggesting new explanatory ventures.

(Salmon, 1978, in Bannister and Fransella, 1980)

These views regarding the nature of psychological research are echoed in feminist psychology (see Chapter 6) and in collaborative/new paradigm research (see Chapter 11).

HOMO PSYCHOLOGICUS: HUMAN BEINGS AS NATURAL PSYCHOLOGISTS

According to Humphrey (1986), 'The minds of human beings are part of nature. We should ask: What are minds for? Why have they evolved in this way rather than another? Why have they evolved at all, instead of remaining quite unchanged?'

Language, creativity, and self-awareness are unique to human beings (although many would challenge this; see, for example, Gross, 2003), and human societies are infinitely richer, more stable and more psychologically demanding than anything that exists elsewhere in nature. Nowhere on earth, though, can human beings survive outside society. Consequently, nowhere on earth can we survive without a deep sensitivity to, and understanding of, our fellow creatures. Humphrey asks:

Did people . . . then evolve to be psychologists by nature? Is that what makes our families and commitments work? Has that been the prime mover behind the evolution of *our* brains and *our* intelligence? If so, it would mean that almost all the earlier theories of human evolution had got it upside down. Fifteen years ago, nothing in the textbooks about evolution referred to man's need to do psychology: the talk was all of tool-making, spear-throwing and fire-lighting – practical rather than social intelligence.

It has been argued that the mark of the first man-like ape was the ability to walk on his hind legs, to eat and digest a wide range of grassland food, and to relate his fingers to his thumb. However, according to Humphrey, as important as these were: 'Not fingers to thumb, but person to person. The real mark of a man-like ape would have been his ability to manipulate and relate himself – in human ways – to the other apes around him.'

Humphrey argues that there's sufficient archaeological evidence to suggest that by two million years ago the fundamental pattern of human social living had already been established. While the Kalahari bushmen may be biologically modern, in many respects their lifestyle hasn't changed in the last million years. By observing them, we can still see just how far the success of a hunter-gatherer community depends on the psychological skills of its individual members. Their social system works, but only because they, like all human beings,

. . . are . . . supremely good at understanding one another. They come of a long, long line of natural psychologists whose brains and minds have been slowly shaped by evolution . . . Small wonder human beings have evolved to be such remarkable psychological survivors, when for the last six million years their heavy task has been to read the minds of other human beings.

Figure 1.3 Self-awareness/consciousness and the ability to understand and predict the behaviour and responses of others may be the essential characteristics of human beings which make them distinctive from all other species

But how do we do it? Essentially, as intelligent social beings we use knowledge of our *own* thoughts and feelings (through 'introspection'; see Chapter 11) as a guide for understanding how others are likely to think and feel, and, therefore, behave. Humphrey goes even further and claims that we are conscious (that is, we have self-awareness) *because* this is so useful to us in this process of understanding others and thus having a successful social existence. Consciousness is a biological adaptation, which has evolved to enable us to perform this introspective psychology.

Consistent with Humphrey's discussion of the evolution of human beings as nature's psychologists (*phylogenesis*) is the recent interest among developmental psychologists in how an understanding of other people's minds develops in the individual child (*ontogenesis*). This capacity appears, on average, between the ages of three and four, and is called the child's 'theory of mind'. Humphrey's theory of consciousness, plus the child's theory of mind, are discussed further in Chapter 13 (see also Gross, 2003).

CONCLUSION

To begin a book on psychology by looking at people as psychologists seems, in many ways, the only logical way to start. Since most of us are, by definition, neither professional psychologists nor any other kind of 'literal' scientist, the person-as-psychologist is a metaphor: let's 'pretend' that everyone's a psychologist/scientist and see where that takes us in understanding ourselves.

Compared with other metaphors (such as people-as-information-processors; see Chapters 12 and 13), it feels intuitively 'right'. After all, science, including psychology, is done by people, scientists are people, and, as far as we know, science is a uniquely human behaviour. By contrast, information-processing machines are designed by people, and it seems odd to liken people to something they have designed. At the same time this makes us unique among such machines, because we design machines as part of our scientific activity. We are organisms that 'do science', which also makes us unique within the biological world.

SUMMARY

○ **Psychology is part of the sum total of what people do, a (rather special) human activity.**

○ **One of the things that makes psychology unique as a science is that the investigator and the subject matter are, essentially, the same.**

○ **A useful way of trying to understand 'ordinary' (lay) people is to regard them *as psychologists/scientists*, as in *person perception*. Ordinary people can already do the kinds of things that psychologists as scientists are trying to do (such as reflecting on the causes of behaviour).**

○ **Heider was interested in *common-sense* (or folk) *psychology*, i.e. how the lay person acts as a *naïve scientist*, by linking observable behaviour to unobservable causes. The causes of behaviour are what give *meaning* to what people do.**

○ **Social life requires that members of a particular culture *share* the same basic version of everyday psychology.**

○ **Heider distinguished between *personal* or *dispositional* (internal) and *situational* or *environmental* (external) causes, which is the central feature of *attribution theory*. Assigning internal or external causes to behaviour is called the *attribution process*.**

○ **Influential psychological theories, notably Freud's psychoanalytic theory, may become part of our taken-for-granted beliefs about the causes of behaviour.**

O According to Wellman, *desire*, *belief*, *thinking* and *intention* are key constructs involved in everyday *mentalistic* psychology.

O Everyday *social* psychology refers to *social norms, rules and conventions*, and *social roles*, and also includes understanding of *event/scripted episodes*.

O The lay person's theories are called *intuitive/implicit personality theories*, an important example being *stereotypes* (and the related process of *stereotyping*). Stereotypes are a kind of *person schema*.

O Schemas and other implicit theories make the world more *manageable*, through making it more *predictable*; this is more important than their *accuracy*.

O Many sociologists, psychologists and philosophers of science argue that our knowledge of the world is *constructed* by us; this challenges the *positivist* view of science, according to which science is *objective*.

O Scientific observation is always pre-structured and directed; data are always collected in the light of a particular theory, and 'facts' do not exist independently of theory.

O Scientists, but not everyday psychologists, are obliged to follow the rules of *scientific method*, including *falsification* (as opposed to mere *verification*); the former are also obliged to make them *explicit*.

O Psychologists as scientists are trying to construct laws of behaviour/psychological processes *as an end in itself*, while the lay person's theories serve a *practical/pragmatic* purpose ('recipe knowledge').

O According to Kelly's PCT, people can be thought of as intuitive scientists (*man-the-scientist*), who use their *personal constructs* to make predictions about, and to explain, behaviour. To understand other people's behaviour, we must know what constructs they are putting to the test.

O In the experimental situation, subjects formulate hypotheses about the experimental hypothesis being tested; this relates to Orne's *demand characteristics*.

O In traditional psychology, the experimenter is of higher status and 'in charge', while within a PCT framework, research is a cooperative venture between 'equals'; the *process* of research is much more important than the results obtained.

O According to Humphrey, human beings have evolved as natural psychologists (*homo psychologicus*). What makes humans distinctive as a species is our ability to *read the minds of other human beings*. Based on introspection, we use knowledge of our *own* thoughts/feelings as a guide for understanding how others are likely to be thinking/feeling.

O Consciousness is a biological adaptation that has evolved to enable us to perform this introspective psychology. The development in children of a 'theory of mind' is consistent with this evolutionary view.

Useful websites

- O http://www.apa.org/
- O http://www.bps.org.uk
- O cogsci.soton.ac.uk/~hamad/Papers/Py104/Anderson.every.html

(See also the 'Useful websites' listed at the end of Chapter 2.)

Recommended reading

Bannister, D. and Fransella, F. (1980) *Inquiring Man* (2nd edn). Harmondsworth: Penguin.

Gross, R. (2003) *Key Studies in Psychology* (4th edn) (Chapter 3 on theory of mind). London: Hodder & Stoughton.

Humphrey, N. (1986) *The Inner Eye* (especially Chapter 2). London: Vintage.

Kelly, G.A. (1955) *A Theory of Personality: The Psychology of Personal Constructs.* New York: Norton.

ATTRIBUTION

ATTRIBUTION AND EVERYDAY PSYCHOLOGY

As described in Chapter 1, Fritz Heider (1958) regarded the 'ordinary' person (the non-psychologist) as a *naïve scientist*, someone who actively tries to make sense of the world, in particular, the social world, the world of behaviour. He claimed that a fundamental feature of *common-sense psychology* is the belief that underlying people's overt behaviour are *causes*, and it's these causes, and not the observable behaviour itself, that represent the meaning of what people do.

Causes can be of two main kinds, *dispositional* or *personal* (internal), and *situational* or *environmental* (external), and a major 'task' that we face as everyday psychologists is to decide which type of cause (abilities, emotions, personality, motivation, attitudes or other internal causes, *or* the behaviour of other people, demands of the situation, physical aspects of the environment or other external causes) best accounts for the behaviour we're trying to explain. This decision process is called the *attribution process*, and Heider's insights into the process form the basis for *attribution theory*; the latter is the scientific psychologist's attempt to explain the former.

CAUSES AND PERCEIVED CAUSES

Before getting any deeper into the details of attribution theory and how it has been used in psychology, we should note a distinction that is crucial for appreciating the nature of the attribution process and psychologists' attempts to explain it.

When we talk about 'the causes' of behaviour, the implication is that we *know* what is responsible for the observed behaviour, that our explanation is accurate, adequate and sufficient. By contrast, when we talk about 'perceived causes', we refer to what we *believe* is responsible for the observed behaviour, acknowledging that our explanation might be mistaken. While we might be willing to accept this distinction at the theoretical level, in practice we often confuse our beliefs with 'the truth'. For example, we may be 'convinced' that someone acted for a particular reason, or that 'so-and-so is the murderer', subsequently only to be proved wrong. There are really two issues involved here:

1 However sure we are about the truth of something, this doesn't in itself mean that it *is* true; subjective certainty doesn't guarantee objective truth.

2 It is often very difficult to say in an objective way exactly what is the cause (or causes) of behaviour. Indeed, the whole of psychology can be seen as an attempt to find out 'what makes us tick', with different theories offering very different (and sometimes conflicting) accounts (see Chapters 11 and 15).

When attribution theorists try to explain the lay person's explanations of behaviour, they are *not* concerned with the *accuracy* or validity of these everyday explanations, but simply with *how* they're reached – the *process* rather than the product. In fact, some of the most important research and theory dealing with the attribution process has focused on the *biases* involved in people's attempts to make sense of behaviour (their own as well as others'), implying that the resulting explanations aren't accurate or objective. Hence, 'Attribution theory is concerned with the cognitive processes individuals use to understand and predict their own behaviour, as well as that of others. Specifically, the focus is on the perceived "cause" of a person's behaviour' (Moghaddam *et al.*, 1993).

Figure 2.1 It's impossible not to make some interpretation of the picture in terms of the causes of the behaviour of the people shown. There are clues which suggest the context is some kind of riot, which is likely to influence your interpretation.

ATTRIBUTION THEORY AND THEORIES OF ATTRIBUTION

Fiske and Taylor (1991) distinguish between attribution theory and theories of attribution. *Attribution theory* deals with the general principles that govern how the social perceiver selects and uses information to arrive at causal explanations or judgements for events (i.e. behaviour) in a wide variety of domains. *Theories of attribution*, on the other hand, draw on the principles of attribution theory and make predictions about how people respond in particular life domains.

However, attribution theory doesn't refer to a single body of ideas and research, but to a collection of diverse theoretical and empirical contributions that share several common concerns. Fiske and Taylor identify six different theoretical traditions, which form the backbone of attribution theory, namely:

1 Heider's (1958) *common-sense psychology* (see Chapter 1)

2 Jones and Davis's (1965) *correspondent inference theory*

3 Kelley's (1967, 1972, 1973) *covariation model*

4 Schachter's (1964) theory of *emotional lability* (better known as 'cognitive labelling theory')

5 Bem's (1967, 1972) *self-perception theory*, and

6 Weiner's (1979, 1985) *motivational theory of attribution*.

Identifying these major theoretical strands also helps to identify some of the major *life domains* (to use Fiske and Taylor's term) to which attribution principles have been applied.

Common-sense psychology

The title of Heider's 1958 book was *The Psychology of Interpersonal Relations*. In it, he attempted to apply the Gestalt theory of physical object perception to the perception of people (social perception or, more specifically, *interpersonal perception*, the perception of *others*). Most of our impressions of others are based on what they actually do, and the situations in which they do it. Unless we're able to make a judgement as to the internal or external causes of someone's behaviour, we cannot really use behaviour as a basis for forming impressions – only when we make an *internal attribution* are we using behaviour as an indication of what the actor is like.

According to Fiske and Taylor (1991), Heider's major contribution was to 'define many of the basic issues that would later be explored more systematically in further theoretical ventures', in particular, those of Jones and Davis, and Kelley, which will be summarized below.

Cognitive labelling theory

Schachter's cognitive labelling theory represents perhaps one of the first attempts to apply attributional principles to a domain other than interpersonal perception, namely the subjective experience of emotion. Specifically, how do we come to label our physiological arousal in one way rather than another? Although the behaviour of other people may influence this labelling process, Schachter is concerned with the individual's emotional experience, *not* our perception of emotion in others. We will discuss Schachter's research below.

Self-perception theory

While Bem's 'self-perception theory' suggests that it is directly relevant to social perception (albeit not to the perception of others), it is in fact a theory of *attitude change* that draws on Heider's basic distinction between internal and external causes. This, too, will be discussed later in this chapter.

Stability and controllability as self-attributions

Whether the cause is judged to be internal (generated by the actor) or external (produced by the situation) is referred to as the *locus* of a cause. As important as this is, it is not a sufficient explanation. For example, if you fail an exam, even if you accept that it was 'your fault' (it wasn't a particularly difficult paper, and you weren't badly taught), the specific internal cause that you believe was responsible is important. If you had a really bad headache on the morning of the exam, at least you can console yourself that you may well have passed *had it not been for the headache*, and others are likely to take a similar view. However, if you believe that you failed simply because you lack the necessary ability, the implications for the future are very different from the first explanation. Although both headaches and lack of ability are *internal* causes, the former is a transient, temporary state, while the latter is a stable, permanent feature of a person's make-up. Both Jones and Davis, and Kelley, argue that causal analysis is most informative when stable causes are identified, such as personal dispositions (of which academic ability is one). So we have now identified a second important dimension of causality, namely *stability*.

However, the attribution process isn't just about understanding why something has happened, it's also about trying to:

○ *predict* what will happen in the future (understanding/explanation and prediction are two major aims of science), and

○ understand what *controls* future events (Heider, 1958; Kelley, 1967) (control being the third main aim of science; see Chapters 3 and 11).

If you attribute your exam failure to not working hard enough and allowing yourself to be distracted by social life instead of revising, at least that's something you have control over, whereas your (perceived) lack of ability isn't. So *controllability* is a third important dimension of causality.

Such *self-attributions* are important for behaviour because they are associated with differences in feelings of self-confidence, and expectations of future success and failure. If you believe that not working hard enough was the reason for your failure, you're likely to try harder next time, because removing the cause of failure should improve the chances of success. However, there's not much you can do to 'remove' your basic lack of ability! Much the same can be shown for a number of challenges that people face in the field of health. For example, cigarette smokers who see themselves as more 'addicted' have lower expectations of their ability to give up and may be less likely to try: 'Thus, the way we describe ourselves will reflect what we think others expect, or are entitled to expect, of us as well as what we expect of ourselves' (Eiser, 1994).

Drawing on these observations and assumptions, Weiner's motivational theory of attribution has explored domains such as impression management (our attempts to influence the impressions formed of us), achievement motivation, and helping behaviour. These are discussed later in the chapter. (Bem's self-perception theory could be renamed *self-attribution* theory – see below.)

Figure 2.2 Cigarette smokers who see themselves as more addicted have lower expectations of their ability to give up and may be less likely to try – despite increasingly strong health warnings

Other domains to which attribution principles have been applied include prejudice, depression and marital relationships (see Figure 2.3).

Figure 2.3 Some of the domains to which attribution theory principles have been applied

Correspondent inference theory

Jones and Davis (1965) were concerned primarily with whether a person's behaviour will be attributed to some disposition (i.e. a stable cause) of the actor, rather than to accidental or extenuating (situational) factors. An attribution or inference is 'correspondent' when the disposition attributed to an actor 'corresponds' to the behaviour from which this disposition is inferred.

For example, if someone gives up his/her seat on the bus to allow a pregnant woman to sit down, and we infer that the actor is 'kind and unselfish', we're making a correspondent inference: both the behaviour and the disposition can be labelled in the same way ('kind and unselfish'). But if we attribute the behaviour to compliance with someone else's behaviour (the person giving up his seat is a man whose wife has *told* him to give up his seat), then we might infer some other disposition about him (e.g. 'he's weak and likes to be dominated by others'). This disposition *doesn't* correspond to the behaviour from which it is inferred (it is *not* a correspondent inference).

According to Jones and Davis, a precondition for a correspondent inference is the attribution of *intentionality* (the behaviour was deliberate), and they specify, in turn, two criteria or conditions for this: the actor must be perceived as having (i) *knowledge* that the act would have the observed effects, and (ii) the *ability* to produce the observed effects. The aim of the attribution process is to infer that both the observed behaviour, and the intention to behave in that way, correspond to the actor's dispositions. Briefly, this is done through *the analysis of uncommon* (or non-common) *effects*, and the use of other cues – in particular, *choice*, *social desirability*, *social role* and *prior expectations*.

Covariation model

Kelley's (1967, 1972, 1973) covariation model is concerned primarily with whether the cause of some behaviour is internal or external. The latter can refer either to the external target of the behaviour (usually, but not invariably, another person) or the external circumstances surrounding the behaviour (Zebrowitz, 1990). However, this describes the end result of a process; the model really begins with the question 'What information do people use to arrive at one or other kind of attribution?'

When the perceiver has information from multiple sources, the principle of *covariation* is used: an effect (the behaviour to be explained) is attributed to a condition (cause) that is present when the effect is present and absent when the effect is absent. (This is based on a statistical technique, analysis of variance, or ANOVA, which examines the changes in a dependent variable (the *effect*) in an investigation involving two or more independent variables (the *conditions*).)

There are three main conditions and three kinds of *causal information* that correspond to them: *consensus*, *distinctiveness* and *consistency*. The permutation of high or low consensus/distinctiveness/consistency is what leads the perceiver, logically, to make an internal or external attribution. But what happens when all three kinds of information aren't available?

Kelley (1972) himself acknowledged that the ANOVA model was 'idealized', and that there are many occasions when the perceiver lacks the information, time or motivation to examine multiple observations. In these cases, the perceiver uses *causal schemata*, ready-made beliefs, preconceptions and even theories, built up from experience, about how certain kinds of causes interact to produce a specific kind of effect (Hewstone and Antaki, 1988).

Some difficulties for attribution theory

As just noted, Kelley recognized a major limitation of his original model, and introduced the concept of causal schemata in an attempt to 'plug the hole'. Despite this, Gahagan (1991) believes that scant attention has been paid to a very important issue for attribution theorists, namely under what circumstances does the lay psychologist act like a scientific psychologist, carefully and systematically drawing inferences about the causes of behaviour, and when does s/he simply use some ready-made explanation?

Lalljee *et al.* (1982) showed that explanations of *unexpected* behaviour tend to be more complex than those of expected behaviour. If the situation is familiar and the behaviour is unexpected, we're likely to make an *internal* attribution, while if the situation is unfamiliar and the behaviour is also unfamiliar, we're likely to make an *external* attribution. Lalljee

(1981, in Gahagan, 1991) argues that even something as apparently straightforward as *consistency* information (i.e. is the behaviour we are trying to explain a 'one-off' or does the person regularly behave like this?) is problematical. Even assuming that we have knowledge of the actor's previous behaviour, 'consistency' can mean very different things depending on the nature of the behaviour. For example, getting divorced four times in five years would strike us as much *more* frequent than, say, jogging four times in three years! We might draw very different inferences about the actor in these two cases if that were all we knew about them.

All three major theories (those of Heider, Jones and Davis, and Kelley) adopt the perspective of the perceiver as a naïve scientist, and as such all three tend to see everyday psychologists as logical and rational thinkers, who arrive at attributions in much the same way as their professional counterparts. Indeed, Kelley's ANOVA model was presented as a *normative* model – that is, it showed how perceivers *should* make accurate causal attributions. However, the research has shown that perceivers *don't* usually act like scientists, following such detailed, formal, logical rules. Instead, they make attributions quickly, using much less information, and showing clear preferences for certain sorts of explanation.

What is needed, therefore, are more *descriptive* models, more accurate accounts of how people actually go about making attributions, and this has been at least partly achieved by exploring the *biases* involved in the attribution process. These include the *fundamental attribution error* (FAE) (Ross, 1977), the *actor–observer effect* (AOE) (Jones and Nisbett, 1971), and the *self-serving bias* (SSB) (Miller and Ross, 1975). Together, they seem to provide a better descriptive analysis of causal attribution than do complex, normative models (Hewstone and Antaki, 1988).

When attribution principles are applied to particular domains of behaviour, such as emotional experience and attitude change, the fundamental distinction between internal and external causes is used in more or less the way that Heider originally made it. In other cases, such as impression management, achievement motivation and helping behaviour, depression and marital relationships, the more complex analysis proposed by Weiner (where the *locus, stability and controllability* of causes are all taken into account) is used. In the examples of depression and marital relationships, the SSB is also used to explain the nature of the behaviour involved, while the FAE has been used to help explain certain aspects of prejudice.

The rest of this chapter discusses how all these different aspects of attribution theory and research have been applied to a wide range of behaviour and experience.

ATTRIBUTION AND EMOTION

Two of the earliest theories of emotion were the James-Lange (1878, 1890) and the Cannon-Bard (1929). According to the former, our emotional experience is the *result* of perceived bodily changes (not their *cause*, as would be claimed by the 'common sense' view). So, for example, we feel *frightened* of the bear *because we run away from it*, whereas common sense would say that we run away *because we are frightened*: 'the bodily changes follow directly the perception of the exciting fact, and … our feeling of the same changes as they occur *is* the emotion' (James, 1890).

According to Cannon, there are four major faults with the James-Lange theory, two of which are of particular relevance here.

1 It implies that for each subjectively distinct emotion there's a corresponding set of physiological (bodily) changes which enable us to attach a label to the emotional experience. Against this, Cannon (1927) argued that 'the same visceral changes occur in very different emotional states and in non-emotional states'.

2 Even if there were identifiable patterns of physiological response associated with different subjective emotions, such physiological changes themselves don't necessarily produce emotional states; in other words, there's more to emotion than just bodily arousal.

The Cannon-Bard theory proposes that the emotional experience is *independent* of the physiological changes involved. The emotion-producing stimulus is processed by the thalamus (the part of the brain through which all sensory information is processed), which sends impulses to the cortex, where the emotion is consciously experienced, *and* to the hypothalamus (a different part of the brain, which plays a major role in controlling the activity of the autonomic nervous system and the endocrine-hormonal-system), which sets in motion certain autonomic physiological changes.

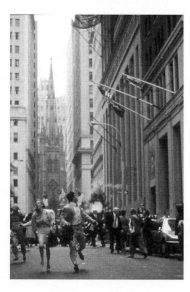

Figure 2.4 According to the James-Lange theory, we feel frightened because we are running away from something and are not running away because we are frightened

According to Schachter (1964), Cannon was wrong in thinking that bodily changes and emotional experience are independent, while the James-Lange theory was mistaken in claiming that physiological changes cause the feeling of emotion. But the James-Lange theory correctly sees physiological changes as *preceding* the emotional experience, because the latter depends on *both* physiological changes *and* on the interpretation made of those changes. We have to *decide* which particular emotion we're feeling, and how we label our arousal depends on what we *attribute* that arousal to. This is demonstrated in what is now considered one of the classic experiments of psychology (see Box 2.1, page 25).

The mis-attribution effect

Despite failures to replicate the 1962 study, and criticisms of the methodology and the conclusions drawn from it, Schachter's cognitive labelling theory has had a considerable influence on the study of emotion (Parkinson, 1987).

One of the implications of the theory is that emotional reactions induced by, say, a threatening experience, can be *re-attributed* to a neutral or less threatening source.

Box 2.1 Schachter and Singer's (1962) 'adrenaline' experiment

Schachter and Singer gave participants what they were told was a vitamin injection in order to see its effects on vision; in fact, it was adrenaline.

○ *Group A* participants were told the *real* side-effects of the injection (palpitations, tightness in the throat, tremors, sweating, etc.).

○ *Group B* were given *false* information (itching and headache).

○ *Group C* were given *no* information (true or false).

○ *Group D* were given a saline injection (and were otherwise treated like Group C).

While waiting for a 'vision test', each participant sat in a waiting room with a confederate (supposedly another participant). For half the participants in each condition, the confederate acted *either* in a happy, frivolous way (*euphoria*) *or* very angrily (*anger*). The dependent variable – the participants' emotional experience – was measured by (i) how much they joined in with the confederate's behaviour, and (ii) self-report scales.

The results were very much in line with predictions.

1 If an individual experiences a state of physiological arousal for which there is no immediate explanation (it *cannot be attributed to* the injection), s/he will 'label' this state and describe it in terms of the cognitions available. This means that exactly the *same* state of arousal could receive very *different* labels (euphoria or anger – *Groups B and C*).

2 If an individual experiences a state of physiological arousal for which there is a completely appropriate explanation (it *can be attributed* to the injection), s/he will 'label' this state accordingly, and will largely ignore other available cognitions (*Group A*).

3 Given the same circumstances, an individual will react emotionally or describe his/her feelings as emotions, only to the extent that s/he experiences a state of physiological arousal (*Groups A, B* and *C*).

So, according to prediction 3, physiological arousal is *necessary*. According to prediction 1, *both* the arousal *and* cognitive labelling are necessary: the nature of the arousal is unimportant, and it is how we *interpret* that arousal that is crucial (hence, the theory sometimes being called the 'two factor theory of emotion'). Our interpretation depends on the attribution we make: what *caused* that state of arousal? If we can attribute it to an injection (which has elements of both internal and external causation), then we need go no further in looking for an explanation.

Group A participants experienced arousal that didn't need to be given an *emotion-interpretation*: it could be given a perfectly adequate *physiological* one. But for Groups B and C, their arousal wasn't adequately explained; neither group could attribute it to the injection, because *either* they experienced symptoms that were different from those they had been told to expect *or* they *didn't know* what to expect. For them, their arousal was *ambiguous*; there was no ready-made explanation available (the injection). This explains their 'susceptibility' to the cognitive cues provided by the (rather extreme) behaviour of the confederate.

Schachter has demonstrated that our attributions for our emotional arousal are malleable – that is, it is possible for us to mis-label our feelings and to draw mistaken conclusions about the causes of those feelings: the *mis-attribution effect* (Ross and Nisbett, 1991). The Group B and C participants in the adrenaline experiment all attributed their arousal to something other than the drug that was the actual cause.

A classical demonstration of the mis-attribution effect is a study by Nisbett and Schachter (1966). Participants were given a sugar-pill placebo, which they were told was a drug, and would affect them in one of two ways, either (i) tremors, shaky hands, pounding heart and other symptoms associated with fear arousal, or (ii) itching, headache and other symptoms unrelated to fear. The 'drug' was given just before the participants experienced a series of intense electric shocks, and they had to indicate at what point the shocks became painful and when they became intolerable. As predicted, those in the first group reported first experiencing pain at a *higher* shock level and showed a *higher* tolerance level than those in the second group. Why? Because they *mis-attributed* their fear symptoms to the drug (when they were, in fact, induced by the shock), actually *reducing* the fear.

This suggests that, by inducing people to re-attribute their arousal from a threatening source to a neutral or less threatening one, they can be helped to function more effectively in settings that currently induce anxiety (Fiske and Taylor, 1991). So what began as a laboratory-based, experimental approach to emotional arousal – *the mis-attribution* paradigm (Valins, 1966) – has important *clinical* implications, since it provides the potential for a general model for the treatment of emotional disorders (Valins and Nisbett, 1972).

One criticism of the mis-attribution effect is that laboratory studies seem to be more successful than actual clinical investigations (Fiske and Taylor, 1991). A possible *reason* for this difference is itself to do with attribution, namely that people with real problems already have a stable explanation for their arousal and don't search for alternatives, making them less susceptible to mis-attribution. Reference to the treatment of clinical problems through re-attribution techniques is also relevant to an analysis of depression (see below).

ATTRIBUTION AND ATTITUDE CHANGE

Bem's *self-perception theory* (1967, 1972) is best understood as a major alternative to Festinger's *cognitive dissonance theory* (1957), one of the most widely debated and tested theories of attitude change. Briefly, Festinger proposed that whenever we simultaneously hold two (or more) cognitions that are psychologically inconsistent, we experience dissonance. This is a negative drive state, a state of 'psychological discomfort or tension', which motivates us to reduce it and so achieve consonance. For example, if we've acted in a way that is inconsistent with our beliefs or attitudes, we are likely to experience dissonance; one cognition will correspond to the behaviour, and the other(s) will correspond to the relevant belief or attitude. According to the theory, dissonance may be reduced by changing our cognitions, often through adding one or more (such as coming to see our behaviour in a different light). This is what is meant by attitude change.

Perhaps the most famous dissonance experiment is the '1 dollar–20 dollar' experiment (Festinger and Carlsmith, 1959), in which college students spent 30 minutes working on two extremely dull and repetitive tasks. Later, they were offered either 1 or 20 dollars to try to convince the next 'participant' (a confederate) that the tasks were interesting and enjoyable. Finally, they were asked to assess the tasks, and this was taken to indicate the extent of their *attitude change* (based on the assumption that their initial attitude was that the tasks were extremely dull and boring). As predicted by dissonance theory – but contrary to the common-sense prediction of incentive theory (Janis *et al.*, 1965) – the 1-dollar group showed the greater attitude change.

The explanation is that the large, 20-dollar incentive gave those participants ample *justification* for their counter-attitudinal behaviour, so that they experienced very little dissonance (and, therefore, little motivation to change their attitude). The 1-dollar group, on the other hand, experienced considerable dissonance (and, therefore considerable motivation to reduce it through attitude change), because they could hardly justify their counter-attitudinal behaviour in terms of the negligible reward.

Despite several successful replications of these findings, the theory has been criticized, and one of its most outspoken critics is Bem. He claims that dissonance as such is neither a necessary nor sufficient explanation, and (as a behaviourist) he rejects any reference to hypothetical, intervening variables (which, by definition, cannot be directly observed and measured: see Chapter 15).

According to self-perception theory,

> ... 'self-attributions' follow much the same logic as the attributions we make about other people. In other words, statements about our *own* mental or personal characteristics do not reflect any 'privileged access' ... but are simply *explanations* of our own observable behaviour, no different in principle from those that could be made by a fully informed outside observer. We see ourselves ... as *we* would see someone else who behaved as we did in the same situation ...
> *(Eiser, 1994)*

Any self-report of an attitude is an inference from observation of one's own behaviour and the situation in which it occurs. If the situation contains cues (for example, the offer of a large, 20-dollar reward) which imply that we might have behaved that way regardless of how we personally felt (we tell someone else how interesting the task is even though it's terribly boring), then we make no inference that our behaviour reflected our true attitude. But in the absence of obvious situational pressures (we're only offered 1 dollar), we assume that our attitudes are what our behaviour suggests they are.

In attributional terms, those in the 20-dollar group can easily make a *situational attribution* ('I did it for the money'), whereas those in the 1-dollar group have to make a *dispositional attribution* ('I did it because I must have really enjoyed it').

Bem's way of testing his theory is a form of experiment that he calls *interpersonal simulation*. He presents 'observer' participants with a summary description of the procedure used in some well-known dissonance experiments (such as the 1-dollar–20-dollar study) and then asks them to estimate the original participants' attitudinal response. Usually, this is done quite accurately, with the 'observers' being less likely to assume a match between the behaviour and attitude of the 20-dollar participants than in the case of the 1-dollar group.

The reasoning is, if a non-involved observer (simulator) can reproduce the results obtained with actual experimental participants, then it isn't necessary to believe that any internal, motivational state (i.e. dissonance) is involved in the 1-dollar group's change in attitude. They simply observe their own behaviour, find no obvious situational explanation and ask themselves, in effect, 'What must my attitude have been in order for me to describe the task as enjoyable?' Answer? 'I must have enjoyed it after all!' (This is a *dispositional attribution*.)

The responses given by real and observer participants should, according to Bem, be identical, because, in an important sense, they're *all* only observers (Shaver, 1987). However, the actual participants are observers *of their own behaviour*, while the 'observers' are assessing *someone else's behaviour*, and, according to the AOE, the former are more likely to make a *situational attribution*, and the latter a *dispositional attribution*. (Remember, this is one of the major sources of bias in the attribution process, more of which below.)

THE SELF-SERVING BIAS (SSB) AND DEPRESSION

The AOE refers to the actor's tendency to explain his/her own behaviour in terms of situational factors, and the observer's tendency to explain the actor's behaviour in terms of dispositional factors. The observer's bias corresponds to the FAE (or *lay dispositionism*; Ross and Nisbett, 1991), defined as the tendency to underestimate the impact of situational factors and to overestimate the role of dispositional factors in controlling behaviour.

Despite empirical support for the AOE (e.g. Nisbett *et al.*, 1973; Storms, 1973), it sometimes simply fails to fit the facts. If something goes wrong or we receive negative feedback about something we've done, we typically blame it on the situation (or somebody else), as predicted by the AOE. But what about *positive* feedback and achievements – do we normally attribute these to the situation as well, rather than to our own efforts and abilities? No – we usually want to take the credit for our successes (*self-enhancing bias*) while not wishing to accept the blame for our failures (*self-protecting bias*). Together, these constitute the *self-serving bias* (SSB) (Miller and Ross, 1975):

... in an attempt to maintain or improve self-esteem, self- attributions may deny responsibility (i.e. externalize) for failure and take credit for (i.e. internalize) success. It has been shown that there is a predictable pattern between the dimensions of self-esteem and self-attribution in adults ... and in children ...
(Burgner and Hewstone, 1993)

An interesting exception to this general rule is the clinically depressed person. Based on his research with dogs, Seligman (1974) explained depression in people in terms of *learned helplessness*. When faced with repeated, uncontrollable, aversive stimulation (usually electric shocks), all attempts to escape eventually stop, even after escape has become practically possible. Seligman observed many similarities between the helplessness syndrome in laboratory animals and depressed patients, including passivity in the face of stress, and a number of experiments with humans seemed to replicate the original animal findings.

However, the *helplessness model* of depression was seen as inadequate, for a variety of reasons. For example, the experience of being unable to control the outcome of one particular situation (helplessness) doesn't inevitably lead to clinical depression in most people, and some studies involving people indicated that helplessness sometimes actually *improves* performance (Davison and Neale, 2001). So what other factors are involved?

The original model was revised, the major change being the introduction of *attribution principles* (Abramson, Seligman and Teasdale, 1978; Abramson and Martin, 1981). When we experience failure, we try to explain it (just as we try to explain our successes), and this is perfectly 'normal'. What is associated with depression is a particular *pattern* of attributions, or *attributional style* – 'a tendency to make particular kinds of causal inferences, rather than others, across different situations and across time' (Metalsky and Abramson, 1981, in Fiske and Taylor, 1991).

This 'depressed attributional style' is based on three key dimensions, namely *locus* (internal or external), *stability* (stable or unstable), and *global* or *specific*. (This overlaps with Weiner's theory, outlined above, but his includes 'controllability' instead of global/specific.) The depressed person believes that his/her failure:

○ is caused by *internal* factors

○ reflects *stable*, long-term, relatively permanent, factors

○ reflects a *global*, pervasive, deficiency – that is, failure applies to all or most aspects of his/her life (see Figure 2.5).

People diagnosed as clinically depressed are more likely to display this pattern when given, for example, the *Attributional Style Questionnaire* (Seligman *et al.*, 1979). But just as importantly, the person who is *prone* to become depressed may display this attributional style. It is thought to play a mediating role between negative life events and adverse physical and mental health outcomes. When such depression-prone people experience stressors, they're more likely to develop the symptoms of depression and their self-esteem is shattered (Peterson and Seligman, 1984, in Davison and Neale, 1994).

	Successes	**Failures**
Depressed	*External* *Unstable* *Specific*	*Internal* *Stable* *Global*
Non-depressed	*Internal* *Stable* *Global*	*External* *Unstable* *Specific*

Figure 2.5 Attributional styles for success and failure in depressed and non-depressed people (Based on Abramson *et al.*, 1978; Abramson & Martin, 1981)

Davison and Neale (1994) also refer to studies that show characteristic differences in how men and women cope with stress. Men typically engage in activities that distract them from their depression, while women are less active, tending to ponder over their situation, and blaming themselves for being depressed. This reinforces the state of depression and negative mood, perhaps by interfering with attempts to solve problems.

ATTRIBUTIONAL STYLE, ACHIEVEMENT MOTIVATION AND GENDER

The gender difference in depression noted above, in particular the tendency of women to blame themselves for their problems, is very relevant for an understanding of achievement motivation (need for achievement, or nAch) (Murray, 1938; McClelland *et al.*, 1953). This is the need to be successful, especially where it entails doing as well as or better than someone else (Paludi, 1992).

According to Weiner's (1972) *cognitive attribution theory of achievement motivation*, the key difference between high- and low-achievement individuals is the different attributions they make regarding the causes of their success and failure. High nAch scorers make *internal* attributions for their success. They take charge of their own achievements – that is, they believe themselves to be the cause of their successes (because of ability and hard work). By contrast, low scorers attribute their successes to *external* causes (such as an easy exam., luck, or a mistake in the marking) and their failures to *internal* ones (such as lack of ability).

These patterns of attribution are, of course, consistent with those for non-depressed and depressed people respectively. What is particularly interesting is the finding that there are gender differences in both domains. Women are about twice as likely as men to suffer from depression – with learned helplessness, and lack of personal and political power being popular explanations for this difference (Davison and Neale, 1994). They are also more likely to make external attributions for success and internal attributions for failure. Women also tend to reverse this pattern when explaining men's successes and failures (Paludi, 1992).

This pattern of self-attribution (typical of depression-prone people and women, who are often the same) is *self-derogatory/self-derogating*. If self-attributions reflect, and affect, self-esteem, then we might expect that individuals belonging to social groups perceived as inferior (e.g. women), would have low self-esteem and a self-derogatory pattern of attributions compared with those who belong to the dominant social group (e.g. men) (Burgner and Hewstone, 1993). As we've seen, women are more likely to display a self-derogating pattern, and men are more likely to display a self-enhancing pattern (consistent with the SSB).

Burgner and Hewstone refer to studies that show these gender differences among children as young as four (such as Lochel, 1983). In their own research, they tried to extend Lochel's findings to ethnic minorities (Asians in Britain), predicting that members of such groups would show the same self-derogating pattern as girls, and that there would be an interaction between gender and ethnic background. They gave Asian and white children (mean age five years, three months) a number of (non-sex-stereotyped) tasks to perform, and then asked them to explain their successes and failures.

Lochel's original findings were confirmed, but there was *no* evidence of an ethnic difference. Both boys and girls used 'can' and 'know' attributions, but boys used these to explain their success only, while girls used them for both success and failure. This is likely to increase boys' experience of positive affect and self-esteem following success ('I succeeded because I know how to do it'), while protecting them from negative affect following failure. However, girls used these attributions less than boys to explain success and slightly more to explain failure ('I failed because I don't know how to do it'), which may account for increased negative affect and lower self-esteem following failure. According to Burgner and Hewstone (1993):

The rather depressing picture of self-enhancing attributions for boys and self-derogating attributions for girls parallels the results from the adult literature and needs to be considered within the broader context of sex-role socialization and the social divisions between the sexes.

(See also Chapter 6.)

ATTRIBUTIONAL STYLE AND MARITAL RELATIONSHIPS

If depressed people, and women and girls, display similar attributional styles when explaining their successes and failures, another domain in which such a style has been found is in married couples' relationships.

Research has shown that when members of married couples try to account for their partner's behaviour, both positive and negative, they tend to use a pattern of attribution that is associated with the overall state of the marital relationship (Bradbury and Fincham, 1990; Brehm and Kassin, 1990, in Brehm 1992).

Figure 2.6 shows the typical attributions made for happy and unhappy couples. These patterns match exactly those for depressed and non-depressed people when explaining their successes and failures (see Figure 2.5).

Figure 2.7 shows these patterns in a different way, and also indicates that the patterns of happy couples are *relationship-enhancing*, while those of unhappy couples are *distress-maintaining*.

Partner's behaviour

	Positive	**Negative**
Unhappy couples	*External* *Unstable* *Specific*	*Internal* *Stable* *Global*
Happy couples	*Internal* *Stable* *Global*	*External* *Unstable* *Specific*

Figure 2.6 Attributional styles for partner's behaviour in happily and unhappily married couples (Based on Bradbury & Fincham, 1990)

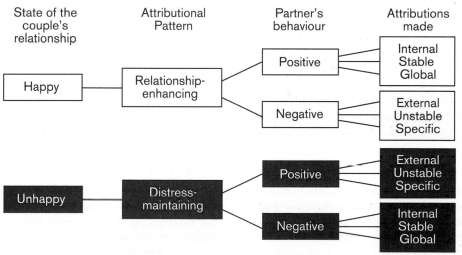

Figure 2.7 Attributions made by happy and unhappy couples (From Brehm, 1992)

Like depressed people, those involved in unhappy marriages tend to make attributions that are contrary to what the SSB implies is 'normal', while those who are happily married (like non-depressed people) show attributional styles that are consistent with it. (Strictly, the SSB refers to self-attributions, but by extension it can also be applied to others who are emotionally significant for us.)

Shaver (1985) makes the important distinction between *causal* attributions and *responsibility* attributions, the former referring to factors seen as *producing* an event (morally neutral), the latter referring to a person's perceived *accountability* for an event (not morally neutral). So, for example, you might have caused the fire (causal attribution), but it might not have been your fault, because it was an accident, or somebody else's negligence or carelessness was to blame (responsibility attribution).

Figure 2.8 Unhappy couples tend to attribute selfish motives and negative behaviour to their partner, which intensifies the unhappiness in the relationship over time

In general, *unhappy couples* are more likely to regard their partner as selfishly motivated and behaving with negative intent, in other words, they *blame* their partner for negative events, making both a causal and a responsibility attribution (Bradbury and Fincham, 1990). These findings suggest that:

... these attributions act as a screen – magnifying behaviours consistent with the state of the relationship while filtering out discrepant relationships. Over time, such a screen should intensify the initial emotional quality of the relationship. The happy should get happier, and the miserable more miserable ...
(Brehm, 1992)

However, this assumes that the kind of attributions made to the partner can produce differences in satisfaction. Is it possible that attributions are simply *produced* by the state of the relationship without having any direct influence themselves? Brehm believes that the available research raises the possibility that causal attributions for the partner's behaviour *may* have an influence on subsequent satisfaction with the relationship.

There's also considerable evidence that dissatisfaction with one's marriage leads to depression, so could distress-maintaining attributions made by unhappy couples stem from their depressed mood? Although this is unlikely, such attributions may become associated with depression over time, and are likely to increase hostile, non-cooperative behaviour at times of conflict. This is likely to increase stress which may, in turn, lead to depression (Brehm, 1992). It would certainly be very unusual if one partner's attributions about the other partner's behaviour didn't influence the former's cognitive, affective and behavioural reactions to the latter. As noted earlier, attributions can also be seen as expectancies about future behaviour, and there's considerable evidence that an observer's expectancies may influence perceptions of, and behaviour towards, the actor; which, in turn, may alter the actor's behaviour, mood and attitudes, including self-concept (Sacco *et al.*, 1993)

Sacco and Dunn (1990, in Sacco *et al.*, 1993) studied the attributions made within naturally occurring relationships involving a clinically depressed partner. In line with their prediction, they found that husbands of depressed wives (compared with those with non-depressed wives) made more dispositional attributions about negative events occurring to their wives, but, contrary to predictions, they didn't make more situational attributions for positive events. They also reported more negative affect in reaction to negative events, and indicated less marital satisfaction. While previous research focused on attributions about marital behaviours directed at the partner making the attributions (e.g. 'your spouse criticizes something you do'), here the relationship between attributions and marital distress was also found for negative events that *didn't* directly affect the partner (e.g. 'a friend acts in a hostile way towards your wife') (Sacco *et al.*, 1993).

THE SELF-SERVING BIAS AS A CULTURAL PHENOMENON

Discussing the attributional patterns of groups of people (such as depressives, women and unhappily married couples) as deviating from the SSB implies that it represents a *norm*, an expected, 'natural' way of explaining one's successes and failures (and those of one's husband or wife). However, could it be that this bias is only normal in particular cultures, rather than being a universal norm (see Chapter 8)?

According to Moghaddam *et al.* (1993), there are two assumptions about culture involved in the apparently straightforward self-serving principle:

1 people have a strong need to judge themselves favourably

2 a positive self-image is derived from biased attributions related to the *self*.

Are there entire cultures where a self-derogating (or self-effacing) attributional style (that is, where it is self-derogating/effacing only *relative* to the norm of the SSB) is normal?

When discussing cross-cultural psychology, a basic distinction is made between *individualist* and *collectivist* cultures (corresponding to western and eastern cultures respectively), and a major distinguishing feature is how much focus is put on the self relative to the in-group. If people derive much of their esteem not from individual achievement but from collective or group identity, then esteem can well be maintained by attributions serving the group rather than the individual. Kashima and Triandis (1986), for example, found that Japanese students are less likely to be self-serving than American students, reflecting the much greater emphasis on mutual support and effort towards group aims, rather than individual achievement. As predicted by the SSB, American students explained their successes more in terms of ability than they did their failures, but the Japanese students showed the *reverse* pattern: they attributed their failures to lack of ability more than they attributed their successes to ability.

In a comparison of American and Asian students (from Hong Kong, Japan, Korea, the Philippines, Vietnam, Indonesia and Malaysia), all attending a large US university, Yan and Gaier (1994) found that Americans attributed academic achievement significantly more often to ability, and they also seemed to believe that effort is more important for success than lack of effort for failure. By contrast, the Asian and South-East Asian students attributed effort much more equally to success and failure; if anything, it was seen as more important in relation to failure.

These findings are consistent with the individualist nature of the USA and the collectivist nature of eastern cultures. In the latter, the individual is not 'inner directed', but is controlled by the need not to lose face: 'Face is lost when the individual, either through his action or that of people closely related to him, fails to meet essential requirements placed upon him by virtue of the social position he occupies' (Hofstede, 1980, in Yan and Gaier, 1994).

According to Moghaddam *et al.* (1993):

The minute an examination of the self-serving bias in other cultural contexts suggests a more collective orientation, it forces consideration of the whole internal/external distinction, which lies at the heart of attribution theory . . .

If we now add a person's group as a potential unit of attribution, a new classification scheme for attribution becomes necessary, comprising four categories, as shown in Figure 2.9.

1 Internal:

Perceived cause = **Self**

2 In-group/self-inclusion:

Perceived cause = **In-group, including oneself**

3 In-group/self-exclusion:

Perceived cause = **In-group, but *not* oneself**

4 External:

Perceived cause = **An agent, external to oneself *and* in-group**

Figure 2.9 A four-way classification of the self-serving bias (Based on Moghaddam *et al.*, 1993)

This more group-oriented classification can accommodate more collectivist cultures, where the group — family, role or cultural — takes precedence over the self as a unit of analysis. It allows for the traditional SSB (e.g. internal attribution for positive events), a group-serving bias (e.g. in-group/self-exclusion attribution for positive events), or a SSB in a more collective cultural context (e.g. in-group/self-inclusion for positive events) (Moghaddam *et al.*, 1993).

According to Markus and Kitayama (1991), perceiving a boundary between the individual and the rest of the social environment (as involved in the internal/external cause distinction) is distinctly *western* in its cultural orientation. They describe this western view as one where the individual is 'an independent, self-contained, autonomous entity who (a) comprises a unique configuration of internal attributes (e.g. traits, abilities, motives and values) and (b) behaves primarily as a consequence of these internal attributes'. (This is relevant to the trait/situation debate; see Chapter 4.) Markus and Kitayama use the term *connectedness* to describe the perspective of non-western cultures (instead of the more common 'collectivist'). (See Box 2.2, page 35.)

What these observations suggest is that the internal/external distinction, the very cornerstone of attribution theory, needs to be re-examined. This isn't meant to discredit attribution, but to try to understand it as a culturally relative phenomenon (Moghaddam *et al.*, 1993).

ATTRIBUTIONAL BIAS, PREJUDICE AND DISCRIMINATION

Discussion of this more group-oriented classification of attribution is relevant to the work of Crocker and Major (1989, in Moghaddam *et al.*, 1993), who are particularly interested in the

---

Box 2.2 Allocentrism and idiocentrism

To avoid confusion between analysing attributions at the level of culture and the individual, Triandis *et al.* (1985) distinguished between 'allocentric' and 'idiocentric'.

○ *Allocentric* describes an individual who endorses *collectivist* values. Statistically, it is likely that s/he would be found in a collectivist culture, but there will also be a minority of such people living in individualist cultures.

○ *Idiocentric* describes a cultural member who endorses *individualist* values. Again, it is likely that such a person will be living in an individualist culture, but there will also be a small minority found in collectivist cultures.

According to Smith and Bond (1998), how we compare our attitudes and behaviours with those of others has long been a central topic in social psychology. However, the reasons for comparing ourselves may differ, depending on whether we endorse allocentric or idiocentric values. In an individualist cultural group, social comparison could provide feedback about our personal qualities and abilities, and so reinforce or undermine our sense of a distinctive, unique self. But in a collectivist culture, social comparison can assume different meanings depending on the target of the comparison (other members of our own group or strangers/members of other known groups).

However, most studies showing differences in attribution patterns between collectivist and individualist cultures haven't distinguished between the cultural and individual levels that Triandis *et al.* distinguished. More recently, it has been shown that individuals may define themselves as allocentric in particular life domains (such as the family) but idiocentric in others (such as work) (e.g. Matsumoto *et al.*, 1996, for Japan and the USA).

The difference might emerge through how individuals are socialized to *direct their attention in different ways* (Smith and Bond, 1998). For example, an idiocentric individual would try to identify the active element in any situation and its effect on other elements − consistent with Kelley's covariation model (see above). An allocentric person would attend to the pattern/configuration of elements. However, this way of analysing *cultural* differences in terms of how *individuals* direct their attention would be a serious oversimplification:

Culture is a system of *shared* meanings. This implies that any differences there may be in how we as individuals direct our attention, or behave in other distinctive ways, is not just a matter of something that we as individuals happen to do. It occurs because we grow up in particular groups, which teach us how to construe the world.
(Smith and Bond, 1998)

---

attributions of those who belong to groups that are potential victims of discrimination. They argue that members of stigmatized groups are constantly confronted with attributional ambiguity: they are never sure if their bad (or, indeed, their good) treatment from others is due to their own behaviour or the fact that they belong to that particular group. Such constant ambiguity can result in feelings of insecurity and frustration, but surprisingly, it is precisely this ambiguity that allows members of stigmatized groups to maintain a positive self-image. How? Instead of *internalizing* failure and other negative experiences, they can attribute them to discrimination (an *external* attribution, consistent with the SSB).

An extension of the SSB can help us understand prejudice and discrimination from the point of view of the prejudiced person (the bigot). There appears to be a *positivity bias for intimate others*, such that we grant them the benefit of the doubt by attributing positive actions to dispositional causes and negative actions to situational causes (Taylor and Koivumaki, 1976, in Pettigrew, 1979).

However, granting members of a disliked out-group the benefit of the doubt may not be so common. Taylor and Koivumaki suggest that:

A person who is disliked or hated may well be viewed as responsible for bad behaviours and not responsible for good ones. In other words, we may find a corresponding 'negativity' effect for disliked others.

The ultimate attribution error

The positivity and negativity biases illustrate *group-serving attribution* (Hewstone, 1990), and these prejudice-sustaining styles form the basis of what Pettigrew (1979) calls the *ultimate attribution error* (UAE).

Often, when race and ethnicity are involved, attributions will take the form of believing that the negative behaviours of the individual are the result of immutable, genetic characteristics of the group in general. The UAE, which Pettigrew describes as 'the bedrock assumption of racist doctrine', is the FAE when it operates at the group level (Moghaddam, 1998) 'blended' with the SSB at the group level.

ATTRIBUTION AND IMPRESSION MANAGEMENT

We noted early in this chapter that making dispositional attributions is an integral part of the process of forming impressions of others. But it would be mistaken to think that we just let others form impressions of us without our trying to influence that process. Because we usually wish to make a *favourable* impression, we try to present ourselves to others 'in such a way as to obtain favourable reactions or more generally to look good in terms of cultural ideals or their private values' (Turner, 1991).

This process of trying to influence how others see us is called *impression management* (or *self-presentation*), and two ways of trying to create favourable impressions, both explicable in terms of attributional principles, are *excuse giving* and *confessing* (Weiner, 1992). It is often in our own interests to manipulate others' perceptions of our responsibility for our behaviour, in order to control or alter their affective reactions towards us. If we've 'broken a social contract' by, for example, arriving late for an appointment, a lesson or even a date, we usually blame our lateness on something (or somebody) else. What we call 'making an excuse' involves 'substituting a false cause for a true cause', the word 'excuse' meaning 'from' (*ex*) 'cause' (*cuse*) (Weiner, 1992).

Through trying to get the other person to make an *external attribution* about our socially unacceptable behaviour, we try to reduce/prevent an angry, disapproving, response.

To ward off these negative consequences, people may withhold the truth (lie), substituting explanations they anticipate will lessen anger. These good or functional excuses relieve the transgressor of personal responsibility. That is,

excuses for a broken social contract are given to foster the perception that the wrongdoer is a 'moral person'. This certainly increases the likelihood that the relationship will be maintained ...
(Weiner, 1992)

When we confess (as when we apologise), we're actually accepting responsibility and personal blame, 'Yet this admission of responsibility has the paradoxical effect of reducing responsibility and eliciting forgiveness' (Weiner, 1992). In terms of Jones and Davis's *correspondent inference theory*, 'the behaviour and the intention that produced it are less likely to be perceived as corresponding to some underlying dispositional property of the person'.

ATTRIBUTION AND HELPING BEHAVIOUR

In one of the most famous field experiments of *bystander intervention*, Piliavin *et al.* (1969) had actors stage a collapse in a New York subway train compartment. They manipulated several variables in order to see their effect on helping behaviour, the most relevant to our discussion of attribution being whether the 'victim' who collapsed was either apparently ill or apparently drunk.

It was found that an individual who appeared to be ill was significantly more likely to receive help than one who appeared to be drunk, even when the immediate help needed was of the same kind. Piliavin *et al.* explained this finding by arguing that the costs of helping the drunk are higher (greater disgust) and the costs of not helping are lower (less self-blame and censure, since he's partly responsible for his own plight).

Figure 2.10 Getting drunk is perceived as a controllable cause of need, and alcoholics are often seen as the most responsible for their own predicament

One of the major determinants of the decision to go to the aid of another person is the *perceived cause* of the need for help (Weiner, 1992). Piliavin *et al.* proposed this explanation of the greater help received by the ill victim as an 'after-the-fact interpretation' (they didn't predict this outcome). But is there any evidence that perceived causes are an element in the 'cost–reward matrix' involved in the decision to help or not to help?

A common experimental procedure is for a student to receive a request for academic help from a supposed classmate, with the reasons for the request being manipulated. One early study (Berkowitz, 1969) involved two reasons: experimenter error (*external locus*) or the classmate taking it easy (*internal locus*). More help was offered in the former case. Barnes *et al.* (1979) varied two dimensions of causality independently:

1 *controllability* – the classmate asked to borrow notes either because of low ability (uncontrollable) or lack of effort (controllable)

2 *stability*.

The uncontrollable cause was much more likely to elicit help, especially if this was seen as a stable characteristic. Since *both* controllability and stability involve an internal locus, the results suggest that *controllability* is the crucial variable (rather than internal locus).

As applied to the Piliavin *et al.* study, getting drunk is perceived as a controllable cause of a need – people typically are held responsible for their alcohol consumption. When alcoholics are rated along with other stigmatized groups (such as the mentally ill, homosexuals and obese people) they are often seen as the most responsible for their own predicament (Weiner, 1992). This is highlighted in campaigns against drink-driving. Although the driver clearly isn't *intentionally* harming his/her victim, because the harm is a consequence of a freely chosen, controllable act, s/he is held responsible – both legally and morally – for those consequences.

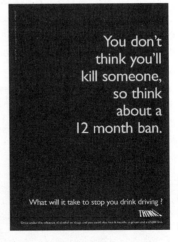

Figure 2.11 Drink-drivers are held legally and morally responsible for the consequences of their actions

According to Weiner (1992), if witnesses regard the behaviour of the victim as uncontrollable (e.g. the victim is ill), they are more likely to respond sympathetically, which, in turn, makes it more likely that they will help. But if they consider it to be controllable (the victim is drunk), they are more likely to respond angrily, and help is less likely to be forthcoming.

Clearly, not all forms of illness will be seen as equally uncontrollable, and some may be seen as highly controllable (i.e. preventable), as in the case of lung cancer or heart disease, which are linked to smoking. There is an ongoing debate in the UK concerning the rights and wrongs of accepting patients for heart surgery (and other forms of treatment for major illnesses) when they continue to smoke or otherwise reduce the chances of the treatment being successful.

While these are clearly *ethical* issues, an understanding of the cognitive and affective processes involved when people debate them may throw light on the opinions expressed and the conclusions reached. Prominent among those cognitive processes are the *attributions* made concerning causation, controllability and responsibility.

SUMMARY

○ The *attribution process* refers to the *naïve psychologist's* attempt to explain behaviour in terms of *dispositional/personal* (internal) or *situational/environmental* (external) causes.

○ *Attribution theory* refers to the attempt by psychologists to understand the attribution process. It is the process itself (and the 'perceived' cause), rather than its accuracy ('the' cause), that they're interested in.

○ Attribution theory comprises a collection of diverse theoretical traditions, notably Heider's *common-sense psychology*, Jones and Davis's *correspondent inference theory*, Kelley's *covariation model*, Schachter's *cognitive labelling theory*, Bem's *self-perception theory*, and Weiner's *motivational theory of attribution*.

○ Attribution principles have been applied to interpersonal perception, the subjective experience of emotion, attitude change, self-attributions, impression management, achievement motivation, helping behaviour, prejudice, depression, and marital relationships.

○ According to Jones and Davis, an attribution or inference is *correspondent* when the disposition attributed to an actor 'corresponds' to the behaviour from which it is inferred.

○ A precondition for a correspondent inference is the attribution of *intentionality*, which, in turn, depends on *knowledge* that the act would have the observed effects and the *ability* to produce them.

○ According to Kelley, the three kinds of causal information people use to arrive at an internal or external attribution, are *consensus*, *distinctiveness* and *consistency*. *Causal schemata* are also used to supplement these.

○ Attribution theory is criticized for portraying naïve scientists as being much more rational and logical than they really are. *Attributional biases*, such as the FAE, AOE and SSB, seem to provide a better descriptive analysis of causal attribution.

○ According to Schachter, emotional experience depends on *both* physiological changes *and* on how these are interpreted. The famous 'adrenaline' experiment shows that we have to 'decide' which particular emotion we're feeling, the label we give to our arousal depending on what we *attribute* that arousal to.

○ An important implication of Schachter's theory is the *mis-attribution effect*, which, in turn, has therapeutic/clinical implications, especially in the treatment of anxiety disorders.

O Bem's *self-perception theory* is a major alternative to Festinger's *cognitive dissonance theory* of attitude change. It claims that '*self-attributions*' are explanations of our own observable behaviour, essentially the same as attributions we make about *others*.

O An exception to the SSB is the person who is *clinically depressed*. The earlier *helplessness model* of depression was replaced by a model based on attributional principles, namely an *attributional style*, in which failures are explained in terms of *internal*, *stable* and *global factors*.

O This *self-derogatory/self-derogating* pattern of self-attribution is also more common among females in general, and women are also more likely to be depressed and to score low on nAch.

O Happily married couples show *relationship-enhancing*, and unhappily married couples *distress-maintaining* patterns of attribution when explaining their partner's positive and negative behaviour. Unhappy couples are also more likely to *blame* their partner (*responsibility attribution*).

O The SSB may be a characteristic of *individualist* cultures, and not a universal norm. Indeed, the whole internal/external cause distinction is distinctly *western* in its cultural orientation.

O Members of minority groups can maintain a positive self-image by attributing their failures to discrimination and other *external* factors.

O A *negativity effect* applied to whole groups forms the basis of the UAE, the fundamental assumption of racist doctrine.

O Two forms of *impression management/self-presentation* are *excuse giving* and *confessing*. Both involve the attempt to lead the other person to make an external attribution about our socially unacceptable behaviour, thus reducing our personal responsibility.

O One of the major influences on people's decision to offer help to another person is the *perceived cause* of the need for help, with *controllability* being a crucial variable.

Useful websites

- O http://www.psych.purdue.edu/~esmith/scarch.html
- O http://www.vcu.edu/hasweb/psy/faculty/fors/ratt1.html
- O http://www.midcoast.com.au/~lars/Attribution_Bias
- O http://www.as.wvu.edu/~sbb/comm221/chapters/attrib.htm

Recommended reading

Gross, R. (2003) *Key Studies in Psychology* (4th edn) (Chapter 11 on the actor–observer effect). London: Hodder & Stoughton.

Ross, L. and Nisbett, R.E. (1991) *The Person and the Situation: Perspectives of Social Psychology* (especially Chapter 3). New York: McGraw-Hill.

Weiner, B. (1992) *Human Motivation: Metaphors, Theories and Research* (especially Chapters 6 and 7). Newbury Park, CA: Sage.

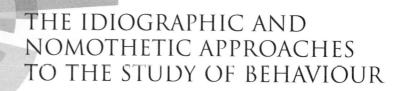

THE IDIOGRAPHIC AND NOMOTHETIC APPROACHES TO THE STUDY OF BEHAVIOUR

PSYCHOLOGY: THE STUDY OF INDIVIDUALS OR THE STUDY OF PEOPLE?

Of all the methods traditionally used by psychologists to study human beings, the case study is the one most often criticized for being unscientific (or the *least* scientific). The reason usually given is that, since only one 'case' is being studied, it isn't possible to *generalize* the results. In other words, we can't base our theories of what *people* are like on the study of *individuals*.

According to the same argument, the *experiment* is the most powerful method of research, partly because it *does* allow us to generalize (notwithstanding the criticisms of artificiality, and so on). This is possible only because the characteristics of *particular* subjects/participants, being controlled through the use of experimental design, are irrelevant: it is *group averages* that are statistically analysed and that the investigator is interested in, not *individual performance*.

Consequently, if psychologists want to find out about *people*, the last thing they should do is study … *people*! This might seem like an absurd conclusion to draw, but is it also an inevitable one?

A number of points need to be made here.

○ Imagine a chemist refusing to generalize the results of an investigation on the grounds that the particular sample of the chemical used wasn't typical or representative. However bizarre that may sound, it's the equivalent of the situation with regard to the psychological case study.

○ It follows from this first point that human beings are different from chemicals (and other aspects of the physical world) in at least one major respect, namely they aren't all identical or interchangeable but display great variability and variety.

○ Different psychologists have interpreted (and studied) the nature and extent of this variability and variety in different ways. A convenient way of identifying these different approaches is to quote Kluckhohn and Murray (1953): 'Every man is in certain respects like all other men, like some other men, and like no other men.'

How we are *all like each other* is a way of referring to *general psychology*, the study of basic psychological processes, with the emphasis very much on the *process* (such as memory, perception and learning). It's almost as if the process occurs in some disembodied way, with the memorizer, perceiver or learner being almost irrelevant, or at least unnecessary, for an understanding of the process under investigation. This is part of what goes on in the name of psychology, so it must be to do with the study of people, mustn't it?

The nomothetic approach

Ways in which we are like *some* other human beings is the subject matter of *individual differences*. While this approach acknowledges that humans are definitely not like chemicals, it also claims that there's only a limited, relatively small number of ways in which people differ from each other, sometimes referred to as *group norms*. Examples include personality, intelligence, age, gender, and ethnic and cultural background.

This way of studying people is called the *nomothetic approach* (from the Greek *nomos*, meaning 'law'). If psychologists can establish the ways in which we're like *some* others, then they can also tell us how we're *different from* others – these are two sides of the same coin. In either case, people are *compared* with each other, and this is usually done using *psychometric tests*. The results of these tests are then analysed using a statistical technique called *factor analysis*, which is used to identify the basic factors or dimensions that constitute personality, intelligence etc. Once these have been identified, the basis for comparing people with each other has been established. Factor-analytic theories of intelligence include Spearman's *two-factor theory* (1904, 1927), Burt's (1949, 1955) and Vernon's (1950) *hierarchical model*, Thurstone's *primary mental abilities* (1938), and Guilford's *structure of intellect* (1959). Eysenck (1953, 1965) and Cattell (1965) are probably the best-known factor-analytic personality theorists.

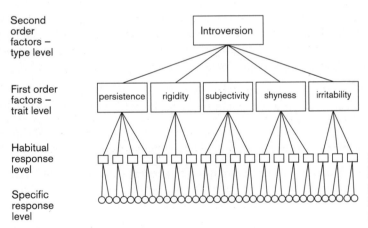

Figure 3.1 Eysenck's hierarchical model of personality in relation to the introversion dimension (After Eysenck, 1953)

According to Jones and Elcock (2001):

An important effect of the use of such statistical methods [factor analysis] on scores from groups of subjects was to create an idealized 'average' person. Psychology was to become the scientific investigation of such hypothesized average 'individuals', rather than investigating individuals themselves.

The idiographic approach

Ways in which we are *unlike anyone else* is the subject matter of those psychologists who adopt an *idiographic approach* (from the Greek *idios*, meaning 'own' or 'private'). This is the study of *individual norms*, of people as unique individuals. Gordon Allport (1937, 1961) is arguably the main advocate of an idiographic approach. The humanistic personality theories of Maslow (1954, 1968) and Rogers (1951, 1961), and Kelly's (1955) *personal construct theory* (PCT; see Chapters 1 and 12) also represent this approach and embody many of its basic principles and assumptions.

Some questions for consideration

1 Are the nomothetic and idiographic approaches mutually exclusive – that is, do we have to choose between them? Are there any theories of personality that embody *both* approaches?

2 Does it make sense to talk about a totally unique person, someone whose personality has *nothing* in common with that of any other?

3 Must we agree with Allport (1937) that, since all science is nomothetic, and since psychology should be concerned with the study of individuals, therefore psychology cannot be a science?

4 Have we found a solution to the riddle concerning the study of people (that psychologists, in order to learn about people, shouldn't study people)? If we distinguish between *people as individuals* and *people as groups*, then perhaps we have; we have to be clear whether our aim is to find out about this *particular* person, or how this person *compares with others*. The *idiographic* approach takes *the individual* as its basic unit of analysis, while for the *nomothetic* approach it is *groups of individuals* (see Figure 3.2, page 46). In the former, the data that are obtained represent a sample of the individual's total set ('population') of emotions, cognitions, personality traits, and so on, while in the latter, the obtained data are a specified trait or behaviour as measured in a sample of individuals drawn from some larger population of individuals. It is the difference between a *population of many* (nomothetic) and a *population of one* (idiographic).

If the answers to the first question (1) are 'no' and 'yes' respectively, and if the answer to the second (2) is 'no', then we should regard the process of studying individuals *as individuals* as being inseparable from the process of *comparing individuals* with each other. By the same token, if the answer to the third question (3) is 'no', then we should be willing to accept that generalizing from the individual case, as well as generalizing *about the same individual*, are legitimate scientific activities: the nomothetic and idiographic approaches are compatible with each other.

HISTORICAL BACKGROUND

The idiographic/nomothetic distinction is related to another distinction made, independently, by two nineteenth-century German philosophers, Dilthey and Windelband, between two kinds of science:

○ the *Naturwissenschaften* (natural sciences), such as physics and chemistry, aim to establish general laws, allowing predictions based on statements about cause-and-effect relationships

○ the *Geisteswissenschaften* ('moral sciences'), such as philosophy, the humanities, history, biography and literary criticism, and 'social science', involve *Verstehen*, an intuitive, empathic understanding (see Figure 3.3, page 47).

The natural sciences are concerned with the natural world, and so quite appropriately *explain* it in terms of 'natural laws' ('laws of nature'), and analyse it into elements. But the moral or human sciences require an *understanding* of human mental activity (i.e.

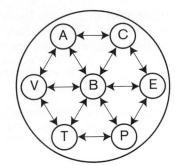

a) Basic unit of study = the individual

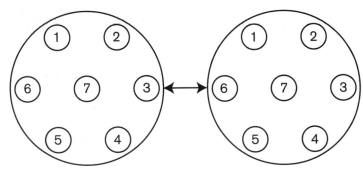

b) Basic unit of study = the group

Figure 3.2 Differences in the kind of generalization involved in the (a) idiographic and (b) nomothetic approaches. In the idiographic approach, data collected represent samples from an individual's total population of characteristics (A, attitudes; B, behaviour; C, cognition; E, emotion; P, physiological make-up; T, traits; V, values), and the norms that operate are **individual norms** (generalizing *within* the individual). In the nomothetic approach, data collected represent either (i) samples from the total population of the characteristic in question (e.g. 'How do high E (extroversion) scorers compare with low E scorers on some task?'), or (ii) samples from the total population of performance on some task with individual differences held constant. In both cases, this gives **group norms** (generalizing *across or between* individuals).

consciousness), stressing the inner unity of individual life and the person as an articulated whole (Valentine, 1992). Rather than treating the individual case as incidental to the discovery of general laws, the social sciences focus primarily on the particular (whether this be a person, historical event, or literary work). Windelband, together with another German, Rickert, went on to argue that all the disciplines concerned with 'man and his works' should not – and by their very nature cannot – generalize, but must devote themselves to the understanding of each particular case (Holt, 1967). Corresponding to the distinction between the natural and human sciences is that between a *variable-centred* and *person-centred* approach (Bem, 1983; Mischel, 1983), and a *normative* ('compared with others') and *ipsative* ('compared with the self') approach (Cattell, 1944) respectively (see Figure 3.3, page 47).

According to Holt (1967), there are a number of false beliefs, still widely held, about the nomothetic/idiographic distinction. He points out that (i) these are false beliefs as held by those of an idiographic persuasion, and (ii) a distinction is commonly made between *personology* (the psychology of personality) and *differential psychology* (the psychology of individual differences). These correspond to the idiographic and nomothetic approaches respectively.

The goal of personology is understanding, while that of nomothetic science is prediction and control

According to Holt (1967), all the highly developed sciences aim at prediction and control *through* understanding, and these three goals cannot be separated. He argues that:

Windelband/Dilthey

**Natural Sciences
(Naturwissenschaften)**

**Moral (human) Sciences
(Geisteswissenschaften)**

General laws
Nomothetic

Verstehen
Idiographic

*Group norms
(Differential
psychology/Individual
differences)*

Stern (1921)

Allport (1937)

*Individual norms
(Personology/Psychology
of personality)*

Normative

Cattell (1944)

Ipsative

Variable-centred

Bem (1983)

Mischel (1983)

Person-centred

Figure 3.3 The nomothetic-idiographic distinction and its relationship to other, corresponding distinctions

Figure 3.4 The nomothetic and idiographic distinction is related to the distinction made in the nineteenth century between *Naturwissenschaften* (natural sciences) and *Geisteswissenschaften* (moral sciences), which can be recognised as the distinction between the scientist in the laboratory and the philosopher in his/her armchair

Most scientists, as contrasted with technologists, are themselves more motivated by the need to figure things out, to develop good theories and workable models that make nature intelligible, and less concerned with the ultimate payoff, the applied benefits of prediction and control that understanding makes possible . . .

Holt believes that many psychologists, based on this misconception of natural science as totally rigorous, objective and machine-like, try to emulate this nomothetic approach. It is because of, rather than despite, the 'intrinsically difficult and ambiguity-ridden' nature of psychology that this view of natural science is so appealing, especially to behaviourist psychologists (see Chapters 11 and 15). But at the 'opposite extreme' lies *Verstehen* (see above), an attempt to know something from the inside, by non-intellectual means, as directly as possible, through trying to gain an empathic feeling for it. This is *non-explanatory*, 'a subjective effect properly aimed at by artists, not scientists' (Holt, 1967).

But even accepting Holt's argument regarding the importance of understanding in natural science, and the important difference between 'scientific' and 'non-scientific' understanding, isn't this only half the story? Does it necessarily follow that prediction and control are appropriate aims for psychology (as they clearly are for physics and chemistry, along with explanation/understanding)?

George Miller (1969) for one believes that control is *inappropriate*, at least in the sense of one person (the experimenter/investigator/therapist) assuming a powerful, directing, role in relation to another (subject/patient) (see Chapter 10). Critics of mainstream psychology (especially Skinner's *radical behaviourism*; see Chapter 15) see the attempt to apply principles and methods derived from the laboratory study of rats and pigeons to human behaviour as the ultimate kind of mechanistic, dehumanizing approach (e.g. Shotter, 1975: Heather, 1976). Not only is *understanding* the appropriate aim for psychology (as opposed to control), but Miller argues that *self*-understanding is what psychology should be striving to provide people with. This is what he means when he advocates 'giving psychology away'. Attempts to realize these aims are perhaps best seen in psychotherapy, much of which is an attempt to change individuals' perception of themselves and increase their self-understanding/insight. It also aims at increasing autonomy and independence (Lindley, 1987, in Fairbairn, 1987). *Taking control of one's own life* is a very different form of control compared with its meaning in the natural sciences (see Gross, 2003).

The proper methods of personology are intuition and empathy, which have no place in natural science

Holt (1967) rejects this claim by pointing out that *all* scientists make use of intuition and empathy as part of the most exciting and creative phase of their work, namely when deciding what to study, what variables to control, what empirical strategies to use, and when making discoveries within the structure of empirical data. To the extent that such processes are inevitably involved in science, which is, first and foremost, a human activity, no science can be thought of as wholly objective (see Chapters 1 and 11). The failure to recognize the role of these processes, and the belief in the 'objective truth' produced by the use of the 'scientific method', can result in theories and explanations that can work to the detriment of certain individuals and social groups (as in the 'race and IQ debate'; see Chapter 10).

While 'hard science' may appear softer when the role of intuition is acknowledged, it is also nomothetic psychology that has been most guilty of the 'crimes' of racism, ethnocentrism and sexism (see Chapters 6 and 8).

The concepts of personology must be individualized, not generalized as are the concepts of natural science

General laws aren't possible in personology, because its subject matter is unique individuals that have no place in natural science

These two beliefs are dealt with together, because they lie at the very heart of the nomothetic/idiographic debate. They relate to two fundamental questions.

○ Does it make sense to talk about a wholly unique individual?

○ What is the relationship between individual cases and general laws/principles in scientific practice?

THE WHOLLY UNIQUE INDIVIDUAL

Allport (1961) distinguished between three types of personal traits or dispositions: *cardinal, central* and *secondary*. Briefly, *cardinal traits* refer to a particular, all-pervading disposition (for example, greed, ambition or lust) that dictates and directs almost all of an individual's behaviour. In practice, these are very rare. *Central traits* are the basic building blocks that make up the core of the personality and constitute the individual's characteristic ways of dealing with the world (such as honest, loving, happy-go-lucky). A surprisingly small number of these is usually sufficient to capture the essence of a person. *Secondary traits* are less consistent and influential than central traits, and refer to tastes, preferences, and so on, that may change quite quickly and don't define 'the person' as central traits do.

These *individual traits* are peculiar (idiosyncratic) to each person, in at least three senses.

1 A trait that's central for one person may only be secondary for another, and irrelevant for a third. What makes a trait central or secondary isn't what it *is*, but how often and how strongly it influences the person's behaviour (Carver and Scheier, 1992).

2 Some traits are possessed by only one person; indeed, there may be as many separate traits as there are people.

3 Even if two different people are given (for convenience) the same descriptive label (for example, 'aggressive'), it may not *mean* the same for the individuals concerned, and to that extent, it is *not* the same trait.

For Allport, since personality dispositions reflect the subtle shadings that distinguish a particular individual from all others, they must often be described at length (for example, 'little Susan has a peculiar anxious helpfulness all her own') instead of by a single label ('helpful'). What all this means is that it's very difficult to compare people:

Suppose you wish to select a roommate or a wife or a husband, or simply to pick out a suitable birthday gift for your mother. Your knowledge of mankind in general will not help you very much ... [Any given individual] is a unique creation of the forces of nature. There was never a person just like him and there will never be again ... To develop a science of personality we must accept this fact.
(Allport, 1961)

While the idiographic approach contends that people aren't comparable (everyone is, in effect, on a 'different scale'), comparing people in terms of a specified number of traits or dimensions (in order to determine individual differences) is precisely what the nomothetic approach involves. According to this view, traits *have the same psychological meaning* for everyone, so that people only differ in the extent to which the trait is present. For example, everyone is more or less introverted, which means that everyone will score somewhere on the introversion–extroversion scale: the difference between individuals is one of degree only (*a quantitative difference*). By contrast, the idiographic approach sees differences between people as *qualitative* (a difference in kind).

Allport himself recognized that people *can* be compared with each other, but in terms of *common traits* (as distinct from individual traits). Although every person is unique, there are basic modes of adjustment that are applicable to *all* members of a particular cultural, ethnic or linguistic group. These basic modes of adjustment are called common traits, and are

... those aspects of personality in respect to which most people within a given culture can be profitably compared ... [and are] indispensable whenever we undertake to study personality by scales, tests, ratings, or any other comparative method.
(Allport, 1961)

At best, they can only provide a rough approximation to any particular personality. For example, many individuals are predominantly outgoing or shy, yet

... there are endless varieties of dominators, leaders, aggressors, followers, yielders, and timid souls ... When we designate Tom and Ted both as *aggressive*, we do not mean that their aggression is identical in kind. Common speech is a poor guide to psychological subtleties.
(Allport, 1961)

The nomothetic approach, for Allport, can only portray human personality in an oversimplified way: even the traits that people seem to share with one another always have a personal flavour that differs from individual to individual. So how valid is the notion of a wholly unique person?

According to Holt (1967), to describe an individual trait we either have to create a new word (neologism) for each unique trait, or we use a unique configuration of already existing words. While the former would make ordinary communication impossible, let alone science, the latter is a concealed form of nomothesis, a 'fallacious attempt to capture something ineffably individual by a complex net of general concepts' (Allport, 1937, quoted in Holt, 1967).

Disagreement between Allport and those of a nomothetic persuasion isn't so much to do with whether or not they believe in the idea of uniqueness, but rather *how it is defined*. Eysenck, for example, sees uniqueness as reflecting a *unique combination* of levels on trait dimensions, with the dimensions themselves being the same for all: 'To the scientist, the unique individual is simply the point of inter-section of a number of quantitative variables' (Eysenck, 1953).

As we have seen, this is a definition of uniqueness in terms of *common* traits. But, for Allport, this is a contradiction in terms, since only *individual* traits capture the individuality of individuals. Agreeing with Holt, Brody (1988, in Eysenck, 1994) argues that:

If the trait applies only to one person, then it cannot be described in terms that apply to more than one person. This would require one to invent a new language to describe each person or, perhaps, to develop the skills of a poet to describe an individual.

According to Krahé (1992), the idiographic claim that there are unique traits that apply to only one individual is undoubtedly false, if taken literally. Traits are defined as differential constructs referring to a person's position on a trait dimension relative to others. But at the other extreme, Krahé believes that the traditional (nomothetic) view of traits as explanatory constructs that apply to everyone, is equally misguided.

Holt believes that the nomothetic/idiographic distinction is based on a *false dichotomy*. All descriptions involve some degree of generalization, so that when we describe an individual case, there is always (at least implicitly) a comparison being made with other instances of the category or class to which the individual belongs. To describe *this* person, we must already have (and be applying) our *concept of a person*. If our concept of a person includes their uniqueness, this at least is something that everyone has in common and is perfectly consistent with Eysenck's (nomothetic) concept of uniqueness. Indeed, could we even *recognize* a person who was totally unlike any other, in any respect, *as a person*?

THE RELATIONSHIP BETWEEN INDIVIDUAL CASES AND GENERAL PRINCIPLES

When Windelband distinguished between *Naturwissenschaften* and *Geisteswissenschaften* in 1894, the mechanistic science of the time operated on the principle that science doesn't deal with individual cases. The individual case isn't lawful, since laws were seen as empirical regularities; an *average* is the only fact and all deviations from it are merely errors (Holt, 1967). Since it isn't possible to generalize from a single case, and since the aim of science is to formulate general laws and principles, the study of single cases isn't a valid part of scientific practice.

But is this a valid view of science as it is practised today? Are there different senses in which generalization can take place? Given the false dichotomy between the nomothetic and idiographic approaches, how should we understand the relationship between individual cases and general laws or principles?

Finding the general in the particular

Holt (1967) himself pointed out that, while we cannot carry out the *complete* scientific process by the study of one individual,

> . . . in certain of the disciplines concerned with man, from anatomy to sensory psychology, it has usually been assumed that the phenomena being studied are so universal that they can be located for study in any single person . . .

However, no matter how intensively prolonged, objective and well controlled the study of a single case may be, we can never be sure to what extent the findings will apply to other people. Unless and until the investigation is repeated with an adequate sample, we cannot know how 'typical' the single case actually is. This is the logic behind the study by psychologists of *groups* of people, so that personality and other individual differences don't 'get in the way' of the key individual variable under investigation. But while the reasons behind this practice may be clear, are they necessarily valid?

The objections from an idiographic theorist like Allport should now be obvious, but a nomothetic theorist such as Eysenck will also object, although for very different reasons. Precisely because he emphasizes the basic dimensions of personality, in terms of which every person can be compared, he believes that any investigation that attempts to exclude them or render them irrelevant (through rigorous use of experimental design) is inadequate. For example:

O main experimental effects apply only to *means*, preventing predictions about individual cases

O any theories or explanations based on such studies may only have very limited validity – that is, they may not generalize to samples with particular scores on important personality dimensions

O failure to take individual differences into account may result in main experimental effects being swamped or obscured.

Eysenck (1966) sees the dimensional approach (or typologies; see above) as a compromise between (i) the false extremes of the experimentalist, who seeks to establish general functional relationships (the nomothetic approach), where personality differences are largely excluded, and (ii) the idiographic personality theorist, who 'embraces the concept of the individual so whole-heartedly that it leaves no room for scientific generalization, laws, or even predictability of conduct' (Eysenck, 1966, in Valentine, 1992).

Single-subject designs are OK

The distinction between single case and group studies may be another false dichotomy. An individual case can be, and often is, the subject of scientific investigation. Where data from individual subjects are seen as reliable and representative, single-subject designs are considered acceptable (Valentine, 1992).

From the idiographic perspective, the very notion of an individual being 'representative' is contentious (because it implies the opposite of unique). But the fact that the study of individual cases goes on at all within 'mainstream', nomothetic psychology indicates that the study of individuals may not, in and of itself, be incompatible with the aim of psychological science to *generalize* about behaviour.

Indeed, for Thorngate (1986, in Hilliard, 1993), the study of averages is often ill-suited to providing information about what people 'in general' do, since it typically cancels out systematic patterns in individual persons. (This is similar to Eysenck's criticism of experimental psychology, discussed above, regarding the irrelevance of individual differences.) Rather than searching for nomothetic laws based on averaged data, their discovery requires a strategy in which the uniqueness of individuals is preserved. As Thorngate says:

> To find out what people do in general, we must first discover what each person does in particular, then determine what, if anything, these particulars have in common ... Nomothetic laws lie at the intersection of idiographic laws; the former can be discovered only after we find the latter.

In other words, the generality of the findings wouldn't be determined through group aggregates (finding the average for a large number of individuals), but *by replication on a case-by-case basis*. Thorngate is arguing that the two approaches are complementary and interdependent. According to Hilliard (1993):

> Although single-case methodology has been identified with an exclusive idiographic focus in the minds of many, this identification is simply not warranted. Most single-case research clearly involves determining the generality across subjects of the relationships uncovered at the individual, or idiographic, level ...

Hilliard gives as a prime example of such methodology Skinner's use of single-case research to study the principles of operant conditioning (see Box 3.1, page 53).

Sometimes, single cases may be all that's available to the investigator, as in neuropsychology, where patients who suffer brain injury and disease are *patients* first, and *subjects/participants* second. While they may be intensely interesting in themselves, they are usually studied for what they can tell us about the *normal* functioning of the brain and nervous system. Unless an adequate baseline for comparison is provided, such as the patient's performance before the illness/injury, or scores from the normal population on standardized tests, the results are scientifically uninterpretable. Without replication, it is

Box 3.1 Skinner's single-subject experimental design

Skinner typically studied the behaviour of *one subject* at a time. 'Experimental' denotes that only *one variable* is manipulated at a time. This allowed him to uncover causal (functional) relationships. Behaviourist researchers wish to detect principles that have generality – that is, cover a large number of cases and situations. The goal of research isn't to discover idiosyncratic information about the particular situation being studied, but general principles that allow accurate prediction and control in a wide variety of situations.

Part of Skinner's rationale for using individual organisms was that *groups don't behave* – only individuals do. Therefore, it makes more sense to study single organisms. Although general principles may apply to a group, the specifics of these principles may vary between organisms.

The natural/physical sciences *don't* face the problem of the individuality of the entities under study, but this isn't true for most biological entities. An appropriate research design in behavioural science must account for individual differences in a way that still produces general principles. Skinner argued that the single-subject design achieves this goal. Derived measures such as group averages are artificial contrivances that obscure important information about actual behaviour. The extent to which principles generally hold is discovered through replications with other single subjects.

One feature of such research is the fact that the individual rat or pigeon acts as its own control, since its behaviour is measured before, during and after the reinforcement contingencies are applied.

(Based on O'Donohue and Ferguson, 2001)

Figure 3.5 The individual pigeon acts as its own control in the Skinner Box and represents single-case research

difficult to know if the results are generalizable: such data are insufficient to establish general laws. However, even if the study of individual cases doesn't allow the *testing* of hypotheses, it may at least help to *formulate* them (Valentine, 1992).

Generalizing within the individual

The results from studies of individuals may also offer the potential for generalizing to other attributes or behavioural characteristics *of the individual being studied*. We noted earlier that idiographic research is aimed at generalizing *within* the individual, while nomothetic research seeks to generalize *across* individuals. According to Krahé (1992), there's no inherent conflict between these aims – they are complementary, rather than mutually exclusive, research strategies:

Nomothetic procedures are important for investigating individual differences and differences in performance among groups of subjects, but provide no information on processes within individuals. Idiographic approaches, on the other hand, provide information about processes within individuals, but provide no information on individual differences or on the generality of findings across individuals. Thus, each procedure has its advantages and limitations, and neither is a substitute for the other.
(Epstein, 1983, in Krahé, 1992)

We saw earlier that the nineteenth-century scientific belief that the average is the only fact, and that the individual case isn't lawful, led Windelband to make the distinction between the natural and 'human' sciences. It is from this distinction that the whole nomothetic/idiographic debate emanates. Logically, there's no reason to equate 'generalization' with the study of 'groups', although that's exactly what the nomothetic approach does. Allport was interested in the study of *individual norms* (as distinct from *group norms*), but both involve 'going beyond' the data that have actually been collected and making predictions about future 'performance'. This can either be the future performance of other individuals not included in the sample studied (group norms/nomothetic approach), or the future performance of the same individual (individual norms/idiographic approach).

According to Hilliard (1993), there has been a recent widespread resurgence of interest in single-case designs within psychotherapy research. Various terms are used for such designs, including: *single case*, *N of 1*, *case study*, *small N*, *idiographic*, *intensive*, *discovery-oriented*, *intrasubject* and *time-series*. These can be confusing, and single-case research is best viewed as a sub-class of *intrasubject* research, in which the focus is on the unfolding, over time, of variables within individual subjects.

Consistent with this revival is the view that it is perfectly possible to apply systematic, reliable, quantitative or experimental methods to the study of individual cases. For example, factor analysis can be applied to individual as well as to group data (Krahé, 1992). Not only is this a scientifically valid approach, but there has been a proliferation of quantitative and experimental studies of the single case (Runyan, 1983, in Krahé, 1992).

RECONCILING THE NOMOTHETIC/IDIOGRAPHIC APPROACHES

From the preceding discussion, it seems that psychologists are increasingly coming to believe that the two approaches, far from being opposed and mutually exclusive, are in fact complementary and interdependent. As Krahé (1992) puts it:

Thus, there seems to be a growing consensus that it is possible, in principle, for idiographic and nomothetic approaches to join forces so as to contribute to a more comprehensive analysis of the issues of personality psychology ...

Even Allport himself, the leading advocate of the uniqueness of the individual, didn't reject the nomothetic approach out of hand. For example, when discussing the nature of psychology as a science, he says that:

Science aims to achieve powers of understanding, prediction and control above the level of unaided common sense. From this point of view it becomes apparent that only by taking adequate account of the individual's total pattern of life can we achieve the *aims* of science. Knowledge of general laws . . . quantitative assessments and correlational procedures are all helpful: but with this conceptual (nomothetic) knowledge must be blended a shrewd diagnosis of trends within an individual . . . Unless such idiographic (particular) knowledge is fused with nomothetic (universal) knowledge, we shall not achieve the *aims* of science, however closely we imitate the methods of the natural and mathematical sciences.
(Allport, 1960)

Also related to the aims of science, Jaccard and Dittus (1990, in Krahé, 1992) argue that a strictly idiographic approach *isn't* directly opposed to the identification and development of universal laws of human behaviour. The idiographic researcher, like the nomothetic, is interested in *explaining* behaviour, and to do this *both* seek a general theoretical framework that specifies the constructs that should be focused upon and the types of relationship expected among these concepts. The essential difference between them is that one applies the framework to *a single person*, while the other applies it to *people in general*. They share the same scientific aim.

Both Allport and Windelband made it very clear that one and the same issue can, in principle, be considered either from an idiographic or nomothetic perspective, depending on the nature of the question under investigation (Krahé, 1992). According to Epstein (1983, in Krahé, 1992), the two approaches 'do not present different solutions to the same problem but solutions to different problems'. Lamiell's (1981, 1982, 1987) *idiothetic* approach is an attempt to integrate the aims of both approaches.

IDIOGRAPHIC METHODS, OLD AND NEW

We began the chapter by pointing out the limitations (as judged from a nomothetic point of view) of the *case study*. A standard criticism of Freud's psychoanalytic theory is that he relied on the case study for the collection of his 'data'. But we have also seen that this method is central to neuropsychology. Perhaps it isn't the case study method itself that is of limited scientific value, but rather the use researchers make of it, the data that are obtained, and the resulting theories and hypotheses.

A more specific idiographic method is the *Q-sort*, originally devised and developed by Butler and Haigh (1954) and Stephenson (1953), but best known as it was used by Carl Rogers for assessing an individual's self-concept, especially in the context of psychotherapy. Although there are many variations, the basic procedure involves giving people a large set of cards that contain self-evaluative statements (such as 'I am intelligent', 'I often feel guilty', 'I am ambitious'), phrases or single words. The person is asked to sort the cards into piles, one pile containing statements that *are most like you*, another that *are least like you*, and other piles representing gradations in between these two extremes. While each of the two 'extreme' piles may comprise only a single card, those in between are allowed to have more, with those in the middle having the most.

The technique forces the sorter to decide what s/he is like by *comparing qualities with each other*, while in (nomothetic) rating scales, each response is separate and unrelated to the others (all the descriptions apply equally well). This is impossible in the Q-sort (Carver and Scheier, 1992).

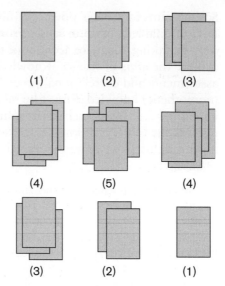

(1) (2) (3)

(4) (5) (4)

(3) (2) (1)

Figure 3.6 The Q-sort is used to assess an individual's self-concept

This same basic technique can be used to assess: 'The kind of person I am (now)', 'The kind of person I used to be' (allowing an assessment of changes in the self-image over time), and 'The kind of person I would like to be', a measure of the person's ideal self. Comparing self-image and ideal-self can be used as a measure of the progress of therapy, since the greater the similarity between the two, the greater the degree of *congruence*, one of the goals of Rogers' *client-centred therapy* (see Chapter 12). The Q-sort is repeated several times during the course of therapy.

The *repertory grid technique* (or 'rep grid') was used by Kelly to investigate a person's system of constructs – the individual's unique set of concepts and perceptions through which the world, both social and physical, is interpreted and predicted (see Box 3.2, page 57, and Chapter 12).

According to Krahé (1992), the traditional range of methodologies (both idiographic and nomothetic) for studying personality has been substantially enriched by the growing acceptance of idiographic research methods. Building on the work of Allport (1937) and Murray (1938): 'the study of individual lives has recently been rediscovered as a central task for personality theorists committed to the personological tradition'.

Krahé discusses several new concepts and units of analysis designed to capture an individual's characteristic way of dealing with the multiple tasks, themes and events of life, including *personal projects* (Little, 1989), *personal strivings* (Emmons, 1989) and *life tasks* (Cantor and Langston, 1989).

CONCLUSIONS: A DIFFERENT WAY OF LOOKING AT THE RESEARCH PROCESS

Regardless of the details of particular new methodologies, the major implication of the resurgence of interest in the idiographic approach is a new conception of the relationship between the investigator and the person 'under investigation' (Krahé, 1992).

The traditional (nomothetic) perception of the process of psychological inquiry involves a clear-cut division of roles, whereby the investigator formulates hypotheses, produces

Box 3.2 Kelly's repertory grid technique

While there are different forms of the test, the basic method involves:

1 writing a list of the most important people in your life (*elements*)

2 choosing three of these elements

3 deciding how two of these are alike and different from the third; the resulting description is a *construct*, expressed in a *bipolar* way (e.g. affectionate–not affectionate)

4 applying the construct to all the other elements

5 repeating steps 2, 3 and 4, until either the person has produced all the constructs s/he can, or until a sufficient number has been produced as judged by the investigator.

All this information can be collated in the form of a *grid*, hence the name. The grid can be factor analysed, in order to reveal any overlap between the person's constructs. Although the rep grid is primarily an idiographic technique, it can be used nomothetically. For example, Bannister and Fransella's *Grid Test of Thought Disorder* (1966, 1967) is designed for use with thought-disordered schizophrenics. It contains standardized elements and constructs (these are supplied by the investigator), and the test has been standardized on large numbers of similar patients, allowing individual scores to be compared with group norms.

Like the Q-sort, the rep grid has been used to study how patients participating in group psychotherapy change their perception of each other (and themselves) during the period of therapy. The group members and themselves are the elements, and constructs are supplied (Fransella, 1970). The method has been used extensively by Fransella (1972) with people being treated for severe stuttering.

operational definitions and selects appropriate measuring instruments, while the *subject* delivers valid data by dutifully completing the measuring instruments. Interaction between the two is limited to (i) instructions, and (ii) debriefing. From the idiographic perspective, this role division is neither appropriate nor fruitful: it makes little use of the competence of the individual as an expert on his/her own personality.

Some investigators have explicitly advocated that the person whose personality is being studied should play a more active and cooperative role in the research process. For example, Hermans and Bonarius (1991, in Krahé, 1992) use the term *co-investigator* (compare this with Kelly's personal construct therapy, in which the client is likened to a PhD student, with the therapist his/her supervisor; see Chapter 12). *Collaborative* and *new paradigm research* are becoming increasingly influential (see Chapter 11).

The very use of the term *participant*, instead of 'subject' (e.g. British Psychological Society, 1990, 1993, 2000) reflects a change in the thinking of psychologists about the research process, especially its *ethical* features. Not only is the term 'subject' degrading and dehumanizing (e.g. Heather, 1976), but if a person isn't studied as a unique individual (individual norms), but only in order to establish group norms, then s/he is not being treated fully *as a person* (see Chapter 10).

This, of course, is an ethical criticism of the *nomothetic* approach to research from an *idiographic* perspective. But just as there has been considerable reconciliation in recent years between the methodologies of the two approaches, so there is the promise that this reconciliation will make the study of human personality a more meaningful, and a more ethically acceptable, enterprise.

SUMMARY

O Human beings aren't all identical or interchangeable, but display great variability and variety.

O The ways in which we are *like some other people* is the concern of *individual differences*, which is concerned with *group norms*, such as personality, intelligence, age, gender, ethnic and cultural background.

O The study of individual differences involves a *nomothetic approach*, according to which people are *compared* in terms of a limited number of factors or dimensions, established by *factor analysis*. Examples include the personality theories of Eysenck and Cattell.

O The ways in which we are *unlike anyone else* is the concern of the *idiographic approach*, which studies *individual norms*. Examples include Allport's trait theory, Maslow and Rogers' humanistic personality theories, and Kelly's *personal construct theory*.

O The idiographic and nomothetic approaches are related to the *Geisteswissenschaften* ('moral sciences') and the *Naturwissenschaften* (natural sciences) respectively. The latter are concerned with establishing general laws that enable predictions to be made about the natural world, while the former involve *Verstehen*, which focuses on individual cases and doesn't permit generalization.

O Holt argues that the three goals of prediction and control (*differential psychology/individual differences*) and understanding (*personology/psychology of personality*) cannot be separated.

O There is much debate as to whether prediction and control are appropriate aims for psychology, and *self-understanding* may be more appropriate than *understanding* (best seen in psychotherapy).

O Intuition and empathy aren't unique to personology, but play a part in all scientific work, making science less than wholly objective.

O Allport distinguished between three kinds of *individual traits*, namely *cardinal*, *central* and *secondary*. Because these are peculiar (idiosyncratic) to each person, it is impossible to use them to compare people; however, they can be compared in terms of *common traits*.

O The idiographic approach sees differences between people as *qualitative*, while the nomothetic approach sees them as merely *quantitative*.

O Uniqueness can be defined in different ways. Eysenck sees uniqueness as reflecting a *unique combination* of levels on trait dimensions (which are the same for everybody).

O Eysenck criticizes the (extreme nomothetic) attempt to eliminate individual differences from experimental studies, in order to establish general functional relationships, as well as the (extreme idiographic) emphasis on the individual that prevents generalization, laws, or even the prediction of behaviour.

O The dichotomy between *single case* versus *group* studies is a false one, with individual cases often being used in psychological research, indicating that the study of individuals may not be incompatible with making *generalizations* about behaviour.

O Most single-case research involves determining the *generality across subjects* of the relationships uncovered at the individual level, such as in Skinner's study of operant conditioning.

O Sometimes, single cases may be all that's available to the investigator, as in neuropsychology. But an adequate baseline must be provided if data from such single cases are to be scientifically useful.

O There has been a widespread revival of interest in single-case designs within psychotherapy research, as well as a proliferation of quantitative (including factor analysis) and experimental studies of the single case.

O Allport advocated the use of *both* idiographic and nomothetic methods/knowledge in the pursuit of science's aim to achieve powers of understanding, prediction and control *above the level of unaided common sense*.

O The *Q-sort* is an idiographic method, best known as used by Rogers for assessing an individual's self-concept in the context of psychotherapy.

O Kelly's *repertory grid technique* (or 'rep grid') is used to identify a person's unique set of constructs. It *can* be used nomothetically, as with thought-disordered schizophrenics, patients in psychotherapy, and people being treated for severe stuttering.

O The major implication of the resurgence of interest in the idiographic approach is a new view of the relationship between the investigator (who used to be 'in control') and the person being studied ('the subject'). The latter is now seen as an expert on his/her own personality, and is much more of a *co-investigator* or *collaborator/colleague* in the research process.

Useful websites

- O **www.cafes.net/mathis/effect.htm**
- O **www.cycad.com/cgi-bin/Brand/quotes/qO2.html**
- O **homepage.mac.com/vickilee/unitsOfPractice.htm**

Recommended reading

Allport, G.W. (1962) The general and the unique in psychological science. *Journal of Personality, 30*, 405–22.

Holt, R.R. (1962) Individuality and generalization in the psychology of personality. *Journal of Personality, 30*, 377–404. (An alternative reference is 1967, which is a revised version of the 1962 article in R.S. Lazarus and E.M. Opton (eds) *Personality.* Harmondsworth: Penguin).

Krahé, B. (1992) *Personality and Social Psychology: Towards a Synthesis* (especially Chapters 6, 7 and 9). London: Sage.

TRAITS AND SITUATIONS AS CAUSES OF BEHAVIOUR

COMMON-SENSE VIEWS OF PERSONALITY

Part of 'common sense' psychology (the lay person's everyday understanding of behaviour; see Chapter 1) is the belief that people behave in a largely reliable (that is, consistent) and hence predictable way. As a general rule, if you ask someone to predict another person's behaviour, the response will depend on how well (or otherwise) s/he knows (or feels they know) the other person: complete strangers are (almost) impossible to predict, while with close relatives and friends it is much easier. Why?

Part of what we mean by saying we know somebody well is to be able to identify the traits and characteristics which comprise that person's *personality*. In turn, we take these traits to be relatively permanent features of the person, which, collectively, make someone the person s/he is. Logically, it follows that people will behave consistently, and predictably, on different occasions and in different situations. Since personality is constant, behaviour will also be consistent:

Personality traits → Consistency of behaviour → Predictability of behaviour

As Krahé (1992) puts it: 'Our experience with other people – as well as with ourselves – tells us that there is a certain regularity, consistency and uniqueness in the behaviours, thoughts and feelings of a person which define his or her personality.' But is this all there is to it? Even in terms of our common-sense psychology, aren't things more complex than the picture presented so far?

Surely they are, since another feature of our common-sense psychology is the view of people as being less than 100 per cent predictable. Indeed, we might regard someone who was so predictable as somehow being robot-like, more of an automaton than a person. We *expect* people to be different at different times, to show changes in mood, thought and behaviour, *within certain limits*. And what sets those limits? To some degree they are set by our general concept of a person ('people are not robots', etc.), but also by our familiarity with particular individuals (which relates to what we said above about what it means to say we know someone well). Our knowledge of (or, perhaps more accurately, our beliefs about) another's personality is based on interactions with that person and observations of his/her behaviour over a large number of occasions, in a variety of situations. So, we will have witnessed the variations in their behaviour, as well as the regularities, with the latter being used to draw our inferences about 'the kind of person' s/he is.

Figure 4.1 We might regard someone who was one hundred per cent predictable as somehow not quite human, more of an automaton than a person

CONSISTENCY OF BEHAVIOUR AND PSYCHOLOGICAL ABNORMALITY

If part of our concept of a person is the element of unpredictability/inconsistency, then anyone who shows excessive consistency may, to that extent, be judged as displaying abnormal behaviour (see above). Indeed, the behaviour of individuals whom clinicians tend to work with may be highly predictable on the basis of some underlying trait or disposition. Clinical problems may, in fact, be associated with a rigidity or inflexibility to changing conditions (Wachtel, 1977). But at the other extreme, people who 'shift with the wind' may also be subject to emotional disorder, such as overdependence on the environment as a guide to behaviour: 'To be totally at the mercy of one's surroundings, like a rudderless ship, would seem to pose as many problems as being insensitive to varying environmental demands' (Phares, 1979, in Davison and Neale, 1994).

So, we could suggest that a criterion of psychological normality is a balance between consistent behaviour (usually taken to reflect the influence of personality traits) and inconsistent behaviour (usually taken to reflect the influence of situational factors).

PERSONALITY AND SOCIAL PSYCHOLOGY

Traditionally, it has been personality psychologists who have been committed to the view that individuals can be characterized by enduring qualities that distinguish them from others, and that make their behaviour highly consistent and predictable across a range of situations (high *intra-individual consistency*). By contrast, social psychologists have emphasized the impact on individuals of social situations, which can account for high *inter-individual consistency*. Since social psychologists are less interested in individual differences, and more interested in the social influences on behaviour, they tend to stress how different people behave *in similar ways* in particular situations.

These two kinds of consistency relate to *weak* and *strong situations* respectively (Mischel, 1977):

○ weak situations allow people to express their personal qualities easily – that is, they 'leave room' for individual differences (such situations are fairly 'open-ended')

○ strong situations force behaviour into specific channels, making individual differences largely irrelevant – that is, most people behave in the same way in that (kind of) situation (such situations are highly structured).

Some of the most famous (and controversial) studies in the whole of social psychology, if not psychology as a whole, involve strong situations: Asch's studies of conformity, Milgram's studies of obedience, and Zimbardo's study of a simulated or 'mock' prison (see Box 4.1 below). While there *is* evidence of individual differences in all three studies, what they have in common is their focus on the power of social situations to make individuals behave in similar ways (to create *inter-individual consistency*).

 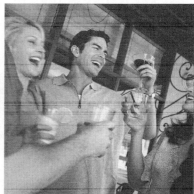

Figure 4.2 Zimbardo's prison simulation experiment showed that it is the prison environment which makes inmates and guards behave as they do and not their predispositions or character traits, whereas at a party everyone is free to behave as they please; the environment is open or weak

---

Box 4.1 The prison simulation experiment (Haney *et al.*, 1973)

This study investigated why prisons induce destructive, dehumanizing and pathological behaviour in both staff and inmates. The conventional, widely held view is that prison guards are 'sadistic, uneducated and insensitive', while prisoners, by definition, are antisocial. It is these personal qualities of the people who populate prisons that makes them the kinds of institutions they are (the *dispositional hypothesis*). What the prison experiment aimed to do was to *reject* the dispositional hypothesis in favour of a *situational* explanation: it is the physical, social and psychological conditions of prisons that are to blame, *not* the people in them.

Haney *et al.* believed that they'd found very convincing evidence in support of the situational explanation, based largely on the abnormal reactions of both prisoners and guards who were volunteers, selected for their non-criminal, non-sadistic, psychologically well-adjusted personalities, and randomly selected to their respective roles. In this way, the characteristics of the people were being controlled, leaving only the prison environment to account for the pathological reactions that developed. Like Milgram's obedience studies before it, the prison simulation experiment provoked considerable criticism, both from other psychologists and the general public. But Zimbardo (1973) believes that this was caused only in part by ethical concerns: 'another part of their [experiments like those of Milgram and Zimbardo] power lies precisely in their demonstration of how strong situational determinants are in shaping behaviour'.

What such dramatic studies demonstrate is that predicting the behaviour of individuals based on personal dispositions has its limits, set by the demands of strong situations. Equally strong, although far less dramatic, are all kinds of everyday situations in which the norms or rules of behaviour are very clearly defined and widely accepted (at least by those familiar with the culture), thus making *conformity* the 'easy' thing to do, and making the expression of personal qualities almost irrelevant. Personality psychologists don't deny the role of situational factors, and social psychologists acknowledge the part played by individual differences. There has also been some convergence between them in recent years. However, there is still a great divergence between them, social psychology still being very strongly biased towards *situationist* models of explanation, and personality psychology still favouring *dispositionism* (Krahé, 1992).

SOME KEY ISSUES IN THE STUDY OF PERSONALITY

Consistency

As we have already seen, central to the concept of personality is the consistency and predictability of behaviour. What is commonly referred to as the *consistency controversy* was sparked in 1968, when Walter Mischel declared that, based on his review of a wide range of personality domains, there was very little support for intra-individual consistency. He argued that the average correlation between different behavioural measures designed to tap the same personality trait was typically between 0.1 and 0.2, often lower. He also claimed that correlations between (i) scores on personality scales designed to measure a given trait, and (ii) behaviour in any particular situation meant to tap that trait, rarely exceed 0.2 to 0.3. Hardly any studies produced correlations (either between individual pairs of behavioural measures or between personality scale scores and individual behavioural measures) exceeding the 0.3 'barrier'.

This effectively undermined the whole concept of a *personality trait*, since it is the possession of traits that (according to personality theorists) accounts for consistency and predictability. According to Mischel, if you remove the usefulness of the trait concept, you're left only with situational influences to account for the inconsistency of individual behaviour. In other words, the same person behaves differently in different situations because different situations *require* different behaviour, are associated with different kinds of reinforcement, and so on. So, from this (rather extreme) *situationist* perspective, intra-individual *inconsistency* is exactly what you'd expect!

Interactionism

While Mischel's attack on the concept of consistency produced a severe crisis of confidence in the field of personality (Krahé, 1992), Mischel came in for criticism of his own, largely in terms of the methodological flaws in many of the studies he reviewed in reaching his conclusions. These criticisms helped him to modify his views, so that he moved away from situationism and towards an *interactionist* perspective. Essentially, this sees behaviour as a joint function of both the person and the situation:

$$\text{Behaviour} = \text{Person} \times \text{Situation}$$

According to Ross and Nisbett (1991), Mischel *never did* argue that the absence of behavioural consistency across situations proves that there are no measurable or predictable individual differences. On the contrary, he stressed that individuals might show responses that are very consistent within the same situation (i.e. *specific* responses to *specific* situations might be very stable over time, such as a child's tendency to copy from an answer book during a general knowledge test when, apparently, not being watched, as in Hartshorne and May's 1928 study). Indeed, stability coefficients (correlations between two measures of the same behaviour on different occasions) often exceed 0.4. However, he did believe that strong individual differences between people are limited to these very specific responses and situations, while the 'consistency debate' seemed to be about broad, cross-situational traits (such as 'honesty').

The 'formula' above for interactionism is also relevant to another major debate within social psychology, namely *attribution theory*, specifically the *actor–observer effect* (AOE) and the *fundamental attribution error* (FAE; see Chapter 2). This mirrors the current debate within the field of personality.

The AOE (Jones and Nisbett, 1971) refers to the lay person's bias towards explaining other people's behaviour in terms of *dispositional or internal* causes – this, in fact, is the FAE (Ross, 1977) – and his/her own behaviour in terms of *situational or external* causes. By describing these as biases – the 'error' in the FAE is itself rather inaccurate (Fiske and Taylor, 1991) – we are implying that an unbiased, logical, objective analysis of social behaviour will always show that *both* the personal dispositions of the actor *and* features of the situation contribute to what the actor does, albeit in different ways and to varying degrees and proportions. This can be seen in terms of weak and strong situations: dispositional factors play a much greater role in the former compared with the latter, but even here not everyone behaves in an identical way (see above).

THE MEANINGS OF 'INTERACTIONISM'

Interactionism seems to be the only logical, as well as empirically reasonable, view to take (as opposed to extreme dispositionism or extreme situationism). But are there different kinds of interactionism, or at least different ways of thinking about what an interaction between the person and the situation might mean?

According to Carver and Scheier (1992), there are four main ways in which the term has been used. One of these relates to the distinction between weak/strong situations, which we discussed earlier. A second relates to the 'formula' we considered above; this is probably the most common understanding of the term and is associated with the research of psychologists such as Endler and Magnusson (1976), Pervin (1985), and Snyder and Ickes (1985). It is tied to the ANOVA (analysis-of-variance) understanding of how two (or more) variables (or classes of variables) influence an outcome (as used in Kelley's covariation model of attribution, for example; see Chapter 2). When a situation and a trait are examined in the same study, three systematic sources of influence on behaviour result.

1 Sometimes, variations in the situation have an overall (and fairly predictable) effect (corresponding to *strong* situations and high *inter-individual consistency*).

2 Sometimes, variations on a trait dimension have an overall effect (corresponding to *weak* situations and *low* inter-individual consistency).

3 Sometimes, variations in the situation affect different people in different ways. This may be *instead of* the first two sources of influence, or *in addition to* them. Either way, it's the interaction between person and situation that produces weak overall effects (or correlations) for both trait and situation. While the traditional dispositional view of behaviour (as held by personality theorists) sees the trait as being the crucial factor (for example, the tendency to dominate others), interactionists argue that the expression of this tendency will inevitably be influenced by situational factors. For example, authoritarian personalities bully less powerful or less important people, but are submissive to more powerful or more important people (Argyle, 1983).

A typical study aimed at testing the trait and interactionist models involves observing, or asking for reports of, the behaviour of a number of individuals in a number of situations, and calculating how much of the variation can be explained by person factors, how much by situational factors, and how much by interaction between them. The general pattern of results that emerges from this kind of study, involving a variety of different populations, traits and situations, is very clear: situations are at least as important as persons, and $P \times S$ interactions are more important than either (Bowers, 1973; Argyle, 1983). While it is now recognized that this kind of research cannot determine whether personality or situation is more important, the results nevertheless clearly favour the interactionist position (Argyle, 1983).

The third of Carver and Scheier's definitions describes how one of the limitations of the ANOVA approach to studying interaction effects is that it is largely laboratory-based, with people put into identical situations. While this might be very convenient for the investigators, it may not be ecologically valid – that is, it may not reflect what goes on outside the laboratory situation, where people exercise considerable choice over which situations or environments they expose themselves to. Because the choices people make depend partly on personality differences, the choosing of situations represents a kind of interaction that is very different from what's involved in the ANOVA model.

In their fourth definition, Carver and Scheier cite evidence that people differ in the kinds of responses they evoke in others, that introverts and extroverts tend to steer conversations in different directions, and that people manipulate one another, using charm, coercion, 'the silent treatment', and other tactics. All these *effects of people* serve to *change the situation*, so that the situation is different for different individuals involved. This reciprocal influence between persons and situations is another way of looking at person–situation interaction (Carver and Scheier, 1992).

The psychological situation

Although other actors are an important part of any situation, individual differences between actors, as we've seen, also contribute to how a particular situation is *experienced* by the various participants. In other words, not only are personality differences essential for any understanding of people's behaviour in particular situations, but there's a very real sense in which *the situation is defined in terms of the individuals involved*.

Trying to define the situation in an objective way, independently of the actors involved, has only limited value. A critical determinant of behaviour is the 'psychological situation' – that is, the psychological meaning of a situation for the individual (how it's perceived). This represents a crucial factor in predicting behaviour and accounting for regularities in behaviour across situations (Krahé, 1992).

The trait dimension

Reference to the 'psychological situation' suggests at least a partial explanation of the lack of behavioural consistency claimed by Mischel. If people fail to show consistent behaviour across situations, couldn't this be because those situations might not all have the same meaning for the individuals concerned (which they 'should' have – and need to have – according to the researchers who define those situations in an objective way)? Only if the perceptions of actors and those of researchers coincide, can there be any possibility of finding consistency.

A solution to this problem was proposed by Bem and Allen (1974). They basically conceded Mischel's claim about low consistency when a random sample of people responds to some fixed set of trait-relevant situations. But they argued that a rather more restricted trait theory might still be valid, namely the view that at least *some* traits can be appropriately applied to at least *some* people. That is, instead of claiming that everyone is more or less equally consistent and predictable according to whichever traits one chooses to measure, Bem and Allen argued that most people are probably consistent on *some* behavioural dimensions but not others, and people will differ regarding *which* traits are consistent for them and which aren't.

The traditional trait approach (the target of Mischel's attack) adopts a *nomothetic* approach, assuming that every person can be meaningfully assigned a score on every personality dimension. Bem and Allen, on the other hand, were advocating an *idiographic* approach, focusing on the unique aspects of a given individual's personality configuration (Ross and Nisbett, 1991; see Chapter 3). To do this, one must first identify the particular traits that 'apply' for the individual in question (or, alternatively, identify particular individuals for whom the trait of interest is truly applicable) – that is,

. . . one must conduct one's search for behavioural consistency recognizing that only a subset of trait dimensions usefully characterizes any given individual, and that only a subset of individuals can be characterized in terms of any given trait dimension.

(Ross and Nisbett, 1991)

What made Bem and Allen's theoretical approach different was the assumption that: consistency will be shown only by people striving to meet personal standards, trying to convey a consistent impression to others or actively monitoring their behaviour in an attempt to achieve consistency, and that it will only be manifested in the particular situations perceived as relevant by those individuals. However, what Bem and Allen advocated, and what they actually did, were not the same thing. What they did is described in Box 4.2.

Box 4.2 Bem and Allen's (1974) study of trait consistency

Bem and Allen stipulated two specific traits, *friendliness* and *conscientiousness*, then classified all the available actors as high or low in consistency on these traits (based on self-ratings, and ratings by peers and parents). This is essentially a nomothetic approach. The idiographic alternative, which is what they originally advocated, would have involved deriving trait dimensions and situations relevant to those dimensions, from the participants themselves.

As far as both traits are concerned, the high-consistency individuals' peer ratings, parent ratings and self-ratings correlated highly *with each other* (the average correlation coefficient being 0.61 for friendliness and 0.48 for conscientiousness) *and* (although less highly) with the relevant behavioural measures (the average for friendliness being 0.47 and for conscientiousness, 0.36). In all cases, coefficients for the low-consistency individuals were lower.

Regarding correlations *between* the relevant behavioural measures, (i) for *friendliness*, the high-consistency individuals scored 0.73, compared with 0.30 for the low-consistency individuals (clearly in line with predictions). However, (ii) for *conscientiousness*, the results were −0.04 and −0.19 respectively (clearly *not* what they expected or hoped to find).

MODERATOR VARIABLES

Carver and Scheier (1992) point out that attempts to replicate Bem and Allen's results have met with very mixed fortunes. However, their view of consistency represents an important *moderator variable*, which links personal dispositions and actual behaviour, and can account for the very low levels of consistency found in earlier studies (and on which Mischel based his attack of the trait approach).

Another such moderator variable is *self-monitoring* (Snyder, 1987). *High* self-monitors are expected to show *low* cross-situational consistency, since these individuals adapt their behaviour to suit the demands of the situation, while *low* self-monitors are expected to show *high* cross-situational consistency, since they tend to 'be themselves' regardless of the demands of the situation. If people can validly be classified as high or low self-monitors, this means that some people are less or more consistent *in general* than others.

Aggregated observations

Bem and Allen were trying to defend the trait concept against Mischel's attack. Another response has been to argue that, instead of measuring *single* instances of behaviour and calculating the correlations between these (individual) instances, we should take the *average* of several different individual measures ('items') and calculate the correlations between these *aggregated* observations. The main advocate of this view is Epstein (e.g. 1979), who argues that only by taking an average can we obtain a reliable or accurate measurement of a disposition. Only by doing this will random or extraneous factors partially cancel each other out: individual behaviours, like single items on a test of any kind, are highly unreliable, and are likely to reflect the influence of several systematic and random factors other than the underlying personality disposition under investigation. This is a purely statistical argument, one that Mischel himself had made in 1968 (Ross and Nisbett, 1991).

According to the Spearman-Brown 'prophecy formula', championed by Epstein, if we took 25 measures of, say, extroversion, for each individual, found the mean, then correlated this mean with that for a different set of 25 measures, we would obtain a correlation of 0.83. If we did the same for a mere nine measures, we would still obtain a correlation of 0.63.

Not surprisingly, Epstein's argument was greeted enthusiastically by personality test researchers. It seemed to explain why standardized pencil-and-paper self-reports, and peer ratings generally produce high levels of stability over time, and at least moderate levels of inter-rater agreement; these kinds of assessment are likely to be the product of *many* observations, made on *different* occasions, in a *variety* of situations (Ross and Nisbett, 1991).

Long-term consistency

One very important implication of Epstein's argument is that to measure consistency in the *short term* (based on one or two observations made close together in time) misses the point. The widely held definition of a personality trait is that it's a latent tendency or disposition that plays a causal role in determining both specific patterns of individual behaviour and individual differences in people's reactions to a given situation. Gordon Allport (1937), one of the pioneers of personality research and a major trait theorist, argued that a person with a particular disposition will only behave in a particular way if s/he meets with situations that actualize that disposition (allow it to be expressed).

Not only does this represent a form of interactionism, it implies that if we observe a person on just one or two occasions, we won't have given particular traits 'enough of a chance' to manifest themselves; it is only in the *long term* that intra-individual consistency can be meaningfully measured. Short-term inconsistency, but long-term consistency, is exactly what's predicted by trait theories of personality.

The constructionist approach

Another strand in the complex fabric of the 'trait debate' is to shift the focus away from the actor and onto the observer. Instead of traits denoting dispositional qualities of the individual, they are conceptualized as cognitive categories used by the perceiver to interpret an individual's behaviour across different situations. Therefore, consistency is *construed* by the perceiver, as much as *manifested* by the actor: judgements of an individual's personality depend as much on the interpretative activity of the perceiver as on the observed behaviour itself (Krahé, 1992).

While not rejecting the trait concept, the constructionist view maintains that personality doesn't have an objective reality independent of the observer, or of the cultural and historical context in which both the actor and observer are located. According to Hampson (1988), the process of personality construction is seen as a form of communication through which the actor, observer and the self-observer ideally arrive at a shared impression about the actor: 'In this sense, personality should not be located *within* persons, but *between* and *among* persons' (Hampson, 1988).

In relation to our role of self-observer, *self-monitoring* is a key process (see above). Also, the constructionist approach has led to a revival of research on *social desirability scales*, which may be measuring two distinct qualities: self-deception and impression management (Deary and Matthews, 1993).

An alternative constructionist re-interpretation of the trait concept is even more radical. This challenges the very notion of 'the individual' itself.

Box 4.3 Deconstructing the self

Mainstream psychology as a whole, and personality theory in particular, takes the idea of the *individual* as its point of departure. The 'self' is a construct used in cognitive, psychoanalytic, social and humanistic theories, and all more or less share a view of the self as separate, self-contained, independent, consistent, unitary and private (Wetherell and Maybin, 1996). This view corresponds with our everyday/common-sense view, which seems to be the only view our culture permits (McGhee, 2001).

However, some *social constructionists* (including Wetherell and Maybin) and *critical* psychologists, influenced by anthropology and sociology, have challenged this view (see Chapter 15). They criticize the psychological focus on the individual for ignoring how society shapes people in various ways (e.g. Shotter and Gergen, 1989). Role theory is used to highlight the impact of social expectations and situations on the self, which must be 'managed' in order to fulfil social norms and obligations (Goffman, 1971). Such an analysis implies a self that is flexible and dynamic, adopting and discarding 'multiple roles' as the situation demands – that is, a fragmented rather than a unitary self.

For social constructionists, the self is *emergent* (not reducible to a lower biological or cognitive level), *contextual* (constructed in and for different situations and

---

circumstances), *discursive* (constructed through language), *multiple* (has variable rather than unitary forms), *relational* (constructed through interaction with others), and *distributed* (participates in many roles, relationships and representations simultaneously). This more fluid, socially constructed self makes it difficult to answer questions such as 'What are the main underlying, stable differences between individual personalities?' (McGhee, 2001). This isn't because there is insufficient empirical evidence with which to answer it, but because it's the wrong kind of question to ask.

Some social constructionists, especially those critical psychologists influenced by Foucault (see Chapter 15), argue that the very sense of 'individual' is an illusion created by language and perpetuated by a society that has a vested interest in encouraging us to take responsibility for ourselves ('subjectivity'). According to Gough and McFadden (2001), one criticism of the concept of self predominant in western culture is that: 'the Western capitalist spotlight on individuals rather than societies facilitates a politics where individuals are blamed for problems which might otherwise be conceived in terms of social factors'.

Gough and McFadden give the example of the murder of the black teenager Stephen Lawrence in 1993, and the subsequent bungled police inquiry. This sparked a debate about *institutionalized racism*, as opposed to the racial prejudice of a few extreme minds.

Personality factors

Finally, let's return to 'the beginning of the story', so to speak. According to Krahé (1992), despite its troubled history, 'the trait concept presents itself in remarkably good shape at the beginning of the '90s'. Since the 1980s, there's been a vast amount of research involving a search for a small but comprehensive number of basic trait dimensions that can account for the structure of personality and individual differences. The results suggest that personality can be adequately described by five broad constructs, commonly referred to as the 'Big Five', namely: *Neuroticism (N), Extroversion (E), Openness (O), Agreeableness (A)* and *Conscientiousness (C)* (McCrae and Costa, 1989). The first two are almost identical to these dimensions as used in Eysenck's personality theory.

While different versions of the 'Big Five' have been proposed, the five-factor model has provided a unified framework for trait research (Costa and McCrae, 1993). However, this approach faces some of the same basic problems as more traditional theories, notably those of Eysenck and Cattell, and this stems from the fact that they all rest upon the use of the statistical technique of *factor analysis* (FA).

One of the sources of debate and disagreement between, say, Eysenck and Cattell has been to do with the 'best' method of FA to use, which in turn determines the *number* of factors (or basic trait dimensions) to be extracted from the mass of data derived from self-reports, observer ratings, and so on. There is much more general agreement now among personality psychologists than there used to be about the number of factors that should be sought (i.e. five). But there remains the fundamental problem of the *meaning* of the factors that are extracted (Krahé, 1992; Kline, 1993):

The labelling of factor solutions is a largely intuitive process whereby the investigator typically inspects the items with high loadings on a given factor and then chooses a label that, in his or her view, contains the gist of the total range

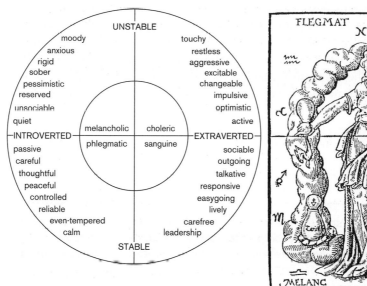

Figure 4.3 Personality has been dissected into component parts for thousands of years; what is interesting is how these ideas relate to the modern concept of personality traits, as shown by Eysenck's dimensions of personality (From Eysenck, 1965)

of items making up the factor. Thus, it is not surprising that different studies have arrived at different qualitative interpretations of their obtained five factor solutions . . .
(Krahé, 1992)

Ultimately, personality factors, however many or few, must be identified from their correlations with *external criteria* (Kline, 1993).

Finally, Bentall (1993), a clinical psychologist, asks if personality theory has anything to offer in the context of helping or understanding people with psychological problems. He argues that the 'Big Five' seem to suffer from many of the disadvantages of traditional diagnostic approaches in psychopathology, for the following reasons:

○ While these personality dimensions are described as 'natural' categories, the labels used to designate them seem to reflect the value-systems of the researchers. For example, the anxious (neurotic), introverted, reserved person 'stands condemned as a lesser human being. Should any liberal society tolerate this way of classifying individuals?' The use of assessment techniques derived from the 'Big Five' model in job selection, for example, raises serious ethical and political questions.

○ While the 'consistency debate' has focused almost exclusively on 'normal' behaviour, as far as problem behaviour is concerned, it is often the *inconsistencies* that are most striking, such as the breakdown in normal functioning following some major life event.

CONCLUSIONS

Surely, for a theory of personality to even begin to be adequate, it must apply to both the consistencies and inconsistencies, the short and the long term, the predictable and the unpredictable features of behaviour. It must also be able to explain both normal and abnormal behaviour, as well as the emotional, cognitive, social and interpersonal components of behaviour, all within the cultural and historical context in which a person's personality is perceived and judged. Carver and Scheier (1992) sum things up like this:

Today's view isn't a picture in which traits exert a *constant* influence on behaviour . . . Rather, trait differences sometimes matter a lot and sometimes don't matter at all. People also display traits by choosing situations, not just by reacting to situations forced on them. This dynamic approach to understanding the role of traits in the constantly varying social environment recognizes complexities in behaviour that formerly were ignored. As a result, this picture is widely seen as a distinct improvement over simpler conceptions of the effects of traits.

SUMMARY

○ Part of our common-sense understanding of behaviour is the belief that people behave in fairly consistent, and hence predictable, ways, across a range of situations (high *intra-individual consistency*). This is attributed to their *personality*, which refers to the relatively permanent features of a person's make-up.

○ Another common-sense belief is that people are *not completely predictable*; they are changeable, *within certain limits*, those limits being set by (a) our general concept of a person, and (b) our familiarity with particular individuals.

○ Both excessive predictability/consistency and excessive unpredictability/inconsistency may be indicators of psychological abnormality.

○ Personality psychologists have tended to stress high *intra-individual consistency*, while social psychologists have stressed the impact of social situations, accounting for high *inter-individual consistency*. These relate to *weak* and *strong situations* respectively.

○ Many famous (and controversial) studies in social psychology involve strong situations, such as the prison simulation experiment. Such studies show that the validity of predicting the behaviour of individuals on the basis of personal dispositions is limited by the demands of strong situations.

○ Despite recent convergence between personality psychology and social psychology, the former still strongly favours *dispositionism* and the latter *situationism*.

○ Mischel sparked the *consistency controversy* by claiming that there was very little evidence of intra-individual consistency. This undermined the whole concept of a *personality trait* and introduced a *situationist* perspective into personality psychology, which predicts intra-individual *inconsistency*.

○ Criticisms of Mischel led him towards an *interactionist* perspective, which sees behaviour as a joint function of *both* the person *and* the situation. However, there are different ways of thinking about what a person–situation interaction might mean.

○ The general pattern of results found in studies aimed at testing the trait and interactionist models is that situations are at least as important as persons, and person × situation interactions are more important than either.

○ In real life, people *choose* the situations to which they expose themselves. This represents a kind of interaction. Also, people *change the situation* by virtue of their personality, and the responses they evoke in others, which represents another form of interaction.

O Rather than trying to define situations independently of the actors involved, it is the *psychological situation* that is the crucial influence on behaviour.

O Bem and Allen proposed a restricted trait theory, according to which most people are probably consistent on *some* behavioural dimensions but not others. People will differ regarding which traits are consistent for them and which are not, depending on the *personal relevance of different traits*.

O Empirical support for Bem and Allen is mixed, but their view of consistency represents an important *moderator variable*, another example being *self-monitoring*.

O We should take the *average* of several individual observations and calculate correlations for these *aggregated* measures. We also need to recognize that intra-individual consistency is a *long-term* phenomenon.

O Consistency is also viewed as *construed by the perceiver*, as much as *manifested by the actor*. This constructionist approach maintains that personality does *not* exist *objectively*, but is a form of *communication*.

O Social constructionists also challenge the concept of the individual and the self as traditionally understood. They propose both theoretical and political reasons for not seeing people as separate, self-contained, unitary and private.

O Although the 'Big Five' personality trait dimensions/factors have provided a framework for trait research, there remains the fundamental problem of the *meaning* of the factors extracted by the use of factor analysis.

O The value of personality theory in relation to people with psychological problems has been questioned – in particular the 'Big Five', which seem to reflect the value-systems of the researchers and overemphasize consistency relative to inconsistency.

Useful websites

- http://muskingum.edu/~psychology/psycweb/history/milgram.htm
- http://pmc.psych.nwu.edu/personality
- members.truepath.com/Counselme/Self-con.htm
- http://www.ship.edu/~cgboeree/perscontents.html
- http://www.prisonexp.org/

Recommended reading

Krahé, B. (1992) *Personality and Social Psychology: Towards a Synthesis* (especially Chapters 1–5 and 8). London: Sage.

Mischel, W. (1968) *Personality and Assessment.* New York: Wiley.

Mischel. W. (1977) The interaction of personality and situation. In D. Magnusson and N.S. Endler (eds) *Personality at the Crossroads: Current Issues in Interactional Psychology.* Hillsdale, NJ: Lawrence Erlbaum.

HEREDITY AND ENVIRONMENT

5

FRAMING THE QUESTIONS

The debate about the roles of heredity and environment (or *nature* and *nurture*) is one of the most enduring, as well as one of the most heated and controversial, both inside and outside psychology. Whether in a religious, philosophical, political or scientific context, the debate is concerned with some of the most fundamental questions that human beings (at least those from western cultures) ask about themselves: 'How do we come to be the way we are?' 'What makes us develop in the way we do?'

I have deliberately expressed these questions in a very general, abstract way, in order to highlight an ambiguity involved: are they concerned with *the human species* as a whole, relative to other species, or are they concerned with *individual differences* between human beings, i.e. individuals relative to each other? In a broad, general sense, the nature–nurture debate involves *both* types, or level, of question. For example, 'Is language an innate (inborn) ability that is unique to the human species?' and 'Is it a "natural" (biologically given) ability that will appear, under "normal" environmental conditions, in people with normal brains?' represent the first (species) level. Clearly, if language is a species-specific ability, then the focus of theory and research will be on the nature of that ability, exactly what it is that is innate or biologically 'given', how the brain is specialized for language, and so on. Chomsky's (1965, 1968) *Language Acquisition Device (LAD)* is perhaps the prime example within modern psychology of such an approach. A related example is Pinker's (1994) view of language as an instinct (see the discussion of evolutionary psychology in Chapter 15).

Similar questions have been asked about perception and aggression. In the case of aggression, both types of question have been posed: 'Are human beings the naturally most aggressive species on the planet?' represents the same level as the first question regarding language; while 'Why are some people more aggressive than others?' represents the other level, the one that focuses on individual differences. According to Plomin (1994), it is in the *latter* sense (i.e. individual differences) that the nature–nurture debate takes place.

However, there's another, equally important distinction that needs to be made between the kinds of questions that are asked relating to heredity and environment. In order to appreciate this distinction we need to take a brief look at the philosophical roots of the nature–nurture debate.

NATIVISM, EMPIRICISM AND INTERACTIONISM

As the word implies, *nativism* refers to the philosophical theory that sees nature (i.e. heredity) as determining certain abilities and capacities, rather than learning and experience. A well-known nativist, who has had an enormous impact on psychology, is the French philosopher, René Descartes (1596–1650). At the opposite philosophical extreme is *empiricism*, associated mainly with seventeenth-century British philosophers, in particular John Locke (1632–1704). Locke believed that, at birth, the human mind is a *tabula rasa* (or 'blank slate'), which is gradually 'filled in' by learning and experience.

At risk of some oversimplification, these two doctrines represent polar opposites – that is, they take the view that it is *either* nature (nativism) *or* nurture (empiricism) that accounts for human abilities: they are either innate *or* learnt.

Most present-day psychologists (and biologists) would reject such an extreme either/or approach to such a complex issue, mainly on the grounds that the two theories are attempts to answer *the wrong question*: to ask 'Is it nature or nurture?' is to ask an oversimplified question that will inevitably produce an oversimplified answer. Also, Descartes and Locke were asking the question at the level of 'the whole species', and *not* at the level of individual differences.

However, despite these two observations, nativism and empiricism have had a considerable impact on psychology – particularly, but by no means exclusively, in the early days of the discipline. The *Gestalt* psychologists (notably, Wertheimer, Kohler and Koffka, during the 1920s and 1930s) believed that the basic principles of perceptual organization are innate, with perceptual experience having very little, if any, influence. One of the American pioneers of child psychology, Arnold Gesell (1925), introduced into psychology the concept of maturation. This refers to genetically programmed sequential patterns of change (Bee, 1989), according to which all babies and children will pass through the same series of changes, in the same order, and at more or less the same rate. A third, and more recent, example of a nativist theory is Chomsky's *LAD* (see above).

Empiricism has had its impact within psychology in many different forms. An early and extremely influential theory is *behaviourism*, whose American founder, John Watson (1878–1958), leaves the reader in no doubt as to the behaviourist position regarding the nature–nurture debate when he declares:

Give me a dozen healthy infants, well-formed, and my own specified world to bring them up in and I'll guarantee to take any one at random and train him to become any type of specialist I might select – a doctor, lawyer, artist, merchant-chief and, yes, even into beggar-man and thief, regardless of his talents, penchants, abilities, vocations and race of his ancestors.
(Watson, 1925/1926, in Soyland, 1994)

He also claimed that 'there is no such thing as an inheritance of capacity, talent, temperament, mental constitution and character', and again:

The behaviourists believe that there is nothing from within to develop. If you start with the right number of fingers and toes, eyes, and a few elementary movements that are present at birth, you do not need anything else in the way of raw material to make a man, be that man genius, a cultured gentleman, a rowdy or a thug.
(Watson, 1928, in Plomin, 1994)

This extreme form of empiricism (or *environmentalism*) was perpetuated in the behaviour analysis work of B.F. Skinner (1904–90; see Chapter 15).

So, if extreme nativism and empiricism, whether in the form of philosophical or psychological theories, choose between nature and nurture, a more complex question is to ask 'How much?' This, of course, presupposes that *both* nature and nurture are involved, a view that, as we noted above, most psychologists would subscribe to. Indeed, for most behavioural scientists, it is probably inconceivable that there is no *interaction* between them (Plomin, 1994).

In turn, the 'How much?' question is linked, almost inevitably, to the 'individual differences' form of the debate. For Francis Galton (a cousin of Charles Darwin), the issue was clearly about the *relative importance* of heredity and environment, and he left us in no doubt as to which he considered the more important: 'There is no escape from the conclusion that nature prevails enormously over nurture when the differences in nurture do not exceed what is commonly to be found among persons of the same rank in the same country' (Galton, 1883, in Plomin, 1994).

Finally, even though 'How much?' represents an improvement on the rather crude, oversimplified 'Which one?', it is still concerned with trying to measure or *quantify* the contributions of genetic and environmental factors. This has been the main focus of *behavioural* (or quantitative) *genetics*, which attempts to establish the extent to which individual differences (such as intelligence or personality) are due to differences in people's genetic make-up (i.e. *heritability estimates*). The methods used in behavioural genetics include *twin studies*, *adoption studies* and other studies of *family resemblance*. One reason for the emphasis on 'How much?' is the availability of these methods, which make it relatively straightforward to establish heritability estimates. We shall discuss behaviour genetics (and the related *molecular genetics*) in more detail later in the chapter.

A much more difficult *third question* about the nature–nurture relationship, which follows logically from the second, is 'How do they interact?' (Anastasi, 1958; Plomin, 1994). This is concerned with *qualitative* issues – that is, the ways in which heredity and environment influence each other. Much of the rest of this chapter will be concerned with some of the different attempts to understand this interaction, many of which also derive from behaviour genetics research.

THE NATURE OF 'NATURE'

Within *genetics* (the science of heredity), 'nature' refers to what is typically thought of as inheritance. This denotes (differences in) genetic material (chromosomes and genes), which are transmitted from generation to generation (i.e. from parents to offspring). The 'father' of genetics, Gregor Mendel, an Austrian monk, explained the difference between smooth and wrinkled seeds in garden peas in terms of different genes (1865). Similarly, in modern human genetics, the focus is on genetic differences among individuals. 'Nature' in this context does *not* refer to the nature of the human species, what we all have in common genetically with other human beings (and indeed with other primates), but rather to genetically produced differences among individuals within the (human) species. This was certainly how the term 'nature' was used by Galton, who coined the phrase *nature–nurture* in 1883 as it is used in the scientific arena (Plomin, 1994).

Genetics and evolution

The raw material of evolution is genetic variability: individuals with genes that help them to survive changing environmental conditions will be more likely to produce offspring (who also

Figure 5.1 Gregor Mendel (1822–1884) the 'father' of genetics

possess those genes), while those individuals lacking such genes will not. In this way, new species develop, and species-specific characteristics (including behaviours) are those that have enabled the species to evolve and survive.

However, the links between such species-typical evolution and genetic sources of individual differences are much looser than is often assumed (Plomin, 1994). Plomin cites the examples of *sociobiology* (e.g. Wilson, 1975), *evolutionary psychology* (e.g. Buss, 1991), and *developmental psychology* (e.g. Harper, 1992), all of which are mainly concerned with differences between species, although attempts have been made to incorporate individual differences (e.g. by Dawkins, 1983). It is easy to make the mistake of assuming that evolution implies genetic variation *within* a species, and vice-versa. Taking the example of language again, if acquisition of language is a human species-specific behaviour, hardwired by evolution to occur if the minimal environment encountered by our species during development is present (most importantly, other language users), then we can say that we are natural language users. However, this *doesn't* imply that differences among individual language users in their language ability are also genetic in origin — such differences could be entirely due to environmental factors (Plomin, 1994).

The causes of average differences between species are not necessarily related to the causes of individual differences within groups. Moreover, characteristics that have been subject to strong directional selection will not show genetic variability because strong selection exhausts genetic variability. In other words, when genetic variability is found among individuals within our species for a particular trait, it is likely that the trait was not important evolutionarily, at least in terms of directional selection . . .
(Plomin, 1994)

HEREDITY: CHROMOSOMES, GENES AND DNA

Now that we've established what nature *isn't*, let's take a closer look at what it *is*; clearly this is important if we are to try to understand the relationship between nature and nurture.

The basic units of hereditary transmission are *genes*. Genes are large molecules of deoxyribonucleic acid (DNA), extremely complex chemical chains, comprising a ladder-like, double-helix structure (discovered by Watson and Crick in 1953, see Figure 5.2, page 79). Genes occur in pairs, and are situated on the *chromosomes*, which are found within the nuclei of living cells. The normal human being inherits 23 pairs of chromosomes, one member

Figure 5.2 The structure of a DNA molecule represented schematically. This shows its double-stranded coiled structure and the complementary binding of nucleotide bases, guanine to cytosine and adenine to thymine (From Pinel, 1993)

| thymine | is bound to | adenine |
| cytosine | is bound to | guanine |

of each pair from each parent. These consist of 22 pairs of *autosomal chromosomes* (the same in males and females) and two *sex chromosomes* (pair 23), which comprise two Xs in the case of females, and an X and a Y in males (see Figure 5.3, page 80).

The steps of the gene's double helix (or spiral staircase; Plomin, 1994) consist of four nucleotide bases (adenine, thymine, cytosine and guanine), which can occur in any order on *one* side of the double helix, while the *other* side is fixed, such that adenine always pairs with thymine, and cytosine always pairs with guanine. Taking just *one* member of each of the 23 pairs of chromosomes, the human *genome* (the total complement of genes) comprises more than 3 billion nucleotide base pairs (Plomin, 1994). Genes can range in size from fewer than 100 base pairs to several million. Two major functions of genes are *self-duplication* and *protein synthesis*.

Self-duplication

DNA copies itself by 'unzipping' in the middle of the spiral staircase, with each half forming its complement. In other words, when a cell divides, *all* the genetic information (chromosomes and genes) contained within the cell nucleus is reproduced, so that the 'offspring' cells are identical to the 'parent' cells. This process is called *mitosis* and applies only to non-gonadal (non-reproductive) cells (such as skin, blood and muscle cells).

Figure 5.3 A sample karyotype. The 21st chromosome has one too many chromosomes, a common problem. This is called a 'trisomy'. The 23rd chromosome pair is shown with both male and female versions. In a normal karyotype, only one such pair would be found (From Ruch, 1984)

The reproductive or germ cells (ova in females and sperm in males) duplicate through *meiosis*, whereby each cell only contains *half* the individual's chromosomes and genes (*haploid*); which member of a chromosome pair goes to any particular cell seems to be determined randomly. The resulting germ cells (called *gametes* in their mature state), therefore, contain 23 chromosomes, one of which will be either an X (female) or a Y (male). When a sperm fertilizes an ovum, the two sets of chromosomes combine to form a new individual with a full set of 46 chromosomes: if both parents contribute an X chromosome, it will be female, while if the father contributes a Y (remember, the mother only has Xs) it will be male. It is the father, therefore, who determines the baby's sex (see Figure 5.4, page 81).

Protein synthesis

The 'genetic code' was cracked in the 1960s. Essentially, DNA controls the production of RNA (ribonucleic acid) within the cell nucleus. This 'messenger' RNA moves outside the nucleus, into the surrounding cytoplasm, where it is converted by ribosomes into sequences of amino acids, which are the building blocks of proteins and enzymes. Genes that code for proteins and enzymes are called *structural genes*, and they represent the foundation of classical genetics (Plomin, 1994). The first single-gene disorders discovered in the human species involved metabolic disorders caused by mutations (spontaneous changes) in structural genes. A much-cited example is phenylketonuria (PKU), which is discussed below in relation to gene–environment interaction.

However, most genes are *regulator genes*: they code for products that bind with DNA itself, and serve to regulate other genes. Unlike the structural genes, which are 'deaf' to the environment, the regulator genes communicate closely with the environment and change in response to it (Plomin, 1994).

THE NATURE OF NURTURE: WHAT IS THE ENVIRONMENT?

When the term 'environment' is used in a psychological context, we normally think of all those influences, or potential sources of influence, that lie outside the individual's body, in the form of other people, opportunities for intellectual stimulation and social interaction, as well as the physical circumstances of the individual's life ('environs' = 'surroundings').

For most babies and young children, the immediate family is the environmental context in which their development takes place, although the nature of this immediate environment is itself coloured and shaped by the wider social and cultural setting in which the family exists. In other words, we normally view the environment as:

○ external to the individual

○ post-natal (i.e. something that becomes important after birth)

Sperm cells are created by Meiotic Division

The father's body cells have 23 pairs of chromosomes; 1 pair is shown here.

The chromosomes duplicate themselves to create 46 pairs.

The cell divides to create two cells, each with 23 pairs.

Each cell divides to create 4 sperm cells, each with 23 chromosomes, half the normal number.

Egg cells are created by Meiotic Division

The mother's body cells have 23 pairs of chromosomes; 1 pair is shown here.

The chromosomes duplicate themselves to create 46 pairs.

The cell divides to create two cells, each with 23 pairs of chromosomes. One of these cells dies.

Bingo! Fertilization.

The fertilized cell divides to create two cells, each with 23 chromosomes, half the usual number. The cell without the sperm dies.

The sperm and the egg combine to form a zygote with 23 pairs of chromosomes.

The Zygote Grows by Mitotic Division

The zygote has 23 pairs of chromosomes.

The chromosomes duplicate to create 46 pairs.

The cell divides to create two cells, each with 23 pairs of chromosomes.

Mitotic division occurs over and over until an adult organism is created.

Figure 5.4 Mitotic and meiotic cell division (From Pinel, 1993)

○ a way of referring to a whole set of (potential) influences that impinge on a passive individual, who is *shaped by his/her environment*, without in any way *shaping* or contributing to that environment (see Figure 5.5, page 82).

On all three counts, this view seems to be mistaken.

Regarding the first two points, while the nature–nurture debate is normally conducted at the level of the immediate family, and the society and culture within which it is embedded: 'opportunities for gene–environment interaction arise long before the birth process … [and] individual differences in environmental conditions have a modifying influence upon the expression of genetic inheritance' (McGurk, 1975).

For example, with repeated mitosis, any one cell has a specific location within a cluster of other cells, but that location is forever changing as the cell's environment (the total number

Figure 5.5 Traditional, extreme behaviourist/ environmentalist view of the environment as a set of external, post-natal influences acting upon a purely passive individual

Figure 5.6 For the nucleus of an individual cell, the environment is the surrounding cytoplasm

of cells in the cluster) continues to grow. At an even more micro level, the cell nucleus (which contains the genetic material) has as its environment the cytoplasm of the cell.

Strictly speaking, 'heredity' refers only to the particular set of chromosomes and genes that combine at the moment of fertilization; anything that occurs from that moment on is environmental (Kirby and Radford, 1976). This, of course, includes all the influences acting on the developing embryo (as the 'baby' is called during the first eight weeks of pregnancy, thereafter the 'foetus'), such as hormones, drugs taken by the mother, accidents, mother's diet, and so on. From a psychological perspective, the importance of this pre-natal, *biological* environment, relates to the damaging effects it can have on the unborn child's brain development. For example, of commonly taken (and legal) drugs, alcohol is the most harmful. It is toxic to brain cells during the first ten weeks of pregnancy, and *foetal alcohol syndrome* refers to intellectual impairment, hyperactivity and attention difficulties associated with very high levels of alcohol consumption during pregnancy (Rutter and Rutter, 1992).

The view of the environment as impinging on a passive individual applies to the *social* (and *cultural*) environment (as opposed to the biological), as well as the *physical*. This, as we've seen, is the level at which the nature–nurture debate normally takes place. If it is inaccurate to see the individual as at the mercy of the environment (as Watson, for one, would have us believe), then we need to ask, 'In what ways does the individual influence/contribute to his/her environment?'

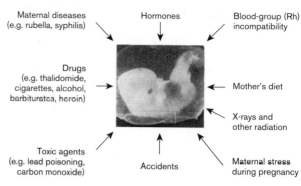

Maternal diseases (e.g. rubella, syphilis)

Hormones

Blood-group (Rh) incompatibility

Drugs (e.g. thalidomide, cigarettes, alcohol, barbiturates, heroin)

Mother's diet

X-rays and other radiation

Toxic agents (e.g. lead poisoning, carbon monoxide)

Accidents

Maternal stress during pregnancy

Figure 5.7 Alcohol consumption during pregnancy can result in Foetal Alcohol Syndrome; the baby may be intellectually impaired, hyperactive and suffer from a very short span of attention. Physical abnormalities can also be present such as a relatively small head, a short nose and low nasal bridge

Figure 5.8 The pre-natal, biological environment

Watson's extreme brand of environmentalism sees 'the environment' as existing largely *independently* of the individual, a passive receptacle for environmental influences. As we saw earlier, it relates to the 'Which one?' question regarding the nature–nurture debate. An alternative view of what the environment is, relevant to the 'How?' question (which, remember, assumes that *both* heredity and environment contribute to the development of individual differences), is to see people as *making their own environments* (Scarr, 1992). This runs counter to what most parents believe about the impact they have on their children, as well as what mainstream developmental psychology teaches. Scarr argues that '. . . each child constructs a reality from the opportunities afforded by the rearing environment, and . . . the constructed reality does have considerable influence on variations among children and differences in their adult outcomes'.

Eliciting a response

One way in which people influence/contribute to their environments is through *evoking* or *eliciting* certain responses from other people. This may be due either to their *behaviour* or to particular *biological characteristics*. An example of the latter is *gender*. If people have stereotyped views and expectations regarding differences between boys and girls, then these are likely to be expressed through different ways of relating to boys and girls, *simply because they are male or female*. This is demonstrated in the 'baby X' experiments (Smith and Lloyd, 1978, in Rutter and Rutter, 1992). Toddlers were dressed in unisex snowsuits and then given names to indicate gender, half the time in line with their actual gender, half the time not. When adults played with the toddlers, they treated them differently according to what they *believed* the toddler's gender to be.

What this demonstrates is that a person's biological make-up (or, at least, others' *perception* of it) becomes part of that person's environment, because other people's reactions to our biological make-up is part of our (social) environment. Indeed, anything about us that may form the basis for others' stereotyped perceptions and reactions towards us (such as physical attractiveness, ethnic, racial or national background, or any physical disability) is as much a part of our environment as it is part of our biological make-up.

However, these examples all relate to *static* aspects of our make-up. What about more *dynamic* aspects, such as temperament and behaviour?

For example, children with a very sunny, easy-going and cheerful disposition are more likely to elicit friendly interactions with others than children perceived as miserable or 'difficult'; it is widely accepted that some children are easier to love (Rutter and Rutter, 1992). Research has shown that aggressive boys not only behave more aggressively, but also *elicit* more hostile behaviour in other boys. Their actions help to create a vicious cycle of negative interactions: when aggressive behaviour meets with a hostile response, this makes it more likely that further aggression will occur, and so on (Rutter and Rutter, 1992).

To the extent that all these characteristics are, to some degree, influenced by genetic factors, all the above examples illustrate *gene–environment correlations* (Rutter and Rutter, 1992; Scarr, 1992): aggressive children tend to experience aggressive environments because they tend to evoke aggressive responses in others. This illustrates *reactive gene–environment correlations*, while the 'static' examples of gender and physical appearance illustrate *passive gene–environment correlations* (Plomin *et al.*, 1977). Looking at the environment in this way helps to explain why it is that different individuals have different experiences.

Shared and non-shared psychosocial environments

When the environment is being discussed as a set of (potential) influences that impinge on the individual, it is often 'broken down' into factors such as overcrowding, poverty, social class or socioeconomic status (SES) (which is correlated with the first two, as well as with other indicators), family break-up, marital discord, and so on. In studies of, say, intelligence or aggression, children are often compared with each other in terms of these environmental factors, which are then correlated with the behaviour or ability. So, for example, it may be concluded that children from low-SES backgrounds are more likely to behave in antisocial ways and to be labelled as juvenile delinquents.

When families are compared in this way, it is assumed that children from the *same* family will all be similarly and equally affected by those environmental factors (*shared environment*). However, for most characteristics, most children within the same family *aren't* very similar – in fact, they're often extremely varied in personality, abilities and psychological disorders. This observation is most striking when two adopted children are brought up in the same family: 'they're usually very little more alike than any two people chosen at random from the general population' (Rutter and Rutter, 1992; Plomin, 1996).

This substantial within-family variation is exactly what we'd expect to find if *non-shared influences* are the crucial ones: *differences* between children in the same family will be associated systematically with differences between their *experiences*. One of the few major studies of this relationship is Dunn and Plomin's (1990) *Separate Lives*. In that book they argue that family-wide influences (such as SES and marital discord) cannot influence behavioural development *unless* their impact is experienced differently by each child.

A more specific way of trying to account for these findings is by distinguishing between relative and absolute differences between children in how they are treated. Dunn and Plomin found that the ways in which parents respond differently to their different children (*relative differences*) are likely to be much more influential than the overall characteristics of the family (*absolute differences*). For example, it may matter very little whether children are brought up in a home that is less loving or more punitive than average, whereas it may matter considerably that one child receives less affection or more punishment than his/her brother or sister.

These findings imply 'that the unit of environmental transmission is not the family, but rather micro-environments within families' (Plomin and Thompson, 1987). Consistent with these findings is the view that, provided children are brought up in good-enough, supportive, non-deprived/abusive/neglectful environments, the *particular* family in which they are raised makes very little difference to their personality and intellectual development. Most families provide sufficiently supportive environments for children's individual genetic differences to develop (Scarr, 1992). This *could* account for:

○ temperamental differences between children

○ why parents treat different offspring differently (the *relative differences*)

○ differences in the experiences of different children.

Even though Dunn and Plomin's findings are only preliminary, they represent a very important explanation of how the experiences of different individuals might differ; and to the extent that people's experiences differ, their environments are different.

The constructionist view

What Dunn and Plomin's findings show is that it is futile to try and define the environment *independently* of the person experiencing it, since every person's experience is different. An extreme *behaviourist* approach would see the structure of experience as given in the environment, which provides stimuli that impinge and shape the individual *regardless of who they are*. According to *constructionist* views, however, people shape their own experiences: we don't merely *respond* differently to our environments (which implies a fairly *passive* role), we *actively create* our own experiences. Cross-cultural psychology is based on the assumption that no sociocultural environment exists separately from the meaning that human participants give it (Shweder, 1990). Nothing real 'just is'; realities are the product of how things get represented, embedded, implemented and reacted to (Scarr, 1992; see Chapters 8 and 15). The same applies to individual differences *within* the same culture. According to Scarr:

Different people, at different developmental stages, interpret and act upon their environments in different ways that create different experiences for each person. In this view, human experience is a construction of reality, not a property of a physical world that imparts the same experience to everyone who encounters it.

This constructionist view relates to what Plomin *et al.* (1977) call *active gene–environment interactions*.

Facilitativeness

A further way of trying to answer the 'How?' question is to consider the idea of vulnerability or susceptibility to environmental influence; this represents an important kind of *gene–environment interaction* (Rutter and Rutter, 1992).

According to Horowitz (1987, 1990) a highly *facilitative* environment is one in which the child has loving and responsive parents, and is provided with a rich array of stimulation. When different levels of facilitativeness are combined with a child's initial vulnerabilities or susceptibilities, there is an *interaction* effect. For example, a resilient child (one with many protective factors and few vulnerabilities) may do quite well in a poor environment; equally, a vulnerable child may do quite well in a highly facilitative environment. Only the vulnerable child in a poor environment will do really poorly.

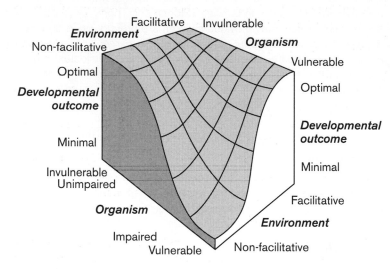

Figure 5.9 Horowitz's model of the interaction of a child's environment with protective factors and vulnerabilities. The surface of the curve illustrates the level of a developmental stage, such as IQ or social skills. According to this model, if a low-birthweight child is reared in a poor environment then it is likely that that child will do less well than other children reared with a different combination of vulnerabilities and environment

This interactionist view is demonstrated in a 30-year, longitudinal study, which took place on the Hawaiian island of Kauai (see Box 5.1, page 87).

These findings challenge the traditional assumption that there is a simple and direct link between early experiences and later development (Werner, 1989).

SOME PROVISIONAL CONCLUSIONS REGARDING THE GENE–ENVIRONMENT RELATIONSHIP

Although we are not free to choose the womb we're born in or the school we go to, this is clearly *not* because it's our genes that determine these things (Dobzhansky and Penrose, 1955, cited in Plomin, 1994). However, as we have seen, the environment comprises more than such *macro* environments: we *are* free to choose and create the *micro* environments that form the bulk of our immediate, ongoing experience. As Plomin (1994) says:

> Socially as well as cognitively, children select, modify, and even create their experiences. Children select environments that are rewarding or at least comfortable, *niche-picking*. Children modify their environments by setting the background tone for interactions, by initiating behaviour, and by altering the impact of environments ... Children can make their own environments. That is, they can create environments compatible with their own propensities, *niche-building* ... (see Figure 5.10, page 88.)

BEHAVIOUR GENETICS: GOING BEYOND THE NATURE–NURTURE DEBATE

Much of what we have said above about gene–environment correlations and interactions (which relate to the 'How?' question) derives from the work of behaviour geneticists, such as Scarr and Plomin. But Pike and Plomin (1999) define behaviour genetics (BG) as exploring 'the origins of individual differences ... in complex behaviours' and, more specifically, as attempting to quantify how *much* of the *variability* for any given trait (such as intelligence, schizophrenia or aggressiveness) can be attributed to:

Box 5.1 Werner's 'Children of the Garden Island' (1989)

Starting in 1955, Werner and her colleagues studied all the children born on the island (nearly 700 of them) in a given period, following them up when they were one, two, ten, 18 and 31/32 years old.

Werner became interested in a number of 'high risk' or 'vulnerable' children. Despite exposure to four or more of the following:

○ reproductive stress (either difficulties during pregnancy and/or during labour and delivery)

○ discordant and impoverished home lives (including divorce, uneducated, alcoholic or mentally disturbed parents)

before the age of two, these children went on to develop healthy personalities, stable careers and strong interpersonal relationships. There were two main kinds of protective factor that contributed to their resilience.

Constitutional factors

These included temperamental characteristics that elicit positive responses from family and strangers, such as a fairly high activity level, a low degree of excitability and distress, and a high degree of sociability. They were typically described, as infants, as 'active', 'affectionate', 'cuddly', 'easy-going', and 'even-tempered', with no eating or sleeping habits that caused distress to their carers.

Environmental factors

Their families had four or fewer children, with two or more years between the child being studied and the next child. In spite of poverty, family discord, or parental mental illness, they had established a close attachment to at least one carer, who might be a grandparent, older sibling, aunt or uncle, or a regular baby-sitter. They also found a great deal of emotional support from outside the family, were popular with their classmates and had at least one close friend. School became a home away from home, a refuge from a disordered household.

Of the 72 children who were classified as resilient, 62 were studied after reaching their thirties. As a group, they seemed to be coping well with the demands of adult life, three-quarters had received some college education, and nearly all had full-time jobs and were satisfied with their work. Werner (1989) concluded that, 'As long as the balance between stressful life events and protective factors is favourable, successful adaptation is possible. When stressful events outweigh the protective factors, however, even the most resilient child can have problems.'

○ genetic differences between people (*heritability*)

○ *shared environments*, and

○ *non-shared environments*.

So, BG addresses *both* the 'How?' *and* the 'How much?' questions.

According to Jones (1993), most modern geneticists regard the 'Which one?' question as largely meaningless and the 'How much?' question as dull. The reason for this is that:

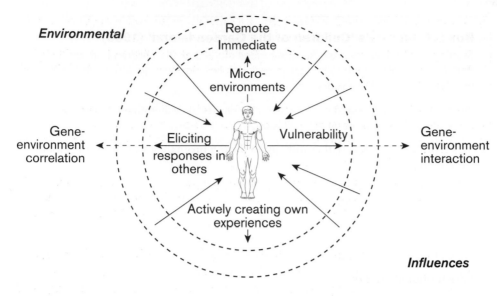

Figure 5.10 The post-natal, socio-cultural environment with the individual portrayed as actively influencing the environment as much as he/she is influenced by it

Nearly all inherited characteristics more complicated than a single change in DNA involve gene and environment acting together. It is impossible to sort them into convenient compartments. An attribute such as intelligence is often seen as a cake which can be sliced into so much 'gene' and so much 'environment'. In fact, the two are so closely blended that trying to separate them is more like trying to unbake the cake . . .

Plomin (2001) agrees with Jones that the nature–nurture debate has largely faded, but for different reasons. Plomin argues that during the 1980s and 1990s, psychologists became much more accepting of genetic influence (the controversy between 'geneticists' and 'environmentalists' having been at its fiercest); BG research became much more 'mainstream'. But as well as demonstrating what behaviour geneticists had always believed – 'the ubiquitous importance of genetics throughout psychology' – BG research also demonstrated that individual differences in complex psychological traits are due at least as much to environmental influences as they are to genetics. In fact, Plomin maintains that BG research 'provides the strongest available evidence for the importance of environmental factors'.

While this may seem paradoxical, we've seen how the concepts of gene–environment correlation and interaction try to explain environmental influences *in terms of* genetic factors. So, there's still a sense in which genes are 'primary', but Plomin's way of tying them into the environment, rather than looking at them in isolation, satisfies most psychologists' need to put 'the environment' into the equation. As Claridge and Davis (2003) put it, 'The balanced view is that behaviour genetics is as much about determining environmental, as genetic, effects; though it is naturally the latter that mostly interests . . . [behaviour geneticists].' Ironically, Plomin also believes that in some areas, especially psychopathology, the pendulum representing the accepted view may be swinging too far from environmental to genetic determinism.

Molecular genetics: going back to nature

A relatively recent new direction taken by researchers trying to explain individual differences biologically involves the attempt to identify (some of the) *specific genes* that are responsible.

This is the aim of *molecular genetics*. Some of this research is directed at psychological disorders, such as schizophrenia and autism. For example, an international research team led by Rutter and Monaco has identified a region of chromosome 7 that may be linked with vulnerability to autism (International Molecular Genetic Study of Autism Consortium, 1998). According to Plomin and Rutter (1998):

Finding specific genes that contribute to vulnerability to autism and other behaviour disorders and dimensions will provide the strongest evidence for genetic influence and will make it easier to explore the developmental interplay between nature and nurture.

Claims to have discovered the gene(s) for complex behavioural traits (what Rose, 1997, calls *reductionism as ideology*) are currently widespread, both in popular writing and in scientific publications; but these are very misleading. According to Claridge and Davis (2003):

Genes code for very precise, literally microscopic, bits of biological material (proteins) that are both physically and conceptually very distant from the complex behavioural and psychological characteristics which they are supposed to – and perhaps in some sense do – influence. But it is unlikely that there are genes, or sets of genes, 'for' impulsivity, the preference for gay relationships, religiosity, anxiety, or even serious mental disorders, such as schizophrenia. The route from genes to behaviour is likely to be much more tortuous than that and, for any particular characteristic, to involve a multitude of genes and interactions among them – as well as an interplay between genes and environmental factors . . .

Claridge and Davis identify the rationale behind molecular genetic research as the belief that *phenotypic characteristics* (such as observable behaviour) can be found to be associated with a particular sequence of DNA at a given locus on a particular chromosome. But a DNA sequence can show variability (*polymorphisms*), and it is this variation that can be expressed phenotypically as a certain behaviour. Similarly, a single gene can have several different effects (*pleiotropic expression*), and the particular effect it produces depends on other genes (*contingent expression*). According to Rose (2001), the more we learn about pleiotropic and contingent expression:

. . . the more the assumption that the expression is simply an additive one becomes implausible. Gene expression changes depend both on the internal environment (including the other genes present in the organism), and the external one in which the organism develops . . .

BG as a whole is based on what Rose sees as the naïve belief that complex human psychological characteristics and behaviours can be quantified (see Chapters 3 and 11) and their origins partitioned into dichotomous 'genetic' and 'environmental' components. Underlying this belief is the assumption that the two factors are almost entirely *additive*, with little interaction between them. In other words, the similarity between individuals is *linearly* related to the proportion of genes they share: the fewer genes they share, the greater the psychological and behavioural differences between them. But often genes simply don't operate this way (Claridge and Davis, 2003).

The problem with phenotypes: what is schizophrenia?

While identifying the connections between genes and phenotype is relatively straightforward for recognizable, easily definable 'big effects' (such as well-known diseases), it is much more difficult for the kinds of phenotypes found in psychological research (such as personality and intelligence). This is partly because the core features that need explaining may not be all that obvious or agreed, and partly because, even if they are, they don't represent such huge differences between people that these will be discoverable above the 'noise' in the system (Claridge and Davis, 2003).

It is widely accepted that twin and other family resemblance studies show the contribution of genetic influences in schizophrenia (Gottesman, 1991), even in the absence of specific genes. Claridge and Davis claim that this is one of the few factual certainties about schizophrenia. But by the same token (and echoing Plomin; see above), they also claim that it is equally certain that environmental factors must also be important. So far, so good.

However, they cite studies that have produced some rather intriguing and puzzling findings. The *same* sets of monozygotic (MZ), or identical, twins were assessed for schizophrenia twice, once according to Schneider's (1959) *first rank symptoms* (passivity experiences and thought disturbances, auditory hallucinations and primary delusions) and on a separate occasion using broader criteria. In the latter case, the heritability estimate was 50 per cent, while using the first rank symptoms it was zero! This suggests, of course, that when we ask about the heritability of schizophrenia, our answer should be couched in 'well, it depends what you mean by . . .' terms. In other words, defining – and diagnosing – schizophrenia is more complex and less straightforward than for physical diseases.

Again, different studies have produced heritability estimates ranging from zero to 90 per cent. According to Claridge and Davis (2003): 'Is it possible that the value of 50 per cent now generally quoted is merely some average of a range of heritabilities for entirely different psychotic disorders, different variants of schizophrenia, or just illnesses of different severity?'

One notable development in genetics research on schizophrenia is the realization that clinical diagnosis is a very blunt, inaccurate phenotype for exploring heritability (Claridge and Davis, 2003). Instead, we should substitute or look for the genetics of intermediate phenotypes (or *endophenotypes*; Gottesman, 1991). These are measures that don't at first glance seem to have much to do with psychotic symptomatology. Instead, it is assumed that they tap more basic, but quite narrow, behaviours that might underlie the clinical state. A widely cited example is *smooth pursuit eye movement* (SPEM). It has been found that a proportion of schizophrenic patients show abnormal ability to follow, effectively, a swinging pendulum. It doesn't follow, of course, that everyone who shows this inability is likely to be schizophrenic!

DRAWING SOME CONCLUSIONS AND RAISING SOME IMPORTANT ISSUES

Watson, the co-discoverer of the double-helix structure of DNA and the former head of the Human Genome Project (the massive international attempt to identify every single human gene), claimed that 'We used to think that our fate was in our stars. Now we know, in large part, that our fate is in our genes' (in Horgan, 1993).

According to Koshland, an eminent biologist and editor of the influential journal *Science* (the journal of the American Association for the Advancement of Science), the nature–nurture debate is 'basically over', since scientists have shown that genes influence many aspects of human behaviour. He also claims (in Horgan, 1993) that genetic research may help to eliminate society's most intractable problems, including drug abuse, homelessness and violent crime. Horgan believes this illustrates that 'Eugenics is back in fashion.'

The term *eugenics* (from the Greek for 'good birth') was coined by Galton in 1883, and it embodied the idea that human society could be improved through 'better breeding'. Beginning in the 1920s, the American Eugenics Society sponsored 'Fitter Families Contests' at state fairs; just as cows and sheep were judged, so were people. Eugenicists helped to persuade more than 20 states to authorize the sterilization of men and women in prisons and psychiatric hospitals, and they also urged the federal government to restrict immigration of 'undesirable' races. Intelligence tests, which had been developed for the selection of soldiers during the First World War, were then used to justify the exclusion of certain nationalities, including those from eastern Europe, from entry into America during the 1920s and 1930s. It was, of course, precisely these groups that suffered at the hands of the Nazis, who took eugenics to its horrifying extreme, by exterminating six million Jews and other 'undesirables' in the gas chambers (see Gould, 1981; Gross, 2003).

Figure 5.11 These young German men from 1934 demonstrate the stereotype of the Nazi ideal of fitness and health

Research into the genetics of homosexuality also raises some quite fundamental social and political issues, which go beyond homosexuality itself (see Box 5.2, page 92).

As we have already noted, genes in themselves specify proteins, *not* behavioural or psychological phenomena. Although we know virtually nothing about how complex psychological phenomena are embodied in the brain, it is conceivable that particular DNA sequences might somehow cause the brain to be wired specifically for homosexual orientation. However, Byrne (1994) warns that:

... we should also be asking ourselves why we as a society are so emotionally invested in this research ... Perhaps the answer to the most salient questions in this debate lie not within the biology of human brains but rather in the cultures those brains have created.

The genetic theory of intelligence, especially the claim that racial differences are due to genetic variations (e.g. Jensen, 1969), has always been condemned by those of a left-wing persuasion; they see it as reinforcing, and even fuelling, the racism and racial inequalities that are responsible for the intellectual differences in the first place. However, in the case of homosexuality, things are much less clear-cut. If scientific evidence shows that

Box 5.2 Is homosexuality genetically determined?

LeVay and Hamer (1994) discuss research that claims to have identified a segment of the X chromosome likely to be the site of the genes responsible for 'swaying', if not 'determining', sexual orientation. This research is a *linkage study* based on the finding that genes that are close together on a chromosome are almost always inherited together. So, if there's a gene that influences sexual orientation, it should be 'linked' to a nearby DNA *marker* (segments of DNA that indicate locations on a chromosome) that tends to travel along with it in a 'family'. Out of 40 pairs of gay brothers, 33 showed the same marker, located at the tip of the long arm of the X chromosome, in a region known as Xq28.

X Chromosome **Xq28 (Shared region)**

According to LeVay and Hamer:

> The most straightforward interpretation of the finding is that chromosome region Xq28 contains a gene that influences male sexual orientation. The study provides the strongest evidence to date that human sexuality is influenced by heredity because it directly examines the genetic information [in] the DNA . . .

However, LeVay and Hamer recognize that these are only initial findings, and that, as well as the need for replication, the gene itself hasn't yet been isolated. Xq28 is about 4 million base pairs in length; although this represents less than 0.2 per cent of the total human genome, it's still long enough to contain several hundred genes. Searching for 'gay genes' is like looking for the proverbial 'needle in a haystack' (LeVay and Hamer, 1994).

Figure 5.12 The Xq28 region of the X chromosome (From LeVay and Hamer, 1994)

homosexuality is genetically determined, this means that gays (and, presumably, lesbians too) don't *choose* their sexual orientation: they 'cannot help it'. This could, however, be used *against* gays and lesbians: if they cannot choose to be different (i.e. *heterosexual*), then they are *more* of a threat, rather than less. The genetic view is usually a chance to blame the victim, a way of excusing injustice (Byrne, 1994).

Many gays and lesbians fight for the right to choose their sexual preference, so it may be very surprising to find LeVay, a homosexual and eminent biologist, advocating the search for 'gay genes'. He believes that, if successful, the scientific evidence will make society as a whole *more*, not less, tolerant, precisely because it will show that homosexuals don't choose to 'be that way'. However, LeVay and Hamer (1994) recognize that:

> . . . increasing knowledge of biology may eventually bring with it the power to infringe on the natural rights of individuals and to impoverish the world of its human diversity. It is important that our society expand discussions of how new scientific information should be used to benefit the human race in its entirety.

SUMMARY

○ The debate about heredity and environment (or the *nature–nurture debate*) is concerned with some of the most fundamental questions that human beings ask about themselves.

○ In its broadest sense, the debate is concerned with *both* the *human species as a whole* (compared with other species) *and* with *individual differences* between people. It's in the latter sense that the nature–nurture debate takes place.

○ *Nativists* believe that heredity determines certain abilities/capacities, while *empiricists* believe that the mind, at birth, is a *tabula rasa*, which is gradually 'filled in' by learning and experience.

○ Examples of nativism in psychology include the Gestalt psychologists, Gesell's concept of *maturation*, and Chomsky's *LAD*. *Behaviourism* represents a very influential and extreme form of empiricist theory within psychology.

○ 'Is it nature or nurture?' is an oversimplified question, while 'How much?' is a more complex question, concerned with the *relative importance* of heredity and environment. It presupposes that *both* are involved, consistent with an *interactionist* position, and is linked to the 'individual differences' form of the debate.

○ Attempts to *quantify* the relative contributions of genes and environment is the main focus of *behavioural genetics*, which uses methods such as *twin studies*, *adoption studies* and other studies of *family resemblance*.

○ Within *genetics*, 'nature' refers to 'inheritance', i.e. *differences* in chromosomes and genes transmitted from parents to offspring.

○ While genetic variability is the raw material of evolution, evolution *doesn't* imply genetic variation *within* a species, and vice-versa.

○ The basic units of hereditary transmission are *genes*, large molecules of *DNA*. They occur in pairs and are situated on the *chromosomes*.

○ Genes have two major functions: *self-duplication* and *protein synthesis*. The body's non-reproductive cells duplicate through *mitosis*, while the reproductive/germ cells duplicate through *meiosis*.

○ *Structural* genes code for proteins and enzymes, and form the basis of classical genetics. *Regulator* genes (the majority) communicate closely with the environment and change in response to it.

○ In a psychological context, 'environment' usually implies external, post-natal influences impinging on a passive individual. Instead of seeing the environment as independent of/separate from the individual, however, people may be seen as *making their own environments*. This is demonstrated by *gene–environment correlations, non-shared psychosocial experiences*, attaching their own *meaning* to events/experiences, and *gene–environment interaction*. Related to these are *niche-picking* and *niche-building*.

O Behaviour genetic research not only shows beyond doubt that genetic factors are involved in complex human behaviour and psychological characteristics, but it also provides the strongest evidence for the importance of environmental factors. To this extent, the nature–nurture debate is 'over'.

O *Molecular genetics* involves the attempt to identify specific genes responsible for individual differences. Many such claims have been made, but the research on which they're based seems to ignore *polymorphisms*, and *pleiotropic* and *contingent expression*. It also assumes the *additive* nature of genetic influence.

O Another problem with molecular genetics is defining and measuring the *phenotype* for which the genes are being sought. Heritability estimates for schizophrenia are influenced by what criteria for diagnosing it are used, a problem that rarely occurs with physical diseases. One solution to this problem is to look for the genetics of *endophenotypes*.

O Genetic research into homosexuality raises several (more general) important social and political issues, including: *eugenics*; why the research is seen as so important in the first place; and whether society becomes *more* or *less* tolerant of homosexuality if it is found that gays 'can't help it'.

Useful websites

O http://www.apa.org/releases/mother.html
O http://www.learner.org/exhibits/personality/genes.html
O http://www.sanger.ac.uk
O http://objana.com/frog/natnurt.html
O http://genetics.nature.com
O guardian.co.uk/genes

Recommended reading

Ceci, S.J. and Williams, W.M. (eds) (1999) *The Nature–Nurture Debate: The Essential Readings.* Oxford: Blackwell.

Gross, R. (2003) *Key Studies in Psychology* (4th edn) (Chapters 23 and 24 on intelligence). London: Hodder & Stoughton.

Plomin, R. (1994) *Genetics and Experience: The Interplay between Nature and Nurture.* Thousand Oaks, CA: Sage.

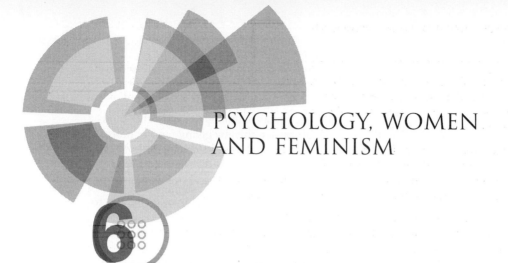

PSYCHOLOGY, WOMEN AND FEMINISM

At first sight, it may not seem obvious what a chapter with the title 'Psychology, women and feminism' would be about, or why such a chapter should be necessary. But in a very real sense, what it's *about* is what makes it *necessary*, namely the very strong and pervasive *masculinist bias* within psychology, which, in turn, reflects – and to some degree may contribute to – the superior power and status of males in western society.

While *feminism* is a social and political movement that arose outside of psychology (often used synonymously with the women's movement of the 1970s in particular), many who would describe themselves as feminists were, and are, academics who criticized their particular discipline for being 'gender blind' (Kelly, 1988). If what feminists have in common is a condemnation of the oppression of women (in any and all its forms), then we'd expect that those engaged in occupations and professions (including psychology) would be critical of such treatment of women as it goes on within their occupation or profession.

However, feminist thinkers and writers aren't just *against* oppression of and discrimination against women, they're also *for* the recognition of the achievements, contributions and experience of women as being valid and important *in their own right*, and not just as matters to be understood and evaluated *in comparison with men*. *Feminist psychologists*, therefore, are female psychologists who criticize psychology as a discipline – both its methods, its theories and its applications – from a feminist perspective.

WHAT IS FEMINIST PSYCHOLOGY?

According to Wilkinson (1989), definitions of feminist psychology vary widely, in both substance and inclusiveness. For example, in the USA, the terms 'feminist psychology' and the 'psychology of women' are often used synonymously: psychological research on women, and its practitioners, are automatically described as 'feminist'. However, in the UK, these areas are generally more clearly distinguished.

This chapter as a whole explores some of the major criticisms of psychology made from a feminist perspective. Briefly, these include:

○ a great deal of psychological research is conducted on all-male samples, but then it either fails to make this clear or reports the findings as if they applied to women and men equally

○ some of the most influential theories within psychology as a whole are based on studies of males only, but are meant to apply equally to women and men

○ if women's behaviour differs from men's, the former is often judged to be pathological or abnormal or deficient in some way, since the behaviour of men is, implicitly or explicitly, taken as the 'standard', the norm against which women's behaviour is compared

○ psychological explanations of behaviour tend to emphasize biological (and other internal) causes, as opposed to social (and other external) causes, thereby giving (and reinforcing) the impression that *psychological sex differences* are inevitable and unchangeable, at the same time reinforcing widely-held stereotypes about men and women. As well as being objectionable in themselves, such stereotypes contribute to the oppression of women

○ heterosexuality – both in women and men – is taken (either implicitly or explicitly) to be the norm, so that homosexuality is seen as abnormal.

In short, feminist psychologists see psychology as being *sexist* – that is, women are regarded as inferior to men and are discriminated against *because* they are women – and *heterosexist* – that is, gay men and lesbian women are considered to be abnormal and are discriminated against *because* they're gays or lesbians. Feminist psychologists also consider that while psychology, as a science, claims to be 'neutral', 'objective' and 'value-free', it is in fact *value-laden*, taking men as the 'universal' standard, the centre around which everything else revolves. So, apart from being sexist and heterosexist, psychology is also *androcentric* (male-centred).

SEXISM WITHIN THE PSYCHOLOGY PROFESSION

In 1974, Bernstein and Russo published an article in *American Psychologist* called 'The history of psychology revisited: Or, up with our foremothers'. It consisted largely of a quiz, which their psychology colleagues failed miserably! The questions were as follows

(i)   Who were the first persons to use the term 'projective technique' in print?

(Answer: Lois Murphy and Ruth Horowitz)

(ii)   Who was the first person to develop child analysis through play?

(Answer: Hermine von Hug-Hellmuth)

(iii)   Who developed the Cattell Infant Intelligence Test Scale?

(Answer: Psyche Cattell)

(iv)   What do the following have in common?

The Bender–Gestalt Test, the Taylor Manifest Anxiety Scale, the Kent–Rosanoff Word Association Test, the Thematic Apperception Test (TAT), and the Sentence Completion Method.

(Answer: A woman was either the senior author or the sole author of each test/method)

(v)   The following are the last names of individuals who have contributed to the scientific study of human behaviour. What else do these names have in common?

Ausubel, Bellak, Brunswick, Buhler, Dennis, Gardner, Gibson, Glueck, Harlow, Hartley, Hoffman, Horowitz, Jones, Kendler, Koch, Lacey, Luchins, Lynd, Murphy, Premack, Rossi, Sears, Sherif, Spence, Staats, Stendler, Whiting, Yarrow.

(Answer: They are the surnames of female social scientists)

While you may have recognized some of the names in the last question, this may only be because they had more famous and familiar husbands with whom they jointly published research (e.g. Gardner and Gardner, Harlow and Harlow, Kendler and Kendler, Luchins and

Luchins, and Sherif and Sherif): we automatically infer that the 'Harlow' in the list is Harry Harlow (of rhesus monkey fame) and that the 'Sherif' is Muztafer Sherif (of the autokinetic effect in conformity fame). We are *all* guilty!

Similarly, there's a strong tendency to assume that a psychologist whose name is unfamiliar to you is *male*. Even though *statistically* it's very likely that you'll be correct, this *isn't* the basis for making such assumptions. Instead, it reflects a *masculinist bias*, the belief that the contributions made by men to psychology are more important than those made by women. As Scarborough and Furumoto (1987, in Paludi, 1992) state, the history of psychology is the history of male psychology.

If the names in the answers to questions i–iii aren't what you'd call 'household names', this is precisely because the psychological literature's treatment of women psychologists has kept them invisible (Paludi, 1992):

> The histories written by psychology's academicians are neither accurate nor complete, neglecting as they do the most important contributions made by women ... they do not include Mary Calkin's theory of self nor her invention of the method of paired associates, they do not mention Christine Ladd-Franklin's developmental theory of colour vision ... Additionally, they fail to mention the monumentally important books of Margaret Washburn on animal behaviour ... and they totally ignore Magda Arnold's comprehensive theory of emotions and Margaret Harlow's contribution to an understanding of the importance of tactile stimulation in mothering.
> *(Stevens and Gardner, 1982, in Paludi, 1992)*

Figure 6.1 Mary Calkins and Margaret Washburn; if these women are not household names, it is because psychological literature's treatment of women psychologists has kept them invisible

Mary Calkins was also the first person to explicitly recognize, and vividly describe, primacy-recency effects in memory (although she never actually used these terms) (Jackson, 1992).

Jackson (1992) points out that during the earliest days of the discipline of psychology (the mid-1800s), discrimination against women was overt: they were simply banned from participating. Calkins was excluded, in 1890, from a graduate psychology programme on the grounds that she was a woman. Similarly, both Calkins and Ladd-Franklin were refused their PhDs, even though they had completed their theses.

Washburn was the first white American woman to receive a PhD in psychology, in 1908 (1904, according to Paludi); Inez Prosser was the first black American woman, receiving her

PhD in 1933 (Jackson, 1992)! Washburn was also the second woman President of the American Psychological Association (APA), in 1921, but despite this, she was denied an academic post at a research university (Paludi, 1992).

The rediscovery of women psychologists

Their colleagues' poor performance on their quiz led Bernstein and Russo (1974) to conclude that women psychologists needed to be *rediscovered*. According to Paludi (1992), in response to the neglect of women's contributions to psychology and to the recognition that women's history has the potential to transform women's self-understanding, a sub-field of *women's history in psychology* has evolved in recent years. This draws on Lerner's (1979) model, namely (i) finding lost or overlooked women and putting them back into the history (*compensatory history*), (ii) noting women's contributions (*contribution history*), and (iii) noting how history is constructed through a male (*androcentric*) perspective and reconstructing it from the perspective of women (*reconstruction history*) (see Chapter 11).

In the USA, the Association for Women in Psychology (AWP) was formed in 1969, and in 1973, the APA formed the Division of the Psychology of Women (Division 35), which publishes its own journal, *The Psychology of Women Quarterly* (*PWQ*). Parlee (1991) asks how far the *PWQ* has helped to develop a psychology for women or a psychology of gender that is different from mainstream (or 'malestream') psychology. Compared with mainstream journals, articles in the *PWQ* have (i) more often involved women of different ages, sexual orientations and from different ethnic backgrounds, (ii) less often involved just experimental research designs, and (iii) have paid somewhat more attention to the context of behaviour (as opposed to biological or personality variables). (Both (ii) and (iii) are discussed in more detail below.) However, Parlee feels that these differences represent only a superficial change.

This view is endorsed by Wilkinson (1989), who asks why there has been a lack of change within mainstream psychology in response to the 'feminist critique'. The answer, she says, is essentially to do with *legitimacy*: feminist research isn't seen by the mainstream to be 'legitimate science' and so is largely dismissed. Not only is it not seen as legitimate, but, because of the commitment of feminist research to social and political change for the benefit of women, it provides a convenient 'handle' for the labelling of feminist research as 'purely political'. This false polarization of 'science' and 'politics' removes the need to take feminist arguments seriously, and protects mainstream researchers from having to acknowledge the political dimension of his/her practice (Wilkinson, 1989) (see Chapters 5, 11 and 15). The Division of the Psychology of Women also has a Section on the Psychology of Black Women, as well as Committees on the Psychology of Latinas and Asian-American Women.

In her Presidential Address to the APA in 1987, Bonnie Stricklund pointed out that women now constitute about one-third of all employed psychologists and more than half of those gaining PhDs in psychology each year. Compared with the overt discrimination of the early years of psychology, this represents a radical change. She predicted that psychology will become the first science to be 'feminized' – that is, it will have more women than men. This will allow the investigation of a set of research problems that weren't consistent with, or couldn't be solved by, the *androcentric paradigm* – such as women's friendships with other women, rape, sexual harassment, battered women, eating disorders, and sexism within psychopathology (Paludi, 1992).

One manifestation of sexism within psychology is the devaluation (by men) of the areas of the discipline in which women are traditionally more numerous and which they seem to prefer, compared with the traditionally 'male' areas. The former include person-oriented/service-oriented fields, such as educational, developmental and clinical psychology, and counselling, while the latter are the academic/experimental areas, including learning and cognitive psychology, which are regarded (by men) as more scientifically rigorous and intellectually demanding (Paludi, 1992). This is consistent with the more general observation that professions dominated by women are seen as low status (at least by male practitioners) (Wilkinson, 1989).

Could it be that women are 'channelled' into certain fields of psychology, which are then defined as 'inferior', simply because they are populated mainly by women? People who play a key role in this process are *gatekeepers* – individuals, such as heads of university psychology departments, with the power and authority to decide who is employed to teach and do research, and in what areas of the discipline. In psychology, the gatekeepers are usually men.

HETEROSEXISM IN THE PSYCHOLOGY PROFESSION

Many radical feminists, both within and outside psychology, are lesbians. Not surprisingly, lesbian feminist psychologists tend to focus their criticisms on the neglect of the topic of homosexuality, and discrimination against lesbians and gays, both staff and students.

According to Celia Kitzinger (1990), homosexuality hardly features in undergraduate psychology courses. She quotes Louise Clarke (1989), a lesbian student at one of the 'new' universities in London, who says that, 'There are ... lesbians/gay men in every college of higher education, whose needs are barely acknowledged, let alone met. Our existence should be acknowledged and reflected not just in the lecture room, but also in the curriculum.'

Kitzinger goes on to say that for gay and lesbian students and staff alike, academic psychology departments can be deeply oppressive places. Although teaching unions have anti-discrimination policies and oppose Section 28 of the Local Government Act (outlawing the 'promotion' of homosexuality and the teaching of the 'acceptability of homosexuality as a pretended family relationship'), universities still embody anti-gay attitudes. Psychologists who 'come out' run the risk of verbal abuse and threats of violence. Kitzinger advocates that policies should be implemented comparable to those dealing with gender, race and disability discrimination, to protect lesbians and gays wherever psychologists work.

The APA Gay and Lesbian Studies Division was established in 1984. In the UK, the British Psychological Association (BPS) has a Psychology of Women Section (POWS), set up in 1987, and there also exists the more informal *Women in Psychology* organization. According to Kitzinger and Coyle (2002), publication of their book (*Lesbian and Gay Psychology: New Perspectives*) marks the 'coming of age' of British lesbian and gay psychology. It celebrates the founding of the BPS's Lesbian and Gay Psychology Section in 1998, after nine years of campaigning and three rejected proposals.

THE FEMINIST CRITIQUE OF SCIENCE

If certain areas of psychology (such as cognitive) are regarded (by men) as scientifically more rigorous and intellectually demanding, we need to ask just what is meant by 'scientifically rigorous'. What view of science is assumed by those who would make such a claim? What is the 'malestream' or androcentric account of the nature of science?

Basically, it sees the scientist as pursuing 'the truth' through the use of highly controlled, experimental methods. The scientist is able to discover 'what the world is really like', in some objective sense (how things are when they are *not* being observed and measured by scientists). Because the scientist is only interested in objective truth ('facts'), science, according to this perspective, is said to be *value-free*: the scientist's values, biases, and so on, have no influence on the scientific process. This *positivist* approach applies as much to the study of people as it does to the physical world (see Chapters 11 and 15).

But can scientific enquiry be neutral, totally free of bias, wholly independent of the value-system of the human scientists who are doing the science? According to Prince and Hartnett (1993):

Decisions about what is, and what is not, to be measured, how this is done, and most importantly, what constitutes legitimate research are made by individual scientists within a socio-political context, and thus science is ideological. Science is perhaps better viewed as 'a discourse that narrates the world in a special way' ... Scientific psychology has reified concepts such as personality and intelligence – and the scientific psychology which 'objectively' and 'rationally' produced means of measuring these reifications has been responsible for physical assaults on women such as forced abortions and sterilizations ...

Prince and Hartnett point out that, between 1924 and 1972, over 7500 women in the state of Virginia alone were forcibly sterilized – in particular, 'unwed mothers, prostitutes, the feeble-minded, children with discipline problems'; the criterion in all cases was the woman's mental age as measured by the Stanford–Binet intelligence test (Gould, 1981).

When some human ability or quality, such as intelligence, is treated as if it had a separate, independent, objective, existence (when it is *reified*), such that it can be measured in an objective way, scientific 'findings' relating to that ability/quality can then be used to promote and justify discrimination against groups in society. But intelligence, personality and so many more of the 'things' psychologists study are *hypothetical constructs*, abstract concepts used to help explain and predict behaviour, but *not* directly, or literally, observable.

The very decision to study intelligence, and to develop tests designed to measure it, indicates that (some) psychologists believe that not only is this possible, but (much more relevant to the view of science as value-free) that it is *important* to do so! Such decisions aren't made in a politico-cultural vacuum, and so cannot be seen as objective, neutral and value-free. As Weisstein (1993b) says, 'our ideas are filtered through our cultural and social categories, the ongoing social context and our own social rank'.

According to Nicolson (1995), *the scientific method is gender-biased* (see Chapters 11 and 15). She argues that:

Psychology relies for its data on the practices of socialized and culture-bound individuals, so that to explore 'natural' or 'culture-free' behaviour (namely that behaviour unfettered by cultural, social structures and power relations) is by definition impossible, which is a state of affairs that normally goes unacknowledged ...

'Normally' denotes mainstream, positivist psychology.

Far from advocating that psychology should be value-free, objective and 'scientific', many feminist psychologists argue that we should stop denying the role of values, and acknowledge that psychological investigation must always take wider social reality into account. They call for a new *value-laden approach to research*: unless and until psychology 'comes clean' about its values and biases, it will never be able to adequately reflect the reality of its subject matter, namely human beings.

In the 1993 'Preface' to her classic *In A Different Voice* (first published in 1982), Carol Gilligan says that at the core of her work on moral development in women and girls was the realization that within psychology, and in society at large, 'values were being taken as facts'. She continues:

> In the aftermath of the Holocaust . . . it is not tenable for psychologists or social scientists to adopt a position of ethical neutrality or cultural relativism – to say that one cannot say anything about values or that all values are culturally relative. Such a hands-off stance in the face of atrocity amounts to a kind of complicity . . .
> *(Gilligan, 1993)*

While the example she gives is clearly extreme, it helps to illustrate the argument that, not only do psychologists (and other scientists) have a responsibility to make their values explicit about important social and political issues, but their failure to do so may (unwittingly) *contribute* to prejudice, discrimination and oppression.

THE MASCULINIST BIAS

The major 'sin' of mainstream psychology has been to *deny* the part played by values, resulting in the *masculinist bias* that permeates so much of the discipline. This takes a number of forms.

'Women want first and foremost to be mothers'

As we have seen, most psychologists are male, and the predominant research methodology used is the experiment, which is supposed to be objective and value-free. But we've also seen that deciding what's worth investigating is itself a value judgement, and this is particularly clear when male psychologists investigate aspects of female behaviour, such as motherhood.

For example, according to Bettelheim (1965), 'we must start with the realization that, as much as women want to be good scientists or engineers, they want first and foremost to be womanly companions of men, and to be mothers'. Similarly, Bowlby (1953) linked motherhood inextricably to being at home, white, 20–30 years old, middle class and married. But what about the parent and infant studies of non-married, single, gay, lesbian and black parents (Jackson, 1992)?

In the twenty-first century, a lesbian sexual orientation is no longer considered to be a reason to deny a mother custody of her children. At present in the UK lesbian women are individually eligible to adopt children, and MPs have recently voted to allow unmarried couples, whatever their sexual orientation, to adopt children jointly. Lesbian mothers also have access to assisted reproduction clinics to allow them to conceive a child without the involvement of a male partner. This change in social attitudes has come about largely through the efforts of the women's movement and the gay liberation movement beginning in the 1970s (Golombok, 2002).

Golombok believes that psychology has also had a part to play. There will always be some people who believe that it is morally wrong for lesbian women to rear children – whatever the outcome for the child. Others object on the grounds that the children would suffer. But psychological research (including Golombok's own) to the contrary has brought about a change of mind:

Mothers no longer have to choose between their partner and their child, and children who would otherwise have remained in care are being adopted or fostered into loving homes. Psychological research has helped tackle the injustices and prejudice that has damaged people's lives. That is why I study lesbian mothers.
(Golombok, 2002)

(See 'Essentialism revisited', page III.)

The male standard

Men are taken as some sort of *standard* or *norm*, against which women are compared and judged. According to Tavris (1993):

In any domain of life in which men set the standard of normalcy, women will be considered abnormal, and society will debate woman's 'place' and her 'nature'. Many women experience tremendous conflict in trying to decide whether to be 'like' men or 'opposite' from them, and this conflict is itself evidence of the implicit male standard against which they are measuring themselves. This is why it is normal for women to feel abnormal.

Figure 6.2 The fact that Eve was made from Adam's rib illustrates the point that men are the standard by which women are all too often judged

She gives three examples.

1 Women and men have the same moods and mood swings, but only women get theirs packaged into a syndrome. Women's hormones have never been reliably related to *behaviour*, competence or anything to do with work, while men's *are* related to a variety of antisocial behaviours. Despite this, women may suffer from PMS (pre-menstrual syndrome), but there's no male equivalent (such as 'hyper-testosterone syndrome').

2 In 1985, the American Psychiatric Association proposed two new categories of mental disorder for inclusion in the revised (third) edition of *DSM (Diagnostic and Statistical*

Manual of Mental Disorders), the official classification system used by American psychiatrists. One of these was *masochism*, which in *DSM II* was one of the psychosexual disorders, in which sexual gratification requires being hurt or humiliated. The proposal was to extend the term so that it became a more pervasive personality disorder, in which a person seeks failure at work, at home and in relationships, rejects opportunities for pleasure, puts others first, thereby sacrificing his/her own needs, playing the martyr, and so on. While not intended to apply to women exclusively, these characteristics are associated predominantly with the female role. Indeed, Caplan, in 1985, appeared before an American Psychiatric Association hearing on the proposed disorder, and argued that it represented a way of calling psychopathological the behaviour of women who conform to social norms for a 'feminine woman' (the 'good wife syndrome'; Caplan, 1991). In short, such a diagnostic label was biased against women and perpetuated the myth of women's masochism.

After a year-long debate, the label was changed to *self-defeating personality disorder* and was put in the Appendix of *DSM-III-R*, under the heading 'Proposed Diagnostic Categories Needing Further Study'. As Zimbardo (1992) argues, this example shows the political and ideological implications of diagnosing certain behaviour patterns as mental disorders (see Chapter 7). At the same time, there was no proposal for a parallel diagnosis for men who conform to social norms for a 'real' man (the John Wayne type, or 'macho personality disorder'). However, in 1991, Pantony and Caplan formally proposed that *delusional dominating personality disorder* be included in *DSM IV*, which was at the time being prepared (and was subsequently published in 1994). The Committee soundly rejected the proposal, on the grounds that 'there is no clinical tradition' for such a disorder (Caplan, 1991; Tavris, 1993).

Figure 6.3 John Wayne is seen by many as the ultimate 'macho man'

3 When men have problems (such as drug abuse), and behave in socially unacceptable ways (as in rape and other forms of violence), the causes are looked for in their upbringing. Women's problems, on the other hand, are the result of their psyche or their hormones. This corresponds roughly to an *internal attribution* in the case of women, and an *external attribution* in the case of men. The further implication is that for men, *it could have been different* (*they* are the victims of their childhoods, etc.), while for women it couldn't (because 'that's what women are like') (see Chapter 2).

According to Tavris (1993), the view that man is the norm and woman is the opposite, lesser or deficient (*the problem*), constitutes one of three currently competing views regarding what she calls the 'Mismeasure of Woman' (meant to parallel Gould's *The Mismeasure of Man* (1981), a brilliant critique of intelligence testing; see Gross, 2003). It's the view that underlies so much psychological research designed to discover why women aren't 'as *something*' (moral, intelligent, rational) as men. According to Tavris (1993): 'The bias of seeing women's behaviour as something to be explained in relation to the male norm makes sense in a world which takes the male norm for granted.'

Moreover, the male norm *frames the very questions* investigators ask; the answers to these questions then create the impression that women have 'problems', 'deficiencies', etc. if they differ from the norm (see Box 6.1, page 105).

The male standard as the norm also underlies the enormous self-help industry, whereby women consume millions of books advising them how to be slimmer, more beautiful, independent or whatever. Men, being normal, feel no need to 'fix' themselves in corresponding ways (Tavris, 1993).

Consistent with this view is a study by Broverman *et al.* (1979, in Jackson, 1992), which asked several psychiatrists to define a *healthy adult*, a *healthy adult male* and a *healthy adult female*. The first two definitions were very similar, being defined by traits such as assertiveness, aggression, ambition and task-orientation. But healthy women were viewed as being caring, expressive, nurturing and affiliative. Women, therefore, are in a double bind. As healthy *women*, they fall outside the norm for healthy *adults*; if they assume male characteristics, they step outside the definition of a *healthy woman* (Jackson, 1992).

Accentuating the sex differences

In psychology in general, but perhaps in the study of gender in particular, there is a strong bias towards publishing studies that have produced 'positive' results (where there is a significant difference). So, in the case of gender, studies that find *sex differences* will be published, while those that don't, won't. The far more convincing evidence for 'sex similarity' is, therefore, ignored, creating the very powerful impression that differences between men and women are real, widespread and 'the rule'. Indeed, the very term 'sex similarities' sounds rather odd (Unger, 1979; Jackson, 1992; Tavris, 1993).

Sexism in research

Pointing out the sexist bias in psychological research is as much an *ethical* as a scientific/practical criticism: we've already seen how damaging to women sexist research can be (see also Chapter 10).

The APA Board of Social and Ethical Responsibility for Psychology set up a Committee on Nonsexist Research, which reported its findings as *Guidelines for Avoiding Sexism in Psychological Research* (Denmark *et al.*, 1988).

According to Denmark *et al.*, gender bias is found at all stages of the research process: (i) question formulation; (ii) research methods and design; (iii) data analysis and interpretation; (iv) conclusion formulation. The principles set out in the *Guidelines* are meant to apply to other forms of bias too: race, ethnicity, disability, sexual orientation and socioeconomic status.

Box 6.1 Some examples of typical findings from the literature on psychological sex differences (Tavris, 1993)

○ Women have lower self-esteem than men do.

○ Women do not value their efforts as much as men do.

○ Women are less self-confident than men.

○ Women are more likely to say they're hurt than to admit they're angry.

○ Women have more difficulty developing a 'separate sense of self'.

Most people would agree that it is desirable for women to have high self-esteem, to value their efforts more, and so on. So such studies usually conclude with discussion of 'the problem' of why women are so insecure and what can be done about it.

But had these studies used *women* as the basis of comparison, the same findings might have produced different conclusions about what the 'problems' are.

○ Men are more conceited than women.

○ Men overvalue the work they do.

○ Men are not as realistic as women in assessing their abilities.

○ Men are more likely to accuse/attack others when unhappy, instead of stating that they feel hurt or looking for sympathy.

○ Men have more difficulty in forming and maintaining relationships.

If these 'translations' of the first set of statements sound biased and derogatory, this is precisely the point Tavris is trying to make: describing *women's* deficiencies isn't usually seen as biased and derogatory, because the *male norm* is the standard against which women are being judged. As soon as a *female norm* is used to set the standard, the bias becomes apparent; only then do we become aware of the bias that was there all the time!

'Why has it been so difficult to notice the same negative tone in the way we talk about women? The answer is that we are used to seeing women as the problem, and to regarding women's differences from men as deficiencies and weaknesses' (Tavris, 1993).

Tavris argues that, after centuries of trying to 'measure up', many women feel exhilarated by having female qualities and experiences valued and celebrated. *Cultural feminists*, while regarding man as the norm, see woman as *opposite but better* ('the solution'); this represents the second current version of the 'mismeasure of woman'.

QUESTION FORMULATION

Gender stereotypes associated with the topic being studied can bias the questions that are asked (and the research outcomes). For example, leadership is often defined in terms of dominance, aggression, and other styles that stress stereotypically male characteristics. To correct this problem, researchers should recognize the existence of a range of leadership styles, including those that stress egalitarian relationships, negotiation, conflict resolution and consideration of others.

Again, questions derived from, or constrained by, existing theory and research based on male samples, thus not taking women's experiences into account, are likely to result in explanations of female behaviour that aren't very meaningful. For example, the hypothesis that aggressive stimuli increase sexual arousal is based on results using male participants only; it is essential either to use female participants as well as male, or to point out the difficulties of generalizing these results to women.

Finally, it is assumed that topics relevant to white males are more important and 'basic', whereas those relevant to white females, or ethnic-minority females or males, are more marginal, specialized or applied. For example, research on the effects of TV violence on aggression in boys is considered basic, while research on the psychological correlates of pregnancy or the menopause isn't. (This relates to what we noted earlier regarding the value-laden nature of psychology and the need to recognize the biases involved in research, instead of trying to deny them.)

RESEARCH METHODS AND DESIGN

The selection of research participants is often based on stereotypic assumptions, and doesn't allow for generalizations to other populations. For example, in studies of contraception, female-only samples are used, on the assumption that males aren't (or needn't be) responsible for contraception. But both sexes should be studied before drawing any conclusions about the factors that influence the use of contraception.

Sometimes male samples are used because of practical convenience. For example, male animals are often preferred as subjects in experiments because the oestrous cycle in females disrupts responses in certain types of behavioural or biological tests. Generalization to females must then be made only with great caution.

In a surprisingly large number of studies, the sex and race of the participants, researchers and any confederates who may be involved, aren't specified. As a consequence, potential interactions between these variables aren't accounted for. For example, men tend to display more helping behaviour than women in studies involving a young female confederate who needs help. These findings could be a function of either the sex of the confederate or an interaction between the confederate and the participant, rather than sex differences between the participants (which is the usual conclusion that is drawn).

DATA ANALYSIS AND INTERPRETATION

As we noted in the section on 'Accentuating the sex differences', above, when sex differences *aren't* found, the findings tend to remain unreported. Not only should they be, but conversely when any *non-hypothesized* sex differences *are* found they should be reported. In both cases, the findings should be reported so that replications can be carried out.

Sex differences are sometimes claimed to be present when a significant correlation is found between two variables for, say, men, but not for women. Instead of testing to see if there is a significant difference between the two correlations, it is simply *assumed* (because the findings fit the stereotypes).

Finally, significant sex differences may be reported in a very misleading way, because the wrong sort of comparisons are being made. For example, 'The spatial ability scores of women in our sample are significantly lower than those of men, at the 0.01 level.' We might conclude from this that women cannot/should not become architects or engineers.

However, 'Successful architects score above 32 on our spatial ability test ... engineers score above 31 ... 12 per cent of women and 16 per cent of men in our sample score above 31; 11 per cent of women and 15 per cent of men score above 32.' What conclusions would you draw now?

CONCLUSION FORMULATION

Results based on one sex only are then applied to both. This can be seen in some major psychological theories, notably Erikson's theory of life-span development and Kohlberg's theory of moral development. Grosz (1987, in Wilkinson, 1989) would describe these as 'phallocentric' theories, involving 'the use of general or universal models to represent the two sexes according to the interests and terms of one, the male'.

Discussing Erikson's theory, which was based on the study of males only, Gilligan (1982) states that: 'psychological theorists ... Implicitly adopting the male life as the norm ... have tried to fashion women out of a masculine cloth ... In the life cycle ... the woman has been the deviant ...'.

Erikson (1950) describes a series of eight developmental stages meant to be *universal* – that is, they apply to both women and men, in different cultures, and so on. For example, the conflict between *identity* and *role confusion* (which occurs during adolescence) precedes that between *intimacy* and *isolation* (young adulthood). But he acknowledges (Erikson, 1968) that the sequence is *different* for the female: she holds her identity in abeyance as she prepares to attract the man by whose name she will be known, by whose status she will be defined, the man who will rescue her from emptiness and loneliness by filling 'the inner space'. For men, achieving a sense of identity precedes intimacy with a sexual partner; but for women, these tasks seem to be fused, and intimacy goes along with identity: 'the female comes to know herself as she is known, through her relationships with others' (Gilligan, 1982)

Yet despite his observation of sex differences, Erikson's *epigenetic chart* of the life-cycle stages remains unchanged: 'identity continues to precede intimacy as male experience continues to define his [Erikson's] life-cycle concept' (Gilligan, 1982).

Similarly, Kohlberg's six-stage theory of moral development was based on a 20-year longitudinal study of 84 boys (starting in 1955), but he claims universality for his stage sequence. Girls and women rarely attain a level of moral reasoning above the third stage (*good boy–nice girl orientation*), which is supposed to be achieved by most adolescents and adults. This leaves females looking decidedly morally deficient. But Gilligan argues, based on her own studies of females, that men and women have qualitatively different conceptions of morality. When presented with hypothetical moral dilemmas, such as the famous case of Heinz (whose wife is dying from cancer and can only be saved by a drug which Heinz can only obtain through stealing it), both boys and girls typically want his wife to live. But the 'female' solution is to 'find some other way' besides stealing the drug, and the emphasis is put on the notions of care, responsibility and relationships. By contrast, males are more likely to condemn the druggist for asking so much money for the drug (which is his invention), stressing rights and rules.

Also, sex differences in performance on a specific task or behaviour are interpreted as reflecting sex differences in a global ability or characteristic. For example, it is concluded that males are more *field-independent* than females (i.e. they have the ability to ignore the context by picking out part of a picture/diagram from the picture/diagram as a whole). But this is found only for embedded figure tests and rod-and-frame tests, and *not* for tactile and auditory tests.

Finally, *group* (mean) scores indicating sex differences often obscure important *individual differences* within each sex. Group averages mustn't be used to justify any inequality of opportunities.

WHAT'S DIFFERENT ABOUT FEMINIST RESEARCH?

From a feminist standpoint, researchers must become actively involved in the research process, taking the perspective of the participants; they're not detached investigators but became an integral part of the whole process. According to the Task Force of APA Division 35, feminist research in psychology tends to be '... co-operative, participative ... interdisciplinary [and] non-hierarchical ... [beginning] with personal experience' and recognizing that 'truth is not separate from the person who speaks it' (in Wilkinson, 1989).

The very terms used by psychologists – such as *subject, manipulate* and *control* – imply the masculinist-biased nature of the field: the dominance, status and power of the experimenter and the subordinate role of the participant (Paludi, 1992) (see Chapter 10). Most psychologists have been, and still are, trained within a paradigm that is positivistic and behaviouristic, being taught that

... effects derived from orderly determinist causes, that the subjective aspects of behaviour were irrelevant, and that the best studies required maximal distance between experimenter and subject ... If I thought of sex professionally at all, I saw it as a variable which could neither be manipulated or controlled and therefore of very little scientific interest. Even the rats were male.
(Unger, 1984, in Unger, 1993)

According to Tavris (1993), two new directions taken by feminist researchers in recent years are (i) looking outward at gender in context, and (ii) looking inward at gender as narrative.

Gender in context

This relates to the debate within the psychology of personality as to the relative influence of individual traits and situational factors on behaviour (see Chapter 4). It can be seen as the application of that debate to the particular issue of gender differences.

It is widely believed among feminist psychologists that a major figure in the debate is Weisstein (1971, in Weisstein, 1993a). While she wasn't the first person to discuss the role of ideology and social context in the construction of the female psyche (that person probably being Simone de Beauvoir, 1953), her article entitled 'Psychology constructs the female' was the first to provide a challenge to psychology's *essentialist views* regarding maleness and femaleness (Unger, 1993).

The central argument in Weisstein's critique was that psychology can have 'nothing of substance to offer' to either 'a study of human behaviour' (male or female) or a vision of 'human possibility', because it insists on looking for 'inner traits' when it ought to be looking 'for social context'. In doing so, psychology has functioned as 'a pseudo-scientific buttress for our cultural sex-role notions', which include not only our ideas about the 'nature of women', but also about 'the nature of homosexuality'. Consequently, psychology has helped to justify and reinforce many of the prejudices inherent in a 'patriarchal social organization', such as the USA (and western culture generally).

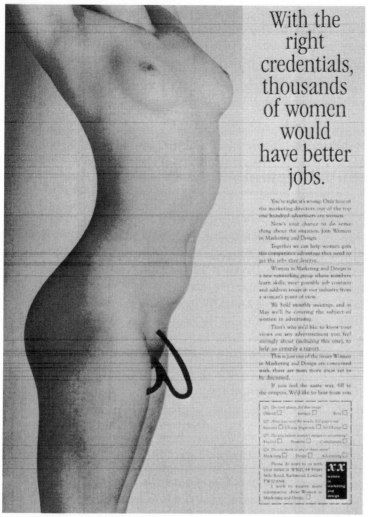

Figure 6.4 This Cowan Kemsley Taylor advertisement was censored by every national newspaper. It appeared once, in *Girl about Town* magazine

By placing the emphasis on internal, individual causes of behaviour, psychologists, unwittingly, help to promote a view of society as composed of so many individuals removed from the political, economic and historical context in which human behaviour takes place. It reinforces the popular view that 'people are as they are', including, of course, the 'nature' of women and men, making behavioural *change* virtually impossible. According to Bem (1993):

Psychology may be so predisposed as a discipline to individualize and decontextualize the phenomena it studies (including gender, sexuality, race and class) that it necessarily depoliticizes those phenomena and thereby functions both as a collaborator in the social reproduction of the status quo and as an obstacle to social change.

Bem gives the example of 'battered woman's syndrome' (see Box 6.2, page 140).

Bem is probably best known for her work (during the 1970s) on *androgyny*, the blending within the same individual man or woman of masculine and feminine characteristics. Her later *gender schema theory* (1984) sees androgyny as a disposition to process information

---

Box 6.2 'Battered woman's syndrome'

Creation of the concept of 'battered woman's syndrome' has helped battered women in the USA to conduct a legal defence when accused of murdering their batterers, and has captured some of the helplessness they undoubtedly feel. But it has achieved this by *pathologizing* the women themselves, rather than trying to expose the institutional context in which they live and in which their ultimate act of self-defence occurs.

A less individualized and depoliticized approach would be to argue *not* that the woman herself is sick (which necessarily deflects attention away from the 'sickness' of her institutional context), but to argue that there is something fundamentally male-centred about the US legal definition of self-defence. A defendant may be found innocent of homicide (murder) only if s/he perceived imminent danger of great bodily harm or death, and responded to that danger with only as much force as was necessary to defend against it. Feminist legal scholars point out that this definition fits the scenario in which two men are involved in an isolated episode of sudden violence much better than the battered woman scenario. She is put at an immediate and fundamental disadvantage by virtue of the fact that her victimization has been taking place over an extended period of time: the perceived danger may be no greater at the time the killing takes place than on many previous occasions. In other words, the act is the culmination of (usually) years of terror.

(based on Bem, 1993)

---

in accordance with relevant non-sex principles (in contrast with traditional, 'masculine' men and 'feminine' women, who spontaneously think of things in sex-typed terms).

By the mid-1980s, Bem began to feel 'theoretically hemmed in', partly because of her own 'overly narrow focus on how gender stereotypes in the head constrain both sexes' (Bem, 1993). This left out the social institutions that push women and men into different and unequal roles, and the (rather obvious) fact that, because most societies are male-dominated, women are a lot more constrained by these social institutions than men are. She describes her 1993 book *The Lenses of Gender* as 'a contextualized and constructivist analysis of how biology, culture, and individual psyche all interact in historical context to systematically reproduce not only the oppression of women, but of sexual minorities too'.

In it, she argues that there are hidden assumptions embedded in cultural discourses, social institutions and individual psyches, which shape not only perceptions of reality, but the material aspects of reality itself (for example, unequal pay, inadequate daycare facilities for children). These assumptions take the form of three kinds of lenses:

1 *androcentrism,* or male-centredness (see above)

2 *gender polarization,* which superimposes a male/female dichotomy on almost every aspect of human experience (such as modes of dress, social roles, ways of expressing emotion, experiencing sexual desire)

3 *biological essentialism,* which rationalizes and legitimizes the other two lenses by treating them as the inevitable consequences of the intrinsic biological nature of women and men.

Her *enculturated lens theory* tries to explain how we either acquire the culture's lenses and construct a conventional gender identity, or we construct a gender-subversive identity: 'We must reframe the debate on sexual inequality so that it focuses not on the differences between women and men but on how male-centred discourses and institutions transform male–female difference into female disadvantage' (Bem, 1993).

SO HOW *IS* GENDER CONSTRUCTED?

Weisstein's (1971, 1993a) article foreshadowed the paradigm shift within psychology, from the view that reality constructs the person to the view that the person constructs reality (Buss, 1978, in Unger, 1993). She, together with a few other pioneers, explicitly used the term 'social constructionism' to question the bases of psychological knowledge.

One form that this construction of gender can take is *social expectations* of behaviour, both other people's expectations of our behaviour and *our* expectations of our own behaviour. More specifically, expectations can influence behaviour through the *self-fulfilling prophecy*, and Weisstein cites classic studies by Rosenthal and his co-workers (Rosenthal, 1966; Rosenthal and Jacobson, 1968), which demonstrate how expectations can change experimental outcomes (see Chapter 11): '… even in carefully controlled experiments, and with no outward or conscious difference in behaviour, the hypotheses we start with will influence enormously the behaviour of another organism' (Weisstein, 1971, 1993a).

Weisstein also discusses Milgram's obedience experiments as demonstrating the very powerful influence of the social situation on the behaviour of individuals (see Chapter 4).

In line with this continuing shift towards studying the importance of context, more recent studies of gender have consistently shown that the behaviour we associate with 'gender' depends more on what an individual is doing than on biological sex (e.g. Eagly, 1987). For example, Maccoby (1990, in Tavris, 1993) re-analysed studies that used to show that little girls are 'passive' and little boys are 'active'. She concluded that boys and girls *don't* differ, as groups, in some consistent, trait-like, way: *their behaviour depends on the gender of the child they're playing with*. Girls (as young as three) are only passive when a boy is present, but they're just as independent as boys when in an all-girl group. According to Tavris (1993), results like these suggest that:

… gender, like culture, organizes for its members different influence strategies, ways of communicating and ways of perceiving the world. The behaviour of men and women often depends more on the gender they are interacting with than on anything about the gender they are – a process that West and Zimmerman (1987) call 'doing gender'.

However, a major aspect of the context of people's lives is the *power* they have (or lack) in influencing others, and in determining their own lives. Clearly, the 'two cultures' of women and men *aren't* equal in power, status and resources. Tavris (1993) believes that many behaviours and personality traits thought to be typical of women (such as the ability to 'read' non-verbal cues, and the tendency to blame themselves for their shortcomings and to have lower self-esteem than men), turn out to be typical of women – *and men* – who lack power; they seem to be the *result* of powerlessness, *not* the cause.

Essentialism revisited

According to Kitzinger and Coyle (2002), 'The social constructionist/essentialist debate has been described as the "hottest" philosophical controversy to hit psychology in years … and it is a controversy in which lesbian and gay psychology has been deeply enmeshed.'

It is sometimes difficult to see certain research as 'essentialist', because it is simply good psychology as traditionally done. An example of such research is a study by Tasker (2002) of lesbian and gay parenting. Its essentialism is indicated by its aim: 'empirically to evaluate the basis on which lesbian mothers were commonly refused custody' – that is, to compare children from lesbian families with those from heterosexual-mother families in terms of family relationships, mental health, peer relationships and psychosexual development. In effect, the questions Tasker addresses are whether or not children of lesbians have worse family relationships, suffer more mental health problems, have to endure more bullying and are more likely to be homosexual themselves (these being factors that are often cited as reasons for denying custody to lesbian mothers). Her findings are reported as offering new 'facts' about family life, such as 'the quality of family relationships is more important than family structure in terms of the child's psychological well-being'.

Kitzinger and Coyle (2002) see Tasker's study as *contributing* to 'positive' representations of lesbian parenting. They contrast this with a study by Clarke (2002), which *interrogates* such representations. Clarke proceeds *not* from the 'neutral' position of the scientist, but from a politically engaged feminist perspective. She asks about the political *effects* of making the kind of argument that Tasker makes (scientific evidence concerning the development of children raised by lesbian mothers). Rather than asking about the truth value of claims made in support of lesbian and gay families (are they empirically true or false?), Clarke explores the strategies people use to defend lesbian and gay parenting, and discusses the political costs and benefits of these different strategies.

So, for example, where Tasker claims that the quality of family relationships is more important than parents' sexual orientation, Clarke represents this kind of claim as a 'discourse', which emphasizes the importance of love, security and stability over any particular family structure. Accordingly, families can assume any shape or form, provided they are loving and stable environments. Clarke's assessment of this discourse isn't in terms of 'truth', but rather the rhetoric; for example, she argues that it runs the risk of being 'defensive' and judgemental of lesbian and gay families in accordance with 'heterosexual norms and expectations' (see Chapter 7).

In sum, whereas Tasker is aiming to uncover something approximating to 'truths' about lesbian and gay parenting, Clarke treats these truth claims as 'discourses' to be assessed not in terms of their facticity, but in terms of their rhetorical force and political implications (Kitzinger and Coyle, 2002).

Gender as narrative

The other major recent direction that feminist research has taken is to focus on the *life story*, which Sarbin (1986) describes as the key metaphor in understanding human behaviour. Our plans, memories, love affairs and hatreds are guided by narrative plots, with women and men differing greatly in the narrative plots they tell about their lives. (These can be seen as an important move towards *idiographic* methods of studying gender, and away from the *nomothetic* methods used by psychologists wanting to establish gender *differences* from the androcentric perspective; see Chapter 3.)

Where do the narratives come from? What functions do they serve for the story-teller? Why do so many women today feel safe telling stories that place their fate in the stars or PMS rather than in their own hands – or society's? However, life stories can change; how and why they do is at the heart of psychology and politics (Tavris, 1993).

SO ARE WOMEN AND MEN DIFFERENT – AND, IF SO, HOW?

According to the third of the current versions of the mismeasure of woman, there is no problem, because man is the norm and woman is just like him. According to Tiefer (1992, in Tavris, 1993), this assumption pervades the diagnosis of sexual disorders in *DSM*: 'Men and women are the same, and they're all men.'

Tavris believes that the study of gender has entered a 'transformationist' era (citing Crawford and Mararcek, 1989), whereby we should 'stand back from the fray' and accept that we shall never know the essence of male and female. These are endlessly changing, and depend both on the eye of the observer and the conditions of our lives. Instead of asking 'Do men and women differ?' (which is literal and limited), this approach asks, 'Why is everyone so interested in differences? Which differences? What function does *belief* in differences serve? What are the *consequences* of believing that women are emotionally and professionally affected by their hormones, but men aren't, or that women are the love experts and that men are incapable of love and intimacy? Where do these beliefs come from, and who benefits (and loses) from them?'

While *cultural feminism* is an important step forward in the study of gender, it runs the risk of replacing one set of stereotypes with another: the 'woman-is-better' school, like the 'woman-is-deficient' school, assumes a fundamental opposition between the sexes. Thinking in opposites leads to what philosophers call 'the law of the excluded middle': most actual women and men fall somewhere in between the stereotypical opposites regarding psychological qualities, abilities, traits, and so on.

The debate about gender and gender differences is not whether or not women and men differ. Of course they do. As in the debate about racial differences in IQ, what is controversial is how such differences (when they're found) should be *interpreted*. Do they reflect permanent, biological, intra-individual traits and characteristics, or should they be understood in relation to life experiences, social contexts, resources and power, which can and do change culturally and historically? 'By setting aside predetermined categories, we have learned that there is no one right way to be lesbian, straight or gay, no one right way to *be*' (Tavris, 1993).

CONCLUDING COMMENTS: WHAT'S BETTER ABOUT FEMINIST PSYCHOLOGY?

Wilkinson (1989) maintains that there are three major improvements that feminist psychology can make to mainstream psychology:

1 it identifies hitherto unrecognized sources of bias (such as Gilligan's critique of Kohlberg)

2 it increases critical thinking

3 it broadens the scope of research by (i) looking at under-researched areas (such as violence against women), and (ii) by generating new ways of looking at old problems.

This, in turn, offers the possibility of an 'extra dimension' to psychological knowledge: by looking at human experience from women's perspective, we can enrich and extend our understanding of the whole of human functioning and its possibilities (Wilkinson, 1989).

SUMMARY

O *Feminism*, as a social and political movement, condemns the oppression of women and strives for the recognition of women's achievements, contributions and experience as valid and important *in their own right*.

O Feminist psychologists see psychology as *sexist* and *heterosexist, value-laden* and *androcentric*.

O The *masculinist bias* holds the contributions made by men to psychology to be more important than those made by women; the history of psychology is the history of *male* psychology.

O *Women's history in psychology* comprises: *compensatory history, contribution history,* and *reconstruction history*.

O The 'feminist critique' has had little impact on mainstream psychology, because it isn't seen as *legitimate science* and is dismissed as 'purely political'.

O Despite the growing numbers of female psychologists, they still work in predominantly *person-oriented/service-oriented* areas, compared with the traditionally male *academic/experimental* areas.

O This could reflect sexism among male psychologists, who regard 'female' areas of psychology as scientifically/intellectually inferior; *gatekeepers* are also predominantly male.

O Many radical feminist psychologists are lesbians, who criticize mainstream psychology for its *heterosexism*.

O The feminist critique of science challenges the fundamental assumptions of the *positivist* approach, which sees scientific enquiry as objective and value-free. But psychologists' decisions about what they should study reflect *values*, and are related to a particular politico-cultural context.

O Feminist psychologists advocate a *value-laden approach* to research, so that values will no longer be mistaken for facts. If psychologists fail to make their values explicit about important social/political issues, they may (unwittingly) *contribute to* prejudice and discrimination.

O The *masculinist bias* can take the form of: (i) deciding what is worth investigating about women; (ii) taking men as a *standard/norm* against which to compare and judge women; and (iii) only publishing the results of studies that have found evidence of *sex differences*.

O Gender bias can be found at all stages of the research process: *question formulation, research methods/design, data analysis/interpretation,* and *conclusion formulation*.

O Results regarding sex differences are often reported/interpreted in line with stereotyped expectations, or they may be reported in a very misleading way, because the wrong sort of comparisons are being made.

O Sex differences in performance on a *specific* task/behaviour are often interpreted as reflecting a difference in some *global* ability/characteristic.

O *Group* (mean) scores indicating sex differences often obscure important *individual differences* within each group.

O Feminist researchers become actively involved in the research process, taking the perspective of the participants; they reject the detached experimenter role, and don't see themselves as of higher status, or more powerful, than the 'subject'.

O Feminist critics of mainstream psychology believe that it has overemphasized *internal*, individual causes of behaviour and neglected social context; this helps to reinforce the status quo and the belief that people cannot change.

O Bem's *enculturated lens theory* sees gender/gender identity as being *constructed* in a way that disadvantages women. Three 'lenses' through which this is done are *androcentrism, gender polarization,* and *biological essentialism*.

O One way in which gender is constructed is through *social expectations* of behaviour, specifically *self-fulfilling prophecies*.

O Many behaviours/personality traits thought to be typical of women are, in fact, typical of *people* who lack power, and so are the *result, not* the cause, of powerlessness.

O Feminist research tends towards *idiographic methods*, such as the recent focus on the *life story*.

O According to *cultural feminism*, women are *opposite but better* than men, who are the norm. This threatens to replace one set of stereotypes with another, and assumes a fundamental opposition between the sexes.

O The crucial question isn't whether sex differences exist, but how they should be interpreted.

Useful websites

- O www.bps.org.uk/sub-syst/POWS/powsweb.htm
- O http://web.lemoyne.edu/~hevern/narpsych.html
- O http://www.nova.edu/ssss/QR/web.html
- O http://www.vix.com/men/articles/genderbiastest.html
- O http://www.socialpsychology.org/social.htm#sexuality
- O http://www.socialpsychology.org/social.htm#lesbigay

Recommended reading

Coyle, A. and Kitzinger, C. (eds) (2002) *Lesbian and Gay Psychology: New Perspectives.* BPS/Blackwell.

Paludi, M.A. (1992) *The Psychology of Women.* Debuque, Iowa: WCB Brown & Benchmark.

Tavris, C. (1993) The mismeasure of women. *Feminism & Psychology, 3*(2), 149–68. (There are several other important articles in the same issue.)

Trew, K. and Kremer, K. (eds) (1998) *Gender and Psychology.* London: Arnold.

NORMALITY AND ABNORMALITY

7

Most of this chapter is devoted to trying to *define* the terms 'normal' and 'abnormal', and to establish the relationship between them. While it is always important to be clear about the meaning of the terms we use in discussion of any psychological topic, here it is essential, because the whole field of *abnormal psychology* rests upon the assumption that a distinction can be made between normality and abnormality.

As with many terms and concepts, *examples* can help to get a discussion started and may help to raise some of the important issues. So, if you were asked to give some examples of the kinds of behaviour and experience that fall under the heading of abnormal psychology, you would probably include *schizophrenia*, *anxiety*, *panic attacks*, *homosexuality*, *sexual fetishes*, *depression* and *hallucinations*. While the list of possible examples is very much longer, these make it reasonably clear what the field of abnormal psychology is about (its 'scope'). However, giving examples is the easy bit! What we really want to know is: What do they all have in common that makes us want to call them abnormalities in the first place? Does there have to be anything that links them, or can they all illustrate abnormality for different reasons? Do psychologists and psychiatrists consider the meaning of normality and abnormality, or do they just *assume* that, say, schizophrenia is abnormal and concentrate on investigating its causes, diagnosing and treating it? Is it possible to define and diagnose abnormality in an objective way, without allowing our values to bias the judgements we make? What are some of the practical and ethical implications of labelling a person's behaviour as abnormal?

The attempt to give answers to these very complex questions forms the basis of this chapter.

ABNORMALITY, DEVIANCE AND DIFFERENCE

According to Littlewood and Lipsedge (1989), every society has its own characteristic pattern of normative behaviour and beliefs – that is, expectations about how people should behave as well as what they should think. These norms define what's acceptable and permissible, as well as what's desirable. It might be useful to think of this as a scale or continuum, as shown Figure 7.1.

Figure 7.1 The continuum of normative behaviour

Unacceptable.......Tolerable.......Acceptable/permissible.......Desirable.......Required/obligatory

At the left-hand end of the scale, behaviour is either illegal (such as burglary or fraud) or breaches fundamental moral or religious principles (adultery, abortion) or both (child sexual abuse, rape, bigamy). There is usually little room for disagreement as to whether or not something is illegal, but there will usually be more debate about the immorality of (illegal) acts: the vast majority of people will condemn child abuse and rape (including, very often, the perpetrator of the act), but people have very different views regarding the smoking of marijuana. (The current climate of opinion in the UK, including that of the police, is towards the legalization of soft drugs, but whether this reflects a change in *moral* opinion is another issue.)

Behaviour that is deemed *tolerable* is at the fringes of illegality and/or immorality; examples might include gambling, drinking (large amounts of) alcohol, going to pole-dancing clubs, joining a squat, and living with one's sexual partner (as opposed to getting married).

Getting married is, of course, also *acceptable/permissible*, and *desirable*, as far as most people are concerned (despite the very high divorce rate). To the extent that most people will get married (at least once in their lives), that we usually assume that adults *are* married (unless we have good reason to believe otherwise), and that there's an implicit judgement made about people who don't get married ('there must be something wrong with them'), getting married can also be seen as *required/obligatory*.

This example brings us back full circle to what is *unacceptable*. This was defined earlier in terms of illegality and immorality, but perhaps there's another criterion by which we make this judgement. Clearly, it isn't illegal to remain single (there's no actual, literal, law against it), and nor is there any religious or moral law that's being broken (assuming that instead of being married one isn't cohabiting or 'living in sin'). But it's still somehow socially unacceptable, it's 'not quite right', it may make us feel a little uneasy, less sure about how to relate to this person than when we're interacting with individuals who are married.

Our first reaction to learning that someone is unmarried might be to wonder if s/he's gay or lesbian. This may be a perfectly logical explanation, but at the same time it raises even more fundamental questions about acceptability and normality (see below). Similarly, if the person is painfully shy, or badly disfigured or has a disability, or a nun or a priest, we can easily understand his or her unmarried state.

But what if none of these explanations is available to us? This is when the unacceptability of the 'behaviour' becomes an issue: being married is, for most people, part of their definition of 'reality', the 'natural order' of things.

Perhaps the unacceptability of schizophrenia, homosexuality, and the other examples given above, also lies in the way they threaten and challenge our basic view of the world, what Scheff (1966) called *residual rules*: the 'unnameable' expectations we have regarding such things as 'decency' and 'reality'. Because these rules are themselves implicit, taken for granted, and not articulated, behaviour that violates them is found strange and sometimes frightening – but it's usually very difficult to say *why*!

Similarly, Becker (1963) believes that the values on which psychiatric intervention is based are, generally speaking, middle-class values regarding decent, reasonable, proper behaviour and experience. These influence the process of diagnosis of patients, who, in state-funded – National Health Service (NHS) – hospitals, at least, are mainly working class. (We return to the question of the objectivity of psychiatric diagnosis below.)

In addition to the breaking of residual rules, the mere fact of being different may contribute to the unacceptability of schizophrenics and others deemed 'abnormal'. If every society has its own characteristic pattern of normative behaviour and beliefs, then 'outsiders' (those who deviate from these norms), even if they're not seen as physically dangerous, are threatening simply because they are different. As a way of confirming our own identity (which is so much bound up with these norms), we push the outsiders even further away, and 'By reducing their humanity, we emphasize our own' (Littlewood and Lipsedge, 1989).

'Outsiders in our midst' include criminals (those who break the 'law of the land'), those whose behaviour and beliefs conflict with our moral code, and those, like the mentally ill, who break residual rules. All three groups can be regarded as *deviants*, since their behaviour is considered to deviate from certain standards as held by the person making the judgement. While criminal behaviour is sometimes seen as being caused by psychological disturbance, it is important to distinguish between *social deviance* (non-conformity) and mental disorder or abnormality (Zimbardo, 1992).

Neither deviant behaviour, e.g., political, religious, or sexual, nor conflicts that are primarily between the individual and society, are mental disorders unless the deviance or condition is a symptom of a dysfunction (i.e. impairment of function) in the person.

The above is a quote from the revision of the third edition of the *Diagnostic and Statistical Manual (of Mental Disorders)*, published by the American Psychiatric Association (1987), abbreviated to *DSM-III-R*. It is the official system for classifying and diagnosing mental disorders used by American psychiatrists. This – and the latest edition, *DSM-IV* (1994) – is discussed throughout the rest of the chapter (see also Chapter 6).

Although some *clinical psychologists* and *psychiatrists* are interested in the causes and treatment of criminality as a form of social deviancy, the main focus of abnormal psychology is the kinds of unacceptable behaviour and experience that are variously called *mental illness*, *emotional disturbance*, *behaviour disorder*, *mental disorder*, or *psychopathology* (literally, 'disease of the mind', or psychological abnormality).

CRITERIA FOR DEFINING PSYCHOLOGICAL ABNORMALITY

So far, the discussion has suggested a number of possible criteria for defining psychological abnormality, and has considered their usefulness and validity. In this section, we take another look at these criteria (although from a slightly different angle), as well as discuss some additional ones. Many of these have been proposed by a number of different writers (e.g. Miller and Morley, 1986; Rosenhan and Seligman, 1989; Davison and Neale, 2001), and so particular points will not always be attributed to specific writers.

The statistical infrequency criterion (or deviation from the average)

According to this criterion, what is average determines what is normal: behaviour is abnormal to the extent that it falls outside the middle ranges (what the majority of people do). In other words, it is *extreme*.

Take the example of people with learning difficulties ('mental retardation'). As measured by intelligence (IQ) test scores, those with a score below 70 or 75, who represent the lowest 2 per cent of the whole population, are considered to be retarded; their scores are, clearly, extremely low and so, according to this criterion, their intelligence is *abnormally* low (see Figure 7.2, page 120).

But what about those individuals whose scores are extremely *high*? According to the statistical criterion, they should be thought of as equally abnormal because their scores (the 2 per cent scoring 130 and above) are as extreme as those scoring 75 and below. Those

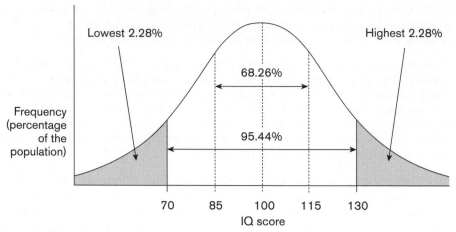

Figure 7.2 Normal distribution curve for IQ, given a mean of 100 and a standard deviation of 15 IQ points

who score extremely high are usually described as 'gifted', a somewhat more positive label than 'mentally retarded', *yet the two groups are statistically equally abnormal.* Clearly, there is more to abnormality than mere statistics!

Also, just how far from the population mean does an individual need to be to be considered abnormal? As Miller and Morley (1986) point out, any chosen cut-off point is necessarily arbitrary: what is the significance of 75/70 as the boundary between mental normality and retardation?

A further problem with this criterion is that most kinds of abnormality that psychologists are interested in (see the list above) simply cannot be measured in the way that intelligence can (or, at least, is). In other words, the statistical criterion assumes that psychological characteristics in general can be viewed as *dimensional* (measured on at least an ordinal scale), such that individual scores can all be placed somewhere on the same scale. This in itself is a complex and controversial issue in relation to the normality/abnormality debate, which we return to below.

Abnormality as personal distress

From the perspective of the individual, abnormality is the subjective experience of intense anxiety, unhappiness, depression or a whole host of other forms of personal distress or suffering. While this may often be the only indication that anything is wrong (and may not necessarily be obvious to others), it may be a sufficient reason for someone to seek professional help. As Miller and Morley (1986) say, 'people do not come to clinics because they feel that they have met some abstract definition of abnormality. For the most part they come because their feelings or behaviour cause them distress.'

However, the converse may also sometimes be true. Someone whose behaviour is obviously 'mad' as far as others are concerned, may be unaware of how others see him/her and may experience little or no subjective distress. This 'lack of insight' (self-awareness or understanding) is often taken to be a characteristic of *psychotic mental disorder* (as opposed to neurotic disorder), and is a kind of 'the fish is the last to discover water syndrome'.

Abnormality as others' distress

It might at first seem very strange, if not illogical, to define *one* person's abnormality in terms of *another person's* distress. But, as we have seen in discussing the personal distress criterion, the person seen by others as behaving abnormally may be the last to recognize that there is a problem, so others' concern acts as a counterbalance to the former's lack of concern.

This criterion also suggests that, as with all behaviour, abnormality is *interpersonal*, and not simply *intrapersonal/intrapsychic*. Behaviour takes place *between* people, in social situations, and isn't merely a reflection of the personal qualities or characteristics of the individual actor (see Chapters 1 and 15).

From a practical and ethical point of view, this criterion can be seen as double-edged. Others' distress may be both a 'blessing' (literally a life-saver on occasions, for someone lacking insight into his/her own self-destructive behaviour, for example) and a curse (for example, parents' distress regarding a child's homosexuality, with which the child him/herself may feel perfectly comfortable). While the former may be termed *empathic concern*, where the 'helper' has an *altruistic desire* to reduce the *other's distress*, in the latter, *personal distress* produces an *egoistic desire* to reduce *one's own distress*. The question is, *whose distress* is really the focus of the attempt to intervene?

Box 7.1 Laing and anti-psychiatry

One of the most outspoken critics of conventional, medical, psychiatry during the heyday of the *anti-psychiatry* movement in the 1960s was the Scottish psychiatrist R.D. Laing. According to his *family interaction model* (1961), schizophrenia can only be understood as something that occurs *between* people, rather than as something taking place *inside* a person (as the medical model maintains; see below). Schizophrenia refers to an *interpersonal ploy* used by some people (parents, doctors, psychiatrists) in their interactions with others ('the schizophrenic').

To understand individuals, we must study not individuals but interactions between individuals, and this is the subject matter of *social phenomenology*. The family interaction model was consistent with research by Bateson *et al.* (1956), which showed that schizophrenia arises within families that use 'pathological' forms of communication, in particular, contradictory messages (*double binds*).

More directly relevant to the 'distress criterion' is a later explanation of schizophrenia, namely Laing's (1967) *conspiratorial model*, according to which schizophrenia is a *label*, a form of violence perpetrated by some people against others. The family, GPs and psychiatrists conspire against the schizophrenic in order to keep him/her in check: by treating them as patients who are sick, 'imprisoning' them in a psychiatric hospital, where they are degraded and invalidated as human beings, these people are able to maintain their definition of reality (the *status quo*). (*Residual rules* again?) The threat posed by the behaviour and experience of the 'patient' is contained within a medical framework: 'If they act and think like that they *must be sick*, which means that we're all right and everything is still all right with the world as we know it.'

According to Laing's *psychedelic model* (1967), the schizophrenic is, in fact, an exceptionally eloquent critic of society and schizophrenia is 'itself a natural way of healing our own appalling state of alienation called normality'.

Abnormality as unexpected behaviour

According to Davison and Neale (2001), it is abnormal to react to a situation or an event in ways that couldn't be predicted, or reasonably expected (given what we know about human behaviour). For example, anxiety disorders are diagnosed when the anxiety is 'out of proportion to the situation'.

While this might seem like a very reasonable and useful criterion, it could be claimed that it raises as many questions as it answers. In particular, who is to say what is 'in proportion'? Is this just another form of the statistical criterion, whereby what is a reasonable, acceptable, response is simply how *most people* would be expected to respond? By this criterion, *under*reacting is just as abnormal as *over*reacting, and yet the way Davison and Neale describe it suggests very strongly that it is only an *over*reaction that is seen as a problem. So, *by what other criteria* do we judge a reaction to be normal or abnormal?

Abnormality as highly consistent/inconsistent behaviour

If we have generalized expectations about how people are typically going to react to particular (kinds of) situation, as when we define abnormality as unexpected behaviour, then a person's behaviour is predictable to the extent that we know about the situation. However, not all situations are equally powerful influences on behaviour, and so cannot be used equally to predict a person's behaviour. In some situations, individual differences play a much larger role in influencing behaviour, and this makes behaviour *less* predictable. Consequently, it is 'normal' for any individual's behaviour to be partially predictable (high *intra-individual consistency*) and, at the same time, partially unpredictable (low *intra-individual consistency*).

If we accept this argument, then we can reasonably further argue that it is abnormal for a person to display *either* extremely predictable *or* extremely unpredictable behaviour. If someone acts so consistently that they seem to be unaffected by a situation, including the other people involved, this would strike most people as very odd; it's almost as if we're dealing with more of a machine than a person! Someone who's paranoid, for example, might see the world almost entirely in terms of others' malevolent intentions, which may, in turn, elicit certain kinds of responses in others; these responses may reinforce the attribution of negative intent, thus producing a vicious cycle.

Equally, it's difficult to interact with someone who, for whatever reason, is very unpredictable, since our dealings with others require us to make assumptions and have expectations about their responses. Schizophrenics are often perceived, by the lay person, as embodying this kind of unpredictability, which is unnerving and unsettling. Again, this perception, together with the related expectation of unpredictability, may to some degree contribute to that unpredictability.

In both cases, the assessment being made is as much a reflection of the perceiver making the judgement as of the person whose behaviour is being judged. Perhaps the term *consistency* should be applied to the actor's behaviour, and *predictability* to the perceiver's judgement. But regardless of the term that's used, the basic argument is the same: to understand behaviour we must always take the actor *and* the situation (including other people) into account (see Chapter 4). We return to this point later on when we look at the process of psychiatric diagnosis.

Abnormality as maladaptiveness or disability

When people's behaviour prevents them from pursuing and achieving their goals, or doesn't contribute to their personal sense of well-being, or prevents them from functioning as they'd wish in their personal, sexual, social, intellectual and occupational lives, it may well be seen as abnormal for that reason.

For example, substance use disorders are defined mainly by how the substance abuse produces social and occupational disability, such as poor work performance and serious marital arguments. Phobias can be maladaptive or disabling in this way; for example, fear of flying might prevent someone from taking a job promotion (Davison and Neale, 2001).

So, according to this criterion, it is the *consequences* of the behaviour that lead us to judge the behaviour to be abnormal, rather than the behaviour itself. At the same time, such behaviours may be very distressing for the person concerned; by their nature, phobias are negative experiences because they involve extreme fear, regardless of any practical effects of the fear.

AN INTERIM SUMMING UP: WHAT HAVE WE LEARNT SO FAR?

We've now considered six criteria for defining behaviour as abnormal:

1 statistical infrequency involves a *comparison* with other people's behaviour

2 abnormality as personal distress involves the *consequences for self* of the behaviour in question

3 abnormality as others' distress involves looking at the *consequences for others* of the behaviour in question

4 abnormality as unexpected behaviour involves another kind of *comparison* with others' behaviour

5 abnormality as highly consistent/inconsistent behaviour also involves making comparisons, this time between both the actor and others, and between the actor and him/herself on different occasions

6 abnormality as maladaptiveness or disability is concerned with the *consequences for the actor* of his/her behaviour.

But what is different about abnormality as personal distress (the second criterion)? While the other criteria could be seen as having an *external* focus (they look outwards from the behaviour in question towards something else), the personal distress criterion has an *internal* focus (it begins and remains with the person whose behaviour is in question).

While it is generally agreed that it's impossible to give a simple definition of abnormality that captures it in its entirety (see, for example, Davison and Neale, 2001), and that no single criterion is necessary (see Zimbardo, 1992), this distinction between external and internal focus is important. Discussions of abnormality often seem to assume that certain behaviours and experiences are abnormal *in and of themselves*, without any reference to any external criterion. Examples might include all those in our original list, although some of these – such as homosexuality (see below) – will be considerably more controversial than others when seen from this perspective. None of the criteria discussed so far addresses this issue.

THE CASE OF HOMOSEXUALITY: NORMAL OR ABNORMAL?

Let's apply the criteria we've discussed so far to the case of homosexuality, in order to expose their limitations and to introduce some important additional ones.

As far as statistical infrequency is concerned, it's very likely that most people, especially perhaps those who believe that homosexuality is abnormal, also believe that lesbians and gay men (especially lesbians!) represent a very small minority of the adult population. But even if it turned out that the majority of adults were homosexual (or had had at least one homosexual relationship), most people would continue to believe it to be abnormal – the very use of the term 'queer' conveys a negative attitude towards homosexuals (its other main meaning is 'ill'). In other words, there's more to judging homosexuality to be abnormal than 'deviation from the average'.

In relation to personal distress, while there are undoubtedly some homosexuals who experience conflict and distress about their sexuality, there are probably as many for whom being gay or lesbian feels as 'right' as being heterosexual does for most 'straights'. This, together with the fact that many of those who are in conflict are so because of society's *homophobic* attitudes (the irrational fear and extreme intolerance of homosexuality) and *heterosexism* (inequality and discrimination based on people's sexual preference or orientation), suggests that 'being homosexual' isn't distressing *in itself*. It isn't an inherent feature of preferring members of one's own sex as sexual partners to experience distress, unlike the person with a phobia, for example (but see Box 7.2). Indeed, it is as likely to be as pleasurable as a heterosexual's attraction to someone of the opposite sex. (The 'flip side' of the belief that being homosexual isn't inherently distressing is the homophobic assumption that any gay man will 'fancy' any male (gay or straight), so that no one is 'safe'.)

Assuming that homosexuals themselves don't, typically, or inevitably, experience distress, why should other people do so 'on their behalf', which is what happens, according to 'abnormality as other people's distress'? It is clearly false (as well as patronizing) to claim that homosexuals 'don't realize what they're doing' (as in, say, the case of drug addicts or

---

Box 7.2 Is homosexuals' distress homosexual distress?

According to Taylor (2002), men (and by the same token women) who identify – or are struggling to identify – as gay (or lesbian) appear to be more vulnerable to certain forms of psychological and emotional distress than men and women who identify as heterosexual. Much of this distress is, undoubtedly, the result of factors that have nothing to do with sexual identity or orientation and everything to do with being human. Indeed:

... an insistence upon consistently sexualising the emotional difficulties of gay men would constitute naïve reductionism and would be potentially oppressive. While sexuality may be a constituent part of a person's identity – especially when the sexuality is constructed as being in some way 'different' – we are not simply the uncomplicated product of our sexualities ...
(Taylor, 2002)

Nevertheless, this unequal distribution of psychological distress suggests that certain processes are operating here. As a clinical psychologist, Clarke observes that many men present with difficulties, dilemmas and conflicts that are intrinsically tied to their sexual identities. Sometimes, these difficulties seem to be a direct response to negative societal representations of and behaviour towards homosexuality (homophobia and heterosexism). Sometimes they appear to be the consequence of participation within a specific sub-culture and the internalizing of negative stereotypes and other representations of 'gayness' (Taylor, 2002).

others engaging in self-destructive behaviour), such that they need to be 'saved from themselves'. We need to look elsewhere for the source of others' distress.

Such an explanation is most unlikely to be found in 'abnormality as unexpected behaviour': it doesn't make very much sense to see homosexuality as an overreaction to some event. What could such an event be? If it were discovered, for example, that homosexuals have typically experienced some kind of trauma in early childhood that caused their homosexuality, we wouldn't then want to call this outcome an *over*reaction; it would be seen as a 'normal' reaction to that kind of trauma. (Although 'normal' here might seem to beg the question, the idea of homosexuals *as a group* all reacting in the same way at least suggests that homosexuality as a reaction to certain childhood trauma isn't a deviation.)

While research may not have found any evidence for traumatic events as a causal influence on the development of homosexuality, Bieber *et al.* (1962) claim to have found a difference between male homosexuals and heterosexuals, namely that the former are brought up by a 'close-binding intimate mother' and a father who displays 'detachment-hostility'. This difference is referred to as a *pathogenic* ('disease-producing') factor, which is responsible for the pathological condition of homosexuality. But we only judge this pattern of child-rearing to be pathological if we have already judged its outcome to be pathological. In other words, only if we already regard homosexuality to be abnormal will we regard any difference between homosexuals and heterosexuals (and which we think causes homosexuality) as itself abnormal (Davison and Neale, 1994). This is clearly a *circular argument* which begs the whole question of the normality or abnormality of homosexuality.

Regarding the abnormality as highly consistent/inconsistent behaviour criterion, there is no reason to believe that homosexuals, as a group, compared with heterosexuals, are any more or less consistent or predictable in their overall behaviour. So, this criterion doesn't move us on any further in our search for the reasons behind the belief that homosexuality is abnormal.

This leaves just abnormality as maladaptiveness or disability. Unlike the case of someone with a phobia, the negative consequences suffered by homosexuals aren't to do with being homosexual, but stem from society's response to the homosexual. Whereas someone with a phobia of flying might be unable to visit faraway lands as a direct result of the phobia (almost as an *extension* of the phobia), quite independently of any external factors or influences, the homosexual is confronted by homophobia and heterosexism, which aren't part of being homosexual. It is social attitudes towards homosexuals that constitute the maladaptiveness/disability of homosexuality, *not* the 'handicapping' nature of being gay. (However, homophobia and heterosexism can become internalized to form part of the individual homosexual's self-concept; see Box 7.2 above.)

So, we're left still needing to know by what criteria homosexuality is judged to be abnormal (and where homophobia and heterosexism 'come from'). This brings us on to the *deviation from the norm* criterion.

Abnormality as deviation from the norm

This implies that, regardless of how other people behave (the statistical criterion), abnormality involves not behaving, feeling or thinking as one *should*. 'Norms' have an 'oughtness' about them: they convey expectations about behaviour, such that what's normal is *right, proper, natural, desirable*, and so on (see Figure 7.1) Clearly, these terms all convey *value judgements*. They aren't neutral, value-free, objective descriptions or assessments of behaviour, but reflect beliefs concerning what are essentially *moral/ethical* issues.

Sometimes, it's very obvious how a particular behaviour deviates from a norm, and it's equally obvious what the norm is. For example, murder is a crime, and the law that makes it a crime embodies the moral law – 'Thou shalt not murder'. As with most crime, the behaviour is labelled as 'bad', making clear that legal/moral norms have been breached. However, there's no *law* against being schizophrenic, or having panic attacks, or being depressed, nor is it obvious what *moral law or ethical principle* is being broken in these cases. It seems that we might be dealing, once more, with *residual rules* (see above).

Up until the 1960s in the UK, homosexuality among consenting adults *was* illegal. That law, presumably, embodied the pre-Christian Jewish and early Christian condemnation of sex outside marriage and for any purpose except reproduction, even as an expression of love between husband and wife (Doyle, 1983). Now it is legal (at least between consenting adults over the age of 18), but homophobia and heterosexism continue to reflect these *religious* roots. (Interestingly, repeated attempts in the UK to bring down the age of consent between consenting homosexuals to 16, and hence bring it in line with that for heterosexuals, have failed!)

So, behaviour may be judged abnormal quite independently of its legal status (including its legal history), because it seems to breach certain fundamental religious–moral principles (even though it may not be easy to identify these principles or even to articulate them). However, in western culture, unlike many non-western cultures, a sharp distinction is made between legal, religious and *medical* aspects or definitions of normality. Disease, illness and pathology (bodily and psychological) are dealt with by the medical profession, they are the province of doctors and psychiatrists (as opposed to priests): mental disorder has become *medicalized*. Religion and illness are in separate 'cultural compartments'; illness is an entirely secular matter.

However, many human situations and forms of human distress that are conceptualized in the West as 'illness' are seen in religious and/or philosophical terms in Indian culture, for example, which also stresses harmony between the person and his/her group as indicating health. In African culture, the concept of health is more *social* then biological:

In the mind of the African, there is a more unitary concept of psychosomatic interrelationship, that is, an apparent reciprocity between mind and matter. Health is not an isolated phenomenon but part of the entire magico-religious fabric; it is more than the absence of disease. Since disease is viewed as one of the most important social sanctions, peaceful living with neighbours, abstention from adultery, keeping the laws of gods and men, are essentials in order to protect oneself and one's family from disease.
(Lambo, 1964, in Fernando, 1991)

The spiritual and physical worlds aren't separate entities, as they are in western culture; mind and body don't exist separately, and no distinction is made between 'bodily illness' and 'mental illness' (see Chapter 13).

However, although ideas about health and illness vary across cultures on a number of parameters, every culture possesses a concept of illness as some kind of departure (or deviation) from health. Yet, according to Fernando (1991), 'The overall world view within a culture, appertaining to health, religion, psychology and spiritual concerns determines the meaning within that culture of "madness", mental illness and mental health'. So, thinking about, and treating, psychological abnormality from a medical, biological, perspective, is itself a cultural phenomenon. This leads onto an eighth major criterion of abnormality, namely *abnormality as mental illness or mental disorder* (see below).

Abnormality as an exaggeration of normality

A ninth criterion emerges from the study of personality. According to Claridge and Davis (2003), the development of a psychological disorder can be seen as a particularly dramatic example of how 'apparently quite stable propensities to action, motivations, and other characteristics that constitute the personality can be thrown into disarray'. This is especially true in the case of serious (psychotic) mental illness (such as schizophrenia), but also in other (neurotic) disorders (such as obsessive-compulsive disorder).

As discussed in Chapter 4, psychologists tend to see personality as composed of a collection of traits, relatively stable tendencies, inherent within the individual, which define 'typical' ways of behaving, thinking and feeling. Some – notably Eysenck – prefer to define and measure personality in terms of a small number of dimensions (such as introversion–extroversion), which subsume a larger number of traits (they summarize 'underlying' traits). These dimensions apply to everyone, allowing people to be compared with each other (a nomothetic approach), but people can also be regarded as unique, in that they differ in the profiles they display across these various dimensions (an idiographic approach; see Chapter 3).

What both the trait and dimensional approaches assume is *continuity* in the features (broad or narrow) they use to describe personality. In other words, individuals are *more or less* X, Y or Z, being ranged at various points along a continuum ('more or less extrovert', or 'more or less sociable'). Claridge and Davis (2003) believe that this approach is tailor-made for helping us understand psychological disorders: 'The clinically abnormal can easily be visualized as, in some regard, an extension of the normal, defining the extremes of the dimensions that describe personality'. In other words, there is only a *quantitative* difference (one of degree) between 'normal' people and those who are diagnosed with mental disorders (in rather less 'technical' language, 'we're all a little bit mad' or 'some of us are madder than others'). Eysenck was very critical of the psychiatric construction of psychological abnormality as discrete (distinct) disease entities that prevailed in the 1960s. Unlike the anti-psychiatrists (such as Laing; see Box 7.1), Eysenck very much argued for the essentially *biological* roots of mental disorder. But unlike most psychiatrists, he argued that the biology of mental illness was an extension of the biology of the personality dimensions that *predispose* to illness (Eysenck, 1960).

Some empirical support for this dimensional approach, from a rather surprising quarter, is described in Box 7.3 on page 128.

However, the picture isn't quite as simple as Steel paints it.

○ Claridge and Davis (2003) point out that people with mental disorders aren't *merely* individuals occupying one end of some normal personality dimensions (even if the latter do describe part of their condition). For example, someone with agoraphobia would almost certainly score high on a rating scale or personality inventory of *trait anxiety*. But by the time they have been formally diagnosed as agoraphobic (and probably even before), such individuals will have developed new, pathological behaviours (symptoms), such as refusal to leave home and expressing irrational fears they didn't previously have. In other words, 'they are now *more* than just people of very anxious personality; so new facts are needed to explain the transition from extreme *trait* anxiety to *symptomatic* anxiety' (Claridge and Davis, 2003).

Box 7.3 Are we all a little bit schizophrenic?

Ochert (1998) describes research by Steel (at the Institute of Psychiatry in London) into schizophrenia-like personality traits ('schizotypy'). He regards the symptoms of schizophrenia as a 'severe manifestation of personality traits that exist within the normal population'.

Everyone has some degree of schizotypy, as assessed by the Oxford–Liverpool Inventory of Feelings and Experiences (O–LIFE). 'High schizotypes' are normal people who answer questions in much the same way as schizophrenics, and who may be particularly vulnerable to schizophrenia. Their brains may operate in similar ways to schizophrenics' brains, and there is evidence that both groups have difficulty weeding out irrelevant information. They also share a tendency to be less affected by expectations built up from past events. Steel believes that this and other schizotypal traits may make people more creative, but he has no doubt that schizophrenics are actually suffering. He hopes that greater understanding might translate into better therapies, not least by making it 'more normal to be abnormal' (Ochert, 1998).

○ The preferred approach amongst psychiatrists is the *categorical* approach, which forms the basis of attempts to classify mental disorders, such as *DSM* and *ICD* (see below). But the authors of *DSM* themselves admit that it falls short of standards for a strictly categorical model of the kind that works well in physical medicine. They defend it largely on *practical* grounds (such as providing a system for communication between clinicians and others involved in the care of psychiatric patients), but its *scientific* value is much more doubtful (see Box 7.4, page 129).

○ Claridge and Davis also draw attention to a distinction between psychological disorders and *neurological* diseases (such as Alzheimer's and Huntington's). (This relates to the further distinction between functional and organic mental disorders discussed below.) Both categories appear in the major classification systems (*DSM* and *ICD*), but there are important differences in how the nervous system is implicated in the two types of disorder. (i) In *neurological* disorders, illness results from some pathological process, either one that's already known or that can be confidently assumed, and, therefore, at some future point, discovered. They are just like any other physical disease – they just happen to affect the brain, often producing progressive deterioration in mental functioning. They *destroy* healthy brain, partly or completely, and are incompatible with full health. (ii) In *psychological* disorders, the biology is much more continuous with the biology of health.

○ According to McGhee (2001), discussion of mental disorders often focuses on *absences*, while actual diagnostic categories for specific disorders focus on the *presence* of symptoms. For example, the mentally ill are often described as *not* following society's behavioural norms (they are deviant), *not* functioning effectively (they are dysfunctional), and so on. But diagnosis is made in terms of present, identifiable symptoms, such as hearing voices, anxiety, anger outbursts, and so on. So, specific disorders may be distinguishable *from each other* in terms of what the sufferer displays, but:

... according to psychologists, the mentally ill do not seem to have anything in common *with one another*, apart from the fact that they are different from

some notional standard of normal functioning. If this is the case, then we should treat very sceptically any *general* claims about the 'mentally ill'.
(McGhee, 2001)

Box 7.4 Some problems with the diagnosis of mental disorders

(i) When someone with cystitis suffers hair loss, there's factual evidence that each disease/condition has a distinct aetiology (causation) – and they also *look* very different. But in psychiatry, 'comorbid disorders can often seem suspiciously similar, as though they share some common cause or underlying mechanism' (Claridge and Davis, 2003). So, *comorbidity* refers to having more than one disorder/disease, and Claridge and Davis give the example of eating disorders and substance use disorder, which often occur together.

(ii) The distinction between illness or dysfunction and health is an issue in relation to physical disease, but in the context of psychological disorders it takes on even greater force. Psychological disorders are uniquely different:

In physical diseases the primary fault lies in just one part of the organism and the evidence for its failure or deficiency is usually fairly objective. Psychological disorders, on the other hand, are defined more in terms of the person's *whole* behavioural and mental functioning . . .
(Claridge and Davis, 2003)

This means that what's judged psychologically abnormal can sometimes seem quite arbitrary and may often depend on changing social criteria regarding what's healthy and unhealthy. In other words, 'the idea of 'disease process' as the *sole* cause of psychological disorders is less helpful than in the case of physical illness' (Claridge and Davis, 2003).

THE OBJECTIVE NATURE OF MENTAL DISORDERS: DO THEY EXIST?

At the heart of the 'abnormality as mental illness' criterion is the *medical model*. The use of the term *psychopathology* to refer to the particular kind of deviancy that psychiatrists and clinical psychologists are concerned with ('mad', not 'bad') reflects the medical model. Also central to the model is the classification and diagnosis of mental disorders, the treatment of psychiatric patients in psychiatric hospitals, and the use of other medical terminology and practices (Maher, 1966).

All systems of classification stem from the work of Emil Kraepelin (1913), who published the first recognized textbook of psychiatry in 1883. He proposed that certain groups of symptoms occur together sufficiently often to merit the designation 'disease' or 'syndrome', and he went on to describe the diagnostic indicators associated with each syndrome. His classification helped to establish the *organic* (bodily) nature of mental disorders, and this is an integral feature of the medical model. See Box 7.5 (page 130).

Most biologically orientated psychiatrists (the large majority of psychiatrists as a whole) have always believed that schizophrenia (as well as the other functional psychoses) is actually organic, and that it is only a matter of time until medical science discovers the biological causes and mechanisms involved. This argument is supported by classic cases such as

---

Box 7.5 Organic vs functional disorders

Kraepelin's system laid the foundation for all subsequent classification systems (in particular *DSM* in America, and the World Heath Organization's *ICD – International Classification of Diseases*). Until recently, psychiatrists distinguished between:

○ *organic mental disorders*, in which *biological factors* are clearly involved (usually taken to be *causal* factors), such as Alzheimer's disease and senile dementia; and

○ *functional mental disorders*, in which the role of biological factors is much less obvious.

What 'functional' conveys is that there is no demonstrable physical basis for the abnormal behaviour, and that something has gone wrong with the way the person functions in the network of relationships that make up his/her world (Bailey, 1979).

This distinction is related to another that has traditionally been made (and that has also recently been dropped), namely that between *neurosis* and *psychosis*.

The great majority of neuroses and psychoses have traditionally been thought of as functional disorders; the examples given above of organic disorders have usually been referred to as *organic psychoses*. Although neuroses and psychoses haven't been *defined* in terms of the role of biological factors (otherwise *all* psychoses would be organic, and all neuroses functional), the difference in the way they've typically been *treated* strongly suggests the underlying view regarding their likely causes. While neuroses (such as phobias, panic attacks, obsessive-compulsive disorder) are mainly treated using *psychological techniques* (psychotherapy, behaviour therapy), psychoses (such as schizophrenia, manic depression) are mainly treated using *physical methods* (major tranquillizing, and other powerful drugs, and electro-convulsive therapy/ECT).

---

general paresis of the insane (GPI). This was recognized as a clinical syndrome (in summary, dementia) long before the physical cause was discovered (namely, untreated syphilis). This discovery represents an important landmark in the history of psychiatry because it stimulated a search for organic causes of other syndromes (Gelder *et al.*, 1989). Also, many illnesses that were once thought to have a supernatural or psychological origin, have now become generally accepted as physical; for example, epilepsy was for centuries thought to be of divine origin (Littlewood and Lipsedge, 1989).

Contrary to this view, however, socially orientated psychiatrists argue that mental disorders, such as GPI, always had an 'organic feel' about them – they are only found associated with easily recognized bodily abnormalities. Conversely, Charcot and Freud helped hysteria (for so long thought to be caused by abnormalities of the womb) to be generally accepted as psychological in origin (Littlewood and Lipsedge, 1989).

If mental disorders 'exist' in some objective sense – that is, independently of cultural norms, values and worldviews – then the most likely candidates will come from those believed to be organic in origin. Just as modern medicine is based on the assumption that *physical disease* is the same throughout the world, and that definition, classification, causation and diagnosis are largely unaffected by cultural factors, so biologically orientated psychiatrists contend that psychoses, in particular schizophrenia and depression, are also 'culture-free'.

THE CROSS-CULTURAL STUDY OF MENTAL DISORDER

During the 1970s and 1980s, psychiatrists and clinical psychologists became increasingly interested in 'cultural psychiatry' (otherwise known as 'transcultural psychiatry', or 'comparative psychiatry'). Bhugra and Bhui (2001) define comparative psychiatry as: 'the study of the relations between psychiatric disorder and the psychological traits and characteristics of people, the cultures and societies they come from and the interaction between various factors arising from this'. It also deals with cultural factors in the genesis and management of psychiatric disorders. Although comparative psychiatry was originally proposed as an academic discipline, it is essential that any academic findings and views are put into practice in the delivery of healthcare to people from ethnic minorities and even to members of ethnic majority groups that differ from those to which the clinicians themselves belong (Bhugra and Bhui, 2001) (see below).

According to Berry *et al.* (1992), the central issue in the cross-cultural study of psychopathology is whether phenomena such as schizophrenia are (i) *absolute* (found in all cultures in precisely the same form), (ii) *universal* (present in some form in all cultures, but subject to cultural influence regarding what factors bring them on, how they're expressed, and so on), or (iii) *culturally relative* (unique to particular cultures and understandable only in terms of those cultures).

Absolute phenomena

Of the three possibilities, this is the only one that corresponds to a 'culture-free' view of abnormality. But even in the case of a disorder that may appear to be totally 'biological', such as the physiological response to alcohol, cultural factors seem to play a part. For example, cultural norms regarding what, where and how much to drink result in quite different expressions of alcohol use across cultural groups: 'We may conclude that it makes little sense to even consider a culture-free abnormal behaviour, since cultural factors appear to affect at least some aspects of mental disorders, even those that are so closely linked to human biology' (Berry *et al.*, 1992) (see Chapter 8).

Universality

This is a more likely candidate for capturing the nature of psychopathology, and is supported, in particular, by studies of schizophrenia and depression. We will look at the former here.

Schizophrenia is the most commonly diagnosed mental disorder in the world, and of the major disorders, the largest number of *culture-general symptoms* has been reported for schizophrenia (e.g. World Health Organization, 1973, 1979; Draguns, 1980, 1990). These two findings constitute one of the major arguments for the biological basis of this disorder.

The core symptoms include: (i) poor insight into the reasons for one's problems and one's current thinking; (ii) thinking aloud; (iii) incoherent speech, one phrase or sentence apparently bearing no relationship to others; (iv) giving unrealistic information that would be contradicted by objective facts if the person were able to consider them; (v) widespread, bizarre and/or nihilistic delusions (feeling that existence is useless and nothing is worth living for); (vi) flattened mood and limited ability to form emotional ties with others (Brislin, 1993). But even with this large core of culture-general symptoms, there are at least three possible ways in which culture-specific factors can influence schizophrenia: (a) the form that symptoms will take; (b) the specific reasons for the onset of the illness; (c) the prognosis.

THE FORM THAT SYMPTOMS WILL TAKE

When schizophrenics complain that their minds are being invaded by unseen forces, in North America and Europe these forces keep up to date with technological developments. So, in the 1920s, these were often voices from the radio, in the 1950s they often came from the television, in the 1960s it was satellites in space, and in the 1970s and 1980s spirits were transmitted through microwave ovens. In cultures where witchcraft is considered common, the voices or spirits would be directed by unseen forces under the control of demons.

Citing Katz *et al.* (1988), Brislin points out that the exact form taken by the symptoms of schizophrenia can be understood by looking at predominant cultural values. In Ibadan, Nigeria, the symptoms shown by schizophrenics emphasized a highly suspicious orientation towards others, with many bizarre fears and thoughts. For many Nigerians it is normal to view illness as caused by unseen evil forces, and sometimes those forces are directed at a person by enemies and witches. This paranoid aspect of the schizophrenic's symptoms is an exaggeration of this normal view, a distortion of the 'normal' state. This, of course, is directly relevant to the *dimensional* vs *categorical* views of abnormality discussed earlier.

REASONS FOR THE ONSET OF ILLNESS

One view of schizophrenia is that we inherit a predisposition towards the disorder (we are 'at risk'), while the actual symptoms are triggered by stress (see Draguns, 1990).

Day *et al.* (1987, in Brislin, 1993) studied schizophrenia in nine different locations in the USA, Asia, Europe and South America. Acute schizophrenic attacks were associated with stressful events, which could be described as external to the patients (and not initiated by them), and they tended to cluster within a two- to three-week period before the onset of obvious symptoms (such as the unexpected death of a spouse, losing one's job, and parental divorce). Some stressful events were interpretable only if the researchers had considerable information regarding the cultural background of the sample.

THE PROGNOSIS

Lin and Kleinman (1988, in Brislin, 1993) found that the prognosis for successful treatment of schizophrenia was better in non-industrialized than industrialized societies. Why should this be? Wouldn't we expect the opposite to be true, given the superior resources available in the latter?

To be a functioning member of a 'highly industrialized' nation, certain skills are needed that are very difficult for the schizophrenic to demonstrate, and many of the core symptoms involve relating to others. Individualism is valued in highly industrialized societies (see Chapter 8), and it is up to the *individual* to develop rapport and emotional ties with others. Yet there's no automatic support group available to help with this. In the past, there might have been the nuclear family, but its members are often so affected by divorce and intra-familial conflict that it can be a source of stress rather than support.

Along with this heavy emphasis on independence, self-reliance, and personal freedom, individualistic value orientations also tend to foster fierce competition, frequent life changes, and alienation, and they do not usually provide the kind of structured, stable, and predictable environments that allow schizophrenic patients to recuperate at their own pace and to be reintegrated into the society.
(Lin and Kleinman, 1988, in Brislin, 1993)

132

In contrast, the slower lifestyle and more integrated collectives commonly found in less industrialized nations may provide a more supportive environment for schizophrenics; this includes the greater likelihood of finding productive work (for example, in the family farm or business). This is clearly important for developing a sense of self-worth. Also, 'colleagues' will be more tolerant of mistakes than would an employer or colleagues in large, impersonal organizations. Brislin concludes by saying: 'As part of their socialization, people learn to express psychological disturbances in ways that are acceptable within their culture, in ways that will be understood, and in ways that will evoke sympathy from others.' What Brislin seems to be implying is that: (i) there is a crucial element of *learning* involved in abnormality, although this doesn't, of course, rule out the role of biological factors; (ii) abnormal behaviour and experience aren't random or arbitrary or meaningless, but make perfectly good sense in terms of the culture in which they are manifested; and (iii) there is a continuity between normal and abnormal behaviour (including schizophrenia), since both are, at least in part, acquired through the same process of socialization.

Although these observations are consistent with how *universal* abnormality has been defined by transcultural psychiatrists, Berry *et al.* (1992) point out two major limitations of the studies that provide the bulk of the evidence.

1 Studies such as the International Pilot Study of Schizophrenia (World Health Organization, 1973), which compared the prevalence of schizophrenia in Columbia, (the former) Czechoslovakia, Denmark, India, Nigeria, Taiwan, the UK, USA, and (the former) USSR, involved the use of diagnostic instruments, concepts and researchers that all belonged to western psychiatry.

2 The patient populations involved weren't representative of world cultural variation (and were themselves, to some extent, acculturated to a western way of life).

Cultural relativity

A large number of studies have found that, in a wide range of non-western cultures, there are apparently unique ways of 'being mad' (Berry *et al.*, 1992): there are forms of abnormality that aren't documented and recognized within the classification systems of western psychiatry. These 'exotic' disorders are usually described and interpreted in terms that relate to the particular culture in which they are reported. The local, indigenous, name is used, which then gradually enters the (western) psychiatric literature. They are commonly referred to as *culture-bound syndromes* (CBSs; see Box 7.6, page 134).

Again, researchers distinguish between modern, scientific, psychiatry and traditional *ethnopsychiatry* (the study of culture-relative/culture-specific disorders), seeing the former as telling us about *authentic* illness, while the latter tells us about illness that is *contaminated/distorted* by culture. Fernando (1991) believes that anthropology and psychiatry have colluded in regarding psychiatric disorders seen in western (white) societies as being on a different plane from those seen in non-western (black, 'primitive') societies:

When culture 'distorts' a syndrome beyond a certain point, a CBS is identified. Practitioners go along with this approach seeing symptom constellations in the West as the standard and those in *other* cultures as anomalies . . .

This represents a form of *ethnocentrism* within western psychiatry, and in keeping with this view, Fernando believes that the concept of a CBS has a distinctly racist connotation.

Similarly, Littlewood and Lipsedge (1989) argue that it is wrong to look at beliefs about madness in other cultures as if they are only more or less accurate approximations to a

---

Box 7.6 Culture-bound syndromes (CBSs)

Culture-bound syndromes are studied mainly by anthropologists, who focus on 'culture-specific' disorders, stressing the differences between cultures. This contrasts with the approach of traditional (biological) psychiatrists, who tend to focus on 'universal' disorders, stressing the similarities. So, when a 'new' condition is observed in some non-western society (people perceived as being alien to western culture), the syndrome itself is perceived as alien to the existing classification system, sufficiently 'outside' the mainstream that it may be *unclassifiable*. The fact that they may be quite common within a particular culture makes no difference – if they are (apparently) limited to *other* cultures, they are excluded from the mainstream classification of mental disorder. Since the disorder occurs in groups seen as alien in primarily *racial* terms, the concept of a CBS is, therefore, one that has been generated by the ideology of western psychiatry: 'psychopathology in the West is seen as culturally neutral and psychopathology that is distinctively different (from that seen in the West) as "culture-bound"' (Fernando, 1991).

'scientific' (accurate, objective) description. A cultural understanding of mental disorder is as important in western as in any other culture, and, indeed, some general features of those 'ritual patterns' usually classed as CBSs are applicable to western neurosis (Littlewood and Lipsedge, 1989). It has been suggested that anorexia nervosa and pre-menstrual syndrome (PMS; see Chapter 6) may be western CBSs (Fernando, 1991).

Ironically, in at least two cases, CBS names have become part of the common vocabulary in English-speaking, western societies. *Amok* involves wild, aggressive behaviour, usually short-lived, and usually confined to males, involving attempts to kill or injure. It was identified in Malaysia, Indonesia and Thailand, the Malay word 'amok' meaning 'to engage furiously in battle'. It has obvious similarities to the Viking behaviour called *berserker*, practised just before going into battle (Berry *et al.*, 1992). You don't have to come from South-East Asia, or be a Viking, in order to 'run amok' or 'go berserk!

Figure 7.3 A modern-day interpretation of the 'berserker'; Michael Douglas in *Falling Down*, where a 'normal' man goes on the rampage in retaliation against the frustrations of everyday life

Figure 7.4 During the Middle Ages, what we would now call mental disorder was seen as possession by the Devil or as witchcraft

THE CULTURE-BOUND NATURE OF PSYCHIATRY

If western psychiatry is, inevitably, influenced by western cultural beliefs and values (since it is part of that culture), then it cannot claim to be objective, scientifically 'detached' and value-free. If we accept this argument, it should follow that: (i) psychiatric definitions and the classification of mental disorders will change over time, reflecting changes in cultural beliefs and values; and (ii) the process of psychiatric diagnosis will be influenced by wider cultural beliefs and values.

Changing views of homosexuality

Psychological abnormality hasn't always been explained and dealt with in western culture by medicine. During the Middle Ages (roughly AD 500–1500), when religion was the dominant force in almost all aspects of European life, what we now call mental disorder was seen as possession by the Devil. It was the time of witch-hunts and burning witches at the stake, the Spanish Inquisition, and brutal exorcisms to drive out the Devil (Holmes, 1994). The 1500s marked the beginning of widespread recognition that disturbed people needed care, not exorcism and condemnation, but it wasn't until the middle of the 1800s that 'modern' psychiatry began to emerge, seeing psychological abnormality as comparable to bodily, physical, illness with organic origins (*somatogenesis*).

In *DSM-IV* (1994), the category 'Organic Mental Disorders', which had appeared in *DSM-III-R* (1987), was omitted and replaced by 'Delirium, Dementia, Amnesic and Other Cognitive Disorders'. According to Davison and Neale (1994), the thinking behind this change is that the term 'organic' implies that the other major categories *don't* have a biological basis. Since research has shown the influence of biological factors through a whole range of disorders, it is no longer considered appropriate to use the term 'organic' (it is now thought to be misleading). To this extent, mental disorder is even *more medicalized* than it has ever been.

What this shows is that mental disorders and how they're classified aren't 'set in stone'. Assuming that the behaviour and experience of people with disorders don't change radically (at least within the same cultural group) over relatively short periods of time, it isn't the 'reality' of mental disorder that changes but how psychiatrists define and interpret that reality. We've seen how those definitions and interpretations reflect wider cultural beliefs and values, and there's perhaps no better demonstration of this process than the example of homosexuality.

DSM-II (1968) included homosexuality as a sexual deviation. In 1973, the Nomenclature Committee of the APA, under pressure from many professionals and gay activist groups, recommended to the general membership that the category should be removed and replaced with *sexual orientation disturbance*. This was to be applied to gay men and lesbians who are 'disturbed by, in conflict with, or wish to change their sexual orientation'. The change was approved, but not without vehement protests from several eminent psychiatrists, who maintained the traditional view that homosexuality is inherently abnormal.

When *DSM-III* was published in 1980, another new term, *ego-dystonic homosexuality* (EDH), was used, referring to a person who is homosexually aroused, finds this arousal to be a persistent source of distress, and wishes to become heterosexual. Since homosexuality *itself* was no longer a mental disorder, there was no discussion in *DSM-III* of *pre-disposing factors* (as there was for all disorders). But pre-disposing factors for EDH *were* included, and were, primarily, those negative societal attitudes (homophobia and heterosexism) that have been internalized by the homosexual individual. So, according to *DSM-III*, a homosexual is abnormal if s/he has been persuaded by society's prejudices that his/her sexual orientation is inherently abnormal, but at the same time denies that homosexuality in itself is abnormal (Davison and Neale, 2001)!

For whatever reasons, very little use was made of the EDH category. Less surprisingly, no such category as 'ego-dystonic *heterosexuality*' has ever been used (Kitzinger, 1990)!

When *DSM-III* was revised (*DSM-III-R*, 1987), the APA decided that even the watered-down EDH should no longer be included. Instead, 'Sexual Disorder Not Otherwise Specified' includes 'persistent and marked distress about one's sexual orientation'. This has been retained in *DSM-IV*. This new category doesn't specify a sexual orientation, so ego-dystonic heterosexuality is a diagnostic possibility; however, Davison and Neale (2001) believe that, in practice, this is as unlikely to be made as ego-dystonic homosexuality.

Psychiatric diagnosis as a social process

According to Fernando (1991), the diagnostic interview consists, primarily, of (i) taking the patient's history, and (ii) assessing the patient's current 'mental state'.

The history is often thought of as comprising objective facts, but, in reality, it's a highly selective account of whatever information has been acquired from the patient and others, and it is the psychiatrist who does the crucial sorting out. The psychiatrist also influences the content of the history, in two interrelated ways.

1 First, the type and extent of information given by the patient and others are fashioned by the perceptions of the psychiatrist about the people providing the information, and vice-versa. For example, if a black Asian patient says little about an arranged marriage (because s/he thinks it will be disapproved of by the white psychiatrist), this will usually be interpreted as a negative quality of the patient (secretiveness or deviousness), rather than a quality of the doctor.

2 Second, the picking and choosing that occurs during the history-taking depends on the beliefs, value judgements, understanding and knowledge of the psychiatrist. White, middle-class psychiatrists are unlikely to have personal experience of predominantly black areas (such as Harlem in New York, Tower Hamlets in London, and St Paul's in Bristol), and so will be unaware of the pressures impinging upon black people who live there. This is likely to result in a misinterpretation of their lifestyles and behaviour, which often reinforces their racist attitudes.

The assessment of the patient's 'mental state' is probably the major determinant of the final diagnosis. What the patient reports of his/her experiences is taken to depict an inner state of mind. The validity of such an inference is dubious even when there's excellent rapport and full understanding between patient and psychiatrist, but in a multi-cultural setting this is highly unlikely. Fernando (1991) argues that:

The meanings attached to experiences and perceptions, the concept of illness, and the overall significance of the interview situation ... are but some of the parameters along which variation must occur when cultural differences are present between the participants of an interaction.

Deductions made from an 'examination' of the mental state cannot be viewed as equivalent to a medical description of the state of a bodily organ: 'What a doctor "finds" in a "mental state" is as much a reflection of the observers as the so-called patient. It is the result of an interaction rather than a one-sided observation' (Fernando, 1991).

According to Kareem (1978, in Mohamed, 2000): 'The fact of being from another culture involves both conscious and unconscious assumptions, both in the patient and the therapist ... for the successful outcome of therapy it is essential to address these ... assumptions from the beginning.' To help patients change, therapists must possess an understanding of the psychology, pathology and social experiences of individuals, including themselves. They need a deep level of self-awareness that enables them to recognize all the assumptions they bring with them. This includes facing the oppression, discrimination, stereotyping and racism within their society and their role in it. However, ignoring someone's blackness (as with their gender or sexual orientation) as if it were irrelevant, involves denying major aspects of that person's experiences. In order to avoid having to deal with material that *white therapists* might perceive as frightening or too challenging, they may tend to try to match culturally different clients with therapists from a similar background, instead of developing their own *transcultural skills*. However, the 'idea that black clients can *only* be seen by black therapists may serve to protect white therapists from having to confront issues about their own prejudices and racism' (Mohamed, 2000).

SUMMARY

○ The whole field of *abnormal psychology* rests upon the assumption that a distinction can be made between *normality* and *abnormality*.

○ It is relatively easy to give *examples* of psychological abnormality, but much more difficult to provide precise *definitions*.

○ All behaviour can be placed somewhere on a continuum, running from *unacceptable*, through *tolerable, acceptable/permissible*, to *desirable* and *required/obligatory*.

○ 'Unacceptable' conveys 'not decent and proper' (*residual rules*). Because these rules are implicit, we cannot easily say *why* schizophrenia or homosexuality is strange and frightening.

○ It is important to distinguish between *social deviance* and *mental disorder/abnormality*; only the latter involves an *impairment of function* in the person.

○ The *statistical infrequency criterion* (or *deviation from the average*) assumes that psychological characteristics in general are *dimensional*.

○ Those judged to be suffering from *psychotic mental disorder* may not experience any *personal distress* at all.

○ Defining abnormality as *other people's distress* suggests that abnormality, like normality, is *interpersonal*. According to Laing's *conspiratorial model* of schizophrenia, schizophrenia is a *label* applied by other people to protect them against the threat posed by the patient's behaviour/experience.

○ *Abnormality as maladaptiveness/disability* focuses largely on the *consequences* of behaviour, namely what it prevents the individual from achieving – personally, sexually, socially, intellectually or occupationally.

O According to the *deviation from the norm* criterion, abnormality involves not behaving, feeling or thinking as one *should*. This involves *value judgements* and relates to *residual rules*.

O The *abnormality as exaggeration of normality* criterion is based on the *dimensional* view of mental disorder, as opposed to the *categorical* view. These are favoured by (western) psychologists and psychiatrists respectively.

O Although now no longer illegal, homosexuality still breaches certain fundamental religious–moral principles; homophobia and heterosexism continue to reflect these *religious* roots.

O In western culture, unlike many non-western cultures, a sharp distinction is made between legal, religious and *medical* definitions of normality; mental disorder has become *medicalized*. In African culture, however, no distinction is made between bodily and mental illness.

O At the heart of the *abnormality as mental illness criterion* is the *medical model*. This involves the classification/diagnosis/treatment of *psychopathology*, stemming from the work of Kraepelin.

O Two traditional distinctions made within psychiatry are *organic* vs *functional* disorders, and *neurosis* vs *psychosis*.. Psychoses are mainly treated using *physical methods*, which implies a belief that they are biologically caused.

O The central issue in comparative psychiatry is whether phenomena such as schizophrenia are *absolute* ('culture-free'), *universal* ('culture-general') or *culturally relative* (unique to particular cultures).

O Although schizophrenia is the most commonly diagnosed mental disorder in the world, culture-specific factors could influence schizophrenia in relation to: (i) *the form the symptoms will take*; (ii) *the specific reasons for the onset of the illness*; (iii) *the prognosis*.

O The evidence that supports the view of abnormality as *universal* is of limited value because of the use of culturally biased diagnostic instruments and samples.

O Many studies have found unique ways of 'being mad' in a wide range of non-western cultures. These *culture-bound syndromes* (CBSs) are excluded from mainstream, western psychiatric classification, according to which psychopathology is seen as *culturally neutral*.

O This exclusion of culture-bound syndromes represents a form of *ethnocentrism*, since 'western symptoms' are seen as the 'standard'.

O Western psychiatry is influenced by western cultural beliefs and values, and so isn't objective and value-free. This is reflected in changing definitions among psychiatrists regarding the 'status' of homosexuality as a mental disorder.

O The cultural nature of psychiatry can also be seen if psychiatric diagnosis is understood as a *social process*. Assessment of the patient's 'mental state' isn't equivalent to a medical description of a bodily organ, but is the product of an *interaction* between individuals who often possess widely divergent beliefs, values and cultural experiences.

Useful websites

O   www.understandingpsychosis.com
O   www.nsf.org.uk
O   www.hants.gov.uk/istcclr/cch33222.html
O   cebmh.warne.ox.ac.uk/cebmh
O   http://www.sterling.holycross.edu/departments/psychology/

Recommended reading

Davison, G.C. and Neale, J.M. (2001) *Abnormal Psychology* (8th edn). New York: John Wiley & Sons.

Gross, R. (2003) *Key Studies in Psychology* (4th edn) (Chapter 20 on Rosenhan's pseudo-patient experiment). London: Hodder & Stoughton.

Miller, L. and Morley, S. (1986) *Investigating Abnormal Behaviour.* London: Lawrence Erlbaum Associates.

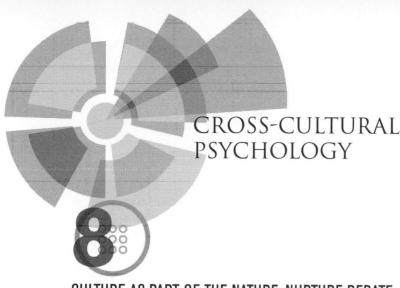

CROSS-CULTURAL PSYCHOLOGY

CULTURE AS PART OF THE NATURE–NURTURE DEBATE

When discussing the *heredity–environment* (nature–nurture) issue in Chapter 5, a distinction was made between two levels at which the debate has taken place:

1 the *species level*

2 the *individual* (or, more accurately, the *individual differences*) level.

The former relates to questions such as: Are particular abilities, such as language, unique to human beings, and if so, is it part of our biological make-up? Or Is It an acquired ability? Or does it involve an interaction between biological factors and environmental ones?

The latter relates to questions such as: How do we account for the fact that people vary in, say, intelligence? Are these differences largely due to differences in genetic make-up between people, or to differences in their environmental experience, or to an interaction between the two?

The concept of *culture* and *cultural differences* provides a third level at which the nature–nurture issue may be debated, intermediate between the other two. All human beings are born into a particular cultural environment, and culture (to be defined below) may be regarded as unique to human beings (also see below). This corresponds to level 1. To the extent that different cultures provide their members with different experiences, they represent an important source of individual differences; this, of course, corresponds to level 2.

So, culture is part of the experience of every human being (and is a distinctive feature of human behaviour), but at the same time cultures differ, providing people with different experiences. To ask in what ways differences in culture are related to differences in behaviour is to ask about nature–nurture at level 3.

Accepting that most psychologists believe that *both* nature *and* nurture are always involved in any human behaviour, cross-cultural psychologists argue for the *centrality of learning*. According to Segall *et al.* (1999):

Human behaviour can best be understood as the product of learning, particularly learning that results from experiences with other people or with ideas, institutions, or other products of the behaviour of other people. In short, we are largely what we are because of culturally based learning . . .

Our sociocultural nature reflects a highly developed capacity to benefit from the lessons of experience, our own and our culture mates'. No other animal has this capacity to the same extent ... No other animal learns as much. As a result, we display many forms of behaviour that are uniquely human, many of which are part of what we call *culture* ...'

As the creation of culture, each person is the product of the twin processes of *enculturation* and *socialization*.

○ *Enculturation* (Herskovits, 1948) refers to all the learning that occurs in human life because of what's available to be learned – that is, without any direct, deliberate teaching. This is demonstrated in observational learning (e.g. Bandura, 1971), where we (especially children) learn through modelling the behaviour of others (in particular, adults). Conformity (e.g. Asch, 1951) is another example.

○ *Socialization* was defined by Child (1954) as:

the whole process by which an individual, born with behavioural potentialities of enormously wide range, is led to develop actual behaviour which is confined within a much narrower range – the range of what is customary and acceptable for him according to the standards of his group.

This definition reminds us that all human beings are capable of a far greater repertoire of behaviours than any single person ever displays. As Segall *et al.* (1999) put it: 'Each of us, because of the accident of birth, begins life in a particular social context, within which we learn to make certain responses and not others.' They say that the most dramatic illustration of this is our language (see below).

A useful way of thinking about culture and environment is Bronfenbrenner's (1979, 1989) *ecological model*, intended mainly to help explain child development. According to this model, there are four levels, with interactions possible both within and between:

1 *the microsystem* – the immediate setting in which the individual is directly involved; for instance, face-to-face interactions between a mother and child

2 *the mesosystem* – the total system of microsystems that impinge on a particular child; for example, experiences at school and at home are bound to influence each other

3 *the exosystem* – interactions between settings in which at least one setting doesn't directly involve the individual; for example, the child's home and the parents' place of work

4 *the macrosystem* – the overall system of micro-, meso- and exosystems that characterizes a particular culture or sub-culture. 'The ecological environment is conceived as a set of nested structures, each inside the next, like a set of Russian dolls' (Bronfenbrenner, 1979). So, interactions between two individuals, such as mother and child, are influenced by the social context within which they occur (usually the family). In turn, the family exists and functions within a broader social setting (for example, socioeconomic status, racial background), which is itself part of an even broader, cultural, context.

WHAT IS CROSS-CULTURAL PSYCHOLOGY?

The study of microsystems has mainly been carried out by psychologists, while the 'larger' units (mesosystems and exosystems) have traditionally been the focus of sociologists and anthropologists. To the extent that *cross-cultural psychologists* are interested in studying variability in behaviour among the various societies and cultural groups around the world (Smith and Bond, 1998), they have more in common with sociologists and social anthropologists than with other (more traditional) psychologists. In terms of Bronfenbrenner's model, it is the *interrelationship* between the different levels that makes the cross-cultural approach different from that of other psychological approaches to the study of behaviour.

Absolutism vs relativism

According to Jahoda (1978), the immediate (and modest) goals of cross-cultural psychology are (i) to describe varieties of social behaviour encountered in different cultural settings and to try to analyse their origins, and (ii) to sort out what is similar across different cultures and, thus, likely to be our common human heritage (the *universals* of human behaviour).

Segall *et al.* (1999) see cross-cultural psychologists as trying to determine how sociocultural variables influence human behaviour. To do so, they sometimes focus on behavioural differences across cultures, and sometimes on universal patterns of behaviour. But the ultimate goal is always to discover how culture and individual behaviour relate. To reach this goal, cross-cultural psychologists are confronted by different general orientations, which they refer to as extreme *absolutism* and *relativism*.

Box 8.1 Absolutism vs relativism

Absolutism is associated with much traditional, 'mainstream', scientific psychology as it has been conducted in most European and US universities during the twentieth century; *relativism* is the approach central to anthropology during this same time-frame.

Cross-cultural psychology is located between the two, borrowing some aspects of each. For example, *cultural relativism* (Boas, 1911), extended by Herskovits (1948), was meant primarily to warn against invalid cross-cultural comparisons, flavoured by ethnocentric value judgements (see text below). Berry *et al.* (1992) 'borrowed' the term *relativism* to denote one pole of a dichotomy, with absolutism at the other pole.

○ *Relativists* give more weight to cultural factors than to biological ones, while the reverse is true for *absolutists*.

○ *Relativists* attribute group differences mainly to cultural differences, while *absolutists* attribute them mainly to non-cultural factors.

○ *Relativists* have little/no interest in intergroup similarities, while *absolutists* believe that species-wide basic processes cause many similarities between groups ('the search for the psychic unity of mankind').

○ *Relativists* advocate strictly 'emic' research, arguing that context-free categories and their measurement are impossible. They try to avoid all comparisons, which, if made at all, would be as non-evaluative as possible. *Absolutists* attempt to use context-free measurements, using standardized psychological instruments, which results in 'imposed etics' (see text below).

Based on Segall *et al.*, 1999

As with most dichotomies, few scholars are either *extreme* relativists or absolutists. For years, however, many US and European experimental psychologists stubbornly denied that cultural factors affected psychological processes. They proceeded to accumulate culture-bound findings they believed to be universally valid for all humankind. In parallel, some *cultural psychologists* place themselves quite close to the relativism end, emphasizing that psychological processes and structures vary in such fundamental ways in different cultural contexts that they are beyond comparison (or nearly so). Or they'll suggest that culture shouldn't be treated as existing outside individuals, where it can influence their behaviour, but *inside* (Greenfield, 1997; Miller, 1997; see below).

Segall *et al.* conclude by saying that most cross-cultural psychologists are somewhere in between these two extremes, where they try to strike a balance:

... revealing an orientation that borrows from both of the poles. Cross-cultural psychologists expect both biological and cultural factors to influence human behaviour, but, like relativists, assume that the role of culture in producing human variation both within and across groups (especially across groups) is substantial.

Like absolutists, cross-cultural psychologists allow for similarities, due to species-wide basic processes, but consider their existence subject to empirical demonstration. When doing our research among different human groups, we adapt standard instruments to local conditions and make controlled nonevaluative comparisons, employing 'derived etics' ...

(Trans)cultural and cross-cultural psychology: emphasizing differences

If knowledge is culturally created, then we shouldn't assume that our ways of understanding are necessarily any better (closer to 'the truth') than other ways. Yet this is precisely what mainstream (social) psychology has done. According to Much (1995), a new *(trans)cultural psychology* has emerged in North America (e.g. Bruner, 1990; Cole, 1990; Shweder, 1990) as an attempt to overcome the bias of *ethnocentrism* that has too often limited the scope of understanding in the social sciences (see below).

Shweder (1990) makes the crucial distinction between 'cross-cultural psychology', which is a branch of experimental social, cognitive and personality psychology, and *cultural psychology*. Most of what has been known as 'cross-cultural' psychology has presupposed the categories and models that have been based on (mostly experimental) research with (limited samples of) Euro-American populations. It has mostly either 'tested the hypothesis' or 'validated the instrument' in other cultures, or 'measured' the social and psychological characteristics of members of other cultures with the methods and standards of western populations, usually assumed as a valid universal norm. The new 'cultural psychology' rejects this *universalist* model (Much, 1995).

Cole (1996) refers to the results of the last 100 years of psychological research, including cross-cultural experimental studies, as the 'first psychology'. We shouldn't discard these results, since:

Cross-cultural studies, especially when they are sensitive to the local organization of activity, can serve to refute ethnocentric conclusions that 'those people' suffer from general cognitive deficits as a consequence of cultural inadequacies. From time to time they may even induce adherents of the first psychology to rethink their conclusions and their experimental methods . . .

However, he advocates a return to the early decades of psychology, particularly Wundt's *Volkerpsychologie* (see Chapter 11). Wundt argued that the methods of natural science could only be applied to the most elementary, universal, and therefore *timeless*, aspects of human behaviour. Genetic (historical and developmental) methods are needed to study culturally mediated and historically dependent 'higher psychological processes'. He seemed to have anticipated modern objections to cross-cultural research even before the first such study was conducted. But the road Wundt advocated wasn't taken – that is,

. . . the road along which culture is placed on a level with biology and society in shaping individual human natures. The name correctly given to that enterprise is *cultural psychology*, a major late twentieth-century manifestation of the second psychology.
(Cole, 1996)

The biases of mainstream psychology: emphasizing similarities

It has become almost a standing joke that experimental (social) psychology is really the psychology of the American undergraduate/psychology major. Apart from their accessibility, the main argument used to justify the practice of studying mostly student behaviour is based upon a sweeping *universalist assumption*: since we're all human, we're all fundamentally alike in significant psychological functions, and cultural/social contexts of diversity don't affect the important 'deep' or 'hardwired' structures of the mind. The corollary of this assumption is that the categories and standards developed on western European and North American populations are suitable for 'measuring', understanding, and evaluating the characteristics of other populations.

By contrast, a genuinely transcultural psychology ('the interplay between the individual and society and [symbolic] culture' (Kakar, 1982, in Much, 1995)) would base its categories, discriminations and generalizations upon empirical knowledge of the fullest possible range of existing human forms of life, without privileging one form as the norm or standard for evaluation. This is related to the *emic–etic* distinction (see below).

Cross-cultural psychology (despite the criticism from (trans)cultural psychologists) is important because it helps to correct the fundamental *ethnocentrism* within psychology as a whole (including social psychology, which 'ought to know better'). This refers to the strong human tendency to define 'reality' by using our own ethnic/cultural group's norms and values to define what is 'natural' and 'correct' for everyone (Triandis, 1990).

Psychology as a discipline has been largely dominated by psychologists from the USA, the UK and other western cultures, and the large majority of participants in psychological research have been members of those same cultures.

Historically, both researchers and subjects in social psychological studies have shared a lifestyle and value system that differs not only from that of most other people in North America, such as ethnic minorities and women, but also the vast majority of people in the rest of the world.
(Moghaddam et al., 1993)

Yet the findings from this research, and the theories based upon it, have been applied to *people in general*, as if culture makes no difference. An implicit, assumed, equation is made between 'human being' and 'human being from western culture', and this is commonly referred to as the *Anglocentric* or *Eurocentric bias*.

When members of other cultural groups *have* been studied, it has usually been so that they can be compared with western samples, using the behaviour and experience of the latter as the *standard*. (This is an exact parallel to the *masculinist* or *androcentric bias* in mainstream psychology, whereby men's behaviour and experience have been taken, by male psychologists, as the standard against which women have been judged; see Chapter 6.)

In both cases (the *Anglocentric* and *masculinist biases*), the failure to recognize and acknowledge the bias creates the misleading and false impression that what is being said about behaviour can be generalized without qualification. Cross-cultural psychologists *don't* equate 'human being' with 'member of western culture' because, for them, cultural background is the crucial *independent variable*.

Smith and Bond (1998) analysed the best-selling US social psychology textbook (Baron and Byrne, 1994) and the best-known European social psychology text (Hewstone *et al.*, 1996), to see in which countries the studies referred to were carried out. In the former, a full 94 per cent are American, and even in the latter 75 per cent are American. The same figures apply to another widely used text, written by social psychologists from Australia and New Zealand (Hogg and Vaughan, 1995). In all three cases, all but 2–3 per cent of the non-American studies were conducted outside western Europe, Australia or New Zealand. This means that only about 10 per cent of the world's population is being sampled (Smith and Bond, 1998).

While this may not be a problem in, say, physics, it very definitely is in the study of behaviour (particularly social behaviour). Instead of an objective, universal account of behaviour, what is presented is a predominantly North American, and to a lesser degree European, picture of human behaviour!

This isn't to say that the search for universal principles of human behaviour is, in itself, invalid; it is certainly consistent with the 'classical' view of natural science, according to which the scientist's ultimate goal is to discover laws of nature, to which there are no exceptions (see Chapters 3 and 11). Furthermore, if universal principles of behaviour are to be found, they can be found by anyone, regardless of race, gender or social class. But this could only be achieved if the researchers adopted a *non-ethnocentric* approach. Unfortunately,

... ethnocentrism, involving a belief in the superiority of one's own cultural group, has influenced research in social psychology so that even some of the most established findings in social psychology do not stand up to the test when assessed in cultures outside North America ...
(Moghaddam et al., 1993)

Some examples of these apparent social psychological 'facts' are considered later in the chapter.

WHAT IS THIS THING CALLED CULTURE?

Based on Herskovits (1948), culture is usually defined as the 'man-made part of the environment' (Segall *et al.*, 1999), or (more politically correctly) the 'human-made part of the environment' (Moghaddam *et al.*, 1993). According to Triandis (1990), it has two major aspects: *objective* (e.g. roads, bridges, cooking pots and military weapons, musical symphonies and poetry — examples given by Moghaddam *et al.*) and *subjective* (e.g. beliefs, attitudes, norms, roles and values). The examples of objective aspects suggest that this category should be sub-divided into *physical/material* and *social/non-material*.

So, culture is the part of the environment made by humans; but, in turn, culture helps to 'make' humans: 'In essence, humans have an interactive relationship with culture: we create and shape culture, and are in turn influenced by our own cultural products' (Moghaddam *et al.*, 1993).

While our culture is already 'there' when we arrive in the world (we're born into our culture), this doesn't mean that it is static. Jahoda (1978) cites the famous geneticist, Waddington, who referred to culture as an 'information-transmitting system', which provides humans with an evolutionary system distinct from the biological one governing the animal world:

There is no evidence that our Stone Age ancestors were biologically very different from modern man, and most of the vast transformations that have taken place appear to have been the outcome of cultural evolution which is social rather than genetically transmitted . . .
(Jahoda, 1978)

Of course, the rate of cultural evolution is far greater in some societies than others. A common distinction is made between western culture, which is characterized by very rapid change (of both material and social/non-material aspects), and traditional (non-western) culture, where the rate of change is very much slower. In turn, 'traditional' has come to mean something like 'resistant to the influence of western culture', but this seems to be a matter of degree only: *nowhere* is immune from western influence.

Broadly speaking, 'culture' can refer to groups of nations (e.g. the USA, Canada and all the member states of the European Community, are 'western'), or a single one, or it can refer to sub-units (or sub-cultures) within a nation, such as tribes, social classes and castes. Rohner (1984, in Smith and Bond, 1998) makes the important distinction between *culture* and *social system*. The former refers to an organized system of meanings that members attribute to the persons, objects and events comprising that culture, while the latter refers to the behaviours found within a culture. *Society* is defined as 'the largest unit of a territorially bounded, multi-generational population, recruited largely through sexual reproduction, and organized around a common culture and a common social system' (Rohner, in Smith and Bond, 1998). This definition acknowledges the degree to which culture and social system are interwoven.

Much cross-cultural research is in fact based on 'national cultures', which, of course, often comprise a number of separate sub-cultures. These may be demarcated by religion (as in Northern Ireland), by language (as in Belgium) or by race (as in Malaysia and Singapore). But studies in this area often provide little more detail about the participants than the name of the country (national culture) in which the study was done.

According to Smith and Bond (1998), this involves two 'penalties'. First, when we compare national cultures we can lose track of the enormous *diversity* found within many of the major nations of the world, and differences found *between* any two countries might well also be found between carefully selected sub-cultures *within* those countries. Second, there is the danger of implying that national cultures are unitary systems, free of conflict, confusion and dissent. This, of course, is rarely the case.

Figure 8.1 The national culture of Northern Ireland is dominated by the subculture of religion

So, if we should distinguish between *culture* and *country/national culture*, how can we define 'culture'? Or, as Brislin (1993) puts it, what are the *fundamental features* of culture? Brislin proposes a checklist of 12 features (see Box 8.2, page 149), some of which overlap with the definitions we've already considered.

Since Brislin's checklist is to do with the fundamental features of culture, the emphasis is on *what different cultures have in common*. Only point 12 relates to *differences between cultures*; one way of trying to distinguish between cultures is to see how the concept of time is used and understood in different cultures (see Gross, 2003). However, as important as it is, time represents a fairly specific feature of cultural life. Are there any more general features or dimensions that can help us to understand the differences between cultures?

Dimensions of cultural difference

Two very useful attempts to identify the key dimensions in terms of which cultures differ, allowing them to be compared, are those of Hofstede (1980) and Triandis (1990). For Hofstede (1980), culture is 'the collective programming of the mind which distinguishes the members of one group from another'. He conducted a large-scale study of several thousand IBM employees in 40 different countries, and identified four dimensions:

1 *power distance*: the amount of respect and deference shown by those in both superior and subordinate positions

2 *uncertainty avoidance*: the focus on planning and stability as ways of dealing with life's uncertainties

3 *individualism-collectivism*: whether one's identity is defined by personal choices and achievements (individualism) or by characteristics of the collective groups to which one is more or less permanently attached (collectivism)

4 *masculinity–femininity*: the relative emphasis on achievement (masculinity) or interpersonal harmony (femininity).

When a culture is described as, say, collectivist, we *don't* mean that any two members of the culture must be equally collectivist, or that either one of them must necessarily be more collectivist than someone from an individualist culture (see Chapter 2). We're looking at the *mean score* of a large number of individual scores, such that a collectivist culture displays

---

Box 8.2 A checklist of fundamental features of culture

1 Culture consists of ideas, values and assumptions about life that guide specific behaviour.

2 Culture consists of those aspects of the environment that people make. (But people's *responses* to aspects of the environment that are *natural*, such as the climate, also constitute part of the environment).

3 Culture is transmitted from generation to generation, with the responsibility being given to parents, teachers, religious leaders and other respected elders in a community.

4 There will be childhood experiences that many people in a community remember happening to them.

5 Aspects of one's culture aren't commonly discussed by adults; since culture is widely shared and accepted, there's little reason to.

6 Culture can become clearest in well-meaning clashes – that is, interactions among people from very different backgrounds. Each may behave quite 'normally' as far as their own culture is concerned, but not as judged by the other culture.

7 Culture allows people to 'fill in the blanks' when presented with a basic sketch of familiar behaviours or situations.

8 Cultural values remain despite compromises and slip-ups. Even though we can list exceptions, the cultural value is seen as a constant that continues to guide specific behaviours.

9 People react emotionally when cultural values are violated, or when a culture's expected behaviours are ignored.

10 There can be both acceptance and rejection of a culture's values at different times in a person's life. For example, rebellious adolescents and young adults come to accept a culture's expectations after having children of their own.

11 When changes in cultural values are contemplated, people are likely to react by saying, 'this will be difficult and time-consuming'. In other words, people tend to resist cultural change.

12 When comparing proper and expected behaviour across cultures, it is possible to observe certain sharply contrasting beliefs or orientations; for example, the treatment of time, and the clarity of rules or norms for certain complex behaviours.

(Based on Brislin, 1993)

---

collectivism to a greater degree than individualism, and more than an individualist culture does. These are *dimensions* rather than categories or types; it is the manifestation of these characteristics and behaviours *relative* to each other and *relative* to other cultures that matters (see Figure 8.2, page 150).

In 1983, Hofstede expanded his sample to include 50 national cultures, although he omitted the former Soviet Bloc countries, as well as most of Africa. However, in terms of global coverage, his study is unrivalled, and the individualism–collectivism dimension has attracted many cross-cultural researchers in recent years (Smith and Bond, 1998).

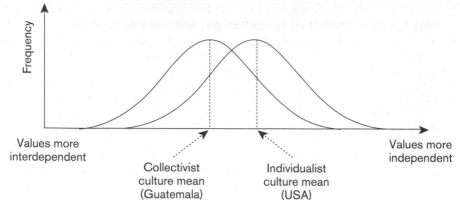

Figure 8.2 Hypothetical distributions of interdependent/independent value scores in a collectivist and an individualist national culture

Cultural syndromes

One of these cross-cultural researchers is Triandis, who replicated some of Hofstede's results with 15 samples from different parts of the world (Triandis *et al.*, 1986, in Triandis, 1990). Triandis sees 'culture' as comprising *cultural syndromes*, which he defines as 'a pattern of values, attitudes, beliefs, norms and behaviours that can be used to contrast a group of cultures to another group of cultures'. Three major cultural syndromes are *cultural complexity*, *individualism–collectivism* and *tight vs loose cultures*.

CULTURAL COMPLEXITY

The more complex the culture, the more people must pay attention to *time*, which is one of the examples given by Brislin (1993; see above). This is related to the number and diversity of roles that members of the culture typically play: the more numerous and diverse the roles, the more important it is that time be allocated in an appropriate way.

Cultures that are more industrialized and technological, such as Japan, Sweden and the USA, tend to be more focused on time. To this extent, therefore, more industrialized and technological cultures are more complex cultures. The *concept* of time also differs between cultures. Typically, in the West, time is seen as *linear* (i.e. it 'travels' in a straight line, from past, through present, to future), while in many non-western cultures it is seen as *circular* (i.e. it occurs in recurring cycles).

Another feature of complexity is *specificity vs diffusion*: the more complex, the more specific roles become. For example, because of the role of religion in certain cultures (e.g. the Arab world in general, and Iran), a person's religion is a major determinant of his/her social behaviour. But in western cultures, there's a fairly clear demarcation between the religious and the non-religious (i.e. the secular).

INDIVIDUALISM VS COLLECTIVISM

Triandis believes that this is the most promising of the many dimensions of cultural variation that have been proposed, in the sense of being the most likely to account for a great deal of social behaviour. As we saw earlier, people in every culture have both types of tendency, but the relative emphasis in the West is towards individualism, and in the East towards collectivism.

When Triandis *et al.* (1986, see Triandis, 1990) replicated some of Hofstede's findings, they found four additional factors related to the main construct. *Family integrity* (e.g. 'Children should live at home with their parents until they get married'), and *interdependence* (e.g. 'I like to live close to my good friends') are both related to *collectivism*, while *self-reliance with hedonism* (e.g. 'If the group is slowing me down, it's better to leave it and work alone; the most important thing in my life is to make myself happy') and *separation from in-groups* (indicated by agreement with items showing that what happens to extended family members is of little concern) are both related to *individualism*. Other 'defining attributes' (Triandis, 1990) include the following:

○ Collectivists pay much more attention to an identifiable in-group and behave differently towards members of that group compared with out-group members. The in-group can best be defined by the *common fate* of members; often, it is the unit of survival, or the food community, so that if there's no food, all in-group members starve together. In most cultures, the family is the main in-group, but in some the tribe or country can be just as important, and in still others, the work group (e.g. Japan), reflecting the incredible economic success enjoyed by that culture.

○ For collectivists, in-group goals have primacy over individual goals. For individualist cultures, it's the other way round, and the former often perceive the latter as 'selfish'.

○ Collectivists' behaviour is regulated largely by in-group norms, while that of individualists is regulated largely by personal likes and dislikes and cost–benefit analyses. Thus for 'traditional' behaviours, such as having children, *norms* (which have an outward-looking, group reference) should be more important in collectivist cultures, while *attitudes* (which have an inward-looking, personal reference) should be more important in individualist cultures. Lower-class groups, in most societies, are more collectivist than upper-class groups.

○ Collectivists emphasize social hierarchy much more than individualists; usually the father is 'head of the household' and women are generally subordinate.

○ Collectivists emphasize harmony and 'saving face'. They favour homogeneous in-groups, in which there are no internal disagreements, so that a 'united front' is shown to out-groups. But in individualist cultures, disagreements within the in-group are acceptable and often help to 'clear the air'.

○ Collectivist cultures stress in-group fate and achievement, and interdependence within it. *Self-reliance* implies 'I'm not a burden on the in-group', while in individualist cultures it conveys 'I can do my own thing.' There's generally much more emotional detachment from the larger in-group in individualist cultures.

○ For collectivists, the *self* is an appendage, or extension, of the in-group, while for individualists it is a separate and distinct entity (see Chapter 3). When asked to complete statements that begin 'I am', collectivists typically give more in-group-related answers (e.g. 'I am a son', 'I am a Roman Catholic'), while individualists typically give more personal-attribute answers (e.g. 'I am kind', 'I am hard-working'). In collectivist cultures, people usually belong to a small number of in-groups that influence them significantly; but in individualist cultures, behaviour is rarely greatly influenced by any one in-group in particular, because there are usually so many, and they often make conflicting demands on the individual.

○ In collectivist cultures, *vertical relationships* (e.g. parent–child) take priority over *horizontal relationships* (e.g. spouse–spouse) when there is conflict between them. The reverse is true in individualist cultures. Collectivists stress family integrity, security, obedience and conformity, whereas individualists stress achievement, pleasure and competition. Consistent with these differences, individualist cultures use child-rearing methods that encourage autonomy and self-reliance, while collectivist cultures encourage children to be obedient and dutiful, and to make sacrifices for the in-group.

Roughly speaking, *capitalist* politico-economic systems are associated with *individualism*, and *socialist* societies are associated with *collectivism*. There is also evidence which shows that urban environments, compared with rural ones, *within* the same societies, seem to encourage competitiveness, one of the major features of individualism (Smith and Bond, 1998).

TIGHT VS LOOSE CULTURES

In *tight* cultures, people are expected to behave according to clearly defined norms, and there is little tolerance of deviation from those norms; in *loose* cultures, there's a good deal of freedom to deviate. (This is relevant to the whole question of *normality/abnormality*, including mental disorder; see Chapter 7.)

The concept of *tightness* has much in common with Hofstede's (high) *uncertainty avoidance* (see above). Japan is the prototype of a tight culture (although tightness isn't a feature of every aspect of social life), and Thailand is the prototype of a loose culture. Tightness is also associated with *cultural homogeneity* – that is, there is very little mixing of ethnic groups from a variety of cultural backgrounds, and the culture is relatively 'pure'. By contrast, looseness is associated with *cultural heterogeneity*. Hofstede found evidence of looseness (low uncertainty avoidance) in Hong Kong and Singapore, two cultures in which East (China) meets West (Britain).

In addition to these three major dimensions of cultural diversity, Triandis (1990) discusses three more specific dimensions.

1 *Masculinity vs femininity* is also one of Hofstede's four main dimensions, which he described in terms of work-related goals (Japan is masculine and Sweden feminine). There is an interesting similarity between masculinity and *individualism*, on the one hand, and femininity and *collectivism* on the other. *Masculine* cultures stress getting the job done, achievement, progress, advancement, and being strong and effective, while *feminine* cultures stress quality of life, good interpersonal relationships, nurturing, concern for others, and being kind and caring (see Chapter 6).

2 Regarding *emotional control vs emotional expressiveness*, in cultures such as Japan, where people are expected to express mostly pleasant emotions (even in unpleasant situations), people do very well in controlling their emotions, By contrast, in cultures such as southern Europe, where people aren't expected to control their emotions, they often feel good about expressing themselves openly.

There is some evidence that people in Africa, and places near Africa, express their emotions freely, and that the further people live from where human beings first developed, the more emotional control they have. If human beings originated in Africa (a widely held belief among anthropologists), then as they migrated to remote corners of the world, they had to learn to control the unfriendly environments they encountered – and themselves. Self-control became a value, and emotional control was a manifestation of that value.

3 *Contact vs no-contact cultures* refers to cultural differences in terms of what Hall (1959, 1966) called *proxemic rules*. These prescribe the amount of physical distance between people in everyday interactions, according to the situation and the relationship between the people involved. How close we're 'allowed' to sit or stand next to others (particularly strangers) constitutes an important feature of non-verbal communication. Misunderstandings between members of different cultural groups (and unfavourable first impressions) can arise from a failure to appreciate the appropriate proxemic rules that apply on a particular occasion.

Table 8.1   Major dimensions of cultural difference

Power distance	Hofstede (1980)
Uncertainty avoidance	Hofstede (1980)
Tight vs loose cultures	Triandis (1990)
	Triandis *et al.* (1986)
Individualism–Collectivism	Hofstede (1980)
	Triandis (1990)
	Triandis *et al.* (1986)
Masculinity–Femininity	Hofstede (1980)
	Triandis (1990)
	Triandis *et al.* (1986)
Cultural complexity	Triandis (1990)
	Triandis *et al.* (1986)
Emotional control vs emotional expressiveness	Triandis (1990)
	Triandis *et al.* (1986)
Contact vs no-contact cultures	Triandis (1990)
	Triandis *et al.* (1986)

DOING CROSS-CULTURAL RESEARCH: CONCEPTUAL AND METHODOLOGICAL ISSUES

The emic–etic distinction

As we have seen, cross-cultural psychology (like psychology as a whole) involves the study by (mostly) members of one cultural group (western psychologists) of members of non-western cultural populations. This perhaps makes it inevitable (even if it doesn't make it justifiable) that, when a western psychologist studies members of some other culture, s/he will use theories and measuring instruments that have been developed in the 'home' culture. These can be used for studying *both* cross-cultural *differences* and *universal* aspects of human behaviour (the 'psychic unity of mankind'). For example, aggression is a cultural universal – but *how it is expressed* may be culturally specific.

Similarly, there are good reasons for believing that a mental disorder such as schizophrenia is universal, with core symptoms found in a wide range of cultural groups, but also with culture-specific factors influencing the *form* the symptoms will take, the specific reasons for the onset of the illness, and the likely outcome of the illness (the prognosis) (Brislin, 1993; see Chapter 7).

The distinction between culture-specific and universal behaviour is one version of what has come to be known in cross-cultural psychology as the *emic–etic* distinction. This also refers to problems inherent in the cross-cultural use of instruments developed in a single culture (Segall *et al.*, 1999).

Box 8.3 The emic–etic distinction

The terms 'emic' and 'etic' are based on the distinction made in linguistics between *phonemics* (the study of sounds as they contribute to the *meaning* of a language) and *phonetics* (the study of *universal sounds* used in human language, independently of their relationship to meaning) (Pike, 1954). As applied to the study of cultures, *etics* refers to culturally general concepts, which are easier to understand (because, by definition, they are common to all cultures), while *emics* refers to culturally specific concepts, which include all the ways that specific cultures deal with etics. It is the emics of another culture that are often so difficult to understand (Brislin, 1993).

According to Pike (1954), the terms should be thought of as referring to two different viewpoints regarding the study of behaviour: the etic approach studies behaviour from *outside* a particular cultural system, and the emic approach studies behaviour from the *inside* (Segall *et al.*, 1999).

While both viewpoints represent part of cross-cultural psychology, does the distinction help us to understand how research is actually carried out? According to Berry (1969), research has to begin somewhere and, inevitably, this usually involves an instrument or observational technique rooted in the researcher's own culture (an *emic* for that culture). When such an emic is brought in from an outside culture, is assumed to be valid in the alien culture and so is seen as a valid way of comparing the two cultures, an *imposed etic* is being used (Berry, 1969).

Many attempts to replicate American studies in other parts of the world involve an imposed etic; they all assume that the situation being studied has the *same meaning* for members of the alien culture as it does for members of the researcher's own culture (Smith and Bond, 1998). The number of failures to replicate the findings obtained using American samples illustrates very clearly that this assumption is often false! (Some examples of such failures are discussed at the end of the chapter.)

An (imposed) etic approach is more likely to be used, since the researcher brings with him/her ready-made theories and measuring instruments in an attempt to identify universal behavioural patterns. But this is also the approach that involves the danger of the researchers imposing their own cultural biases and theoretical framework on the behaviour of people from a different cultural group. The danger is that the biases and framework may simply not 'fit' the phenomena being studied, resulting in their distortion.

Brislin (1993) gives the example of 'raising responsible children' as an etic, and 'encouraging independent thinking' as an emic designed to achieve it. While the etic may be reasonable (relevant to all cultures), it is simply wrong to believe that the emic will also be: different cultures may use very different means to achieve the same goal. We cannot simply *assume* that 'one's own emics are *part of* the culturally common etic'. This is, of course, an imposed etic.

Another example is the concept of intelligence. Brislin suggests that the etic is 'solving problems, the exact form of which hasn't been seen before', a definition likely to be generally acceptable across cultures (partly because it is at least consistent with the fact that what constitutes a 'problem' differs from culture to culture). However, is the emic of 'mental quickness' (for example, as measured by timed IQ tests) universally valid? Among the Baganda people of Uganda, intelligence is associated with slow, careful, deliberate thought

(Wober, 1974, in Brislin, 1993), nor is it necessarily valid for all schoolchildren *within* a culturally diverse country like the USA (Brislin, 1993).

Some possible solutions to the 'imposed etic' problem

Instead of using imposed etic measures, Berry (1969) outlines a strategy for reaching a more valid set of *derived etic* generalizations; this strategy basically consists of a number of parallel emic studies within a series of national cultures. This focuses on culture-specific phenomena, such as the behaviours, values, customs and traditions of the particular national cultures included. This is the approach typically used in ethnographic anthropological research (*ethnography* being 'fieldwork'), which provides a rich source of information about the culture, which can then be used as a basis for cross-cultural psychology (Berry *et al.*, 1992). Typically, participant observation is used, together with local people serving as informed observers, as well as local test construction, in an attempt to tap the culture's own indigenous system of classification or 'subjective culture' (Triandis, 1972).

If the 'subjective cultures' of different national cultures show similarities (that is, there is a convergence between the results obtained within each culture), we can be more confident that we have identified processes that are equivalent, and we are in a position to make a derived etic generalization, at least with regard to the particular cultures that have been sampled (Smith and Bond, 1998).

The problem of equivalence

The emic—etic distinction implies that social psychology cannot discover cultural universals unless it adopts a cross-cultural approach. The methods used by psychologists need to be adapted, so that researchers can study the *same* processes in *different* cultures (Moghaddam *et al.*, 1993).

But how do we know that we are studying the same processes? What does 'same' mean in this context? For Brislin (1993), the question is: 'Do the concepts being investigated, and especially the way the concepts are being measured, have the same meaning in the different cultures?' He describes three approaches that have been used to deal with this fundamental issue of *equivalence*: translation equivalence, conceptual equivalence and metric equivalence.

TRANSLATION EQUIVALENCE

Discovering if concepts can be easily expressed in the languages of the different cultures being studied represents a first step in dealing with the issue of equivalence. If material doesn't translate well, this might be because emic aspects are involved with which the translators are unfamiliar. Alternatively, there may not be readily available terms in the language to capture certain aspects of the concept being translated.

A common method used in trying to overcome this problem is *back-translation*. The material in the original language (usually English) is carefully prepared (e.g. a questionnaire on child-rearing practices), then a bilingual person translates it into the target language. A second bilingual person (unfamiliar with the efforts of the first) then translates it from the target language (back) into English. The two English versions are then examined in order to see what 'comes through' clearly. If the two English versions are equivalent, it is *assumed* that the target-language version is adequate. By studying the back-translated original-language (English) version, researchers can gain insights into what can and cannot easily be expressed in the target language (see Figure 8.3).

Figure 8.3 An example of back-translation between English and Chamorro (the native language of Guam, an island in the northern Pacific) (From Brislin, 1993)

CONCEPTUAL EQUIVALENCE

The material that proceeds smoothly through the multiple steps of back-translation is said to be *translation equivalent*. Conceptual equivalence begins with the assumption that there will probably be *different* aspects of a concept that serve the same purpose in different cultures. This often begins by identifying the *etic* aspects, followed by a further identification of the *emic* aspects related to the etic in the various cultures being studied.

To take an earlier example, the etic for 'intelligence' might be 'solving problems the exact form of which haven't been seen before', while the emic might include 'mental quickness' (USA and western Europe), 'slow, careful, deliberate thought' (the Baganda people of Uganda; Wober, 1974), and 'responsibility to the community (getting along well with others)' (the Chi-Chewa people of Zambia; Serpell, 1982).

All these emics are conceptually equivalent – that is, they all form part of the definition of intelligence as used by respected adults in the various cultures, and might be elicited by asking such adults, 'Which young people in your community are considered intelligent?'

METRIC EQUIVALENCE

While conceptual equivalence centres on the analysis of different behaviours that can all demonstrate the same general concept, *metric equivalence* centres on the analysis of the *same* concepts across cultures, based on the assumption that the same scale (after proper translation procedures have been carried out) can be used to measure the concept.

For example, after careful translation, an IQ test produces a score of, say, 120 for an American woman *and* for a woman in Chile. The assumption is that the intelligence scale (metric) is measuring exactly the same concept (intelligence) in the two countries, and that a score in one country can be directly compared with that in another. But even if translation has been carried out satisfactorily, this is no guarantee of *conceptual equivalence* and, surely, this is the most important criterion by which to assess the cross-cultural equivalence of an IQ test (as well as being a requirement for metric equivalence). While translation equivalence has actually been used in cross-cultural research (and isn't particularly controversial), conceptual and metric equivalence are largely *theoretical* and are much more controversial (they beg more questions than they answer).

Even if conceptual equivalence *can* be established, there remains the question of *who constructs the test* – a western psychologist (in which case the test must be translated, still begging the question of *metric equivalence*) or a local test constructor (which removes the need for translation). In either case, we seem to be left with the question of whether the test is *culture-fair*.

> ## Box 8.4 Are culture-fair tests possible?
>
> According to Frijda and Jahoda (1966, in Segall *et al.*, 1999), a culture-fair test could: (i) be a set of items that are equally unfamiliar to all possible persons in all possible cultures, so that everyone would have an equal chance of passing (or failing) the items; or (ii) comprise multiple sets of items, modified for use in each culture to ensure that each version of the test would contain the same degree of familiarity. This would give members of each culture about the same chance of being successful with their respective version. While (i) is a virtual impossibility, (ii) is possible in theory, but in practice very difficult to construct.
>
> Clearly, culturally mediated experience *always* interacts with tests' content to influence test performance.
>
> The root of all measurement problems in cross-cultural research is the possibility that the same behaviours may have different meanings across cultures or that the same processes may have different overt manifestations. As a result, the 'same' test, be it a psychometric one or another type of instrument, might be 'different' when applied in different cultures. Therefore the effort to devise culturally fair testing procedures will probably never be completely successful. The degree to which we are measuring the same thing in more than one culture, whether we are using the same or different test items, must always worry us.
> *(Segall et al., 1999)*

The view that 'tests of ability are inevitably cultural devices' (Cole, 1985) is related to Segall *et al*'s claim that the 'same' test might actually be 'different' when applied across cultures. What none of the three types of equivalence takes into account is the *meaning of the experience of taking an intelligence test* (what we could perhaps call 'experiential equivalence'). Taking tests of various kinds is a familiar experience for members of western culture, both within and outside the educational context, but what about cultures in which there is no generally available schooling? How can we measure intelligence independently of people's responses to taking the test itself? The very nature or form of the *tasks* involved in an intelligence test (as distinct from the content) has a cultural meaning, as illustrated by Glick's report of research with the Kpelle people (1975, in Rogoff and Morelli, 1989).

Participants were asked to sort 20 objects into groups. They did this by using *functional* groups (e.g. knife with orange, potato with hoe), instead of *category* groups, which the experimenter thought more appropriate. When their way of classifying the objects was challenged, they often explained that this was how a wise man would do it. 'When an exasperated experimenter asked finally, "How would a fool do it?", he was given back sorts of the type that were initially expected – four neat piles with food in one, tools in another, and so on' (Glick, 1975, in Rogoff and Morelli, 1989).

This is a kind of 'putting two fingers up' at the researcher for being ethnocentric, imposing an etic, and making culturally inappropriate assumptions. Being asked to perform a task outside of its usual context (from practical to abstract) could so easily produce the conclusion that the people being studied lack the basic ability to classify, when it is the inappropriateness of the task that is at fault.

Advantages of cross-cultural research

It has become almost a truism among cross-cultural researchers that the development of concepts and theories of human behaviour demands that behaviour be studied all over the world. This might seem like common sense, but we've seen already in this chapter that psychologists often seem to believe it is perfectly legitimate to investigate behaviour in one culture (or using one gender; see Chapter 6), and then generalize to other cultures (or to the other gender).

HIGHLIGHTING IMPLICIT ASSUMPTIONS

An important function of cross-cultural research is to allow investigators to look closely at the impact of their own belief systems ('folk psychology') on scientific theories and research paradigms. When participants and researchers are from the same population, interpretations of the behaviour under investigation may be constrained by implicit cultural assumptions.

Working with people from a quite different background can make us aware of aspects of human activity that we normally wouldn't notice, either because they are missing in the 'new' culture, or because they are arranged differently. In this way, we become aware of our assumptions, helping us to recognize that human functioning cannot be separated from its contexts, both cultural and more immediate (Rogoff and Morelli, 1989). The case of the Kpelle being asked to sort objects is an insightful (and very amusing) example of this.

SEPARATING BEHAVIOUR FROM CONTEXT

One consequence of researchers being unable to stand back from their own cultural experience is that, when studying behaviour within their own culture, they tend to focus on the behaviour rather than on the situation or context. This results in the *fundamental attribution error* (FAE; Ross, 1977) – that is, seeing the behaviour as reflecting the personal dispositions of the actor (see Chapter 2). The researchers are so familiar with these situations and contexts, it is difficult for them to appreciate the impact that they have on behaviour. For example, researchers comparing minority-group children in the USA with mainstream children often assume that mainstream (white, middle-class) skills and upbringing are normal and superior. This results in a 'deficit model' view of minority groups, who are seen as needing intervention to compensate for their deficiencies (Rogoff and Morelli, 1989).

However, when studying other cultures, it may be far easier to make this separation of behaviour from situational context, since many situations will be new, unfamiliar and fresh in their eyes (Brislin, 1993). This increased sensitivity to context may help to counteract the ethnocentrism found when studying minority groups within the researcher's own national culture.

EXTENDING THE RANGE OF VARIABLES

Studying members of only one, or a small number and range of cultures, limits the range of variables and concepts that can be explored. For example, trying to find out what effect having a TV set in the home has on school achievement is very difficult to do just by studying American or British samples, since the vast majority of families have (at least) one!

Again, research suggests that members of individualist cultures (which includes the vast majority of psychologists) are much more likely to explain behaviour in terms of personality traits (and so see behaviour as consistent across situations), while those from collectivist

Figure 8.4 A researcher would have to go a long way to find a corner of the Earth which did not have access to television

cultures use a more complex analysis, whereby the same person may act differently in different situations (e.g. Schweder, 1991, in Brislin, 1993). The point here is that, if only individualist cultures were studied, we would regard the explanation of behaviour as reflecting personality traits as a universal tendency (Brislin, 1993; see Chapters 2 and 4).

SEPARATING VARIABLES

Cross-cultural research can also help to separate out the effects of variables that may usually be confounded within a particular culture. According to Rogoff and Morelli (1989): 'Cross-cultural research ... allows psychologists to use cultural variation as a natural laboratory to attempt to disentangle variables that are difficult to tease apart in the US and to study conditions that are rare in the US'. For example, how do gender differences manifest themselves under different cultural conditions? To what extent is cognitive development a function of schooling as distinct from age (two variables that cannot be separated where schooling is freely available and compulsory)?

A very famous example is Freud's theory of the Oedipus complex, as it applies to little boys, according to which the son experiences extreme jealousy of his father (over the father's 'possession' of the mother), and at the same time extreme fear of the father (who is more powerful and, in the child's view, will punish him by castration if he continues to compete with the father for the mother's affections). Among the Trobriand islanders of the South Pacific, Malinowski (1929) found that it is the mother's brother, *not* the child's father, who is the major figure of authority, although the father continues to have a normal sexual relationship with the mother. Under these circumstances, sons tend to have a very good relationship with their father, free of the love–hate ambivalence Freud saw as an inevitable feature of the Oedipus complex. But the relationship with the uncle is not usually so good.

What this suggests is that, not only is the Oedipus complex *not* universal, as Freud claimed, but that sexual jealousy and rivalry, as a major component in the whole 'family drama', may play a much less important role than he believed.

TESTING THEORIES

Finally, a major function of cross-cultural research is to test out theories developed in the West, in order to see whether they apply to other cultural groups. Most of the major theories within psychology, such as those of Freud and Piaget, are meant to be universal, but we have just considered one example of a cross-cultural study that casts doubt on one of the fundamental elements of Freud's psychosexual theory of personality.

While the USA is still the world centre of psychology, and of social psychology in particular, some of the models of social behaviour that have come out of the USA may have little relevance or appeal in a different cultural context. For example, Thibaut and Kelley's (1959) analysis of social relationships in terms of the exchange of rewards is a:

... kind of rational, market-based model ... [which] is shaped by the values of middle-class, US culture, and often it is only when people from other backgrounds become familiar with middle-class, US culture that such models make sense to them.
(Moghaddam et al., 1993)

Since the late 1960s, European social psychology has developed its own character, with Tajfel (regarded generally as the 'father' of European social psychology) and Harré in England, Moscovici in France, and Doise in Switzerland, among the leading figures. It has become more *social* than its American counterpart: there is a greater focus on larger societal issues, such as intergroup relations, unemployment and ideology (Moghaddam *et al.*, 1993).

Festinger's (1957) *cognitive dissonance theory* has generated an enormous amount of research and theorizing in America, but it doesn't explain behaviour very well in some non-western cultures, including Japan. For example, how well a person handles a supposed 'inconsistency' is considered a sign of maturity and broad-mindedness. Japanese children are brought up to *accept* inconsistency, whereas the focus of the theory is on how people attempt to *reduce* the dissonance that results from perceived inconsistencies (see Chapter 2).

According to one estimate, only about 13 per cent of all the research reported in the leading American journals of social psychology are field studies. Because these are conducted in contexts that are culturally richer than laboratory studies, we need to be even more attentive to the role of cultural factors when interpreting the results (Moghaddam *et al.*, 1993). A good example of this is the famous 'Robber's Cave' experiment of intergroup conflict involving boys at a summer camp in America (Sherif *et al.*, 1961). The very fact that it was conducted in this setting is significant, since boys' summer camps play a certain role in North American culture not found elsewhere.

The study also illustrates the importance of taking into account what the participants see as the appropriateness of different types of behaviour in certain settings. The boys interpreted the situation as one where *both* competition *and* cooperation for scarce resources were appropriate; which strategy was used depended on which best served their material interests (e.g. they competed for the knives awarded to the winners of the tournament, but cooperated by, literally, pulling together to get their bus out of the mud). Such interpretations have a cultural bias (Moghaddam *et al.*, 1993. See Box 8.5, page 161).

SOME CONCLUDING COMMENTS

As we noted when discussing culture-fair intelligence tests, the participant's familiarity with taking tests *of any description*, together with his/her *concept* of a test and understanding of the test situation, are all crucial factors when evaluating test performance. Similarly, the tradition of political polls, consumer surveys, and so on, cannot be taken for granted when conducting research outside western countries; social science may not be practised at all, or it may be highly politicized.

Figure 8.5 The famous 'Robbers' Cave' experiment of intergroup conflict involved boys at summer camp in America, a culturally significant factor

---

Box 8.5 Non-American replications of the Robber's Cave field experiment

Diab (1970, in Smith and Bond, 1998) replicated this study in Lebanon and tried to follow the procedure used by Sherif *et al.* as closely as possible (using a summer camp setting, with 11-year-old boys, and the same planned stages of group formation, intergroup competition and, finally, group cooperation). Two randomly created groups of nine (Muslims and Christians in each group) developed very different 'cultures': 'The Friends' were warm and cooperative, while 'Red Genie' were highly competitive, and stole things from one another, not just from The Friends. It proved impossible to get the two groups to cooperate in stage three (as Sherif *et al.* had managed to do); when 'Red Genie' lost the tournament, they stole the knives, threatened The Friends with them, and tried forcibly to leave the camp. The study had to be abandoned.

Tyerman and Spencer (1983) failed to find any spirit of competition in their replication involving English boy scouts. They point out that the culture of each specific group will depend not just on externally imposed incentives of competition and cooperation, but also on established traditions and local cultures that form a background to specific events within each group.

The summer camp is a North American phenomenon, although we could find 'stimulus equivalents' in other cultures. However, the formation of friendships rigidly within one's own age group is more characteristic of industrialized societies, compared with traditional cultures, where friendships tend to be extensions of family networks. Such cultural differences help to explain why it has proved so difficult to replicate Sherif *et al.*'s study outside of North America (Moghaddam *et al.*, 1993).

These factors make it essential that novel methodologies are developed (instead of questionnaires, laboratory experiments, etc.), relationships with cultural informants are carefully nurtured, and participants carefully trained before data collection begins. The cultural context of 'doing social science' must be thoughtfully assessed by the social scientist to ensure that the outcome of the resulting research has a claim to validity (Smith and Bond, 1998).

But it is not just methods of investigation that may be inappropriate or invalid when used outside of the western cultural context from where they have arisen. According to Danziger (1997),

There is a substantial body of cross-cultural evidence which throws doubt on the universal validity of many of the categories with which the discipline of Psychology has been operating ... these categories do not occupy some rarefied place *above* culture but are embedded in a particular professional sub-culture. There is a certain arrogance in taking it for granted that, alone among a myriad alternative ways of speaking about individual action and experience, the language of twentieth century American Psychology accurately reflects the natural and universal structure of the phenomenon we call 'psychological' ...

SUMMARY

O **The concept of *culture/cultural differences* represents a third level at which the nature–nurture debate takes place, intermediate between (i) the *species* level and (ii) the *individual differences* level.**

O **According to Bronfenbrenner's *ecological model*, there are four interacting levels: *microsystem*, *mesosystem*, *exosystem* and *macrosystem*.**

O **Cross-cultural psychologists study variability in behaviour among the various societies/cultural groups around the world, as well as the *universals* of human behaviour. They fall somewhere between the extremes of *absolutism* (associated with experimental psychology) and anthropology's *relativism*.**

O **Learning, in the form of *enculturation* and *socialization*, is fundamental to human behaviour.**

O **Cross-cultural psychology helps to correct *ethnocentrism* within psychology, whereby an implicit equation is made between 'human being' and 'human being from western culture' (the *Anglocentric/Eurocentric bias*).**

O ***Culture* is usually defined as the man/person-made part of the environment, both the *material* and *non-material/social aspects*. Human beings both create culture and are influenced by it.**

O **Culture isn't static, but provides humans with an evolutionary system distinct from the biological system of animals. Cultural evolution is social rather than genetically transmitted.**

O **Much cross-cultural research is based on *national cultures* (denoted by the name of a country). This obscures the enormous diversity *within* a national culture and implies that national cultures are unitary, harmonious systems.**

O Hofstede identified four central dimensions of culture: *power distance, uncertainty avoidance, individualism–collectivism* and *masculinity–femininity.*

O Overlapping with these are Triandis's *cultural syndromes,* namely *cultural complexity, individualism–collectivism* and *tight vs loose cultures.* He also discusses three more specific cultural dimensions: *masculinity vs femininity, emotional control vs emotional expressiveness,* and *contact vs no-contact cultures.*

O The distinction between culture-specific/universal behaviour is one version of the *emic–etic* distinction. *Etics* refers to culturally *general* concepts, while *emics* refers to culturally *specific* concepts.

O The etic approach studies behaviour from *outside* a particular cultural system, while the emic approach studies behaviour from the *inside.*

O When western psychologists use an instrument/observational technique from their own culture (an *emic* for that culture) to study another culture, an *imposed etic* is being used.

O An imposed etic approach is involved when attempts to replicate American studies are made in other countries. It assumes that the situation being studied has the same *meaning* in all the cultures being tested.

O One solution to the 'imposed etic problem' is to reach a more valid set of *derived etic* generalizations, by conducting a number of parallel emic studies in a variety of national cultures, focusing on culture-specific phenomena.

O Psychologists need to adapt their methods so that they study the *same* processes in *different* cultures. This raises the fundamental issue of the *equivalence of meaning.*

O Three approaches used to deal with this issue are *translation equivalence* (often using *back-translation*), *conceptual equivalence,* and *metric equivalence.* The first is actually used and not particularly controversial, while the other two are largely theoretical proposals and are much more controversial.

O Cross-cultural research allows investigators to examine the influence of their own beliefs/assumptions, revealing how behaviour cannot be separated from its cultural context and the impact of situational factors.

O Cross-cultural research expands the range of variables/concepts that can be explored, and allows the separation of the effects of variables that may be confounded within a particular culture.

O Only by conducting cross-cultural research can western psychologists be sure that their theories and research findings apply outside of their own cultural context. Sherif *et al.*'s 'Robber's Cave' experiment has failed the 'replication test' outside of North American settings.

O Research methods need to be made relevant to the particular cultural setting in which they are used, and western psychologists mustn't assume that their concepts and categories capture the nature of human behaviour and experience in non-western cultures.

Useful websites

○ http://www.socialpsychology.org/social.htm#cultural
○ http://www.iupui.edu/#authkb/ewthnocen.htm

Recommended reading

Brislin, R. (1993) *Understanding Culture's Influence on Behaviour*. Orlando, FLA: Harcourt Brace Jovanovich.

Cole, M. (1996) *Cultural Psychology: A Once and Future Discipline*. Cambridge, MS: Harvard University Press.

Moghaddam, F.M. (1998) *Social Psychology: Exploring Universals Across Cultures*. New York: W.H. Freeman & Co.

Segall, M.H., Dasen, P.R., Berry, J.W. and Poortinga, Y.H. (1999) *Human Behaviour in Global Perspective: An Introduction to Cross-Cultural Psychology* (2nd edn). Needham Heights, MA: Allyn & Bacon.

Smith, P.B. and Bond, M.H. (1998) *Social Psychology across Cultures* (2nd edn). Hemel Hempstead: Prentice Hall Europe.

ATTACHMENT AND SEPARATION THROUGH THE LIFE CYCLE

9

Considering how often we use the word 'attached' in everyday language when referring both to people and objects, it is surprising that psychologists have, at least until quite recently, confined the term to the earliest emotional ties that human (and non-human) beings form to those who care for them. While the *primary* use of the term in everyday life is related to our feelings for our parents, we also describe ourselves as being attached to a whole range of people, including romantic partners, friends (of both sexes), as well as our own children. In a *secondary* use of the term, we often confess to being attached to our pets, as well as a whole variety of physical objects (including books, souvenirs and mementoes, houses and motor cars).

So, what do all these attachment 'objects' have in common? Perhaps it is the significance these things have for our self-concept, our sense of who we are as a person; they help define who we are. Clearly, some will be much more important in this way than others, and it is when we are separated from them, either temporarily or permanently, that we realize just how important they are. Indeed, if attachments are vital to our self-concept, it follows that *loss* of these attachment objects threatens that self-concept, requiring an adjustment on our part, a re-definition of our sense of ourselves. Permanent loss of our most significant attachments will require a major, perhaps fundamental, adjustment, while some losses may upset us only briefly, especially if we are able to replace what we have lost.

Figure 9.1 People can become very emotionally attached to their pets, resulting in emotional trauma if the pet should die or be lost

The most significant attachments in our lives are to the people who are irreplaceable, and it is this feature of our relationships that makes the process of readjustment so essential. Attachment and separation (or loss) are two sides of the same emotional coin, interrelated processes that aren't confined to infancy and early childhood, but that recur throughout our lives.

WHAT IS ATTACHMENT?

According to Ainsworth (1989), an attachment is an affectional bond: 'a relatively long-enduring tie in which the partner is important as a unique individual and is interchangeable with none other'. In common with other affectional bonds, there is a desire to stay close to the partner, be in their company and spend time with them (*proximity maintenance*). A unique feature of attachments, though, is that the attachment figure provides a sense of security, a *safe base* from which to explore and investigate the environment, approaching what is unfamiliar, unknown and even threatening.

This feature of attachments can be seen very clearly in the case of *securely attached* one-year-olds in the 'Strange Situation' (Ainsworth *et al.*, 1978). They typically play quite happily in an unfamiliar room, with unfamiliar toys and in the presence of a stranger, provided the mother is present. However, when the mother leaves the room, the child is distressed, stops playing and cannot be comforted by the (female) stranger. When the mother returns, the child greets her very warmly, and only after being picked up and cuddled by her does playing resume. The mother's ability to comfort the child when it is upset represents the third major feature of attachments, namely the attachment figure provides a *safe haven*, a source of support and reassurance at times of distress and threat (either to the self, the attachment figure, or the relationship).

A securely attached child will largely ignore its mother in her presence (although it will need reassurance every so often that she's still there). This lack of attention to the mother is evidence of the security and safety she provides ('she's there if I need her'). An *anxious-avoidant* child also ignores its mother, but this time because of *indifference* towards her; the child's play and general behaviour are hardly affected by whether she is present or absent.

Just as the securely attached child largely takes the attachment for granted, so do adults (Weiss, 1991). However, even relatively brief separations result in *separation protest*, and the death of a partner usually results in deep, persisting grief, in which separation protest is a major component. In turn, one feature of separation protest is a sense of hopelessness and fear: 'In adults as well as children, attachments appear to be relationships critical to continuing security and so to the maintenance of emotional security' (Weiss, 1991). In fact, Weiss defines attachments as relationships whose loss produces grief, and defines loss as 'an event that produces persisting inaccessibility of an emotionally important figure'.

Clearly, then, young children and adults seem to have much in common regarding both attachments and reactions to their loss. Bowlby and Ainsworth are best known (and perhaps known exclusively) for their study of attachment and separation in young children (they both used the term *safe base* in that context). Although Bowlby made repeated reference to attachment as a lifespan phenomenon ('attachment behaviour is held to characterise human beings from the cradle to the grave' (Bowlby, 1977)), the main focus of his theorizing was 'the nature of the child's tie to his mother' (Bowlby, 1958). But attachment *theory* (which Bowlby and Ainsworth developed both independently and together) leads to two very significant hypotheses:

1 attachment behaviour characterizes human beings throughout life; and

2 patterns established in childhood parent–child relationships tend to structure the quality of later bonds in their adult relationships, and may account for why some people even seem to avoid this presumably 'natural' inclination (Bartholomew, 1993).

Is there an adult counterpart to the anxious-avoidant child? We will return to this question later in the chapter.

ATTACHMENTS, AFFECTIONAL BONDS AND OTHER RELATIONSHIPS

While attachments are affectional bonds, not all affectional bonds are necessarily attachments. For example, one of the defining features of an attachment is security and safety, which parents are expected to provide for their children. But children aren't expected to provide this for their parents, and any such relationship would probably (and justifiably) be regarded as unhealthy. In other words, the child's attachment to its mother is *asymmetrical* (complementary); essentially, the mother 'gives' and the child 'takes', and the relationship lacks *mutuality* (Hazan and Zeifman, 1999). Perhaps the most fundamental change that takes place in attachment relationships is that the asymmetrical attachments of early life are replaced by more symmetrical, *reciprocal* attachments (Hazan and Zeifman, 1999). According to Bowlby, the *sexual pair bond*, where sexual partners *mutually* derive and provide security, is the prototype of adult attachment.

For these reasons, Ainsworth (1989) prefers to say that children are *attached* to their mothers, but mothers have *bonds with* their children. However, it is quite appropriate to describe the affectional bonds between sexual partners as attachments, since they share so many basic features with children's attachments to their parents. Bowlby maintained that, while parental figures tend to remain permanent members of an individual's attachment hierarchy, they eventually assume a position of secondary importance to pair-bond partners. Attachment theory doesn't specify exactly when or how this change from complementary (parental) to reciprocal (peer) attachment takes place (Hazan and Zeifman, 1999) (see Box 9.1, page 171).

Although parents of young children are appropriately described as bonded (rather than attached) to their children, it might be useful to think of the relationship as becoming more

Figure 9.2 A child's attachment to its parents is most evident when the child is distressed, for whatever reason

Figure 9.3 Renoir 'Dance at Bougival' 1883. Most individuals find a new principal attachment figure in the form of their sexual partner

Figure 9.4 Edward Munch 'Death in the Sick Chamber' 1895 (detail.) A person's response to the death of a parent usually demonstrates that the attachment has endured

attachment-like, particularly when the parents are elderly, widowed and more dependent, both emotionally and materially, on their adult children. Elderly parents may seek real safety and security from their grown-up children, representing a kind of 'crossing-over' or exchange of roles (see below).

This change in the nature of the parent–child relationship is consistent with the view that in *all* relationships with attachment properties, contact with the attachment figure may be sought if there is some kind of threat to (i) the self, (ii) the attachment figure, or (iii) the relationship. In all three cases, attachment feelings and behaviours are aroused (Weiss, 1991).

Threat to the self

When children are afraid or unwell, attachment behaviours become more evident; the need for reassurance, which can normally be taken for granted (at least when the attachment is secure), is heightened. Similarly, elderly parents, especially when widowed and thus deprived of their major life-long source of safety and security (again assuming a stable, happy marriage), experience an increased need for emotional support (see below).

Threat to the attachment figure

Children are, of course, very distressed by the illness of a parent, just as a husband or wife is by the illness (or suffering of whatever kind or cause) of the partner. Similarly, even though most individuals are likely to have found a new primary attachment figure in the form of their sexual partner, this doesn't mean that attachment to the parents no longer exists. As we noted earlier, most adults continue a meaningful association with their parents, regardless of the fact that they penetrate fewer aspects of their lives than they did before. A person's response to the death of a parent usually demonstrates that the attachment has endured, and even after grieving has been resolved, internal models of the lost parent continue to be an influence (Ainsworth, 1989; see below). While parents no longer provide the security for their grown-up children that they did when the children were physically and emotionally dependent on them, the death of a parent makes the likelihood of one's own death seem greater. While they are still alive, our parents serve as a 'psychological buffer' against death (Moss and Moss, 1983, in Hayslip and Panek, 1993):

As long as a parent is alive, one can still feel protected, cared for, approved of, and even scolded. Stripped of this 'protection', one must acknowledge that he or she is now a senior member of the family and that death is a certainty. The orderliness of life and death – that those who are older should die first – is reinforced when a parent dies.
(Hayslip and Panek, 1993)

Could it also be that when our second parent dies, we finally lose our childhood, and perhaps this is grieved for along with the loss of the unique individuals who were one's parents? We become – psychologically and emotionally – an orphan.

Threat to the relationship

When married couples engage in intense quarrelling, involving threats of abandonment and/or the discovery of infidelity, it is the relationship itself that is under threat, independent of the well-being of the partner or the self (Weiss, 1991). In many ways, divorce is as much a death as is the actual death of a spouse (Raphael, 1984); the end of the marital relationship may be grieved for in its own right. If the former spouse dies, there may be intense grief, especially if feelings about the divorce haven't been properly resolved (Doka, 1986, in Hayslip and Panek, 1993). And if the deceased spouse was also the mother or father of your children, grief may be heightened: you've lost the mate with whom you produced your offspring and with whom, presumably, you had intended to spend the rest of your life.

According to Ainsworth (1989), a sexual pair bond involves three basic behavioural systems: *reproductive*, *attachment* and *caregiving* (both to the partner and offspring). These become integrated as the relationship with the sexual partner develops (Hazan and Zeifman, 1999). Although sexual attraction may be the most important component at the start of a relationship, those relationships that depend entirely on the sexual component are likely to be short-lived. As the relationship continues, the caregiving and attachment components are likely to become relatively more important, and these will tend to sustain the bond even when sexual interest has waned (see Box 9.1).

Ainsworth also points out that the caregiving and attachment components may not always be symmetrical and reciprocal: one partner may do most of the giving and the other most of the taking. This resembles the parent–child relationship. Members of a sexual pair bond are 'meant' to engage in a mutual 'give and take' (unlike the parent–young child pair, in which the parent is all-giving and the child all-taking). Another important difference between an adult's and a child's attachment is the extent to which the attachment figure is seen as wiser and stronger and, therefore, able to be protective at times when the self seems inadequate. In the sexual pair bond, neither partner seems established as wiser and stronger, although each may now and again be seen in this way (Weiss, 1991).

According to Hazan and Shaver (1987), romantic love is usually a 'two-way street', with both partners sometimes anxious and security-seeking, and at other times the providers of security and care. Weiss (1991) also suggests that patients may often see their therapists or counsellors in this way, again resembling the child's dependency on its parents. (This, in turn, is very similar to Freud's concept of *transference*; see Chapter 15.)

SIMILARITIES BETWEEN ADULT AND CHILDHOOD ATTACHMENTS

Despite the differences we have just noted between the attachments of children to their parents and adults to each other, 'the underlying dynamics may be surprisingly similar' (Bartholomew, 1993). Indeed, Weiss (1991) notes three major similarities:

1 As we noted earlier, the loss of an attachment figure, both in childhood and adulthood, produces a grief reaction. *Separation protest*, as a component of grief in adults, is similar to that of the child in its behavioural expression. The syndrome includes calling and crying, a determined and sometimes frantic search, persistent perceptual recall of the lost figure, restlessness, and eventual despair.

2 It seems that the emotional elements that have become associated with childhood attachment are expressed in adult attachments. In particular, there is evidence that children who lose confidence in their parents as attachment figures (perhaps because of divorce) are likely to have difficulties in pair bonding later on, because of this distrust of their parents. No such effects are seen in their work relationships.

3 Pair bonding and bonding (in Ainsworth's terms) to one's own children both appear only *after* parents have largely faded as attachment figures. This is consistent with the claim that adult attachment represents a later stage of the childhood attachment system.

The securely attached child is able, most of the time, to take the attachment figure for granted; this reflects the child's trust, *not* indifference (see above). Similarly, as courtship continues between two adults, and the relationship becomes more reliable and stable, less energy need be given over to assuring the continuation of the attachment relationship. Instead, the secure base of the attachment can be taken for granted, freeing up effort and attention for achieving goals in the world outside the self (Weiss, 1991).

For most adults (especially men, in western culture), the major feature of their lives, other than their attachments and other affectional bonds, is their work. If a secure attachment with the mother (figure) provides the young child with a safe base from which to explore and investigate unfamiliar surroundings, might work represent the adult equivalent of the child's explorations, and could it be similarly related to the security provided by the attachment figure?

According to Freud, the goal of psychotherapy is to allow the patient to love and to work (*Lieben und Arbeiten*). The themes of love and work are central to some of the most influential theories of psychological well-being, such as those of Erikson (1963), Maslow (1954) and Rogers (1961) (Hazan and Shaver, 1990) (see Chapters 6 and 11). They are the key to a successful adult life (Bee, 1994), and there is evidence that adults who are satisfied with their work and their intimate relationships are also satisfied with their lives in general. Furthermore, love may be the more important of the two. Bee (1994) refers to studies which suggest that the single best predictor of overall life satisfaction in adults, of any age, is a person's reported happiness in marriage and other family relationships.

According to Hazan and Shaver (1990), work is the equivalent in the adult of the child's exploration. According to Bee (1994):

It [work] is the major source of a sense of competence, just as is true of a child's exploration. And like the child's exploration, adult work is best accomplished when the adult has a safe emotional base from which to move outward into the world.

Box 9.1 Are romantic relationships true attachments?

Hazan and Zeifman (1999) cite two interview studies (Hazan and Zeifman, 1994), which were designed to shed some light on how and when the transition from parental to adult romantic relationships takes place.

In Study 1, almost all the 100 6–17-year-olds were peer-oriented in terms of *proximity-seeking* (they preferred to spend time with their peers rather than their parents). There was an apparent shift between 8–14 with regard to the *safe haven*: peers came to be preferred as sources of comfort and emotional support. For the majority, parents continued to serve as a *secure base*, and were their primary source of *separation distress*. Only among the 15–17-year-olds were there full-blown attachments to peers (displaying all four components of attachments), and these attachment figures were usually a *romantic* partner.

Previous research on the formation and development of romantic relationships suggested that whether attachment components were present (and if so, which ones) would depend on how long the couple had been together. For example, couples typically experience a strong desire for physical proximity in the early stages ('they can't keep their hands off each other' (Berscheid, 1985)), whereas providing mutual care and support becomes important later on (Reedy *et al.*, 1981; Sternberg, 1986). Reaction to separation also seems to vary according to the length and stage of a relationship (Weiss, 1988).

Study 2 involved 100 18–82-year-olds, divided into three relationship status groups: 'not in a romantic relationship'; 'in a romantic relationship for less than two years'; and 'in a romantic relationship for more than two years'. All the participants were clearly peer-oriented in both proximity-seeking and safe-haven behaviours; partners and friends were preferred to parents and siblings. But the 'over two years' group overwhelmingly named their partners in response to separation distress and secure base. These findings were replicated by Fraley and Davis (1997).

Hazan and Zeifman (1999) conclude, on the basis of their findings, that adult romantic relationships *are* true attachments.

We return to the connection between work and attachment in a later section.

ROMANTIC LOVE CONCEPTUALIZED AS AN ATTACHMENT PROCESS

This is the title of an article by Hazan and Shaver, published in 1987, in which they reported the findings of a study that has come to be seen as breaking new ground, and has stimulated a growing body of research into adult love relationships from the perspective of attachment theory. In fact, during the 1990s investigations of adult attachment proliferated at a rate comparable to infant attachment studies during the years following Ainsworth's Uganda study (1967). (This was replicated and modified in the USA, resulting in the Strange Situation method for studying infant attachment; see below.) According to Hazan and Zeifman (1999):

Adult attachment research has proceeded largely on the faith that Bowlby was right about two things: that patterns of attachment established early in life are relatively stable across development, and that pair-bond relationships are the prototypical adult instantiation of attachment.

The first point is discussed later in the chapter; the second has already been discussed (see Box 9.1).

Hazan and Shaver's purpose was (i) to explore the possibility that attachment theory offers a valuable perspective on adult romantic love, and (ii) to create a coherent framework for understanding love, loneliness and grief at different points in the life cycle. They argued that attachment theory can help to explain both healthy and unhealthy forms of love, encompassing both positive emotions (caring, intimacy and trust) and negative emotions (fear of intimacy, jealousy, and emotional ups and downs). It also deals with separation and loss, and helps to explain how loneliness and love are related.

The study was the first attempt to apply the three basic *attachment styles* identified by Ainsworth *et al.* (1978) in their study of 12-month-olds using the Strange Situation, to adult–adult sexual/romantic relationships. These three styles are described in Table 9.1.

Table 9.1 Classification of attachment styles based on the 'strange situation' (Ainsworth *et al.*, 1978)

Classification	Percentage of sample	Description
Securely attached	70	Baby shows sign of missing mother on her departure, seeks proximity on her return, then returns to play. Associated with 'sensitivity to infant signals and communications'.
Anxious–avoidant	15	Baby shows no or few signs of missing the mother and actively ignores or avoids her on reunion. Associated with maternal insensitivity to baby's signals, and specifically with rejection of attachment behaviour.
Anxious–ambivalent	15	Baby is distressed and highly focused on the mother, but cannot be settled by mother on return, often expressing anger and seeking contact in quick succession and generally failing to return to play. Associated with maternal insensitivity and unpredictability of maternal responsiveness.

When describing the three styles, Ainsworth *et al.* refer to the child's *expectations* regarding the mother's accessibility and responsiveness. This is similar to Bowlby's claim that infants and young children construct *inner working models* (internal representations or *mental models*, to use Hazan and Shaver's term) of themselves and their major social-interaction partners. These working models become integrated into the personality structure of the individual, thereby providing a prototype for later relationships and representing some of the most important sources of continuity between early and later feelings and behaviours.

If what we acquire from our early attachment experiences is a set of fundamental expectations about romantic relationships, we'd expect these expectations to have some influence over our initial choice of partner, as well as the course of the relationship. We bring with us into our relationships an inner working model (IWM), which may be as influential as anything to do with the partner him/herself or with the 'objective' nature of the relationship.

So what did Hazan and Shaver find? The three attachment styles (based on observational studies of young children) had to be 'translated' in a way that would make them suitable for the study of adult attachments. This was done as shown in Table 9.2, where respondents to a 'love quiz' in a local newspaper were asked to indicate which of three descriptions best applied to their feelings about romantic relationships.

They were also asked to complete a simple adjective checklist describing their childhood relationships with their parents. The correlation between the attachment style they chose as best describing their feelings, and their recollections of the kind of parenting they received, mirrors remarkably closely the findings of Ainsworth *et al.* (see Table 9.3 below).

Hazan and Shaver tested two separate samples as part of the same 1987 study.

1 *Sample one* comprised 205 men and 415 women, aged between 14 and 82 (mean age 36), 91 per cent describing themselves as 'primarily heterosexual'. At the time of the survey, 42 per cent were married, 28 per cent were divorced or widowed, 9 per cent were 'living with a lover', and 31 per cent were dating. (Some checked more than one category.)

2 *Sample two* was a *non*-self-selected sample of 108 undergraduate students, comprising 38 men and 70 women (mean age of 18), who completed the questionnaire as a class exercise. They answered additional items that focused more on the *self* side of the mental model (as opposed to the partner), as well as additional items measuring loneliness.

Table 9.2   Responses to the question 'Which of the following best describes your feelings?' in Hazan and Shaver's (1987) study

Classification	Percentage of respondents	Response
Securely	56	I find it relatively easy to get close to others and am comfortable depending on them and having them depend on me. I don't often worry about being abandoned or about someone getting too close to me.
Anxious–avoidant	23–25	I am somewhat uncomfortable being close to others; I find it difficult to trust them completely, difficult to allow myself to depend on them. I am nervous when anyone gets too close, and often, love partners want me to be more intimate than I feel comfortable being.
Anxious–ambivalent	19–20	I find that others are reluctant to get as close as I would like. I often worry that my partner doesn't really love me or won't want to stay with me. I want to merge completely with another person, and this desire sometimes scares people away.

Table 9.3 Correlation between attachment style and type of parenting of respondents in Hazen and Shaver's (1987) study

Attachment style	Type of parenting
Securely attached	Readily available, attentive, responsive
Anxious–avoidant	Unresponsive, rejecting, inattentive
Anxious–ambivalent	Anxious Fussy, out of step with child's needs Only available/responsive *some* of the time

Based on Ainsworth's original studies, and later studies involving young children (62 per cent securely attached, 23 per cent anxious–avoidant and 15 per cent anxious–ambivalent), Hazan and Shaver predicted that about 60 per cent of adults would classify themselves as secure, with the other two types being fairly evenly split (but a few more anxious–avoidant). The results went very much as expected: in both samples, 56 per cent were secure, 23 and 25 per cent were anxious–avoidant (samples one and two respectively), and for anxious–ambivalent the figures were 19 and 20 per cent respectively.

When asked to describe the 'most important love relationship you have ever had, why you got involved in it, and why it turned out the way it did … It may be a past or a current relationship, but choose only the most important one', both samples produced very similar responses. Those classified as secure described this special relationship as especially happy, friendly and trusting, being able to accept and support their partner despite his/her faults. Their relationships also tended to last longer and, if married, were less likely to end in divorce.

Questions designed to measure the IWM of self and relationships were answered in line with the prediction only in the case of sample one, whose items were more focused on the partner or relationship than on the self. The *secure* types expressed belief in lasting love. Even though romantic feelings wax and wane, only sometimes reaching the intensity experienced at the start of the relationship, genuine love is enduring. They also generally find others trustworthy and have confidence in their self as likeable.

The *anxious–avoidant* types are much more doubtful about the existence or durability of romantic love: the kind of head-over-heels love that is portrayed in fiction doesn't happen in real life, and it is rare to find a person you can really fall in love with. They also maintain that they don't need a love partner in order to be happy.

The *anxious–ambivalent* types fall in love easily and often, but they rarely find what they would call true love. They also express more self-doubts (compared with both the other types), but compared with the anxious–avoidants, they don't repress or try to hide their feelings of insecurity.

Finally, the two insecure types, compared with the secure, were found to be the most vulnerable to loneliness, but the anxious–ambivalent (in sample two) obtained the highest scores of all. Hazan and Shaver believe that this reflects the greater defensiveness of the anxious–avoidants (they only *appear* to be less lonely), together with the yearning of the anxious–ambivalent types for a love relationship in which they can merge with their partner who shares their intense passion – something that they are extremely unlikely to find.

Hazan and Shaver acknowledge several methodological and theoretical limitations of their study, but they conclude that the results overall provide encouraging support for an attachment perspective on romantic love. One such note of caution is to do with the *continuity* between early childhood and adult experience. They say that it would be overly pessimistic – at least from the point of view of the insecurely attached person – if continuity were the rule rather than the exception. While correlations between parent variables and current attachment style were statistically significant, they weren't strong. Also, they were higher for sample two, who were much younger, suggesting that continuity *decreases* as one gets further into adulthood. The average person participates in several important friendships and love relationships, which provide opportunities for revising IWMs of self and others.

Support for this more optimistic view comes from a study by Main *et al.* (1985). Despite an impressive association between adults' attachment history and the attachment styles of their own young children, some adults who reported being insecure in their relationships with their parents, managed to produce children who were securely attached at one and six years of age. They had mentally worked through their unpleasant experiences with their parents, and now had mental models of relationships that are more typical of secure types (Hazan and Shaver, 1987).

ADULT ATTACHMENT RESEARCH SINCE 1987

Hazan and Shaver's findings have been replicated and extended in several studies. According to Bartholomew (1993), their method of operationalizing adult attachment patterns as self-report measures has stimulated a thriving new area of research, such as attachment patterns among dating couples, interactive behaviours of couples in the laboratory, the sociocognitive processes associated with attachment patterns, the process of relinquishing parents as attachment figures, attachment patterns and work satisfaction, and attachment styles and religious beliefs and fear of death. Some of these research areas are described below.

Bartholomew herself has expanded Hazan and Shaver's model of adult attachment patterns provided in the 1987 study. Based on a series of intensive interviews with young adults about their close relationships (1990, cited in Bartholomew, 1993), she distinguished between two types or *patterns of avoidance* in adults:

1 *fearful avoidant,* whose desire for social contact is inhibited by fears of rejection

2 *dismissive avoidant,* who defensively deny the need or desire for intimate contact.

This distinction reflects different *models of the self:* people who fearfully avoid intimacy view themselves as undeserving of the love and support of others, while those who dismiss intimacy possess a positive model of the self that minimizes the subjective awareness of distress and social needs. Only the former (*fearful avoidant*) correspond to Hazan and Shaver's avoidant style.

Bartholomew distinguishes between two other styles, this time reflecting different *models of (or orientation towards) others,* namely: (i) *preoccupied,* in which people view themselves negatively but possess a positive model of others that motivates them to strive to find self-validation and fulfilment through their intimate relationships; (ii) *secure,* in which people possess positive models of both themselves and others, and enjoy both personal autonomy and satisfying intimate relationships. This produces a four-way classification, as shown in Table 9.4, page 176.

To take the secure style to explain what the table means, a positive model of self is defined in terms of low dependence on others for self-esteem and fulfilment, while a positive model of the other is defined as low avoidance of intimacy. So, at one extreme, the secure type (positive models of self and others) has the 'best of both worlds', while at the other, the

Table 9.4   Four category model of adult attachment from Bartholomew, K. (1993)

Model of other (Avoidance)	Model of self (Dependence)	
	Positive (Low)	**Negative** (High)
Positive (Low)	**Secure,** comfortable with intimacy and autonomy	**Preoccupied** Preoccupied with relationships
Negative (High)	**Dismissing** Dismissing of intimacy	**Fearful** Fearful of intimacy

fearful avoidant (negative models of self and others) needs intimacy for self-esteem, but cannot achieve it through fear – the 'worst of both worlds', perhaps?

According to Collins and Read (1990), when *both* members of dating couples are asked about their IWMs, the securely attached tend to choose other securely attached partners, but the anxiously attached are no more likely to choose one another than one of the other types. The least happy among young dating couples seem to be (i) any combination involving an anxiously attached woman (perhaps because they tend to be clingy and jealous, thereby producing the unstable, unhappy, relationship she expects), and (ii) any combination involving an avoidant man (again, because his IWM may result in fulfilment of the expectation that relationships have little to offer) (Bee, 1994).

Paley *et al.* (2002) studied married couples making the transition to parenthood. They were interviewed prenatally, then three, 12 and 24 months after the baby's birth. The researchers concluded that a secure attachment may confer a protective advantage on spouses during stressful periods in their marriage, such as the birth of a first child.

ATTACHMENT, EXPLORATION AND WORK

As noted earlier, the child's exploration (using the mother as a safe base) can be seen as having its adult counterpart in work. According to Bowlby, to learn about and become competent at interacting with the physical and social environment, one must explore. But exploration can be tiring and even dangerous, so it's desirable to have a source of protection (a safe haven) available if needed. According to attachment theory, while both the tendency to form an attachment and the tendency to explore the environment are innate, attachment needs are primary – that is, they must be met before exploration can proceed normally (Hazan and Shaver, 1990).

Adult work activity can be seen as functionally parallel to the young child's exploration: they both represent a major source of actual and perceived competence. Based on these features of attachment theory, as well as on their own previous research, Hazan and Shaver (1990) derived and tested three hypotheses concerning the relationship between attachment style and orientation towards work, using a questionnaire design.

○ In line with Hypothesis 1, secure respondents approach their work with the confidence associated with secure attachments. They enjoy work activity and are relatively free of fears of failure. Although they value work, they tend to value relationships more, and generally don't allow work to interfere with those relationships. They don't, typically, use work to satisfy unmet needs for love, nor do they use work to avoid social interaction.

○ In line with Hypothesis 2, anxious–ambivalent respondents reported that love concerns often interfere with work performance and that they often fear rejection for poor performance. They also reported a tendency to ease up after receiving praise, which may indicate that their main motivation at work is to gain respect and admiration from others. They have the lowest average income of the three groups, even when differences in education are controlled.

○ Consistent with Hypothesis 3, anxious–avoidant respondents use work activity to avoid social interaction. They reported that work interferes with having friends and having a social life. While their average income is equal to that of the secure group, they are less satisfied with their jobs; they are also the least likely to take enjoyable holidays.

Secure attachment was also associated with greater overall well-being. Relative to the two insecure groups, the secure respondents report less loneliness and depression, anxiety or irritability, as well as fewer colds or incidences of flu.

As with their original study, Hazan and Shaver are well aware of the limitations of their research, among them the very conceptualization of work as exploration. Clearly, although work is probably the major form of exploratory behaviour in adulthood, it is far from being the only form. Also, attachment type (in this and the earlier study) and orientation to work were treated more as *traits* than as products of unique person–situation interactions (see Chapter 4). As Feeney and Noller (1996) point out, we need to look at work-related measures with more established, objective, psychometric properties, such as job involvement, job-related stress, and patterns of supervisor–peer interaction.

However, despite these and other limitations, Hazan and Shaver's findings suggest that one's approach to work is deeply affected by the strengths or deficiencies of one's IWM of attachments and relationships in general (Bee, 1994). Feeney and Noller (1996) believe that Hazan and Shaver's findings suggest that 'attachment style is meaningfully related to the ways in which people balance their investments in work, leisure activities and love relationships', and according to Hazan and Shaver (1990): 'Scientists often treat love and work as two separate realms, but being deeply social creatures, humans cannot easily separate the two … Attachment theory offers a way of explaining why love and work are so closely intertwined.'

RELIGIOUS BEHAVIOUR: GOD AS A SECURE BASE AND SAFE HAVEN

According to Kirkpatrick (1999), many aspects of religious belief and experience, especially those related to perceived relationships with God and other supernatural figures, reflect (at least in part) the operation of psychological attachment processes. God can be regarded as demonstrating all the defining features of an attachment figure. For example, many believers use prayer as a way of maintaining contact with God (*proximity seeking*), and belief in the existence or presence of God seems to allay fear and anxiety, and provide a sense of confidence and emotional security (*secure base*). Perhaps most strikingly, religion plays an important role in times of stress (such as the loss of a loved one), providing comfort, support and strength (*safe haven*) (Kirkpatrick, 1992, 1994).

Box 9.2 (page 178) gives examples from Christian hymns, showing how they are related to these three defining features of attachment.

Kirkpatrick (1992, 1994) claims that most Christians see themselves as having a personal relationship with God, which represents the core of their religious faith. From an individual-

---

Box 9.2 How first lines of hymns are related to the defining features of attachment

Defining feature	First line of hymn
Proximity seeking	Abide with me, fast falls the eventide O' for a close walk with God, a calm and heavenly frame
Secure base	Forth in Thy name, O Lord I go, my daily labour to pursue Awake my soul and with the sun Thy daily stage of duty run
Safe haven	Rock of ages, cleft for me, let me hide Myself in Thee Jesus, lover of my soul, let me to Thy bosom fly

(From Feeney and Noller, 1996)

---

differences perspective, IWMs of God appear to parallel current IWMs of (other) close interpersonal relationships.

Kirkpatrick suggests that the attachment perspective enables researchers to investigate two apparently contradictory sets of findings regarding the correlates of religious behaviour.

1 *Compensation model.* People are most likely to turn to religion during times of emotional stress, or in the absence of adequate human relationships. Studies of religious conversion suggest that converts typically report a period of turmoil and distress, often marked by serious difficulties with parental and other personal relationships prior to the conversion. This is consistent with the view that the attachment system is most strongly activated under conditions of stress, and those who fail to establish secure attachments with parents are likely to seek substitute attachment figures (Ainsworth, 1985).

2 *Correspondence hypothesis.* Individual differences in relationship styles parallel differences in religious behaviour. For example, perceptions of God tend to be positively correlated with perceptions of self and the preferred parent. Using a simple measure of individual differences in attachment to God (based on Hazan and Shaver's 1987 study; see Table 9.2), Kirkpatrick and Shaver (1992) found that secure individuals (compared with anxious-avoidants) see God as more loving, less distant and less controlling. Anxious-avoidants show less religious commitment, and are more likely to be agnostic than both securely attached and anxious-ambivalent individuals.

Kirkpatrick (1992) believes that the compensation model and the correspondence hypothesis can be integrated by taking into account the time dimension. At any one point in time, security of (human) attachment is linked to security of attachment to God: people seem to hold similar models of human and divine relationships. But insecure attachment predicts conversion experiences at a later point in time, in which people turn to God as a substitute attachment figure. There is evidence to suggest that attachment to God may confer the kinds of psychological benefit associated with secure interpersonal attachments (Kirkpatrick, 1999).

Although attachment processes cannot explain all aspects of religious behaviour, Kirkpatrick (1999) believes that: 'no model of adult interpersonal relationships in general, or attachment relationships in particular, will be complete without explicit acknowledgement of the role of God and other supernatural figures in people's relationship networks'. Consideration of the role of religion may also help to shed new light on developmental processes, such as the transition from parental to peer attachments during adolescence (see above) and responses to the loss of significant attachments in (especially late) adulthood (see below) (Kirkpatrick, 1999).

ATTACHMENT AMONG OLDER ADULTS

Despite the research interest in adult attachments inspired by Hazan and Shaver's (1987) groundbreaking study, relatively little attention has been paid to attachment phenomena specifically among older adults. Some theorists and researchers have begun to recognize the unique significance that attachment issues might hold among older adults, as the potential for distressing separations and loss experiences (such as illness and death) increases with old age. The rapid growth of the world's elderly population has stimulated many social scientists to seek greater understanding of issues such as (i) the role of attachment bonds in caregiving and chronic illness, (ii) the influence of attachment in coping with bereavement and loss, and (iii) the relationship of attachment to adjustment and well-being in old age (Bradley and Cafferty, 2001).

Attachment, caregiving and chronic illness

Caregiving in relation to the elderly involves a reversal of how it has previously been described, namely parental (in particular, maternal) care for their children. Here, the caregiver is the middle-aged child, and the recipient of the care is the elderly parent. This represents a normative developmental task of middle age (Sorenson et al., 2002). Although attachment theory doesn't suggest that individuals' attachment histories determine their patterns of caregiving behaviour, it is assumed that IWMs are likely to be closely related to IWMs of caregiving (George and Solomon, 1999).

ATTACHMENT AND CARE-RECEIVING

An elderly person's loss of self-sufficiency associated with illness produces a growing sense of fear, vulnerability and insecurity. This is like the infant's dependency on a caregiver to function and survive in a strange environment (Wright et al., 1995). At both developmental stages, this dependency may be accompanied by separation protest/anxiety, and fears of abandonment by attachment figures. These feelings, in turn, result in behaviours aimed at maintaining proximity to attachment figures, such as clinging, demanding and proximity-seeking. These behaviours are commonplace among Alzheimer's patients. As chronic illnesses become more severe, needs often change from psychological to more basic physical ones, again mirroring the mother–child caregiving relationship (Bradley and Cafferty, 2001).

Miesen (1992, 1993, 1998) describes 'parent fixation' that is common in dementia and Alzheimer's disease. These patients behave as if their parents were still alive (asking about them, crying out to them). While this is often seen as a specific type of delusion or memory distortion, it is best explained in attachment theory terms (Bradley and Cafferty, 2001). These patients feel threatened by feelings of vulnerability, disconnection from safety and the familiarity of everyday surroundings, so they become more prone to engage in proximity-seeking behaviours aimed at family and caregivers in an attempt to re-establish feelings of safety. As dementia progresses, attachment behaviour declines, but parent fixation (which represents an *internal* source of security) increases dramatically.

ATTACHMENT AND CAREGIVING

According to Cicirelli (1996), adult children feel threatened by ageing parents' increased susceptibility to illness and death. The desire to protect them (and, as such, delay the imminent separation and loss of a key attachment figure) provides the motivation for caregiving behaviour. Although others have proposed alternative motives (such as a sense of obligation and a desire to avoid guilt), Cicirelli has tried to define the unique contribution of the continuing attachment to parents.

In a series of studies, Cicirelli (1983, 1993, 1995) reported that secure attachment to a parent was more strongly related to caregiving behaviour and commitment to provide future care than was a sense of obligation. '*Stronger*' attachment was related to a lower sense of subjective burden, while feelings of obligation were related to a greater sense of burden.

ATTACHMENT, SEPARATION AND LOSS

Earlier in the chapter, we drew attention to the belief that, while attachment to the parents is retained throughout our adult lives, we need to transfer our major attachments away from our parents to our partner in a sexual pair bond. Only such a major shift in our emotional ties will allow us to achieve psychological adulthood, which, in turn, is necessary for us to become attachment figures for our children in turn.

According to Rutter (1981), the essential function of (secure) attachment is *detachment* – that is, the young child gradually learns to tolerate greater and longer-lasting physical separations from the mother. However, the most crucial time in our life for achieving the separation from parents is during adolescence. Leaving home is more than just setting up a separate place to live – it also involves a highly significant psychological emancipation process, whereby the young person distances him/herself emotionally from the parents to at least some degree (Hazan and Shaver, 1991, in Bee, 1994).

Similarly, if children are eventually to form their own households, their bonds of attachment to the parents must become attenuated and eventually end. Otherwise, independent living would be emotionally troubling. According to Weiss (1986, in Bee, 1994), 'The relinquishing of attachment to parents appears to be of central importance among the individuation-achieving processes of late adolescence and early adulthood.' Some writers take the view that this cutting of the emotional tie to the parents must be total if the adolescent is to achieve emotional independence (see, for example, Blos's 1967 theory of adolescence as a *second individuation process*). However, we noted earlier that adult grief reactions to the death of their parents is a clear indication that those ties are never severed once and for all. Perhaps a feature of maturity is the ability to balance the need for separateness, on the one hand, and the need for attachment on the other, without having to adopt extreme behavioural or emotional strategies.

In attachment theory terms, the agoraphobic patient is reacting (albeit in an extreme way) to the (threatened) loss of his/her safe base. While the patient may lack insight into the nature and cause of their symptoms (they make a *mis-attribution*; see Chapter 2), the symptoms reveal the importance of attachment figures throughout our lives (see Box 9.3, page 181).

Studies of psychosocial transitions that commonly precede the onset of mental illness suggest that the most dangerous life changes are those that (i) require people to undertake

---

Box 9.3 Agoraphobia as a response to loss

Agoraphobia is a common mental disorder, affecting between 1 and 6 per cent of the adult population (Liotti, 1991). Such patients seem to have lost the ability to tolerate temporary and explainable separations from attachment figures. They typically tend to avoid staying alone, either in public places or in their own home. In moderately severe cases, they will stay on their own at home only when a trusted family member can be called back easily; in more severe cases, only having a familiar person within immediate reach keeps their anxiety in check.

They are usually distressed when they find themselves in daily situations that, while objectively safe, make escape to a familiar place difficult or impossible, such as joining a queue, being in a traffic jam, in the hairdresser's chair, on a motorway, and so on.

While any attempt to explain the syndrome based on attachment theory would focus on these clinical features, a more subtle feature is that the patient finds it difficult to attribute meaning to any emotions related to the threatened separation from a significant other. In order to properly understand these features, it is necessary to understand (i) the nature of the patient's interpersonal relationships at the time the symptoms first appeared, and (ii) how the patient accounts for his/her symptoms (Liotti, 1991).

As far as the patient's relationships are concerned, many psychotherapists and researchers believe that the onset of agoraphobia may be related to life events (*psychosocial transitions*; Parkes, 1993) that imply changes in the patient's network of affectional bonds. These might include threats of loss or separation from parents or spouse, marital quarrels and perceived rejection from a loved one. These aren't simply linked in time to the onset of panic attacks and agoraphobic avoidance behaviour, but are very likely the *cause* (Liotti, 1991).

Regarding patients' accounts of their symptoms, many don't acknowledge the possibility of a link between such (potential) changes in their life and the appearance of their symptoms. They insist that their distress is due to something totally unrelated to their interpersonal life, typically to an impending illness, either physical or mental (a process that is totally alien to their experience of the self). A common feature of every agoraphobic patient is a blindness to the meaning of a certain class of their own emotions, which, in a sense, lose their psychological status and are transformed into the symptoms of a disease (Liotti, 1991).

---

a major revision of their *assumptive world* ('everything that we assume to be true on the basis of our previous experience ... the internal model of the world that we are constantly matching against incoming sensory data in order to orient ourselves, recognize what is happening, and plan our behaviour accordingly' (Parkes, 1993)), (ii) have lasting implications, and (iii) take place over a relatively short period of time, allowing little time for preparation (Parkes, 1993).

According to Mikulincer and Florian (1996), different types of relationships are generally associated with different levels of severity of grief reactions. While loss of a child is generally regarded as having the most devastating effects, loss of spouse is also regarded as highly stressful. In terms of Parkes' third point (the unexpectedness of the loss), to the extent that old age is associated with greater likelihood of death, the loss of an attachment figure may be viewed as a natural developmental event; this may make it less devastating than the 'same' loss at an earlier stage of the life cycle. For example, distress following the death of an elderly parent is generally less than that following other losses, and where the elderly person has suffered long-term illness, their death may be seen as a happy release (Mikulincer and Florian, 1996).

Parkes and Weiss's (1983) research suggests that IWMs formed on the basis of early experiences with caregivers and maintained by adult relationships, play a significant role in determining the nature and severity of grief reactions to loss of spouse. Scharlach (1991) extended this to adult children who had lost a parent. Those who felt emotionally dependent on older adult parents, and perceived a lack of autonomy in their relationships with them, suffered more severe grief reactions. But their reported levels of closeness to parents *weren't* related to their distress.

According to Steele (2002), much further research is needed to reveal which early experiences are carried over into later life, and what is most likely to be reworked, updated or otherwise changed as a function of later experience:

Clearly, the language we use, the story we tell, and the meaning we derive from our lives must be open to revision across the life cycle. At the same time, there may be spontaneous modes of responding to the world, and automatic interpretations of emotional and social stimuli that remain with us as a consequence of earliest experiences.
(Steele, 2002)

SUMMARY

○ While the *primary* use of the term 'attachment' is related to other people, a *secondary* use relates to our 'ties' to our pets and possessions.

○ The common factor in all these attachments may be their importance to our *self-concept*, which would explain why *loss* requires us to redefine our self-concept.

○ In Ainsworth's 'Strange Situation', *securely attached* one-year-olds largely ignored their mother, indicating the security that her presence provides. By contrast, the *anxious–avoidant* child largely ignores the mother because of *indifference* towards her.

○ While attachments are affectional bonds, not all affectional bonds are attachments. Children are *attached* to their parents, but mothers have *bonds* with their children.

○ Adult romantic relationships (*sexual pair bonds*) display all the major features of children's attachments to parents, namely *proximity maintenance*, *secure base*, *safe haven* and *separation protest*.

○ Perhaps the major developmental change in attachments concerns their *mutuality*. Asymmetrical (complementary) parent–child attachments are replaced by more symmetrical (reciprocal) adult–adult attachments.

○ Attachments to parents are maintained in adult life. The death of one's parents makes our own death seem closer, as well as finally ending our childhood.

○ Divorce is as much a death as the actual death of a spouse, and the end of the marital relationship may be grieved for in its own right, especially if there are children from the marriage.

○ Hazan and Shaver applied the three *attachment styles* first identified by Ainsworth *et al.* in their study of 12-month-olds (*secure*, *anxious–avoidant* and *anxious–ambivalent*) to adults' romantic relationships.

○ These attachment styles are related to the child's *expectations* regarding the mother's accessibility/responsiveness (Ainsworth). Children construct *inner working models* (IWMs) (Bowlby) of themselves and their major attachment figures, which become integrated into their personalities.

○ Hazan and Shaver found that the correlation between (i) the attachment style adults chose as best describing their feelings about their adult relationships and (ii) their recollections of the kind of parenting they received is remarkably similar to Ainsworth *et al.*'s findings for young children.

○ The continuity between current attachment style and the kind of parenting received as a child may *decrease* as one progresses into adulthood. Most adults have opportunities for revising their internal working models of self and others.

○ Bartholomew distinguishes between *fearful avoidant* and *dismissive avoidant*, reflecting *negative* and *positive* models of the self respectively. Another distinction is between *preoccupied* and *secure* orientation towards others.

○ Securely attached individuals tend to choose other securely attached individuals as partners. The least happy, stable, combinations involve an anxiously attached woman or an avoidant man.

○ Work represents a major feature in the life of most adults (especially men). It can be seen as the adult equivalent of exploration in the child, and is best achieved when there is a safe emotional base.

○ One's approach to work seems to be deeply affected by the strengths and deficiencies of one's IWM of attachments.

○ Many aspects of religious belief and experience reflect the operation of attachment processes. Belief in God and prayer can fulfil attachment needs, such as proximity seeking, secure base and safe haven.

○ The apparent contradiction between the *compensation model* and *correspondence hypothesis* of religious behaviour can be resolved by taking the time dimension into account.

○ Illness may increase the elderly person's sense of vulnerability and insecurity, which may increase attachment behaviours directed towards grown-up children. 'Parent fixation' in Alzheimer's patients represents an *internal* source of security.

○ Adult children's desire to protect their ageing parents and delay their loss motivates caregiving behaviour. Attachment to the parents is more strongly related to caregiving than is a sense of obligation.

○ We have to transfer our primary attachment from our parents to our sexual partner in order to achieve psychological adulthood. While *detachment* is achieved in early childhood, the crucial time for achieving emotional separation from parents is during adolescence.

○ The onset of agoraphobia is commonly linked to *psychosocial transitions*, such as involvement in marital quarrels and threats of separation from one's spouse.

○ The most dangerous life changes are those that (i) require a major revision of our *assumptive world*, (ii) have lasting implications, and (iii) allow little time for preparation.

○ To the extent that death is normative in old age, the loss of elderly parents will probably be less distressing than it would have been earlier in life, especially if they have suffered long-term illness.

Useful websites

○ http://129.49.73.3/ewaters
○ www.attachmentnetwork.org
○ http://galton.psych.nwu/great ideas/attachment.html
○ http://www.bereavement.org.uk
○ http://www.johnbowlby.com

Recommended reading

Ainsworth, M.D.S. (1989) Attachments beyond Infancy. *American Psychologist, 44*(4), 709–16.

Cassidy, J. and Shaver, P.R. (eds) (1999) *Handbook of Attachment: Theory, Research and Clinical Applications*. New York: Guilford Press.

Hazan, C. and Shaver, P.R. (1987) Romantic love conceptualized as an attachment process. *Journal of Personality & Social Psychology, 52*(3), 511–24.

Holmes, J. (1993) *John Bowlby and Attachment Theory*. London: Routledge.

Parkes, C.M., Stevenson-Hinde, J. and Martin, P. (eds) (1991) *Attachment across the Life Cycle*. London: Routledge.

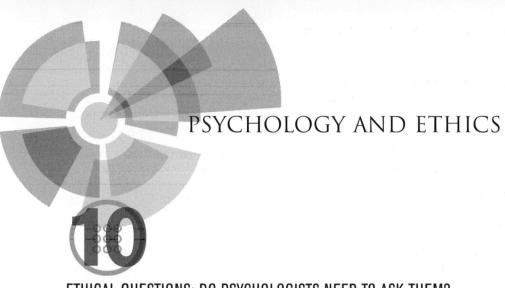

PSYCHOLOGY AND ETHICS

ETHICAL QUESTIONS: DO PSYCHOLOGISTS NEED TO ASK THEM?

Perhaps the most general question we can ask about ethics is 'Why do ethical issues arise at all?' Answers to this question might include the following:

1 Human beings and non-human animals have feelings and sensations. They are capable of experiencing pain, fear, and so on (they are *sentient*, living, things), and so are capable of reacting with pain and fear to certain kinds of aversive (painful) stimulation.

2 Humans aren't just sentient, they're also *thinking* beings. This means that situations that aren't literally, or physically, painful or dangerous, may still be experienced as threatening, stressful, offensive, belittling or embarrassing, or may evoke feelings of guilt, self-doubt, inadequacy or incompetence.

3 Any attempt on the part of one person to induce any of the above feelings or sensations in another person (or animal), or the inducement of any of these feelings or sensations in one person (or non-human animal) as a result of the neglect or negligence of another, is usually condemned as immoral or morally unacceptable.

These points may seem perfectly reasonable, and perhaps fairly 'obvious' (at least once they're pointed out), and it may seem fairly clear in what ways they are relevant to psychology. But we should still ask 'Why do ethical issues arise for psychologists?' Answers to this question might include the following:

1 Psychologists study human beings and non-human animals.

2 Psychologists often subject – deliberately or otherwise – the human beings and non-human animals they study to situations and stimulation that induce pain, embarrassment, and so on.

3 Just as every psychology experiment is primarily a *social* situation (Orne, 1962; see Chapter 11), so every psychological investigation may be thought of as an *ethical* situation. In other words, whenever one person (the researcher) deliberately creates a situation intended for the investigation of the behaviour and/or experience of another person (the 'subject' or participant), there is always the possibility that the person being studied will experience one or more of the feelings and sensations identified above. This may be what the researcher is expecting to happen (it may be a crucial feature of the study), or it may genuinely not be anticipated by the researcher, who is as surprised as everyone else by how the participants respond.

But while we normally associate 'deliberately created situations' with laboratory studies (whether experimental or not), ethical issues aren't confined to such settings. Indeed, *naturalistic* studies face ethical problems of their own, despite the fact that the researcher isn't creating a situation into which other people are brought so that s/he may study their behaviour (see below).

Perhaps the common feature linking the laboratory and naturalistic settings, which makes them both 'ethical 'situations, is the difference in the *power* associated with the roles of researcher and researched. If this is true in the case of humans studying other humans, it's even more true in the case of humans studying non-human animals! (Again, we will return to this issue later in the chapter.)

PSYCHOLOGISTS AS INVESTIGATORS AND AS PRACTITIONERS

So far, we have been discussing ethics in relation to the psychologist's role as *scientist* or *investigator* – that is, someone who wishes to find out more about human behaviour and experience. Sometimes this is done for its own sake (because of its intrinsic interest: *pure research*), sometimes as part of an attempt to solve a practical problem (*applied research*). While there is no hard-and-fast distinction between these two kinds of research, the distinction between psychologists as scientists/investigators and as practitioners is important in relation to understanding ethical issues. While many psychologists are both researchers and practitioners, the difference in these two roles needs to be understood when ethics is being discussed.

○ The practitioner role refers to the work of clinical, counselling, educational, forensic and industrial/occupational psychologists, who work in applied, naturalistic settings, such as psychiatric hospitals, schools, the prison service and commercial organizations.

○ While all psychologists have responsibilities and obligations towards those they 'work' with, which are common to both the scientist and practitioner roles, there are also important differences in these responsibilities and obligations that are related to the different roles. This is reflected in the various codes of conduct and ethical guidelines that are published by the major professional bodies for psychologists: the British Psychological Society (BPS) and the American Psychological Association (APA).

As shown in Figure 10.1 (see page 187), the *Code of Conduct for Psychologists* (British Psychological Society, 1985) and the *Code of Conduct, Ethical Principles and Guidelines* (BPS, 2000) apply to both of the main areas of research and practice, while there are additional documents designed for the two areas separately. The *Ethical Principles for Conducting Research with Human Participants* (British Psychological Society, 1990, 1993; now incorporated into the *Code of Conduct*, 2000) and the *Guidelines for the Use of Animals in Research* (BPS, 1985) clearly cover the former. The *Code of Conduct* (2000) includes a section on 'Guidelines for psychologists working with animals'. The *Division of Clinical Psychology Professional Practice Guidelines* (British Psychological Society, 1995) apply to the latter.

Clinical psychologists are by far the most numerous single group of psychologists: more than one-third of all psychologists classify themselves as clinical, and a further 10 per cent call themselves 'counselling psychologists'. The latter tend to work with younger clients in colleges and universities, rather than in psychiatric hospitals (and other mental health facilities), which, typically, accommodate a much greater age range of adults (including many who are psychogeriatric). What clinical and counselling psychologists have in common is responsibility for people with psychological problems.

The psychologist as scientist/investigator

Human participants

Animal subjects

The psychologist as practitioner

Psychotherapy
Counselling
Psychiatry

The psychologist as an agent of change

Ethical Principles for Research on Human Subjects (BPS, 1978)

Ethical Principles for Conducting Research with Human Participants (BPS, 1990, 1993)

Guidelines for Ethical Conduct in the Care and Use of Animals (APA, 1985)

Guidelines for the Use of Animals in Research (BPS, 1985)

Ethics in Psychological Research: Guidelines for students at Pre-Degree Levels (Association for the Teaching of Psychology, 1992)

Report of working Party on Behaviour Modification (BPS, 1978)

Principles Governing the Employment of Psychological Tests (BPS, 1981)

Code of Conduct for Psychologists (BPS, 1985)

Code of Conduct, Ethical Principles & Guidelines (BPS, 2000)

Division of Clinical Psychology Professional Practice Guidelines (BPS, 1995)

Guidelines for Avoiding Sexism in Psychological Research (APA, 1988) (see Chapter 6)

Ethical Principles of Psychologists and Code of Conduct (APA, 1992)

Figure 10.1 Major codes of conduct/ethical guidelines published by the British Psychological Society (BPS) and American Psychological Association (APA) (Adapted from Gross, 1992)

Because their clients are seeking professional help for a whole range of mental disorders, clinical and counselling psychologists have much in common with psychotherapists, in terms of both therapeutic methods/techniques used, and ethical issues raised by their work. While psychologists are trained largely to use *behaviour therapy/modification*, based on the principles of learning theory, counselling psychologists (and other trained counsellors) mainly use methods based on Rogers' *client-centred therapy*. Psychotherapists may have trained initially as psychiatrists, social workers or even psychologists, but all undergo special psychotherapy training (which includes their own psychotherapy). They use *psychodynamic* techniques derived from Freud's *psychoanalytic* theory and therapy (see Chapter 15).

The important point here is that, regardless of the particular training the practitioner has received and the particular therapeutic techniques s/he uses, the nature of the relationship between 'helper' and 'helped' is very different from that between researcher and researched. In particular, the helper is attempting to *change* something, presumably for the benefit of the helped, while the researcher is 'merely' trying to find out (more) about what the researched is already like. This changes the nature of the respective situations from an ethical point of view.

In the remainder of this chapter, we explore some of the major ethical issues and debates that take place in relation to both psychologists as researchers and as practitioners.

RESEARCH WITH HUMAN PARTICIPANTS

Guidelines such as the *Ethical Principles for Conducting Research with Human Participants* are intended, *primarily*, to protect the 'rights and dignity' of those who participate in psychological research. The ability to test human participants in research is referred to as a 'privilege', which will be retained only if 'all members of the psychological profession abide by the Principles' (British Psychological Society, 2000).

Violation of the principles could also form a basis of disciplinary action, and the Introduction to the *Ethical Principles* points out that:

In recent years, there has been an increase in legal actions by members of the general public against professionals for alleged misconduct. Researchers must recognise the possibility of such legal action if they infringe the rights and dignity of participants in their research.
(British Psychological Society, 2000, Paragraph 1.4)

As a *secondary* aim, therefore, the *Ethical Principles* are designed to protect psychologists themselves; but this protection only becomes necessary if the primary aim is not fulfilled.

The document lists nine major principles that are meant to be followed by *anyone* engaged in psychological research: all professional psychologists, whether members of the BPS or not, research assistants, and all students, from GCSE, through A-Level and undergraduate, up to postgraduate. These principles concern the following:

- consent
- deception
- debriefing
- withdrawal from the investigation
- confidentiality
- protection of participants
- observational research
- giving advice
- colleagues.

While these are listed separately, many are overlapping. Also, while the sixth principle is called 'Protection of participants', *all* the principles are aimed, in different ways, at protecting participants.

What are participants being protected from?

As we noted at the beginning of the chapter, people are sentient and thinking creatures, which means that they are capable of experiencing a wide range of negative emotions in response to situations that psychologists may create as part of their research. This danger is increased when we consider the difference in the power inherent in the roles of researcher and researched (also noted above).

From a feminist perspective (see Chapter 6), researchers should try to reverse the traditional, orthodox, masculine-dominated approach, whereby the experimenter, who is dominant and has superior status and power, *manipulates* and *controls* the experimental situation to which the subordinate *subject* reacts (e.g. Paludi, 1992). This difference in status and power creates a social and emotional distance between them. The 'subject' is, in fact, regarded and treated more as 'object', which is what is required from the positivistic, behaviouristic paradigm (Heather, 1976; Unger, 1984; see Chapter 11). According to Harré (1993):

> To speak of people as 'males' and 'females', to write of 'running subjects in an experiment' and so on is morally troublesome. It denigrates the men and women who give up their time to assist one in one's studies. It displays a contempt for them as people that I find quite unacceptable. I find it deeply disturbing that students are encouraged to adopt this scientific rhetoric . . .

When the BPS changed its *Ethical Principles for Research with Human <u>Subjects</u>* (1978) to *Ethical Principles for Conducting Research with Human <u>Participants</u>* (originally in 1990):

> In the forefront of its considerations was the recognition that psychologists owe a debt to those who agree to take part in their studies and that people who are willing to give up their time, even for remuneration, should be able to expect to be treated with the highest standards of consideration and respect. This is reflected in the change from 'subjects' to 'participants'.
> *(British Psychological Society, 2000)*

While recognizing that to psychologists brought up on the jargon of their profession the term 'subject' isn't derogatory, 'to someone who has not had that experience of psychological research it is a term which can seem impersonal'.

Feminist research requires the researcher to become actively involved in the research process, taking the perspective of the participants: they are not detached investigators but become an integral part of the whole process (see Chapter 11). Similarly, Eysenck (1994) argues that the human participant is in a rather vulnerable and exploitable position. He quotes Kelman (1972), who believes that 'most ethical problems arising in social research can be traced to the subject's power deficiency'. As well as possessing knowledge and expertise relating to the experimental situation that isn't shared with the participant, the experimenter is on 'home ground' (i.e. the laboratory), and the situation is under his/her control.

Deception, consent and informed consent

The experimenter's 'being in charge' is potentially most detrimental to participants when what they *believe* is going on in the experimental situation (for example, a study of perceptual judgement, as in Asch's 1951 conformity experiments, or a study of the effects of punishment on learning, as in Milgram's 1963 obedience experiments) isn't what is *actually* going on, as defined by the experimenter. Because it is the experimenter who manipulates the situation, the participant cannot know that s/he is being deceived; this is a feature of the experimenter's greater power.

The key ethical questions here are: 'Can failure to inform the participant of the true purpose of the experiment ever be justified?', 'Can the end (what the experimenter is hoping to find out) justify the means (the use of deception)?'

If informed consent involves the participant knowing everything that the experimenter knows about the experiment, and if giving informed consent (together with the *right to withdraw* from the experiment once it has begun) represents some kind of protection against powerlessness and vulnerability, should we simply condemn all deception and argue that it is always, and by its very nature, unacceptable?

According to Milgram (1977, 1992), many regard this as the cornerstone of ethical practice in human experimentation. According to some estimates, more than half the research published in social psychology journals involves some sort of misinformation or lack of disclosure, and although the 'topic' has received less attention in recent years (compared with the 1960s), the debate still goes on (Krupat and Garonzik, 1994).

Milgram cites Kelman (1974), who identifies two quite different reasons for not fully informing the participant.

1 The experimenter believes that if the participant knew what the experiment was like, s/he might refuse to participate (the *motivational* reason). Milgram believes that, 'Misinforming people to gain their participation appears a serious violation of the individual's rights, and cannot routinely constitute an ethical basis for subject recruitment.'

2 More typically, many social psychology experiments cannot be carried out unless the participant is ignorant of the true purpose of the experiment. Milgram calls this the *epistemological* reason; it is the psychologist's equivalent to what the author of a murder mystery does by not revealing the culprit until the very end of a novel – to do so would undermine the psychological effect of the reading experience!

But is this sufficient justification? While readers of murder mysteries *expect* not to find out 'whodunnit' until the very end (indeed this is a major part of the appeal of such literature), people who participate in psychology experiments do *not* expect to be deceived, and if they did, they presumably wouldn't agree to participate! But are things as cut and dried as this?

What if we found that, despite expecting to be deceived, people still volunteered, or that, not expecting to be deceived, they said that the deception didn't particularly bother them? Would this change the ethical 'status' of deception?

A number of points need to be made in response to this question.

1 Mannucci (1977, in Milgram, 1977, 1992) asked 192 lay people about ethical aspects of psychology experiments. They regarded deception as a relatively minor issue, and were far more concerned about the quality of the experience they would undergo as participants.

2 Most of the actual participants who were deceived in Asch's conformity experiments were very enthusiastic, and expressed their admiration for the elegance and significance of the experimental procedure (Milgram, 1977, 1992).

3 In defence of his own obedience experiments, Milgram (1974) reports that all participants received a comprehensive report when the experiments were over, detailing the procedure and the results, as well as a follow-up questionnaire concerning their participation. (This was part of a very thorough debriefing or 'dehoax'.) Of the 92 per cent who returned the questionnaires (an unusually high response rate), almost 84 per cent said they were glad or very glad to have participated, while less than 2 per cent said they were sorry or very sorry; 80 per cent said they felt that more experiments of this kind should be carried out, and 74 per cent said they had learned something of personal importance.

More specifically, the 'technical illusions' (Milgram's preferred term for 'deception') are justified for one reason only – they are in the end accepted and endorsed by those who are exposed to them:

The central moral justification for allowing a procedure of the sort used in my experiment is that it is judged acceptable by those who have taken part in it. Moreover, it was the salience of this fact throughout that constituted the chief moral warrant for the continuation of the experiments.
(Milgram, 1974)

Milgram goes on to say that any criticism of the experiment (or any other, for that matter) that doesn't take account of the tolerant reactions of the participants is hollow: 'Again, the participant, rather than the external critic, must be the ultimate source of judgement' (Milgram, 1974).

4 In a review of several studies focusing on the ethical acceptability of deception experiments, Christensen (1988, cited in Krupat and Garonzik, 1994) reports that, as long as deception isn't extreme, participants don't seem to mind. He suggests that the widespread use of mild forms of deception is justified – first, because apparently no one is harmed and, second, because there seem to be few, if any, acceptable alternatives.

5 Krupat and Garonzik (1994) found that, among 255 university psychology students, those who had had at least one experience of being deceived while participating in some psychological research, compared with those who hadn't, were significantly more likely to expect to be deceived again. But the experience of being deceived *doesn't* have a significant impact on the students' evaluation of other aspects of participation, such as enjoyment and interest. Consistent with Christensen's and Mannucci's findings, previously deceived participants weren't terribly upset at the prospect of being deceived again. Indeed, those who had been deceived at least once said they would be *less* upset at being lied to or misled again. According to Krupat and Garonzik (1994):

It almost seems that these people are accepting deception as par for the course and, therefore, not worthy of becoming upset. To the extent that the ethical issue revolves around subjects' negative reactions to deception, our findings are consistent with that of prior research . . .

6 Milgram (1977, 1992) acknowledges that the use of 'technical illusions' (a morally neutral term that he prefers to the morally biased, or 'loaded', 'deception') poses ethical dilemmas for the researcher. By definition, the use of such illusions means that participants cannot give their informed consent, and he asks whether this can ever be justified. Clearly, he says, they should never be used unless they are 'indispensable to the conduct of an inquiry', and honesty and openness are the only desirable bases of transactions with people in whatever context.

But does the judgement that they *are* indispensable justify their use? In other words, while believing that they are crucial may be a *necessary* reason for using them, is it a *sufficient* reason? Milgram gives examples of professions in which there exist exemptions from general moral principles, without which the profession couldn't function. For example, male gynaecologists and obstetricians are allowed to examine the genitals of female strangers, because they are their patients. Similarly, a lawyer may know that a client has committed a murder but is obligated *not* to tell the authorities, based on the principle of 'privileged communication'. We return to this very important issue when we discuss psychologists as practitioners later in the chapter.

In the case of gynaecology and the law, the underlying justification for 'suspending' more generally accepted moral principles ('It is wrong to examine the genitals of female strangers' and 'If you know that someone has committed a serious crime, you should tell the police'), is that, in the long run, society as a whole will benefit (women need gynaecologists and people need lawyers whom they can trust implicitly). But there is a crucial difference between these two instances. In the case of gynaecology and the law, *both* 'society in general' *and* the individual patient or client benefit. But in the case of the psychology experiment, the individual participant clearly *isn't* the beneficiary. So how do we resolve this moral dilemma?

The ethical status of psychological research

Any research that psychologists do is carried out within a whole range of constraints – methodological, ethical, financial, social, cultural and political. As the discussion of feminist and cross-cultural psychology shows (see Chapters 6 and 8), the very questions that psychologists ask about human behaviour and experience reflect a whole range of beliefs, values, presuppositions and prejudices, which, in turn, reflect the particular cultural, gender and other groups to which they belong. While this raises important questions about the objective nature of psychological inquiry (see Chapter 11), it also raises very important ethical issues. If sexism, heterosexism, the androcentric/masculinist bias, eurocentrism and racism are all inherent features of what psychologists do when they study human beings, then it could be argued that traditional, mainstream, western, academic, psychology (as well as the applied areas, such as clinical and educational psychology) is inherently unethical. In other words, most psychologists, most of the time, are trying to answer questions which stem from all kinds of prejudices. Most of the time, the psychologists themselves are unaware of these prejudices, but this doesn't by itself absolve them of the 'crime' ('ignorance of the law is no defence').

Protecting the individual vs benefiting society

The debate about the ethics of psychological research usually focuses on the vulnerability of individual participants and the responsibility of the psychologist towards his/her participants to ensure that they don't suffer in any way from their experience of participating. As we have seen, codes of conduct and ethical guidelines are designed to do just that. According to the BPS's *Ethical Principles* (2000):

Participants in psychological research should have confidence in the investigators. Good psychological research is possible only if there is mutual respect and confidence between investigators and participants. Psychological investigators are potentially interested in all aspects of human behaviour and conscious experience. However, for ethical reasons, some areas of human experience and behaviour may be beyond the reach of experiment, observation or other form of psychological investigation. Ethical guidelines are necessary to clarify the conditions under which psychological research is possible.
(British Psychological Society, 2000, Paragraph 1.2)

But how useful and effective are they in achieving these aims? See Box 10.1, page 193.

Wider issues about the 'morality' of the questions the researcher is trying to answer through the research are much less commonly asked. These would include the fundamental issue of the *values* that are, often unconsciously, helping to shape the research questions. If the questions themselves are limited and shaped by the values of the individual researcher, they

Box 10.1 How useful are codes of conduct and ethical guidelines?

According to Gale (1995), the fact that both the BPS and the APA codes are regularly reviewed and revised indicates that at least some aspects don't depend on absolute or universal ethical truths. Guidelines need to be updated in light of the changing social and political contexts in which psychological research takes place. For example, new issues, such as sexual behaviour in the context of AIDS, might highlight new ethical problems. Information revealed by participants can create conflict between the need to protect individuals and the protection of society at large. For instance, despite the confidentiality requirement, should a researcher inform the sexual partner of an HIV-positive participant? As Gale (1995) points out: 'One consequence of such breaches of confidentiality could be the withdrawal of consent by particular groups and the undermining of future research, demonstrating ... how one ethical principle fights against another.'

Taking the example of *informed consent*, Gale argues that however much information is given in advance of the procedure, this can never *guarantee* that informed consent is given. There is a sense in which you don't truly know what something is like until you've actually experienced it – and that goes for the researchers as much as the participants. Also, how much information can children, the elderly or disabled, or emotionally distressed people be expected to absorb? Even if this wasn't a problem, the status of the experimenter, the desire to please and 'be a good subject' (see Chapter 11) all detract from truly choosing freely in the way that is assumed by the BPS's *Ethical Principles* (Gale, 1995).

The BPS *Code of Conduct* (which incorporates the *Ethical Principles*) is an important guide in monitoring ethical standards and professional practice. But because it applies to *all* psychologists, regardless of the nature of their work, it is of necessity more general than is always helpful (Joscelyne, 2002). It is specific about some issues, but vague about others, and this can be confusing. For specific issues, such as disclosing an adult client's prior child sexual abuse if there are indications that s/he might be currently abusing a child, the *Division of Clinical Psychology Professional Practice Guidelines* (1995) are far more useful. Another issue that arises within clinical psychology is having a (sexual) relationship with a former client. Again, the *Code of Conduct* is very vague, and so unhelpful, on this (Joscelyne, 2002).

It is worth pointing out that the *Code of Conduct* (2000) consists of several sections (apart from the *Ethical Principles*). These include 'Guidelines for psychologists working with animals', 'Guidelines on advertising the services offered by psychologists', and 'Guidelines for penile plethysmography (PPG) usage'. The latter refers to the measurement of sexual arousal and involves apparatus being attached to the penis and sexual stimuli being presented. This might be used in the context of assessing paedophilia and sexual dysfunction, so its use is highly sensitive. But it is amusing to note that point nine of the Guidelines states that: 'Stimuli material for PPG assessment should be kept secure and access limited to those using it for professional purposes.'

are also limited and shaped by considerations of *methodology* – that is, what it is possible to do, practically, when investigating human behaviour and experience. According to Brehm (1992):

Given the clarity with which experiments allow us to test our causal ideas, it may seem strange that anyone would ever use anything other than an experimental design. Unfortunately, the same factor that defines an experiment also limits its use: the manipulation of the independent variable. Researchers can control the information that subjects receive in the laboratory about people they have never met, but they cannot manipulate many of the truly important factors in intimate relationships. We cannot create love in the laboratory. We don't know how to do it … For the most part, laboratory experiments are limited to explaining relatively emotionless interactions between strangers. Yet, in the study of relationships, we often want to understand intense encounters between intimates.

Brehm is saying that, in the context of interpersonal attraction, the laboratory experiment *by its nature* is extremely limited in the kinds of questions it will allow psychologists to investigate. Conversely, and just as importantly, there are certain aspects of behaviour and experience that *could* be studied experimentally, but it would be unethical to do so. Brehm gives 'jealousy between partners participating in laboratory research' as an example. Indeed,

… all types of research in this area [intimate relationships] involve important ethical dilemmas. Even if all we do is to ask subjects to fill out questionnaires describing their relationships, we need to think carefully about how this research experience might affect them and their partner …

So, the research that psychologists do is partly constrained by practical (methodological) considerations, and also partly by ethical ones: what it may be *possible* to do may be *unacceptable* but, equally, what may be *acceptable* may not be *possible*. As shown in Figure 10.2, the *what* of research is constrained by both the *how* and the *should*.

Figure 10.2 Ethical and methodological constraints on the questions that psychologists can try to answer through the research process

As we have seen, ethical debates (the 'should') are usually confined to protecting the integrity and welfare of the individual participant. This is what the various codes of conduct and ethical guidelines are designed to try and ensure. But are there wider ethical issues involved? For example, is it possible that by focusing on the protection of (individual) participants, the social groups to which they belong may be harmed in some way? This possibility, and the reasons underlying it, are discussed in Box 10.2.

Box 10.2 The ethics of ethical codes: underlying assumptions

According to Brown (1997), a core assumption underlying ethical codes is that what psychologists do as researchers, clinicians, teachers, and so on, is basically harmless and inherently valuable, because it is based on (positivist) science. Consequently, it is possible for a psychologist to conduct technically ethical research but still do great harm. For example, a researcher can adhere strictly to 'scientific' research methodologies, obtain technically informed consent from participants (and not breach any of the other major ethical principles), but still conduct research that claims to show the inferiority of a particular group. Because it is conducted according to 'the rules' (both methodological and ethical), the questions of whether it is ethical *in the broader sense* to pursue such matters is ignored.

For example, neither Jensen (1969) nor Herrnstein (1971) was ever considered by mainstream psychology to have violated psychology's ethics by the questions they asked regarding the intellectual inferiority of African-Americans. Individual black participants weren't harmed by being given IQ tests, and might even have found them interesting and challenging; however, Brown (1997) argues that how the findings were interpreted and used:

... weakened the available social supports for people of colour by stigmatising them as genetically inferior, thus strengthening the larger culture's racist attitudes. Research ethics as currently construed by mainstream ethics codes do not require researchers to put the potential for this sort of risk into their informed consent documents.

Jensen's and Herrnstein's research (highlighted by Herrnstein and Murray in *The Bell Curve*, 1994) has profoundly harmed black Americans. Ironically, the book has received a great deal of methodological criticism, but only black psychologists – such as Hilliard (1995) and Sue (1995) – have raised the more fundamental question of whether the mere fact of conducting such studies might be ethically dubious.

Herrnstein and Murray, Rushton (1995), Brand (in Richards, 1996) and others, like the Nazi scientists of the 1930s, claim that the study of race differences is a purely 'objective' and 'scientific' enterprise (Howe, 1997).

Also, as important as it surely is to protect individuals, does the 'should' relate to something beyond the particular experimental situation in which particular participants are involved?

The other side of the ethical coin: research that must be done

In our necessary concern with treating subjects well and protecting them from any harmful effects, we must not overlook the other side of the ethical issue: the ethical imperative to gain more understanding of important areas of human behaviour. Intimate relationships can be a source of the grandest, most glorious pleasure we human beings experience; they can also be a source of terrible suffering and appalling destructiveness. It is, I believe, an inherently ethical response to try to learn how the joy might be increased and the misery reduced. *(Brehm, 1992)*

Although specifically discussing the study of intimate relationships, Brehm's argument applies to psychology as a whole, but perhaps to social psychology in particular. Her argument is that not only are psychologists obliged to protect the welfare of individual participants, they are also under obligation to carry out socially meaningful research: research that, potentially, may improve the quality of people's lives. Social psychologists in particular, have a two-fold ethical obligation: to individual participants *and* to society at large (Myers, 1994). Similarly, Aronson (1992) argues that, in a real sense, social psychologists are under an obligation to use their research skills to advance our knowledge and understanding of human behaviour for the ultimate aim of 'human betterment'. But they face a dilemma when this general ethical responsibility to society comes into conflict with their more specific ethical responsibility to each individual experimental participant.

In talking about the aim of 'human betterment', we are raising many important questions to do with basic values. This opens up the ethical debate in such a way that *values must be addressed and recognized as part of the research process* (something that feminist psychologists advocate very strongly; see Chapter 6). Discussion of values may also have provided a solution to the dilemma that we noted earlier, whereby the individual participant isn't the beneficiary (unlike the gynaecology patient or the lawyer's client). The short-term deception of individual participants (and the distress this might cause) may be necessary if psychologists are to learn things about human behaviour and experience which can then be used to benefit *people in general*. What form might such benefits take?

In some of the early, and very famous, studies of bystander intervention, people were deceived as to the 'emergency' that was supposedly taking place. In the Latané and Darley (1968) experiment, steam, which was meant to resemble smoke, poured into the room where the participants were filling out questionnaires, and in a second study (Darley and Latané, 1968), participants believed that another participant (supposedly in another part of the building and heard via an intercom system) was having an epileptic fit.

Many participants were very distressed by their experience, especially those in the latter experiment. Yet when asked to complete a post-experiment questionnaire (which followed a very careful debriefing), *all* said they believed the deception was justified and that they would be willing to participate in similar experiments again. None reported any feelings of anger towards the experimenter.

A later study, by Beaman *et al.* (1978, in Myers, 1994) built on these earlier experiments. They used a lecture to inform some students about how bystanders' refusal to help can influence both one's interpretation of an emergency and one's feelings of responsibility. Two other groups of students heard either a different lecture or no lecture at all. Two weeks later, as part of a different experiment in a different location, the participants found themselves walking (accompanied by an unresponsive confederate) past someone slumped over or sprawled under a bike. Of those who had heard the lecture about helping behaviour, 50 per cent stopped to offer help, compared with 25 per cent of those who had not.

What this suggests, of course, is that the results of psychological research can be used to make us more aware of the influences that affect our behaviour, making it more likely that we will act differently armed with that knowledge from how we might otherwise have done. In the case of bystander intervention, this 'consciousness-raising' is beneficial in a very tangible way to the person being helped. As for the helper, being more sensitive to the needs of others and the feeling of satisfaction from actually having helped another person may be seen as benefits too.

We should note that in the Beaman *et al.* experiment, the participants were being deceived, both as to the identity of the unresponsive confederate and the apparent 'victim'. But this can be justified in the same way as any experiment using deception.

How do we decide when to deceive?

The preceding argument implies rejection of the view that deception can never, under any circumstances, be justified. But that doesn't inevitably lead us to the opposite view, namely that almost any price is worth paying for results that may have profound benefits for humankind (Aronson, 1992). So what is the middle ground?

I believe the science of social psychology is important, and I also believe experimental subjects should be protected at all times. When deciding whether a particular experimental procedure is ethical or not, I believe a cost–benefit analysis is appropriate. That is, how much 'good' will derive from doing the experiment and how much 'bad' will happen to the experimental subjects should be considered. Put another way, the benefits to society are compared with the costs to the subjects, and this ratio is entered into the decision calculus . . .
(Aronson, 1992)

Unfortunately, this comparison is often very difficult to make, because neither the benefits nor the harm are known or calculable. McGhee (2001) identifies several problems faced by any cost–benefit analysis (see Box 10.3, page 198).

Our judgement about the acceptability of any experimental procedure (including any deception involved), may be (unconsciously) influenced by the results that are obtained. If the results tell us something pleasant or flattering about human nature, the procedure is *less* likely to be criticized as unethical, while the reverse is true if the results tell us 'something we'd rather not know' (Aronson, 1992). This is to *confuse* the procedure with the outcome, when they need to be assessed *independently* before being weighed against each other.

There is little doubt that Milgram's experiments told us something about ourselves that 'we'd rather not know'. Aronson agrees with Milgram himself, who is convinced that:

. . . much of the criticism [of his obedience experiments], whether people know it or not, stems from the results of the experiment. If everyone had broken off at slight shock or mild shock, this would be a very reassuring finding and who would protest?
(Milgram, 1977, 1992)

Ironically, our current codes of ethics are a direct consequence of the public and academic debates that followed Milgram's research (McGhee, 2001).

Consistent with this argument is Aronson's observation that the dilemma faced by social psychologists (regarding their obligations to society and to their individual participants) is greatest when investigating such important areas as conformity, obedience and bystander intervention. In general, the more important the issue, (i) the greater the potential benefit for

> ## Box 10.3 Some problems with cost–benefit analysis (McGhee, 2001)
>
> Both costs and benefits are multiple and subjective, some are immediate, others are longer term, and there are difficulties in 'adding them up'.
>
> Regarding *multiplicity*, every psychology experiment (like every complex social activity) has many outcomes. It is difficult, if not impossible, to *identify* them, let alone assess them. Even if they can be assessed individually, they need to be *aggregated* in some way, because we are trying to assess the experiment as an overall package. For example, how much is deception 'worth' relative to 'new data'?
>
> Ultimately, costs and benefits can only be *subjectively* assessed. Each individual values different kinds of experiences (gains and losses) differently. Indeed, one person's cost might be another's benefit.
>
> In theory-driven research such as Milgram's (as distinct from applied research), costs tend to be real, while benefits tend to be *potential*: 'The distress to the participants in Milgram's studies is real but the prospect of reducing the possibility of another Auschwitz is remote − even if extraordinarily desirable.' Similarly, although the benefits may outweigh the costs, for individual participants it is mostly all costs: time, effort, stress, and occasional humiliation and deception; any tangible or practical benefits are unlikely to be for them. The costs, therefore, are linked to specific people, while the identity of those who will benefit is much less obvious.
>
> We need to decide *before* a study takes place whether or not it should go ahead. But very often the full range and extent of costs and benefits will only become apparent *retrospectively*.
>
> Finally, who should have the right to *decide* whether the benefits outweigh the costs?

society and (ii) the more likely that an individual participant will experience distress and discomfort. The 'missing middle' from this observation is that the more important the issue, the more essential it becomes that *deception* (or 'technical illusion') is used. Why? Because the psychologist wants to know how people are likely to behave were they to find themselves in that situation *outside of the laboratory* (or, at least, outside of the experimental situation).

This raises a number of crucial *methodological* questions (to do with experimental realism, external validity or mundane realism; see Chapter 11). But the key *ethical* issue hinges on the fact that the use of deception *both* contributes enormously (and perhaps irreplaceably) to our understanding of human behaviour (helping to satisfy the obligation to society) *and at the same time* may significantly increase the distress of individual participants (detracting from the responsibility to protect individuals).

So what is the psychologist to do?

Some suggested solutions to the 'double obligation' dilemma

USING DECEPTION ONLY WHEN ESSENTIAL

Having accepted that, under certain circumstances, deception is permissible, most psychologists still advocate the principle that it shouldn't be used unless it is considered to be *essential* to do so (Milgram, 1977, 1992; Aronson, 1992). This is consistent with the BPS's *Ethical Principles*, according to which:

> Intentional deception . . . over the purpose and general nature of the investigation should be avoided whenever possible. Participants should never be deliberately misled without extremely strong scientific or medical justification. Even then there should be strict controls and the disinterested approval of independent advisors.

(British Psychological Society, 2000, Paragraph 4.2)

ACCURATELY REFLECTING HUMAN EXPERIENCE

Milgram (1977, 1992) also believes that if we excluded, *on principle*, the experimental creation of stress or conflict, and only allowed studies that produced positive emotions, 'such a stricture would lead to a very lopsided psychology, one that caricatured rather than accurately reflected human experience'. Historically, the most deeply informative experiments in social psychology include those that examine how participants resolve *conflicts* of one kind or another, such as the Asch studies of conformity (truth vs conformity), the Latane and Darley bystander intervention studies (getting involved in another's troubles vs not getting involved), and Milgram's own obedience experiments (internal conscience vs external authority). If we excluded the study of such core human issues, we would be causing an 'irreparable loss' to any science of human behaviour.

But what of the accusation that Milgram's experiment may produce diminished self-esteem, or sense of self-worth, in those participants who obey the experimenter all the way up to 450 volts? Milgram's reply is to agree that it is the experimenter's responsibility to make the laboratory session as constructive an experience as possible, and to explain the experiment in a way that allows participants to integrate their performance into their self-concept in an insightful way. However, if the experimenter were to hide the truth from the participant, even if this is negative, this would set the experiment completely apart from other life experiences (and, we could add, would simply be dishonest).

ALTERNATIVES TO INFORMED CONSENT

Two compromise solutions to the problem of not being able to obtain informed consent are (i) *presumptive consent* (of 'reasonable people') and (ii) *prior general consent*.

In the former, the views of a large number of people are obtained about the acceptability of an experimental procedure. These people wouldn't participate in the actual experiment (if it went ahead), but their views could be taken as evidence of how people *in general* would react to participation. In the latter, prior general consent could be obtained from people who might, subsequently, serve as experimental participants. Before volunteering to join a pool of volunteers to serve in psychological research, people would be explicitly told that sometimes participants are misinformed about the true purpose of the study and sometimes experience emotional stress. Only those agreeing, in the light of this knowledge, would be chosen for a particular study (Milgram, 1977, 1992).

This is a compromise solution, because people would be giving their 'informed consent' (i) well in advance of the actual experiment, (ii) only in a very general way, and (iii) without knowing what specific manipulations/deceptions would be used in the particular experiment in which they participate. It seems to fall somewhere between 'mere' consent and full 'informed consent', and could perhaps be called *semi-* or *partially informed consent*.

THE USE OF ANIMALS IN PSYCHOLOGICAL RESEARCH

Why do psychologists study animals?

Because of the very close relationship between the *ethical* and the *practical* aspects of animal experimentation, they are discussed together here.

1 Experiments that wouldn't be *allowed* (or would be very impractical if they were) if they involved human participants, are permitted (or have been in the past) using animal subjects. This, of course, begs the question as to the *ethics* of such animal experiments.

2 Even if animals aren't subjected to ethically unacceptable procedures, such as severe sensory deprivation (e.g. Riesen, 1947; Blakemore and Cooper, 1970), total social isolation (e.g. Harlow and Zimmerman, 1959), extreme stress (e.g. Brady, 1958; Seligman, 1974), or surgical procedures and eventually 'sacrifice' (e.g. Olds and Milner, 1954), greater *control* can still be exerted over the variables under investigation compared with the equivalent human experiment. For example, the Skinner box is an environment totally controlled by the experimenter (see Chapter 15).

3 There is an underlying *evolutionary continuity* between humans and other species, which gives rise to the assumption that differences between humans and other species are merely *quantitative* (as opposed to *qualitative*): other species may display more simple behaviour and have more primitive nervous systems than humans, but they are not of a different order from humans (see Chapter 15). In fact, the mammalian brain (which includes rats, cats, dogs, monkeys and humans) is built on similar lines in all these species, and neurons (nerve cells) are the same in all species, and work in the same way. These similarities of biology are, in turn, linked to behavioural similarities. So, it is argued, studying the more simple cases is a valid and valuable way of finding out about the more complex ones. Skinner's analysis of behaviour is a good example of this approach (again see Chapter 15).

4 Animals are (mostly) smaller and, therefore, easier to study in the laboratory. They also have much shorter lifespans and gestation periods, making it much easier to study their development: many generations can be studied in a relatively short time.

5 Animal studies can provide useful hypotheses for subsequent testing with human participants. For example, Bowlby's theory of attachment (see Chapter 9) was partly influenced by Lorenz's study of imprinting in geese. Equally important, animals can be used to test cause-and-effect relationships where the existing human evidence is only correlational, as in smoking and lung cancer. This, of course, raises fundamental *ethical* questions.

The *Guidelines for Psychologists Working with Animals* (British Psychological Society, 2000) point out that research isn't the only reason psychologists work with animals, even though, not surprisingly, it is what has caused the most controversy and media attention. Animals are sometimes used in practical teaching within psychology degree courses, and increasingly animals are being used in various forms of psychological therapy, including companion animal visiting schemes in hospitals or hospices, pet-keeping within prison rehabilitation schemes, and in behaviour therapy for the treatment of specific animal phobias: 'In all these cases, considerations concerning the general care and welfare of therapeutic animals are similar to those ... for experimental animals. In addition, however, a number of specific considerations can be noted ...' (Section 9). These include issues relating to the temperament and training of the animals, and their need for protection and rest.

Figure 10.3 Darwin was ridiculed by the media of the day for his 'outrageous' ideas of evolution

The case for animal experimentation

The main justifications for using animals in experiments are (i) the pursuit of scientific knowledge, and (ii) the advancement of medicine. To justify the use of animals, especially when the procedures used are likely to be very stressful, the research must be rigorously designed and the potential results must represent a significant contribution to our knowledge of medicine, pharmacology, biopsychology or psychology. This is a safeguard against distressing research being carried out for its own sake, or at the whim of the researcher.

Much of the controversy surrounding animal research is focused on its use in medical research. Despite the safeguards that are in place, including the BPS *Guidelines* and the Animals (Scientific Procedures) Act 1986, opponents object to animal experimentation *in principle*. Supporters – who, not surprisingly, are mainly medical researchers and physiologists – stress the many human diseases and psychological disorders that are now successfully treated or controlled using drugs whose development would have been impossible without animal research (see Gross, 2001).

Some would take the 'medical justification' argument even further. For example, Gray (1991) argues that most people (both experimenters and animal rights activists) would accept the ethical principle that inflicting pain is wrong. However, we are sometimes faced with having to choose between different ethical principles – that is, we have to make moral choices, which may mean having to choose between human and animal suffering. Gray believes that *speciesism* (discriminating against and exploiting animals because they belong to a particular (non-human) species (Ryder, 1990)) isn't only justified, but it is our *duty* to carry out animal research if this may lead to the (long-term) alleviation of human suffering.

Bateson (1986, 1992) proposes a 'decision cube' (similar to Aronson's cost–benefit analysis in human research; see above), involving (i) the quality of the research, (ii) the certainty of medical benefit, and (iii) the degree of animal suffering. The latter should only be tolerated if (i) and (ii) are high.

Chimpanzees and animal rights

In recent years, the ethics debate in relation to non-humans has become focused on chimpanzees and other primates, and in the process its scope has widened to include the notion of equality under the law. One strand to this debate involves psychologists' attempts to teach language to chimpanzees (and other great apes). A famous example is described in Box 10.4.

Box 10.4 Washoe and the Gardners

In 'Teaching sign language to a chimpanzee' (1969), Gardner and Gardner report their famous research with Washoe, estimated to be between 8 and 14 months when she arrived at their laboratory.

When she was five years old, Washoe was sent away with Roger and Deborah Fouts. The Gardners next saw her 11 years later; when they unexpectedly entered the room Washoe was in, she signed their name, then 'Come, Mrs G', led her to an adjoining room and began to play a game with her which she hadn't been observed to play since she left the Gardners' home (Singer, 1993).

Observations like this, as well as supporting the argument that non-humans really are capable of language (see Gross, 2003), also raise important ethical questions – in particular:

○ How justifiable is the whole attempt to study language in non-humans, since this involves removing the animals from their natural habitat in which they don't spontaneously use language?

○ What happens to the chimpanzees after they have served their purpose as experimental subjects?

While these kinds of study aren't usually the target for attacks against cruel treatment of animals in psychological research, they nonetheless involve animals that haven't chosen to become involved. But perhaps it's the fact that they're great apes, and not just 'other animals', which makes these ethical questions so fascinating and important. This also applies to the other 'strand', which involves the several hundred chimpanzee 'veterans' of American research during the 1970s aimed at developing vaccines for hepatitis B and C. While euthanasia was being considered, the AIDS epidemic in the mid-1980s came to their 'rescue'. Once again, because of their genetic similarity to ourselves, they became 'surrogate human beings' again (Mahoney, 1998).

By the mid-1990s, scientists began turning to human volunteers for the initial testing of HIV vaccines, leaving large numbers of 'redundant' chimpanzees (which have a lifespan of up to 40 years). A report of the US National Research Council (1997) concluded that chimpanzees should be afforded special consideration, on ethical grounds, over other non-humans, and that euthanasia isn't an acceptable means of population control (Mahoney, 1998).

The Great Ape Project (GAP) is (i) the title of a book (subtitle: *Equality Beyond Humanity*, edited by Singer and Cavalieri, 1993), (ii) a simple but radical idea, to extend the 'community of equals' beyond human beings to all great apes (chimps, gorillas and orang-utans), and (iii) an organization, comprising 34 academics and others, set up to work internationally for the immediate inclusion of the great apes within the community of equals. This refers to the moral community within which we accept certain basic moral rights/principles as governing our relationships with each other and which are enforceable at law.

The central tenet of the GAP is that it is ethically indefensible to deny the great apes the basic rights of (i) the right to life, (ii) protection of individual liberty, and (iii) prohibition of torture (collectively, the *Declaration of Great Apes*).Wise (2000), in a book entitled *Rattling the Cage: Towards Legal Rights for Animals*, argues that animals should have full rights under the law. Goodall describes Wise's book as the 'animals' Magna Carta' (Mee, 2000). Taylor (2000) considers that Singer has established the basis for a revolution in ethics. Traditional approaches have rested on the belief in the unique value of human life, but Singer insists that this no longer works, and that ethics must be concerned instead with *reducing suffering*. This applies equally to humans and to non-humans.

PSYCHOLOGISTS AS AGENTS OF CHANGE

We noted at the beginning of the chapter that there are both important similarities and differences as regards the ethical problems faced by psychologists as scientists and as practitioners. We also noted that there is considerable overlap between clinical and counselling psychologists, and psychotherapists, in terms of the ethical dimensions of their work.

The major ethical issues that relate to these applied areas of psychology (and related professions) include:

- informed consent
- the influence of the therapist
- behavioural control
- the abuse of patients by therapists
- confidentiality and 'privileged communication' (we have already touched on this above).

Informed consent

Where someone is voluntarily seeking help from a psychologist or psychotherapist (as opposed to the position of an involuntary, sectioned, patient in a psychiatric hospital), it might seem that there wouldn't be an issue regarding informed consent. However, if we think about what this means in relation to participants in research (namely, being fully aware of the purpose of the study), things begin to look a little less straightforward.

According to Holmes (1992), this is a problem throughout the caring professions. The law in Britain and the USA differs regarding the extent to which doctors are expected to explain in advance every detail of the possible adverse consequences of a procedure or treatment. In the case of psychotherapy this is especially problematic, for four main reasons:

1 the patient may well be in a vulnerable and emotionally aroused state and, thus, unlikely to be able to make a balanced judgement as to the suitability of the particular form of therapy on offer and/or his or her compatibility with the therapist

2 unlike medical procedures, the range of different forms of psychotherapy available tends to be poorly understood by the general public and the media

3 the lack of any generally agreed standards of training, practice or regulatory procedures within psychotherapy as a whole, means that there are no external criteria against which a particular therapy can be assessed

4 there are special problems of informed consent associated with particular therapies. For example, in psychoanalysis, some degree of 'opacity' is necessary if certain techniques, such as transference, are to be effective. In other words, the therapist must remain partially 'obscure' or 'non-transparent' if the patient is to be able to transfer onto the therapist unconscious feelings for parents (or other key relatives), which are then discussed and interpreted. When assessing patients for treatment, analysts must strike a balance between providing legitimate information on the one hand, and maintaining their 'professional distance' on the other.

Despite these difficulties, the problems of consent can be overcome. Holmes (1992) believes that recognized standards of training and practice would help. Indeed, most psychotherapy organizations in Britain favour a state-recognized profession of psychotherapy, and are actively trying to achieve this goal through the UK Standing Conference on Psychotherapy. Masson (1992) proposes that there should be a 'psychotherapy ombudsman'.

Most patients probably gravitate towards the therapies and therapists they feel comfortable with, and word-of-mouth recommendations are very important in private practice. At least you only pay for one session at a time – it's not like buying a used car (Holmes, 1992)!

The influence of the therapist

Psychologists are aware of the subtle coercion that can operate on hospitalized psychiatric patients – even voluntary ones. The in-patient is subjected to strong persuasion to accept the treatment recommendations of professional staff. As Davison and Neale (2001) observe, 'even a "voluntary" and informed decision to take psychotropic medication or to participate in any other therapy regimen is often (perhaps usually) less than free'. The issue of the influence of the therapist on the patient/client has been central to a long-standing debate between traditional (psychodynamic) psychotherapists and behaviour therapists (who, as we saw earlier, are usually clinical psychologists by training).

Many psychotherapists believe that behaviour therapy is unacceptable (even if it works), because it is manipulative and demeaning of human dignity. By contrast, their own methods are seen as fostering the autonomous development of the patient's inherent potential, helping the patient to express his/her true self, and so on. Instead of an influencer, they see themselves as a kind of psychological midwife, present during the birth, possessing useful skills, but there primarily to make sure that a natural process goes smoothly (Wachtel, 1977).

According to Wachtel, however, this is an exaggeration and misrepresentation of both approaches. For many patients, the 'birth' probably wouldn't happen at all without the therapist's intervention, and s/he undoubtedly does influence the patient's behaviour. Conversely, behaviour therapists are at least partly successful because they establish an active, cooperative relationship with the patient, who plays a much more active role in the therapy than psychotherapists believe.

Wachtel argues that *all* therapists, of whatever persuasion, if they are at all effective, influence their patients. Both approaches comprise:

... a situation in which one human being (the therapist) tries to act in such a way as to enable another human being to act and feel differently than he has, and this is as true of psychoanalysis as it is of behaviour therapy.

For Wachtel, the crucial issue is the *nature* of this influence (*not* whether it occurs), and there are four crucial questions that need to be asked:

1 Is the influence exerted in a direction that is in the patient's interest, or in the service of the therapist's needs?

2 Are some good ends (such as reduction in anxiety) being achieved at the expense of others (such as the patient's enhanced vision of the possibilities that life can offer or an increased sense of self-directedness)?

3 Is the patient fully informed about the kind of influence that the therapist wishes to exert and the kind of ends being sought? (This, of course, relates to informed consent.)

4 Is the patient's choice being excessively influenced by a fear of displeasing the therapist, rather than by what s/he would really prefer?

The *neutrality* of therapists is a myth; they influence their clients in subtle yet powerful ways:

Unlike a technician, a psychiatrist cannot avoid communicating and at times imposing his own values upon his patients. The patient usually has considerable difficulty in finding the way in which he would wish to change his behaviour, but as he talks to the psychiatrist his wants and needs become clearer. In the very process of defining his needs in the presence of a figure who is viewed as wise and authoritarian, the patient is profoundly influenced. He ends up wanting some of the things the psychiatrist thinks he should want.
(Davison and Neale, 1994)

In the above extract, we can add the terms 'psychologist' and 'psychotherapist' to 'psychiatrist'.

Behavioural control

While a behavioural technique such as *systematic desensitization* (SD, based on classical conditioning) is largely limited to the reduction of anxiety, at least this can be seen as enhancing the patient's freedom, since anxiety is one of the greatest restrictions on freedom. By contrast, methods based on *operant conditioning* can be applied to almost any aspect of a person's life (largely because they are applied to *voluntary* as opposed to *reflex* or *autonomic* behaviour; see Chapter 15).

Those who use operant methods, such as the *token economy*, often describe their work rather exclusively in terms of *behavioural control*, and they subscribe to Skinner's (1971) view that freedom is only an illusion (see Chapter 12). Wachtel (1977) believes that when used in institutional settings (as with long-term schizophrenic patients in psychiatric hospitals), the token economy is so subject to abuse that its use is highly questionable. It may be justifiable (i) if it works, and (ii) if there's clearly no alternative way of rescuing the patient from an empty and destructive existence. But as a routine part of how society deals with deviant behaviour, this approach raises very serious ethical questions.

One of these relates to the question of *power*. Just as we noted earlier when discussing the role of the 'subject' in experiments, the patient is powerless relative to the institutional staff responsible for operating the token economy programme, According to Wachtel:

. . . reinforcement is viewed by many – proponents and opponents alike – as somehow having an inexorable controlling effect upon the person's behaviour and rendering him incapable of choice, reducing him to an automaton or duly wound mechanism . . .

The alarming feature of the token economy is the reinforcing agent's power to physically deprive un-cooperative patients of 'privileges'.

APPLIED BEHAVIOUR ANALYSIS (ABA) AND PUNISHMENT

Another application of operant conditioning is applied behaviour analysis (ABA), often referred to simply as 'behaviour modification'. This is commonly used with autistic and brain-damaged children and adults, and punishment techniques may be involved, especially when the client displays self-injurious behaviour. O'Donohue and Ferguson (2001) believe that a common misconception about ABA is that it uses a great deal of punishment such as electric shock: 'The caricature of these approaches is a cattle-prod-wielding Nurse Ratchett who shocks and threatens to punish in order to coerce behaviour change . . .'.

Although punishment is sometimes used, psychologists who use ABA follow Skinner's recommendations and rarely use it as a first choice (see Chapter 15). It often induces escape and avoidance behaviour, anger and fear. Also, it's not a constructive learning mechanism: while it decreases the frequency of some behaviours, it doesn't increase the frequency of more desirable behaviours. So, applied behaviour analysts prefer to use a reinforcement-based intervention. Reinforcement doesn't always work, though, and sometimes the undesirable behaviour is so serious that punishment *must* be used (O'Donohue and Ferguson, 2001).

Leslie (2002) observes that, although punishment is a 'normal' part of everyday attempts to modify others' behaviour, it becomes controversial in applied settings. While it can be effective, 'it should be a technique of last resort, both because the situation in which it occurs may become aversive and lead to escape or aggression, and because of the public debate that surrounds its use'. Some critics have condemned punishment in particular, and ABA in general, as evil and controlling. But these attacks are based partly on misinformation, partly on a small number of cases of abuse, and partly on ideological objections to all scientific accounts of human behaviour (see Chapter 15). But this only strengthens the need for applied behaviour analysts to explain how and why their practices *are* ethical (Leslie, 2002).

Leslie refers to ethical guidelines that have been developed for the use of behavioural treatments (citing Van Houten *et al.*, 1988) These are primarily intended to protect the human rights of the clients involved, and comprise six fundamental rights of individuals for whom behavioural intervention is provided. These are the rights to:

- a therapeutic environment
- services whose overriding goal is personal welfare
- treatment by a competent behaviour analyst
- programmes that teach fundamental skills
- behavioural assessment and ongoing evaluation, and
- the most effective treatment procedures available.

As the guidelines indicate:

. . . professionals who practise applied behaviour analysis are fundamentally interested in improving the lives of the people they work with and of society in

general. Regrettably, there will, from time to time, be individuals in any discipline who will violate professional guidelines, and such individuals should not be allowed to practise behaviour analysis
(Leslie, 2002)

The abuse of patients by therapists

In recent years, there has been a wave of criticism of psychotherapy (especially of the Freudian variety) from a number of directions, and these have included criticism of its ethical shortcomings. One of its most outspoken critics is an American, ex-Freudian psychoanalyst, Jeffrey Masson.

Masson (1992) believes that there is an imbalance of power involved in the therapeutic relationship. Individuals who seek therapy need protection from the constant temptation to abuse, misuse, profit from and bully on the part of the therapist. The therapist has almost absolute emotional power over the patient, and in his *Against Therapy: Emotional Tyranny and the Myth of Psychological Healing* (1988), he catalogues example after example of patients' abuse – emotional, sexual, financial – at the hands of their therapists.

Naturally enough, Masson's attack has stirred up an enormous controversy. Holmes (1992) agrees with the core of Masson's argument, namely that:

. . . no therapist, however experienced or distinguished, is above the laws of the unconscious, and all should have access to supervision and work within a framework of proper professional practice.
(Masson, 1992)

In defence of psychotherapy, Holmes (1992) points out that exploitation and abuse are by no means confined to psychotherapy: lawyers, university teachers, priests and doctors are also sometimes guilty. All these professional groups have ethical standards and codes of practice (often far more stringent than the laws of the land), with disciplinary bodies that impose severe punishments – usually expulsion from the profession. As Leslie (2002) argues in the case of ABA, we shouldn't condemn an entire profession because of the transgressions of a small minority.

SUMMARY

O Ethical issues arise because (i) human beings and animals are *sentient*, living things, and (ii) human beings are *thinking* creatures, capable of experiencing embarrassment, guilt, and so on.

O Ethical issues arise for psychologists because (i) they study human beings and animals, (ii) they often subject the people/animals they study to painful/embarrassing situations/stimulation, (iii) every psychological investigation can be thought of as an *ethical* situation.

O The BPS and APA both publish various codes of conduct and ethical guidelines, some of which apply to the roles of both *scientist/investigator* and *practitioner* jointly, while others apply to one *or* the other.

O Guidelines such as the BPS's *Ethical Principles* are intended, primarily, to protect the 'rights and dignity' of participants. These include *deception*, *consent/informed consent*, *withdrawal from the investigation,* and *debriefing*.

O Feminists argue that the *power difference* between researcher and researched should be reversed by the researcher becoming actively involved in the research process, as opposed to a detached manipulator/controller of the experimental situation.

O According to Milgram, the *motivational* reason for deceiving participants is quite unacceptable, but the *epistemological* reason is justified.

O Milgram believes that 'technical illusions' are justified only if they are in the end accepted/endorsed by those exposed to them. But since their use prevents participants from giving their *informed consent*, they should only be used if absolutely essential.

O The questions that psychologists try to answer through their research are shaped partly by their *values*, and partly by *methodological* considerations. The research itself is constrained by *what is possible* and *what is ethically acceptable*.

O Ethical debates usually concentrate on the need to protect the integrity/welfare of the individual participant. But psychologists are also obliged to carry out *socially meaningful research* (the 'ethical imperative'). This two-fold obligation can present psychologists with a dilemma over whether or not they should use deception.

O Generally, the more socially significant the issue, the greater the need for deception, and the more likely that an individual participant will experience distress.

O Some possible solutions to this dilemma include: (i) only use deception if the scientific/medical justification is extremely strong; (ii) the use of *presumptive consent* and *prior general consent*.

O While ethical codes serve to protect individual participants, underlying assumptions may harm the *social groups* they represent. Formal codes neglect wider issues regarding the ethical acceptability of *socially sensitive research*.

O In the case of animal experimentation, *ethical* and *practical* issues are **very** closely tied.

O Some of the *reasons* for using animals in research include: (i) the greater *control* over variables; (ii) the *evolutionary continuity* between humans and other species; (iii) the convenience and speed of studying animals' development; and (iv) the testing of cause-and-effect hypotheses from human correlational research.

O The main justifications for using animals are: (i) *the pursuit of scientific knowledge*; (ii) *the advancement of medicine*.

O Many drugs used in the treatment of human diseases couldn't have been developed without animal research, and this may be seen as a *sufficient* justification for the use of animals.

O According to Gray, not only is *speciesism* justified, it is our *duty* to carry out animal research if this may result in the alleviation of human suffering.

O Safeguards for animals used in research include the BPS's *Guidelines*, and the Animals (Scientific Procedures) Act. The *Great Ape Project* argues that the great apes should be given the basic rights of life, freedom and protection from torture.

O As *agents of change*, clinical psychologists (along with psychotherapists) face the ethical issues of *informed consent*, *the influence of the therapist*, *behavioural control*, *the abuse of patients*, *confidentiality*, and '*privileged communication*'.

O Subtle forms of coercion can operate on hospitalized psychiatric patients (including voluntary ones) to accept particular forms of treatment.

O Many psychotherapists see behaviour therapy as manipulative and demeaning of human dignity, but view their own methods as helping patients to become autonomous. *All* therapists influence their patients, however, and it is the *kind* of influence involved that matters.

O The *token economy*, as a form of *behavioural control*, is ethically highly dubious. One objection is the *powerlessness* of patients relative to the staff operating the programme; another is the patient's reduction to an *automaton*, who lacks choice.

O *Applied behaviour analysis* (ABA) has been condemned for its use of punishment techniques. However, these are only used as a last resort to stop seriously harmful behaviour.

O Masson condemns psychotherapists for abusing the power they have over their patients. However, exploitation/abuse can be found in a small minority within all professions.

Useful websites

○ http://www.apa.org/ethics/code.html
○ www.bps.org.uk/documents/Code.pdf
○ www.bps.org.uk/sub-syst/dcp/publicat.cfm
○ http://www.informin.co.uk/LM/LM119/LM119_AnimalExp.html
○ http://altweb.jhsph.edu
○ http://www.aalas.org
○ http://www.apa.org/science/anguide.html

Recommended reading

Milgram, S. (1974) *Obedience to Authority* (especially Appendix 1: 'Problems of ethics in research'). New York: Harper & Row.

Milgram. S. (1992) *The Individual In a Social World: Essays and Experiments* (2nd edn) (especially Chapters 10, 12 and 15). New York: McGraw-Hill.

Wise, R. (2000) *Rattling the Cage: Towards Legal Rights for Animals*. London: Profile Books.

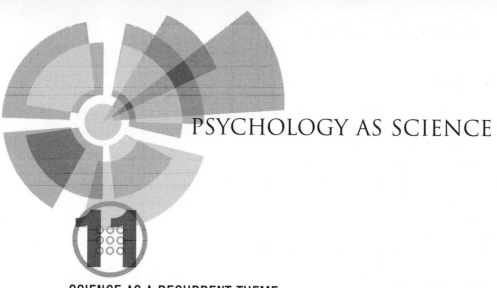

PSYCHOLOGY AS SCIENCE

SCIENCE AS A RECURRENT THEME

Explicitly or implicitly, the nature of science and psychology's status as a science are discussed throughout this book. Chapter 1 looks at the ways in which everyone may be thought of as a psychologist, by examining common-sense psychology, and how this is both similar to, and different from, scientific psychology. In Chapter 2 on attribution, some of the issues raised in the first chapter are explored in greater detail, in particular, the attribution process, according to which the lay person assigns *causes* to behaviour and, to that extent, acts like a naïve scientist.

Identifying the causes of a phenomenon as a way of trying to *explain* it (as well as a means of predicting and controlling it) is a fundamental part of 'classical' science (see below). This is related to *determinism*, which is discussed in relation to free will in Chapter 12.

The three aims of explanation/understanding, prediction and control are discussed in Chapter 3 in terms of their appropriateness for a science of psychology. The *idiographic* and *nomothetic* approaches refer to two very different views as to what it is about people that psychologists should be studying, and the methods that should be adopted to study them. These two approaches correspond to the *social sciences/humanities* and *natural/physical sciences* respectively. This distinction is much less clear-cut than it was once thought to be; indeed, the view of natural science current at the time that Windelband originally made the distinction between the *Geisteswissenschaften* ('moral sciences') and the *Naturwissenschaften* ('natural sciences') is now considered by many scientists and philosophers to be outmoded. Ironically, psychologists may still be trying to model their discipline on a view of physics (in particular, and natural science in general) which physicists themselves no longer hold. More of this below.

Chapter 6 considers how feminist psychologists have exposed a major source of bias within both the research and theorizing of 'mainstream' academic psychology, as well as within the psychology profession itself. That bias is *androcentrism*, or male-centredness. From the perspective of classical, orthodox, mainstream scientific psychology, there are very powerful reasons for 'keeping quiet' about it, namely that science is meant to be *unbiased*, *objective* and *value-free*. This view of science is called *positivism*, something that feminist psychologists explicitly reject when they advocate a study of human beings, in which the researchers 'come clean' about their values.

Positivism is also involved in the attempts of clinical psychologists and psychiatrists to define, classify, diagnose and treat psychological disorders in an objective, value-free or value-neutral way (comparable to what goes on in general medicine; see Chapter 7). In other words, definitions of abnormality are influenced by a wide range of cultural beliefs, values, assumptions and experiences, but as long as practitioners remain unaware of their influence, they will perceive what they do as being objective. The belief that it is *possible* to be objective about psychological disorders reflects the positivist scientific training of clinical psychologists and psychiatrists.

The fact that the cultural (as well as the class, ethnic and gender) background of practitioners is usually different from that of the majority of their patients/clients, introduces a strong *ethnocentric* bias to the area of abnormal behaviour. This is often even more apparent when western psychologists travel to other cultures in order to study the behaviour and experience of members of those other cultures (see Chapter 8). While cross-cultural psychology can serve as an important counterbalance to the equation of 'human' with 'member of western culture', it is even more difficult (both theoretically and in practice) for a member of one culture to objectively study a person from another culture than it is when the researcher and the person being investigated share a common culture (although even here the differences may be greater than the similarities).

In Chapter 10 on ethics, reference is made to Orne's (1962) claim that every psychology experiment is a *social situation*. Whatever topic is being investigated or hypothesis tested, there is an interaction between two (or more) people who bring with them to the experimental situation a whole set of expectations, questions, and other cognitive processes (both conscious and unconscious) and behaviours, just as they do to other social situations. In other words, what is going on in the minds, and between the minds, of the people involved inevitably affects the outcome, making the experiment something less than a wholly objective situation. This is often contrasted with experiments in the natural sciences, which are interpreted according to the classical, positivist view of science in which objectivity plays such a crucial role. But this, in turn, is considered by many to be an oversimplification – indeed a misrepresentation – of what goes on even in the natural sciences (see below).

Chapter 14 considers some of the issues surrounding the study of paranormal ('unusual' or anomalistic) phenomena and experiences. These issues include some basic questions about the nature of science and the validity of using scientific methods to study human experience.

Finally, Chapter 15 considers major theoretical approaches within psychology. One of the major criteria used to assess these is how 'scientific' their methods (and the resulting theories) are. But this criterion is only applied by those who adopt a positivist approach, and both psychodynamic and social constructionist approaches show that there are different 'takes' on what science means. Importantly for parts of this chapter, social constructionists argue that not only is knowledge (including scientific knowledge) socially constructed, but science itself is a socially constructed, socially mediated activity. Theories about 'the world' are as much a reflection of the social nature of science as they are a reflection of the world itself.

A BRIEF SKETCH OF THE HISTORY OF SCIENCE

Many of the basic principles and assumptions of modern science, as well as some fundamental 'common sense' assumptions we make about the world, can be attributed to the French philosopher Descartes (1596–1650). He divided the universe into two fundamentally different realms, or 'realities': physical matter (*res extensa*) is extended in time and space; and non-material, non-extended mind (*res cogitans*), which isn't. This is known as *philosophical dualism*, and the opposed view that only matter exists is called *materialism*; both views (and others relating to the mind–body issue) are discussed in detail in Chapter 13.

Figure 11.1 René Descartes

This distinction between matter and mind allowed scientists to treat matter as inert and completely distinct from themselves, which meant that the world could be described objectively, without reference to the human observer. Objectivity became the ideal of science; Comte's extension of it (in the mid-1800s) to the study of human behaviour and social institutions became known as *positivism* (see below).

Descartes believed that the material world comprised objects assembled like a huge machine and operated by mechanical laws that could be explained in terms of the arrangements and movements of its parts. This view of the world is called *mechanism* ('machine-ism'). Descartes extended this mechanistic view of matter to living organisms. He compared animals to clocks composed of wheels and springs, and later extended this view to the human body, which he saw as a machine, part of a perfect cosmic machine, controlled, at least in principle, by mathematical laws. Descartes also believed that complex wholes may be understood in terms of their constituent parts, and so was one of the first advocates of *reductionism* (see below and Figure 11.3).

Figure 11.2 Describing the world objectively became easier with the invention of such instruments as the ruler of Ptolemy for measuring the distance from the ground to the zenith

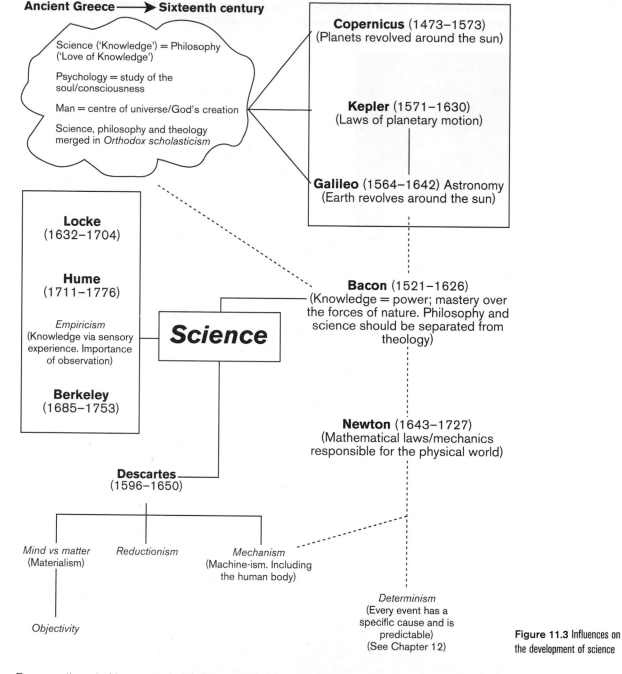

Figure 11.3 Influences on the development of science

Because the mind is non-material, it cannot be studied in the way that the physical world is studied; Descartes believed that the mind could only be approached by *introspection* – that is, looking inwards at one's own thoughts and ideas.

Newton later formulated the mathematical laws and mechanics that were thought to account for all the changes observable in the physical world. The mechanical model of the universe subsequently guided all scientific activity for the next 200 years. By the end of the nineteenth century, Nietzsche (1844–1900) captured the spirit of the age by declaring that 'God is dead', meaning that traditional religious values had been largely negated, replaced by science as the ultimate authority within western culture.

Science and empiricism

In addition to positivism, determinism, mechanism, materialism and reductionism, *empiricism* represented another fundamental feature of science (and a major influence on its development). This refers to the ideas of the seventeenth-century British *empiricist* philosophers – in particular, Locke, Hume and Berkeley. They believed that the only source of true knowledge about the world is *sensory experience* – that is, what comes to us through our senses or what can be inferred about the relationships between such sensory facts. This belief proved to be one of the central influences on the development of physics and chemistry.

The word 'empirical' is often used synonymously with 'scientific', implying that what scientists do is carry out experiments and observations as means of collecting data or 'facts' about the world. This, in turn, implies other very important assumptions about the nature of scientific activity and its relationship to the phenomena under investigation:

O an empirical approach is different from a *theoretical* one, since the latter doesn't involve the use of experiment, measurement and other forms of data collection

O philosophers, rather than scientists, use theory and rational argument (as opposed to data collection) to try to establish the truth about the world

O the truth about the world (the objective nature of the world – what it's 'really like') can be established through properly controlled experiments and other empirical methods. In other words, science can tell us about reality as it is *independently* of the scientist and of the activity of trying to observe it.

While the first point is true and non-controversial, the second and third points are much more the subject of debate among scientists and philosophers of science. Although the use of empirical methods is a defining feature of science and does distinguish it from philosophy, the use of theory is *also* crucial. This explains why many would reject the view of science as involving the discovery of 'facts' about the world, which are uninfluenced by the scientist's *theories*. These may be to do with what causes the phenomenon under investigation (corresponding perhaps to most people's understanding of what a 'scientific theory' is), but in a broader sense they also 'include' and reflect the biases, prejudices, values and assumptions of the individual scientist, as well as the scientific community in general to which s/he belongs. To the extent that such characteristics of the scientist influence the scientific process, it cannot be regarded as objective.

If this is true in the cases of physics and chemistry, it's even more likely to be true of Psychology (with a capital 'P'), where human beings are studying other human beings. Unconscious biases (such as androcentrism, sexism and ethnocentrism) come into play here, which is less likely to be true of the physicist or chemist investigating aspects of the physical world. But in Psychology's attempt to model itself on the natural sciences, people have been regarded and treated *as if* they were part of the natural world. The difficulties of using this approach are discussed later in the chapter.

An unbroken lineage: origin myth 1

Just as psychological concepts and categories are *culturally relative* (see Chapter 8), so they are *historically relative*. The notion of an 'unbroken lineage' reinforces the idea that Psychology has a history as long as any other science, with the Ancient Greek philosophers being seen as concerned with the same problems and issues as present-day psychologists (Jones and Elcock, 2001). People are praised or criticized according to how their ideas fit with modern conceptions of Psychology. But Jones and Elcock describe this as an 'origin myth'.

According to Danziger (1997), modern Psychology is deeply *ahistorical* – that is, it fails to see psychological categories and concepts from a historical perspective. Why? One reason is Psychology's wishful identification with natural science. As Danziger says:

Psychological research is supposed to be concerned with natural, not historical, objects, and its methods are considered to be those of natural science, not those of history. Psychology is committed to investigating processes like cognition, perception and motivation, as historically invariant phenomena of nature, not as historically determined social phenomena. Accordingly, it has strongly favoured the experimental approach of natural science and rejected the textual and archival methods of history . . .

Related to this is the implicit belief in scientific progress. As a scientific discipline develops, so knowledge accumulates and we move closer to 'the truth':

. . . the past simply consists of that which has been superseded. The main reason for bothering with it all [the historical course of science] is to celebrate progress, to congratulate ourselves for having arrived at the truth which the cleverest of our ancestors could only guess at.
(Danziger, 1997)

Implicit in this view is the assumption that psychological domains, such as 'intelligence', 'personality' and 'motivation', truly reflect the actual structure of a timeless human nature. So, even though pre-twentieth-century writers may not have organized their reflections around such topics, they are still presented as having had theories about them. If changes in such categories are recognized at all, it is their *present-day form* that is taken to define their true nature: older work is interesting only in so far as it 'anticipates' what we now know to be true. But as Danziger says:

The essence of psychological categories (insofar as they have one) lies in their status as historically constructed objects. There are no 'perennial problems' driving through the history of Psychology through the ages . . . At different times and in different places psychologically significant categories have been constructed and reconstructed in attempts to deal with different problems and to answer a variety of questions, many of them not essentially psychological at all . . .

Even the categories of physics are historical constructions, and so are subject to change.

Danziger (1997) examines how Aristotle, one of the Ancient Greek philosophers, used concepts such as 'psyche', which have become equated with 'mind' through translation from Greek into Latin, then into various modern languages. He concludes that:

Many of the fundamental categories of twentieth-century Psychology are, to all intents and purposes, twentieth-century inventions. Such concepts as 'intelligence', 'behaviour' and 'learning' were given such radically changed meanings by modern Psychology that there simply are no earlier equivalents.

In other cases, such as 'motivation' and 'social attitudes', use of the terms themselves is new, describing previously unsuspected phenomenological domains:

The coming of modern Psychology was associated with a revolutionary restructuring of the network of categories employed in the conceptualization of human experience and conduct.

But some, unquestionably psychological, categories were retained with little or no change in meaning from an earlier period, such as 'emotion', motive', 'consciousness' and 'self-esteem'. These examples point to an older layer of psychological concepts that predated the emergence of Psychology as a discipline. However:

The very notion of 'Psychology' does not exist before the eighteenth century. Of course, there was no lack of reflection about human experience and conduct, but to imagine that all such reflection was 'psychological' in our sense is to project the present on to the past. Before the eighteenth century there was no sense of a distinct and identifiable domain of natural phenomena that could be systematically known and characterized as 'psychological'. There were theological, philosophical, rhetorical, medical, aesthetic, political categories, but no psychological categories.

Danziger's analysis implies that psychological concepts and categories *don't* refer to 'natural kinds' – that is, 'groups of naturally occurring phenomena that inherently resemble each other and differ crucially from other phenomena'. In other words, they are *constructions*, used to make sense of observable behaviour. But while they may not refer to 'real', objectively existing phenomena, they nevertheless have the power to influence people's behaviour and experience (that is, their psychology). This unique feature of Psychology is discussed below.

SOME (OTHER) INFLUENCES ON THE DEVELOPMENT OF PSYCHOLOGY

Philosophy

Richards (2002) identifies a number of major philosophical theories, prior to 1850, which made significant contributions to the body of psychological concepts that psychologists had to work with. These include *associationism*, which is logically distinct from, but commonly linked with, empiricism (see above), and Scottish 'common sense' realism.

According to Locke (1690) and other British empiricists, all psychological phenomena originate in, and consist of, atom-like, 'corpuscular' sensations, which are built up into complex ideas through a few simple 'laws of associationism'. Although meant to explain how the mind operates, associationism was, ironically, first seized upon by Watson, the founder of behaviourism. The conditioned response represented the 'atom', or basic unit, from which all (learned) behaviour is ultimately derived, but mental processes should be removed from a scientific psychology altogether (see below). Scottish 'common sense' realism identified several innate 'powers' of the mind, but perhaps its more important contribution to

217

psychology was its *practical* orientation, including an interest in child development and social psychological phenomena (Richards, 2002).

Physiology

These philosophical theories weren't trying to account for psychological phenomena as we understand them today – that is, they *weren't* an early form of 'scientific' (or 'natural philosophical') psychology. For the beginnings of 'research', as we now use the term, we need to look to physiology (Richards, 2002). By the late 1700s, physiology was making serious progress in conceptualizing biological processes, and as it did so, various psychological issues took shape. These included a growing debate about brain functioning, with Gall's 'craniology' or 'phrenology' assuming great popularity as a 'scientific' approach to 'character' from about 1800 to the early 1850s (especially in Scotland, where it mapped onto 'common sense' realism's belief in innate mental powers).

Figure 11.4 A phrenology map of the brain

Richards believes that, in many ways, phrenology was a 'dry run' for psychology. Although traditionally dismissed as naïve pseudo-science, phrenology is now understood to have played a vital contextual role in popularizing the idea of a secular 'science of the mind', as well as pioneering the 'functionalist' approach (as reflected in the localization of brain function).

Other physiological discoveries that had important implications for psychology included:

○ the distinction between afferent and efferent nerves (1820s)

○ reflex action (1830s–1840s), which put the possibility of 'unconscious' (automatic) action clearly on the map, as well as the possibility of theorizing about the biological basis of learning

○ experimental study of the senses.

In the case of the latter, Weber, in the early 1800s, brought the experimental approach across from physiology to psychological issues, such as reaction times and sensory thresholds. This laid the foundation for the work of Fechner and Wundt in the 1850s, which is generally held to represent the birth of experimental psychology (see below). Richards believes that Fechner's (1966) *Elements of Psychophysics* marked the advent of experimental psychology. Psychophysics is the study of the relationship between sensory stimuli and people's experience of them.

From around 1800, such developments in physiology began to make increasing inroads into philosophy's academic monopoly on psychological issues. But both philosophy and physiology 'may be seen as Psychology's major roots' (Richards, 2002).

Evolutionary theory

According to Richards, something was needed to integrate these various developments, and this came in the form of evolutionary thought, triggered by Spencer and Darwin in the 1850s. Richards argues that: 'The role of evolutionary thought is absolutely crucial to the birth of modern Psychology and modern "psychology" too in fact.' Throughout Richards' account, he distinguishes between the academic discipline of 'Psychology' and what this discipline attempts to explain, namely people's behaviour and experience (their 'psychology'). This 'Big P'/'Little P' distinction (as made, in particular, in this chapter) is actually quite crucial in discussing the uniqueness of Psychology as a scientific discipline (see below).

Some key evolutionary ideas are summarized in Box 11.1 (see page 220).

THE DEVELOPMENT OF PSYCHOLOGY AS A SCIENCE: THE EARLY DAYS

The secularization of science and philosophy had profound implications for the western perspective on human beings. According to Graham (1986):

By the nineteenth century, thinking was essentially analytic, reductionist, objective and positivistic in the sense that it was held that the only valid knowledge is scientific knowledge or positive fact which is objectively verifiable . . .

The emergence of Psychology as a separate discipline, distinct from philosophy, clearly reflected this scientific 'mentality' or *Zeitgeist* ('spirit of the time'), but at first the *subject matter* was what it had traditionally been, namely 'non-material consciousness' (Graham, 1986).

University courses in scientific psychology were first taught in the 1870s, before which time there were no laboratories explicitly devoted to psychological research. According to Fancher (1979), the two professors who set up the first two laboratories deserve much of the credit for the development of academic psychology, namely Wilhelm Wundt (1832–1920) in Germany and William James (1842–1910) in the USA.

Wundt's contribution: founding father or origin myth 2?

In the light of physiology's influence on the development of Psychology, it is not too surprising to learn that Wundt was a physiologist. He (sometimes along with James, sometimes alone) is generally regarded as the 'founder' of the new science of experimental psychology. As he wrote in the 'Preface' to his *Principles of Physiological Psychology* (1974 [1874]), 'The work I here present to the public is an attempt to mark out a new domain of science' (in Fancher, 1979). In 1879, he converted his 'laboratory' at Leipzig University (in fact, a small, single room used as a demonstration laboratory, in a rather run-down old building) into a 'private institute' of experimental psychology. For the first time, a place had been set aside for the explicit purpose of studying psychology and conducting psychological

---

Box 11.1 Some key examples of evolutionary theory's ideas

○ Humans are descended from primates, and so can be considered *zoologically*. We aren't semi-divine or beyond the scope of scientific enquiry.

○ The raw material for natural selection is the occurrence in each generation of *random variations* ('spontaneous variation'). The 'gene' concept later clarified this, but the lack of genetic understanding handicapped evolutionary theory until the 1920s (see Chapter 5).

○ Each individual's development, from conception to maturity, repeats ('*recapitulates*') the evolutionary stages of the species ('ontogeny reflects phylogeny'). This is referred to as the 'biogenetic law'.

These ideas galvanized interest in 'human nature', which took various forms, including the following:

1 Investigating the evolution of 'mind': how far are human characteristics present in rudimentary form in 'lower' animals, and, conversely, how far have humans retained 'lower' traits? This led to the development of Comparative Psychology, one aspect of which was a fascination with *instincts* (see Chapter 15).

2 Focusing attention on the diversity of human 'stock' as raw material from which future generations would be 'naturally selected'. This underlay Galton's pioneer studies of *individual differences* and the development of statistical procedures for analysing them. Galton was also the founder of *eugenics* (see Chapter 5).

3 Studying children as a means of looking back in time and tracking the evolution of humankind. A good example is G. Stanley Hall's (1904) recapitulation theory of adolescence.

4 Understanding the structure of the brain in terms of older and newer components; the human brain has evolved by successive additions/modifications to those of lower organisms.

(Based on Richards, 2002)

---

research. Hence, 1879 is the year that is commonly cited as the 'birth date' of Psychology as a discipline in its own right. The institute soon began to attract people from all over the world, who returned to their own countries to establish laboratories modelled on Wundt's.

In his 'Preface' to *Contributions to the Theory of Sensory Perception* (1862), Wundt outlined the possibility of an experimental Psychology, whose aim would be to vary systematically the stimuli and conditions that produce differing mental states. It should be possible to manipulate and observe the facts of consciousness, just like those of physics, chemistry or physiology. In his *Principles of Physiological Psychology*, he argued that conscious mental states could be analysed by carefully controlled techniques of *introspection*. Introspection was a rigorous and highly disciplined technique designed to analyse conscious experience into elementary *sensations* and *feelings*. Participants were always advanced Psychology students who had been carefully trained to introspect properly. Wundt founded the journal *Philosophische Studien* ('Philosophical Studies'), which, despite its name, was the world's first to be primarily devoted to experimental Psychology. This indicated the popularity and success of the 'new psychology'.

Figure 11.5 In 1879, Wilhelm Wundt founded the first proper laboratory devoted to experimental Psychology.

Wundt believed, however, that introspection was only applicable to psychophysiological phenomena (sensations, reaction times, attention and other 'lower mental processes' – that is, immediate objects of conscious awareness). Memory, thinking, language, personality and social behaviour belong to the *Geisteswissenschaften* (social sciences), rather than the *Naturwissenschaften* (natural sciences). Specifically, he argued that human minds exist within human communities, so in order to study memory, thinking and other 'higher' mental processes, as well as cultural practices, one needs to study communities of people (*Volkerpsychologie*); introspection under controlled laboratory conditions isn't an option and can only be used to study the 'lower' mental processes.

By making these distinctions, Wundt was limiting the scope of scientific/experimental Psychology. But, according to Jones and Elcock (2001), the experiment and the laboratory are portrayed as being of paramount importance in Psychology's construction of itself as a natural science like physics and chemistry. Consequently, Wundt's advocacy of this approach for the study of certain psychophysiological processes has been inflated, creating an 'origin myth', a distorted account of how Psychology 'began'. As we have seen, there was a lot more to Wundt's picture of Psychology as a whole than the aspects the origin myth has focused on.

Even those American students who came to Leipzig to study under Wundt failed to establish his introspective methodology permanently back in their own country. Wundt has dominated English-speaking Psychologists' picture of late nineteenth-century psychological thought *without* good foundation (Richards, 2002). He left no lasting legacy, in terms of either theory or empirical discoveries, and although he helped to put experimental Psychology 'on the map', beyond that:

... his status appears to derive more from the symbolic significance he acquired for others than the success of his Psychology. The discipline *wanted* a founding father with good experimental scientific credentials, and his American ex-students naturally revered him as their most influential teacher even while subsequently abandoning most of what he taught them ...
(Richards, 2002)

The best-known criticism of Wundt's approach to scientific psychology came from Watson, the American founder of *behaviourism* (more of which below). But there were underlying cultural differences between Germany and America, which made it difficult for American psychologists to accept Wundt's work wholeheartedly. Wundt, as a representative of the German intellectual tradition that was interested in the mind *in general*, wanted to discover the universal characteristics of the mind that can account for the universal aspects of human experience. But Fancher (1979) argues that, by contrast:

Americans, with their pioneer tradition and historical emphasis on individuality, were more concerned with questions of *individual differences* . . . and the usefulness of those differences in the struggle for survival and success in a socially fluid atmosphere. These attitudes made Americans especially receptive to Darwin's ideas about individual variation, evolution by natural selection, and the 'survival of the fittest' when they appeared in the nineteenth century . . .

The contribution of James

James was 'perhaps the greatest writer and teacher psychology has ever had' (Fancher, 1979). He trained to be a doctor, never founded an institute for psychological research, and in fact did relatively little research himself. But he used his laboratory to enrich his classroom presentations, and his classic textbook, *The Principles of Psychology* (1890), was a tremendous popular success, making Psychology interesting and personally relevant. *The Principles* includes chapters on brain function, habit, the stream of consciousness (see Chapter 13), the self (see Chapter 4), attention, association, the perception of time, memory, perception, instinct, free will (see Chapter 12), and emotion (see Chapter 2). The book has given us the immortal definition 'Psychology is the science of mental life'.

After its publication, James became increasingly interested in philosophy, and thought of himself less and less as a psychologist. However, he was (in 1894) the first American to call favourable attention to the recent work of the then still rather obscure neurologist from Vienna, Sigmund Freud (Fancher, 1979). According to Fancher, James didn't propose a theory so much as a *point of view* (as much philosophical as psychological), which directly inspired *functionalism*. This was particularly popular with American psychologists. According to functionalism, ideas had to be meaningful to people's lives, and James emphasized the functions of consciousness over its contents. He believed in free will, but this conflicted with his belief in Psychology as a natural science (see Chapter 12). Functionalism, in turn, helped to stimulate interest in *individual differences*, since they determine how well or poorly individuals will adapt to their environments.

James's theory of emotion (see Chapter 2) proposed that behaviour (such as running away) produces changes in our conscious experience (such as the emotion of fear). This implied that consciousness might be less important to Psychology than had previously been thought. While this conflicted with James's belief in free will, it helped lead American Psychology away from a focus on mentalism and towards behaviour (Leahey, 2000).

Behaviourism: revolution or origin myth 3?

When John B. Watson first took over the psychology department at Johns Hopkins University in 1909, he continued to teach courses based on the work of Wundt and James, while conducting his own research on animals. But he became increasingly critical of the use of introspection. In particular, he argued that introspective reports were unreliable and difficult to verify. It is impossible to check the accuracy of such reports, because they are based on purely *private* experience, to which the investigator has no possible means of access. Surely this is no way for a *scientific* Psychology to proceed!

The only solution, as Watson saw it, was for psychology to redefine itself (see Box 11.2).

In 1915, Watson was elected president of the American Psychological Association (APA), and his presidential address dealt with his recent 'discovery' of Pavlov's work on conditioned reflexes in dogs. He proposed that the conditioned reflex could become the foundation of a full-scale *human* Psychology:

. . . encompassing everything from habit-formation to emotional disorders. Whereas his behaviourism had been at first little more than a point of view, it promised to become a full-fledged program of research with apparently limitless horizons. *(Fancher, 1979)*

Box 11.2 Watson's 'Behaviourist Manifesto'

In his 1913 article, 'Psychology as the behaviourist views it' (often referred to as the 'Behaviourist Manifesto'), Watson declared that:

Psychology as the behaviourist views it is a purely objective natural science. Its theoretical goal is the prediction and control of behaviour. Introspection forms no essential part of its methods, nor is the scientific value of its data dependent upon the readiness with which they lend themselves to interpretation in terms of consciousness. The behaviourist, in his efforts to get a unitary scheme of animal response, recognizes no dividing line between man and brute. The behaviour of a man, with all its refinement and complexity, forms only a part of the behaviourist's total scheme of investigation.

Three features of this 'behaviourist manifesto' deserve special mention.

1 Psychology must be purely objective, excluding all subjective data or interpretations in terms of conscious experience. Whereas traditional Psychology used objective observations of behaviour to *supplement* introspective data, Watson argued that these should be the *sole* and *exclusive* subject matter. He was redefining Psychology as the 'science of behaviour', instead of the traditional 'science of mental life'.

2 Whereas traditional Psychology aimed to *describe* and *explain* conscious mental states, Watson's goals were to *predict* and *control* overt behaviour, as they were for the other major behaviourist psychologist, B.F. Skinner (see Chapters 3, 10 and 12).

3 Watson wanted to remove the traditional distinction between human beings and non-human animals. If, as Darwin had shown, humans evolved from more simple species, then it follows that human behaviour is simply a more complex form of the behaviour of other species. In other words, the difference is merely *quantitative* (one of degree), rather than *qualitative* (one of kind; see Chapter 10). Consequently, rats, cats, dogs and pigeons became the major source of psychological data. Since 'psychological' now meant 'behaviour' rather than 'consciousness', animals that were convenient to study, and whose environments could easily be controlled, could replace people as experimental subjects.

Although Wundt had been influenced by empiricism through its impact on science as a whole (including physiology), it was behaviourism that was to embody empiricist philosophy within Psychology. The extreme environmentalism of Locke's empiricism (the mind at birth is a *tabula rasa*, or 'blank slate', on which experience makes its imprint) lent itself very well to the behaviourist emphasis on *learning* (through the process of conditioning). Despite rejecting the mind as valid subject matter for a scientific Psychology, what the environment shapes simply moves from 'the mind' to observable behaviour (see Chapters 5 and 15).

Behaviourism also embodied the positivism of the Cartesian–Newtonian tradition (Cartesian = from Descartes), in particular the emphasis on the need for scientific rigour and objectivity. Human beings were now being conceptualized and studied as 'natural phenomena', with their subjective experience, consciousness and other characteristics that had for so long been taken as distinctive human qualities being removed from the 'universe'. There was no place for these things in the behaviourist world.

But was Watson really, single-handedly, responsible for redefining/reinventing Psychology as the science of behaviour? According to Jones and Elcock (2001):

When behaviourism arose as an identified school of Psychology, the discipline had already adopted a behaviourist orientation. This shift was driven in part by a desire for application and by the wider social context . . .

There had been increasing acceptance of reflex theories derived from physiology, which was reinforced by Dewey's (1896) 'The reflex arc concept in Psychology'. He saw stimulus, sensation and response as coordinated behaviours that allowed the organism to adapt to the environment. Sensation was a form of behaviour that interacted with other concurrent behaviours. There was evidence of associations between incoming afferent (sensory) and outgoing efferent (motor) nerves without the intervention of consciousness. This suggested that consciousness was a mere *epiphenomenon* (see Chapter 13) with no causal powers. By 1905, functionalism had replaced introspectionism (Wundt's structuralism) as the dominant approach within American Psychology, which was now seen as allied to biology rather than philosophy. By 1911, Angell proposed that Psychology should be 'a general science of behaviour' (Jones and Elcock, 2001).

So, rather than a revolutionary break with the past, behaviourism is best regarded as the logical culmination of changes that had been taking place during the preceding 15–20 years. Historians of Psychology have exaggerated the shift to behaviour as a way of strengthening behaviourism's claims to validity. Its claimed dominance was both less complete and more gradual than usually presented. The claims based on the famous case of 'Little Albert' (Watson and Rayner, 1920) became exaggerated over time and added to behaviourism's origin myth (Jones and Elcock, 2001).

Despite challenges from both the psychometric (mental testing) approach and Gestalt Psychology during the 1920s, behaviourism did come to dominate experimental Psychology from the 1930s onwards. According to Jones and Elcock, this was due partly to Watson's attempts to persuade the public through magazines, popular books and radio broadcasts, and the introduction of Pavlov's work to the US audience (it wasn't translated into English until the mid-1920s). According to Danziger (1997), there were also more deep-rooted, 'political', and conceptual reasons for behaviourism's appeal.

The two categories of 'learning' and 'behaviour' came to establish the claim that there were phenomena of importance common to all fields of Psychology. Then these common phenomena could be studied in order to discover the principles that unified the discipline. Of the two, 'behaviour' was the more foundational: it became the category the discipline used to define its subject matter. As Danziger (1997) puts it:

> Whether one was trying to explain a child's answers on a problem-solving task, an adult's neurotic symptomatology, or a white rat's reaction to finding itself in a laboratory maze, one was ultimately trying to explain the same thing, namely, the behaviour of an organism. Classifying such diverse phenomena together as instances of 'behaviour' was the first necessary step in establishing the claim that Psychology was one science with one set of explanatory principles ...

'Learning' and 'behaviour' became almost inseparable for several decades, and the 'laws of learning' 'provided the core example of those behavioural principles that were supposed to unify the discipline'. But Danziger is at pains to distinguish between 'behaviour' and 'behaviourism'. The history of the *category* must not be confused with the history of the *movement*. Historically, behaviourists had no monopoly on the category of behaviour: it existed as a scientific category before they picked it up and 'nailed it to their masthead'; but 'One did not have to be a card-carrying member of one of the behaviourist schools to agree to the definition of Psychology as the science of behaviour.' Though influenced by behaviourism, most psychologists *didn't* identify themselves as behaviourists, and indeed rejected many of its specific claims (Danziger, 1997).

WHAT SHOULD THE SUBJECT MATTER OF PSYCHOLOGY BE?

The need to study the whole person

According to Ornstein (1975), in the process of refining its methods Psychology discarded its essence, namely consciousness. Fromm (1951, in Graham, 1986) argues that Psychology, in

> ... trying to imitate the natural sciences and laboratory methods of weighing and counting, dealt with everything except the soul. It tried to understand those aspects of man which can be examined in the laboratory, and claimed that conscience, value judgements, and knowledge of good and evil are metaphysical concepts, outside the problems of psychology; it was often more concerned with insignificant problems which fitted the alleged scientific method than with devising new methods to study the significant problems of man. Psychology thus became a science lacking its main subject matter, the soul.

According to Graham (1986), eastern psychology is rooted in the tradition of mysticism, with an emphasis on the spiritual, the subjective and the individual, and its dominant ethos is necessarily *humanistic*. By contrast, as we have seen, western psychology is rooted in the tradition of science, stressing the material, the objective and the general, and its predominant ethos (especially since the rise of behaviourism) is *mechanistic* and *impersonal*. Graham regards the fundamental difference between them as one of perspective: mystical *insight* (observing from within) and scientific *outlook* (observing from without). While traditional eastern psychologies fully recognize the double aspect of human existence – that is, the inner world of subjective experience, and the outer, public world of overt behaviour (an essential dualism) – western psychologists have failed to acknowledge these two fundamentally different realities. In order to gain acceptance as a science, it was seen as necessary to 'suppress the human face of psychology, thereby extinguishing its essence, and as Heather (1976) suggests, effectively murdering the man it claims to study ' (Graham, 1986).

Since scientific method is implicitly *reductionist* (from the Latin *reductio*, meaning to 'take away'), Psychology, in

... reducing the study of man to those of his aspects which are 'objective facts' – his physical behaviours – and precluding any examination of his experience, takes away from man what is essentially and fundamentally his humanness. Man is thereby reduced to a mere thing or object, from which, Heather (1976) suggests, it is but a small step to accepting the idea that man is a machine, and nothing but a machine.
(Graham, 1986)

The importance of free will

The popular definition of psychology as the study of 'what makes people tick' reflects this mechanistic view of the person, which derives from the nineteenth-century mechanistic view of the universe central to the physical sciences.

Figure 11.6 The term 'subject' reduces a person to something less than human; 'man as a machine'

To the extent that both Freud's psychoanalytic theory and behaviourism see people as being controlled by forces over which they have little or no control, they both depict people as machine-like. The person is pulled, in a puppet-like way, either by internal (unconscious) or external (environmental contingencies of reinforcement) 'strings'. In this way, both theories are *deterministic* (see Chapter 12). The debate regarding whether people have free will is crucial in trying to establish the appropriate subject matter of psychology. If we believe that people have personal agency and are responsible for their actions, that they are not mere passive responders to forces beyond their control (internal or external) but actively influence what they do and what happens to them, then a deterministic account (such as Freud's or Watson's) simply will not do. A mechanistic view of people, whether this is meant to be taken literally ('people *are* machines') or just metaphorically ('people are *like* machines'), reduces them to something less than human, and this is implied by the use of the term 'subject' (see Chapter 10).

Humanistic psychology

It was as a reaction against such a mechanistic, dehumanizing view of the person that *humanistic psychology* emerged, mainly in America, during the 1950s. In fact, the term was first coined by John Cohen, a British psychologist, who wrote a book called *Humanistic Psychology* in 1958, aimed at condemning 'ratomorphic robotic psychology' (Graham, 1986).

Abraham Maslow, in particular, gave wide currency to the term in America, calling it a 'third force' (the other two being behaviourism and psychoanalytic theory). However, he didn't reject these approaches, but hoped that his approach would act as a unifying force, integrating subjective and objective, the private and public aspects of the person, and providing a complete, *holistic* psychology. He insisted that a truly scientific Psychology must embrace a humanistic perspective, treating its subject matter *as fully human*. This meant:

○ acknowledging individuals as perceivers and interpreters of themselves and of their world, trying to understand the world from the perspective of the perceiver (a *phenomenological* approach), rather than trying to study people from the position of a detached observer; other psychologists whose ideas were influenced by phenomenology include Kelly (see Chapter 1) and Allport (see Chapter 3)

○ recognizing that people help determine their own behaviour, and are not simply slaves to environmental contingencies or to their past

○ regarding the self, soul or psyche, personal responsibility and agency, choice and free will, as legitimate issues for psychology.

Maslow's theory is commonly referred to as a 'psychology of being', while Carl Rogers' (the other key humanistic psychologist) theory is a 'psychology of becoming'. Although both saw human beings as possessing the need for *self-actualization* (a unique human characteristic), for Maslow this represented an end in itself, while for Rogers it was the *process* of becoming a 'fully functioning person' that was of major interest and importance. Rogers (1961) described self-actualization as: 'the mainspring of life ... It is the urge which is evident in all organic and human life – to expand, extend, become autonomous, develop, mature.'

Just as Maslow hoped to be able to bring behaviourism and Freudian theory together through his humanistic approach, so Rogers never rejected the rigour of empirical methods. Indeed, he used and advocated the use of empirical methods in the assessment of psychotherapy, in particular the *Q-sort* (see Chapter 3). But he did maintain that *experience* must be included in any attempt to understand man and the universe: there can be no scientific knowledge without experiential knowledge.

Similarly, Rollo May (1967) argued that humanistic psychology isn't hostile to science, although he urged that psychologists need to recognize the limits of traditional scientific methods, and that they should try to find new methods that will more adequately reveal the nature of man. Although not derived from a humanistic perspective as defined above, new methods for studying people are increasingly being used and developed that represent a significant move away from the traditional, mechanistic, laboratory-based methods that are seen as distorting our understanding of human beings. Some of this *new paradigm research* will be discussed later in the chapter.

THE SOCIAL NATURE OF SCIENTIFIC RESEARCH

Experimenters and participants are people first

A major criticism of traditional empirical methods, especially the laboratory experiment, has focused on the *artificiality* of the laboratory situation and the tasks that people are often asked to perform there in the name of science. The experimental set-up is so far removed from what people are likely to encounter in everyday situations, that their behaviour *inside* the laboratory is a very poor indicator of how they are likely to behave *outside*, in the real world. Since it is the real world we are interested in, experiments can tell us very little of any value. This relates to the *external validity* of experiments.

However, this criticism assumes that what happens in the experiment is valid *within the parameters of the laboratory situation*. In other words, the observed behaviour (the dependent variable) is affected by the experimental manipulation (the independent variable) *and nothing else* (a well-controlled, properly run experiment has *internal validity*). This assumption is necessary as part of the objectivity that is claimed for empirical research. The experimenter doesn't influence the participants' behaviour (the outcome of the experiment) except to the extent that s/he decides on what hypothesis/hypotheses to test, which variables to operationalize (and how to do this), which design to use, who the participants are to be (and how many), how to run the procedure, collate and interpret the results, and so on. But isn't this a very significant 'except'?

OBSERVING THE WORLD AS IT IS?

The whole situation is the creation of the experimenter and, to this extent, s/he cannot be considered to be objective within that situation. All kinds of biases, preferences, attitudes, beliefs, expectations, and so on, are reflected in the choices and decisions that go to create the experiment. If 'objectivity' requires that the researcher observe the world *as it is*, playing no part in what is studied and how it is studied, then clearly objectivity is a non-starter, whether it is in physics, chemistry or Psychology.

Is it *possible* for science to be a 'cool, passionless, absolutely objective exploration of an external reality' (Gould, 1987)? Since all scientists are people, and since science is a human activity, part of human behaviour (at least in western culture), the answer would seem to be 'No!' Gould argues that:

We scientists are no different from anyone else. We are passionate human beings, enmeshed in a web of personal and social circumstances . . . unless scientists understand their hopes and engage in vigorous self-scrutiny, they will not be able to sort unacknowledged preference from nature's weak and imperfect message . . .

In other words, the world *doesn't* reveal itself to us *as it is*; scientists have to discover ways of explaining the world that best enable them to predict and control it (at least in the case of the natural sciences). To do this most efficiently, they must be able to separate their biases and prejudices from the 'accuracy' of those explanations. Related to this is what Kitzinger (1987) calls the 'mythologizing of expertise'. Scientific expertise brings with it the power to define reality. Of all the accounting strategies open to scientists, it is the myth of the unbiased, neutral scientific expert that credits scientists with access to knowledge denied to ordinary mortals. She gives examples from research into homosexuality of how 'scientific' and 'lay' concepts have been related in a way that serves to reinforce the status of the scientist. 'Stereotypes often depict . . . but current research shows . . !' and 'It is a popular myth that . . . but the data indicate . . !'. The scientist clearly has access to 'the truth' through his/her expertise, which is denied to the lay person. This myth ignores the essentially *social* and *sociological* nature of scientific activity and knowledge (see below).

THE EXPERIMENTAL DRAMA

What makes the laboratory experiment such an unnatural and artificial situation is the fact that it is almost totally structured by one 'participant' (the experimenter). (See Chapter 10 for a discussion of the ethical implications of the *power* differences between the people involved in psychological research.)

As important as the assumption regarding the objectivity of the experimenter, is the assumed 'objectness' of the human 'subject', who is implicitly denied subjectivity, agency and intentionality (Graham, 1986). For the experimental situation to be considered an objective study of human behaviour, the person being studied must be thought of, and treated as, a passive responder to whatever stimuli are presented. The only factors that matter (that influence his/her responses) are the variables manipulated by the experimenter, and that are objectively defined (operationalized). This view of the person really does suggest that 'object' would be a more fitting term than 'subject'; it would be no more offensive and dehumanizing than 'subject' and a lot more descriptively accurate!

EXPERIMENTER BIAS AND THE SELF-FULFILLING PROPHECY

But is this a valid representation of the actors involved in the experimental drama? Might the experimenter be contributing something more to the situation than what has already gone into the planning and design of the experiment, things to do the fact that s/he is a human being, a social animal? And might the 'subject' be rather more actively involved, ultimately influencing the outcome of the experiment, contrary to his/her 'object-ness'?

According to Rosenthal (1966),

It appears indisputable that the humanness of both the experimenter and the subject interact in numerous ways which are likely to have a profound effect on experimental outcomes. The experimenter's appearance, sex, age, mood, manner, race, social class, dialect and dress are all likely to influence the subject so that instead of the experimenter being an external 'objective' observer, he is, in effect, a participant who actively contributes to the behaviour that he wishes passively and objectively to observe and record . . .

Rosenthal uses the word 'actively' to describe the way that various characteristics of the experimenter may affect the subject's behaviour, but those characteristics are essentially *static*, unchanging characteristics, over which s/he has little control (what the experimenter is *like*). However, such characteristics *are* correlated with the experimenter's *behaviour*, and will also influence the subject's perception of, and response to, the experimenter. (This is what 'actively' implies.) For example, Rosenthal (1967, in Valentine, 1992) described the pattern of behaviour that female experimenters show towards male subjects as 'interested modesty', while that shown by male experimenters towards female subjects was described as just plain 'interested'. They took significantly longer to prepare stimulus materials for presentation to female subjects than to males. Sex differences reveal themselves in a wide range of non-verbal behaviours.

Perhaps of even greater significance is the way that the experimenter's expectations can influence the outcome of the experiment, serving as a *self-fulfilling prophecy*. This is referred to as *experimenter bias*. Such effects have been demonstrated in a wide range of experiments, including reaction time, psychophysics, verbal conditioning, personality assessment, person perception, learning and ability, involving both humans and rats

(Rosenthal and Rubin, in Valentine, 1992). What they consistently show is that, if one group of experimenters is testing one hypothesis, and another group tests the opposite hypothesis, both groups will obtain results in line with their respective hypotheses. These results are *not* due to the mishandling of data by biased experimenters, but, somehow, the bias of the experimenter *creates a changed environment in which subjects actually behave differently*. Perhaps the most famous demonstration of such bias involving humans is the 'Pygmalion' experiment by Rosenthal and Jacobson, 1966 (written up in book form as *Pygmalion in the Classroom*, 1968; see Box 11.3).

Box 11.3 Rosenthal and Jacobson's (1968) 'Pygmalion' experiment

In a natural classroom situation, children whose teachers were told that they would show academic 'promise' during the next academic year showed significantly greater gains in IQ than children for whom such predictions weren't made (although this group also showed substantial improvements). The children were, in fact, *randomly allocated* to the 'academic promise' and the control (no such prediction) conditions. The teachers' expectations of gains in the first group actually produced the predicted improvements, demonstrating a *self-fulfilling prophecy*.

As to the mechanism, it is likely that the children who were expected to excel received more attention, encouragement, praise, and so on, than those who weren't. This, in turn, affected their self-concept and motivation in a positive way, reflected in the actual gains in IQ.

DEMAND CHARACTERISTICS

A way of trying to understand what the subject contributes to the experiment is through the concept of *demand characteristics* (Orne, 1962). Whereas the mechanistic model stresses what is *done to* the (passive) subject, Orne is interested in what the human subject/participant *does*, which implies a far more *active* role. Participants' performance in an experiment could almost be thought of as a form of *problem-solving behaviour* since, at some level, they try to work out the true purpose of the experiment and to respond in a way that will support the hypothesis being tested. In this context, the totality of *cues* that convey an experimental hypothesis to the participant become significant influences on his/her behaviour. It is the sum total of these cues that Orne calls the *demand characteristics of the experimental situation*.

These cues include:

... the rumours or campus scuttlebut [gossip] about the research, the information conveyed during the original situation, the person of the experimenter, and the setting of the laboratory, as well as all explicit and implicit communications during the experiment proper.
(Orne, 1962)

Orne goes on to point out that the experimental procedure itself may provide cues. For example, if a task is presented twice, with some intervening task (in other words, a repeated measures design), then even the dullest college student will realize that some change in performance is expected on the second task compared with the first.

It is very difficult in practice to find truly naïve participants who don't believe they have at least some familiarity with Psychology, or who cannot work out the purpose of the experiment from the procedure. The crucial point is not whether participants are correct in their attempts to 'suss out' what is going on, but the mere fact that such an attempt is being made at all. It means that participants *aren't* the passive responders implied by the mechanistic model.

This tendency to identify the demand characteristics is related to the tendency to play the role of 'a good experimental subject', wanting to please and cooperate with the experimenter, and not to 'upset the experiment'. It is mainly in this sense that Orne sees the experiment as a *social situation*, in which the participants (experimenter and subject) play different, but complementary, roles; for the interaction to proceed relatively smoothly, each participant must have some idea of what the other(s) expect of him/her.

THE CULTURAL NATURE OF EXPERIMENTS

The experiment is a rather special type of social situation, with its own rules and norms (some explicit, some implicit). As Moghaddam *et al.* (1993) point out, when we agree to participate in a laboratory experiment, we are not entering a cultural vacuum. We have a host of ideas and expectations about what an experiment is, the role and nature of psychologists, science, and so on. What makes an experiment 'possible' is a set of shared understandings as to the nature of science, and the respective roles of investigator and 'subject'. This, in turn, detracts from science's claim to complete objectivity: *science itself is a culture-related phenomenon*.

THE SOCIOLOGY OF SCIENTIFIC KNOWLEDGE

The sociology of scientific knowledge (SSK) focuses on the practices that help construct scientific knowledge. While it has been aimed mainly at physics and biology, Danziger (e.g. 1990, 1997), Richards (e.g. 2002) and others have applied it to Psychology. As with feminism (see Chapter 6), SSK has influenced both how science is understood, and how some researchers within Psychology work (Jones and Elcock, 2001). Edwards (1997) and Potter (1996) use SSK within their social constructionist approaches (see below and Chapter 15).

According to Danziger (1997):

A scientific fact is always a fact under some description. The discursive framework within which factual description takes place is as much a part of science as its hardware and its techniques of measurement. To be effective, such a framework must be shared ... Any reference to the 'facts of the world' has to rely on some discursive framework in use among a particular group of people at a particular time. Facts are there to be displayed, but they can only be displayed within a certain discursive structure ...

Strictly speaking, there are no 'raw data' in science: by the time measurements and observations are made and recorded, an enormous amount of selection, classification, prediction and so on have already taken place. Consistent with what we have said above about experimenter bias and demand characteristics, Danziger (1990) claims that

... neither experimenters nor their subjects enter the investigative situation as social blanks to be programmed in an arbitrary manner. Both are the products of a distinctive historical development that has left a heavy sediment of blind faith and unquestioned tradition . . .

Experimenters' expectations and participants' search for demand characteristics operate within a particular social framework that has to be taken for granted in such studies. The framework is provided by the traditions and conventions of psychological experimentation, which, over time, are now well understood by all experimenters and most participants:

In those societies in which it is practiced on any scale, the psychological experiment has become a social institution recognized by most people with a certain level of education. As in all social institutions the interaction of the participants is constrained by institutional patterns that prescribe what is expected and permitted for each participant . . .
(Danziger, 1990)

If the experiment is to be 'successful', everyone must follow the same 'rules'. Hardly more than a hundred years ago, the institution of the psychological experiment was as unknown everywhere as it might be now in parts of the 'Third World' (see Moghaddam *et al.*'s point above about the cultural nature of experiments). Ultimately, the experiment is part of the history of those societies that produced it (Danziger, 1990).

Figure 11.7 The social contexts of investigative practice (based on Danziger, 1990)

THE UNIQUENESS OF PSYCHOLOGY

According to Jones and Elcock (2001), studying Psychology as a social activity has one 'reflexive twist' that isn't involved in the case of other sciences. This is to do with how 'Psychology' affects 'psychology'.

According to Richards (2002), the boundaries between the history of science, the philosophy of science, and the sociology of knowledge have become blurred, partly because they have acquired an increasingly 'psychological' character. Understanding 'scientific behaviour' raises issues of *perception* (e.g. how one makes sense of what one is seeing when it has not been seen before), *cognition* (e.g. how scientists really create their theories and decide what their results mean), *personality* (e.g. what motivates scientists to devote their lives to a particular topic), *communication* (e.g. how scientists succeed or fail in getting their work accepted as valid, and how controversies are resolved), and *group dynamics* (e.g. how scientific disciplines are organized and managed). Richards believes this puts Psychology itself in a rather odd position relative to other sciences, because 'as the science of human behaviour, its subject matter logically includes scientific behaviour'.

Compared with the natural sciences, Psychology is in a quite ambiguous position, since 'while trying to operate as a normal science, it is also on the outside looking in'. Looking at science as a product or expression of specific social contexts has been developed into a way of looking at human behaviour and ideas in general, and this has merged into *social constructionism* (see Chapter 15). According to Richards:

... psychology itself must be one of the routes by which this process of 'social construction' operates. The history of Psychology thereby becomes one aspect of the history of its own subject-matter, 'psychology'. The historian of Psychology is not only looking at the history of a particular discipline, but also at the history of what that discipline purports to be studying. Whereas in orthodox sciences there is always some external object of enquiry – rocks, electrons, DNA, stars – existing essentially unchanging in the non-human world (even if never finally knowable 'as it really is' beyond human conceptions), this is not so for Psychology. 'Doing Psychology' is the human activity of studying human activity, it is human psychology examining itself – and what it produces by way of new theories, ideas and beliefs about itself is also part of our psychology ...

Richards is describing the 'reflexivity' or self-referring relationship that is unique to Psychology as a (scientific) discipline. The discipline of Psychology actually contributes to the dynamic psychological processes by which human nature constantly 'recreates, re-forms, and regenerates itself, primarily in western cultures'. Again, 'Psychology is produced by, produces, and is an instance of its own subject-matter.'

Language and the nature of psychological kinds

Changes in psychological terminology signify psychological changes in their own right. In one sense, what we are studying is quite literally language: it is only in this form that previous accounts of psychological phenomena are available. In discussing science in general, Danziger (1997) makes a similar point when he says that the most basic instrument of scientific investigation is language. The entire investigative process is so immersed in language that it is simply taken for granted, and its role becomes invisible. But if this is true of science in general, in the case of Psychology it becomes absolutely critical.

According to Danziger, the notion of 'natural kinds' may be peculiarly inappropriate for Psychology:

If we change our identification of a chemical compound as a result of advances in techniques of analysis, this changes our knowledge of the compound but the compound itself remains the same compound it always was. But the objects represented in psychological language are generally not like that. A person who learns not to think of his or her actions as greedy or avaricious but as motivated by a need for achievement or self-realization has changed as a person ... The sorts of things that Psychology takes as its objects, people's actions, experiences and dispositions, are not independent of their categorization.

Identifying actions, dispositions and so on isn't like sticking labels on fully formed specimens in a museum. So many psychological categories have a taken-for-granted quality about them because the labels we use *appear* to describe something 'essential' – that is, 'emotions', 'motives', 'cognitions' look as though they are really distinct in some objective, fundamental way. But they only seem 'natural' to members of that particular linguistic community. This sense of natural mustn't be confused with the concept of 'natural kinds'. For Danziger (1997), 'Natural kinds have nothing to do with culture, whereas the natural-appearing kinds of Psychology have everything to do with it.' Similarly, Richards (2002) argues that, 'To classify and explain the psychological in a new way is to be involved in changing the psychological itself. To think about oneself differently is to change oneself.' Richards doesn't believe in some independent psychological 'reality' beyond the language used to describe it more or less 'accurately'. This doesn't mean that language is all there is, but 'Psychological language is itself a psychological phenomenon – a psychological technique for both talking about other psychological phenomena *and* for giving them form and meaning.'

One implication of this view is that nobody prior to Freud had an Oedipus complex, and nobody before Pavlov or Watson was ever classically conditioned. If we disagree with this conclusion it is because (in Danziger's terms) we are confusing natural kinds with natural-appearing kinds. However similar to such phenomena previous ones appear to be in retrospect, 'they were not terms in which the psychology of people prior to their introduction was actually structured. They had no psychological reality' (Richards, 2002).

The very act of introducing such concepts provided people with new terms in which to experience themselves; only *then* can they properly be said to refer to really occurring psychological phenomena. The same holds true for much of everyday psychological language ('folk psychology'): nobody 'went off the rails' before the advent of railways, and people who agreed with each other weren't 'on the same wavelength' before radios were invented (Richards, 2002).

A SHIFT TOWARDS STUDYING PEOPLE AS PEOPLE

The various criticisms of the positivist, mechanistic, behaviourist-dominated scientific Psychology began to be drawn together during the late 1960s, culminating in Harré and Secord's (1972) *The Explanation of Social Behaviour*. This book is widely seen as marking the beginning of a 'new paradigm' in Psychology (Harré, 1993). Harré and Secord called their new approach *ethogenics*, partly to indicate the break from experimentation they were advocating, but also to acknowledge the importance of context and convention in everyday life. They had been particularly influenced by Garfinkel's (1967) *Ethnomethodology* and Goffman's *dramaturgical* analysis of social interaction (in books such as *Stigma*, 1963, and *The Presentation of Self in Everyday Life*, 1971). Both Garfinkel and Goffman had developed methodologies that were appropriate to the nature of the phenomenon they were studying, namely human beings.

New paradigm research

New paradigm research (NPR; Reason and Rowan, 1981) refers to the attempt to integrate naïve enquiry (the kind of ordinary day-to-day thinking that everyone engages in; see

Chapter 1) and orthodox research, making it 'objectively subjective'. It openly opposes the positivist, deterministic, reductionist, mechanistic approach (which they call 'quantophrenia'), which typically produces statistically significant but humanly insignificant results. They insist that in the field of human enquiry, it is preferable to be deeply interesting than accurately boring. They oppose deception and debriefing, manipulation and mystification. But at the same time they advocate that certain aspects of conventional methods and procedures, in particular certain aspects of report-writing, be expanded and developed. For example, the 'Introduction' and 'Discussion' sections should be written with as much care and attention as is usually given to the main part of the investigation ('Procedure' and 'Results'), involving literature searches within sociology, the natural sciences, literature, philosophy, theology and history. They should become part of the research process itself, so that research reports become:

... a statement of where the researchers stand, not only theoretically, but politically, ideologically, spiritually and emotionally in as much that they discuss the many influences which have shaped the thinking and feeling which has led to the current investigation.
(Graham, 1986)

Another new direction taken by NPR is *collaborative/participative* research, or *cooperative enquiry*, in which both the researcher and the participant actively contribute to the planning, execution and interpretation of the research. According to Heron (1982, in Graham, 1986):

The way of co-operative enquiry is for the researcher to interact with the subjects so that they do contribute directly both to hypothesis making, to formulating the final conclusions, and to what goes on in between. This contribution may be strong, in the sense that the subject is co-researcher and *contributes* to creative thinking at all stages. Or it may be weak, in the sense that the subject is thoroughly *informed* of the research proposals at all stages and is invited to assent or dissent, and if there is dissent, then the researcher and subject negotiate until agreement is reached. In the complete form of this approach, not only will the subject be fully fledged co-researcher, but the researcher will also be co-subject, participating fully in the action and experience to be researched. (The continued use of 'subject' seems totally incompatible with the approach being advocated, with 'participant' being the obvious alternative.)

Another major innovation within NPR is *discourse analysis* (DA; see Box 11.4, page 236).

According to Edwards and Potter (1992), DA extends beyond a specific method into a fairly radical rethink about traditional psychological topics, which they call *discursive psychology* (DP; see Chapter 15). So, memory and attribution theory are treated as processes of *discourse* between people: memories are *not* close or not-so-close attempts at recalling 'the facts', but are motivated constructions by people with a 'stake' in producing an 'account' that may, for example, suit their defence against blame and accountability (Coolican, 1994). We cannot simply take what people *say* as revealing what they *think*, as if their talk provided a window through which we could peer at their cognitive processes: we must first understand what their talk is trying to *do*, what it is trying to achieve in a particular social context, at a particular time.

Box 11.4 Discourse analysis (DA)

DA brings together a wide variety of perspectives and influences, from philosophy, linguistics, artificial intelligence, anthropology and sociology (as well as various aspects of Psychology). Some of its main features include the following:

1 'Talk' (both conversation between people and written language) is worthy of study *in its own right*, and as a way in which people (attempt to) achieve their goals. This contrasts sharply with the traditional view of language as an index of external reality or of a person's inner states.

2 The prime source of data in DA is conversation, either in natural settings or in interviews, but the emphasis is very different from that of traditional social psychological methods; for example, instead of treating what people say in interviews as acceptable *substitutes* for actual observation of behaviour, it is the interview data *itself* that is of interest (the 'subject matter').

3 DA also avoids hypothesis testing and the use of pre-defined coding schedules (as is usual in observational studies). In this sense, it is mainly *inductive* (as opposed to hypothetico-deductive) and *data-driven* (as opposed to theory-driven).

4 One use of DA is in the scrutiny of psychological theories (such as Freud's, Skinner's, and Piaget's) in order to show how they use language to create a convincing theoretical account of human behaviour. One 'strategy' is to use *metaphors* in such a way that they are taken *literally*, apparently referring to the 'external reality' of behaviour that the theory is trying to account for. (See Soyland's (1994) *Psychology As Metaphor*.)

5 In everyday life, as well as in putting forward psychological theories and politics, we are often trying to get our account/version of the truth accepted by others as 'fact' or '*the* truth'. This is one sense in which language is seen primarily as a form of *social action* (rather than primarily a *representation* of reality, including what people *really* think about the issue being discussed).

(Based on Lalljee and Widdicombe, 1989)

THE CHANGING FACE OF SCIENCE

In his 1983 Presidential Address to the British Psychological Association, Hetherington (cited by Graham, 1986) stressed the need for a paradigm shift in Psychology and the development of its own methods. The methods of natural science can at best only provide a partial knowledge of why people behave as they do, and since Psychology is part natural science and part interpretative science, it needs to develop methods that are adequate for the study of human beings as organisms, as members of social organizations, and as people with whom we engage in dialogue.

Hetherington cited James's (1890) observation that 'the natural science assumptions are provisional and revisable things'. In other words, scientific 'facts' are not 'set in stone' but are constantly being changed, not because the world changes but because our theories and explanations change.

As we have seen, new methods of studying people are being developed, and no doubt Hetherington would approve of these developments. However, the great irony about this new paradigm, is that what it is replacing (or partially replacing, since most psychologists still subscribe to the positivist methodology) may itself have been out of date for some time. The natural science on which Watson so explicitly and vigorously based Psychology (originally in 1913) is in many ways *not* the natural science of the present day (or even of the recent past).

A number of physicists and other scientists, philosophers of science and other academics (beginning probably with Einstein's 1905 theory of relativity) are moving away from the Cartesian–Newtonian view of a clockwork universe, which is completely predictable and determinate, towards a view of the universe as much more uncertain and unpredictable. A major 'ingredient' in this 'new physics' is Heisenberg's *Uncertainty Principle*. According to this, there are limits beyond which there can be no certainty, not because of the lack of precision in our measuring instruments or the extremely small size of the entities being measured – but by nature itself. More specifically, all attempts to observe sub-atomic particles, such as electrons, *alter* them; at the sub-atomic level, we cannot observe something without changing it, because the universe doesn't exist independently of the observer trying to measure it.

If most psychologists are still trying to model themselves on a physics based on Descartes and Newton, then they are out of date and out of touch, and if they want their science to reveal what people are 'really like', in some absolute, objective, way, they are also out of luck.

SUMMARY

O Mainstream, academic psychology has been very strongly influenced by the classical, *positivist*, view of science, according to which science is meant to be *unbiased*, *objective* and *value-free*. This can also be seen in the practice of psychiatry and clinical psychology.

O Ironically, while psychology has always modelled itself on 'classical physics', physics itself no longer adopts a 'classical' view of science.

O Descartes divided the universe into *res extensa* (physical matter) and *res cogitans* (non-physical mind). This is *philosophical dualism*. Dualism allowed scientists to describe the physical world objectively, without reference to the human observer.

O Descartes also introduced *mechanism* into science and extended this view of matter to living organisms, including the human body. He was also one of the first people to advocate *reductionism*.

O As applied to the study of human behaviour/social institutions, objectivity came to be called *positivism* (Comte). Another fundamental feature of science is *empiricism*, which claims to be able to tell us about reality independently of scientific activity.

O Psychological concepts are both culturally and historically *relative*. Many current psychological concepts/processes are *historically constructed social phenomena*, rather than part of a timeless human nature. The notion of 'Psychology' itself didn't exist before the eighteenth century.

O Philosophy, physiology, and evolutionary theory were the major influences on Psychology's emergence as a separate discipline. Physiology contributed experimental research methods, as well as the discovery of biological processes that helped shape various psychological issues.

O Wundt is traditionally regarded as Psychology's founding father. But he advocated the use of introspection under controlled conditions only for the investigation of psychophysiological phenomena ('lower mental processes'). 'Higher mental processes', including social and cultural behaviour, required different methods. His place in the history of Psychology seems to be an origin myth.

O While Wundt was interested in *universal* aspects of the mind, American psychologists were influenced by Darwin's theory of evolution and James's theory of *functionalism*, which helped to stimulate interest in *individual differences*.

O Watson rejected introspectionism on the grounds that it is based on purely *private* experience. To be an objective, natural science, Psychology must replace consciousness with *behaviour* as its subject matter. *Behaviourism* combined the extreme environmentalism of Locke's *empiricism* and the *positivist* emphasis on objectivity.

O The idea that Watson was responsible for the 'behaviourist revolution' represents another origin myth. The concept of 'behaviour' had been used by psychologists long before Watson's 'behaviourist manifesto'. Though most psychologists were influenced by behaviourism, they didn't identify themselves as such.

O Traditional psychologies of the East recognize the double aspect of human existence: the inner world of subjective experience/the outer world of overt behaviour. But western psychologists, by excluding the former, reduce 'man' to a mere thing/object/machine.

O Humanistic psychology emerged as a reaction against the mechanistic, dehumanizing image of the person that was contained in both behaviourism *and* Freud's psychoanalytic theory. Both Maslow and Rogers advocated a *phenomenological* approach, and believed in the fundamental human need for *self-actualization*.

O Humanistic psychologists don't reject science, but urge that there can be no scientific knowledge without experiential knowledge, and that appropriate methods must be found to study people as they are.

O Even if laboratory experiments lack *external validity*, they are still seen as having *internal validity*; this assumption is necessary if empirical research is to be considered *objective*. But the world *doesn't* reveal itself to us *as it is*.

O Both the experimenter and the 'subject'/'object' contribute much more to the outcome of the experiment than is compatible with the positivist account of scientific research. Examples of the social dimension of psychological experiments include *experimenter bias*, which can produce a *self-fulfilling prophecy*, and *demand characteristics*.

O There also needs to be a shared understanding of what 'science' is for an experiment to be possible, making science itself a *culture-related* phenomenon. The psychological experiment has become a social institution in many western countries, so it is also *history-related*.

O Psychology is unique among the sciences, because the study of scientific activity is part of its subject matter. It is also unique because changes in Psychology the discipline affect psychology the subject matter. This refers to Psychology's *reflexivity*.

O Psychological concepts and categories *aren't* 'natural kinds', as is the case in the natural sciences. But they often *appear* to be describing something that has an objective, independent, existence.

O Criticisms of the positivist approach in psychology culminated in Harré and Secord's *ethogenics*, which marked a new paradigm. *New paradigm research* (NPR) attempts to integrate 'everyday psychology' and orthodox research.

O Reason and Rowan advocate that research reports make clear the researcher's theoretical/political/other values, and how these have shaped the current investigation.

O *Collaborative/participative research/co-operative enquiry* involves both the researcher and the participant actively contributing to the planning/execution/interpretation of the research.

O *Discourse analysis* (DA) sees the study of conversation/written language as important *in its own right*. Edwards and Potter have extended DA from a method, to a new way of thinking about traditional topics – *discursive psychology* (DP) – which sees language as a form of *social action*.

O Ironically, the positivist view of science, which the new paradigm is (partially) replacing, may itself have been out of date for some time. Physicists now believe that the world cannot be studied objectively, independently of attempts to measure it.

Useful websites

O www.yorku.ca/dept/psych/orgs/apa26/apadiv26.htm
O http://psychology.dur.ac.uk/eshhs
O www.salve.edu/~walsch/psych.history.html
O www.chss.montclair.edu/psychology/museum/museum.html
O www.chelt.ac.uk/ess/sess/hps
O www.staffs.ac.uk/schools/divisions/psychology/chop.html
O http://elvers.stjoe.udayton.edu/history/people/Wundt.html

Recommended reading

Danziger, K. (1990) *Constructing the Subject: Historical Origins of Psychological Research*. New York: Cambridge University Press.

Danziger, K. (1997) *Naming the Mind: How Psychology Found its Language* (especially Chapters 1–4, 6 and 9–10). London: Sage.

Deese, J. (1972) *Psychology as Science and Art*. New York: Harcourt Brace Jovanovich.

Fancher, R.E. (1996) *Pioneers of Psychology* (3rd edn). New York: Norton.

Gough, B. and McFadden, M. (2001) *Critical Social Psychology: An Introduction*. Basingstoke: Palgrave.

Jones, D. and Elcock, J. (2001) *History and Theories of Psychology: A Critical Perspective*. London: Arnold.

Rosnow, R.L. and Rosenthal, R. (1997) *People Studying People: Artifacts and Ethics in Behavioural Research*. New York: W.H. Freeman & Co.

Richards, G. (2002) *Putting Psychology in its Place: A Critical Historical Overview* (2nd edn) (especially Chapters 1–5 and 7). Hove: Routledge.

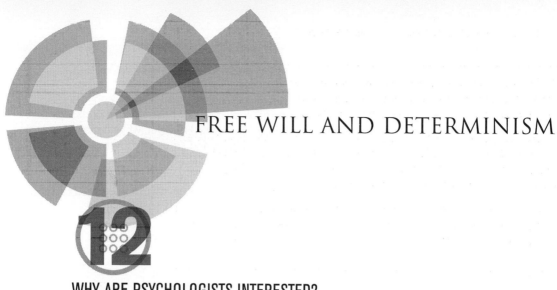

FREE WILL AND DETERMINISM

WHY ARE PSYCHOLOGISTS INTERESTED?

Historical reasons

The debate about free will and determinism has been a central feature of western philosophy, at least since Descartes (1596–1650; see Chapter 11). Given psychology's intellectual and historical roots in philosophy, it would be very surprising if psychologists weren't interested in the issue for this reason alone.

To understand the causes of behaviour

As Chapter 11 shows, identifying the *causes* of phenomena, as part of the attempt to explain them, is a fundamental part of 'classical' science. According to the philosophical doctrine of *determinism*,

> . . . in the case of everything that exists, there are antecedent conditions, known or unknown, given which that thing could not be other than it is . . . More loosely, it says that everything, including every cause, is the effect of some cause or causes; or that everything is not only determinate but causally determined . . . if true, it holds not only for all things that have existed but for all things that do or ever will exist.
> *(Taylor, 1963)*

'Everything that exists' includes people and their thoughts and behaviour, so a 'strict' determinist believes that thought and behaviour are caused no differently from (other) 'things' or events in the world. But this, of course, begs the question 'Are thoughts and behaviour the same *kind of thing or event* as chemical reactions in a test tube, a volcanic eruption, or the firing of neurons in the brain?' We don't usually ask ourselves if the chemicals 'agreed' to combine in a certain way, or if the volcano just 'felt like' erupting, or if the neurons 'decided' to fire. To do so (assuming we weren't being witty or in some other way not wanting to be taken literally) would involve us in the 'sin' of *anthropomorphizing* – that is, attributing human abilities and characteristics to non-human things (including animals). No one *seriously* believes that chemicals can agree, or that volcanoes have feelings, or that neurons can make decisions. But we *do* attribute these abilities to people, they are part of our *concept of a person*, and this concept forms an essential part of 'everyday' or common-sense psychology (see Chapter 1).

For these reasons, psychologists who study the attribution process, for example (see Chapter 2), must take seriously the common-sense view that people make decisions, agree (or not) with each other, and, in a whole host of ways, exercise their *free will*. And having free will depends upon having 'a mind': deciding, agreeing and so on are precisely the kinds of things we do with our minds; they are mental processes or events. However, while it may be *necessary* to 'have a mind' in order to be able to decide, agree, and so on (free will implies having a mind), having a mind *doesn't* imply free will: our decisions, agreements/disagreements, and so on, may be *caused* (determined) even though they don't seem to be. These kinds of observations lead us directly into the realm of philosophy, where the arguments become extremely complex, abstract and technical. We shall try to keep to more psychological paths.

To investigate the influence of mental events on behaviour

Even if we accept that human thinking and behaviour are different from natural, physical phenomena, and that they are not determined (caused) in the same way (or that a different kind of explanation is required), for most of its history as a separate discipline, psychology has operated *as if* there were *no difference*. Since 1913, anyway, when Watson launched the behaviourist 'movement', psychologists have been trying to emulate the natural sciences, and the most obvious form this has taken has been the use of empirical methods, in particular the laboratory experiment. The use of such methods to study people *implicitly* adopts a view of human behaviour as determined, and is closely related to the positivist and mechanistic nature of experimental research (see Chapter 11). But does this mean that all, or most psychologists, are behaviourists?

In one important sense, the answer is 'yes'. *Methodological behaviourism* refers to the belief in the importance of empirical methods, especially the experiment, as a way of collecting data about human thought and behaviour which can be quantified and statistically analysed. Most psychologists today would probably describe themselves as behaviourists in this sense.

However, most psychologists since the late 1950s, would deny that they are behaviourists in the other important sense, namely *philosophical behaviourism*. In its most extreme form, as represented by Watson, the very existence of mind is denied; thinking, for example, is nothing but a series of vocal or sub-vocal and verbal responses (i.e. 'mind' is *reduced* to behaviour). As we saw above, if you reject the mind, you consequently reject free will too: without a mind, there can be no deciding, choosing, and so on (see Chapters 11 and 15).

A less extreme view is adopted by Skinner. Despite his extreme environmentalism, and calling his approach *radical behaviourism*, Skinner *doesn't* deny the existence of mental processes. What he denies is the common-sense explanation of the role of mental events in relation to behaviour (see Chapter 15). For Skinner, they are *irrelevant* in trying to predict and control behaviour; they are mere *epiphenomena*, 'by-products' of behaviour, totally lacking any influence over behaviour. This is one attempt to solve the 'mind–body' (or 'mind–brain') problem (see Chapter 13). The important point here is that, along with his denial of the influence of mental events over behaviour, Skinner rejected the notion of free will. While not denying that people *believe* they make choices, he argued that this belief is an *illusion* (see below).

While philosophical and radical behaviourism involve an *explicit* rejection or denial of free will, this is *implicit* in the case of methodological behaviourism. Some, perhaps a majority, of methodological behaviourists might actually express a belief in free will and *at the same time* believe in the validity of the experimental methods they use to study human behaviour, and this might seem contradictory. They may reject their critics' claim that the use of those methods implies a deterministic, mechanistic model of people, in which case there is no contradiction. Alternatively, they may draw a distinction between (i) 'people as they live their lives on a day-to-day basis', where free will is certainly assumed, and (ii) 'people as subjects in psychological experiments', where the question of free will doesn't arise or isn't relevant. William James drew a similar distinction himself (see below).

These 'solutions' raise more problems and questions in their turn, but the best we can hope for is 'solutions', rather than 'the solution' (which is true of all major philosophical issues and debates).

To diagnose mental disorders

When psychologists and psychiatrists discuss abnormality, and diagnose and treat mental disorders, they often make judgements about free will and determinism, either implicitly or explicitly (see Chapter 7).

In a general sense, mental disorders can be seen as the partial or complete breakdown of the control a person normally has over his/her behaviour, emotions and thinking. For example, compulsive behaviour, by definition, is behaviour the person cannot help but is 'compelled' to do. People are 'attacked' by panic, obsessed by thoughts of germs, become the victims of thoughts that are inserted into their minds from outside and are under external influence (one kind of passivity experience and thought disturbance in schizophrenia). In all these examples, things are happening to or being done to the individual (instead of the individual doing them), both from the point of view of the individual concerned and that of the psychologist or psychiatrist.

Being judged to have lost the control that we think of as a major feature of normality ('being of sound mind'), either temporarily or permanently, is a legally acceptable defence in cases of criminal offences.

Forensic psychiatry deals with the assessment and treatment of mentally abnormal offenders. There are several clauses within the Mental Health Act (1983) that provide for compulsory detention of prisoners (either while awaiting trial or as part of their sentence) in hospital. Psychiatrists, as expert witnesses, can play an important role in advising the court about: (i) fitness to plead; (ii) mental state at the time of the offence; (iii) diminished criminal responsibility (Gelder et al., 1989; see Box 12.1, page 244).

In the case of Peter Sutcliffe, the 'Yorkshire Ripper', the jury found him guilty of the murder of 13 women and the attempted murder of seven others, despite the defence that he heard the voice of God telling him to get rid of prostitutes. He was sentenced to 20 concurrent terms of life imprisonment, which he served initially in an ordinary prison before being sent to Broadmoor Special Hospital.

To discuss moral accountability

Underlying the whole question of legal – and, by the same token, moral – responsibility, is the presupposition that people are, at least some of the time, able to control their behaviour and to choose between different courses of action. Otherwise, how could we ever be held responsible/accountable for any of our actions? We only need expert witnesses (like psychiatrists) to help juries decide whether or not the accused was suffering from a mental abnormality that, at the time the crime was committed, substantially impaired his/her responsibility, because it isn't clear in this particular case. But usually it is. In most everyday

---

Box 12.1 The McNaughton Rules and diminished responsibility

The defence of *diminished responsibility* (for murder) was introduced in England and Wales in 1957 and has largely replaced 'Not guilty by reason of insanity' (NGRI), which was based on the so-called McNaughton Rules. In 1843, Daniel McNaughton shot and killed Edward Drummond, Private Secretary to the then Prime Minister, Sir Robert Peel. He shot Drummond by mistake, intending to shoot Peel. In the Old Bailey trial, the defence of NGRI was made on the grounds that McNaughton had suffered delusions for many years; his paranoia focused on the Tory Party and he decided to kill Peel. In accordance with the judge's summing-up, he was found NGRI. However, he was admitted to Bethlehem Hospital and later transferred to the Criminal Lunatic Asylum, Broadmoor, soon after it was opened.

There was a public outcry at the decision, which was debated in the House of Lords. This resulted in the McNaughton Rules, which although having no statutory basis were given the same status by the courts as an actual law. However, they were considered to present far too narrow a concept of insanity (working to the disadvantage of the mentally ill), and the Homicide Act 1957 introduced the plea of *diminished responsibility* for murder charges. If accepted, there is no trial and a sentence of manslaughter is passed; if not, a trial is held and the jury must decide whether at the material time (the time when the actual crime(s) was committed) the accused was suffering from an abnormality of mind and, if so, whether it was such as to *substantially impair his/her responsibility.*

---

situations and interactions, we *assume* responsibility – our own as well as others' – unless we have reason to doubt it. Imagine having to consult an 'expert' every time we had to blame, criticize, praise, thank, accuse, warn or in any other way perform a social act that implies responsibility on the part of the person being blamed, criticized, and so on.

Descartes made the fundamental distinction between mind and body – the former being non-physical, the latter being physical and essentially a machine (philosophical *dualism*; see Chapters 11 and 13). According to Descartes, the person is an agent whose behaviour is governed by no other law than that which the agent himself creates:

But the will is so free in its nature, that it can never be constrained . . . And the whole action of the soul consists in this, that solely because it desires something, it causes a little gland to which it is closely united to move in a way requisite to produce the effect which relates to this desire.
(Descartes, 1649, in Flanagan, 1984)

The 'little gland' that Descartes refers to is in fact the pineal gland/body, situated near the corpus callosum (which joins the two hemispheres of the brain). This is now generally accepted as playing an important role in sleep, but *not* as the 'seat of the mind', the meeting point between the mind and the body, as Descartes believed.

The mind, via the pineal body, uses its immaterial (non-physical) powers to move the material body; this is what happens every time we behave in a voluntary way. The mind itself, however, is self-moved. Flanagan (1984) believes that one of the main consequences of dualism, and what most people would regard as its main advantage, is that it makes sense of the intuitive (common sense) distinction between (i) conscious, purposeful, voluntary actions, and (ii) mechanical, unintentional, involuntary actions.

Figure 12.1 The influence of the soul on the machinery of the brain, according to René Descartes, from the 1664 French edition of the *Treatise of Man*. Descartes thought of the pineal gland (the pear-shaped object in the middle of the head) as the point of connection between the soul and the brain. It receives messages from the senses (the eyes in this diagram) by means of waves of vibration through the fluid in the chambers of the brain. In turn, by subtle movements and deflection, conveying the will of the mind, it influences the transmission of signals from the brain to the muscles

This distinction in turn makes sense of moral discourse:

> When we speak morally ... we employ an idiom which assumes certain things about human behaviour. At the most general level, the moral idiom assumes that people are capable of controlling their actions – it assumes that we are not mere reflex machines ... it seems silly to have any expectations about how people ought to act, if everything we do is the result of some inexorable causal chain which began millennia ago. 'Ought', after all, seems to imply 'can', therefore, by employing a moral vocabulary filled with words like 'ought' and 'should', we assume that humans are capable of rising above the causal pressures presented by the material world, and, in assuming this we appear to be operating with some conception of freedom, some notion of free will.
> *(Flanagan, 1984)*

This may seem to describe the common-sense understanding of how moral responsibility and free will are related (namely that it is only because we believe that people have free will that we attribute them with moral responsibility for their actions). But is it necessarily the *only* view that one could take?

Skinner (1971) claims (consistent with his argument that free will is an illusion) that all the practical sense of doling out rewards and punishments, and speaking in moral terms would be maintained even if we gave up our shared belief that human nature is free: we would simply be using them to shape, control and maintain behaviours that we (as a society, as well as individually) find pleasing. In other words, the fact that we *do* usually attribute responsibility to people (based on the assumption that they have free will), doesn't mean that we *have to*. (A common argument in support of free will, which could be used against Skinner, is what is called the 'appeal to experience', which we shall consider later on in the chapter.)

Perhaps we need to distinguish between a purely *philosophical* position (one based on logical analysis, the meaning of concepts, and so on) and a more *practical* position (based on everyday, intuitive, subjective experience). As Koestler (1967) says, whatever one's philosophical convictions, 'in everyday life it is impossible to carry on without the implicit belief in personal responsibility; and responsibility implies freedom of choice'.

To understand the theories of major figures in psychology

Most of the major theorists in psychology have addressed the issue of free will and determinism, including James, Freud, Skinner (as we have already seen), Fromm, Kelly and Rogers. The issue has also been discussed by those working in the field of artificial intelligence, such as Johnson-Laird, and sociobiologists, principally Wilson and Dawkins. This represents perhaps the single major reason for including a chapter on free will and determinism in a book on psychology: to fully appreciate the theories of these major figures we must understand the position they adopt regarding this fundamentally important feature of human beings.

According to Morea (1990), the 'story' of Adam and Eve losing their innocence in the Garden of Eden when they chose to eat the fruit from the forbidden tree, is a myth suggesting that humans are free. It also suggests how like a god they become in knowing right from wrong and in having a mind. Morea believes that any adequate explanation of human personality must confront these age-old puzzles of free will, morality and mind.

Mind, or consciousness, is discussed in Chapter 13. Much of the rest of this chapter concentrates on what a number of eminent psychologists, and other scientists, have said about free will and determinism.

Figure 12.2 Adam and Eve were expelled from the Garden of Eden when they chose to eat the forbidden fruit, a choice which, Morea suggests, indicates that humans are free

WHAT DO WE MEAN BY FREE WILL?

Valentine (1992) identifies a number of different definitions or senses in which the term is used. These are described below.

Having a choice

The common-sense, lay person's, understanding of the term is that the actor *could have behaved differently* given the same circumstances; this is what 'having a real choice' means. This is something that we normally 'take on trust', it is an 'article of faith', because it can never be *shown* to be true.

Not being coerced or constrained

Behaviour is 'free' if it is *uncaused*, implying that if behaviour is caused (i.e. determined), then it cannot be free. However, 'free' and 'determined' aren't opposites: the opposite of 'determined' is 'random' (occurring by pure chance). Clearly, when we speak of human actions being 'free', we certainly *don't* mean that they are 'random'. So, what is the true opposite of 'free'? The answer is 'coerced' or 'constrained': if someone puts a loaded gun to your head and tells you to undress (otherwise you'll be shot), no one – magistrate, priest or onlooker – could condemn your behaviour, since it is obviously done *against your will*, you were forced into it, your behaviour wasn't freely chosen.

The view that all acts are caused, but only those that aren't coerced or constrained are free, is called *soft determinism* (first proposed formally by James, 1890; see below).

Voluntary

We noted earlier that the word 'voluntary' is usually meant to convey behaviour over which we have control, while 'involuntary' implies the opposite. In one sense, the opposite of voluntary is 'reflex', as in the knee-jerk response to a tap on the patella, or the eye-blink response to a puff of air directed at the eye. It is very difficult, if not impossible, to prevent these from happening, however hard you try. Clearly, when you undress at gunpoint, your behaviour *isn't* involuntary in this sense, but it *is* involuntary in the sense that you have been forced into it (it is *against your will*). So, if behaviour is neither a reflex response to a specific stimulus (knee-jerk), nor coerced (undressing at gun point), then it is free (at least in the soft determinism sense).

Valentine (1992) observes that there is both *phenomenological* and *behavioural* evidence for the distinction between voluntary and involuntary.

Box 12.2 The phenomenology of free will

Penfield (1958) performed what are now classic experiments involving patients undergoing brain surgery. Their motor cortex was stimulated while they were fully awake, so they could report their experience. Even though the brain region being stimulated was the same as that which is involved when we move our arms and legs under normal circumstances, these patients reported feeling that their limbs were being moved passively, quite a different experience from initiating the movement themselves. This demonstrates that the *subjective experience* (or phenomenology) of the voluntary movement of one's limbs cannot be reduced to the stimulation of the appropriate region of the brain (otherwise Penfield's patients wouldn't have reported a difference) – doing things voluntarily simply *feels* different from the 'same' things just 'happening'.

If this is true for bodily movements, then this adds weight to the claim that having free will is an undeniable part of our subjective experience of ourselves as a person. As Koestler (1967) claims, our sense of self is most acute (and important and real for us) where moral decisions and feelings of responsibility for one's past actions (the problem of free will) are involved.

One demonstration of peoples' *belief* in their free will is *psychological reactance* (Brehm, 1966; Brehm and Brehm, 1981). This refers to a common response to the feeling that our freedom is being threatened, namely the attempt to regain or reassert our freedom. It is related to the need to be free from the controls and restrictions of others, to determine our own actions, and not be dictated to. A good deal of contrary (resistant) behaviour seems to reflect this process ('Don't tell me what to do') (Carver and Scheier, 1992), otherwise known as 'bloody-mindedness'.

Similar to this need to feel free from the controls of others is what has been called *intrinsic motivation* or *self-determination* (Deci, 1975, 1980; Deci and Ryan, 1985, 1987, all in Carver and Scheier, 1992). The central idea is that people have an intrinsic interest in many things, so that they don't need to be offered extrinsic incentives for doing them. Engaging in such activities is motivated by the desire for competence and self-determination.

So what happens if someone is offered an extrinsic reward for doing something that is already interesting and enjoyable in itself? Research by Lepper *et al.* (1973), and others, suggests that the activity will lose its intrinsic appeal, reducing motivation (this is called the *paradox of reward*). In attributional terms, the affect of the extrinsic reward is to change people's explanation for their own behaviour, from an *internal* ('I enjoy it') to an *external* ('I'm only doing it for the reward') explanation. If the reward is withdrawn, they may decide the activity is no longer worth doing (Bem, 1972; Lepper and Greene, 1978; see Chapter 2). In terms of self-determination, the extrinsic reward is 'turning play into work'; it is 'saying' that you haven't chosen the activity freely. You then conclude that you don't have much interest in it, and, given a free choice, you'd rather exercise your will and do something else (Carver and Scheier, 1992).

As far as *behavioural* evidence for the distinction between voluntary and involuntary behaviour is concerned, Valentine cites a study by Kimble (1964), showing that voluntary eye-blinks can be distinguished from involuntary ones in terms of both form and latency. It is generally agreed that voluntary behaviour is learned, flexible (sensitive to consequences), relatively slow and may involve verbal processes, while involuntary behaviour is automatic, inflexible and may be interfered with by verbalization (see, for example, Shiffrin and Schneider, 1977).

Intentional behaviour based on models

Johnson-Laird (1983) identifies three main levels in the evolution (*phylogeny*) of automata ('self-operating machines'), the Cartesian (from Descartes), the Craikian (from Craik), and the self-reflective. (The word 'automaton' is often used in a 'derogatory' sense to describe people who seem to show no emotion or who are efficient or self-controlled to such a degree that they appear less than human, as if 'programmed' to behave in pre-determined, highly predictable ways. This contrasts with the common-sense view of the person as being an emotional being who is less than totally predictable, which seems to imply freedom of choice (see Chapters 4 and 7). This non-technical sense of 'automaton' perhaps relates most closely to the Cartesian level as described by Johnson-Laird.)

○ The *Cartesian automaton* is an open-loop system, such as bacteria and protozoa, whose behaviour is physically mediated by a direct causal link between stimulus and response. It lacks any kind of awareness or symbolism.

○ The *Craikian automaton* is guided by a representation of the external world, constructing a symbolic model of the world in real time – for example, the flight of insects whose flight is controlled by a perceptual model of certain features of the physical environment. This represents a simple kind of awareness or symbolism.

○ *Self-reflective automata* are capable of intentional behaviour, which depends on the 'recursive embedding' [repeating process] of models within models (that is, they have a model of a model of a model, and so on). They are self-aware — that is, they have at least a partial model of how their operating system works. For example, humans know they are capable of generating models of future states of affairs and of deciding to bring them about.

Johnson-Laird (1988) believes that freedom consists in the ability to use models of ourselves to select a method of making choices. When you follow a plan, you don't carry out a rigid sequence of actions, rather you observe the outcomes of your actions and may, as a result, modify your plan; you may even abandon it. You have the freedom to choose between several options at various points in the execution of your plan (especially if you are using your imagination). Sometimes you adopt a course of action ('our next move') without conscious thought:

Level 0: 'You just do it'. For example: Carry on reading
                                     Go for a walk

Sometimes, when you are stuck between two equally appealing (or unappealing?) alternatives, you might say to yourself, 'This is ridiculous; I'll have to choose one of them', and you may then, as a result of this higher-order reflection, make an arbitrary decision (Level 1, Meta-level). You might even make sure that it is arbitrary by resorting to some external method, such as tossing a coin or throwing a die (as did the hero of Luke Rhinehart's *The Dice Man*). At the meta-level, you think about what to do and make a decision based, say, on a simple preference:

Level 1 (Meta-level): By assessing preferences, you choose from:
Level 0:   Carry on reading
           Go for a walk

How did you arrive at this Level 1 method of choice? You didn't think consciously about all the different ways you could make a choice and then choose the 'best' method; it simply came to mind as the right way to proceed. Perhaps most methods of choosing are selected this way. But they needn't be; you *can* confront the issue consciously (Level 2, Meta-meta-level) and reflect on which of the *methods of choice* you will use. You might try to make a rational choice from among them:

Level 2 (Meta-meta-level): Making a rational assessment, you choose from:
Level 1 (Meta-level):   Assessing preferences   ⎫
                         Taking your partner's advice ⎬ to choose from
                         Tossing a coin   ⎭

Level 0:   Carry on reading
           Go for a walk

Why did you decide to choose rationally from among the various methods of choice? Once again, it just came to mind as the right way to proceed. The method of decision at the highest level is always chosen *implicitly* (not consciously): if it were chosen consciously, there would have to be a still higher level at which *that* decision was made. In theory, there would be no end to the hierarchy of decisions about decisions about decisions, etc. (an infinite regress), but the business of everyday life demands that you *do* something, rather than get lost in speculation about how to decide what to do. The buck must stop somewhere! According to Johnson-Laird (1988):

We are free, not because we are ignorant of the roots of many of our decisions, which we certainly are, but because our models of ourselves enable us to choose how to choose. Amongst the range of options are even those arbitrary methods that free us from the constraints of an ecological niche or a rational calculation of self-interest . . . one demonstrates freedom (if not imagination) in acting arbitrarily . . .

This example of a hierarchy of decisions about decisions about decisions, and so on, illustrates the *recursive embedding* of models which is necessary for self-reflection or self-awareness. Johnson-Laird believes that it is an open question whether there is more to self-awareness than this embedding of models, as it is whether cognitive scientists will ever be able to construct computer programs that are self-reflective. Self-awareness is, of course, very closely tied to the concept of *consciousness*, and Johnson-Laird sees the embedding of models as directly relevant to that issue also (see Chapter 13).

Garnham (1991), also a cognitive scientist, agrees with Johnson-Laird that we are unaware of all the factors that influence our decisions. But he reaches the opposite conclusion, namely, that 'It is difficult to see a place for genuinely free will in cognitive science.' But in terms of Johnson-Laird's analysis, it is not obvious in what sense we *aren't* making a free choice: we can still 'choose how to choose' without knowing consciously every 'level' involved in the decision-making process.

Deliberate control

Consistent with Johnson-Laird's analysis is the model of processing capacity proposed by Norman and Shallice (1986). In the context of divided attention (an upper limit to the amount of processing that can be performed on incoming information at any one time), they propose *three levels of functioning*, ranging from:

○ *fully automatic processing*, controlled by organized plans (schemata) that occur with very little conscious awareness of the processes involved, through

○ *partially automatic processing*, which involves *contention scheduling* (a way of resolving conflicts between competing schemata) and generally involves more conscious awareness, but occurs without deliberate direction or conscious control, to

○ *deliberate control* by a supervisory attentional system, which is involved in decision-making and trouble-shooting, and allows flexible responding in novel situations. This corresponds to free will.

Driving a car is a sensori-motor skill performed more or less automatically (at least if you are an experienced driver) and which doesn't require deliberate, conscious control — unless some unexpected event throws the performance 'out of gear', such as putting your foot on the brake pedal when there's an obstacle ahead. According to Koestler (1967), this is a 'rule of the game'. However, on an icy road, this can be risky; the steering wheel has a different feel, the whole strategy of driving must be changed, 'transposed into a different key'. After doing it a number of times, this too may become a semi-automatic routine:

But let a little dog amble across the icy road in front of the driver, and he will have to make a 'top-level decision' whether to slam down the brake, risking the safety of his passengers, or run over the dog. And if, instead of a dog, the jaywalker is a child, he will probably resort to the brake, whatever the outcome. It is at this level, when the pros and cons are equally balanced, that the

subjective experience of freedom and moral responsibility arises.
(Koestler, 1967)

As we move downwards from conscious control, the subjective experience of freedom diminishes: 'Habit is the enemy of freedom ... Machines cannot become like men, but men can become like machines' (Koestler, 1967).

Koestler goes on to say that the second enemy of freedom is very powerful emotions (especially negative ones):

When they are aroused, the control of decisions is taken over by those primitive levels of the hierarchy which the Victorians called 'the Beast in us' and which are in fact correlated to phylogenetically older structures in the nervous system ... It's the arousal of these structures that results in 'diminished responsibility' and 'I couldn't help it'.
(Koestler, 1967)

To complete Koestler's account of free will, let's return to what we earlier called the 'appeal to experience', one of the commonest (if not one of the philosophically most convincing) arguments in support of the existence of free will. He argues that:

The subjective experience of freedom is as much a given datum as the sensation of colour, or the feeling of pain. It is the feeling of making a not enforced, not inevitable, choice. It seems to be working from inside outward, originating in the core of the personality. Even psychiatrists of the deterministic school agree that the abolition of the experience of having a will of his own leads to collapse of the patient's whole mental structure ...

Figure 12.3 The story of Jekyll and Hyde illustrates how the arousal of powerful, primitive emotions can lead to the claim of 'diminished responsibility' and 'I couldn't help it'

THE VIEWS OF WILLIAM JAMES: SOFT DETERMINISM

James was one of the pioneers of psychology as a separate, scientific discipline (see Chapter 11), but he is remembered as much as a philosopher as a psychologist, which perhaps made him especially qualified to express an opinion on the free will and determinism issue.

In his classic *Principles of Psychology* (1890), there is a whole chapter on the 'Will', which he related to attention. He described *effort*, or the sensation of effort, as the primary subjective indication that an act of will has occurred:

The most essential achievement of the will ... when it is most 'voluntary' is to *attend* to a different object and hold it fast before the mind ... Effort of attention is thus the essential phenomenon of will.

But should psychology recognize the existence of free will? Is the feeling of effortful attention strictly a mechanistically determined function of the object of thought, or does subjective consciousness supply certain indeterminate, unpredictable influences of its own, independent of the object? Can a scientific conception of the mind be compatible with our ordinary conception of human nature?

James couldn't find a simple answer to these questions. Belief in determinism seems to fit best with the scientific view of the world, while belief in free will seems to be required by our social, moral, political and legal practices, as well as our personal, subjective experience. In the face of this conflict, James simply distinguished between the scientific and the subjective/everyday realms, claiming that belief in determinism seemed to 'work' best in the former, while belief in free will seemed to work best in the latter. Psychology, as a science, could only progress by assuming determinism, but this doesn't mean that belief in free will must be abandoned in *other* contexts:

Science ... must constantly be reminded that her purposes are not the only purposes, and the order of uniform causation which she has use for, and is, therefore, postulating, may be enveloped in a wider order, on which she has no claims at all.

In other words, there is 'more to life than science'. Scientific explanation isn't the only useful kind of explanation. Psychology didn't, and couldn't, provide all the answers. According to Fancher (1996):

He found he could entertain mechanistic ideas and take them seriously *scientifically*, without fully accepting them *personally*. In personal life it was useful to think and behave as if he had free will, while as a scientist it was useful to accept mechanistic determinism. Both views were essentially articles of faith incapable of absolute proof or disproof. In the absence of any absolute criterion for judging their 'truth', James decided to evaluate ideas according to their *utility* within specified and limited contexts ...

Evaluation of ideas in terms of their practical utility or usefulness is the central idea in the philosophical theory of *pragmatism*, which James helped to establish.

A second 'solution' to the conflict is what Locke, Hume and others have called *compatibilism* (Flanagan, 1984) and what James called *soft determinism*. According to soft determinism, the question of free will depends on the *type(s)* of cause(s) our behaviour has, *not* whether it is caused or not caused (see above). According to James, if our actions have, as their proximate, immediate cause, processing by a system such as *conscious mental life* (CLM – consciousness itself, purposefulness, personality and personal continuity), then they count as free, rational, voluntary, purposive actions (see Chapter 13).

As far as *hard* determinism is concerned, CLM is itself caused, so that the immediate causes are only part of the total causal chain that results in the behaviour we are trying to explain. According to this view, if our behaviour is caused at all, there is no sense in which we can be said to act freely.

James's soft determinism is similar to the views of Johnson-Laird, for whom it is neither necessary, nor possible, to know consciously all the levels involved in the hierarchy of decision-making, in order to say that the decision was made freely; it is sufficient to say that the decision was made at a level higher than *Level 0* (see above). According to Richards (2002), because every experience changes the organism, the organism never has the same experience twice: on the second occasion on which the 'same' stimulus is presented, the organism itself is different. No psychological state recurs in precisely the same form.

THE VIEWS OF SIGMUND FREUD: PSYCHIC DETERMINISM

Although Freud's and Skinner's views on human behaviour are diametrically opposed in most respects, they shared the fundamental view that belief in free will is an illusion. However, in keeping with their theories as a whole, the *reasons* for holding this belief are very different.

According to James Strachey, one of Freud's translators and the editor of the 'Standard Edition' of Freud's collected works:

Freud's discoveries may be grouped under three headings – an instrument of research, the findings produced by the instrument, and the theoretical hypotheses inferred from the findings – though the three groups were of course mutually interrelated. Behind all of Freud's work, however, we should posit his belief in the universal validity of the law of determinism . . . Freud extended the belief [derived from physical phenomena] uncompromisingly to the field of mental phenomena . . .
(Strachey, 1962–1977)

According to Sulloway (1979), Freud's entire life's work in science (and he very much saw himself as a scientist) was characterized by an abiding faith in the notion that all vital phenomena, including psychical ones, are rigidly and lawfully determined by the principle of cause and effect. Together with his belief that dreams have meaning and can, therefore, be interpreted, the extreme prominence he gave to the technique of free association in his clinical work was perhaps the most explicit manifestation of this philosophical theory.

Sulloway points out that '*free association*' is a misleading translation of the German '*freier Einfall*', which conveys much more accurately the intended impression of an uncontrollable 'intrusion' ('*Einfall*') by pre-conscious ideas into conscious thinking. In turn, this pre-conscious material reflected *unconscious* ideas, wishes and memories, which was what Freud was really interested in, since here lay the principal cause(s) of his patients' neurotic problems.

It is a great irony that *free* association should refer to a technique used in psychoanalysis meant to reveal the *unconscious causes* of behaviour. The fact that the causes of our thoughts, actions and supposed choices are unconscious (mostly *actively repressed*, made unconscious because of their threatening, disturbing nature) is what accounts for the illusion that we are free. In other words, we believe we have free will, because we are (by definition) unaware of the *true*, unconscious, causes of our actions. The application of his general philosophical belief in causation to mental phenomena is called *psychic determinism*.

Freud's aim was to establish a 'scientific psychology', and he hoped to be able to achieve this by applying to the human mind the same principles of causality as were in his time considered valid in physics, chemistry and, more recently, physiology. If all mental activity is the result of unconscious mental forces that are instinctual, biological or physical in origin, then human psychology could be formulated in terms of the interaction of forces that were, in principle, quantifiable, and psychology would become a natural science like physics (Rycroft, 1966). (Brown (1961) points out that, strictly speaking, the principle of causality isn't a scientific law, but rather a necessary assumption without which no science would be possible.)

James, Watson, McDougall (1908) and others among Freud's predecessors or contemporaries all assumed the principle of causation (in McDougall's case, instincts were the major cause). But they distinguished between (i) behaviour for which one or more clear-cut cause(s) were known (or could be readily claimed), and (ii) chance or random events that are the result of many separate and apparently trivial causes, which it would be fruitless or impossible to analyse. It was accepted that most psychological events were of the latter kind and, therefore, could only be discussed in broad descriptive terms, as opposed to being analysed in detail in any particular case (Brown, 1961).

Freud took exception to this view. In his early studies of hysterical patients, he showed that the apparently irrational symptoms were in fact meaningful when seen in terms of painful, unconscious, memories. They *weren't* fortuitous or chance events, and their causes could be uncovered by (psycho)analysis. This same reasoning was then applied to other seemingly random, irrational events, to 'parapraxes' (the 'psychopathology of everyday life, such as slips of the tongue and other 'Freudian slips'), and to dreams.

It is a crucial feature of Freud's theory that there are no accidents in the universe of the mind:

In his view of the mind, every event, no matter how accidental its appearance, is as it were a knot in intertwined causal threads that are too remote in origin, large in number, and complex in their interaction to be readily sorted out. True: to secure freedom from the grip of causality is among mankind's most cherished, and hence most tenacious, illusory wishes. But Freud sternly warned that psychoanalysis should offer such fantasies no comfort. Freud's theory of the mind is, therefore, strictly and frankly deterministic.
(Gay, 1988)

However, Gay's conclusion should be qualified.

Some freedom to change

Freud didn't deny that human choices are real and, indeed, one of the aims of therapy is to 'give the patient's ego *freedom* to decide one way or another' (Freud, in Gay, 1988). If we become aware of our previously unconscious memories, feelings, and so on, we are freed from their stranglehold (although there is more to therapeutic success than simply 'remembering'). The whole of psychoanalysis is based on the belief that people *can* change.

However, Freud believed that only very limited change is possible, and among the modest aims of therapy is to convert 'neurotic misery into everyday unhappiness'. Yet even such a limited degree of freedom is incompatible with hard determinism:

Since he believes that humans are largely not free he cannot hold that there is any moral dimension, since one can be moral only if one is free. In Freud's account the difference between a Stalin and a Gandhi comes down to a difference in biology (which is ridiculous) or a difference in childhoods (which may be relevant but is not the whole explanation) . . . If we believed Freud, we would empty all our prisons and turn them into mental hospitals. We do not do this because we suspect that there is a moral element in human beings, and that sometimes they are free and responsible for what they do . . .
(Morea, 1990)

Accidents

Freud *didn't* deny that 'accidents' can and do occur, in the sense of events brought about by intrusions from 'systems' that have nothing to do with the personality of the 'victim'. For example, being struck by lightning or being aboard a ship that sinks are difficult to attribute to the person him/herself; these are clearly to do with forces beyond the victim's control and are true accidents. But repeated 'accidents', particularly of a similar kind, such as the woman who has a string of 'tragic' marriages, with husband after husband dying within a short time of their wedding, or the person who is seen as 'accident-prone', point to the 'victim' as somehow, unconsciously, helping to bring the event(s) about. These *aren't* true accidents.

Multiple causes of behaviour

The Freudian concept of psychic determinism *doesn't* propose a simple one-to-one correspondence between cause and effect. *Overdetermination* refers to the observation that much of our behaviour (as well as our thoughts and feelings) has *multiple* causes, some conscious, some unconscious. By definition, we only know about the conscious causes, and these are what we normally take to be *the* reasons. However, if the causes also include unconscious factors, then the reasons we give for our actions can never tell the whole story and, indeed, the unconscious causes may be more important. According to this view, overdetermination constitutes one aspect of psychic determinism.

The semantic argument

According to Rycroft (1966), the principle of psychic determinism remains an *assumption*, which Freud made out of scientific faith rather than on actual evidence. Nowhere in Freud's writing does he claim to have predicted in advance the outcome of any choice or decision made by a patient. He denied more than once the idea that it is possible to predict whether a person will develop a neurosis, or what kind it will be. Instead, he claimed that all we can do is determine the cause *retrospectively* (not a very scientific way of going about things, as his critics are fond of pointing out, since predictability is seen as a requirement of a scientific theory). As Rycroft says, this is more reminiscent of a historian than a scientist.

However, Freud successfully claimed that he could show that choices made by patients aren't arbitrary, and can be understood as revealing characteristic manifestations of their personality. What he often did, in fact, was to explain patients' choices, neurotic symptoms, and so on, *not* in terms of causes, but by understanding and giving them meaning. The procedure he engaged in wasn't the scientific one of identifying causes, but the *semantic* one of trying to make sense of it:

It can indeed be argued that much of Freud's work was really semantic and that he made a revolutionary discovery in semantics, viz. that neurotic symptoms are

meaningful disguised communications, but that, owing to his scientific training and allegiance, he formulated his findings in the conceptual framework of the physical sciences . . .
(Rycroft, 1966)

The 'semantic argument' is supported by the title of what many people consider to be his greatest book, *The Interpretation of Dreams* (as opposed to *The Cause of Dreams*). He was also well aware that his ideas had been anticipated by writers and poets, not scientists.

THE VIEWS OF B.F. SKINNER: FREE WILL AS AN ILLUSION

Skinner's *radical behaviourism* probably represents the most outspoken and extreme expression among psychologists of the view that people aren't free, and the most explicit and accessible account of this view is his *Beyond Freedom and Dignity* (1971). In it, he argues that *behavioural freedom is an illusion*.

Radical behaviourists regard their view of behaviour as the most scientific, because it provides an account in terms of material causes, all of which can be objectively defined and measured. Mentalistic concepts, such as free will, are '*explanatory fictions*' – that is, they don't account for behaviour (they are not causes, but effects). Also, because they are *private*, they cannot be defined and measured objectively.

If there is some reason, however tentative, for arguing that Freud was something less than a hard determinist, in Skinner's case there is *no* doubt whatsoever – he was as hard as they come! Just as Freud believed that freedom is an illusion to the extent that we are unaware of the unconscious causes of our feelings and behaviour, so Skinner claims that it is because the causes of human behaviour are often hidden from us in the environment that the myth or illusion of free will survives. So what is the nature of those causes?

When what we do is dictated by force or punishment, or by the threat of force or punishment (negative reinforcement), it is obvious to everyone that we are not acting freely. For example, when the possibility of prison stops us from committing a crime, there is clearly no choice involved, because we know what the environmental causes of our behaviour are. Similarly, it may sometimes be very obvious which positive reinforcers are shaping our behaviour, such as a bonus for working extra hours.

However, most of the time we are *not* aware of the environmental causes of our behaviour, so it *looks (and feels)* as if we are behaving freely. When we believe we are acting freely, all this sometimes means is that we are merely free of punishments or negative reinforcements; our behaviour is still *determined* by the pursuit of things that have been positively reinforced in the past. We believe we are free because, most of the time at least, we do what we 'want'; but doing what we want is simply doing what we have previously been rewarded for doing. When we perceive others as behaving freely, we are simply unaware of their reinforcement histories.

But when, for example, people act in a law-abiding way, aren't they *choosing* to do so, and, by the same token, aren't those who take the criminal route also *choosing* the rewards of their crime over the possibility of punishment? In other words, isn't Skinner simply *assuming* that it is the threat of imprisonment and other punishments that determines behaviour, directly, automatically and without the 'mind' of the actor playing any role whatsoever? Skinner does not – and cannot – offer any additional evidence to show that his argument ('when someone appears to be making a choice, we have simply failed to identify the real pay-offs') is more valid than the opposing argument ('when someone appears to be making a choice, it is because *they are* making a choice!'). As Morea (1990) says, Skinner's argument seems to be of the 'Heads I win, tails you lose' variety:

Once this is said, and it is the only behaviourist answer to apparently free choices, what seemed like a scientific account begins to look more like faith ... At least the opposite assertion, of a modest degree of free choice, has the advantage of having common sense and human experience on its side.

Skinner in fact suggests that, instead of our behaviour being determined by rewards and the threat of punishment, it is merely *shaped and modified* by them, allowing for some active part to be played by the actor. This relates to his analysis of behaviour, which is based on operant conditioning. Operant conditioning encompasses what most people think of as *voluntary behaviour* (see above). Indeed, Skinner (1986) stated that 'operant behaviour is the field of intention, purpose and expectation'. Operant behaviour is also purposive: its function is to change the environment and produce particular consequences. However, according to O'Donohue and Ferguson (2001), purposive behaviour *doesn't* imply that the individual has free will, or that behaviour isn't caused, because all behaviour is *determined*. (This argument implies that the opposite of 'determined' is 'free', but recall that the real opposite of determined is 'random'.)

Bettering society and Skinner's attack on 'autonomous man'

As we noted earlier, without free will there cannot be any moral – or legal – responsibility. But Skinner (1971) believes that 'Behaviour is called good or bad ... according to the way in which it is usually reinforced by others.'

He more or less equates 'good' and 'bad' with 'beneficial to others (what is rewarded) and 'harmful to others' (what is punished) respectively. This removes morality from human behaviour, either 'inside' the individual or 'outside', in society. There is only mutual reinforcement, and if we could arrange the reinforcement appropriately, we could create utopia. But in Skinner's utopia (described in his 1948 novel *Walden Two*), how can the planners plan, since you must be free in the first place to be able to plan? For Skinner, 'oughts' *aren't* 'moral imperatives' – that is, they don't reflect moral but *practical* guidelines and rules (Morea, 1990).

Skinner's views on bettering society caused an enormous backlash from critical audiences and the general public. This is reflected in his appearance on the cover of *Time* magazine in September 1971. Carl Rogers claimed that Skinner's utopian vision in *Walden Two* was indistinguishable from George Orwell's *Nineteen Eighty-Four*, a nightmarish *dystopia*, which warns against a punitive society where people are treated as automatons by those in power (O'Donohue and Ferguson, 2001).

Critics saw him as a totalitarian, fascist, 'evil scientist', and at the centre of these attacks was his denial of free will ('autonomous man'). But if we are to improve society, we need to redesign the environment. Only a technology of behaviour can rescue mankind – because social ills are caused by behaviour, it follows that the cure involves changing the variables that control behaviour. For Skinner's critics, *any* attempt to try controlling behaviour is an infringement of personal liberty. But Skinner regarded the dichotomy between freedom and control (or behavioural engineering) as false: *all* behaviour is controlled all of the time. For Skinner (1974),

A scientific analysis of behaviour must, I believe, assume that a person's behaviour is controlled by his genetic and environmental histories rather than by the person himself as an initiating, creative agent ... We cannot prove, of course, that human behaviour as a whole is fully determined, but the proposition becomes more plausible as facts accumulate ... We cannot choose a way of life in which there is no control. We can only change the controlling conditions.

THE VIEWS OF CARL ROGERS: FREEDOM AND THE FULLY FUNCTIONING PERSON

As a humanistic, phenomenological psychologist, Rogers stressed the process of self-actualization and the necessity of adopting the perspective of the other person if we are to understand that person: experience (as distinct from overt behaviour) is all-important (see Chapter 11). In particular, it is crucial to understand the person's *self-concept*, an 'organized, consistent set of perceptions and beliefs about oneself', including our awareness of 'what we are' and 'what we can do'. These influence both our perception of the world and our behaviour. Every experience is evaluated in terms of our self-concept, and most human behaviour can be regarded as an attempt to maintain consistency between our self-image and our actions.

Understanding the self-concept is also central to Rogers' *client-centred therapy*. His experience over many years as a therapist convinced him that real change does occur in therapy; people *choose* to see themselves and their life-situation differently. Therapy, and life, are about free human beings struggling to become more free. While personal experience is important, it doesn't imprison us; how we react to our experience is something we ourselves choose and decide (Morea, 1990).

However, we sometimes fail to acknowledge certain experiences, feelings and behaviours if they conflict with our (conscious) self-image; they are *incongruent* precisely because they are not consistent with our view of ourselves, and they become threatening. So they are denied access to awareness (they remain *unsymbolized*) through actual denial, distortion or blocking. These defence mechanisms prevent the self from growing and changing, and widen the gulf between our self-image and reality (our *true* feelings, our actual behaviour). As the self-image becomes more and more unrealistic, so the incongruent person becomes more and more confused, vulnerable, dissatisfied and, eventually, seriously maladjusted. Defensiveness, lack of congruence, and an unrealistic self-concept may all be seen as a lack of freedom, which therapy is designed to restore.

Humans are growth-oriented, and will naturally progress towards the fulfilment of their innate potential (self-actualize) if psychological conditions are favourable. This contrasts sharply with Freud's view of people as essentially 'savage beasts' (in *Civilization and its Discontents*, 1930), whose aggressive tendencies and unpredictable sexuality can only be controlled by the processes and structures of civilization. Freud was pessimistic about human nature, and saw the instinctual drives of the id (especially sexuality and aggression) as pushing individuals towards the selfish satisfaction of primitive needs or the relief of powerful tensions (the *pleasure principle*). As we saw above, this is a very deterministic view.

However, Rogers' deep and lasting trust in human nature didn't blind him to the reality of evil *behaviour.*

In my experience, every person has the capacity for evil behaviour. I, and others, have had murderous and cruel impulses, desires to hurt, feelings of anger and rage, desires to impose our wills on others . . . Whether I, or any one, will translate these impulses into behaviour depends, it seems to me, on two elements: social conditioning and voluntary choice . . . I believe that, theoretically at least, every evil behaviour is brought about by varying degrees of these elements.

(Rogers, 1982, in Thorne, 1992)

By making the distinction between 'human nature' and 'behaviour', Rogers is able to retain his optimistic view of human beings, but this didn't exclude altogether a deterministic element in his later writings. In *Freedom to Learn for the '80s* (1983), he wrote, 'Yet as we enter this field of psychotherapy with objective research methods, we are, like any other scientist, committed to a complete determinism' (in Morea, 1990). He states that it is becoming clear from science that human beings are complex machines and *not free*. So, how can this be reconciled with self-actualization, psychological growth and the freedom to choose?

One proposed solution is a version of *soft determinism*. Unlike neurotic and incongruent people, whose defensiveness forces them to act in ways they would prefer not to, the healthy, fully functioning person 'not only experiences, but utilizes, the most absolute freedom when he spontaneously, freely and voluntarily chooses and wills that which is absolutely determined' (Rogers, 1983, in Morea, 1990). The fully functioning person *chooses* to act and be the way s/he *has* to: it is the most-fulfilling.

THE VIEWS OF ERICH FROMM: THE FEAR OF FREEDOM

Fromm (1900–80) was, like Freud, a psychoanalytic theorist and therapist, but, like many other *neo*-Freudians, he disagreed with Freud on a number of important issues. One of these was the influence of social, cultural and historical forces on human behaviour, as well as the crucial nature of the child's *relationships*, rather than biological forces within the personality, which were so much stressed by Freud.

In *The Fear of Freedom* (1942; published in 1941 in the USA as *Escape from Freedom*), Fromm argues that we are both part of nature and apart, separate, from it. Human beings created primitive creeds and religious beliefs to enable them to feel less separated from the world, and in Europe, until very recently, the Catholic Church fulfilled this role of providing a sense of security; it mediated between God and humanity, guaranteeing salvation but, in the process, limiting human freedom.

The Reformation and the rise of Protestantism broke the power of the Catholic Church, giving people their freedom, but at what price? According to Morea (1990):

Separation – both physical and psychological separation from nature, and psychological separation from dogma and authority – makes people free. But separation makes people alone, and potentially insignificant and lonely.

At least while Protestantism flourished, people still had a meaningful place in the universe, but with the rise in the nineteenth century of industrialization, capitalism, and science, the universe was turned into a machine, with no room for God. This left people alone and insecure, their lives meaningless.

Figure 12.4 Millions of people lost their identity and 'escaped from freedom' when they submitted to the Nazi regime in Hitler's Germany

What do we do? One solution is to escape from freedom by creating and becoming part of authoritarian organizations and totalitarian regimes, such as those in Hitler's Germany and Stalin's Russia.

People like Hitler and Stalin gave up their freedom by continuously making 'bad' choices; eventually they could *only* choose what was wrong. But a fortunate few, because of living lives in which they have made 'good', right choices, opt only for what is right and good: they are no longer free to choose evil or wrongdoing. At both extremes, human behaviour is caused/determined.

For example, after many years of heavy drinking the alcoholic is no longer free to stop, but most of us aren't yet alcoholics or compulsive gamblers. Only at the end of a long chain of acts does such determinism operate. Earlier along the line we're free, and this is where most of us are, so finely balanced between several contradictory inclinations that we are usually still in a position to choose. But freedom is never absolute; it always depends on the available alternatives.

We all face a fundamental decision: either we accept, even welcome, our freedom, or we can choose to escape from it (our 'ultimate' act of freedom?) by surrendering ourselves and our freedom to a person, ideology or organization. In the *Heart of Man* (1964), Fromm talks about 'soft determinism'. His position is closer to this than to the 'hard' variety, but it often seems that he isn't any kind of determinist at all: 'Fromm has to come down on the side of free-choice because, if humans are moral beings, we must be free − to choose good or bad, right or wrong. And Fromm continually stresses our moral nature . . .' (Morea, 1990).

THE VIEWS OF GEORGE KELLY: FREEDOM AND PERSONAL CONSTRUCTS

According to Kelly (1905–66), people are free to the extent that they have *personal constructs* by which to interpret, predict and control the world. But these constructs also *restrict* freedom, because we can only choose from the constructs we have and, to a very large extent, they *determine* our behaviour:

Constructs are the channels in which one's mental processes run. They are two-way streets along which one may travel to reach conclusions. They make it

possible to anticipate the changing tide of events . . . constructs are the controls that one places on life – the life within him as well as the life which is external to him. Forming constructs may be considered as binding sets of events into convenient bundles which are handy for the person who has to lug them. Events, when so bound, tend to become predictable, manageable, and controlled.
(Kelly, 1955)

So, constructs are needed if the world isn't to seem totally chaotic and unpredictable. But control is a special case of determinism:

A person is to cut a pie. There is an infinite number of ways of going about it, all of which may be relevant to the task. If the pie is frozen, some of the usual ways of cutting the pie may not work – but there is still an infinite number of ways of going about it. But suppose the pie is on the table and there is company present. Certain limiting expectations have been set up about how a meal is to be served. The pie is construed as part of the meal. There are also certain conventions about serving wedge-shaped slices with the point always turned towards the diner. If one accepts all the usual superordinating constructions of the situation, he may, indeed, find his course of behaviour determined and very little latitude left to him. He is not the victim of the pie, but of his notions of etiquette under which the pie-cutting has been subsumed.
(Kelly, 1955)

In Kelly's terms, once we define what we are doing (construe the situation) as 'serving a meal for guests' (a *superordinate construct*), then everything we do as part of that situation, such as cutting a pie, becomes a *subordinate construct* relative to the superordinate one. The way we construe the pie-cutting is *determined* by having subordinated the pie-cutting to the superordinate 'serving a meal for guests'. We are free to define natural events as we wish, but if we want to predict them accurately, we need some kind of construction that will serve the purpose; it is the structure that we erect that rules us.

So, we are free in some respects, but not others. Freedom and determinism are two sides of the same coin; neither is an absolute, but relative to something else. Once I see the world in a certain way, what I do inevitably follows (it is determined), but I am free to *change* my constructs, just as scientists are free to change their theories (see Chapter 1).

SOCIOBIOLOGY: EXTREME BIOLOGICAL DETERMINISM

This section draws on the critique of sociobiology by Rose *et al.* in *Not in Our Genes* (1984), which is a critique of *biological determinism* in general. Here, we concentrate on those aspects that are most relevant to the issue of freedom and determinism.

The central claim of sociobiology is that all aspects of human culture and behaviour, like that of all animals, are coded in the genes and have been moulded by natural selection. Sociobiology is a reductionist, biological determinist explanation of human existence. Its adherents claim, first, that the details of present and past social arrangements are the inevitable manifestations of the specific action of genes. Second, the particular genes that lie at the basis of human society have been selected in evolution; therefore, the traits they determine result in higher reproductive fitness of the individuals that carry them (that is, they are more likely to survive to have offspring that will have genes for those traits; see Chapter 15): 'The academic and popular appeal of sociobiology flows directly from its simple reductionist programme and its claim that human society as we know it is both inevitable and the result of an adaptive process.' What is not always realized is that, if one accepts biological determinism, nothing needs to be changed:

... for what falls in the realm of necessity falls outside the realm of justice. The issue of justice arises only when there is choice ... To the extent that we are free to make ethical decisions that can be translated into practice, biology is irrelevant; to the extent that we are bound by our biology, ethical judgements are irrelevant ...

It is precisely because biological determinism removes guilt and responsibility that it has such wide appeal: it is 'our biology' that is to blame, *not people*, either individually or collectively. This is another instance of one of the recurrent themes of this chapter, namely moral responsibility and responsibility for criminal acts. Aren't sociobiologists obliged to deny them?

To avoid this dilemma, Wilson and Dawkins propose a free will that enables us to go against the dictates of our genes if we so wish. For example, Wilson (1978, in *On Human Nature*) allows that, despite the genetic instructions that demand male domination, we *can* create a less sexist society (at the cost of some loss of efficiency). He then goes on to speculate on the evolution of culture in *Genes, Mind and Culture* (Lumsden and Wilson, 1981). Similarly, Dawkins (1976, in *The Selfish Gene*) proposes independent evolving cultural units or *memes.*

Rose *et al.* object to these attempts to resolve the 'moral responsibility dilemma', on the grounds that they involve a *false dichotomy* between biological and cultural/social, just as 'nature–nurture' (see Chapter 5) and 'mind–brain' (see Chapter 13) are false dichotomies. ('Free will–determinism' is another.) What characterizes human development and actions is that they are the product of an immense array of interacting, intersecting causes. Our actions aren't random or independent with respect to the totality of those causes as an interacting system, for we are material beings in a causal world:

But to the extent that they are free, our actions are independent of any one or even a small subset of those multiple paths of causation: that is the precise meaning of freedom in a causal world. When ... our actions are predominantly constrained by a single cause, like ... the prisoner in his cell ... we are no longer free. For biological determinists we are unfree because our lives are strongly constrained by a relatively small number of internal causes, the genes for specific behaviours or for pre-disposition to those behaviours. But this misses the essence of the difference between human biology and that of other organisms ... Our biology has made us into creatures who are constantly re-creating our own psychic and material environments, and whose individual lives are the outcomes of an extraordinary multiplicity of intersecting causal pathways. Thus, it is our biology that makes us free.
(Rose et al., 1984)

DRAWING SOME CONCLUSIONS: FREEDOM AS AN EVOLUTIONARY REALITY

The same starting point can lead to more than one conclusion. Belief in evolutionary forces and genetic influences may lead sociobiologists to largely deny free will, but it can also lead to the opposite conclusion. According to Dennett (2003):

Free will is an evolved creation of human activity and beliefs, and it is just as real as such other creations as music and money . . . Recognising our uniqueness as reflective, communicating animals does not require any 'human exceptionalism' that must shake a defiant fist at Darwin . . . We may thus concede that material forces ultimately govern behaviour, and yet at the same time reject the notion that people are always and everywhere motivated by material self-interest.

Dennett believes that educated people are trapped in a strange kind of double-think. On the one hand, they believe that natural science implies determinism, which proves they have no control over their lives. But on the other hand, in their actual daily lives, they mostly assume they *do* have this control. The conflict can create deep, underlying anxiety, confusion, guilt and a sense of futility. This is basically the same dilemma faced by William James, who resolved it (i) by adopting a pragmatic approach, and (ii) by arguing for soft determinism (see above).

Consistent with James's position, Dennett argues that determinism *isn't* fatalism, which teaches that human effort makes no difference to what happens. Fatalism is another term for *hard* determinism, which reflects the view of the mind as a mere *epiphenomenon*. This is the view that Skinner adopts: mental processes exist, but they have no causal powers (see Chapter 15). Fatalism, however, is clearly false, based on an oversimplified, largely outdated, scientific view of the world. All the sciences, including physics, now find complexity and variety of patterns everywhere. This is related to *scientific pluralism*: the careful, systematic use of different thinking in different contexts to answer different questions. In particular, we are now finding steadily increasing complexity throughout the developing spectrum of organic life. The more complex creatures become, the wider the range of activities open to them. With this increase comes a steadily increasing degree of freedom. According to Dennett:

The freedom of the bird to fly wherever it wants is definitely a kind of freedom, a distinct improvement on the freedom of the jellyfish to float wherever it floats, but a poor cousin of our human freedom . . . Human freedom, in part a product of the revolution begat of language and culture, is about as different from bird freedom as language is different from birdsong. But to understand the richer phenomenon, one must first understand its more modest components and predecessors.

This evolutionary view of human freedom is similar to the one proposed by Rose (1997, in *Lifelines*). Both make the central point that our conscious inner life isn't some sort of irrelevant supernatural intrusion on the working of our physical bodies (a 'ghost in the machine'; see Chapter 13), but a crucial feature of their design. We have evolved as beings that can feel and think in a way that makes us able to direct our actions. We operate as whole people, our minds and bodies are aspects of us, not separate items. They don't need to compete for the driving seat (Midgley, 2003).

Figure 12.5 The relationship between free will and determinism, showing the link with theories of the mind–brain relationship

SUMMARY

O *Determinism* is a central feature of classical science; according to strict determinism, human thought and behaviour are causally determined along with everything else in the world.

O It is part of common-sense psychology that people have free will, and to believe that people have free will, we must also believe that they have minds. But our thoughts could be caused.

O While most psychologists are *methodological behaviourists*, most aren't *philosophical behaviourists* or *radical behaviourists* who, like Watson and Skinner, *explicitly* deny free will.

O Diagnosis/definition/treatment of psychological abnormality often involve judgements about free will; several kinds of mental disorder seem to involve a loss of control of the patient's behaviour/thinking/emotion.

O The Homicide Act (1957) introduced the plea of *diminished responsibility* for murder charges. This implies that most people, most of the time, *are* responsible for their actions, which, in turn, implies free will.

O *Dualism* helps to make sense of the common-sense distinction between conscious/purposeful/voluntary actions and mechanical/unintentional/involuntary actions. This distinction, in turn, is consistent with our everyday assumption that moral responsibility and free will are related.

O Most major theorists in psychology have addressed the free will/determinism issue, as any adequate account of human personality must.

O The opposite of 'determined' isn't 'free' but *random*, while the opposite of 'free' is *coerced/constrained*.

O According to *soft determinism*, all acts are caused, but only those that aren't coerced/constrained are free.

O Penfield's experiment in which the motor cortex of fully conscious patients undergoing brain surgery is stimulated, provides phenomenological evidence for the distinction between voluntary/involuntary behaviour.

O *Psychological reactance* demonstrates peoples' *belief* in their free will, as does *intrinsic motivation/self-determination*.

O According to Johnson-Laird, despite being unaware of the roots of many of our decisions, we are free because our models of ourselves enable us to choose how to choose (*self-reflective automata*).

O In Norman and Shallice's model of processing capacity, *deliberate control* corresponds to free will. According to Koestler, as we move 'downwards' from conscious control to automatic, habitual behaviour, the subjective experience of freedom diminishes.

O James resolved the conflict between scientific belief in determinism and the common-sense belief in free will by adopting a *pragmatic* approach in distinguishing between the two realms. He also proposed *soft determinism*.

O Freud, like Skinner, saw belief in free will as an illusion. He believed very strongly in *psychic determinism*. While there is no such thing as an accident in the universe of the mind, he accepted that human choices are real, and psychoanalysis is based on the belief that people can change (although only to a very limited degree).

O Much of Freud's work was concerned with trying to *understand/give meaning to* neurotic symptoms and dreams (it was *semantic*), rather than identifying causes.

O Skinner's *radical behaviourism* is probably the most extreme expression among psychologists of the view that people aren't free.

O Skinner argues that most of the time it is not obvious what the environmental causes of our behaviour are, so we *believe* we are acting freely.

O By equating 'good' with 'what is rewarded' and 'bad' with 'what is punished', Skinner seems to have removed morality from human behaviour.

O According to Rogers, people really do change through *client-centred therapy*, and *choose* to see their self and their life-situation differently.

O Defensiveness, lack of congruence, and an unrealistic self-concept all represent a lack of freedom, which therapy is designed to restore.

O In his later writings, Rogers seems to have switched to a deterministic viewpoint, according to which the fully functioning person *chooses* to act and be the way they *have to*.

O For Fromm, the price we pay for our freedom from dogma and authority is isolation and a feeling of being alone, insecurity and meaninglessness. One way of overcoming these feelings is to create/become part of authoritarian organizations/totalitarian regimes (the 'escape' from freedom).

O At the extremes of good and bad, people aren't free. Most of us aren't at these extremes, however, and so are still in a position to choose.

O According to Kelly, people are free in that they have *personal constructs* by which to interpret/predict/control the world. These constructs, however, also *restrict* freedom, because we can only choose from the constructs we have, and they largely *determine* our behaviour.

O *Sociobiology* is a reductionist, biological determinist explanation of human existence. By explaining all individual and social behaviour in terms of genes selected through evolution, sociobiologists seem to be denying guilt and responsibility. But Wilson and Dawkins, in order to allow for moral/legal responsibility, propose a free will that allows us to defy our genes if we so wish.

O Rose *et al.* object to these attempts to resolve the 'responsibility dilemma' on the grounds that they involve a *false dichotomy* between biological and cultural/social. What makes humans unique is that our biology has made us into creatures who are constantly re-creating our own psychic and material environments.

O Dennett rejects fatalism (*hard determinism*) in favour of the view that free will is an evolved creation that is as real as other such creations.

O Fatalism is based on an outmoded scientific view of the world. *Scientific pluralism* shows that freedom is relative, with more complex creatures having greater degrees of freedom.

O Dennett also believes that conscious life is a crucial feature of the design of human beings. Mind and body work together, and neither is dominant relative to the other.

Useful websites

O http://www.determinism.net
O http://www.siu.edu/~philos./faculty/Manfedi/intro/freedom.html
O http://www.ptproject.ilstu.edu/pt/fwdl.htm

Recommended reading

Dennett, D.C. (2003) *Freedom Evolves*. London: Allen Lane.

Flanagan, O.J. (1984) *The Science of the Mind*. Cambridge, MS: MIT Press.

Rose, S. (1997) *Lifelines: Biology, Freedom and Determinism*. Harmondsworth: Penguin.

Rose, S., Lewontin, R.C. and Kamin, L.J. (1984) *Not in Our Genes: Biology, Ideology and Human Nature*. Harmondsworth: Penguin.

CONSCIOUSNESS AND THE MIND–BRAIN RELATIONSHIP

CONSCIOUSNESS AND THE SUBJECT MATTER OF PSYCHOLOGY

For the first 30 or so years of its life as a separate discipline, psychology took consciousness (conscious human experience) as its subject matter, and the process of introspection (observation of one's own mind) was the primary method used to investigate it (see Chapter 11).

Probably the first formal definition of the new discipline of psychology (certainly the most commonly quoted) is William James's 'the science of mental life' (1890), which also probably reflects quite accurately the lay person's idea of what psychology is all about. In his 'Behaviourist Manifesto', John Watson (1913) declared that, 'the time has come when psychology must discard all reference to consciousness ... Its sole task is the prediction and control of behaviour; and introspection can form no part of its method.' On the strength of this doctrine, behaviourists proceeded to purge psychology of all 'intangibles and unapproachables'. The terms 'consciousness', 'mind', 'imagination', and all other mentalistic concepts, were declared unscientific, treated as dirty words and banned from the scientific vocabulary. In Watson's own words, the behaviourist must exclude 'from his scientific vocabulary all subjective terms such as sensation, perception, image, desire, purpose, and even thinking and emotion as they were subjectively defined' (Watson, 1928).

According to Koestler (1967), this represented the first ideological purge of such a radical kind in the domain of science, predating the ideological purges in totalitarian politics, 'but inspired by the same single-mindedness of true fanatics'. This was summed up in a classic dictum by Cyril Burt (1962, in Koestler, 1967):

Nearly half a century has passed since Watson proclaimed his manifesto. Today, apart from a few minor reservations, the vast majority of psychologists, both in this country and America, still follow his lead. The result, as a cynical onlooker might be tempted to say, is that psychology, having first bargained away its soul and then gone out of its mind, seems now, as it faces an untimely end, to have lost all consciousness.

Has it regained consciousness since the early 1960s when this was written? There is no doubt that 'mind' has once again become respectable, legitimate subject matter for psychologists, since the 'cognitive revolution' (usually dated from 1956), and that introspection has at the same time become an acceptable means of collecting data (at least in conjunction with other, more objective methods). These developments have coincided with the decline of behaviourism as the dominant force within British and American academic psychology. However, the dominant view of the mind current among cognitive psychologists and other cognitive scientists, is radically different from the one held by the early psychologists, such as Wundt and James.

Given psychology's philosophical roots, it is not surprising that fundamental philosophical issues continue to be of relevance to modern psychology. *Consciousness* represents one of these issues, and one form this takes is *the problem of mind and brain* (or *the mind–body problem*).

The content of this chapter is drawn from philosophy, neuroscience, artificial intelligence, and biology, as well as psychology itself, since in all these different, but increasingly convergent, disciplines, consciousness and the relationship between mind and brain (or consciousness and brain) represent an increasingly important area of research and debate.

Figure 13.1 René Magritte's painting 'a Reproduction Interdite', 1937, seems to capture the whole idea of psychology being a study of consciousness

KNOWING WHERE TO START: DOES CONSCIOUSNESS EXIST?

Much of the attempt to account for the relationship between mind and brain is taken up by trying to describe, define and generally capture the *nature* of consciousness (and this often takes place separately from the mind–brain issue). But trying to keep them apart is no easy task. For example, Johnson-Laird (1987) states that, 'Consciousness lies at the centre of the mind–body problem, because without it there would be no such problem – or, at least if there were, we would be unaware of it.' Similarly, 'The mind–body problem is the problem of explaining how states of consciousness arise in human brains. More specifically ... it is the problem of explaining how subjective feelings arise in the human brain' (Humphrey, 1992).

It is very difficult in practice, if not also in theory, to begin to describe and define consciousness without trying to relate it to the brain, the 'organ of consciousness'. All psychologists and cognitive scientists, as well as most philosophers, past and present, would accept that without a physical brain, there would be no consciousness (just as without a nervous system of some kind there would be very little in the way of behaviour). That is to say, a brain is *necessary* for conscious experience (or a mind), so that 'no brain means no mind'. But we cannot make the logical jump from saying that minds *need* brains, to claiming that minds *are* brains (although the *mind–brain identity theory* makes exactly this claim; see below). Although 'mind' and 'consciousness' aren't one and the same, many writers *do* equate them (e.g. Wise, 2000).

According to McGinn (1999): 'to any sensible person consciousness is the essence of mind: to have a mind precisely is to endure or enjoy conscious states – inner subjective awareness'. Many would agree with McGinn. It seems 'obvious' that consciousness exists (after all, how could we even begin to discuss it if we didn't already possess it?). But is this a sufficient 'demonstration'? Can things really be so simple?

Wise (2000) believes that the strongest available argument that you (as well as chimpanzees and baboons) are conscious is 'by analogy':

1 I know I am conscious.

2 We are all biologically very similar.

3 We all act very similarly.

4 We all share an evolutionary history.

5 Therefore, you (and other great apes, and other species too) are conscious.

The basic argument is that 'if it walks like a duck and quacks like a duck ...'. If something behaves in all respects as if it is conscious, and there is no good reason to believe otherwise, then it (almost certainly) is conscious. But doesn't this beg the question? Since we don't have direct access to other people's minds (one of Watson's arguments against the scientific study of consciousness), how can I be sure that this human-looking thing isn't a zombie or an android (see Chapters 4 and 7, and Box 13.1, page 270)?

Dennett (1991) has different reasons for rejecting the possibility of humanoids. He denounces anyone who would distinguish non-conscious, humanlike *zombies* from real humans whose consciousness cannot be observed. This kind of argument, he claims:

... echoes the sort of utterly unmotivated prejudices that have denied full personhood to people on the basis of the colour of their skin. It is time to recognize the idea of the possibility of zombies for what it is: not a serious philosophical idea but a preposterous and ignoble relic of ancient prejudices. Maybe women aren't really conscious! Maybe Jews!

Figure 13.2 'Hey, that's *me* in that hat!' Recognizing oneself in a mirror is an early indication of self-awareness or self-consciousness. It usually appears at about 18 months

> ### Box 13.1 Detecting androids
>
> The depiction of androids or humanoids (a synthetic creature made from biological materials, as opposed to a robot's metal, etc.) is quite common in movies. Famous examples include Arnold Schwarzenegger in *Terminator* (1984) and Ian Holm in *Alien* (1979). Although they don't currently exist, except in science fiction, scientists at several research laboratories around the world are trying to construct them (for example, the COG Project at MIT's Artificial Intelligence Laboratory).
>
> If anyone succeeded in manufacturing an undetectable android, it would tell us something important about ourselves. It would prove that we are nothing but machines, whose behaviour can be completely explained in scientific terms (Diller, 1999/2000). Assuming that the engineering aspects an be overcome (for example, sufficiently powerful miniature motors can be made to move the android's limbs, electronic sensors can be devised which mimic how human senses work), Diller argues that, 'it will always be possible to detect an android that has been designed and built by human beings. There will always be some behaviour that distinguishes a manufactured android from a real human being.'
>
> In order for an android to be built, it first has to be designed, and the designer and design team have to make use of a large number of scientific theories. The android's behaviour is produced by means of these theories, and will behave in accordance with them. The psychological theories involved not only describe the behaviour, they also *produce it.* But in the case of human beings, psychological theories are only *attempts* to describe and predict their behaviour: it is impossible for us to know *for sure* how that behaviour is produced. It is this difference between humans and androids which means that there will always be behaviours that allow us to differentiate between 'us' and 'them' (Diller, 1999/2000).

Conscious robots

Dennett also believes that *homo sapiens* is a race of conscious robots, machines with information-processing brains that produce higher-order representations of our lower-order processes. These allow us to describe ourselves as having thoughts, feelings, sensations, and so on, and this is what being conscious means. Any person, animal or machine with the appropriate machinery would be conscious in the way we are, and for the same reasons. Therefore, consciousness isn't something 'extra', added to the processes that produce behaviour; it just 'comes with the territory'.

If we are robots, it is in a rather special, sense. We not only respond knowingly to signals, but we initiate actions in their absence. We can also fail to respond to signals, not because (like mechanical robots) we have broken down, but simply because our attention is elsewhere. As Caldwell (1997) says:

We are not so much programmed as inventors of our programs as we go. We all of us have our own agendas. We as much create our environments as respond to them. In doing so we also – and continuously – create ourselves.

But we are also to a large degree *unconscious*: much of what we do and most of what goes on inside our heads is inaccessible to consciousness, and our behaviour is often automatic. But we are conscious when we *need* to be (Caldwell, 1997). (See Box 13.4, page 279).

Searle (1997) argues that we can never be mistaken (or deluded) about consciousness:

Where the existence of conscious states is concerned, you can't make the distinction between appearance and reality, because the existence of the appearance *is the reality* in question. If it consciously seems to me that I am conscious then I am conscious . . .

Wise (2000) extends this argument to consciousness in non-human animals:

Most mammals and every primate act in ways that cause most reasonable people to think that they have minds of some kinds . . . It is circular thinking to dismiss this belief as mere anthropomorphism . . . , as some do. They begin by assuming that only humans are conscious, then label any contrary claim as anthropomorphic. Why? Because only humans are conscious.

Although behavioural similarity is no *guarantee* of mental similarity:

. . . when animals who are closely related behave in a way that strongly suggests similarity in mental processes to ours, it seems reasonable and fair to shift the burden of proof to those who would argue that what we are seeing is not what we think we are seeing.

Wise uses these arguments to support the case for equality under the law for non-humans (see Chapter 10).

A different approach to demonstrating the existence of consciousness is taken by the novelist David Lodge (2002). He quotes Stuart Sutherland, who states (in the *International Dictionary of Psychology*, 1989) that 'Consciousness is a fascinating but elusive phenomenon; it is impossible to specify what it is, what it does, or why it evolved. Nothing worth reading has been written about it.' In making this claim, Sutherland was, inadvertently, dismissing the entire body of the world's literature, because literature is the richest and most comprehensive record of human consciousness we have. Some of those who work in cognitive science agree with Lodge – for example, Chomsky, who claims that 'It is quite possible . . . that we will always learn more about human life and personality from novels than from scientific psychology.'

Lodge contrasts science's pursuit of universal explanatory laws with literature's description:

. . . in the guise of fiction the dense specificity of personal experience, which is always unique, because each of us has a slightly or very different personal history, modifying every new experience we have; and the creation of literary texts recapitulates this uniqueness . . .
(Lodge, 2002)

Here, Lodge is describing the nomothetic/idiographic debate (see Chapter 3).

Why is consciousness a problem?

As soon as we accept that the physical brain is *involved* in some way in our subjective experience, the philosophical and scientific difficulties start to arise. Why? According to Dennett (1987):

Consciousness is both the most obvious and the most mysterious feature of our minds . . . What in the world can consciousness be? How can physical bodies in the physical world contain such a phenomenon?

One of the fundamental principles of 'classical' science is *objectivity*: the observation and measurement of the world *as it is*, without reference to the human observer (see Chapter 11). As applied to the study of human behaviour and social institutions, this ideal is referred to as *positivism*. Watson clearly didn't believe that the study of consciousness was compatible with such an approach. But most people – scientists and non-scientists alike – would argue that consciousness is an *undeniable, indisputable* 'fact' about human beings, and if it won't 'go away', it has to be explained. But how?

As Dennett (1987) points out, science has revealed the secrets of many initially mysterious natural phenomena, such as magnetism, photosynthesis, digestion and reproduction, but consciousness seems utterly unlike these. Particular cases of magnetism and other phenomena are, in principle, equally accessible to any observer with the right apparatus, but any particular case of consciousness seems always to involve a *favoured* or *privileged observer*, whose access to the phenomenon is entirely unlike, and better than, anyone else's, no matter what apparatus they may use.

By its very nature, consciousness is *private*, while physical objects (and behaviour) are *public*: we don't have any analogies from our shared concepts of the physical world that are at all adequate for describing our experience of it or our experience of ourselves (Gregory, 1981). In other words, we seem to have a view of the physical world in common with others (whether as a lay person with other lay people, or as a scientist with other scientists), but we cannot use that common view for reaching an equivalent view about what goes on inside our heads: the two 'worlds' are simply too different to enable any comparisons to be drawn between them.

WHAT DO WE DO ABOUT QUALIA?

According to Edelman (1992), 'The dilemma is that phenomenal experience is a first person matter, and this seems at first glance, to prevent the formulation of a completely objective or causal account.'

Science is a third-person account. So, how can we produce a scientific account of consciousness that (must) include *qualia*, the collection of personal, subjective experiences, feelings and sensations that accompany awareness? Qualia are phenomenal states, 'how things seem to us as human beings'. Edelman believes that consciousness manifests itself in the form of qualia.

These observations might seem very insightful, although they also confirm just how difficult a concept of consciousness is to 'pin down'. They also appear to raise problems of their own – in particular, the age-old philosophical *problem of other minds*. It is all very well having access to our *own* consciousness (if not to our 'mind'), but how do we know that anybody else is conscious? This, in turn, raises the very important, and controversial, question of whether a machine could have consciousness. Both these issues are discussed in later sections.

Edelman's proposed solution to the 'first-person/third-person dilemma', is to accept that other people and oneself *do* experience qualia, to collect first-person accounts, and to correlate them in order to establish what they all have in common – bearing in mind that these reports are inevitably 'partial, imprecise and relative to . . . personal context'.

A well-known attempt to protect first-person experience (qualia) from reduction to third-person talk (as in neuroscience) is Nagel's (1974) article 'What is it like to be a bat?' The essence of Nagel's argument is that no amount of descriptive knowledge could possibly add up to the experience of how it feels to be a bat, or what it is like to perceive by sonar. Conscious experience *is* 'what it's like' to be an organism *to* the organism. Attempts to reduce that subjective experience must be considered unsuccessful as long as the reducing theory (for example, pain is the firing of neurons in some brain centre) is logically possible without consciousness (the *zombie problem*). A theory of consciousness should be able to distinguish us from zombies (Bem and Looren de Jong, 1997).

Although we may never know animals' or other people's minds, or have an adequate language to describe subjective experience, this doesn't mean it isn't real, complex, rich or highly specific in nature. Nagel argues that any solution to the mind—body problem depends on an attempt to gauge or span the subjective—objective gap.

For Humphrey (1992), the problem of consciousness arises from three obvious facts of human life:

1 my pain, for example, is not part of the objective world, the world of physical material, and can hardly count as a physical event

2 from the fact that there is accompanying brain activity, we could say that my brain-based pain seems to belong nowhere else except in the world of physical material; it is, after all, nothing other than a physical event

3 my pain — that is, my experience of pain — depends wholly on the brain activity.

The problem, specifically, is to explain *how* and *why* and *to what end* the dependence of the non-physical mind on the physical brain has come about (Humphrey, 1992):

Somehow, we feel, the water of the physical brain is turned into the wine of consciousness, but we draw a total blank on the nature of this conversion. Neural transmissions just seem like the wrong kind of materials with which to bring consciousness into the world . . . The mind—body problem is the problem of understanding how the miracle is wrought.
(McGinn, 1989, in Humphrey, 1992)

McGinn (1991) concludes that the problem is probably insoluble — either because there actually *is* no solution, or because human intelligence must always be too limited to grasp it. But Blackmore (2001) argues that, 'there must be something radically wrong with the way we are currently thinking about consciousness or we would not find ourselves with this seemingly intractable problem'. Underlying the views of Humphrey and McGinn, and indeed the whole mind—brain debate, is the fundamental distinction between the physical and the non-physical. It was the French philosopher Descartes who introduced *mind—body dualism* into western thought in the 1600s, where it has remained ever since. Dualism and other theories of the mind—brain relationship are discussed below.

THE NATURE OF CONSCIOUSNESS

'Consciousness', and similar terms, are used in a variety of different ways. Already in this chapter, 'consciousness', 'conscious human experience', 'subjective experience', 'mental life' and 'mind' have all been used interchangeably. 'Awareness', 'self awareness' and 'self-consciousness' can be added to that list. But there are some crucial differences between them.

'Mind' and 'consciousness'

Clearly, 'mind' is a much broader concept than 'consciousness', since there is always much more 'going on' than we can detect through introspection at any one time. According to Humphrey (1992), consciousness refers to what is *felt* and what is *present* to the mind, making it quite limited in scope. Rather than embracing the whole range of higher mental functions (perceptions, images, thoughts, beliefs, and so on), consciousness is uniquely the 'having of sensations' ('what is happening to me' – *qualia*), all other mental activities remaining outside of consciousness.

This view of consciousness can be analysed in terms of three features:

1 consciousness (or conscious awareness) as one level in Freud's psychoanalytic theory of personality

2 consciousness as a form of attention

3 the 'privileged access' of the observer of his/her own mind not being quite so privileged after all.

CONSCIOUSNESS AND PSYCHOANALYTIC THEORY

Freud believed that thoughts, ideas, memories and other psychic material could operate at one of three levels: *conscious*, *pre-conscious* and *unconscious* (see Chapter 15). These are essentially levels of *accessibility*.

What we are consciously aware of at any one time (what we can report) represents the mere tip of an iceberg. Most of our feelings and memories are either not accessible at that moment (pre-conscious), or are totally inaccessible (unconscious), at least without the use of special techniques, such as free association and dream interpretation. The ego (the 'executive', decision-making, rational part of the psyche, governed by the *reality principle*) represents the *conscious* part of the mind, together with some aspects of the superego (the moral part of the psyche and the source of guilt), namely those moral rules and values we are able to express in words.

The ego also controls the *pre-conscious*, a kind of 'ante-room', an extension of the conscious, whereby things we are not fully aware of right now can become conscious fairly

Figure 13.3 Dorethea Tanning 'Eine kleine Nacht Musik', 1944. The impossible nature of the imagery depicted in the painting is what gives dreams and other unconscious phenomena their distinctive flavour

easily if our attention is directed towards them. For example, you suddenly realize that you have had a pain for some time.

The *unconscious* (for Freud the most important type of mental material) comprises (i) impulses arising from the id, the biological, inherited part of the psyche (governed by the *pleasure principle*), (ii) all *repressed* material, (iii) the unconscious part of the ego (the part involved in dream work, neurotic symptoms and defence mechanisms), and (iv) part of the superego, such as free-floating or vague feelings of guilt or shame that are difficult to explain in a rational way.

Freud depicted the unconscious as a *dynamic* force and not a mere 'dustbin' for all those feelings and memories that are unimportant or too weak to force themselves into awareness. This is best illustrated by the process of repression, whereby what is threatening is actively forced out of consciousness by the ego (Thomas, 1985).

Most psychologists would agree that feelings and memories differ in their degree of accessibility: they can be placed on a *continuum* of consciousness, with 'fully conscious' at one end and 'completely unconscious' at the other. However, most wouldn't accept Freud's formulation of the unconscious as based on repression. Indeed, other *psychodynamic* theorists, in particular Carl Jung, disagreed fundamentally with Freud's view. Although he accepted the existence of repression, Jung distinguished between the *personal* and the *collective* unconscious, the former being based on the individual's personal experiences, the latter being inherited and common to all members of particular cultural or racial groups (if not all human beings).

CONSCIOUSNESS AS A FORM OF ATTENTION

One way in which experimental psychologists have studied consciousness is through the concept of *attention*. Although consciousness is difficult to describe because it is fundamental to everything we do (Rubin and McNeil, 1983), one way of trying to 'pin it down' is to study what we are paying attention to — that is, what's in the forefront of our consciousness. According to Allport (1980), 'attention is the experimental psychologist's code name for consciousness'.

Focal attention (or focal awareness) is what we are currently paying deliberate attention to, and what is in the centre of our awareness (corresponding to Freud's 'conscious'). All those other aspects of our environment, and our own thoughts and feelings on the fringes of our awareness, but which could easily become the object of our focal attention, are within our *peripheral attention* (corresponding to Freud's 'pre-conscious').

This distinction between focal and peripheral attention may be seen as overlapping with the model of *processing capacity* (Norman and Shallice, 1986), which is intended to explain divided attention, and which is discussed in relation to free will in Chapter 12.

THE OBSERVER'S 'PRIVILEGED ACCESS'

The concept of focal attention helps us to appreciate how much of our behaviour and mental processes proceed quite automatically, without having to think consciously about what we are doing or deliberately plan each part of our performance.

When we look for examples of 'automatic processing' (Norman and Shallice, 1986), we usually think of the performance of well-practised psycho-motor skills, such as driving, typing and even walking up or down stairs. But just as valid are cases of cognitive processes, such as perception, which usually involves an immediate (and mostly accurate) awareness of something (an object, person or other 'stimulus') in our external environment. In fact, it is difficult to imagine what it would be like if we were aware of exactly *how* we perceive. Our focal attention or awareness is directed at the identified object (the 'finished product'), *not* the process of perception itself. Could it be any other way? Trying to discover how we perceive through introspection is unlikely to throw much light on the matter, which suggests that all the underlying processing that is involved *necessarily* takes place outside our conscious awareness. This ensures that we concentrate on what really matters, namely what's going on around us (rather than all the internal processes).

We can take this a step further, and ask if it's actually necessary to be consciously (focally) aware of an object in order to 'perceive' it?

Box 13.2 Blindsight: can we see without really 'seeing'?

According to Humphrey (1986, 1992), there is increasing evidence that the higher animals, including humans, can in fact show the *behaviour* of perceiving without being consciously aware of what they are doing. During the 1960s, Humphrey worked with a monkey, called Helen, who had had her visual cortex removed (as part of a study of brain damage in humans; see Chapter 10); however, her lower visual centres were intact. Over a six-month period following the operation, she began to use her eyes again, and over the next seven years, she improved greatly. She was eventually able to move deftly through a room full of obstacles, picking up tiny scraps of chocolate or currants, reaching out to catch a passing fly. Her three-dimensional spatial vision and ability to discriminate between objects (in terms of size and brightness) became almost perfect. However, she didn't recover the ability to recognize shapes and colours, and was 'oddly incompetent' in other ways too.

At that time, there were no comparable human cases, but what relevant evidence there was suggested that people *wouldn't* recover vision. Then, in 1974, Weiskrantz *et al.* reported the case of D.B., a young man who had recently undergone surgery to remove a tumour at the back of his brain. The entire primary visual cortex on the right side had been removed, resulting in blindness in the left side of the visual field. So, for example, when he looked straight ahead, he couldn't see (with either eye) anything to the left of his nose. Or could he?

Weiskrantz decided *not* to accept D.B.'s self-professed blindness at face value. While there was no question that he was genuinely unaware of seeing anything in the blind half of his field, was it possible that his brain was nonetheless still receiving and processing the visual information? What would happen if he could be persuaded to discount his own conscious opinion?

Weiskrantz asked him to forget for a moment that he was blind, and to 'guess' at what he might be seeing *if* he could see. To D.B.'s own amazement, it turned out that he could do it: he could locate an object accurately in his blind field, and he could even guess certain aspects of its shape. Yet he continued to deny any conscious awareness. Weiskrantz called this phenomenon *blindsight*: 'visual capacity in a field defect in the absence of acknowledged awareness' (Weiskrantz, 1986). Other cases have since been described, and unconscious vision appears to be a clinical reality (Humphrey, 1986).

A more specific visual deficit, *prosopagnosia*, involves the inability to recognize the human face as such. Although patients with this deficit have no awareness of faces, some, while denying that they can see their spouse's face, will perform on tests in a way that indicates strong discriminative knowledge of that face (Edelman, 1992). What is involved in both this and blindsight is a loss of *explicit conscious recognition*, but the capacity for *implicit behavioural recognition*.

Johnson-Laird (1988) makes a similar point when discussing decision-making (see Chapter 12). At whatever point in the hierarchy (of embedded decisions about decisions, and so on) we make a decision, this will always be made *implicitly* (and not consciously), since if it were chosen consciously, there would have to be a still higher level at which *that* decision was made (and so on, *ad infinitum*). In other words, there is always more going on cognitively ('in the mind') than is available to consciousness (or, to adapt a popular phrase, 'there's more involved than meets the inner eye'; see below).

According to Ross and Nisbett (1991), countless experiments point towards the conclusion that the high-level mental activity taken to be involved in attitude change and emotion (see Chapter 2) in fact goes on outside of awareness. In a much-cited article, Nisbett and Wilson (1977) argued that there is no direct access to cognitive processes *at all*; instead, there is access only to the ideas and inferences that are the *outputs* resulting from such processes.

Sometimes, we do (or could) accompany our performance (such as solving well-formed problems, which have clear rules for their solution) with a verbal commentary, which seems to track the processes as they occur. Hence, our account of how we went about solving the problem may be quite accurate (although even here our introspections aren't likely to tell the whole story). But for many problems, especially novel ones involving social judgement (and most everyday, 'real-life' problems are 'ill-formed'), there is very little conscious representation of underlying cognitive processes:

People have theories about what affects their judgements and behaviour just as they have theories about all kinds of social processes. These theories, rather than any introspective access to mental processes, seem to be the origin of people's reports about the influences on their judgement and behaviour . . .
(Ross and Nisbett, 1991)

Nisbett and Wilson (1977) claim that our common-sense, intuitive belief that we can accurately account for our own behaviour (see Chapter 1) is *illusory*, because what really guides our behaviour is unavailable to consciousness. If true, this conclusion would seem to have serious implications for our belief in *free will*. (Freud's distinction between *our* reasons and *the* reasons has similar implications; see Chapter 12.)

Blackmore (2001) suggests that consciousness per se may not have any function, but simply comes with being the kind of organism we are. This too would seem to threaten our intuitive feeling that our consciousness has some kind of (causal) power – that it *does* things. But does it?

Libet's findings are consistent with previous experiments, carried out on exposed brains. He showed that about half a second of continuous activity in the sensory cortex is needed for us to become aware of a sensory stimulus (Libet, 1981). This implies the odd conclusion that consciousness *lags behind* the events of the world. But, once this period of activity has taken place, these events are referred back to the time of the initial evoked readiness potential. So, even though consciousness takes half a second to build up, events still seem to happen in real time (Blackmore, 2001).

Box 13.3 Is consciousness less important than we think?

Libet (1985) asked people to hold their arms out in front of them, then, whenever they wished, to flex their wrists. They repeated this several times. Libet systematically measured the timing of three things:

1 the start of the action (using electrodes on the wrist)

2 the start of the readiness potential in the motor cortex (using electrodes on the scalp)

3 the decision to move (by a revolving spot on a clock face – participants had to say where the spot was when they consciously decided to act).

(Subsidiary experiments showed that people can time external stimuli this way very accurately, which suggests that they could do the same with their own private decisions.)

The brain activity began about half a second *before* the participant was aware of deciding to act! The conscious decision seemed to come far too late to be the cause of the action; consciousness seemed to be a mere afterthought (Blackmore, 2001).

Critics argue that the voluntary wrist action in Libet's experiments isn't comparable to free (spontaneous) actions in real life, that the clock test is flawed, and that the whole idea of there being a time at which consciousness 'happens' is misguided (Dennett, 1991). But Blackmore asks why we should be surprised: 'If you expected consciousness to have started the process then you are really a believer in magic – in some kind of force that acts on brain stuff.'

Blackmore (2001) cites experiments by Wegner and Wheatley (1999), using modified ouija boards, designed to *induce* feelings of free will. Their findings led them to conclude that free will is an illusion created in three steps:

1 we're ignorant about how our brains plan actions and execute them

2 we become aware of the results of the planning and call these intentions

3 the action occurs after the intention, and we leap – mistakenly – to the conclusion that 'our' intention caused the action.

But what does 'becoming aware of the (brain's) planning' actually mean? How does this awareness happen? Certainly, not everyone agrees with the view that free will is illusory, and there is currently a debate about how neuroscience can contribute to our understanding of free will (Libet *et al.*, 1999; see Chapter 12).

'Consciousness' vs 'self-consciousness'

Edelman (1992) distinguishes between *primary* and *higher order consciousness*, which refer to consciousness and self-consciousness respectively.

○ *Primary consciousness* refers to the state of being mentally aware of things in the world, of having mental images in the present. It isn't accompanied by any sense of being a person with a past and a future. In other words, to be conscious doesn't necessarily imply any kind of 'I' who is aware and having mental images. This is why at least some animal species are likely to be conscious, even though they don't possess

Box 13.4 Where is my mind's 'I'?

To be conscious is also to have a point of view on the world. The 'conscious robot' is conscious of his/her own consciousness (Caldwell, 1997). But Dennett (1991) rejects this idea of a *privileged observer*. There is no mind's 'I' that stands behind all my experience as the condition of its possibility. In the brain's superabundant, often pointless, circuitry, it is impossible to locate a centre, a controller in charge of the whole operation. There's less a 'ghost in the machine' (Ryle, 1949) than a vast, haunted house populated by innumerable ghosts. I don't *have* thoughts – I *am* thoughts. The 'I' is, first and foremost, a *grammatical construction*. In biological terms, our sense of self is no more than a useful fiction (Flanagan, 1992). It would be difficult to live our lives without a sense of self, but it lacks any biological basis, and is merely a superimposition on our biology derived from our social interactions: a solitary human being perhaps would have no self.

Although most psychologists and neuroscientists reject dualism as a philosophical theory (see text below), they still believe in some kind of centre, where everything comes together and 'consciousness happens', some kind of magic finishing line beyond which events 'come into' consciousness, a centre from where 'my' decisions are made and 'my' instructions sent out. But the brain is a massively parallel system with no middle (Blackmore, 2001).

If Dennett, Flanagan and Blackmore are right, who is conscious and what happens to free will and the related legal and moral responsibility? Is free will an illusion after all? But to say that the self doesn't have a biological basis doesn't mean that it is not real in other senses (biology isn't the only reality; see Chapters 11 and 15). For Caldwell (1997), to ask questions about responsibility and other ethical questions is:

. . . to cease to think of ourselves merely as biological organisms, which is the level at which Dennett primarily moves, but rather as creatures who move in the artificial world which they have constructed for themselves. In this sense . . . the mind is not a natural but an artificial construct, and to look for it in terms of biology or brain science is to look where one is least likely to find it . . .

language. Edelman believes that chimpanzees are almost certainly conscious, and in all likelihood, so are most mammals, and some birds; probably those animals without a cortex (or its equivalent) aren't.

Wise (2000) agrees with Edelman, and with Greenfield (1995), who propose that rather than the 'turning on the light' analogy for consciousness, a better one might be the 'dimmer switch'. This captures the idea that consciousness probably ranges across a vast continuum, and allows for non-humans' possession of primary consciousness. According to Wise, the majority opinion boils down to:

Some consciousness tends to allow one to experience the present, another to realize that one is experiencing the present and to anticipate, to some degree, the future and to think about the past. The *International Dictionary of Psychology* (1989) warns against . . . confusing consciousness with self-consciousness – 'to be conscious it is only necessary to be aware of the external world . . .'

O *Higher order consciousness* involves recognition, by a thinking subject, of his/her acts or affections. It embodies a model of the personal, and of the past and future, as well as the present. It shows direct awareness of mental episodes without the involvement of the sense organs or receptors. It is what humans have *in addition* to primary consciousness: we are conscious of being conscious. In order to acquire this capacity, systems of memory must be related to a conceptual representation of a true self (or social self) acting on an environment and vice-versa.

This is rather similar to Johnson-Laird's (1988) description of *self-reflective automata*, which are capable of intentional behaviour, which, in turn, depends on the 'recursive embedding' of models within models. To be self-aware is to have at least a partial model of how our operating system works; we represent to ourselves how we do things (for example, make decisions), rather than 'just doing them'. As well as providing us with self-reflectiveness (or self-consciousness), having 'models of models' also gives us the freedom to make choices (see Chapter 12).

EQUATING 'CONSCIOUSNESS' WITH 'SELF-CONSCIOUSNESS'

Not all descriptions/definitions distinguish between 'consciousness' and 'self-consciousness'. For example, Humphrey (1986) defines 'consciousness' as

the inner picture we each have of what it is like to be ourselves – self-awareness: the presence in each of us of a spirit (self, soul . . .) which we call 'I'. It's 'I' who have thoughts and feelings, sensations, memories, desires. It's 'I' who am conscious of my own existence and my continuity in time. 'I' who am, in short, the very essence of a human being.

This seems to describe Edelman's *higher order consciousness*.

Elsewhere, Humphrey (1992) defines consciousness in a way that seems to combine primary and higher order consciousness: 'To be conscious is essentially to have sensations: that is, to have affect-laden mental representations of something happening here and now to me.'

CAN A MACHINE BE CONSCIOUS? DOES HAVING A BRAIN MATTER?

Many machines 'behave' in ways that, if they were human, would suggest that they had mental states. For example, aeroplanes on autopilot can fly themselves; they respond to external 'sensory' information, make 'decisions' about whether to fly, 'communicate' with other aircraft, and even 'know' when they're 'hungry' for fuel, can 'sense' danger, and so on.

But the very fact that the various words in the previous sentence are in speech marks conveys that they are not to be taken literally: only in a *metaphorical* sense do planes make decisions, and that is because they lack consciousness. It is human beings (and possibly some other animal species) who make decisions, communicate, and so on, not metal machines. Being *sentient* (living, breathing, made of flesh and blood) seems to be a precondition for primary consciousness, just as primary consciousness is a pre-condition for higher order consciousness.

However, isn't there the danger here of confusing (i) the kinds of things in the world that, currently, as far as we know, and according to the criteria that we use to judge consciousness, *are* conscious (human beings and some other species), and (ii) the kinds of things that might, *in the future*, be *considered* conscious (due to advances in our ability to construct certain types of machine)? In other words, should we reject the very idea of a *conscious machine*?

Supporters of what Searle (e.g. 1980) calls *strong artificial intelligence* (AI), believe that 'the future' is already here. Cognitive scientists, such as Turing, Johnson-Laird, Newell, Simon, Minsky and Boden, believe that people and computers turn out to be merely different manifestations of the same underlying phenomenon, namely automatic formal systems. The essence of such systems is the manipulation of symbols according to rules (the *computational theory of mind*, or CTM). CTM is the theory underlying strong AI, according to which the computer isn't merely a tool for formulating and testing hypotheses concerning the human mind, but, if appropriately programmed, *is* a mind: it literally *understands* and has other cognitive states – that is, *it is conscious*.

Some of Searle's objections to strong AI and CTM are discussed later, in relation to the mind—brain issue. But one of his arguments is particularly relevant here. Mental states and processes are real biological phenomena in the world, as real as digestion, photosynthesis, lactation, and so on; they are caused by processes going on in the brain that are entirely internal to the brain. The intrinsically *mental* features of the universe are just higher-level physical features of the brain. Crucially, in principle only a machine (computer, robot) that is made of flesh and blood or *neuroprotein* (a convenient shorthand for the many biochemical substances active in the central nervous system) could be conscious (a view that has been dubbed *carbon/protoplasm* chauvinism by Torrance, 1986).

To Searle it is *obvious* that metal or silicon cannot support intelligence or consciousness. But to Boden (1993), and other advocates of strong AI, as well as for most cognitive psychologists, what matters are the *computational functions* performed by 'neuroprotein' (such as message-passing, facilitation and inhibition). If the neurophysiologist can tell us which cells and chemical processes are involved, so much the better, but any other chemistry would do, so long as it enabled these functions to be performed.

From an intuitive point of view, it is far from obvious how the neuroprotein ('that grey mushy stuff inside our skulls') could possibly support intelligence, so just because it isn't obvious how metal and silicon could, doesn't mean that they *couldn't* do so. Also, what is intuitively obvious may (and does) change as scientific knowledge advances (Boden, 1993; see Chapters 11 and 15).

A different kind of objection to strong AI, but which is relevant here, involves another distinction between different types of consciousness. 'A (access)-consciousness' (Block, 1995) refers to the fact that our minds seem to provide a representation of things, such as the world, the past, our plans, in such a way as to allow us to reason, act and communicate. 'P (phenomenal) consciousness' describes the distinctive *subjective* awareness that seems to be a characteristic *of* those inner representations, but which isn't reducible to them. It is *what it's like* to have the experience of any state (another description of qualia?).

McGhee (2001) believes that, while many systems (including computers) are capable of inner representations that underlie intentional action (A-consciousness), it is more difficult to argue that they have (or ever could have) the subjective awareness that they *have* these representations (P-consciousness). While it is possible to see how the former could *emerge* from physical systems (neuroprotein or silicon), this is much more difficult in the case of the latter (McGhee, 2001).

However, a major difference between how the brain processes information (*parallel processing*) and how most computers have been designed to do it (*serial processing*) is also of key relevance to the whole AI debate. Those who oppose the view that computers could be built to have the kind of consciousness that people naturally have stress this crucial difference.

Supporters of AI argue that, at least in principle, computers could be programmed to use parallel processing. In fact, some cognitive scientists would claim that the objection has already been met *in practice*, in the form of *connectionism*. This approach models itself on the interconnection of the neurons in the brain ('neural networks') and stresses the role of 'parallel distributed processing' (PDP) (Rumelhart *et al.*, 1986). But Boden (1993) continues to maintain that it is the *fact* of the processes being carried out by the machine that is crucial for defining intelligence – not what the machine is made of or how the processes are carried out.

However, Eiser (1994) believes that this emphasis on the processes being carried out is mistaken:

> The error lies in trying to settle the matter by identifying the classes of information-processing operations of which human beings and computers are each capable, whilst ignoring the classes of information with which human and artificial systems actually have to deal . . .

In other words, it is in the *content* of experience (rather than in an exclusive analysis of process) that an understanding of human consciousness is to be found.

CONSCIOUSNESS AND THE IMPORTANCE OF HAVING A BODY

According to Humphrey (1992), the subject of consciousness, 'I', is an embodied self. In the absence of bodily sensations, 'I' would cease: *Sentio, ergo sum* ('I feel, therefore I am' – this is a variant of Descartes' famous *Cogito, ergo sum*, 'I think, therefore I am'; see below). The importance of the body in relation to consciousness and our sense of personal identity is central to Merleau-Ponty's theory, which is outlined later in the chapter.

If there *is* something distinctive about human consciousness, where should we look for it? According to Eiser (1994):

> Even if we could build a machine with this full capacity of a human brain [immensely interactive parallelism] we would still be reluctant to attribute to it the *kind* of consciousness, the sense of self, to which we ourselves lay claim . . . To ask what is special about human consciousness, therefore, is not just a question about process. It is also to ask what is special about our experience of the world, the experience we have by virtue of physical presence *in* the world . . .

Any distinction we try to draw between mind and body (mind–body dualism) is, according to Eiser, objectionable precisely because it divorces mental from physical experience. The most continuous feature of our experience is our own body: personal identity (and that of others) depends on physical identity, we feel our body and we feel the world *through* it, and it provides the anchor and perspective from which we experience other things.

This view is very similar to that of the French phenomenologist, Merleau-Ponty (1962, 1968). He distinguishes between 'one's own body' (the *phenomenal* body) and 'the objective body' (the body as *object*). Experience of our own body isn't, essentially, experience of an object. In fact, most of the time, we are not aware of our body as such – it is, as it were, *transparent* to us. But without our body, we couldn't *be*.

We cannot react to the world without treating it as a more or less meaningful system of situations, contexts and relations. This meaningfulness depends not only on the world's physical properties, but also on *our own* biological, psychological, social and cultural properties. Carrying out goals, plans and intentions necessarily involves our body. We don't 'move' our body like we do other objects: it is as if it moves itself.

Just as sense perception and motor skills function together (as do the different senses), so, for Merleau-Ponty, mind and body, mental and physical, are two aspects of the same thing, namely a person. The mind is embodied in that it can be identified with one aspect of something that has two aspects, neither of which can be reduced to (explained in terms of) the other (Teichman, 1988).

The body provides us with a continuous patterned stream of input, and (simply from the fact that we cannot be in two places at the same time) imposes constraints on the information received by the brain about the outside world (Eiser, 1994). This, in turn, relates to 'aboutness' (or *intentionality*). Mental states (beliefs, desires, perceptions, wishes, fears, ideas, as well as intentions) are *about* things and states in the world apart from themselves. In other words, they have an *external reference* to something outside themselves, and this is (part of) what we mean by saying that the world is *meaningful* to us and that we understand it. According to Searle (1980), intentionality is a fundamental feature of consciousness. The symbols that computers manipulate are *meaningless* for the computer (the meaning has to be applied by a human programmer), which leads to the (inevitable) conclusion that computers (and other machines) do not – and cannot – possess consciousness:

If both the machine's processing operations *and* the information it processed were indistinguishable from those of a human being, so also would be its mind and consciousness. It is the second of these two conditions, rather than the first, which strikes me as the major stumbling block . . .
(Eiser, 1994)

In other words, only information that has meaning for the machine that is carrying out the processing of that information can be considered part of the consciousness of that machine, which is why only human 'machines' can be described as possessing consciousness: 'Computer consciousness – in the sense of self-awareness – is merely science fiction (Eiser, 1994).

WHAT IS CONSCIOUSNESS *FOR*? TAKING AN EVOLUTIONARY APPROACH

If Searle is correct, and Boden and the other *functionalists* are mistaken when they claim that our brains *just happen to be* made from neuroprotein (as opposed to silicon or metal), and that *whatever* they're made of is irrelevant (or incidental) as far as intelligence is concerned, then a useful route to take might be the evolutionary one.

According to Humphrey (1986), when we ask what consciousness *does*, what *difference* it makes to our lives, there are three possibilities that might more or less make sense:

1 it might be making all the difference in the world – it might be a necessary precondition of all intelligent and purposive behaviour, both in humans and animals

2 it might be making no difference whatsoever – it might be a purely accidental feature that happens (at least) sometimes to be present in (some) animals and has no influence on their behaviour

3 it might, for those animals that have it, be making the difference between success and failure in some particular compartment of their lives.

Humphrey believes that common sense must back the first of these. Our everyday experience is that consciousness makes all the difference in the world (just as our experience tells us that we have free will): we are *either* awake, alert and conscious *or* flat on our backs, inert and unconscious, and when we lose consciousness, we lose touch with the world.

But what about those cases in which consciousness *doesn't* seem to be necessary, such as perception, blindsight and automatic processing (see above)? While perception (and other fundamental cognitive and behavioural processes) may not *require* consciousness, the fact remains that they are very often *accompanied* by consciousness, and if (as far as we know) most other species *lack* it, the implication is that it evolved in human beings for some purpose.

Imagine an animal that lacks the faculty of conscious or self-reflexive 'insight'. It has a brain that receives inputs from conventional sense organs and sends outputs to motor systems, and in between runs a highly sophisticated information-processor and decision-maker. But it has no picture of what this information-processing is doing or how it works: the animal is unconscious.

Now imagine that a new form of sense organ evolves, an 'inner eye', whose field of view *isn't* the outside world *but the brain itself*. Like other sense organs, it provides a picture of its informational field (the brain) that is partial and selective; but, equally, like other sense organs, it has been designed by natural selection to give a useful ('user-friendly') picture – one that will tell the subject as much as s/he needs to know: this animal is conscious (see Figure 13.4, page 285).

Suppose our ability to look in upon ourselves and examine our own minds at work is as much a part of human biology as our ability to walk upright or to perceive the outside world. Once upon a time there were animals – our own ancestors presumably – who could not do it. They gave rise to descendants who *could*. Why should those conscious descendants have been selected in the course of evolution?

If Darwin's theory is correct, the only answer can be that, like every other natural ability and structure, consciousness must have come into being because it conferred some kind of biological advantage on those creatures that possessed it:

In some particular area of their lives, conscious human beings must have been able to do something which their unconscious forbears couldn't; something which, in competition with the other members of their species, distinctly improved their chances of survival – and so of passing on the underlying genetic trait for consciousness to the next generation.
(Humphrey, 1986)

If consciousness is the answer to anything at all, it must be to a biological challenge that human beings have had to meet; could the challenge lie in the human need to understand, respond to and manipulate the behaviour of other human beings?

In evolutionary terms I suspect that the possession of an 'inner eye' served one purpose before all: to allow our own ancestors to raise social life to a new level. The first use of human consciousness was – and is – to enable each human being

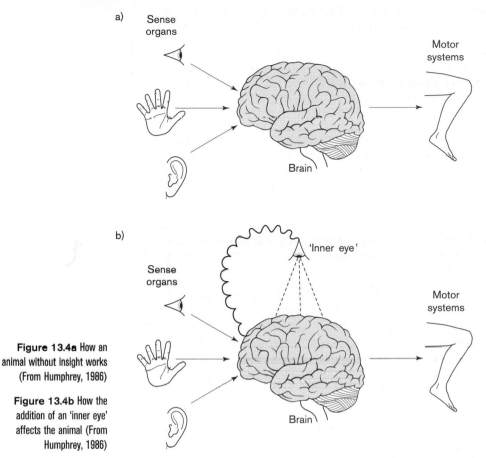

Figure 13.4a How an animal without insight works (From Humphrey, 1986)

Figure 13.4b How the addition of an 'inner eye' affects the animal (From Humphrey, 1986)

to understand what it *feels* like to be human and so to make sense of himself and other people *from the inside* ...
(Humphrey, 1993)

This, of course, is a way of looking at people as *natural psychologists* (see Chapter 1). It is no accident that humans are both the most highly *social* creatures to have evolved and are unique in their ability to use *self-knowledge* to interpret others.

Blakemore (1988) believes that Humphrey's theory raises two important questions.

1 Why does consciousness use such strange symbolism? For example, the biological value of finding a partner obviously has to do with the nitty-gritty of procreation. But we *feel* we are in *love*, a sensation that tells us nothing about the crude necessity of reproduction: 'consciousness translates biological necessities into feelings of pain and pleasure, need and emotion'.

2 Why does the inner eye see so little? It gives us only a tiny glimpse, and a distorted one at that, of the internal world (as we saw above, when discussing unconscious information processing, much of what our brains do is entirely hidden from the 'spotlight' of consciousness).

For Blakemore, our only answers to these questions is in terms of the structure and organization of the brain: 'to understand the organ that allows us to understand would be little short of a miracle. The human brain makes us what we are. It makes the mind' (Blakemore, 1988).

THE RELATIONSHIP BETWEEN MIND AND BRAIN

What Blakemore, Humphrey, Searle, and other physiologists, biologists, psychologists and philosophers, seem to be saying is that consciousness is *real*: it is a property of human beings as much as having a particular kind of body, or walking upright on two legs, or having a particular size and type of brain, are properties of human beings. They also seem agreed that, without the human brain, there would be no consciousness – the two seem to have evolved together. But this *doesn't* mean that the physical brain is in some sense 'primary', with consciousness being 'secondary'.

The logical or philosophical difficulty, as we have seen, is trying to understand how two 'things' are related, when one of them (the brain) is physical (it has size, weight, shape, location in space and time), while the other (consciousness) seems to *lack* all these characteristics.

Closely related to this logical/philosophical difficulty is the *scientific* one of explaining how it is that something non-physical or non-material can influence and produce changes in something physical or material. The classic example given by philosophers of the 'problem' of mind and body is the commonplace, everyday, taken-for-granted act of deciding to lift one's arm. Assuming that it is volitional (an act of free will), how does my 'deciding' or 'intending' to lift my arm bring about the upward physical movement of my arm (which we call 'lifting my arm')?

The problem of causation

The example of lifting my arm is 'classic', partly because it involves the idea of *causation*: how can a non-physical event (my deciding to lift my arm) cause a physical event (the lifting of my arm)? From a strictly materialist, positivistic, scientific perspective, this should be impossible (see Chapter 11 and Box 13.3, page 278). Science, including psychology and neurophysiology, has traditionally rejected any brand of *philosophical dualism*, which stems from Descartes' belief in the essential difference between the physical and the mental (or non-physical).

However, if consciousness evolved because of its survival value, could it have equipped human beings with such survival value unless it had causal properties (Gregory, 1981) – that is, unless it could actually bring about changes in behaviour? This is one of the more *psychologically relevant* questions regarding the mind–brain relationship (as opposed to the philosophically relevant – and interesting – questions). There is no doubt (as with free will, and consciousness in general) that our experience tells us our mind affects our behaviour, that consciousness has causal properties.

Lodge (2002) quotes the physicist James Trefil, who states that,

. . . no matter how my brain works, no matter how much interplay there is between my brain and my body, one single fact remains . . . I am aware of a self that looks out at the world from somewhere inside my skull . . . this is not simply an observation, but the central datum with which every theory of consciousness has to grapple. In the end the theory has to go from the firing of neurons to this essential perception.

An example of the 'reality' of non-physical factors (such as expectations, belief, faith) influencing physical processes (including changes in the brain) is the *placebo effect* (see Chapter 14).

An overview of some of the major theories of the mind–brain relationship

Trying to classify the various attempts to 'solve' the mind–body problem is both complex and a matter of some controversy, but it is necessary to have some general picture of the *types* of theory that have been proposed.

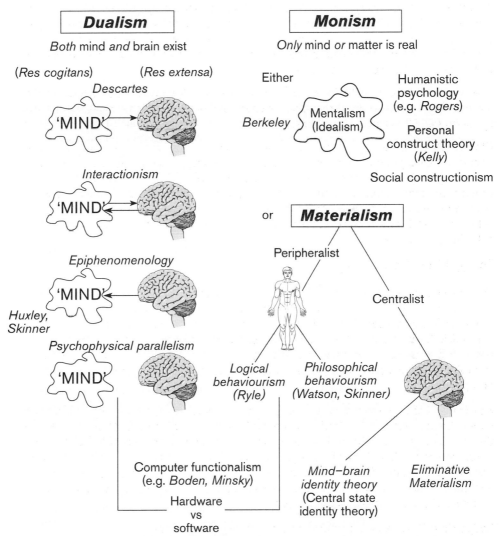

Figure 13.5 An outline of the major theories of the mind-brain relationship

According to Armstrong (1987):

If we think of mind and body as two opponents in a tug-of-war, then we can distinguish between theories which try to drag body, and matter generally, over into the camp of mind; those which try to drag mind over into the camp of body; and those theories where an equal balance is maintained.

DUALISM

The 'equal balance' theories are dualist. It was Descartes' distinction between the physical body and the non-physical mind that really introduced the mind–body problem into philosophy for the first time. Most alternative theories are an attempt to exorcize the 'ghost in the machine', which is how Ryle (1949), an Oxford philosopher with strong behaviourist leanings, attacked Descartes' belief in the non-physical, non-material, mind, with its own separate existence from the body and causal powers to control the body and, hence, behaviour.

Descartes' theory represents a 'pure' form of dualism: the mind can influence the body (through the operation of the pineal gland in the brain), whereas the body cannot influence the mind. By contrast, *interactionists* believe that body and mind influence *each other* (the influence is two-way).

Like Descartes, *epiphenomenologists* believe that the influence is only one-way, but they maintain that it works in the *opposite* direction (the brain influences the mind, but not vice-versa). An epiphenomenon is an accompanying event outside the chain of causation (a 'by-product'), and was first proposed by T.H. Huxley, who claimed that consciousness was simply the 'noise of the brain's engine at work, huffing and puffing as it went about the business of processing the information that controls behaviour (Humphrey, 1986).

Skinner was an epiphenomenologist. While accepting the existence of mental phenomena, his *radical behaviourism* involves a denial that they can have any influence on behaviour (they have no explanatory power; see Chapters 11 and 15).

Dualists who believe that there is no interaction between mind and brain, in *either* direction, are called (psychophysical) *parallelists*.

MONISM

Any theory that isn't dualist is *monist*, implying that there is only *one* kind of reality (not two, as in dualism). Monism can be *mentalist* ('trying to drag the body, and matter generally, over into the camp of mind') or *materialist* ('trying to drag mind over into the camp of body').

According to *mentalism* (or *idealism*), only mental phenomena are real. This idea seems to be contrary to the common-sense belief in the independent existence of an external reality, but it is consistent with psychologists who take a *phenomenological* approach. For example, Carl Rogers puts *experience* (and free will) at the centre of his theory of self, and according to Kelly's *personal construct theory*, the world 'is' how it is defined and interpreted by the individual (see Chapter 12). Also, any *social constructionist* approach has a mentalistic dimension (see Chapters 6 and 15).

The vast majority of monists are *materialists*, who believe that the only kind of reality is physical. It is best interpreted as the doctrine that the fundamental laws and principles of nature are exhausted by the laws and principles of physics (Armstrong, 1987). Armstrong divides materialism into two major forms, *peripheralist* and *centralist*.

PERIPHERALIST MATERIALISM

The peripheralist version is better known as *logical or philosophical behaviourism*, according to which 'the mind' is *reduced* to behaviour. For example, Watson (the founder of behaviourism) claimed that all thought processes are really no more than the sensations produced by tiny movements of the vocal cords, which are too small to produce audible sounds. In fact, he was trying to deny the existence of thought altogether and so reduce it to 'silent speech'.

Ryle's (1949) *logical behaviourism*, which is consistent with Watson's views, claims that mentalistic terms are simply a *grammatical* alternative to terms that describe behaviour: sentences about the mind can be translated into sentences about behaviour, without anything being 'left over'. Sometimes, this will involve reference to *dispositions* to behave — for example, 'John believes it's going to rain' translates into 'John will be disposed to carry an umbrella if he goes out.' According to logical behaviourism, the mind *is* behaviour plus dispositions to behave (Searle, 1992).

For Ryle, the mind—brain problem is a pseudo-problem, resulting from a purely grammatical distinction: matter is normally described using nouns/pronouns, while mind is normally described using verbs/adverbs/adjectives. If, for example, we talk about a person's 'intelligence' instead of his/her 'intelligent behaviour', we create the impression that intelligence exists in some equivalent way to the person's body, because we are using a *noun* when it is more appropriate to use an adjective. These 'category mistakes' have brought about the non-problem of the mind—brain relationship.

CENTRALIST MATERIALISM

Centralist materialism (*mind—brain identity theory* or *central state identity theory*) identifies mental processes with purely physical processes in the central nervous system. According to Place (1956) and Smart (1959), for example, there is no logical absurdity involved in supposing that there might be separate mental, non-physical phenomena, independent of material reality; it just turns out that, as a matter of fact, mental states are identical with states of the nervous system: 'The sciences of biology and psychology ... are an application of physics and chemistry to natural history ... [and] ... organisms are simply very complicated physico-chemical mechanisms' (Smart, 1959, in Teichman, 1988).

A recent example of this rather extreme form of *reductionist* materialism is *The Astonishing Hypothesis: The Scientific Search for the Soul* (1994), by Francis Crick (one of the co-discoverers of the structure of DNA; see Chapter 5). The *Astonishing Hypothesis* states that, 'You, your joys and your sorrows, your memories and your ambitions, your sense of personality and free will, are in fact no more than the behaviour of a vast assembly of nerve cells and their associated molecules' (Crick, 1994, in Smith, 1994).

Crick's objective is to correlate brain activity and consciousness and, more specifically, to identify which neurons are associated with the mere 'water' of automatism and which with the 'wine' of consciousness. But Smith, in a review of Crick's book, asks if Crick's review of all the evidence for the neurophysiological correlates of visual consciousness in primate (including human) brains takes us any further towards a solution to the mind—brain problem: 'How is it that consciousness, that 'wonder of wonders' [Husserl], is correlated with/emerges from/is the 'internal' aspect of all this intricate cerebral activity?' The problem of mind and brain, according to Smith, is radically different from other cases of *contingent identity* it is usually compared with, such as:

○ a cloud is a mass of water droplets or other particles in suspension

○ heat is mean kinetic energy

○ a gene is identical with a section of the DNA molecule.

The difference is to do with *reductionism*, and related to this is the issue of deciding exactly what we mean by *identity*.

Box 13.5 Type and token identity

It has generally been assumed that mind–brain identity implies what philosophers call *type identity*. This involves the claim that whenever a mind-state of a certain type occurs, a brain-state of a certain type occurs, such that we could study the operation of the human system using one or other framework; the results of our studies could be simply translated from one framework directly into the other. 'Mind talk' would just be an alternative way of describing the same thing as we describe using 'brain talk'.

However, the neurophysiological and neuropsychological evidence points instead towards *token identity*. Although there can never be a mind-state that isn't grounded in a brain-state of some kind or other (we cannot have a mind without a brain; see text above), a particular kind of mind-state is sometimes grounded in *one* kind of brain-state and sometimes in *another*. We cannot, therefore, substitute a brain-state description for mind-state descriptions, because these ways of looking at the system *aren't* systematically correlated (Harré *et al.*, 1985).

Broadbent (1981, in Harré *et al.*) has shown that we cannot assume that the same neurophysiological mechanisms will be used by two different people when they engage in the 'same' activity of reading; there may be many ways that 'the brain can perform the same task'. Although in a certain sense everyone 'reads with their brain', a neurophysiological description of brain function cannot displace, or replace, a psychological description: token identity means that there must always be a place for an autonomous psychological account of human action and thought (Harré *et al.*, 1985).

Even if a perfectly systematic correlation between mind-states and brain-states were found, this wouldn't be sufficient *on its own* to support the attempt to replace a psychological account of behaviour with an account in terms of neurophysiology (*eliminative materialism*), which represents an extreme reductionist form of materialism. Apart from the objections to reductionism itself, such correlational evidence would be equally consistent with *psychophysical parallelism* (a form of *dualism*; see above).

Different levels of description

Steven Rose (1992), an eminent biologist interested in the brain, argues in favour of learning how to *translate* between mind language and brain language, and against trying to replace the former with the latter: 'the mind is never replaced by the brain. Instead, we have two distinct and legitimate languages, each describing the same unitary phenomena of the material world.'

Rose is both a materialist and an *anti-reductionist*. While most reductionists are also materialists, they don't necessarily go together. Like Rose, Freud was a materialist who believed that no single scientific vocabulary (such as anatomy) could adequately describe – let alone explain – all facets of the material world. He upheld the *thesis of the autonomy of psychological explanation*: 'psychoanalysis must keep itself free from any hypothesis that is alien to it, whether of an anatomical, chemical or physiological kind and must operate with purely auxiliary ideas' (Freud, 1919, in Flanagan, 1984).

The fact that there are different 'languages' for describing minds and brains (or different *levels of description*) relates to the question of the *relevance* of knowing what is going on inside my brain when I think/am conscious:

The firing of neurons stands to thought in the same relation as my walking across the room (etc.) stands to my getting some coffee. It is absolutely essential in a causal or physical sense, and absolutely superfluous . . . to the logic of the higher-order description. In short, I can accept that it happens, and then happily ignore it . . .
(Eiser, 1994)

This explains how it is possible to be, simultaneously, a materialist (the brain is necessarily implicated in everything we do and the mind doesn't represent a different kind of reality) *and* an anti-reductionist (I can describe and explain my thinking without having to 'bring my brain into it' – two separate levels of description are involved).

IS FUNCTIONALISM A SOLUTION?

In other words, from a *psychological* point of view it is *irrelevant* to establish quite *how*, in physical terms, the brain goes about being a mind. This view isn't too dissimilar from that of the *computer functionalists* (such as Boden, Minsky and others), who, as we noted earlier, stress the importance of the processes carried out by the brain to the exclusion of what the brain is actually made of ('you don't need brains to be brainy'). They attempt to solve the mind–brain problem by distinguishing between *software* and *hardware*: the mind is to software as the brain is to hardware. Since the software/mind is what is important (logical operations involving the manipulation of symbols), the problem of the *relationship* between it and the hardware/brain disappears.

However, as Rose (1992) points out, this separation of mind from its actual material base is in some ways a reversion to Cartesian dualism. At the same time, however, by treating the brain as a sort of 'black box', whose internal biological mechanisms and processes are irrelevant, and insisting that all that matters is matching inputs to outputs, it is also behaviouristic. It seems to (re-)create some of the problems it was designed to solve, and to face the same objections as other attempted solutions. Rose concludes by saying:

Even if minds and brains have an identical *physical* reference, our knowledge of brains as brains is neither similar in kind nor comparable in extensiveness to our knowledge of minds as minds. The task of translating the one kind of knowledge into the other is so difficult – both technically and conceptually – that, for most purposes, it is almost certainly not worth the effort.

Indeed, 'For much of what it conventionally does, psychology might as well be dualist or Cartesian, and might indeed be better for admitting it' (Eiser, 1994).

SUMMARY

O Psychology began its life as a separate discipline taking consciousness/conscious mental life as its subject matter. This was then rejected by Watson's 'Behaviourist Manifesto'.

O 'Mind' has once again become legitimate subject matter and introspection is an acceptable means of collecting data, coinciding with the decline of behaviourism.

O The 'problem of consciousness' arises when we acknowledge that the physical brain is, in some way, involved in our subjective experience.

O 'Mind' is a much broader concept than 'consciousness'; there is always much more mental activity than we can detect through introspection at any one time.

O Freud distinguished between the *conscious*, *pre-conscious* and *unconscious*, which, essentially, are *levels of accessibility* of feelings and memories.

O Most psychologists accept a *continuum* of consciousness, but most wouldn't accept Freud's theory of the unconscious as a *dynamic* force, involving *repression* of threatening material.

O One way in which experimental psychologists have studied consciousness is through the concept of *attention*. An important distinction is made between *focal attention* (or focal awareness) and *peripheral attention*.

O Much of our behaviour/mental processes takes place outside our focal attention/conscious awareness (using *automatic processing*). For example, we don't want to know about *how we perceive*, but what is going on around us in the external world.

O The phenomenon of *blindsight* suggests that it is possible to show the *behaviour* of perceiving without being consciously aware of what we're doing. In blindsight and *prosopagnosia* there is a loss of *explicit conscious recognition* but the capacity for *implicit behavioural recognition*.

O Nisbett and Wilson argued that we have access only to the ideas/inferences that are the *products/outputs* of cognitive processes. This means that our common-sense/'intuitive' accounts of our own behaviour are *illusory*.

O Dennett also rejects the idea of a *privileged observer*. There is no centre in the brain that is the mind's 'I', and our sense of self is a useful fiction. But most psychologists and neuroscientists *do* believe in some kind of centre of consciousness.

O There is empirical evidence which suggests that brain activity *precedes* the conscious decision to act by about half a second. This implies that consciousness isn't, after all, a cause of behaviour.

O Edelman distinguishes between *primary* and *higher order consciousness* (or *self-consciousness*); the latter is similar to Johnson-Laird's *self-reflective automata*.

O One central feature of consciousness is *knowing what it's like to be something/someone*. Consciousness manifests itself as *qualia*: 'how things seem to us as human beings'.

O A person's ability to reflect on the method used to make a choice/decision is a basis for judging him/her to be conscious; this ability is often lacking in mentally ill, or brain-damaged people.

O If an undetectable android could be manufactured, it would prove that we are nothing but machines, whose behaviour can be completely explained scientifically. But humans will always display behaviour that cannot be completely described or explained by psychological theories.

O According to supporters of *strong AI*, people and computers are merely different manifestations of automatic formal systems/symbol manipulators.

O Searle argues that mental states/processes are real *biological* phenomena, caused by brain processes; they are higher-level features of the brain, and in principle, only a machine made of *neuroprotein* could be conscious.

O But for supporters of strong AI, it is the *computational functions* our brain chemistry allows us to perform that matter, *not* the chemistry itself.

O The difference between *parallel* (brain) and *serial processing* (most traditional computer programs) is an argument used by those opposed to strong AI. But *connectionism* is an attempt to meet this objection.

O Another objection to strong AI's exclusive emphasis on the *processes* is that it divorces the mental from the physical. According to Merleau-Ponty, without our body, we couldn't *be*. Mental and physical are both aspects of a person, and neither can be reduced to the other.

O Even though perception (and other cognitive processes) may not *require* consciousness, the fact that consciousness very often *accompanies* them and that most other species *lack* it, suggests that *it evolved in human beings for some purpose*.

O Humphrey describes consciousness as an 'inner eye', which evolved to provide a 'user-friendly' picture of the brain itself. This conferred on human beings the biological advantage of being able to *understand*, respond to and manipulate the behaviour of other human beings. People are *natural psychologists*.

O Different theories of the mind—brain relationship are trying to solve two major 'puzzles': (i) how something physical (the brain) can be related to something non-physical (consciousness); (ii) how something non-physical can influence/produce changes in something physical.

O *Philosophical dualism*, first proposed by Descartes, has traditionally been rejected by positivist, materialist science. But it is unlikely that consciousness evolved unless it had causal properties (which is impossible from a materialist perspective).

O *Interactionism* and *epiphenomenology* are both forms of dualism. They share a belief in some form of interaction between mind and brain, but they differ regarding the *direction* of this influence.

O *Psychophysical parallelists* are dualists who maintain that there is *no* mind–brain interaction.

O Any theory that isn't dualist is *monist*.

O According to *mentalism/idealism*, only mental phenomena are real. *Phenomenological* theories, such as those of Rogers and Kelly, and *constructionist* explanations of behaviour, can be seen as having a mentalist 'flavour'.

O Most monists are *materialists*, who can be divided into *peripheralists* and *centralists*.

O The *peripheralist* version is better known as *logical/philosophical behaviourism*. According to Ryle, the mind–brain problem is a pseudo-problem resulting from a purely *grammatical* confusion.

O *Centralist* materialism (*mind–brain identity theory/central state identity theory*) identifies mental processes with purely physical processes in the central nervous system.

O One of the difficulties with identity theory is that it implies *type identity*, while the available evidence points instead towards *token identity*: 'brain talk' can never displace/replace 'mind talk'.

O *Eliminative materialism* represents an extreme *reductionist* form of materialism.

O It is possible to be *both* a *materialist* and an *anti-reductionist* (such as Freud and Rose), because of the independent existence of different *levels of description*.

Useful websites

O http://psyche.cs.monash.edu.au/
O http://www.consciousness.arizona.edu/
O http://www.fil.ion.ucl.ac.uk/
O www.u.arizona.edu/~chalmers/online.html
O http://assoc.caltech.edu
O http://www.ai.mit.edu/projects/cog.

Recommended reading

Blakemore, C. and Greenfield, S. (eds) (1987) *Mindwaves.* Oxford: Basil Blackwell.

Eiser, J.R. (1994) *Attitudes, Chaos and the Connectionist Mind.* Oxford: Basil Blackwell.

Gross, R. (2003) *Key Studies in Psychology* (4th edn) (Chapter 30 on split-brain patients). London: Hodder & Stoughton.

Humphrey, N. (1992) *A History of the Mind.* London: Vintage.

Ramachandran, V.S. and Blakeslee, S. (1998) *Phantoms in the Brain.* London: Fourth Estate.

Searle, J.R. (1992) *The Rediscovery of the Mind.* Cambridge, MS: MIT Press.

PARAPSYCHOLOGY

PARANORMAL, UNUSUAL AND ANOMALISTIC EXPERIENCES

According to Roberts and Groome (2001):

We live in an age of science. However, there are many types of human experience which continue to defy any scientific explanation, at least in terms of the scientific knowledge that we have at the present time. In some cases we may have a partial explanation, but in other cases the underlying mechanism is completely unknown. These cases which completely defy any normal scientific explanation are referred to as 'paranormal' phenomena. In practice there is considerable overlap between what is regarded as 'paranormal' and what is considered to be merely 'unusual' . . .

Similarly, what Watt (2001) means by 'paranormal' is:

. . . that the phenomena appear to suggest that organisms can interact with the environment in ways that are not explicable with current scientific understanding. This does not mean that paranormal phenomena can never be understood, but it may mean that some of our present scientific knowledge and theories would need to be adjusted to accommodate them . . .

So, we don't yet know exactly how paranormal phenomena operate. Indeed, there is still some debate as to whether such phenomena exist – that is, is there a real anomalous effect occurring. 'Anomalous' here means 'not explainable in terms of our current/conventional scientific knowledge and theories' (which is also how French (2001a) defines 'the paranormal'). But this isn't the same as 'supernatural' or 'beyond nature', which implies 'incompatible with scientific theorizing and investigation' (Watt, 2001). What *do* count as paranormal, unusual or *anomalistic* phenomena are shown in Box 14.1 (see page 296).

This important distinction between 'paranormal ' and 'supernatural' is reflected in the definition of *parapsychology* as 'the scientific study of paranormal phenomena and experiences' (Watt, 2001), with the emphasis on 'scientific'. Watt's distinction between 'phenomena' and 'experiences' allows for situations in which someone might *interpret* their experience as paranormal, even though no anomalous effect is actually taking place (or there is no direct evidence of one). However, this, in turn, begs fundamental questions regarding how we establish that such effects are real. Since 'establish' usually means

Box 14.1 A brief history of parapsychology (PP), and major examples of paranormal/unusual/anomalistic phenomena

According to Blackmore (1995), credit for the founding of PP (in the 1930s) was almost entirely due to J.B. and Louisa Rhine (although Louisa is often overlooked; see Chapter 6). They were biologists who wanted to find evidence against a purely materialist view of human nature (see Chapter 13). They shared the same objectives as *spiritualism*, according to which if souls/spirits survived death of the physical body, they must exist *somewhere* in the universe, and should, in principle, be contactable (such as through mediums). A substantial number of Victorian scientists associated themselves with this religious movement, but the Rhines wanted to be seen as respectable scientists. They renamed the traditional 'psychical research' as 'parapsychology', established a department of PP at Duke University (in the USA), began to develop new experimental methods and defined their terms operationally.

J.B. Rhine introduced the term 'extrasensory perception' (ESP) in 1934. This was a general term used to cover three types of communication that supposedly occur without the use of the senses, and is otherwise called 'paranormal cognition', or 'sixth sense'.

Telepathy is 'the transmission of information from one mind to another, without the use of language, body movements, or any of the known senses' (Evans, 1987). It was previously called 'thought transference'.

Clairvoyance is 'the acquisition by a mind or brain of information which is not available to it by the known senses, and, most important, which is *not known at the time to any other mind or brain*' (Evans, 1987).

Precognition is 'the apparent ability to access information about future events before they happen' (Morris, 1989).

In all the above cases, the direction of influence is from environment to person. In *psychokinesis* (PK), influence goes from person to environment. Evans (1987) defines it as 'the supposed power of the mind to manipulate matter at a distance without any known physical means'. According to Morris (1989), it is the apparent ability to 'influence events simply by a direct volitional act of some sort, by wanting the event to happen in a certain way'.

But there is more to paranormal phenomena than these four examples (collectively known as *psi*). Roberts and Groome (2001) include astrology, sightings of aliens and UFOs, near-death experiences (NDEs; see Gross, 2003), meditation, dreams, unconscious awareness/subliminal perception, and the placebo effect (see below) in their list of paranormal or unusual experiences.

'establish *scientifically*', we have almost come full circle. This and related issues are discussed at various points throughout this chapter.

BELIEF IN THE PARANORMAL

Who believes?

Even if paranormal phenomena don't exist, paranormal *experiences*, and *belief* in paranormal phenomena, certainly do. Surveys have shown that a considerable number of people report experiences they interpret as paranormal in nature (Watt, 2001). While PK experiences are quite rare, ESP is relatively common. One random postal questionnaire survey found that 36 per cent believed in ESP, while 25 per cent had experienced it (Blackmore, 1984). A survey of over 1200 adult Americans (Gallup and Newport, 1991) found that 75 per cent admitted to reading their horoscope in the newspapers, 25 per cent expressed a firm belief in astrology, claimed to have experienced telepathy and believed in ghosts, and almost 17 per cent claimed to have seen a UFO. Responding to an appeal in the *Daily Telegraph*, 59 per cent of respondents expressed some belief in paranormal phenomena (Blackmore, 1997a).

Why do people believe?

For some, an interest in the paranormal represents no more than a bit of harmless fun (Roberts and Groome, 2001), but for many others it plays a major part in helping them to make important decisions, such as deciding to get married or change jobs on the advice of an astrologer, move house to escape a ghost or poltergeist, or take significant actions based on information they believe comes by telepathy or from a clairvoyant. Roberts and Groome maintain that belief in paranormal phenomena may cause fears and anxieties, such as living in constant dread of alien abduction – or believing it has already happened – fear of ghosts, demons and the Devil.

Some accident or catastrophe may be blamed on the intervention of some unknown force: 'The disaster was fated, in the stars, or brought about by demons or the vengeful dead.' This type of attribution can create convenient excuses for those who are actually responsible, and in failing to face up to reality they may also fail to learn from their mistakes. According to Roberts and Groome:

Telepathy, clairvoyance and astrology might all have the potential to enrich and improve our lives, provided that they are valid and genuine. However, if it turns out these paranormal phenomena are not genuine, then they represent a source of considerable confusion, misjudgement and bad decision-making . . .

For these reasons, paranormal phenomena need to be subjected to scientific investigation, in order to determine whether or not they are genuine.

In a more general sense, belief in the paranormal can be seen as one example of how we all try to interpret and make sense of our experience (see Chapters 1 and 2). By definition, unusual or anomalous events 'demand' an explanation in a way that 'ordinary' or expected events do not. So, for some people, belief in paranormal phenomena represents a 'ready-made' explanation for (certain kinds of) unusual experiences. The basic cognitive process(es) involved in explaining the ordinary and the unusual may be identical, but when someone arrives at a conclusion in terms of alien abduction, the actions of poltergeists or merely ESP, we might regard their reasoning as suspect!

According to French (2001a):

People need to make sense of anomalous experiences, and a paranormal explanation is probably seen as preferable to the notion that they are losing their sanity. Once a paranormal explanation has been accepted, it provides various secondary gains (such as a sense of being special) even though the sufferer may be genuinely afraid of further 'attacks'.

Of course, *belief* in the paranormal and reported paranormal *experiences* may be related. Perception and memory are notoriously inaccurate and unreliable, because they are biased by our expectations and beliefs. So, our interpretation of events may be distorted and imprecise. If you have a strong belief in the reality of ESP (you are a 'sheep'), you may interpret an ambiguous occurrence (for example, a coincidence between a dream and a subsequent telephone call) as being due to ESP. But if you are highly sceptical (you are a 'goat'), you are likely to reject the ESP interpretation as improbable or impossible (Watt, 2001).

Who studies paranormal phenomena?

French (2001a) describes himself as an *anomalistic psychologist*, not because he is especially unusual (he's a real human being, not a ghost or an alien), but because he studies *anomalistic psychology* (AP). This attempts to explain:

... paranormal and related beliefs and ostensibly paranormal experiences in terms of known (or knowable) psychological and physical factors. It is directed at understanding bizarre experiences that many people have, without assuming that there is anything paranormal involved ...

One example he gives is that of sleep paralysis. This is a temporary state in which an individual who is either drifting off to sleep or emerging from sleep suddenly realizes that their muscles are totally paralysed. This is frightening enough, but the state is sometimes associated with bizarre and terrifying images of demons, monsters, hags or aliens, and a strong sense of an evil presence. This is a common symptom of narcolepsy, in which the patient suddenly, and uncontrollably, collapses in a state of unconsciousness, any time of the day or night, and in any situation. But many non-narcoleptics suffer from sleep paralysis at least once in their lives.

French argues that while psychology, neurology and other scientific disciplines are rich in explanatory models for many kinds of human experiences, these models are rarely extrapolated to explain unusual experiences. AP tries to do just that. Its aims, he says, would still be valid even if the existence of paranormal forces were to be established beyond doubt, 'because there is little question that most paranormal claims can be plausibly explained in non-paranormal terms'.

Do you have to be a non-believer to study anomalistic psychology?

According to French (2001a), the range and variety of topics covered by AP makes it an excellent tool for teaching critical thinking skills. Most people are familiar with these topics via the media, which create a strong pro-paranormal bias. Students can discuss why some sources of evidence should be treated as more reliable than others, as well as alternative explanations for paranormal experiences. A variety of psychological factors, most notably the limitations and biases of human cognition (see Chapter 2), can lead us into drawing faulty conclusions.

Although AP adopts the working hypothesis that paranormal forces don't exist, it allows for the *possibility* that they *do*. Most sceptics aren't very well informed about parapsychology, and they assume that all apparently positive evidence for psi must be the result of delusion, deception, and incompetence (see above). But techniques used by experimental parapsychologists have become much more refined and sophisticated in the light of previous criticisms. Many are easily on a par with the best psychological studies. Some parapsychologists appear to present evidence in support of the existence of paranormal forces even from such apparently well-controlled experiments. Either these findings should be accepted at face value, or critics should try to specify the subtle methodological flaws responsible for the misleading results (French, 2001a). French argues that:

> Those who attempt to explain away the paranormal are often criticised by believers for being closed-minded. For me, being closed-minded equates to an unwillingness to consider the evidence relating to a particular claim. Attempting to consider all the possible alternative explanations for a particular phenomenon and accepting the need to produce empirical evidence for one's favoured hypothesis is not being closed-minded . . . But non-parapsychological explanations will only be found if one looks for them. If such explanations are found, we will have learned important truths about human nature in the process . . .

In trying to explain the widespread belief in psi and personal experience of it, French says there are only two possibilities: either (i) at least some of these anomalistic experiences really do reflect the operation of paranormal forces, which would have profound implications for our scientific worldview, as well as our understanding of our place in the universe; or (ii) we may be able to explain all aspects of these experiences in terms of knowable psychological and physical factors. Most psychologists adopt a narrow-minded view that paranormal phenomena don't merit serious study. Notable exceptions include Blackmore, Wiseman and Morris in the UK (see Box 14.1 and Gross, 2003), and Spanos, Loftus and Lynn in the USA. However, there is a steadily increasing number of journal articles and books on the topic, and both conferences and undergraduate courses are becoming more common (French, 2001a).

EXPERIMENTAL INVESTIGATION OF PARANORMAL PHENOMENA

Watt (2001) points out that *chance* may play an important part in many spontaneous paranormal experiences. Striking coincidences *will* happen by chance alone, but when they happen to you personally, they can have a very powerful and meaningful effect. Consequently, although spontaneous paranormal experiences are valuable in showing how these experiences occur naturally, parapsychologists also conduct research under laboratory conditions in order to gain a better understanding of psi phenomena.

Studying ESP through altered states of consciousness (ASC)

Probably the strongest evidence for ESP comes from a line of research that uses altered states of consciousness (ASC) to facilitate ESP performance. The underlying idea behind studying ESP through ASC is described in Box 14.2, page 300.

The Ganzfeld

'Ganz' = 'whole' and 'feld = 'field'. The method was first used for psi research by Honorton in 1974. Consistent with the rationale outlined in Box 14.2, Honorton argued that the reason ESP occurs in dreams, meditation and reverie, is that they are all states of reduced sensory input and increased internal attention. He tried to find a way of producing such a 'psi-conducive' state without the expense of a dream laboratory. The basic arrangement is described in Box 14.3, page 301.

THE 'GANZFELD DEBATE'

Honorton (1985) analysed 28 studies using the Ganzfeld procedure (totalling 835 sessions, conducted in ten different laboratories). He reported a 38 per cent correct selection of the

---

Box 14.2 Altered states of consciousness (ASC) and ESP

The basic idea is that normally we live in a very distracting, noisy environment, both internal and external. The ESP information may be like a very weak signal. If it were a strong signal, then we would know all about it already, and there would be no debate as to its existence. In order to help the *receiver* (or recipient) of the ESP to detect the weak ESP signal among the distracting noise, parapsychologists use noise-reduction techniques. These include helping the receiver to relax physically and mentally – the 'noise-reduction model' of ESP (Honorton and Harper, 1974; Braud, 1975).

Parapsychologists used noise-reduction techniques because they noticed several converging lines of evidence, which suggested that such states of consciousness facilitated ESP. In the late nineteenth century, many 'spiritual mediums' claimed to be able to obtain information paranormally through trance. More recently, it has been claimed that ESP could be enhanced by using hypnosis (Honorton and Krippner, 1969). Large-scale surveys of spontaneous psychic experiences have found that about two-thirds of cases occurred during dream states (Rhine, 1969). When parapsychologists tested for ESP using sleep laboratories, the positive results were very encouraging (Ullman *et al.*, 1973). But studying ESP this way is expensive and time-consuming. An alternative method is the 'Ganzfeld' (see Box 14.3, page 301).

(Based on Watt, 2001)

---

target, which compares with a 25 per cent success rate by chance alone (i.e. by guessing). Statistically, this is highly significant: the chance of obtaining a 38 per cent success rate by chance alone is less than one in a billion (Honorton, 1985). However, a critical review by Hyman (in the *Journal of Parapsychology*, 1985) pointed out discrepancies in the scoring systems used, and procedural flaws (such as the failure to use proper randomization for selecting the targets). Hyman also claimed to have found correlations between the quality rating of a study and its outcome: the sloppier studies gave 'better' results. But in the same journal, Honorton claimed to have found *no* evidence of such a correlation. Rosenthal provided a commentary on the debate, generally regarded as favouring Honorton's interpretation (Blackmore, 1995).

Hyman and Honorton issued a joint 'communiqué' in 1986, in which they agreed that the studies as a whole fell short of ideal, but that something beyond selective reporting, or inflated significance levels, seemed to be producing the above-chance outcomes. They also agreed that the significant outcomes had been produced by several different researchers. Further replications would decide which of their interpretations was correct.

This 'debate' – 'an outstanding example of productive interaction between critic and researcher' (Morris, 1989) – brought parapsychologists and sceptics together to try to agree what would constitute an acceptable experiment. As a consequence, Honorton designed a *fully automated* Ganzfeld experiment, leaving little scope for human error or deliberate fraud. Several experiments using this procedure produced significant results. These were published, in the form of meta-analysis, in the *Psychological Bulletin* (Bem and Honorton, 1994), one of the (western) world's most prestigious psychology journals. It meant that 'The Ganzfeld had achieved respectability' (Blackmore, 1997b). However, despite many parapsychologists' belief that the Ganzfeld is a genuinely respectable experiment, and that it provides evidence for ESP (e.g. Utts, 1991; Bem and Honorton, 1994), most other scientists still tend to reject the findings.

Box 14.3 The Ganzfeld

Halved ping-pong balls are taped over the receiver's eyes and red light is shone into them, so all that can be seen is a pinkish glow. Soothing sea-sounds or hissing 'white noise' (like a radio that's not properly tuned in) are played through headphones while the participant lies on a comfortable couch or reclining chair. While this doesn't constitute total sensory deprivation, the Ganzfeld deprives receivers of patterned input, which encourages internal imagery. They typically report a pleasant sensation of being immersed in a 'sea of light'.

A *sender* (an experimenter acting as an agent) is situated in a separate, acoustically isolated, room. A visual stimulus (a picture, slide or brief video sequence) is randomly selected from a large pool of similar stimuli to serve as the *target*. While the sender concentrates on the target (for about 15 minutes), the receiver tries to describe it by providing a continuous verbal report of his/her ongoing imagery and free associations. The sender stays in the room for another ten minutes. From a separate room, the experimenter can both hear (via a microphone) and see (via a one-way mirror) the receiver, and is blind to the target (doesn't know what the target is).

At the end of the experimental session, the receiver is presented with four stimuli (one of which is the target), and asked to rate the degree to which each one matches the imagery and associations experienced during the session. A 'direct hit' is recorded if the receiver assigns the highest rating to the target. The sender is then called in and reveals the target. A typical experiment involves about 30 sessions.

Figure 14.1 Illustration of a Ganzfeld experiment

The Koestler Parapsychology Unit at Edinburgh University is the UK's premier centre for Ganzfeld research. Of the six studies conducted since the unit opened, four have produced statistically significant results. Also, Milton and Wisemen (1999) published a further meta-analysis on Ganzfeld studies that had been conducted prior to 1997. This included 30 studies from seven independent laboratories. The analysis showed only chance success rates – that is, the 'new-generation' studies appeared to provide no replicable evidence for psi. Since then, some more positive findings have emerged. The 'debate' still rages (Watt, 2001).

According to Watt, there is also disagreement among parapsychologists themselves as to what counts as a 'standard' Ganzfeld. For instance, should Ganzfeld experiments using auditory targets be regarded as distinct from those using visual targets? This disagreement suggests that there is a need for systematic research into exactly what features are important in eliciting ESP.

Box 14.4 Proof-oriented versus process-oriented research into ESP

Researchers aren't simply interested in demonstrating the *existence* of ESP (*proof-oriented research*), they also need to understand *how ESP operates* (*process-oriented research*). For example, what types of people perform particularly well at ESP tasks? What is the mechanism that allows ESP to operate? Is extra-sensory information processed in the same way as other types of information?

Progress is slow, but some patterns are beginning to emerge. For example, a study involving students from the Juilliard School for the Performing Arts in New York found remarkably high success rates: 50 per cent of targets were correctly identified (Schlitz and Honorton, 1992). These results would occur by chance alone once in a hundred times. They led to the prediction that creative people would perform well in subsequent studies. This was confirmed by Morris *et al.* (1993: 41 per cent success rate), Morris *et al.* (1995: 33 per cent) and Dalton (1997: 47 per cent). In Dalton's study, musicians had the highest success rates, followed by artists. Actors and writers had the lowest, but they still performed at significantly higher than chance levels.

Research with the Ganzfeld and other techniques has indicated that extra-sensory impressions can be vague and fleeting. Receivers rarely give an exact, unambiguous description of the target. This suggests that they resemble weak sensory impressions, where one obtains only incomplete information that may be distorted or only partially represented in conscious awareness. In fact, some parapsychologists have explicitly suggested that extra-sensory information is processed in a similar way to *subliminal* (i.e. below the threshold of conscious recognition) or weak sensory information.

(Based on Watt, 2001)

PHILOSOPHICAL AND METHODOLOGICAL ISSUES

Science and truth

The Ganzfeld 'debate' is a good example of how bias, prejudice, belief and other attributes of the scientist can influence what research s/he does, and how s/he interprets the research findings of other scientists. This detracts from the positivist nature of science, according to which scientists discover the true nature of the world (i.e. they are objective). According to Roberts (2001), what scientists claim is that the relationships between events that science describes in some way mirror or approximate to events that are assumed to occur in a world that is real and exists independently of any human sensory contact with it. This is the doctrine of *scientific realism* (see Chapter 11).

In the physical sciences, there is a sense in which scientific realism *must* be valid, otherwise the technological applications of scientific theories and research couldn't work. Roberts gives the example of knowledge of the mathematical relationships describing motion, which enable a spacecraft to be put into orbit:

These mathematical descriptions are not arbitrary . . . they do not depend upon a social or public consensus that they are correct. They must fit with reality in some deep sense – otherwise the spacecraft could not remain in orbit, and the practical possibilities of satellite communications and human space travel could not be brought into being.

However, there have been many criticisms of scientific realism and the positivist approach (see Chapter 11 for a detailed discussion). According to Roberts, a recurring issue is whether we should think of science in terms of what scientists *actually* do, or in the ideal, abstract terms of what scientists *ought* to do. As indicated above, scientific activity is influenced by many factors: personal, social and political, apart from/in addition to, the actual phenomenon under investigation. It is essentially *creative*. So, how is it possible that science 'works', as in Roberts' spacecraft example? He argues that there is an article of faith involved in science, according to which the 'laws of nature' are in principle comprehensible and consistent throughout the universe. It is difficult to contemplate how science could be 'done' at all without it. There is also a self-correcting tendency that helps to distinguish science from other disciplines/activities that might also lay claim to the truth: 'what is being corrected is the mismatch (or potential mismatch) between what is predicted from theory and which may be suggested by observation' (Roberts, 2001).

Is scientific study of psi possible?

The preceding discussion has in effect been about natural/physical science. So, how does scientific realism and the notion of scientific objectivity apply to psychology? These issues are discussed in detail in Chapter 11, but suffice it to say here that there are many good reasons for believing that trying to study human behaviour in the way that natural scientists investigate the physical world is a highly complex, problematical and controversial matter (see also Chapter 15). (This perhaps isn't surprising, given that science was originally invented, constructed and elaborated for the study of natural objects.) This is especially true when the 'behaviour' refers to people's self-reported experiences, such as dreams, NDEs, ESP, and alien abductions. (These are, of course, the stuff of para-/anomalistic psychology.) As Roberts (2001) says, 'the private unobservable nature of human experience seems to render it unsuitable for scientific scrutiny'.

Roberts identifies two major ways of systematically investigating (reports of) paranormal experiences.

1 One strategy is to look for correlations between self-reports and other, more easily observable, phenomena, then to try to establish the conditions under which such reports are made. For example, the existence of both sleep and dreaming relies on self-reports of human participants. With sleep, the reports are validated by the appearance of particular *behavioural* or *physiological* indicators (such as brainwave patterns as measured by an electroencephalogram/EEG) linked to levels of arousal occurring immediately prior to a report. But more important as indicators of the existence of a distinct mental state are the *cognitive* correlates of reporting, immediately after waking (such as the detailed description of a dream). These correlates may themselves be correlated, as when eye-ball movements (during rapid eye movement/REM sleep) correspond to events that supposedly occurred in the dream. This inference is supported by the fact that an overwhelming majority of people report such experiences under these conditions. But all of this data might only tell us something about the nature of the reports; by itself it cannot establish the reality/truth of the experiences that the reports supposedly refer to.

2 Once the researchers are satisfied that a particular phenomenon is real, they might turn their attention to the actual contents of the experience, and systematically explore how it can be modified or transformed. For example, this could be done externally through drugs or sensory deprivation, or internally through acts of will or cognition.

HOW DO WE KNOW THAT PRIVATE EXPERIENCES ARE REAL?

Roberts (2001) discusses how we establish the reality of different kinds of experience. The initial stages of scientific investigation must begin with establishing the truth/reality of the experience (i.e. determining its 'boundary conditions'). Science begins with the report as the prime data, *not* by assuming the reality of the reported experience.

Although experiences such as dreaming, remembering and consciously experiencing the world are private, we assume their veracity in others, partly through our mutual identification with them as beings like us who have the same kind of conscious experiences that we do. When it comes to claims of more esoteric experiences (e.g. alien abductions), this type of common ground simply does not exist.

So, in these various ways, science isn't opposed in any fundamental way to the study of experience. What makes science distinctive is in its *interpretative stance* towards reported experience:

By itself experience cannot be and is not regarded as sufficient evidence for the independent reality of what people observe. The difficulties of interpreting reports of certain experiences [especially paranormal phenomena] ... are compounded by virtue of their frequently being presented in terms of an interpretation – an explanation of their origins – rather than an account of only the contents (the phenomenology) of the experience ...

In other words, reports of out-of-body experiences (OBEs), ESP and other paranormal experiences are usually made in terms that presuppose the causes behind them. For example, 'OBEs are caused by the mind leaving the body', or 'people share common thoughts, etc., because thought transmission takes place between them'.

We need to disentangle the process by which people arrive at an interpretation of their experience and just what it was they originally experienced. In the case of people claiming to have seen ghosts, for example, closer questioning should lead to a distinction between (i) perceived physical sensations (such as coldness) and psychological sensations (such as fear or anxiety) experienced at the location; and (ii) the subsequent attribution that these are causally linked to someone having died there. Roberts believes that the psychology of attribution can help shed light not just on the 'wild and wonderful' experiences people report, but also on their beliefs about how the world is structured (see Chapter 2).

Are paranormal experiences a special case?

Roberts (2001) argues that,

The correct attitude of the scientists faced with reports of unusual experiences is to seek further evidence for or against the existence of such experiences. It does not mean that such accounts must *necessarily* be dismissed. Absence of evidence is not of course the same as evidence of absence . . .

This may seem like a fair and reasonable position to adopt in whatever scientific discipline someone may be working, and regardless of the particular phenomena under investigation. But a feature of the history of parapsychological research has been accusations of fraud – the deliberate invention or modification of procedures or results. Arguably, this makes the study of psi unique as an area of psychological enquiry (Gross, 2001). At least as far as 'goats' are concerned, parapsychologists are guilty unless proven innocent. In other words, if psi doesn't exist (as goats maintain), then any claims by 'sheep' that it does must be based on fraudulent (or, at best, unreliable and/or invalid) data. So, rather than simply trying to produce evidence that supports the existence of psi, parapsychologists are constantly having to show that they are *not cheating*! But how can you prove a negative?

The history of PA also seems to highlight a number of methodological issues, which, while they recur throughout all areas of psychological research, assume a more exaggerated or extreme form in relation to psi. These include:

- the question of *the 'conclusive experiment*
- the *replication problem*
- *publication bias* (or the *file-drawer problem*)
- the *inadequacy of controls*
- *experimenter* and *participant effects.*

For a discussion of these, see Gross (2001) and Rao and Palmer (1987).

According to Watt (2001), the 'replication problem' is probably the greatest challenge facing parapsychologists. If psi is a weak and unreliable effect, and PA is a relatively small field with only limited resources, then finding replicable evidence for psi will prove difficult. Where people are involved, it is difficult to find well-established 'laws' of behaviour (unlike the physical sciences). This makes replicability difficult – as it is in behavioural research in general.

As far as experimenter and participant effects are concerned, the experimental system in PP research is a particularly 'open' one. Whenever human participants are involved, they will try to make sense of the experimental situation, which includes trying to work out the aims of the experiment and their role in relation to the aims – they look for the *demand characteristics* in the experimental situation (Orne, 1962; see Chapter 11). The usual 'blind' methods used to prevent or limit the experimenter's unintentional influence on the participants' behaviour, don't apply here. If ESP really exists, can the participant read the experimenter's mind? Can the experimenter use PK to directly influence delicate physical instruments? If this is possible, the experimental environment is even more open than was previously thought. Watt states that, 'If psi is a genuine effect, this has the startling implication that all research is vulnerable to unintended exchange of information and influence.'

It might be impossible to use completely blind methods, because these could be penetrated by ESP: 'This would mean that all experimental findings could be affected, perhaps with the person having most motivation to find a certain outcome (usually the experimenter) being most likely to influence the experiment.'

While this doesn't invalidate all experimental research, it means that researchers have to learn more about its limiting conditions. In general, researchers must become more sophisticated in developing strategies to deal with the study of complex open systems. Parapsychologists are particularly well placed to develop this expertise, as the question of experimenter influence has a particularly high profile. It is already well established that certain experimenters consistently obtain positive results, while others consistently obtain null results. While this could be just a chance pattern, some critics have suggested that the former are either fraudulent or sloppy. However, there is no consistent evidence to support this claim.

As Watt points out, another possibility is that PP's experimenter effects are due to experimenter psi, with some particularly psychic experimenters able to influence a study's outcome according to their desires and expectations. There is some evidence that successful experimenters do tend to perform well on laboratory psi tasks. It is also possible that some experimenters are better at eliciting psi from their participants – perhaps they are more enthusiastic or able to help participants relax and feel confident. Again, some may be better at recruiting the right type of participants (that is, recognizing those who perform well under experimental conditions). Watt concludes by saying that all of these issues may be relevant to other fields of research (both in and outside psychology): 'Regardless of the reality or otherwise of psi, science has much to gain from investigating paranormal phenomena and experiences.'

THE PLACEBO EFFECT: A CASE STUDY IN PARAPSYCHOLOGICAL RESEARCH

As we noted in Box 14.1, Roberts and Groome (2001) include the placebo effect (PE) among paranormal or unusual experiences ('placebo' = Latin for 'I will please'; French, 2001b). They define it as 'the tendency for a therapy to have a beneficial effect which exceeds its known therapeutic mechanisms, sometimes as a result of mere suggestion and expectation on the part of the patient'.

According to Shapiro and Shapiro (1997), the PE is 'the nonspecific, psychological or psychophysiologic therapeutic effect produced by a placebo, or the effect of spontaneous improvement attributed to the placebo'. They define a placebo as 'any therapy prescribed ... for its therapeutic effect on a symptom or disease, but which is actually ineffective or not specifically effective for the symptom or disorder being treated'.

The problem with PEs

The definitions above imply that placebos *shouldn't* work, and that PEs *shouldn't* happen. They represent an attack on the whole scientific paradigm, clearly shaking the foundations of the *biomedical model* (Di Blasi, 2003). According to Ogden (2000), the biomedical model maintains that:

○ diseases come from either outside the body and invade it, causing internal physical changes, or originate as involuntary internal physical changes; such diseases can be caused by chemical imbalances, bacteria, viruses or genetic predisposition

○ individuals aren't responsible for their illnesses, which arise from biological changes beyond their control; people who are ill are victims

○ treatment should consist of vaccination, surgery, chemotherapy or radiotherapy, all of which aim to change the physical state of the body

○ mind and body function independently of each other; the abstract mind relates to feelings and thoughts, and is incapable of influencing physical matter

○ illness may have psychological consequences, but not psychological causes.

Harrington (1997, in Di Blasi, 2003) described placebos as 'ghosts that haunt our house of biomedical objectivity . . . and expose the paradoxes and fissures in our own self-created definitions of the real and active factors in treatment'.

But long before the advent of science and modern medicine, treating disease seemed to rely very largely on the power of placebos. French (2001b) notes that drug treatments used over the centuries included such useless but exotic items as usnea (moss from the skulls of victims of a violent death), Vigo's plaster (viper's flesh, live frogs and worms), parts of the skulls of executed criminals, ants, spiders' webs, the saliva of a fasting man, and sexual organs and excreta of all kinds. Patients were also subjected to such extreme and therapeutically worthless procedures as purging, puking, poisoning, blistering, freezing and heating, leeching, and shocking. All societies throughout recorded history have revered 'healers' (physicians or witch doctors) attributed with special powers. This in itself is an illustration of the power of placebos. According to French (2001b), 'The truth is, of course, that the placebo effect is still a major part of modern medicine, although typically it is not exploited in any systematic way.' However, those who practise complementary and alternative medicine (CAM) could be seen as maximizing the PE.

CAM, conventional medicine and the ethics of PEs

The treatments used in CAM have rarely received strong support, or even been tested with double-blind randomized control trials (RCTs). In RCTs, neither the researcher nor the participants know who has been given the active treatment and who has received the placebo, and participants are randomly allocated to the treatment and placebo conditions. But alternative therapists are invariably convinced that their treatments are effective. This confidence is likely to rub off on the client, raising expectations of recovery. The therapist is also likely to spend a long time listening sympathetically to the client, taking all their symptoms, however vague, very seriously (French, 2001b).

Compare this with the average GP or hospital doctor, who is under great time constraints. S/he probably feels morally obliged to inform the patient of any uncertainties regarding diagnosis, the chances of a particular treatment being effective and the possible side-effects. Most conventional doctors feel it would be unethical not to provide the patient with as much information as possible. But the very act of informing patients of doubts and uncertainties is likely to undermine the PE. Even worse than providing incomplete information would be to give patients *false* information. As French (2001b) says:

Even though a clinician may suspect that prescribing an inert sugar pill might help some patients to feel better, he or she may feel that to do so is a betrayal of the basic trust which should exist between doctor and patient . . .

The dilemma is, if you believe the treatment is inactive, you will be failing to meet one of your obligations as a doctor, namely to give your patient some hope and confidence. This conflicts with another obligation, namely to be honest and trustworthy. But French argues that there is more to the PE than simply giving patients inert treatments. He cites evidence which shows that patients are more likely to improve if: (i) they are thoroughly examined (even if the doctor is certain of the diagnosis); or (ii) given a positive assessment (such as 'I can't find anything seriously wrong with you, and you'll almost certainly feel much better in a week or two') when the doctor cannot give a specific diagnosis. French advocates that:

> If physicians can see placebos – like many conventional drugs – as broadly effective therapies, whose mechanisms of action are not broadly understood and which tend to be more effective for some patients than others, they can then offer placebos both honestly and as plausible treatment.

Are PEs real?

Given how widespread PEs are within medicine, it is perhaps surprising how relatively little research has been done into trying to understand them (French, 2001b). This reflects PEs' negative image in modern western medicine, and their associations with charlatans and quacks. Kienle and Kiene (1998, 2001, in Di Blasi, 2003) reviewed the existing evidence, and concluded that the PE isn't a powerful therapeutic tool but an illusion created by scientific artefacts. This was supported by a separate review (Hrobjartsson and Gotsche, 2001, in Di Blasi) of 114 trials in which 'placebo' and 'no treatment groups' were compared (a 'true' test of PEs according to these researchers). They found 'little evidence in general that placebos had powerful clinical effects'.

However, the PE is an essential ingredient of *all* therapeutic interventions, and it is a conceptual mistake to oppose the placebo (i.e. inactive) effect from the 'true' therapeutic effect of an active treatment (French, 2001b). PEs have been reported in all areas of medicine, including the treatment of depression, anxiety, nausea, diabetes and multiple sclerosis. Most research has been carried out in the area of pain control. Many patients given what they are told is a powerful analgesic will report significant reduction in levels of pain – even if the pain is caused by cancer (French, 2001b).

French identifies several myths surrounding the PE, one of which is the claim that placebos only affect the subjective aspects of *illness* (how people feel about their health, their experience of pain, discomfort, distress etc.), and not objective measures of *disease* (the existence of a pathological process). But this seems to represent only a minority opinion. French cites evidence that objective variables such as the results of blood tests, post-operative tissue swelling, body temperature and the healing of wounds, are all 'placebo-prone'.

Research is now turning to how placebos can induce changes in the brains of patients randomly allocated to placebos. Leuchter *et al.* (2002) wanted to find out exactly what takes place in the brain when someone responds to a placebo in an antidepressant trial. The general assumption has been that placebos work because they somehow activate the same neural pathways that drugs do. This certainly seems to be what happens with placebos used for pain control (Burne, 2002). However, the 32 per cent who responded to the placebo showed quite *different* patterns of brain activation to the 52 per cent who responded to the drug. Placebo responders showed heightened activity in the executive prefrontal lobes, an increase that continued throughout the trial. Drug responders at first showed a decline in the prefrontal area, then a rise, which tapered off. However, once the study was over and the placebo responders were *told* about the treatment allocation, most relapsed and had to be put on drug treatment. Other studies have shown that this doesn't happen with all placebo responders (Di Blasi *et al.*, 2002).

A Canadian study (cited in Burne, 2002) found that the placebo responders showed *similar* brain activity to those given an SSRI antidepressant (of which Prozac is an example). Both groups showed increased activity in the 'thinking' frontal lobes, and a decrease in the 'emotional' limbic system. This mixed evidence suggests that there may not be a general rule about how placebos affect brain activity, but both studies strongly support the claim that the PE is *real* (if, sometimes, short-lived). There's also some evidence that the PE has increased in recent years. A higher percentage of depressed patients improve on placebos than 20 years ago. A major reason for this is almost certainly *rising expectations* (Burne, 2002).

But, equally, negative publicity about drugs can *reduce* their effectiveness. The so-called 'nocebo' (= 'I will harm') has been demonstrated in research where people given a sugar pill were told it would cause headache and drowsiness. A substantial proportion will report such effects. Similarly, patients warned about the gastrointestinal side-effects of taking aspirin were three times more likely to suffer from them (Burne, 2002). Effects can range from slight to extremely strong, and claims that voodoo curses can actually cause death have been explained in terms of extreme nocebo effects (French, 2001b)!

So, what can we conclude about PEs?

According to Di Blasi (2003), the PE, having first been ignored, then controlled for its presumed contaminating effects, is now studied as an important phenomenon in its own right. Researchers increasingly felt that the PE 'was the most magical, mysterious and most widely misunderstood phenomenon in medicine'. Drugs are promoted in ways that try to maximize their effect, with evocative names such as 'Regaine' (for thinning hair), 'Welldorm' (for insomnia) and 'Marvelon' (as a marvellous contraceptive). The colour of drugs has also been shown to affect their perceived effects: red, yellow and orange are perceived as stimulants, while blue and green are perceived as tranquillizers or sedatives (Di Blasi, 2003).

The existence of PEs raises some fundamental questions regarding the interactions between 'mind' and 'body' (see Chapter 13). One explanation of the PE in relation to pain management is that pain relief is achieved through the production of endorphins, the brain's natural pain-killers (Levine *et al.*, 1978; ter Riet *et al.*, 1998, in French, 2001b). But, according to Harrington (1997, in French, 2001b):

Endorphin release, rather, became one more placebo-generated phenomenon to be explained – and we still did not understand the processes whereby a person's belief in a sham treatment could send a message to his or her pituitary gland to release its own endogenous pharmaceutics.

Further research will almost certainly show that we need to speak of placebo *effects*, and that each effect may require a different explanation. But they will all confront the same philosophical conundrum: how can *psychological* factors, such as beliefs and expectations, set in motion *physical/physiological* processes that result in measurable changes in the body and/or the brain?

Perhaps part of the problem is that modern medicine, as well as psychology and 'common sense', all share the same basic *dualism* of 'mind' and 'body'. It is only when we split mind and body in this completely artificial way that we have to try to account for how the physical can be influenced by the non-physical. As Di Blasi (2003) says:

With growing evidence of mind–body interactions in healing and with our current crisis in health care, a revolutionary paradigm shift needs to occur. Rather than fixing the cracks in the biomedical model, we need to break the box, remove the gap between medicine and psychology, and welcome back the discredited sister of scientific medicine.

The 'discredited sister', of course, is the placebo effect.

SUMMARY

O Paranormal or anomalistic phenomena are those that defy explanation in terms of currently available scientific knowledge. *Parapsychology* (PP) is the scientific study of these phenomena, collectively called *psi*.

O *Extra-sensory perception* (ESP) refers to *telepathy*, *clairvoyance* and *precognition*. Other examples of paranormal phenomena include *psychokinesis* (PK), *near-death experiences* (NDEs) and the *placebo effect* (PE).

O PP grew out of *spiritualism*, which stimulated 'psychical research' and which was popular among many Victorian scientists. The Rhines wanted to put this research on a respectable scientific footing.

O Surveys have shown that belief in paranormal phenomena is widespread, with many people interpreting personal experiences as paranormal in nature.

O Belief in the paranormal can influence people's behaviour in important ways, such as making life-changing decisions, and it represents a way of trying to make sense of unusual or *anomalistic* events. But attributing events to paranormal forces may relieve people of responsibility for their actions.

O People who believe in the paranormal ('sheep') are more likely to interpret ambiguous events (such as coincidences) in terms of paranormal forces than are sceptics/non-believers ('goats').

O *Anomalistic psychology* (AP) attempts to understand paranormal/bizarre experiences in terms of known psychological and physical factors, without assuming that there is anything paranormal involved. But it allows for the possibility that paranormal forces do exist.

O If even some anomalistic experiences turn out to reflect the operation of paranormal forces, we would have to change our scientific worldview, as well as our understanding of our place in the universe. Most psychologists are goats, believing that paranormal phenomena don't merit serious study. But this narrow-minded view is being challenged as PP and AP research expands.

O Perhaps the strongest evidence for ESP comes from research that uses *altered states of consciousness* (ASC). This involves the use of noise-reduction techniques, allowing 'weak' ESP signals to be detected by the receiver. The main method used by parapsychologists is the *Ganzfeld*.

O The Ganzfeld involves reduced sensory input combined with increased internal attention. It is a standardized experimental procedure, which has generated many studies since 1974, resulting in the famous 'Ganzfeld debate' in 1985. This brought parapsychologists and sceptics together to try to agree what would constitute an acceptable experiment. The result was a *fully automated* Ganzfeld. But the debate continues.

O *Proof-oriented research* tries to demonstrate the existence of ESP, while *process-oriented research* tries to understand how it operates. The latter has shown that creative people, especially musicians, are most likely to perform well in ESP experiments. Also, extra-sensory information may be processed in a similar way to *subliminal* or weak sensory information.

O In the physical/natural sciences, the doctrine of *scientific realism* must be valid, otherwise technological applications of scientific theories could not work. But scientific activity is driven by many factors other than the phenomenon under investigation, and is essentially creative.

O Science only works because of an article of faith regarding the laws of nature, plus a self-correcting tendency that helps to distinguish science from other attempts to discover the truth.

O Trying to apply scientific realism to psychology is problematical and controversial, especially when the subject matter consists of people's self-reports of paranormal experiences. Looking for correlations between self-reports and more objective, observable phenomena (behavioural/physiological/cognitive) is one solution, although this cannot by itself establish the reality of the reported experiences.

O A problem with establishing the reality of paranormal experiences is that they are often described in terms of an interpretation, which presupposes their causes. We need to disentangle the process by which people interpret their experience from the original experience.

O Throughout PP's history, parapsychologists have been accused of fraud, which makes the study of psi unique as an area of psychological investigation. Its history also highlights certain methodological issues that recur throughout psychological research as a whole, such as the *replication problem* and *experimenter/participant effects*.

O Parapsychological research involves a particularly 'open' experimental system, with the possibility that ESP itself will influence the outcome. This may make experimental control much more difficult to achieve than in other research areas.

O According to the *biomedical model* of disease, *placebos* should not work and *placebo effects* (PEs) shouldn't happen. But illness and disease have always been treated using useless remedies, and the PE is still a major part of modern western medicine.

O Doctors face an ethical dilemma about deliberately using placebos but not informing their patients about them. There is a conflict between their obligation to help patients and to be honest with them.

O Evidence from all areas of medicine suggests very strongly that the PE is a real phenomenon. It affects not only subjective aspects of illness, but also objective measures of disease. There is also growing evidence that placebos can induce changes in patients' brains.

O The PE is exploited by drug companies through the brand names they give to their products, and a drug's colour seems to affect its perceived effects.

O The existence of PEs raises fundamental questions about the mind–body/mind–brain relationship – in particular, how it is possible for something non-physical to influence physiological processes. These questions arise from the *dualism* of mind and body.

Useful websites

O http://placebo.nih.gov
O www.skepdic.com/placebo.html
O www.madscientist.org/features/placebos.html
O www.ednac.uk/~ejua35/parapsy.htm
O www.parapsychology.org/
O www.rhine.org/
O www.psiresearch.org/para1.html

Recommended reading

Gross, R. (2003) *Key Studies in Psychology* (4th edn) (Chapter 32 on near-death experiences). London: Hodder & Stoughton.

Radin, D.I. (1997) *The Conscious Universe: The Scientific Truth of Psychic Phenomena.* New York: Harper Edge.

Roberts, R. and Groome, D. (eds) (2001) *Parapsychology: The Science of Unusual Experience* (especially Chapters 1, 3, 4, 6, 10 and 12). London: Arnold.

THEORETICAL APPROACHES TO PSYCHOLOGY

Different psychologists make different assumptions about the particular aspects of a person that are worthy of study, and this helps to determine an underlying model or image of what people are like. In turn, this model or image determines a view of the nature of development, preferred methods of study, the nature of psychological normality, the major cause(s) of abnormality, and the preferred methods and goals of treatment. However, not all of these apply to all approaches.

An approach is a perspective that isn't as clearly outlined as a theory and that:

... provides a general orientation to a view of humankind. It says, in effect, 'we see people as operating according to these basic principles and we therefore see explanations of human behaviour as needing to be set within these limits and with these or those principles understood'.
(Coolican et al., 1996)

As we shall see, all the major approaches include two or more distinguishable theories or strands but, within an approach, they share certain basic principles and assumptions that give them a distinct 'flavour' or identity. The focus here is on the *behaviourist, psychodynamic, cognitive, social constructionist,* and *evolutionary psychological* approaches.

THE BEHAVIOURIST APPROACH

Basic principles and assumptions

WATSON'S METHODOLOGICAL BEHAVIOURISM

According to Skinner (1974):

The first explicit behaviourist was John B. Watson, who in 1913 issued a kind of manifesto called *Psychology as the Behaviourist Views It*. As the title shows, he was not proposing a new science but arguing that psychology should be redefined as the study of behaviour ... Most of the psychologists at the time believed they were studying mental processes in a mental world of consciousness, and they were naturally not inclined to agree with Watson. Early behaviourists wasted a good deal of time, and confused an important issue, by attacking the introspective study of mental life.

Watson (1913) claimed that only by modelling itself on the natural sciences could psychology legitimately call itself a science. He argued for a certain type of behaviourism, namely *methodological behaviourism*: only events/phenomena that can be *intersubjectively verified* (that is, agreed upon by two or more people) are suitable for scientific investigation. Cognition, thinking, believing, feeling, pain, and so on, are *private* events, and so aren't accessible to anyone else. Therefore, they should be excluded from a science of psychology.

In this sense, what was revolutionary about Watson's behaviourist manifesto has become almost taken-for-granted, 'orthodox' psychology. It could be argued that *all* psychologists are methodological behaviourists (Blackman, 1980). Belief in the importance of empirical methods, especially the experiment, as a way of collecting data about humans (and non-humans), which can be quantified and statistically analysed, is a major feature of mainstream psychology (see Chapter 11).

SKINNER'S RADICAL BEHAVIOURISM

Skinner, generally regarded as the arch-behaviourist, rejected Watson's insistence on 'truth by agreement'. According to his *radical behaviourism*, cognitions are *covert* behaviours ('within the skin') that should be studied by psychologists along with *overt* behaviours (capable of being observed by two/more people). He *wasn't* 'against cognitions', but said that 'so-called mental activities are metaphors or explanatory fictions and ... behaviour attributed to them can be more effectively explained in other ways'.

For Skinner, these more effective explanations of behaviour come in the form of the principles of reinforcement derived from his experimental work with rats and pigeons. What is 'radical' about Skinner's radical behaviourism is the claim that feelings, sensations and other private events cannot be used to explain behaviour but are *to be explained* in an analysis of behaviour (*behaviour analysis*). Since private events cannot be manipulated, they cannot serve as independent variables; but they *can* serve as dependent variables. Some recent studies of consciousness seem to support Skinner's claim that our common-sense belief that we will our actions is an illusion (see Chapter 13). Leslie (2002) argues that cognitive psychological theories are doomed to fail, a distraction or blind alley, arising from a mistaken assumption about the necessary features of psychological explanation:

The mistake is to assume that behaviour (what someone does) is necessarily caused by cognition (what the person thinks). Behaviour analysis instead states that both overt (visible) behaviour and the other apparently 'private' aspects of human psychology arise from interaction with the environment ...

While methodological behaviourism proposes to ignore such inner states (they are *inaccessible*), Skinner ignores them only as variables used for explaining behaviour (they are *irrelevant*) and argues that they can be translated into the language of reinforcement theory (Garrett, 1996). According to Nye (2000), Skinner's ideas are also radical because he applied the same type of analysis to both covert and overt behaviour.

Skinner stressed the importance of identifying *functional relations* between environmental conditions and behaviours. According to Leslie (2002):

... the psychology of an individual consists primarily of an account of those functionally defined behavioural characteristics that occur in the environments typically encountered by that individual. A person, if you like, is primarily to be understood as 'what he or she does' and that account of their behaviour cannot

... be described without also describing the location or occasion of those behaviours and the important consequences of those behaviours ...

From the perspective of behaviour analysis, the key process of psychological change is operant conditioning:

... whereby *those behaviours that are functionally effective* for the individual *become more frequent* (in the corresponding environment) while *other behaviours decline in frequency* ...
(Leslie, 2002)

The behaviour isn't caused by either the individual or the environment. Rather:

... it is the history of interaction between the behavioural repertoire of the individual (that is, the whole range of behaviours shown by the person) and the environment that selects, and in a sense causes, the behaviour ...
(Leslie, 2002)

Skinner also saw his brand of behaviourism as a thorough-going, 'deep' behaviourism (O'Donohue and Ferguson, 2001):

Behaviourism is not the science of human behaviour; it is the philosophy of that science. Some of the questions it asks are these: Is such a science really possible? Can it account for every aspect of human behaviour? What methods can it use? Are its laws as valid as those of physics and biology? Will it lead to a technology, and if so, what role will it play in human affairs?
(Skinner, 1974)

So, radical behaviourism *isn't* a scientific law or set of empirical findings. It is *meta*-scientific – that is, it attempts to define what a science of behaviour should look like. The questions that Skinner asks are essentially philosophical. According to O'Donohue and Ferguson (2001): 'radical behaviourism is a philosophy of science, or more exactly, a philosophy of psychology. Skinner calls the science based on this philosophy the *experimental analysis of behaviour* or *behaviour analysis*.' Given this important distinction between methodological and radical behaviourism, we need to consider some principles and assumptions that apply to behaviourism in general. These are described in Box 15.1 (page 316).

Theoretical contributions

Behaviourism made a massive contribution to psychology, at least up to the 1950s, and explanations of behaviour in conditioning terms recur throughout psychology. For example, apart from learning and conditioning, imagery as a form of organization in memory and as a memory aid is based on the principle of association, and the interference theory of forgetting is largely couched in S–R terms. Language, moral and gender development have all been explained in terms of conditioning, and some influential theories of the formation and maintenance of relationships focus on the concept of reinforcement. The behaviourist approach also offers one of the major models of abnormal behaviour. (Skinner's notorious views on free will are discussed in detail in Chapter 12.)

As with Freud's psychoanalytic theory (see below), theorists and researchers critical of the original, 'orthodox' theories have modified and built on them, making a huge contribution in the process. Noteworthy examples are Tolman's (1948) *cognitive behaviourism* and *social*

Box 15.1 Basic principles and assumptions made by the behaviourist approach

○ Behaviourists emphasize the role of *environmental factors* in influencing behaviour, often to the (apparent) exclusion of innate or inherited factors. In fact, Skinner saw psychology as a branch of *biology*, and was heavily influenced by Darwin's theory of evolution. The environment *selects* certain behaviours over others, and this determines their frequency in future generations. *Operant conditioning* is itself an *evolutionary adaptation*: the ability to learn from the consequences of behaviour is an evolutionary development that proved advantageous. *Classical conditioning* is another learning mechanism that evolution has produced (O'Donohue and Ferguson, 2001).

Figure 15.1 B.F. Skinner

○ Behaviourism is often referred to as 'S–R' (stimulus–response) psychology. However, the stimulus and response relationship can be defined in fundamentally different ways. Only in classical conditioning is the stimulus seen as triggering a response in a predictable, automatic way, and this is what is conveyed by 'S–R' psychology. It is, therefore, a mistake to describe operant conditioning as an 'S–R' approach.

○ Part of Watson's rejection of introspectionism was his belief that it invoked too many vague concepts that are difficult, if not impossible, to define and measure. According to the *law of parsimony* (or 'Occam's razor'), the fewer assumptions a theory makes, the better (more 'economical' explanations are superior).

○ The mechanisms proposed by a theory should be as simple as possible. Behaviourists stress the use of *operational definitions* (defining concepts in terms of observable, measurable, events).

○ The aim of a science of behaviour is to *predict* and *control* behaviour. This raises both *conceptual* questions (about the nature of science – in particular, the role of theory; see Chapter 11) and *ethical* questions (for example, about power *learning theory* (mainly associated with Bandura and Mischel). O'Donohue and Ferguson (2001) state that, '*behaviourism* is not an unequivocal term but rather describes a family of different philosophies'. They claim that, given the variety of forms of behaviourism, Watson's and Skinner's influence is less than you'd think.

Practical contributions

Methodological behaviourism's emphasis on experimentation, operational definitions and the measurement of observable events (see Box 15.1) has had a major influence on the practice of scientific psychology in general, quite unrelated to any views about the nature and role of mental events. Other, more 'tangible' contributions include the following:

○ *Behaviour therapy and behaviour modification* (based on classical and operant conditioning respectively) are major approaches to the treatment of abnormal behaviour (see Chapter 10) and one of the main tools in the clinical psychologist's 'kit bag'. The ethics of some forms of behaviour modification (such as the token economy), and certain aspects of *applied behaviour analysis* (especially the use of punishment with vulnerable individuals), have been seriously questioned (see Chapter 10).

○ *Behavioural neuroscience* is an interdisciplinary field of study, using behavioural techniques to understand brain function and neuroscientific techniques to elucidate behavioural processes. While many believe that behaviour can be reduced to/explained by brain processes, the evidence shows that each is dependent on the other (Leslie, 2002; see Chapter 13).

○ *Behavioural pharmacology* involves the use of *schedules of reinforcement* to assess the behavioural effects of new drugs that modify brain activity. Most importantly, the research has illustrated how many behavioural effects of drugs are determined as much by the current behaviour and reinforcement contingencies as by the effects of the drug on the brain (Leslie, 2002).

○ *Environmental enrichment studies* have produced evidence for *neuronal plasticity* – that is, the brain's capacity for change and adapting to changing environmental conditions. These findings have exciting implications for the treatment of strokes and other conditions involving brain damage. According to Leslie:

The life-long interaction between the behaviour of the individual and the environment produces changes in the brain. This in turn changes behaviour, and so the interaction goes on. Any attempt to deal with a human behavioural problem can involve changes to the nervous system, behaviour or the environment.

An evaluation of behaviourism

Central to Skinner's experimental analysis of behaviour is the famous 'Skinner box', the 'auto-environmental chamber' in which rats' and pigeons' environments can be totally controlled by the experimenter. It has been used with many species, emitting a wide range of operant responses producing a variety of consequences. Yet the same *behavioural processes* are revealed in all the experiments; many of these can be summarized as operant conditioning (Leslie, 2002). Rats pressing a lever was intended to be equivalent to a cat operating an escape latch in Thorndike's puzzle box (1898), so counting the number of lever presses (the response rate) became the standard measure of operant learning. Despite Skinner's claims to not having a *theory*, 'the response' in operant conditioning has largely considered *only* the *frequency* of behaviour, ignoring intensity, duration and quality. As Glassman (1995) observes, 'While the focus on frequency was a practical consideration, it eventually became part of the overall conceptual framework as well – a case of research methods directing theory'. But in everyday life, frequency isn't always the most meaningful aspect of behaviour. For example, should we judge an artist's worth by how many paintings s/he produces, rather than their content?

Skinner's claim that human behaviour can be predicted and controlled in the same way as the behaviour of non-humans is usually only accepted by other behaviour analysts. Possessing language allows us to communicate with each other and to think about 'things' that have never been observed (and may not even exist), including rules, laws and principles (Garrett, 1996). While these can only be expressed in words, or thought about through words, much of people's behaviour is governed by them. According to Garrett, when this happens, 'behaviour is now shaped by what goes on inside their [people's] heads ... and not simply by what goes on in the external environment'. So, what people *think* is among the important variables determining what they do and say, the very opposite of what Skinner's radical behaviourism claims. However, behaviour analysts recognize the limitations of their approach. For example, Leslie (2002) admits that 'operant conditioning cannot provide a complete account of psychology from a behavioural perspective, even in principle'. Leslie argues that classical conditioning, modelling and verbal instruction all help produce *variation* of behaviour, which is vital if selection is to occur.

O'Donohue and Ferguson (2001) acknowledge that the science of behaviour cannot account for creative behaviour, as in music, literature and science. Environmental selection as identified by Skinner merely sets parameters on the range of responding – it doesn't tell us where the novel behaviour comes from in the first place. However, they contend that his psychology is solidly based on hard facts, and that 'The science of behaviour has more empirical evidence supporting its claims than any other area in psychology'.

The impact of behaviourism

According to Richards (2002), it was for a long time believed that behaviourism represented the most advanced 'paradigm' for experimental psychology. But while it certainly pervaded the intellectual atmosphere of American psychology, 'it never in fact dominated psychological practice to the extent which is often claimed'.

Most American researchers between 1918 and 1939 were what Richards calls 'eclectic functionalists', still inclined to include 'experience' alongside 'behaviour' as part of psychology's subject matter. But its impact went beyond theory to influence the whole way of conducting and reporting research (i.e. methodological behaviourism). However, by the 1950s, the tide was turning against behaviourism in favour of cognitive psychology (see below). Richards claims that:

... behaviourism should be considered not so much as a theory in itself but as a conceptual framework in which theorising could be undertaken; a 'unified discourse' and set of methodological practices within which propositions could be formulated and theoretical debates conducted and, hopefully, settled.

This echoes Skinner's own view of radical behaviourism as a philosophy of psychology (see above).

Richards sees behaviourism as leaving behind one of two main images of the psychologist in popular culture, namely the white-coated scientist running rats round mazes, discovering cunning ways to control behaviour ('human beings are maze-bound rats'), and the expert in behavioural control who is subtly affecting our lives using scientific techniques that we are unaware of. He concludes by saying:

> ... as with all psychological doctrines, behaviourism's impact is a psychological fact in its own right and the concepts and images of human nature which it yielded have, for better or worse, irreversibly entered our culture.
> (Richards, 2002)

THE PSYCHODYNAMIC APPROACH

The term 'psychodynamic' denotes the active forces within the personality that motivate behaviour, and the inner causes of behaviour (in particular the unconscious conflict between the different structures that compose the whole personality). While Freud's was the original psychodynamic theory, the approach includes all those theories based on his ideas, such as those of Jung (1964), Adler (1927) and Erikson (1950). Freud's *psychoanalytic theory* (sometimes called '*psychoanalysis*') is psychodynamic, but the psychodynamic theories of Jung and others aren't psychoanalytic. So the two terms *aren't* synonymous. However, because of their enormous influence, Freud's ideas will be emphasized in the rest of this section.

Basic principles and assumptions

Freud's concepts are closely interwoven, making it difficult to know where their description should begin (Jacobs, 1992). Fortunately, Freud himself stressed acceptance of certain key theories as essential to the practice of psychoanalysis, the form of psychotherapy he pioneered and from which most others are derived (see Box 15.2, page 320).

Figure 15.2 Alfred Adler (1879–1937): one of Freud's original 'disciples' and the founder of *Individual psychology*

Theoretical contributions

As with behaviourist accounts of conditioning, many of Freud's ideas and concepts have become part of mainstream psychology's vocabulary. You don't have to be a 'Freudian' to use concepts such as 'repression', 'unconscious', and so on, and many of the vast number of studies of different aspects of the theory have been conducted by critics hoping to discredit it (such as Eysenck and Wilson, 1973, and Eysenck, 1985).

Box 15.2 The major principles and assumptions of psychoanalytic theory

○ Much of our behaviour is determined by *unconscious* thoughts, wishes, memories, and so on. What we are consciously aware of at any one time represents the tip of an iceberg: most of our thoughts and feelings are either not accessible at that moment (*pre-conscious*) or are totally inaccessible (*unconscious*). These unconscious thoughts and feelings can become conscious through the use of special techniques, such as *free association, dream interpretation* and *transference*, the cornerstones of psychoanalysis.

○ Much of what is unconscious has been made so through *repression*, whereby threatening or unpleasant experiences are 'forgotten'. They become inaccessible, locked away from our conscious awareness. This is a major form of *ego defence*. Freud singled it out as a special cornerstone 'on which the whole structure of psychoanalysis rests. It is the most essential part of it' (Freud, 1914). Repression is closely related to *resistance*, interpretation of which is another key technique used in psychoanalysis.

○ According to the *theory of infantile sexuality*, the sexual instinct, or drive, is active from birth and develops through a series of five *psychosexual stages*. The most important of these is the *phallic stage* (spanning the ages three to five/six), during which all children experience the Oedipus complex. In fact, Freud used the German word *Trieb*, which translates as 'drive', rather than *Instinkt*, which was meant to imply that experience played a crucial role in determining the 'fate' of sexual (and aggressive) energy.

○ Related to infantile sexuality is the general impact of early experience on later personality (see Chapter 9). According to Freud (1949):

It seems that the neuroses are only acquired during early childhood (up to the age of six), even though their symptoms may not make their appearance until much later . . . the child is psychologically father of the man and . . . the events of its first years are of paramount importance for its whole subsequent life.

Also like behaviourist theories, Freud's can be found throughout psychology as a whole. His contribution is extremely rich and diverse, offering theories of motivation, dreams, forgetting, attachment and the effects of early experience (see Chapter 9), moral and gender development, aggression, and abnormality (Chapter 7). Psychoanalytic theory has also influenced Gould's (1978) theory of the evolution of adult consciousness, and Adorno *et al.*'s (1950) authoritarian personality theory (a major account of prejudice).

Finally, and as noted earlier, Freud's theories have stimulated the development of alternative theories, often resulting from the rejection of some of his fundamental principles and assumptions, but reflecting his influence enough for them to be described as psychodynamic.

SOME MAJOR ALTERNATIVE PSYCHODYNAMIC THEORIES

○ *Ego psychology*, promoted by Freud's daughter, Anna, focused on the mechanisms used by the ego to deal with the world, especially the ego defence mechanisms. Freud, by contrast, stressed the influence of the id's innate drives (especially sexuality and aggression) and is often described as an instinct theorist (but see the third point in Box 15.2). The ego, as well as the id, originates in basic human inheritance and has its own developmental course. It uses neutralized (non-sexual) energy, which makes possible an interest in objects and activities that aren't necessarily related to underlying sexual and aggressive drives.

According to Nye (2000), the increased attention given to an independent ego has probably resulted partly from a change in the types of patient psychoanalysts are treating. In recent years, patients have tended more often to be troubled by the problems of an increasingly complex society (vague anxieties, insecurities and dissatisfaction), and are seeking ways to find meaning and value in work, family and social roles:

> Since the ego is the part of the personality that must deal with the external world in some rational, decision-making way, it seems natural that more emphasis should be given to it. Perhaps for the contemporary patient it is important to focus more attention on conscious thought processes and coping mechanisms; he or she is less likely to be plagued by unconscious guilt and repressed sexuality than by the uncertainties and rootlessness of modern society that requires the ego to grapple with existential problems.
> *(Nye, 2000)*

○ Erik Erikson, trained by Anna Freud as a child psychoanalyst, also stressed the importance of the ego, as well as the influence of social and cultural factors on individual development. He pioneered the *lifespan approach* to development, proposing eight *psychosocial stages*, in contrast with Freud's five *psychosexual stages* that end with physical maturity.

○ Two of Freud's original 'disciples', Carl Jung and Alfred Adler, broke ranks with Freud and formed their own 'schools' (*analytical psychology* and *individual psychology* respectively). Jung attached relatively little importance to childhood experiences (and the associated *personal* unconscious) but considerable importance to the *collective* (or *racial*) unconscious, which stems from the evolutionary history of human beings as a whole (see below).

○ Like Jung, Adler rejected Freud's emphasis on sexuality, stressing instead the *will to power* or *striving for superiority*, which he saw as an attempt to overcome feelings of inferiority faced by all children as they grow up. He also shared Jung's view of the person as an indivisible unity or whole, and Erikson's emphasis on the social nature of human beings.

○ Melanie Klein (1932) is often seen as a key transitional figure between Freud's instinct theory and the object relations school (see Box 15.3, page 322). Like Anna Freud, she adapted Freud's techniques (such as pioneering *play therapy*) in order to tap a young child's unconscious, and maintained that the superego and Oedipus complex appear as early as the first and second years of life.

Practical contributions

The current psychotherapy scene is highly diverse, with only a minority using Freudian techniques, but, as Fancher (1996) points out:

> Most modern therapists use techniques that were developed either by Freud and his followers or by dissidents in explicit reaction against his theories. Freud

Box 15.3 Object relations theory

The *object relations school* (the 'British school') was greatly influenced by Klein's emphasis on the infant's earliest (pre-Oedipal) relationships with its mother. It places far less emphasis on the role of instincts and more on the relationship with particular love objects (especially the mother), seeing early *relationships* as crucial for later patterns of relationships with others. Fairbairn (1952), for example, saw the aim of the libido as *object-seeking* (as opposed to pleasure-seeking), and this was extended by Bowlby (1969) in his *attachment theory* (see Chapter 9). According to Nye (2000):

> Although both object relations theory and Freudian theory are concerned with childhood experiences and the inner world of the person, the former puts more emphasis on discrepancies between inner-world and real-world persons and situations. The latter puts more emphasis on the role of factors such as instinctual drives and unresolved Oedipus conflicts ...

Object relations theory refers to a number of separate ideas proposed by different theorists. However, they all stress that internal images ('representations') of one's self and of 'objects' (a technical term usually denoting another person toward whom we direct emotion and action: significant others) can have powerful effects on our relationships with others.

Mahler (1975) and Winnicott (1958) stress the movement from the newborn's absolute dependence to the independence and autonomy of adults as the primary and lifelong developmental task. Development proceeds from symbiotic fusion with the mother, through various stages of partial differentiation of the self and other, to a state of increased individuation and independence. The internalized images of others (objects) in the infant (and the psychotic adult; see Chapter 7) are primitive, engulfing, devouring and otherwise menacing. Only when separation from the mother has been successfully achieved, are we capable of empathizing with others and seeing them as they really are (rather than as projections of our primitive fantasies).

(Based on Holmes, 1993; Zeldow, 1995; Nye, 2000)

remains a dominating figure, for or against whom virtually all therapists feel compelled to take a stand.

Both Rogers, the major humanistic therapist, and Wolpe, who developed *systematic desensitization* (a major form of behaviour therapy), were originally trained in Freudian techniques. Perls, the founder of *Gestalt therapy*, Ellis, the founder of *rational emotive therapy* (RET) (see below) and Berne, who devised *transactional analysis*, were also trained psychoanalysts.

Even Freud's fiercest critics concede his influence, not just within world psychiatry but in philosophy, literary criticism, history, theology, sociology, and art and literature generally. Freudian terminology is commonly used in conversations between therapists well beyond Freudian circles, and his influence is brought daily to therapy sessions as part of the cultural background and experience of nearly every client (Jacobs, 1992).

Many mental health practitioners (including psychotherapists, counsellors and social workers), although not formally trained as psychoanalysts, have incorporated elements of Freudian thought and technique into their approaches to helping their patients (Nye, 2000).

An evaluation of the psychodynamic approach

FALSIFIABILITY AND TESTABILITY

A criticism repeatedly made of Freudian (and other psychodynamic) theories is that they are unscientific because they are *unfalsifiable* (incapable of being disproved). For example, if the Freudian prediction that 'dependent' men will prefer big-breasted women is confirmed, then the theory is supported. However, if such men actually prefer *small*-breasted women (Scodel, 1957), Freudians can use the concept of *reaction formation* (an ego defence mechanism) to argue that an unconscious fixation with big breasts may manifest itself as a conscious preference for the opposite, a clear case of 'Heads I win, tails you lose' (Popper, 1959; Eysenck, 1985). However, it is probably a mistake to see reaction formation as typical of Freudian theory as a whole.

Zeldow (1995) observes that the history of science reveals that those theories that are the richest in explanatory power have proved the most difficult to test empirically. For example, Newton's Second Law couldn't be demonstrated in a reliable, quantitative way for 100 years, and Einstein's general theory of relativity is still untestable. Eysenck, Popper and others have criticized psychoanalytic theory for being untestable. But even if this were true:

> ... the same thing could ... (and should) be said about any psychological hypotheses involving complex phenomena and worthy of being tested ... psychoanalytic theories have inspired more empirical research in the social and behavioural sciences than any other group of theories ...
> *(Zeldow, 1995)*

Fisher and Greenberg (1996) conducted an extensive reappraisal of studies of psychoanalytic theory carried out up to the early 1990s. Agreeing with Kline (1989), they argue that Freud's theory should be evaluated in terms of a series of specific hypotheses (or mini-theories), rather than as a whole. They also believe that what should be considered are *overall trends* across studies.

Fisher and Greenberg concluded that there is evidence to support Freud's notion of oral and anal personality tendencies, and some aspects of his ideas on the origins of depression and paranoia. But they found only weak and indirect support for the notion of the Oedipal conflict, and no support for their impact on later development or for his views on women's sexuality and how their development differs from men's (see Chapter 6).

While their review is extremely broad, it is not comprehensive (for example, it doesn't cover repression and other defence mechanisms, or transference). The strength of the evidence presented is variable and sometimes indirect, and where it is supportive it rests on Fisher and Greenberg's interpretation of the results (Andrews and Brewin, 2000). However, for Zeldow (1995) the mere existence of such reviews 'gives the lie to the notion that all psychoanalytic ideas are too vague or abstruse to be tested scientifically'.

Freud's theory provides methods and concepts that enable us to interpret and 'unpack' underlying meanings (it has great *hermeneutic strength*). Popper's and Eysenck's criticism above helps to underline the fact that these meanings (both conscious and unconscious) cannot be measured in any precise way. Freud offers a way of understanding that is different from theories that are easily testable, and it may actually be more appropriate for capturing the nature of human experience and action (Stevens, 1995). Jones and Elcock (2001) make a similar point when they say:

Much more than most approaches in Psychology the approaches in psychoanalysis are explicitly attempting to create a framework of understanding for human experience. In common with other theories of human nature there is a degree of self-fulfilling prophecy about psychoanalysis, as terms, concepts and ideas have become integrated into our cultural common sense. Our awareness of Psychology has to some extent changed at a fundamental level our psychology, and in this psychoanalysis has been much more successful than any approach within Psychology to date.

In other words, Freud's theories aren't merely *about* human behaviour and the mind, they actually help to *change* behaviour and minds. This relates to the broader issue of the nature of psychological constructs, which is discussed further in Chapter 11.

Box 15.4 Is the unconscious a valid concept?

According to Ogden (1989, in Mollon, 2000): 'The unconscious is by definition unknowable ... The psychoanalyst is therefore in the unfortunate position of being a student of that which cannot be known.'

But is Ogden right? Mollon sees the idea of unconscious motivation as an inference that provides an explanation for the gaps and distortions in our conscious awareness. It brings coherence to behavioural and mental data that would otherwise appear incoherent, such as slips of the tongue and other *parapraxes* ('Freudian slips') to which we are all prone. While Freud didn't invent the concept of the unconscious, he was the first to investigate it systematically. Mollon says that, 'His genius was to see that such seemingly trivial phenomena were worth studying, and moreover to recognise the link between these and other mental creations like dreams, jokes and neurotic symptoms.'

One of Freud's great 'discoveries' is that the unconscious operates according to completely different principles from the conscious mind. For example: (i) mutually incompatible ideas or impulses can exist without these appearing contradictory; love and hate could both be expressed at the same time unconsciously, whereas the conscious mind would experience these as conflicting; (ii) meaning may be *displaced* easily from one image to another; (iii) many different meanings may converge in one image (*condensation*); (iv) unconscious ideas and feelings are timeless; ideas aren't ordered temporally and aren't altered by the passage of time; (v) the unconscious doesn't take account of external reality but represents internal psychic reality. Thus, dreams are perceived as real.

Mollon (2000) believes that what remains timelessly valuable in Freud's observations are: (i) the unconscious operates according to a different 'logic' from the conscious mind; and (ii) the cognitive processes of the unconscious are determined partly by the interplay of conflicting emotional forces (*psychodynamics*).

An exciting recent development is the convergence of psychoanalysis and neuroscience (as Freud had always hoped), forming the new discipline of *neuropsychoanalysis*. This is providing many insights into unconscious emotional processing. Basically, the right hemisphere of the brain, which specializes in visual perception, imagery, and emotion, is the basis of the unconscious mind. The left hemisphere, which specializes more in linguistic and sequential/logical processing, is the basis of the conscious mind and matures slightly later than the right (see Mollon, 2000).

According to Reason (2000), Freud was probably wrong to assert that (nearly) all slips (of the tongue) are in some way intended. But he was certainly correct in claiming that 'Freudian slips' represent minor eruptions of unconscious processing. Instead of taking a strictly psychoanalytic interpretation of 'unconscious', Reason prefers one that relates to processes that aren't directly accessible to consciousness, i.e. automatic processing or habitual performance (see Chapter 12).

Similarly, much of modern cognitive psychology and neuropsychology is consistent with the Freudian view that behaviour isn't dependent on conscious experience (Power, 2000). One example is *blindsight* (Weiskrantz, 1986). According to Power (2000):

Whereas cognitive psychology has emphasised the co-operation between conscious and automatic processes (essential, for example, whilst driving), psychoanalysis has always emphasised conflict instead. The most recent models in psychology have come to consider both co-operation and conflict between conscious and unconscious processes.

(Again, see Chapter 12)

Despite mainstream psychology's dismissal of much of psychoanalytic theory as unscientific (see above), Reason (2000), among others, believes that it is time to reacknowledge Freud's greatness as a psychologist. According to Kline (1998):

After 100 years, Freudian theory cannot be uncritically accepted just as it cannot be totally rejected. However, ... Freudian theory contains some profound observations and understanding of human behaviour. These must be incorporated into any adequate human psychology, not only its theory but also its methods ...

HOW CAN WE ACCOUNT FOR FREUD'S GREATNESS?

Grayling (2002) and Richards (2002) identify several reasons for the power of Freudian ideas.

1 Freud's genius as an author and generator of ideas. He had an extraordinary ability to weave together medical knowledge, some genuine insights into the human condition and a powerful imagination. He has the narrative skills of a first-rate novelist, and a knack for devising striking ways to describe psychological phenomena. These included metaphors, often drawn from the science of the day.

2 The immense appeal of any theory that offers to each individual an explanation of his/her own hidden secrets. People spend far more on psychoanalysis than astrology, because it has the 'respectability' of science (but see above).

3 Psychoanalysis seemed to have finally delivered what science had failed to deliver before, namely a proper theory of human nature. Richards considers Freud's to have been the 'first thoroughly *modern* image of human nature'. It coincided with cultural revolutions in painting, music, and literature, a common feature of which was the turning away from 'reason' to emotion. But it was the First World War that was perhaps the historically most crucial factor. This had a profound and traumatic effect on Europeans, making all previous accounts of human nature seem totally inadequate. Only after the war ended in 1918 did psychoanalysis begin to make huge inroads into popular culture and consciousness.

4 Sex was at the centre of his package, 'the most delicious, anxious and titillating of all taboos' (Grayling, 2002). Although it is a myth that sex wasn't discussed before Freud, 'what was distinctive was that sexual discourse (other than the frankly pornographic) was seemingly impossible unless infused with official morality or packaged as something else' (Richards, 2002) such as for medical or scientific male professionals, or in the context of seemingly scientific anthropological studies. According to Richards:

> The Freudian move was unique not only in openly discussing sex but in identifying it as the motivational force underlying all human behaviour from infancy onwards. In effect it sought to enable people to admit and confront their sexuality, identifying the primary aetiological factor in psychopathology as failure to do this . . .

5 Freud's ideas offered both lay people and professional therapists alike a path towards self-reevaluation and exploration.

THE COGNITIVE APPROACH

Basic principles and assumptions

Despite its undoubted influence within psychology as a whole (see below and Chapter 11), it is more difficult to define the boundaries of cognitive psychology compared with the other major approaches. Its identity isn't as clearly established, and it can't be considered to be a specific, integrated set of assumptions and concepts. It has several contemporary forms, with many theories, research programmes and forms of psychotherapy having a 'cognitive tilt' (Nye, 2000).

Also, there is no specific figure who can be identified as central to its development in the same way as Watson, Skinner, Freud and Rogers can with their respective approaches. As Wade and Tavris (1990) say, 'Cognitive psychology does not yet have a unifying theory, and unlike other "brands" of psychology . . . it lacks an acknowledged spokesperson.'

However, there are certain key figures in the developmental history of cognitive psychology. Many of these were not psychologists, but electrical engineers (e.g. Shannon), mathematicians (e.g. von Neumann), and logicians (e.g. Turing), who were at the centre of technological developments in radio, television, and aero-engineering in the 1930s. The Second World War intensified the need for increasingly versatile calculating machines, as used in radar, and from these developments emerged the concepts that would form the basis of the 'cognitive revolution' (Richards, 2002).

Richards identifies three central ideas that were to transform how cognition would be conceptualized.

1 *Information*: in 1948, Shannon used 'binary logic' to give information a precise technical meaning, allowing it to be measured. The key question is: 'How many yes/no decisions are required to specify the information ('bit' = 'binary digit')?' This is easily converted into hardware: yes/no (1/0 in binary) is equivalent to on/off states of electrical switches. Shannon's *information theory* allowed 'channel capacity', 'storage capacity', 'noisy signals' and 'redundancy' (surplus information) to be discussed. This idea of measuring information first entered psychology through psychophysics, and reaction-time studies. It was then applied to memory, attention and other processes: 'The upshot was to recast the study of cognition as the study of human information processing.'

2 *Feedback*: in his *cognitive behaviourism* (1948), Tolman tried to incorporate the concept of 'purpose'. But this was seen as incompatible with that of scientific determinism: how could something later in time (a goal) cause something earlier in time (behaviour)? Causes were supposed to *precede* effects, not follow them. But then Weiner (who founded *cybernetics*) and Craik introduced the concept of *negative feedback*: a system's output is 'fed back' in such a way as to return it to some desired (goal) state (as in a room thermostat maintaining a constant temperature, or the body's homeostatic mechanisms doing the same). The *negative feedback loop* was a way of explaining purposive behaviour in informational terms.

3 *Program*: with the advent of electronic computers (originally in the mid-1940s), 'programming' acquired major significance. For psychologists, the concept of 'program' seemed equivalent to 'plan', which made it possible to handle complex, higher-order behaviour. So:

> By the 1950s humans could thus be viewed as information processing systems operating according to complex sets of programs derived from a variety of sources from genetic to social, and sustained in this way by sophisticated self-monitoring 'feedback' capacities . . .
> *(Richards, 2002)*

Theoretical contributions

Cognitive *behaviourism* and *social learning theory* (see above) both stress the central role of cognitive processes in learning. The influence of the information-processing approach is obvious in relation to attention, pattern recognition and memory (see Box 15.5), but it has permeated many other areas of psychology. *Social cognition* is now a commonly used term to refer to many aspects of the perception of people (see Chapter 1), attribution (see Chapter 2), attitudes and attitude change (including prejudice), and other areas of social psychology. The information-processing approach also represents an increasingly influential view of cognitive development and of the nature of intelligence.

Practical contributions

In relation to counselling and psychotherapy, Ellis's *rational emotive behaviour therapy* (REBT – previously called just rational emotive therapy, or RET) deserves special attention (Nye, 2000). According to Rorer (1998), 'the *cognitive* revolution in psychotherapy began with the publication of [Ellis's 1962 book] *Reason and Emotion in Psychotherapy*'. REBT is the predecessor of the current cognitive and cognitive-behaviour therapies and continues to

---

Box 15.5 Some basic principles and assumptions of the cognitive approach

O According to Parkin (2000), psychologists in general, and cognitive psychologists in particular, face a problem not faced by other scientists:

> The human brain is not like other organs of the body in that looking at its structure does not reveal anything about how it functions. We can see that ... the heart [acts] as a pump, and the kidney as a filter. The brain, however, is a large mass of cells and fibres which, no matter how clearly we look at it, gives no indication of how we think, speak and remember ...

For these reasons, cognitive psychologists are forced to seek *analogies* and *metaphors* when trying to describe a construct within the brain – that is, how the brain works is compared with the operation of something we already understand.

O Many different analogies have been used in cognitive psychology. By far the most dominant is that internal mental abilities are *information processing systems* (the *computer analogy*; see Richards' account above). Included within this overall analogy are several central ideas or concepts, such as *coding, channel capacity* and *serial/parallel processing*.

O Every telecommunication system uses some form of *coding*. For example, a telephone receives and translates our voice into an electromagnetic code, which is then decoded back into our voice at the other end. Cognitive psychologists realized that the concept of coding was central to understanding the representations used by the brain. When we see a picture, for example, we extract information from it that forms a code, which is, therefore, a *symbol* of the original stimulus. But compared with physical communication devices, human coding is more flexible, and can take account of the form of the input in order to reduce the amount and nature of information that is actually formed into a code (as demonstrated in Miller's (1956) concept of *chunking*).

(Based on Parkin, 2000)

---

evolve and gain in popularity. Ellis's emphasis on the primacy of cognition in psychopathology is at the forefront of practice and research in clinical psychology (Nye, 2000).

REBT attempts directly or actively to get clients to dispute their irrational and unscientific beliefs, and replace them with rational beliefs, which are less likely to be associated with extremely negative emotional states or maladaptive behaviours. The key concept underlying REBT (and other cognitive approaches) is that people are disturbed *not* by events but by their *perception* of them.

Although Ellis (1987) believes that people have a biological tendency to think irrationally, REBT is an optimistic approach. It emphasizes that:

... people have enormous power to think about their thinking, to use rationality and the scientific method, and to radically control and change their emotional destiny – providing they really work at doing so.
(Ellis, 1987)

An evaluation of the cognitive approach

The parallels between human beings and computers are compelling (Parkin, 2000). (See Box 15.6, page 330.) According to Lachman *et al.* (1979):

Computers take a symbolic input, recode it, make decisions about the recoded input, make new expressions from it, store some or all of the input, and give back a symbolic input. By analogy that is what most cognitive psychology is about. It is about how people take in information ... recode and remember it, how they make decisions, how they transform their internal knowledge states, and how they translate these states into behavioural outputs.

Information-processing accounts invariably address some specific aspect of mental processing, rather than being all-embracing accounts of cognition. A good example is Bruce and Young's (1986) model of face recognition. A *model* is more than a mere analogy: the proposed information-processing system is specified in sufficient detail to enable clear predictions to be made about how humans would behave in certain situations.

Box 15.6 Some similarities between computers and humans as information processors

O Computers operate in terms of information streams, which flow between different components of the system. This is conceptually similar to how we assume symbolic information flows through human information channels (for example, see Atkinson and Shiffrin's (1971) multi-store model of memory).

O All computers have a *central processing unit*, which carries out the manipulation of information. At the simplest level, a central processor might take a sequence of numbers and combine them according to a particular rule in order to compute an average. This was seen by many as analogous to how a person would perform the same type of mental operation.

O Computers have *data bases* and *information stores*, which are permanent representations of knowledge the computer has acquired. In many ways this is comparable to our permanent (long-term) memory.

O Information sometimes needs to be held for a period of time while some other operation is performed. This is the job of the *information buffer*, which is a feature of computers and information-processing models of human attention and memory (again, see Atkinson and Shiffrin's multi-store model).

(Based on Parkin, 2000)

Cognitive psychologists implicitly adopted, at least initially, a strong *nomothetic* view of human mental processes – that is, they assumed that any information-processing model would apply equally to everyone (see Chapter 3). But the influence of *individual differences* soon became apparent. The general rule is that the more complex the cognitive process, the more likely there are to be individual differences (Parkin, 2000).

Until the mid-1980s, mainstream cognitive psychologists took little interest in the study of how brain damage affects subsequent cognitive and behavioural functioning. *Cognitive neuropsychologists* now study people with acquired cognitive deficits in order to learn about the nature and organization of cognitive functioning in normal people (the *cognitive architecture* of mental processes).

Richards (2002) believes that:

Cognitive Psychology represents a very major example of how novel technologies and scientific discoveries can change how we think about ourselves . . . Some recent writers have also seen its US origins . . . as rooted in a distinctly militaristic view of human nature in which humans are reduced to the status of expendable pieces of equipment . . .

Since the late 1980s there has been a growing criticism of cognitive psychology, both from traditional critics (such as humanistic psychologists and behaviourists) and from various philosophers. phenomenologists and social constructionists.

THE SOCIAL CONSTRUCTIONIST APPROACH

Basic principles and assumptions

Social constructionism (SC) has played a central role in the various challenges that have been made to mainstream, academic psychology during the last 30 years or so, and we have discussed some of these at various points in earlier chapters.

The emergence of SC is usually dated from Gergen's (1973) paper 'Social psychology as history', in which he argued that all knowledge, including psychological knowledge, is historically and culturally specific, and that we therefore must extend our enquiries beyond the individual into social, political and economic realms for a proper understanding of the evolution of present-day psychology and social life. Since the only constant feature of social life is that it is continually *changing*, psychology in general, and social psychology in particular, becomes a form of historical undertaking: all we can ever do is try to understand and account for how the world appears to be *at the present time*.

The paper was written at the time of 'the crisis in social psychology'. Starting in the late 1960s and early 1970s, some social psychologists were becoming increasingly concerned that the 'voice' of ordinary people was being omitted from social psychological research: by concentrating on *decontextualized* laboratory behaviour, it was ignoring the real-world contexts that give human action its meaning. Several books were published, each proposing an alternative to positivist science and focusing on the accounts of ordinary people (e.g. Harré and Secord, 1972). These concerns are clearly seen today in SC.

While there is no single definition of SC that would be accepted by all those who might be described in this way, we could categorize as social constructionist any approach that is based on one or more of the following key assumptions (as proposed by Gergen, 1985). Burr (1995) suggests we might think of these assumptions as 'things you would absolutely have to believe in order to be a social constructionist'.

1. A CRITICAL STANCE TOWARDS TAKEN-FOR-GRANTED KNOWLEDGE

Our observations of the world don't reveal in any simple way the true nature of the world, and conventional knowledge isn't based on objective, unbiased 'sampling' of the world (see Chapter 11). The categories with which we understand the world don't necessarily correspond to natural or 'real' categories/distinctions. Belief in such natural categories is called *essentialism*, so social constructionists are *anti-essentialism*.

Essentialism, in turn, is related to *correspondence theory*, an important element of the positivist view of truth. According to correspondence theory, a description is true if it corresponds to the object or event in the world that it describes. But social constructionists argue that it is an *illusion* to believe that we can establish secure and determinate relationships between words and what the words refer to, that knowledge mirrors nature, and that scientific theory merely reflects or maps reality in any direct or decontextualized way (Bem and Looren de Jong, 1997). In fact, language, and thus our theories, *don't* refer to the world at all: they have no truth-value. The basic function of language 'is not the representation of things in the world ... It works to create, sustain and transform various patterns of social relations' (Shotter, 1991).

2. HISTORICAL AND CULTURAL SPECIFICITY

How we commonly understand the world, and the categories and concepts we use, are historically and culturally *relative*. Not only are they specific to particular cultures and historical periods, they are seen as *products* of that culture and history, and this must include the knowledge generated by the social sciences. The theories and explanations of psychology thus become time- and culture-bound, and cannot be taken as once-and-for-all descriptions of human nature: 'The disciplines of psychology and social psychology can therefore no longer be aimed at discovering the "true" nature of people and social life' (Burr, 1995).

As Bem and Looren De Jong (1997) observe:

> Social constructionists challenge the supposedly objective and universal basis of ... knowledge; they are sensitive to cross-cultural psychological or ethnographic studies which reveal that such psychological concepts differ among wide-ranging cultures because they are produced by and sustain the social, moral, political and economic institutions ...

Cross-cultural and trans-cultural psychology, and the *universalist assumption*, are discussed further in Chapter 8.

3. KNOWLEDGE IS SUSTAINED BY SOCIAL PROCESSES

Our current accepted way of understanding the world ('truth') doesn't reflect the world as it really is (objective reality), but is constructed by people through their everyday interactions. Social interaction of all kinds, and particularly language, is of central importance for social constructionists – it is other people, both past and present, who are the sources of knowledge:

> We are born into a world where the conceptual frameworks and categories used by the people in our culture already exist. These concepts and categories are acquired by all people as they develop the use of language and are thus reproduced every day by everyone who shares a culture and language ... the

way people think, the very categories and concepts that provide a framework of meaning for them, are provided by the language that they use. Language therefore is a necessary pre-condition for thought as we know it . . .
(Burr, 1995)

By giving a central role to social interactions and seeing these as actively producing taken-for-granted knowledge of the world, it follows that language itself is more than simply a way of expressing our thoughts and feelings (as typically assumed by mainstream psychology). When people talk to each other, they (help to) *construct* the world, such that language use is a form of *action* – that is, it has a *performative* role. Topics and concepts such as gender, aggression, person, self, emotion, schizophrenia, child, and mother's love are *social constructions*, products of historically specific interactions between people.

4. KNOWLEDGE AND SOCIAL ACTION GO TOGETHER

These 'negotiated' understandings could take a wide variety of forms, so there are many possible 'social constructions' of the world. But each different construction also brings with it, or invites, a different kind of action: how we account for a particular behaviour (what caused it) will dictate how we react to and treat the person whose behaviour it is (see Chapter 2).

Mainstream psychology looks for explanations of social phenomena inside the person, by, for example, hypothesizing the existence of attitudes, motives, cognitions, and so on (*individualism*; see Chapter 6). This can also be seen as *reductionist* (see Chapters 5 and 13). Social constructionists reject this view: explanations are to be found neither inside the individual psyche, nor in social structures or institutions (as advocated by sociologists), but in the *interactive processes* that take place routinely between people. For Burr (1995), 'Knowledge is therefore seen not as something that a person *has* (or does not have), but as something that people *do* together.'

WHO ARE SOCIAL CONSTRUCTIONISTS?

Burr (1995) and Jones and Elcock (2001) use the label 'social constructionist' to refer to psychologists who may otherwise be referred to as *discursive psychologists* or *critical psychologists*. These represent two quite distinct strands of constructionist theorizing in psychology.

Discursive psychology (DP) has been described as the 'second cognitive revolution' (Harré, 1995). This was marked by the return of the traditional, common-sense idea that psychology is the study of active people, singly or in groups, using material and symbolic tools to achieve all sorts of projects according to local standards of correctness. It is closely related to linguistics, anthropology, and several other disciplines.

According to this approach, the mind *isn't* a mental machine processing information. Rather, 'mind' denotes certain activities – that is, skilled use of symbols, performed both publicly and privately. Since *discourse* is primarily public and only secondarily private, so cognition (the use of various devices for mental tasks) is also primarily public and only secondarily private. Discourse usually implies verbal presentation of thought or argument, but language is just one of many discursive activities we are capable of (see Burr's third point above).

For Potter (1996), the central idea of DP is that the main business of social life is found in interaction, stressing the practical dimension of social life. For example, how does a husband produce a particular narrative (account) of relationship breakdown to show that it is his wife's problem rather than his own? Or how is a rape victim presented as subtly responsible for the attack and how might she resist such a presentation? Through analysis of tape-recordings, transcripts of conversations, videos (and other records of interaction), discursive psychologists have found that they need to rework notions such as attitudes, violence and aggression, and memory (see Gross *et al.* 1997).

Critical psychology (CP) looks more broadly at the structure of the discourse in its cultural context, asks where they come from, and how they constrain people's lives. It also focuses on how selfhood, subjectivity and power are reflected in specific discursive practices. While positivist, mainstream psychology sees 'single parent', 'woman', 'individual', 'self', and so on, as 'natural' categories (see Chapter 11), existing objectively, CP sees them as 'subjective positions' constructed through discourse, providing us with ways of thinking and communicating about ourselves. According to Burr (1995):

The person can be described by the sum total of the subjective positions in discourse they currently occupy. The fact that some of the positions are fleeting or in a state of flux means that our identity is never fixed but always in process, always open to change. The subjective positions that we occupy bring with them a structure of rights and obligations; they legislate for what 'that kind of person' may or may not reasonably do or say ... Not only do our subjective positions constrain and shape what we do, they are taken on as part of our psychology, so that they provide us also with our sense of self, the ideas and metaphors with which we think, and the self-narratives we use to talk and think about ourselves.

CP has been most heavily influenced by Foucault (1926–84), the French philosopher, and Lacan (1901–81), the French psychoanalyst. It has also been more influenced than DP by Marxism and contemporary feminism. Not surprisingly, then, CP is the more explicitly political, advocating empowerment and emancipation of those who are oppressed by psychological and other discourses (McGhee, 2001).

When defining and measuring 'internal' entities, such as 'personality', 'attitude', 'motivation' and 'intelligence', and comparing different groups on these dimensions, psychology paints a rather simplistic, static and de-socialized picture of the phenomenon. In contrast, critical social psychology shows them to be complex, contradictory and constructed, thereby disrupting social psychological narratives of 'objectivity' and 'progress'. Wetherell (1996) advocates:

... a critical 'social psychology' which takes the term 'social' very seriously indeed. We are not isolated individuals but social beings. Our dreams, hopes, fears and expectations may be the products of solitary reflection but they also tell us a great deal about the ways in which we are inserted into society. Social psychology should be a social science, not an imitation natural science. We belong with disciplines such as sociology, politics and cultural studies rather than physics, chemistry and astronomy. Our methods, research aims and theories should reflect the particular nature of social action ... We should work with and study the ambiguities, fluidity and openness of social life rather than try to repress these in a fruitless chase for experimental control and scientific respectability.

Theoretical contributions

SOCIAL CONSTRUCTIONISM AND SOCIAL REPRESENTATION THEORY

According to *social representation theory* (SRT), people come to understand their social world by way of images and social representations (SRs) shared by members of a social group. These representations act like a map that makes a baffling or novel terrain familiar and passable, thereby providing evaluations of good and bad areas. Attitudes are secondary phenomena, underpinned by SRs. SRT tries to provide a historical account of people's understanding of the world (Potter, 1996).

During the 1950s, the French psychologist Moscovici conducted one of the classic pieces of research on SRs. He was interested in how the ideas/concepts of psychoanalysis could be absorbed within a culture (post-Second World War France), based on women's magazines, church publications, and interviews. He concluded that psychoanalysis had trickled down from the analytic couch and learned journals into both 'high' culture and popular common sense: people 'think' with psychoanalytic concepts, without it seeming as if they are doing anything theoretical at all. But rather than the general population of Paris being conversant with/conversing with psychoanalytic theory in all its complexities, they were working with a simplified image of it, with some concepts having a wide currency (such as repression), and others not (such as libido) (Potter, 1996).

SRT is a constructionist theory: instead of portraying people as simply perceiving (or misperceiving) their social worlds, it regards these worlds as constructed, and an SR is a device for doing this construction. It allows someone to make sense of something potentially unfamiliar and to evaluate it. For Moscovici, all thought and understanding is based on the working of SRs, each of which consists of a mixture of concepts, ideas and images; these are both in people's minds and circulating in society.

SRT wasn't published in English until the early 1980s, since when research has snowballed, especially in Europe, Australia and South America (though it has been largely ignored by mainstream North American social psychologists in the experimental cognitive tradition). Potter (1996) suggests that one reason for this may be that the latter's pursuit of general laws and processes is directly challenged by SRT's emphasis on the specific content of a culture's or group's SR as the main object of analysis. (See Box 15.7, page 335.)

Another important theoretical contribution of SC is in the form of the relationship between it and *feminist psychology*. This link is discussed in Chapter 6.

An evaluation of SC

A recurring problem with SC concerns its *relativism* (see Burr's second point above). Relativism here refers to the belief that there is no absolute, ultimate, objective truth (as claimed by mainstream psychology and positivist science in general) or universal values. There are only *truths* – different accounts or versions of the truth as judged from different perspectives and viewpoints, or *different values*, reflecting different group memberships and experiences (i.e. *pluralism*).

But this seems to deny the 'reality' of the world as we experience it: our common-sense understanding of the world seems to correspond to *scientific realism* and the related *correspondence theory* (see above). Is SC claiming, in effect, that the world as we know it doesn't exist at all? One relevant example is emotion. According to Gergen (1997):

Box 15.7 What is social about social representations (SRs)?

According to Potter (1996), SRs are truly social for the following reasons:

○ They are *generated in communication*. When people interact through gossip, argue with one another or discuss political scandals, they are building up shared pictures of the world: 'social representations are the outcome of an increasing babble and a permanent dialogue between individuals' (Moscovici, 1985). The media play a major role in sustaining, producing and circulating SRs, which cannot be reduced to images inside people's heads.

○ They *provide a code for communication*. As a consequence of people sharing SRs, they can clearly understand each other and have free-flowing conversations, since they share a stable version of the world. Communication between people with different SRs is likely to produce conflict.

○ They *provide a way of distinguishing social groups*. According to Moscovici, one way of defining a group is in terms of a shared set of SRs, which provides a crucial homogenizing force for groups.

. . . there are only certain actions that warrant anger as an intelligible response (for example insult, expressions of hostility). And once anger has been *performed*, the other is not free to act in any way; convention requires that one react, for example, with an apology, with an exonerating explanation, or with anger.

In other words, any inner feelings of anger seem to be irrelevant to the *meaning* of anger. Emotion is being characterized as a feature of social interaction, *not* an inner and private experience (McGhee, 2001).

But perhaps we don't have to abandon belief in a real (physical) world altogether. For example, Wetherell and Still (1996) consider the idea of 'New Zealand' and 'hills' as constructed objects. On the one hand, there really is some land in the southern hemisphere of that name, but that shouldn't blind us to how our understanding and knowledge of it is *relative*. They argue that:

. . . the real world is no less constructed for being able to get in the way of planes. How those deaths are understood and what is seen as causing them will still be constituted through our system of social constructions.

Mainstream, positivist psychologists also criticize SC for not being scientific enough. But this is irrelevant as far as SC itself is concerned, because there is little or no attempt at hypothesis-testing, or generalizing from one study to another. So, issues of comprehensiveness, testability, empirical support, and so on, aren't at stake as they are in experimental psychology. Social constructionist analyses are often subtle, novel and imaginative, but their value is only apparent to other social constructionists.

However, just as in experimental psychology, there is good and bad SC research – although it is more difficult to say what criteria are being used to make this judgement (McGhee, 2001). But according to Salmon (2003), the issue as to how we recognize good research, whether it is *qualitative* (as in most SC research) or *quantitative* (as in experimental research) is far from straightforward. He uses the term 'methodologism' to mean judging research to be good if it has been conducted according to certain methods, and argues that 'it's a forlorn belief that quality can be guaranteed simply by following procedures'.

THE EVOLUTIONARY PSYCHOLOGICAL APPROACH

Basic principles and assumptions

Sociobiology (Wilson, 1975) grew out of the work of evolutionary biologists in the 1960s. Wilson set out to explain all non-human and human social behaviour in terms of evolution and other biological principles. It concentrated on the evolutionary origins of behaviour, and tended to imply *rigid genetic control* (Archer, 1996). Since then, many of these principles have been used to study topics covered by the social sciences – including psychology.

Evolutionary psychology (Buss, 1995) is a development of sociobiology (and is often referred to as 'neo- or modern Darwinism'). According to Archer (2001):

Just as the evolutionary approach led ethologists away from concentrating on the immediate causal mechanisms controlling animal behaviour, so evolutionary psychology seeks to lead conventional psychologists away from explanations that concentrate only on immediate mechanisms and mental events. Instead, it offers a single unifying starting point for understanding why we think and behave as we do today: natural selection has made us this way.

Campbell (2001) makes a similar distinction between (i) the *how* question (relating to proximal mechanisms) with which mainstream psychology is preoccupied, and (ii) the *why* question, which distinguishes 'evolutionary hypotheses about adaptations from alternative explanations that view the origins of human behaviour as culturally acquired and nearly infinitely malleable'.

However, contrary to what some critics claim, evolutionary psychologists don't deny the role of cultural factors. But fitness-relevant aspects of culture are seen as being constrained by genetic evolution ('genes hold culture on a leash'). Culture acts as a selecting environment for genotypes (Campbell, 2001).

According to Rose (2000):

The declared aim of evolutionary psychology is to provide explanations for the patterns of human activity and the forms of organization of human society which take into account the fact that humans are animals, and like all other currently living organisms, are the present-day products of some four billion years of evolution . . .

Theoretical contributions

As indicated in Box 15.8, evolutionary psychological (and sociobiological) explanations can be found throughout psychology. For example, the harmful effects of stress have been explained in evolutionary terms. While the body's stress response evolved to help us cope with life-threatening situations ('emergencies'), most 'modern-day' stressors aren't like this. Consequently, our bodies react in an inappropriate, and potentially life-threatening way to 'chronic' stress. This would be accepted by most (bio-)psychologists as a useful, and uncontroversial insight into why stress can be harmful.

Box 15.8 Some basic principles and assumptions of evolutionary psychology (EP)

O EP rejects the *Standard Social Science Model* (SSSM; Tooby and Cosmides, 1992), which makes two broad assumptions about human beings: (i) there's no such things as human nature or, if there is, it has so little effect on people's social lives that it can be ignored; (ii) explanations of social behaviour can be derived from considering only social roles, socialization and culture.

O Human social behaviour, like that of non-humans, can be understood in terms of its past contribution to survival and reproduction. For example, instead of regarding young males' proneness to violence in terms of social learning (modelling) or frustration (Berkowitz, 1993), EP views it as the result of its past contributions to obtaining resources, status and access to women (Daly and Wilson, 1988; see text below).

O While acknowledging their debt to sociobiology, evolutionary psychologists contend that sociobiologists often ignored the role of *mind* in mediating links between genes and behaviour. According to Barkow, Cosmides and Tooby (1992), the mind consists of a collection of specialized, independent mechanisms, or *modules*, designed by natural selection to solve problems that faced our hunter-gatherer ancestors, such as acquiring a mate, raising children and dealing with rivals. The solutions often involve such emotions as lust, fear, affection, jealousy and anger. Together, these modules and the related emotions constitute *human nature*.

O Drawing heavily on the jargon and conceptual framework of computer science and artificial intelligence, evolutionary psychologists see the mind as a cognitive machine, an information-processing device that is 'run' by the brain. It is *not* a general-purpose computer, but (as we have seen) comprises several specific modules.

O EP is, in general, about *universal* features of the mind. In so far as individual differences exist, the default assumption is that they are expressions of the same universal human nature as it encounters different environments. *Gender* is the crucial exception to this rule. Natural selection has constructed the mental modules of men and women in very different ways as a result of their divergent reproductive roles (*sexual dimorphism*; see text below).

O EP *isn't* a form of *genetic determinism* (or *nativism*; see Chapter 5). Like most modern biologists and social scientists, evolutionary psychologists argue that 'nature or nurture' is a false dichotomy, and they distinguish themselves from behaviour geneticists (see Chapter 5).

(Based on Horgan, 1995; Rose, 2000)

Rather more controversially, Buss (1994) claims that men, because they can in principle father a virtually infinite number of children, are much more inclined towards promiscuity than are women. Women, because they can average only one child per year, are choosier in selecting a mate. Men, in all cultures place greater emphasis on youth and physical attractiveness, while women look to men's 'resources'. Similarly, because men can never be sure that a child is theirs, their jealousy tends to be triggered by fears of a mate's sexual infidelity. Women, on the other hand, become more upset at the thought of losing a mate's emotional commitment – and thus his resources. In turn, women make greater 'parental investment' in their children than do men. According to Buss, 'Women's current mate preferences provide a window for viewing our mating past.' Evolution has favoured women who prefer men who possess 'attributes that confer benefits and who dislike men who possess attributes that impose costs'. This female preference is ancient and unlikely to change.

According to Fausto-Sterling (2000), there are four main criteria by which evolutionary biologists would judge the acceptability of hypotheses like Buss's about human reproductive behaviour.

1 Is there a good fit between the hypothesis and the data?

2 Is the evolutionary explanation as good or better than alternative explanations?

3 When using questionnaires to obtain data to support hypotheses about reproduction, do observed and independently documented behaviours correlate with answers to the questionnaires?

4 Do proposed characteristics actually relate to reproductive fitness? For example, does marrying a wealthier man really increase a woman's chance of producing more or fitter children?

Fausto-Sterling believes that only the first criterion has been reasonably met by Buss's hypothesis. McGhee (2001) also argues that we need to ask whether the evidence supports evolutionary explanations to the exclusion of other explanations (so showing that behaviour is *caused* by evolutionary processes), or is it merely *consistent* with evolutionary explanations (showing only that it *could* be).

IS LANGUAGE AN INSTINCT?

According to Pinker (1994), a linguist 'converted' to EP, language is far too complex to be learned: it must stem from an innate programme hardwired into our brains. Language almost certainly arose, he claims, because it was adaptive – that is, it conferred benefits on our hunter-gatherer ancestors. It would have allowed early hominids to share learned toolmaking, hunting and other skills, and those especially adept at language could manipulate others, and form alliances that would increase their chances of producing offspring.

Ironically, these claims are *denied* by Chomsky, a fellow linguist and colleague of Pinker's. Chomsky first argued in the 1950s that language represents a distinct mental module (or 'language organ') unique to human beings and independent of general cognitive ability, and that we all possess an innate language acquisition device (LAD; see Chapter 5). In this way, he laid the foundation for EP, and evolutionary psychologists are, in a sense, his heirs (Horgan, 1995; Kohn, 1998).

However, Chomsky disputes the assumption that language is a 'selected trait': just because language is adaptive now, doesn't mean that it *arose* in response to selection pressures. Given the enormous gap between human language and the relatively simple communication systems of other species, and given our fragmentary knowledge of our evolutionary past, science can tell us little about how language evolved. It may have been an incidental/accidental by-product of a spurt in intelligence or of the human brain's large size (Horgan, 1995; Kohn, 1998). The same may be true of other properties of the human mind.

ARE WE REALLY SEXUALLY DIMORPHIC?

According to Fausto-Sterling (2000), the claim that humans display sexual dimorphism (see Box 15.8) has been largely based on studies of primate societies, such as African baboons. Females were seen as meekly following after the males, who competed with one another for mates and leadership. But over the last 20 years or so, ideas about animal sexual behaviour, and the evolution of sex differences, have undergone a revolution.

During the 1970s, women flooded into the field of animal behaviour, especially the study of primates, and they began, almost for the first time, to watch the behaviour of *females*. Based on studies of a wide range of species, the message is clear: 'female behaviour can determine the pattern of evolution and their activities are every bit as varied, dynamic and complicated as [those] of males'.

Patient observations over many years and several generations, noting which individuals mated, with whom, and which initiated sexual contact, 'refuted the dogmatic assertions that females don't really want sex, females don't gain from exuberant sexual behaviour, and that females do best by choosing their mates prudently and with discrimination'.

The essential point is that, 'in animals and humans alike, male–female interactions around sex and the rearing of offspring are variable matters. Depending on their environments, both sexes can exhibit a wide range of behaviours . . .'.

EP's hardwired view of the inflexibility of human social arrangements flies in the face of the evidence of the *plasticity* of behaviour. Plasticity itself, rather than specific behaviour, may be under genetic control and may have evolved through natural selection (Fausto-Sterling, 2000). Consistent with this view, Karmiloff-Smith (2000) claims that developmental psychologists see plasticity during brain growth as the rule, rather than the exception or a response to brain injury.

An evaluation of EP

OUR HUNTER-GATHERER PAST

EP is based on the belief that the human mind is adapted to cope with life as a Pleistocene hunter-gatherer – which we were for about two million years before the ancient Chinese, Indian, Egyptian and Sumerian civilizations (Abdulla, 1996). Forms of behaviour and social organization that evolved adaptively over many generations in human hunter-gatherer society may or may not be adaptive in modern industrialized society, but have become to a degree fixed by humanity's evolutionary experience in the Palaeolithic *Environment of Evolutionary Adaptation* (EEA), thought to be the African savannah (Rose, 2000).

However, just as Chomsky's argument with Pinker concerned *how* language evolved (rather than whether or not it evolved), so the story of our human hunter-gatherer ancestors is, inevitably, partly a work of fiction (Turney, 1999). According to Rose (2000), the descriptions offered by EP of what hunter-gatherer societies were like read little better than 'Just so' accounts: 'There is a circularity about reading this version of the present into the past, and then claiming that this imagined past explains the present'.

In other words, based on what human beings are capable of now, evolutionary psychologists imagine how these abilities may have evolved, then put forward this constructed past as the cause of these current abilities.

Evolutionary psychologists also claim that the timescale of human history has been too short for evolutionary selection pressures to have produced significant change. But we know very little about just how quickly such change can occur (Rose, 2000). Evolutionarily modern humans appeared 100,000 years ago. Allowing 15–20 years per generation, there have been 5000–6600 generations between human origins and modern times. We really have no idea whether these generations are 'time enough' for substantial evolutionary change:

> However, granted the very rapid changes in human environment, social organisation, technology, and mode of production that have clearly occurred over that period, one must assume significant selection pressures operating ... the automatic assumption that the palaeolithic was an EEA in which fundamental human traits were fixed, and that there has not been time since to alter them, does not bear serious inspection.
> *(Rose, 2000)*

VIOLENT STEPFATHERS AND THE PROBLEM OF UNFALSIFIABILITY

According to Daly and Wilson (1988), children under the age of two were at least 60 times more likely to be killed by a stepparent – and almost always a stepfather – than by a natural parent. This is exactly what evolutionary theory would predict, since stepparents and stepchildren are genetically unrelated, while a child inherits half its genes from each biological parent. However, most stepfathers *don't* kill or abuse, and a minority of biological fathers *do*. And how do they explain the fact that adoptive parents do rather better on the violence/abuse stakes than biological parents (Rose and Rose, 2001)? These findings are difficult to square with any explanation based on shared/non-shared genes.

More seriously, in discussing women who kill their newborn babies, Pinker (1997) claims that when such an act takes place in conditions of poverty, it could be regarded as an *adaptationist* response. The psychological module that normally induces protectiveness in mothers of newborns is switched off by the challenge of an impoverished environment. This means that both killing *and* protecting are explained by evolutionary selection. As Hilary Rose (2000) says, this explains everything and, therefore, nothing.

CONCLUSIONS

The focus of this discussion of various theoretical approaches within psychology has been on how each conceptualizes human beings. Freud's 'tension-reducing person' and Skinner's 'environmentally controlled person' really are quite different from each other (Nye, 2000). The person-as-information-processor, and the person-as-shaped-by-our-evolutionary-past are different again – both from each other and from the first two approaches. Social constructionism's image of the person is rather less concrete and more elusive: what people are like and what they do is *relative* to their culture, historical period, and so on.

However, we have also noted some important similarities between different approaches, such as the deterministic nature of Freud's and Skinner's theories, and the influence of the information-processing approach on evolutionary psychology. Each approach has something of value to contribute to our understanding of ourselves – even if is only to reject the particular explanation it offers. The diversity of approaches reflects the complexity of the subject matter, so, usually, there is room for a diversity of explanations.

SUMMARY

○ Different theoretical *approaches/perspectives* are based on different models/images of the nature of human beings.

○ Watson's *methodological behaviourism* removes mental processes from the science of psychology and focuses on what can be quantified and observed by different researchers. Skinner's *radical behaviourism* regards mental processes as both inaccessible and irrelevant for explaining behaviour.

○ The behaviourist approach stresses the role of environmental influences (learning), especially classical and operant *conditioning*. Psychology's aim is to *predict* and *control* behaviour.

○ Tolman's *cognitive behaviourism* and *social learning theory* represent modifications of 'orthodox' learning (conditioning) theory.

○ Methodological behaviourism has influenced the practice of scientific psychology in general. Other practical contributions include *behaviour therapy* and *modification, behavioural neuroscience, behavioural pharmacology* and *environmental-enrichment studies*.

○ The *psychodynamic approach* is based on Freud's *psychoanalytic theory*. Central aspects are the *unconscious* (especially *repression*), *infantile sexuality* and the impact of early experience.

○ Freud's ideas have become part of mainstream psychology, contributing to our understanding of motivation, sleep and dreams, forgetting, attachment, aggression and abnormality.

○ Major modifications/alternatives to Freudian theory include *ego psychology*, Erikson's *psychosocial* theory, and the *object relations school*.

○ All forms of *psychotherapy* stem directly or indirectly from *psychoanalysis*. Many trained psychoanalysts have been responsible for developing radically different therapeutic approaches, including Rogers, Perls and Wolpe.

○ Criticisms of Freud's theories as unfalsifiable and untestable seem unfounded. There been a vast amount of empirical research into Freudian concepts, and much of modern cognitive psychology and neuropsychology is consistent with Freud's belief that behaviour doesn't depend on conscious experience (as in *blindsight*).

○ Compared with other approaches, the *cognitive approach* lacks both a central figure and a unifying theory. It uses *analogies* and *metaphors* when trying to describe what is going on inside the brain, in particular the *computer analogy* and the view of people as *information processors*.

○ Modern cognitive psychology emerged from a re-conceptualization of cognition in terms of *information, feedback* and *programs*. These concepts derive from electrical engineering, logic, mathematics and telecommunications.

O Other important features include the concepts of *coding, channel capacity* and *serial/parallel processing*.

O A major application of the cognitive approach has been *cognitive behaviour therapy*, as in Ellis's REBT.

O While the computer analogy is a useful way of understanding cognitive processes, there are also some important differences between how computers and people process information.

O One of the goals of *social constructionism* (SC) is to correct the tendency of *mainstream* psychology to *decontextualize* behaviour. Related to this is the *universalist assumption*, which is challenged by *(trans)cultural* (as distinct from *cross-cultural*) psychology.

O SC is also *anti-essentialism*, which involves a rejection of the *correspondence theory* of truth. Other key concepts are *relativism* and a rejection of *individualism*. Two distinct strands within SC are *discursive psychology* (DP) and *critical psychology* (CP).

O *Social representation theory* (SRT) is a social constructionist theory, according to which all thought and understanding is based on the working of SRs; these exist in people's minds and circulate within society.

O *Evolutionary psychology* (EP) grew out of *sociobiology*. Unlike the latter, EP puts the mind centre stage, identifying several independent mental mechanisms or *modules*. These form the core of *human nature*.

O A major assumption of EP is that these mental modules have become fixed by our hunter-gatherer ancestors' experience in the Palaeolithic *Environment of Evolutionary Adaptation* (EEA). But knowledge of the EEA is largely speculative, and there is good reason to believe that human traits have changed since that time.

O The fact that there is empirical evidence consistent with EP hypotheses (such as Buss's explanation of male/female mate preferences) doesn't mean that evolutionary processes actually caused the behaviour in question, only that they might have done.

O *Sexual dimorphism* has been challenged by observations of sexual behaviour among female primates. It seems that behavioural *plasticity*, rather than specific behaviours, may have evolved through natural selection.

Useful websites

- http://www.yorku.ca/dept/psych/orgs/istp
- http://www.uis.edu/~radpsy/
- http://sar.bolton.ac.uk/Psych/default.htm
- http://www.massey.ac.nz/~ALock/virtual/welcome.htm
- http://www.freud.org.uk/
- http://freud.t0.or.at/freud/index-e.htm
- www.psychoanalysis.org.uk
- www.ipa.org
- http://evolution.humb.univie.ac.at/jump.html
- http://www.cogsci.soton.ac.uk
- www.evolpsych/main.htm

Recommended reading

Burr, V. (1995) *An Introduction to Social Constructionism.* London: Routledge.

Glassman, W.E. (1995) *Approaches to Psychology* (2nd edn). Buckingham: Open University Press.

Nye, D. (2000) *Three Psychologies: Perspectives from Freud, Skinner and Rogers* (6th edn). Belmont, CA: Wadsworth/Thomson Learning.

O'Donohue, W. and Ferguson, K.E. (2001) *The Psychology of B.F. Skinner.* Thousand Oaks, CA: Sage Publications.

Rose, H. and Rose, D. (eds) (2000) *Alas, Poor Darwin: Arguments Against Evolutionary Psychology.* London: Jonathan Cape.

REFERENCES

Abdulla, S. (1996) Illuminating the hardware. *The Times Higher*, 1 November, 18.

Abramson, L.Y. and Martin, D.J. (1981) Depression and the causal inference process. In J.H. Harvey, W.J. Ickes and R.F. Kidd (eds) *New Directions in Attitude Research*, Vol. 3. Hillsdale, NJ: Lawrence Erlbaum.

Abramson, L.Y., Seligman, M.E.P. and Teasdale, J.D. (1978) Learned helplessness in humans: critique and reformulation. *Journal of Abnormal Psychology, 87*, 49–74.

Adler, A. (1927) *The Practice and Theory of Individual Psychology.* New York: Harcourt Brace Jovanovich.

Adorno, T.W., Frenkel-Brunswick, E., Levinson, J.D. and Sanford, R.N. (1950) *The Authoritarian Personality.* New York: Harper & Row.

Ainsworth, M.D.S. (1967) *Infancy in Uganda: Infant Care and the Growth of Love.* Baltimore, MD: Johns Hopkins University Press.

Ainsworth, M.D.S. (1985) Attachments across the life span. *Bulletin of the New York Academy of Medicine, 61*, 792–812.

Ainsworth, M.D.S. (1989) Attachments beyond infancy. *American Psychologist, 44*(4), 709–16.

Ainsworth, M.D.S., Blehar, M.C., Waters, E. and Wall, S. (1978) *Patterns of Attachment: A Psychological Study of the Strange Situation.* Hillsdale, NJ: Lawrence Erlbaum.

Allport, D.A. (1980) Attention and performance. In G. Claxton (ed.) *Cognitive Psychology: New Directions.* London: RKP.

Allport, G.W. (1937) *Personality: A Psychological Interpretation.* New York: Holt.

Allport, G.W. (1960) *Personality and Social Encounter.* Boston: Beacon Press.

Allport, G.W. (1961) *Pattern and Growth in Personality.* New York: Holt, Rinehart & Winston.

American Psychological Association (1985) *Guidelines for Ethical Conduct in the Care and Use of Animals.* Washington, DC: American Psychological Association.

American Psychological Association (1992) *Ethical Principles of Psychologists and Code of Conduct.* Washington, DC: American Psychological Association.

Anastasi, A. (1958) Heredity, environment and the question 'How?' *Psychological Review, 65*, 197–208.

Andrews, B. and Brewin, C.R. (2000) What did Freud get right? *The Psychologist, 13*(12), 605–7.

Antaki, C. (1984) Core concepts in attribution theory. In J. Nicholson and H. Beloff (eds) *Psychology Survey, 5*. Leicester: British Psychological Society.

Archer, D. (2001) Evolving theories of behaviour. *The Psychologist, 14*(8), 414–19.

Archer, J. (1996) Evolutionary social psychology. In M. Hewstone, W. Stroebe and G.M. Stephenson (eds) *Introduction to Social Psychology* (2nd edn). Oxford: Blackwell.

Argyle, M. (1983) *The Psychology of Interpersonal Behaviour* (4th edn). Harmondsworth: Penguin.

Armstrong, D.M. (1987) Mind–body problem: philosophical theories. In R.L. Gregory (ed.) *The Oxford Companion to the Mind*. Oxford: Oxford University Press.

Aronson, E. (1992) *The Social Animal* (6th edn). New York: W.H. Freeman & Co.

Asch, S.E. (1951) Effect of group pressure upon the modification and distortion of judgements. In H. Guetzkow (ed.) *Groups, Leadership and Men*. Pittsburgh, PA: Carnegie Press.

Asch, S.E. (1952) *Social Psychology*. Englewood Cliffs, NJ: Prentice-Hall.

Association for the Teaching of Psychology (1992) Ethics in psychological research: guidelines for students at pre-degree level. *Psychology Teaching*, New Series, No. 1, 4–10.

Atkinson, R.C. and Shiffrin, R.M. (1971) The control of short-term memory. *Scientific American, 224*, 82–90.

Atkinson, R.L., Atkinson, R.C., Smith, E.E. and Bem, D.J. (1990) *Introduction to Psychology* (10th edition). New York: Harcourt Brace Jovanovich.

Bailey, C.L. (1979) Mental illness: a logical misrepresentation? *Nursing Times*, May, 761–2.

Bandura, A. (1971) *Social Learning Theory*. New York: General Learning Press.

Bannister, D. and Fransella, F. (1966) A grid test of schizophrenic thought disorder. *British Journal of Social & Clinical Psychology, 5*, 95–102.

Bannister, D. and Fransella, F. (1967) *A Grid Test of Schizophrenic Thought Disorder*. Barnstaple: Psychological Test Publications.

Bannister, D. and Fransella, F. (1980) *Inquiring Man: The Psychology of Personal Constructs* (2nd edn). Harmondsworth: Penguin.

Barkow, J.H., Cosmides, L. and Tooby, J. (1992) Introduction. In J.H. Barkow, L. Cosmides and J. Tooby (eds) *The Adapted Mind: Evolutionary Psychology and the Evolution of Culture*. New York: Oxford University Press.

Barlow, H. (1987) The biological role of consciousness. In C. Blakemore and S. Greenfield (eds) *Mindwaves*. Oxford: Blackwell.

Barnes, R.D., Ickes, W.J. and Kidd, R. (1979) Effects of perceived intentionality and stability of another's dependency on helping behaviour. *Personality & Social Psychology Bulletin, 5*, 367–72.

Baron, R.A. and Byrne, D. (1991) *Social Psychology* (6th edn). Boston: Allyn & Bacon.

Baron, R.A. and Byrne, D. (1994) *Social Psychology: Understanding Human Interaction* (7th edn). Boston, MA: Allyn & Bacon.

Bartholomew, K. (1990) Avoidance of intimacy: an attachment perspective. *Journal of Social & Personal Relationships, 7*, 147–78.

Bartholomew, K. (1993) From childhood to adult relationships: attachment theory and research. In S. Duck (ed.) *Learning about Relationships*. Newbury Park, CA: Sage Publications.

Bateson, G., Jackson, D., Haley, J. and Weakland, J. (1956) Toward a theory of schizophrenia. *Behavioural Science, 1*, 251–64.

Bateson, P. (1986) When to experiment on animals. *New Scientist, 109*(1496), 30–2.

Bateson, P. (1992) Do animals feel pain? *New Scientist, 134*(1818), 30–3.

Becker, H.S. (1963) *Outsiders: Studies in the Sociology of Deviance*. New York: Free Press.

Bee, H. (1989) *The Developing Child* (5th edn). New York: Harper & Row.

Bee, H. (1994) *Lifespan Development*. New York: HarperCollins.

Bem, D.J. (1967) Self-perception: an alternative interpretation of cognitive dissonance phenomena. *Psychological Review, 74*, 183–200.

Bem, D.J. (1972) Self-perception theory. In L. Berkowitz (ed.) *Advances in Experimental Social Psychology*, Vol. 6. New York: Academic Press.

Bem, D.J. (1983) Constructing a theory of the triple typology: some (second) thoughts on nomothetic and idiographic approaches to personality. *Journal of Personality, 51*, 566–77.

Bem, D.J. and Allen, A. (1974) On predicting some of the people some of the time: a search for cross-situational consistencies in behaviour. *Psychological Review, 81*, 506–20.

Bem, D.J. and Honorton, C. (1994) Does psi exist? Replicable evidence for an anomalous process of information transfer. *Psychological Bulletin, 115*, 4–18.

Bem, S. and Looren de Jong, H. (1997) *Theoretical Issues in Psychology: An Introduction*. London: Sage Publications.

Bem, S.J. (1984) Androgyny and gender schema theory: a conceptual and empirical integration. In R.A. Dienstbier (ed.) *Nebraska Symposium on Motivation*. Lincoln, Nebraska: University of Nebraska Press.

Bem, S.L. (1993) Is there a place in psychology for a feminist analysis of the social context? *Feminism & Psychology, 3*(2), 230–4.

Bennett, M. (1993) Introduction. In M. Bennett (ed.) *The Child as Psychologist: An Introduction to the Development of Social Cognition*. Hemel Hempstead: Harvester Wheatsheaf.

Bentall, R.P. (1993) Personality traits may be alive, they may even be well, but are they really useful? *The Psychologist, 6*(7), 307.

Berger, P.L. and Luckmann, T. (1966) *The Social Construction of Reality*. Harmondsworth: Penguin.

Berkowitz, L. (1969) Resistance to improper dependency relationships. *Journal of Experimental Social Psychology, 5*, 283–94.

Berkowitz, L. (1993) *Aggression: Its Causes, Consequences and Control*. New York: McGraw-Hill.

Bernstein, M.D. and Russo, N.F. (1974) The history of psychology revised: or, up with our foremothers. *American Psychologist, 29*, 130–4.

Berry, J.W. (1969) On cross-cultural comparability. *International Journal of Psychology, 4*, 119–28.

Berry, J.W., Poortinga, Y.H., Segall, M.H. and Dasen, P.R. (1992) *Cross-Cultural Psychology*. Cambridge: Cambridge University Press.

Berscheid, E. (1985) Interpersonal attraction. In G. Lindzey and E. Aronson (eds) *Handbook of Social Psychology* (3rd edn). New York: Random House.

Bettelheim, B. (1965) The problem of generations. In E. Erikson (ed.) *The Challenge of Youth*. New York: Doubleday.

Bhugra, D. and Bhui, K. (2001) *Cross-Cultural Psychiatry: A Practical Guide*. London: Arnold.

Bieber, I., Dain, H.J., Dince, P.R., Drellich, M.G., Grand, H.G., Bundlach, R.H., Dremer, M.W., Rifkin, A.H., Wilbur, C.B. and Bieber, T.B. (1962) *Homosexuality*. New York: Vintage Books.

Blackman, D.E. (1980) Image of man in contemporary behaviourism. In A.J. Chapman and D.M. Jones (eds) *Models of Man*. Leicester: British Psychological Society.

Blackmore, S. (1984) A postal survey of OBEs and other experiences. *Journal of the Society for Psychical Research, 52*, 225–44.

Blackmore, S. (1995) Parapsychology. In A.M. Colman (ed.) *Controversies in Psychology*. London: Longman.

Blackmore, S. (1997a) Probability misjudgement and belief in the paranormal: a newspaper survey. *British Journal of Psychology, 88*, 683–9.

Blackmore, S. (1997b) In search of the paranormal. *Psychology Review, 3*(3), 2–6.

Blackmore, S. (2001) Consciousness. *The Psychologist, 14*(10), 522–5.

Blakemore, C. and Cooper, G.F. (1970) Development of the brain depends on the visual environment. *Nature, 228*, 477–8.

Blakemore, C. (1988) *The Mind Machine*. London: BBC Books.

Block, N. (1995) On a confusion about a function of consciousness. *Behavioural & Brain Sciences, 18*, 227–87.

Blos, P. (1967) The second individuation process of adolescence. *Psychoanalytic Study of the Child, 22*, 162–86.

Boas, F. (1911) *The Mind of Primitive Man*. New York: Macmillan.

Boden, M. (1993) The impact on philosophy. In D. Broadbent (ed.) *The Simulation of Human Intelligence*. Oxford: Blackwell.

Bowers, K.S. (1973) Situationism in psychology: an analysis and critique. *Psychological Review, 80*, 307–36.

Bowlby, J. (1953) *Child Care and the Growth of Love*. Harmondsworth: Penguin.

Bowlby, J. (1958) The nature of the child's tie to his mother. *International Journal of Psycho-Analysis, 39*, 350–73.

Bowlby, J. (1969) *Attachment and Loss. Volume 1: Attachment*. Harmondsworth: Penguin.

Bowlby, J. (1977) The making and breaking of affectional bonds: 1. Aetiology and psychopathology in the light of attachment theory. *British Journal of Psychiatry, 130*, 201–10.

Bradbury, T.N. and Fincham, F.D. (1990) Attributions in marriage: review and critique. *Psychological Bulletin, 107*, 3–33.

Bradley, J.M. and Cafferty, T.P. (2001) Attachment among older adults: current issues and directions for future research. *Attachment & Human Development, 3*(2), 200–21.

Brady, J.V. (1958) Ulcers in 'executive monkeys'. *Scientific American, 199*, 95–100.

Braud, W.G. (1975) Psi-conducive states. *Journal of Communication, 25,* 142–52.

Brehm, J.W. (1966) *A Theory of Psychological Reactance.* New York: Academic Press.

Brehm, S.S. (1992) *Intimate Relationships* (2nd edn). New York: McGraw-Hill.

Brehm, S.S. and Brehm, J.W. (1981) *Psychological Reactance: A Theory of Freedom and Control.* New York: Academic Press.

Brislin, R. (1993) *Understanding Culture's Influence on Behaviour.* Orlando, FL: Harcourt Brace Jovanovich.

British Psychological Society (1978) Ethical principles for research with human subjects. *Bulletin of the British Psychological Society, 31,* 48–9.

British Psychological Society (1985) A code of conduct for psychologists. *Bulletin of the British Psychological Society, 38,* 41–3.

British Psychological Society (1990) Ethical principles for conducting research with human participants. *The Psychologist, 3*(6), 269–72.

British Psychological Society (1993) Ethical principles for conducting research with human participants (revised). *The Psychologist, 6*(1), 33–5.

British Psychological Society (1995) *Division of Clinical Psychology Professional Practice Guidelines.* Leicester: BPS.

British Psychological Society (2000) *Code of Conduct, Ethical Principles & Guidelines.* Leicester: BPS.

British Psychological Society Scientific Affairs Board (1985) Guidelines for the use of animals in research. *Bulletin of the British Psychological Society, 38,* 289–91.

Bronfenbrenner, U. (1979) *The Ecology of Human Development: Experiments by Nature and Design.* Cambridge, MS: Harvard University Press.

Bronfenbrenner, U. (1989) Ecological systems theory. *Annals of Child Development, 6,* 187–249.

Brown, J.A.C. (1961) *Freud and the Post-Freudians.* Harmondsworth: Penguin.

Brown, L.S. (1997) Ethics in psychology: cui bono? In D. Fox and I. Prilleltensky (eds) *Critical Psychology: An Introduction.* London: Sage.

Bruce, V. and Young, A.W. (1986) Understanding face recognition. *British Journal of Psychology, 77,* 305–27.

Bruner, J.S. (1990) *Acts of Meaning.* Cambridge, MA: Harvard University Press.

Burgner, D. and Hewstone, M. (1993) Young children's causal attributions for success and failure: 'self-enhancing' boys and 'self-derogating' girls. *British Journal of Developmental Psychology, 11,* 125–9.

Burne, J. (2002) Make-believe medicine. *Guardian Weekend,* 20 June, 10.

Burr, V. (1995) *An Introduction to Social Constructionism.* London: Routledge.

Burt, C. (1949) The structure of the mind: a review of the results of factor analysis. *British Journal of Educational Psychology, 19,* 110–11, 176–99.

Burt, C. (1955) The evidence for the concept of intelligence. *British Journal of Educational Psychology, 25,* 158–77.

Buss, D. M. (1995) Evolutionary psychology: a new paradigm for psychological science. *Psychological Enquiry, 6*(1), 1–30.

Buss, D.M. (1994) Mate preference in 37 cultures. In W.J. Lonner and R.S. Malpass (eds) *Psychology and Culture.* Boston: Allyn & Bacon.

Butler, J.M. and Haigh, G.V. (1954) Changes in the relation between self-concepts and ideal concepts consequent upon client-centred counseling. In C.R. Rogers and R.F. Dymond (eds) *Psychotherapy and Personality Change: Coordinated Research Studies in the Client-Centred Approach.* Chicago: Chicago University Press.

Byrne, W. (1994) The biological evidence challenged. *Scientific American*, May, 26–31.

Caldwell, R. (1997) Dan Dennett and the conscious robot. *Philosophy Now, 18*, Summer, 16–18.

Campbell, A. (2001) Behaviour – Adapted? Adaptive? Useful? *The Psychologist, 14*(8), 426–7.

Campos, J.J., Barrett, K., Lamb, M.E., Goldsmith, H.H. and Stenberg, C. (1983) Socioemotional development. In M.M. Haith and J.J. Campos (eds) *Handbook of Child Psychology. Vol. 2: Infancy and Psychobiology.* New York: Wiley.

Cannon, W.B. (1927) The James–Lange theory of emotions: a critical examination and an alternative theory. *American Journal of Psychology, 39*, 106–24.

Caplan, P. (1991) Delusional dominating personality disorder (DDPD). *Feminism & Psychology, 1*(1), 171–4.

Carver, C.S. and Scheier, M.F. (1992) *Perspectives on Personality* (2nd edn). Boston: Allyn & Bacon.

Cassidy, J. and Shaver, P.R. (eds) (1999) *Handbook of Attachment: Theory, Research, and Clinical Applications.* New York: Guilford Press.

Cattell, R.B. (1944) Psychological measurement: normative, ipsative, interactive. *Psychological Review, 51*, 292–303.

Cattell, R.B. (1965) *The Scientific Analysis of Behaviour.* Harmondsworth: Penguin.

Child, A.L. (1954) Socialization. In G. Lindzey (ed.) *Handbook of Social Psychology*, Vol. 2. Cambridge, MA: Addison-Wesley.

Chomsky, N. (1965) *Aspects of the Theory of Syntax.* Cambridge, MA: MIT Press.

Chomsky, N. (1968) *Language and Mind.* New York: Harcourt Brace Jovanovich.

Cicirelli, V.G. (1983) Adult children's attachment and helping behaviour to elderly parents: a path model. *Journal of Marriage & The Family, 45*, 815–25.

Cicirelli, V.G. (1993) Attachment and obligation as daughter's motives for caregiving behaviour and subsequent effect on subjective burden. *Psychology & Ageing, 8*, 144–55.

Cicirelli, V.G. (1995) A measure of caregiving daughter's attachment to elderly mothers. *Journal of Family Psychology, 9*, 89–94.

Cicirelli, V.G. (1996) Emotion and cognition in attachment. In C. Magai and S.H. McFadden (eds) *Handbook of Emotion, Adult Development and Ageing.* San Diego, CA: Academic Press.

Claridge, G. and Davis, C. (2003) *Personality and Psychological Disorders.* London: Arnold.

Clarke, V. (2002) Resistance and normalization in the construction of lesbian and gay families: a discursive analysis. In A. Coyle and C. Kitzinger (eds) *Lesbian and Gay Psychology: New Perspectives.* BPS/Blackwell.

Clift, S.M. (1984) Should we still teach Freud? *Psychology Teaching*, December, 8–14.

Cole, M. (1985) The zone of proximal development: where culture and cognition create each other. In J. Wertsch (ed.) *Culture, Communication* and *Cognition*. New York: Cambridge University Press.

Cole, M. (1990) Cultural psychology: a once and future discipline? In J.J. Berman (ed.) *Nebraska Symposium on Motivation: Cross-Cultural Perspectives*. Lincoln, NA: University of Nebraska Press.

Cole, M. (1993) Mind as a cultural achievement: implications for IQ testing. In M. Gauvin and M. Cole (eds) *Readings on the Development of Children*. New York: Scientific American Books, W.H. Freeman & Co.

Cole, M. (1996) *Cultural Psychology: A Once and Future Discipline*. Cambridge, MA: Harvard University Press.

Collins, N.L. and Read, S.J. (1990) Adult attachment, working models and relationship quality in dating couples. *Journal of Personality & Social Psychology, 58*, 644–63.

Coolican, H. (1994) *Research Methods and Statistics in Psychology* (2nd edn). London: Hodder & Stoughton.

Coolican, H., Cassidy, T., Chercher, A., Harrower, J., Penny, G., Sharp, R., Walley, M. and Westbury, T. (1996) *Applied Psychology*. London: Hodder & Stoughton.

Costa, P.T. and McCrae, R.R. (1993) Bullish on personality psychology. *The Psychologist, 6*(7), 302–3.

Coyle, A. and Kitzinger, C. (eds) (2002) *Lesbian and Gay Psychology: New Perspectives*. BPS/Blackwell.

Crick, F. (1994) *The Astonishing Hypothesis: The Scientific Search for the Soul*. London: Simon & Schuster.

Dalton, K. (1997) Exploring the links: creativity and psi in the Ganzfeld. In *The Parapsychological Association 40th Annual Convention: Proceedings of Presented Papers*. Durham, NC: Parapsychological Association.

Daly, M. and Wilson, M. (1988) Evolutionary social psychology and family homicide. *Science, 28*, October, 519–24.

Danziger, K. (1990) *Constructing the Subject: Historical Origins of Psychological Research*. New York: Cambridge University Press.

Danziger, K. (1997) *Naming the Mind: How Psychology Found Its Language*. London: Sage.

Darley, J.M. and Latané, B. (1968) Bystander intervention in emergencies: diffusion of responsibility. *Journal of Personality & Social Psychology, 8*, 377–83.

Darwin, C.R. (1859) *The Origin of Species by Means of Natural Selection*. London: John Murray.

Davison, G.C. and Neale, J.M. (1994) *Abnormal Psychology* (6th edn). New York: John Wiley & Sons.

Davison, G.C. and Neale, J.M. (2001) *Abnormal Psychology* (8th edn). New York: John Wiley & Sons.

Dawkins, R. (1976) *The Selfish Gene*. Oxford: Oxford University Press.

Deary, I.J. and Matthews, G. (1993) Personality traits are alive and well. *The Psychologist, 6*(7), 299–311.

Deese, J. (1972) *Psychology as Science and Art*. New York: Harcourt Brace Jovanovich.

Denmark, F., Russo, N.F., Frieze, I.H. and Sechzer, J.A. (1988) Guidelines for avoiding sexism in psychological research: a report of the ad hoc committee on nonsexist research. *American Psychologist, 43*(7), 582–5.

Dennett, D. (1987) Consciousness. In R.L. Gregory (ed.) *The Oxford Companion to the Mind*. Oxford: Oxford University Press.

Dennett, D. (1991) *Consciousness Explained*. London: Little, Brown & Co.

Dennett, D.C. (2003) *Freedom Evolves.* London: Allen Lane.

Dewey, J. (1896) The reflex arc concept in psychology. *Psychological Review, 3,* 357–70.

Di Blasi, Z. (2003) The crack in the biomedical box. *The Psychologists, 16*(2), 72–5.

Di Blasi, Z., Kaptchuk, T.J., Weinman, J. and Kleijnen, J. (2002) Informing participants of allocation to placebo at trial closure: postal survey. *British Medical Journal, 325,* 1329–31.

Diller, A. (1999/2000) Detecting androids. *Philosophy Now, 25,* Winter, 26–8.

Doyle, J.A. (1983) *The Male Experience.* Dubuque, Iowa: Wm C. Brown Co.

Draguns, J. (1980) Psychological disorders of clinical severity. In H.C. Triandis and J. Draguns (eds) *Handbook of Cross-Cultural Psychology, Vol. 6: Psychopathology.* Boston: Allyn & Bacon.

Draguns, J. (1990) Applications of cross-cultural psychology in the field of mental health. In R. Brislin (ed.) *Applied Cross-Cultural Psychology.* Newbury Park, CA: Sage.

Dunn, J. and Plomin, R. (1990) *Separate Lives: Why Siblings are so Different.* New York: Basic Books.

Eagly, A.H. (1987) *Sex Differences in Social Behaviour: A social-role interpretation.* Hillsdale, NJ: Lawrence Erlbaum.

Edelman, G. (1992) *Bright Air, Brilliant Fire: On the Matter of the Mind.* Harmondsworth: Penguin.

Edwards, D. (1997) *Discourse and Cognition.* London: Sage.

Edwards, D. and Potter, J. (1992) *Discursive Psychology.* London: Sage.

Eiser, J.R. (1994) *Attitudes, Chaos and the Connectionist Mind.* Oxford: Blackwell.

Ellis, A. (1962) *Reason and Emotion in Psychotherapy.* Secaucus, NJ: Lyle Stuart (Citadel Press).

Ellis, A. (1987) The impossibility of achieving consistently good mental health. *American Psychologist, 42,* 364–75.

Elms, A.C. and Janis, I.L. (1965) Counter-norm attitudes induced by consonant versus dissonant conditions of role-playing. *Journal of Experimental Research in Personality, 1,* 50–60.

Endler, N.S. and Magnusson, D. (1976) Toward an interactional psychology of personality. *Psychological Bulletin, 83,* 956–74.

Epstein, S. (1979) The stability of behaviour: On predicting most of the people much of the time. *Journal of Personality & Social Psychology, 37,* 1097–1126.

Erikson, E.H. (1950) *Childhood and Society.* New York: Norton.

Erikson, E.H. (1963) *Childhood and Society* (2nd edn). New York: Norton.

Erikson, E.H. (1968) *Identity: Youth and Crisis.* New York: Norton.

Evans, C. (1987) Extra-sensory perception. In R.L. Gregory (ed.) *The Oxford Companion to the Mind.* Oxford: Oxford University Press.

Ewen, R.E. (1988) *An Introduction to Theories of Personality* (3rd edn). Hillsdale, NJ: Lawrence Erlbaum.

Eysenck, H.J. (1953) *The Structure of Human Personality.* London: Methuen.

Eysenck, H.J. (1960) Classification and the problem of diagnosis. In H.J. Eysenck (ed.) *Handbook of Abnormal Psychology.* London: Pitman.

Eysenck, H.J. (1965) *Fact and Fiction in Psychology*. Harmondsworth: Penguin.

Eysenck, H.J. (1967) *The Biological Basis of Personality*. Springfield, Ill.: C.C. Thomas.

Eysenck, H.J. (1970) *Crime and Personality* (revised edn). London: Paladin.

Eysenck, H.J. (1985) *Decline and Fall of the Freudian Empire*. Harmondsworth: Penguin.

Eysenck, H.J. and Wilson, G.D. (eds) (1973) *The Experimental Study of Freudian Theories*. London: Methuen.

Eysenck, M.W. (1994) *Perspectives on Psychology*. Hove: Lawrence Erlbaum.

Fairbairn, G. (1987) Responsibility, respect for persons and psychological change. In S. Fairbairn and G. Fairbairn (eds) *Psychology, Ethics and Change*. London: RKP.

Fairbairn, R. (1952) *Psychoanalytical Studies of the Personality*. London: Tavistock.

Fancher, R.E. (1979) *Pioneers of Psychology*. New York: Norton.

Fancher, R.E. (1996) *Pioneers of Psychology* (3rd edn). New York: Norton.

Fausto-Sterling, A. (2000) Beyond difference: feminism and evolutionary psychology. In H. Rose and S. Rose (eds) *Alas, Poor Darwin: Arguments Against Evolutionary Psychology*. London: Jonathan Cape.

Fechner, G. (1966) *Elements of Psychophysics*, Vol. 1 (trans. H.E. Adler). New York: Holt, Rinehart & Winston (originally published 1860).

Feeney, J. and Noller, P. (1996) *Adult Attachment*. Thousand Oaks, CA: Sage Publications.

Fernando, S. (1991) *Mental Health, Race and Culture*. London: Macmillan, in association with MIND Publications.

Festinger, L. (1957) *A Theory of Cognitive Dissonance*. New York: Harper & Row.

Festinger, L. and Carlsmith, J.M. (1959) Cognitive consequences of forced compliance. *Journal of Abnormal & Social Psychology, 58*, 203–10.

Fisher, S. and Greenberg, R.P. (1996) *Freud Scientifically Reappraised: Testing the Theories and the Therapy*. New York: Wiley.

Fiske, S. and Taylor, S. (1991) *Social Cognition* (2nd edn). New York: McGraw-Hill.

Flanagan, O. (1984) *The Science of the Mind*. Cambridge, MS: MIT Press.

Flanagan, O. (1992) *Consciousness Reconsidered*. Cambridge, MA: MIT Press.

Fraley, R.C. and Davis, K.E. (1997) Attachment formation and transfer in young adults' close friendships and romantic relationships. *Personal Relationships, 4*, 131–44.

Fransella, F. (1970) And there was one. In D. Bannister (ed.) *Perspectives in Personal Construct Theory*. London: Academic Press.

Fransella, F. (1972) *Personal Change and Reconstruction: Research on a Treatment of Stuttering*. London: Academic Press.

Fransella, F. (1980) Man-as-scientist. In A.J. Chapman and D.M. Jones (eds) *Models of Man*. Leicester: British Psychological Society.

French, C. (2001a) Why I study ... anomalistic psychology. *The Psychologist, 14*(7), 356–7.

French, C. (2001b) The placebo effect. In R. Roberts and D. Groome (eds) *Parapsychology: The Science of Unusual Experience*. London: Arnold.

Freud, S. (1930) *Civilization and its Discontents*. London: Hogarth Press.

Freud, S. (1949) *An Outline of Psychoanalysis*. London: Hogarth Press.

Fromm, E. (1942) *The Fear of Freedom*. London: RKP.

Fromm, E. (1964) *The Heart of Man*. London: RKP.

Gahagan, J. (1984) *Social Interaction and its Management*. London: Methuen.

Gahagan, J. (1991) Understanding other people: understanding self. In J. Radford and E. Govier (eds) *A Textbook of Psychology* (2nd edn). London: Routledge.

Gale, A. (1995) Ethical issues in psychological research. In A.M. Colman (ed.) *Psychological Research Methods and Statistics*. London: Methuen.

Gardner, R.A. and Gardner, B.T. (1969) Teaching sign language to a chimpanzee. *Science, 165* (3894), 664–72.

Garfinkel, H. (1967) *Studies in Ethnomethodology*. Englewood Cliffs, NJ: Prentice-Hall.

Garnham, A. (1991) *The Mind in Action*. London: Routledge.

Garrett, R. (1996) Skinner's case for radical behaviourism. In W. O'Donohue and R.F. Kitchener (eds) *The Philosophy of Psychology*. London: Sage.

Gay, P. (1988) *Freud: A Life for our Time*. London: J.M. Dent & Sons.

Gelder, M., Gath, D. and Mayon, R. (1989) *Oxford Textbook of Psychiatry* (2nd edn). Oxford: Oxford University Press.

George, C. and Solomon, J. (1999) Attachment and caregiving: the caregiving behavioural system. In J. Cassidy and P.R. Shaver (eds) *Handbook of Attachment: Theory, Research, and Clinical Applications*. New York: Guilford Press.

Gergen, K.J. (1973) Social psychology as history. *Journal of Personality & Social Psychology, 26*, 309–20.

Gergen, K.J. (1985) The social constructionist movement in modern psychology. *American Psychologist, 40*, 266–75.

Gergen, K.J. (1997) Social psychology as social construction: the emerging vision. In C. McGarty and A. Haslam (eds) *The Message of Social Psychology: Perspectives on Mind in Society*. Oxford: Blackwell.

Gesell, A. (1925) *The Mental Growth of the Preschool Child*. New York: Macmillan.

Gilligan, C. (1982) *In a Different Voice: Psychological Theory and Women's Development*. Cambridge, MA: Harvard University Press.

Gilligan, C. (1993) Letter to readers (Preface). *In a Different Voice* (2nd impression; see entry above).

Glassman, W.E. (1995) *Approaches to Psychology* (2nd edn). Buckingham: Open University Press.

Goffman, E. (1963) *Stigma: Notes on the Management of Spoiled Identity*. Englewood Cliffs, NJ: Prentice-Hall.

Goffman, E. (1971) *The Presentation of Self in Everyday Life*. Harmondsworth: Penguin.

Golombok, S. (2002) Why I study ... lesbian mothers. *The Psychologist, 15*(11), 562–3.

Gottesman, I. (1991) *Schizophrenia Genesis*. New York: W.H. Freeman.

Gough, B. and McFadden, M. (2001) *Critical Social Psychology: An Introduction*. Basingstoke: Palgrave.

Gould, R.L. (1978) *Transformations: Growth and Change in Adult Life*. New York: Simon & Schuster.

Gould, S.J. (1981) *The Mismeasure of Man*. New York: Norton.

Gould, S.J. (1987) *An Urchin in the Storm*. Harmondsworth: Penguin.

Graham, H. (1986) *The Human Face of Psychology: Humanistic Psychology in Historical, Social and Cultural Context*. Milton Keynes: Open University Press.

Gray, J. (1987) The mind–brain identity as a scientific hypothesis: a second look. In C. Blakemore and S. Greenfield (eds) *Mindwaves*. Oxford: Blackwell.

Gray, J.A. (1991) On the morality of speciesism. *The Psychologist, 4*(5), 196–8.

Grayling, A.C. (2002) Scientist or storyteller? *Guardian Review*, 22 June, 4–6.

Greenfield, P.M. (1997) Culture as process: empirical methods for cultural psychology. In J.W. Berry, Y.H. Poortinga and J. Pandey (eds) *Handbook of cross-cultural research*, Vol. 1, *Theory and Method*. Boston, MA: Allyn & Bacon.

Greenfield, S.A. (1995) *Journey to the Centres of the Mind*. New York: W.H. Freeman & Co.

Gregory, R.L. (1981) *Mind in Science*. Hove: Lawrence Erlbaum.

Gross, R. (2001) *Psychology: The Science of Mind and Behaviour* (4th edn). London: Hodder & Stoughton.

Gross, R. (2003) *Key Studies in Psychology* (4th edn). London: Hodder & Stoughton.

Gross, R., Humphreys, P. and Petkova, B. (1997) *Challenges in Psychology*. London: Hodder & Stoughton.

Guilford, J.P. (1959) Three faces of intellect. *American Psychologist, 14*, 469–79.

Hampson, S.E. (1988) *The Construction of Personality: An Introduction* (2nd edn). London: Routledge.

Haney, C., Banks, C. and Zimbardo, P (1973) A study of prisoners and guards in a simulated prison. *Naval Research Reviews, 30*(9), 4–17.

Harlow, H.F. and Zimmerman, R.R. (1959) Affectional responses in the infant monkey. *Science, 130*, 421–32.

Harré, R. (1993) Rules, roles and rhetoric. *The Psychologist, 6*(1), 24–8.

Harré, R. (1995) Discursive psychology. In J.A. Smith, R. Harré and L. Van Langenhove (eds) *Rethinking Psychology*. London: Sage.

Harré, R. and Secord, P.F. (1972) *The Explanation of Social Behaviour*. Oxford: Blackwell.

Harré, R., Clarke, D. and De Carlo, N. (1985) *Motives and Mechanisms: An Introduction to the Psychology of Action*. London: Methuen.

Harrington, A. (1997) Introduction. In A. Harrington (ed.) *The Placebo Effect: An Interdisciplinary Approach*. Cambridge, MA: Harvard University Press.

Harris, P. (1989) *Children and Emotion*. Oxford: Blackwell.

Haworth, G. (1992) The use of non-human animals in psychological research: the current status of the debate. *Psychology Teaching*, New Series No. 1, 46–54.

Hayslip, B. and Panek, P.E. (1993) *Adult Development and Ageing* (2nd edn). New York: HarperCollins.

Hazan, C. and Shaver, P.R. (1987) Romantic love conceptualized as an attachment process. *Journal of Personality & Social Psychology, 52*(3), 511–24.

Hazan, C. and Shaver, P.R. (1990) Love and work: an attachment-theoretical perspective. *Journal of Personality & Social Psychology, 59*(2), 270–80.

Hazan, C. and Zeifman, D. (1999) Pair bonds as attachments: evaluating the evidence. In J. Cassidy and P.R. Shaver (eds) *Handbook of Attachment: Theory, Research, and Clinical Applications.* New York: Guilford Press.

Heather, N. (1976) *Radical Perspectives in Psychology.* London: Methuen.

Heider, F. (1958) *The Psychology of Interpersonal Relations.* New York: Wiley.

Herrnstein, R.J. (1971) IQ. *Atlantic Monthly,* September, 43–64.

Herskovits, M.J. (1948) *Man and His Works: The Science of Cultural Anthropology.* New York: Alfred A. Knopf.

Hewstone, M. (1990) The 'ultimate attribution error'? A review of the literature on intergroup causal attribution. *European Journal of Social Psychology, 20,* 311–35.

Hewstone, M. and Antaki, C. (1988) Attribution theory and social explanation. In M. Hewstone, W. Stroebe, J.P. Codol and G.M. Stephenson (eds) *Introduction to Social Psychology.* Oxford: Blackwell.

Hewstone, M., Stroebe, W. and Stephenson, G. (eds) (1996) *Introduction to Social Psychology: A European Perspective* (2nd edn). Oxford: Blackwell.

Hilliard, A.G. (1995) The nonscience and nonsense of the bell curve. *Focus: Notes from the Society for the Psychological Study of Ethnic Minority Issues,* 10–12.

Hilliard, R.B. (1993) Single-case methodology in psychotherapy process and outcome research. *Journal of Consulting & Clinical Psychology, 61*(3), 373–80.

Hofstede, G. (1980) *Culture's Consequences: International Differences in Work-related Values.* Beverly Hills, CA: Sage.

Hogg, M.A. and Vaughan, G.M. (1995) *Social Psychology: An Introduction.* Hemel Hempstead: Prentice Hall.

Holmes, D.S. (1994) *Abnormal Psychology* (2nd edn). New York: HarperCollins.

Holmes, J. (1992) Response [to Masson's 'The tyranny of psychotherapy']. In W. Dryden and C. Feltham (eds) *Psychotherapy and Its Discontents.* Buckingham: Open University Press.

Holmes, J. (1993) *John Bowlby and Attachment Theory.* London: Routledge.

Holt, R.R. (1967) Individuality and generalization in the psychology of personality. In R.S. Lazarus and E.M. Opton (eds) *Personality.* Harmondsworth: Penguin.

Honderich, T. (1987) Mind, brain and self-conscious mind. In C. Blakemore and S. Greenfield (eds) *Mindwaves.* Oxford: Blackwell.

Honorton, C. (1985) Meta-analysis of psi Ganzfeld research: a response to Hyman. *Journal of Parapsychology, 49,* 51–91.

Honorton, C. and Harper, S. (1974) Psi-mediated imagery and ideation in an experimental procedure for regulating perceptual input. *Journal of the American Society for Psychical Research, 68,* 156–68.

Honorton, C. and Krippner, S. (1969) Hypnosis and ESP: a review of the experimental literature. *Journal of the American Society for Psychical Research, 63,* 214–52.

Horgan, J. (1993) Eugenics. Revisited. *Scientific American*, June, 92–100.

Horgan, J. (1995) The new social Darwinists. *Scientific American*, October, 150–7.

Horowitz, F.D. (1987) *Exploring Developmental Theories: Towards a Structural/Behavioural Model of Development.* Hillsdale, NJ: Erlbaum.

Horowitz, F.D. (1990) Developmental models of individual differences. In J. Colombo and J. Fagan (eds) *Individual Differences in Infancy: Reliability, Stability, Predictability.* Hillsdale, NJ: Erlbaum.

Howe, M. (1997) *IQ in Question: The Truth about Intelligence.* London: Sage.

Humphrey, N. (1986) *The Inner Eye.* London: Faber and Faber.

Humphrey, N. (1992) *A History of the Mind.* London: Vintage.

Humphrey, N. (1993) Introduction. In N. Humphrey, *The Inner Eye* (new edn). London: Faber and Faber.

Hyman, R. (1985) The Ganzfeld psi experiment: a critical appraisal. *Journal of Parapsychology, 49,* 3–49.

Hyman, R. and Honorton, C. (1986) A joint communiqué: the psi Ganzfeld controversy. *Journal of Parapsychology, 50,* 351–64.

International Molecular Genetic Study of Autism Consortium (1998) A full genome screen for autism with evidence for linkage to a region of chromosome 7q. *Human Molecular Genetics, 7,* 571–8.

Jackson, G. (1992) *Women and Psychology – What Might that Mean?* Paper given at Association for the Teaching of Psychology Conference, July.

Jacobs, M. (1992) *Freud.* London: Sage Publications.

Jahoda, G. (1978) Cross-cultural perspectives. In H. Tajfel and C. Fraser (eds) *Introducing Social Psychology.* Harmondsworth: Penguin.

James, W. (1884) What is an emotion? *Mind, 9,* 188–205.

James, W. (1890) *Principles of Psychology.* New York: Holt.

Janis, I.L., Kaye, D. and Kirschner, P. (1965) Facilitating effects of 'eating-while-reading' on responsiveness to persuasive communications. *Journal of Personality & Social Psychology, 1,* 181–6.

Jensen, A.R. (1969) How much can we boost IQ and scholastic achievement? *Harvard Educational Review, 39,* 1–123.

Johnson-Laird, P.N. (1983) *Mental Models.* Cambridge: Cambridge University Press.

Johnson-Laird, P.N. (1987) How could consciousness arise from the computations of the brain? In C. Blakemore and S. Greenfield (eds) *Mindwaves.* Oxford: Blackwell.

Johnson-Laird, P.N. (1988) *The Computer and the Mind.* London: Fontana.

Jones, D. and Elcock, J. (2001) *History and Theories of Psychology: A Critical Perspective.* London: Arnold.

Jones, E.E. and Davis, K.E. (1965) From acts to dispositions: the attribution process in person perception. In L. Berkowitz (ed.) *Advances in Experimental Social Psychology,* Vol. 2. New York: Academic Press.

Jones, E.E. and Nisbett, R.E. (1971) *The Actor and the Observer: Divergent perceptions of the causes of behaviour.* Morristown, NJ: General Learning Press.

Jones, S. (1993) *The Language of the Genes*. London: Flamingo.

Joscelyne, T. (2002) Time for a change? *The Psychologist, 15*(4), 176–7.

Jung, C.G. (ed.) (1964) *Man and his Symbols*. London: Aldus-Jupiter Books.

Karmiloff-Smith, A. (2000) Why babies' brains are not Swiss army knives. In H. Rose and S. Rose (eds) *Alas, Poor Darwin: Arguments Against Evolutionary Psychology*. London: Jonathan Cape.

Kashima, Y. and Triandis, H.C. (1986) The self-serving bias in attributions as a coping strategy: a cross-cultural study. *Journal of Cross-Cultural Psychology, 17*, 83–97.

Kelley, H.H. (1967) Attribution theory in social psychology. In D. Levine (ed.) *Nebraska Symposium on Motivation*, Vol. 15. Lincoln: Nebraska University Press.

Kelley, H.H. (1972) Causal schemata and the attribution process. In E.E. Jones, D.E. Kanouse, H.H. Kelley, R.E. Nisbett, S. Valins and B. Weiner (eds) *Attribution: Perceiving the Causes of Behaviour*. Morristown, NJ: General Learning Press.

Kelley, H.H. (1973) The processes of causal attribution. *American Psychologist, 28*, 107–28.

Kelly, G. (1955) *A Theory of Personality: The Psychology of Personal Constructs*. New York: Norton.

Kelly, L. (1988) *Surviving Sexual Violence*. Cambridge: Polity Press.

Kirby, R. and Radford, J. (1976) *Individual Differences*. London: Methuen.

Kirkpatrick, L.A. (1992) An attachment-theory approach to the psychology of religion. *International Journal for the Psychology of Religion, 2*(1), 3–28.

Kirkpatrick, L.A. (1994) The role of attachment in religious belief and behaviour. In K. Bartholomew and D. Perlman (eds) *Advances in Personal Relationships. Vol. 5. Attachment Processes in Adulthood*. London: Jessica Kingsley.

Kirkpatrick, L.A. (1999) Attachment and religious representations and behaviour. In J. Cassidy and P.R. Shaver (eds) *Handbook of Attachment: Theory, Research, and Clinical Applications*. New York: Guilford Press.

Kirkpatrick, L.A. and Shaver, P.R. (1992) An attachment-theoretical approach to romantic love and religious belief. *Personality & Social Psychology Bulletin, 18*, 266–75.

Kitzinger, C. (1987) *The Social Construction of Lesbianism*. London: Sage.

Kitzinger, C. (1990) Heterosexism in psychology. *The Psychologist, 3*(9), 391–2.

Kitzinger, C. and Coyle, A. (2002) Introducing lesbian and gay psychology. In C. Kitzinger and A. Coyle (eds) *Lesbian & Gay Psychology: New Perspectives*. BPS/Blackwell.

Klein, M. (1932) *The Psycho-Analysis of Children*. London: Hogarth.

Kline, P. (1989) Objective tests of Freud's theories. In A.M. Colman and J.G. Beaumont (eds) *Psychology Survey No. 7*. Leicester: British Psychological Society.

Kline, P. (1993) Comments on 'Personality traits are alive and well'. *The Psychologist, 6*(7), 304.

Kline, P. (1998) Psychoanalytic perspectives. *Psychology Review, 5*(1), 10–13.

Kluckhohn, C. and Murray, H.A. (1953) Personality formation: the determinants. In C. Kluckhohn, H.A. Murray and D.M. Schneider (eds) *Personality in Nature, Society, and Culture* (2nd edn). New York: Knopf.

Koestler, A. (1967) *The Ghost in the Machine*. London: Pan.

Kohlberg, L. (1969) Stage and sequence: the cognitive-developmental approach to socialization. In D.A. Goslin (ed.) *Handbook of Socialization: Theory and Research*. Chicago: Rand McNally.

Kohn, M. (1998) Survival of the chattiest. *The Independent on Sunday*, 5 April, 44–5.

Kraepelin, E. (1913) *Psychiatry* (8th edn). Leipzig: Thieme.

Krahé, B. (1992) *Personality and Social Psychology: Towards a Synthesis*. London: Sage.

Krupat, E. and Garonzik, R. (1994) Subjects' expectations and the search for alternatives to deception in social psychology. *British Journal of Social Psychology*, *32*, 211–22.

Lachman, R., Lachman, J.L. and Butterfield, E.C. (1979) *Cognitive Psychology and Information Processing*. Hillsdale, NJ: Lawrence Erlbaum Associates.

Laing, R.D. (1961) *The Self and Others*. London: Tavistock Publications.

Laing, R.D. (1967) *The Politics of Experience and the Bird of Paradise*. Harmondsworth: Penguin.

Lalljee, M. and Widdicombe, S. (1989) Discourse analysis. In A.M. Colman and J.C. Beaumont (eds) *Psychology Survey*, 7. Leicester: British Psychological Society.

Lalljee, M., Watson, M. and White, P. (1982) Explanations, attributions and the social context of unexpected behaviour. *European Journal of Social Psychology*, *12*(1), 17–29.

Lamiell, J.T. (1981) Toward an idiothetic psychology of personality. *American Psychologist*, *36*, 276–89.

Lamiell, J.T. (1982) The case for an idiothetic psychology of personality: a conceptual and empirical foundation. In B.A. Maher and W.B. Maher (eds) *Progress in Experimental Personality Research*, Vol. 11. New York: Academic Press.

Lamiell, J.T. (1987) *The Psychology of Personality: An Epistemological Inquiry*. New York: Columbia University Press.

Latane, B. and Darley, J.M. (1968) Group inhibitions of bystander intervention in emergencies. *Journal of Personality & Social Psychology*, *10*, 215–21.

Leahey, T.H. (2000) *A History of Psychology: Main Currents in Psychological Thought* (4th edn). Englewood Cliffs, NJ: Prentice-Hall.

Leekam, S. (1993) Children's understanding of mind. In M. Bennett (ed.) *The Child as Psychologist: An Introduction to the Development of Social Cognition*. Hemel Hempstead: Harvester Wheatsheaf.

Lepper, M.R. and Greene, D. (1978) Overjustification research and beyond: towards a means–end analysis of intrinsic and extrinsic motivation. In M.R. Lepper and D. Greene (eds) *The Hidden Costs of Reward*. Hillsdale, NJ: Lawrence Erlbaum.

Lepper, M.R., Greene, D. and Nisbett, R.E. (1973) Undermining children's intrinsic interest with extrinsic reward: a test of the overjustification hypothesis. *Journal of Personality & Social Psychology*, *28*, 129–37.

Lerner, G. (1979) *The Majority Finds Its Past: Placing Women in History*. New York: Oxford University Press.

Leslie, J.C. (2002) *Essential Behaviour Analysis*. London: Arnold.

Leuchter, A.F., Cook, I.A., Witte, E.A., Morgan, M. and Abrams, M. (2002) Changes in brain function of depressed subjects during treatment with placebo. *American Journal of Psychiatry*, *159*(1), 122–9.

LeVay, S. and Hamer, D.H. (1994) Evidence for a biological influence in male homosexuality. *Scientific American*, May, 20–5.

Leyens, J.P. and Codol, J.P. (1988) Social cognition. In M. Hewstone, W. Stroebe, J.P. Codol and G. M. Stephenson (eds) *Introduction to Social Psychology*. Oxford: Blackwell.

Libet, B. (1981) The experimental evidence of subjective referral of a sensory experience backwards in time. *Philosophy of Science*, *48*, 182–97.

Libet, B. (1985) Unconscious cerebral initiative and the role of conscious will in voluntary action. *Behavioural & Brain Sciences*, *8*, 29–539.

Libet, B., Freeman, A. and Sutherland, K. (1999) *The Volitional Brain: Towards a Neuroscience of Free Will*. Thorverton, Devon: Imprint Academic.

Liotti, G. (1991) Insecure attachment and agoraphobia. In C.M. Parkes, J. Stevenson-Hinde and P. Marris (eds) *Attachment across the Life Cycle*. London: Routledge.

Littlewood, R. and Lipsedge, M. (1989) *Aliens and Alienists: Ethnic Minorities and Psychiatry* (2nd edn). London: Routledge.

Locke, J. (1690) *An Essay Concerning Human Understanding*. Oxford: P.H. Nidditch.

Lodge, D. (2002) Sense and sensibility. *Guardian Review*, 2 November, 4–6.

Lumsden, W. and Wilson, E.O. (1981) *Genes, Mind and Culture*. Cambridge, MA: Harvard University Press.

McClelland, D.C., Atkinson, J., Clark, R. and Lowell, E. (1953) *The Achievement Motive*. New York: Appleton-Century-Croft.

McCrae, R.R. and Costa, P.T. (1989) More reasons to adopt the five-factor model. *American Psychologist*, *44*, 451–2.

McDougall, W. (1908) *An Introduction to Social Psychology*. London: Methuen.

McGhee, P. (2001) *Thinking Psychologically*. Basingstoke: Palgrave.

McGinn, C. (1999) *The Mysterious Flame: Conscious Minds in a Material World*. New York: Basic Books.

McGurk, H. (1975) *Growing and Changing*. London: Methuen.

Maher, B.A. (1966) *Principles of Psychopathology: An Experimental Approach*. New York: McGraw-Hill.

Mahler, M. (1975) *The Psychological Birth of the Human Infant*. London: Hutchinson.

Mahoney, J. (1998) Mates past their prime. *Times Higher Educational Supplement*, 25 September, 18.

Main, M., Kaplan, N. and Cassidy, J. (1985) Security in infancy, childhood and adulthood: a move to the level of representation. In I. Bretherton and E. Waters (eds) *Growing Points of Attachment Theory and Research* (Monographs of the Society for Research in Child Development, Vol. 50, Serial No. 209). Chicago: University of Chicago Press.

Malinowski, B. (1929) *The Sexual Life of Savages*. New York: Harcourt Brace Jovanovich.

Markus, H.R. and Kitayama, S. (1991) Culture and the self: implications for cognition, emotion and motivation. *Psychological Review*, *98*, 224–53.

Maslow, A.H. (1954) *Motivation and Personality*. New York: Harper & Row.

Maslow, A.H. (1968) *Toward a Psychology of Being* (2nd edn). New York: Van Nostrand Reinhold.

Masson, J. (1988) *Against Therapy: Emotional Tyranny and the Myth of Psychological Healing.* New York: Atheneum.

Masson, J. (1992) The tyranny of psychotherapy. In W. Dryden and C. Feltham (eds) *Psychotherapy and its Discontents.* Buckingham: Open University Press.

Matsumoto, D., Kudoh, T. and Takeuchi, S. (1996) Changing patterns of individualism and collectivism in the United States and Japan. *Culture & Psychology, 2,* 77–107.

May, R. (1967) *Psychology and the Human Dilemma.* New York: Van Nostrand.

Merleau-Ponty, M. (1962) *The Phenomenology of Perception.* London: RKP.

Merleau-Ponty, M. (1968) *The Visible and the Invisible.* Evanston, Ill.: Northwestern University Press.

Midgley, M. (2003) Fate by fluke. *Guardian Review,* 1 March, 12.

Miesen, B.M.L. (1992) Attachment theory and dementia. In G.M.M. Jones and B.M.L. Miesen (eds) *Care-giving in Dementia: Research and Applications.* London: Tavistock/Routledge.

Miesen, B.M.L. (1993) Alzheimer's disease, the phenomenon of parent fixation and Bowlby's attachment theory. *International Journal of Geriatric Psychiatry, 8,* 147–53.

Miesen, B.M.L. (1998) Attachment behaviour in dementia: parent orientation and parent fixation (POPFID) theory. In G.H. Pollock and S.I. Greenspan (eds) *The course of life: Vol. 7, Completing the Journey.* Madison, CT: International Universities Press.

Mikulincer, M. and Florian, V. (1996) Emotional reactions to interpersonal losses over the life span: an attachment theoretical perspective. In C. Magai and S.H. McFadden (eds) *Handbook of Emotion, Adult Development, and Ageing.* San Diego, CA: Academic Press.

Milgram, S. (1963) Behavioural study of obedience. *Journal of Abnormal & Social Psychology, 67,* 371–8.

Milgram, S. (1974) *Obedience to Authority.* New York: Harper Torchbooks.

Milgram, S. (1977) Subject reaction: the neglected factor in the ethics of experimentation. *The Hastings Centre Report,* October, 19–23. (Reprinted in S. Milgram (1992) *The Individual in a Social World* (2nd edn). New York: McGraw-Hill.)

Miller, D.T. and Ross, M. (1975) Self-serving biases in the attribution of causality: fact or fiction? *Psychological Bulletin, 82,* 213–25.

Miller, E. and Morley, S. (1986) *Investigating Abnormal Behaviour.* London: Weidenfeld & Nicolson/Lawrence Erlbaum.

Miller, G.A. (1956) The magical number seven, plus or minus two: some limits on our capacity for processing information. *Psychological Review, 63,* 81–97.

Miller, G.A. (1969) Psychology as a means of promoting human welfare. *American Psychologist, 24,* 1063–1975.

Miller, J. (1997) Theoretical issues in cultural psychology. In J.W. Berry, Y.H. Poortinga and J. Pandey (eds) *Handbook of Cross-cultural Research, Vol. 1, Theory and Method.* Boston, MA: Allyn & Bacon.

Milton, J. and Wiseman, R. (1999) Does psi exist? Lack of replication of an anomalous process of information transfer. *Psychological Bulletin, 125,* 387–91.

Mischel, W. (1968) *Personality and Assessment.* New York: Wiley.

Mischel, W. (1977) The interaction of person and situation. In D. Magnusson and N.S. Endler (eds) *Personality at the Crossroads: Current Issues in Interactional Psychology.* Hillsdale, NJ: Lawrence Erlbaum.

Mischel, W. (1983) Alternatives in the pursuit of the predictability and consistency of persons: stable data that yield unstable interpretations. *Journal of Personality, 51,* 578–604.

Moghaddam, F.M. (1998) *Social Psychology: Exploring Universals Across Cultures.* New York: W.H. Freeman & Co.

Moghaddam, F.M., Taylor, D.M. and Wright, S.C. (1993) *Social Psychology In Cross-Cultural Perspective.* New York: W.H. Freeman & Co.

Mohamed, C. (2000) Race, culture and ethnicity. In C. Feltham and I. Horton (eds) *Handbook of Counselling and Psychotherapy.* London: Sage.

Mollon, P. (2000) *Freud and False Memory Syndrome.* Cambridge: Icon Books.

Morea, P. (1990) *Personality: An Introduction to the Theories of Psychology.* Harmondsworth: Penguin.

Morris, R.L. (1989) Parapsychology. In A.M. Colman and J.G. Beaumont (eds) *Psychology Survey,* 7. Leicester: British Psychological Society.

Morris, R.L., Cunningham, S., McAlpine, S. and Taylor, R. (1993) Towards replication and extension of Ganzfeld results. In *The Parapsychological Association 36th Annual Convention: Proceedings of Presented Papers.* Durham, NC: Parapsychological Association.

Morris, R.L., Dalton, K., Delanoy, D.L. and Watt, C. (1995) Comparison of the sender/no sender condition in the Ganzfeld. In *The Parapsychological Association 38th Annual Convention: Proceedings of Presented Papers.* Durham, NC: Parapsychological Association.

Moscovici, S. (1985) Social influence and conformity. In G. Lindzey and E. Aronson (eds) *Handbook of Social Psychology* (3rd edn). New York: Random House.

Much (1995) Cultural psychology. In J.A. Smith, R. Harré and L. Van Langenhove (eds) *Rethinking Psychology.* London: Sage.

Murray, H.A. (1938) *Explorations in Personality.* New York: Oxford University Press.

Myers, D. (1994) *Exploring Social Psychology.* New York: McGraw-Hill.

Nagel, T. (1974) What is it like to be a bat? *Philosophical Review, 83,* 435–50.

Nicolson, P. (1995) Feminism and psychology. In J.A. Smith, R. Harré and L. Van Langenhove (eds) *Rethinking Psychology.* London: Sage.

Nisbett, R.E. and Ross, L. (1980) *Human Inference: Strategies and Shortcomings of Social Judgement.* Englewood Cliffs, NJ: Prentice Hall.

Nisbett, R.E. and Schachter, S. (1966) Cognitive manipulation of pain. *Journal of Experimental Social Psychology, 2,* 227–36.

Nisbett, R.E. and Wilson, T.D. (1977) Telling more than we can know: verbal reports on mental processes. *Psychological Review, 84,* 231–59.

Nisbett, R.E., Caputo, C., Legant, P. and Maracek, J. (1973) Behaviour as seen by the actor and as seen by the observer. *Journal of Personality & Social Psychology, 27*(2), 154–64.

Noller, P. and Clarke, S. (1995) Attachment to God: links of religion to attachment theory and mental health. Paper presented as the National Council of Family Relations Conference, Portland, Oregon (November).

Norman, D. and Shallice, T. (1986) Attention to action: willed and automatic control of behaviour. In R.J. Davidson, G.E. Schwartz and D. Shapiro (eds) *Consciousness and Self-regulation: Advances in Research and Theory.* New York: Plenum.

Nye, D. (2000) *Three Psychologies: Perspectives from Freud, Skinner and Rogers* (6th edn). Belmont, CA: Wadsworth/Thomson Learning.

O'Donohue, W. and Ferguson, K.E. (2001) *The Psychology of B.F. Skinner.* Thousand Oaks, CA: Sage Publications.

Oakes, P.J., Haslam, S.A. and Turner, J.C. (1994) *Stereotyping and Social Reality.* Oxford: Blackwell.

Ochert, A. (1998) Madness becomes normal. *Psychology Review, 4*(4), back page.

Ogden, J. (2000) *Health Psychology: A Textbook* (2nd edn). Buckingham: Open University Press.

Olds, J. and Milner, P. (1954) Positive reinforcement produced by electrical stimulation of septal area and other regions of the rat brain. *Journal of Comparative & Physiological Psychology, 47,* 419–27.

Orne, M.T. (1962) On the social psychology of the psychological experiment – with particular reference to demand characteristics and their implications. *American Psychologist, 17*(11), 776–83.

Ornstein, R.E. (1975) *The Psychology of Consciousness.* Harmondsworth: Penguin.

Paley, B., Cox, M.J., Harter, S.M. and Margand, N.A. (2002) Adult attachment stance and spouses' marital perceptions during the transition to parenthood. *Attachment & Human Development, 4*(3), 340–60.

Paludi, M.A. (1992) *The Psychology of Women.* Dubuque, Iowa: Wm C. Brown.

Parkes, C.M. (1993) Bereavement as a psychosocial transition: processes of adaptation to change. In M.S. Stroebe, W. Stroebe and R.O. Hansson (eds) *Handbook of Bereavement: Theory, Research and Intervention.* New York: Cambridge University Press.

Parkes, C.M. and Weiss, R.S. (1983) *Recovery From Bereavement.* New York: Basic Books.

Parkin, A.J. (2000) *Essential Cognitive Psychology.* Hove: Psychology Press.

Parkinson, B. (1987) Emotion – cognitive approaches. In H. Beloff and A.M. Colman (eds) *Psychology Survey,* No. 6. Leicester: British Psychological Society.

Parlee, M.B. (1991) Happy Birth-day to *Feminism & Psychology. Feminism & Psychology, 1*(1), 39–48.

Penfield, W. (1958) *The Excitable Cortex in Conscious Man.* Liverpool: Liverpool University Press.

Pervin, L.A. (1985) Personality: current controversies, issues and directions. *Annual Review of Psychology, 36,* 83–114.

Pettigrew, T.F. (1979) The ultimate attribution error: extending Allport's cognitive analysis of prejudice. *Personality & Social Psychology Bulletin, 5*(4), 461–76.

Pike, A. and Plomin, R. (1999) Genetics and development. In D. Messer and S. Millar (eds) *Exploring Developmental Psychology: From Infancy to Adolescence.* London: Arnold.

Pike, K.L. (1954) Emic and etic standpoints for the description of behaviour. In K.L. Pike (ed.) *Language in Relation to a Unified Theory of the Structure of Human Behaviour,* Pt 1. Glendale, CA: Summer Institute of Linguistics.

Piliavin, I.M., Rodin, J. and Piliavin, J.A. (1969) Good Samaritanism: an underground phenomenon? *Journal of Personality & Social Psychology, 13*(4), 289–99.

Pinker, S. (1994) *The Language Instinct: How the Mind Creates Language.* New York: Morrow.

Pinker, S. (1997) Why they kill their newborns. *New York Times Magazine,* 2 November, 52–4.

Place, U.T. (1956) Is consciousness a brain process? *British Journal of Psychology, 47,* 44–51.

Plomin, R. (1994) *Genetics and Experience: The Interplay Between Nature and Nurture.* Thousand Oaks, CA: Sage.

Plomin, R. (1996) Nature and nurture. In M.R. Merrens and G.C. Brannigan (eds) *The Developmental Psychologists: Research Adventures across the Life Span.* New York: McGraw-Hill.

Plomin, R. (2001) Genetics and behaviour. *The Psychologist, 14*(3), 134–9.

Plomin, R. and Rutter, M. (1998) Child development, molecular genetics and what to do with genes once they are found. *Child Development, 69,* 1221–40.

Plomin, R. and Thompson, R. (1987) Life-span developmental behavioural genetics. In P.B. Baltes, D.L. Featherman and R.M. Lerner (eds) *Life-Span Development and Behaviour,* Vol. 8. Hillsdale, NJ: Erlbaum.

Plomin, R., DeFries, J.C. and Loehlin, J.C. (1977) Genotype-environment interaction and correlation in the analysis of human behaviour. *Psychological Bulletin, 84,* 309–22.

Popper, K. (1959) *The Logic of Scientific Discovery.* London: Hutchinson.

Popper, K. (1972) *Objective Knowledge: An Evolutionary Approach.* Oxford: Oxford University Press.

Potter, J. (1996) Attitudes, social representations and discursive psychology. In M. Wetherell (ed.) *Identities, Groups and Social Issues.* London: Sage, in association with the Open University.

Power, M. (2000) Freud and the unconscious. *The Psychologist, 13*(12), 612–14.

Prince, J. and Hartnett, O. (1993) From 'psychology constructs the female' to 'females construct psychology'. *Feminism & Psychology, 3*(2), 219–24.

Rao, K.R. and Palmer, J. (1987) The anomaly called psi: recent research and criticism. *Behaviour & Brain Sciences, 10,* 539–643.

Raphael, B. (1984) *The Anatomy of Bereavement.* London: Hutchinson.

Reason, J. (2000) The Freudian slip revisited. *The Psychologist, 13*(12), 610–11.

Reason., P. and Rowan, J. (eds) (1981) *Human Inquiry: A Sourcebook of New Paradigm Research.* Chichester: Wiley.

Reedy, M.N., Birren, J.E. and Schaie, K.W. (1981) Age and sex differences in satisfying love relationships across the adult life span. *Human Development, 24,* 52–66.

Rhine, L.E. (1969) Case study review. *Journal of Parapsychology, 33,* 228–66.

Richards, G. (1996) Arsenic and old race. *Observer Review,* 5 May, 4.

Richards, G. (2002) *Putting Psychology in its Place: A Critical Historical Overview* (2nd edn). Hove: Routledge.

Riesen, A.H. (1947) The development of visual perception in man and chimpanzee. *Science, 106,* 107–8.

Roberts, R. (2001) Science and experience. In R. Roberts and D. Groome (eds) *Parapsychology: The Science of Unusual Experience*. London: Arnold.

Roberts, R. and Groome, D. (2001) Preamble. In R. Roberts and D. Groome (eds) *Parapsychology: The Science of Unusual Experience*. London: Arnold.

Rogers, C.R. (1951) *Client-centred Therapy: Its Current Practice, Implications and Theory*. Boston: Houghton-Mifflin.

Rogers, C.R. (1961) *On Becoming a Person: A Therapists' View of Psychotherapy*. Boston: Houghton-Mifflin.

Rogers, C.R. and Dymond, R.F. (eds) (1954) *Psychotherapy and Personality Change: Co-ordinated Research Studies in the Client-Centred Approach*. Chicago: University of Chicago Press.

Rogoff, B. and Morelli, G. (1989) Perspectives on children's development from cultural psychology. *American Psychologist*, *44*, 343–8.

Rorer, L.G. (1998) Attacking arrant nonsense forthrightly. *Contemporary Psychology*, *43*, 597–600.

Rose, H. (2000) Colonising the social sciences? In H. Rose and S. Rose (eds) *Alas, Poor Darwin: Arguments Against Evolutionary Psychology*. London: Jonathan Cape.

Rose, H. and Rose, S. (eds) (2000) *Alas, Poor Darwin: Arguments Against Evolutionary Psychology*. London: Jonathan Cape.

Rose, H. and Rose, S. (2001) Much ado about very little. *The Psychologist*, *14*(8), 428–9.

Rose, S. (1992) *The Making of Memory: From Molecules to Mind*. London: Bantam Books.

Rose, S. (1997) *Lifelines: Biology, Freedom, Determinism*. Harmondsworth: Penguin.

Rose, S. (2000) Escaping evolutionary psychology. In H. Rose and S. Rose (eds) *Alas, Poor Darwin: Arguments Against Evolutionary Psychology*. London: Jonathan Cape.

Rose, S. (2001) DNA is important – but only in its proper place. *The Psychologist*, *14*(3), 144–5.

Rose, S., Lewontin, R.C. and Kamin, L.J. (1984) *Not in Our Genes: Biology, Ideology and Human Nature*. Harmondsworth: Penguin.

Rosenhan, D.L. and Seligman, M.E.P. (1989) *Abnormal Psychology* (2nd edn). New York: Norton.

Rosenthal, D. (1966) *Experimenter Effects in Behavioural Research*. New York: Appleton-Century-Crofts.

Rosenthal, D. and Jacobson, L. (1968) *Pygmalion in the Classroom: Teacher Expectation and Pupils' Intellectual Development*. New York: Holt, Rinehart & Winston.

Ross, L. (1977) The intuitive psychologists and his shortcomings. In L. Berkowitz (ed.) *Advances in Experimental Social Psychology*, Vol. 10. New York: Academic Press.

Ross, L. and Nisbett, R.E. (1991) *The Person and the Situation: Perspectives of Social Psychology*. New York: McGraw-Hill.

Rubin, Z. and McNeil, E.B. (1983) *The Psychology of Being Human* (3rd edn). London: Harper & Row.

Rumelhart, D.E., Hinton, G.E. and McClelland, J.L. (1986) A general framework for parallel distributed processing. In D. Rumelhart, J.L. McClelland and the PDP Research Group (eds) *Parallel Distributed Processing: Vol. 1 Foundations*. Cambridge, MA: MIT Press.

Rushton, J.P. (1995) *Race, Evolution and Behaviour*. New Brunswick, NJ: Transaction Publishers.

Rutter, M. (1981) *Maternal Deprivation Reassessed* (2nd edn). Harmondsworth: Penguin.

Rutter, M. and Rutter, M. (1992) *Developing Minds: Challenge and Continuity across the Life Span.* Harmondsworth: Penguin.

Rycroft, C. (1966) Introduction: causes and meaning. In C. Rycroft (ed.) *Psychoanalysis Observed.* London: Constable,

Ryder, R. (1990) Open reply to Jeffrey Gray. *The Psychologist, 3,* 403.

Ryle, G. (1949) *The Concept of Mind.* London: Hutchinson.

Sacco, W.P., Dumont, C.P. and Dow, M.G. (1993) Attributional, perceptual and affective response to depressed and nondepressed marital partners. *Journal of Consulting & Clinical Psychology, 61*(6), 1076–1982.

Salmon, P. (2003) How do we recognize good research? *The Psychologist, 16*(1), 24–7.

Sarbin, T.R. (1986) The narrative as a root metaphor for psychology. In T.R. Sarbin (ed.) *Narrative Psychology: The Storied Nature of Human Conduct.* New York: Praeger.

Scarr, S. (1992) Developmental theories for the 1990s: development and individual differences. *Child Development, 63,* 1–19.

Schachter, S. (1964) The interaction of cognitive and psychological determinants of emotional state. *Advances in Experimental Social Psychology, 1,* 49–80.

Schachter, S. and Singer, J.E. (1962) Cognitive, social and physiological determinants of emotional state. *Psychological Review, 69*(5), 379–99.

Schank, R.C. and Abelson, R.P. (1977) *Scripts, Plans, Goals, and Understanding.* Hillsdale, NJ: Lawrence Erlbaum.

Scharlach, A.E. (1991) Factors associated with filial grief following the death of an elderly parent. *American Journal of Orthopsychiatry, 61,* 307–13.

Scheff, T.J. (1966) *Being Mentally Ill: A Sociological Theory.* Chicago: Aldine Press.

Schlitz, M.J. and Honorton, C. (1992) Ganzfeld psi performance within an artistically gifted population. *Journal of the American Society for Psychical Research, 86,* 83–98.

Schneider, K. (1959) *Clinical Psychopathology.* New York: Grune & Stratton.

Scodel, A. (1957) Heterosexual somatic preference and fantasy dependence. *Journal of Consulting Psychology, 21,* 371–4.

Searle, J.R. (1980) Minds, brains and programs. *Behavioural & Brain Sciences, 3,* 417–24.

Searle, J.R. (1992) *The Rediscovery of the Mind.* Cambridge, MA: MIT Press.

Searle, J.R. (1997) *The Mystery of Consciousness.* NYREV, Inc.

Segall, M.H., Dasen, P.R., Berry, J.W. and Poortinga, Y.H. (1990) *Human Behaviour in Global Perspective: An Introduction to Cross-Cultural Psychology.* New York: Pergamon.

Segall, M.H., Dasen, P.R., Berry, J.W. and Poortinga, Y.H. (1999) *Human Behaviour in Global Perspective: An Introduction to Cross-Cultural Psychology* (2nd edn). Needham Heights, MA: Allyn & Bacon.

Seligman, M.E.P. (1974) Depression and learned helplessness. In R.J. Friedman and M.M. Katz (eds) *The Psychology of Depression: Contemporary Theory and Research.* Washington, DC: Winston-Wiley.

Seligman, M.E.P., Abramson, L.Y., Semmel, A. and Von Beyer, C. (1979) Depressive attributional style. *Journal of Abnormal Psychology, 88*, 242–7.

Serpell, R. (1982) Measures of perception, skills and intelligence: the growth of a new perspective on children in a Third World country. In W. Hartrup (ed.) *Review of Child Development Research*, Vol. 6. Chicago: University of Chicago Press.

Shannon, C.E. and Weaver, W. (1949) *The Mathematical Theory of Communication.* Urbana, Ill.: University of Illinois Press.

Shapiro, A.K. and Shapiro, E. (1997) The placebo: is it much ado about nothing? In A. Harrington (ed.) *The Placebo Effect: An Interdisciplinary Exploration.* Cambridge, MA: Harvard University Press.

Shaver, K.G. (1985) *The Attribution of Blame: Causality, Responsibility, and Blameworthiness.* New York: Springer-Verlag.

Shaver, K.G. (1987) *Principles of Social Psychology* (3rd edn). Hillsdale, NJ: Lawrence Erlbaum.

Sherif, M., Harvey, O.J., White, B.J., Hood, W.R. and Sherif, C.W. (1961) *Intergroup Conflict and Co-operation: The Robber's Cave Experiment.* Norman, OK: University of Oklahoma Press.

Shiffrin, R.M. and Schneider, W. (1977) Controlled and automatic human information processing: II – perceptual learning, automatic attending and a general theory. *Psychological Review, 84*, 127–90.

Shotter, J. (1975) *Images of Man in Psychological Research.* London: Methuen.

Shotter, J. (1991) The rhetorical-responsive nature of mind. A social constructionist account. In A. Still and A. Costall (eds) *Against Cognitivism: Alternative Foundations for Cognitive Psychology.* Hemel Hempstead: Harvester Wheatsheaf.

Shotter, J. (1992) 'Getting in touch': the meta-methodology of a postmodern science of mental life. In S. Kvale (ed.) *Psychology and Postmodernism.* London: Sage.

Shotter, J. and Gergen, K.G. (eds) (1989) *Texts of Identity.* London: Sage.

Shweder, R.A. (1990) Cultural psychology – what is it? In J.W. Stigler, R.A. Shweder and G. Herdt (eds) *Cultural Psychology.* New York: Cambridge University Press.

Singer, P. (1993) The rights of ape. *BBC Wildlife Magazine, 11*(6), 28–32.

Singer, P. and Cavalieri, P. (eds) (1993) *The Great Ape Project: Equality beyond Humanity.* London: Fourth Estate.

Skinner, B.F. (1971) *Beyond Freedom and Dignity.* New York: Knopf.

Skinner, B.F. (1974) *About Behaviourism.* New York: Knopf.

Skinner, B.F. (1986) Is it behaviourism? *Behavioural & Brain Sciences, 9*, 716.

Smart, J.J.C. (1959) Sensations and brain processes. *The Philosophical Review, 68*, 141–56.

Smith, C.U.M. (1994) You are a group of neurons. *The Times Higher Educational Supplement*, 27 May, 20–1.

Smith, P.B. and Bond, M.H. (1993) *Social Psychology across Cultures: Analysis and Perspectives.* Hemel Hempstead: Harvester Wheatsheaf.

Smith, P.B. and Bond, M.H. (1998) *Social Psychology across Cultures* (2nd edn). Hemel Hempstead: Prentice Hall Europe.

Smith, P.K. and Cowie, H. (1991) *Understanding Children's Development* (2nd edn). Oxford: Blackwell.

Snyder, M. and Ickes, W. (1985) Personality and social behaviour. In G. Lindzey and E. Aronson (eds) *Handbook of Social Psychology*, Vol. 2 (3rd edn). New York: Random House.

Snyder, M. (1987) *Public Appearances/Private Realities: The Psychology of Self-monitoring.* New York: W.H. Freeman.

Sorenson, S., Webster, J.D. and Roggman, L.A. (2002) Adult attachment and preparing to provider care for older relatives. *Attachment & Human Development, 4*(1), 84–106.

Soyland, A.J. (1994) *Psychology as Metaphor.* London: Sage.

Spearman, C. (1904) General intelligence objectively determined and measured. *American Journal of Psychology, 15*, 210–93.

Spearman, C. (1927) The doctrine of two factors. Reprinted in S. Wiseman (ed.) *Intelligence and Ability.* Harmondsworth: Penguin.

Steele, H. (2002) Attachment theory. *The Psychologist, 15*(10), 518–22.

Stephenson, W. (1953) *The Study of Behaviour: Q-technique and its Methodology.* Chicago: Chicago University Press.

Stern, W. (1921) *Die differentielle Psychologie in ihren methodologischen Grundlagen* (3rd edn). Leipzig: Barth.

Sternberg, R.J. (1986) A triangular theory of love. *Psychological Review, 93*, 119–35.

Stevens, R. (1995) Freudian theories of personality. In S.E. Hampson and A.M. Colman (eds) *Individual Differences and Personality.* London: Longman.

Storms, M.D. (1973) Videotape and the attribution process: reversing actors' and observers' points of view. *Journal of Personality & Social Psychology, 27*(2), 165–75.

Strachey, J. (1962–1977) Sigmund Freud: a sketch of his life and ideas. (This appears in each volume of the Pelican Freud Library; originally written for the *Standard Edition of the Complete Psychological Works of Sigmund Freud.* London: Hogarth Press.)

Sue, S. (1995) Implications of the bell curve: whites are genetically inferior in intelligence? *Focus: Notes from the Society for the Psychological Study of Ethnic Minority Issues*, 16–17.

Sulloway, F.J. (1979) *Freud, Biologist of the Mind: Beyond the Psychoanalytic Legend.* New York: Basic Books.

Tasker, F. (2002) Lesbian and gay parenting. In A. Coyle and C. Kitzinger (eds) *Lesbian and Gay Psychology: New Perspectives.* BPS/Blackwell.

Tavris, C. (1993) The mismeasure of woman. *Feminism & Psychology, 3*(2), 149–68.

Taylor, G. (2002) Psychopathology and the social and historical construction of gay male identities. In A. Coyle and C. Kitzinger (eds) *Lesbian and Gay Psychology: New Perspectives.* BPS/Blackwell.

Taylor, R. (1963) *Metaphysics.* Englewood Cliffs, NJ: Prentice Hall.

Taylor, R. (2000) The Singer revolution. *Philosophy Now, 28*, August/September, 10–13.

Teichman, J. (1988) *Philosophy and the Mind.* Oxford: Blackwell.

Thibaut, J.W. and Kelley, H.H. (1959) *The Social Psychology of Groups.* New York: Wiley.

Thomas, K. (1990) Psychodynamics: the Freudian approach. In I. Roth (ed.) *Introduction to Psychology*, Vol. 1. Hove, East Sussex/Milton Keynes: Open University/Lawrence Erlbaum.

Thomas, G.V. and Blackman, D. (1991) Are animal experiments on the way out? *The Psychologist, 4*(5), 208–12.

Thomas, R.M. (1985) *Comparing Theories of Child Development* (2nd edn). Belmont, CA: Wadsworth Publishing Co.

Thorndike, E.L. (1898) Animal intelligence: an experimental study of the associative processes in animals. *Psychological Review Monograph Supplement* 2 (whole No. 8).

Thorne, B. (1992) *Carl Rogers.* London: Sage.

Thurstone, L.L. (1938) Primary mental abilities. *Psychometric Monographs,* 1.

Tolman, E.C. (1948) Cognitive maps in rats and man. *Psychological Review, 55,* 189–208.

Tooby, J. and Cosmides, L. (1992) The psychological foundations of culture. In J.H. Barkow, L. Cosmides and J. Tooby (eds) *The Adapted Mind: Evolutionary Psychology and the Evolution of Culture.* New York: Oxford University Press.

Torrance, S. (1986) Breaking out of the Chinese room. In M. Yazdani (ed.) *Artificial Intelligence: Principles and Applications.* London: Chapman & Hall.

Triandis, H.C. (1972) *The Analysis of Subjective Culture.* New York: Wiley.

Triandis, H.C. (1980) Introduction. In H.C. Triandis and W.E. Lambert (eds) *Handbook of Cross-Cultural Psychology. Vol. 1. Perspectives.* Boston: Allyn & Bacon.

Triandis, H.C. (1990) Theoretical concepts that are applicable to the analysis of ethnocentrism. In R.W. Brislin (ed.) *Applied Cross-Cultural Psychology.* Newbury Park, CA: Sage.

Triandis, H.C., Kashima, Y., Shimada, E. and Villareal, M. (1986) Acculturation indices as a means of conforming cultural differences. *International Journal of Psychology, 21,* 43–70.

Triandis, H.C., Leung, K., Villareal, M. and Clack, F.L. (1985) Allocentric vs idiocentric tendencies: convergent and discriminant validation. *Journal of Research in Personality, 19,* 395–415.

Turner, J.C. (1991) *Social Influence.* Milton Keynes: Open University Press.

Turney, J. (1999) Human nature totally explained. *The Times Higher,* 12 March, 18.

Tyerman, A. and Spencer, C. (1983) A critical test of the Sherifs' Robber's Cave experiment: intergroup competition and cooperation between groups of well-acquainted individuals. *Small Group Behaviour, 14*(4), 515–31.

Ullman, M., Krippner, S. and Vaughan, A. (1973) *Dream Telepathy.* New York: Macmillan.

Unger, R.K. (1979) *Female and Male: Psychological Perspectives.* New York: Harper & Row.

Unger, R.K. (1984) Sex in psychological paradigms – from behaviour to cognition. *Imagination, Cognition & Personality, 3,* 227–34.

Unger, R.K. (1993) The personal is paradoxical: feminists construct psychology. *Feminism & Psychology, 3*(2), 211–18.

Utts, J. (1991) Replication and meta-analysis in parapsychology. *Statistical Science, 6,* 363–403.

Valentine, E.R. (1992) *Conceptual Issues in Psychology* (2nd edn). London: Routledge.

Valins, S. and Nisbett, R.E. (1972) Attribution processes in the development and treatment of emotional disorders. In E.E. Jones, D.E. Kanouse, H.H. Kelley, R.E. Nisbett, S. Valins and B. Weiner (eds) *Attribution: Perceiving the Causes of Behaviour.* Morristown, NJ: General Learning Press.

Valins, S. (1966) Cognitive effects of false heart-rate feedback. *Journal of Personality & Social Psychology, 4,* 400–8.

Vernon, P.E. (1950) *The Structure of Human Abilities.* London: Methuen.

Wachtel, P. (1977) *Psychoanalysis and Behaviour Therapy: Toward an Integration.* New York: Basic Books.

Wade, C. and Tavris, C. (1990) *Psychology* (2nd edn). New York: Harper & Row.

Watson, J.B. (1913) Psychology as the behaviourist views it. *Psychological Review, 20,* 158–77.

Watson, J.B. (1928) *Behaviourism.* Chicago: University of Chicago Press.

Watt, C. (2001) Paranormal Cognition. In R. Roberts and D. Groome (eds) *Parapsychology: The Science of Unusual Experience.* London: Arnold.

Weiner, B. (1972) *Theories of Motivation: From Mechanism to Cognition.* Chicago: Rand McNally.

Weiner, B. (1979) A theory of motivation for some classroom experiences. *Journal of Educational Psychology, 71,* 3–25.

Weiner, B. (1985) An attribution theory of achievement motivation and emotion. *Psychological Review, 92,* 548–73.

Weiner, B. (1992) *Human Motivation: Metaphors, Theories and Research.* Newbury Park, CA: Sage.

Weiskrantz, L. (1986) *Blindsight: A Case Study and Implications.* Oxford: Clarendon Press.

Weiskrantz, L., Warrington, M.D., Sanders, M.D. and Marshall, J. (1974) Visual capacity in the hemianopic field following a restricted occipital ablation. *Brain, 97,* 709–28.

Weiss, R.S. (1988) Loss and recovery. *Journal of Social Issues, 44,* 37–52.

Weiss, R.S. (1991) The attachment bond in childhood and adulthood. In C.M. Parkes, J. Stevenson-Hinde and P. Marris (eds) *Attachment across the Life Cycle.* London: Routledge.

Weisstein, N. (1993a) Psychology constructs the female, or, The fantasy life of the male psychologist (with some attention to the fantasies of his friends, the male biologist and the male anthropologist [this is a revised/expanded version of 'Kinder, Kuche, Kirche as scientific law: psychology constructs the female', 1971]. *Feminism & Psychology, 3*(2), 195–210.

Weisstein, N. (1993b) Power, resistance and science: a call for a revitalized feminist psychology. *Feminism & Psychology, 3*(2), 239–45.

Werner, E.E. (1989) Children of the Garden Island. *Scientific American,* April, 106–11.

Wetherell, M. (1996) Group conflict and the social psychology of racism. In M. Wetherell (ed.) *Identities, Groups and Social Issues.* London: Sage, in association with the Open University.

Wetherell, M. and Maybin, J. (1996) The distributed self. In R. Stevens (ed.) *Understanding the Self.* London: Sage.

Wetherell, M. and Still, A. (1996) Realism and relativism. In R. Sapsford (ed.) *Issues for Social Psychology.* Milton Keynes: Open University Press.

Wilkinson, S. (1989) The impact of feminist research: issues of legitimacy. *Philosophical Psychology, 2*(3), 261–9.

Wilson, E.O. (1975) *Sociobiology: The New Synthesis.* Cambridge, MA: Harvard University Press.

Wilson, E.O. (1978) *On Human Nature.* Cambridge, MA: Harvard University Press.

Winnicott, D.W. (1958) *Through Paediatrics to Psychoanalysis.* London: Hogarth Press.

Wise, R. (2000) *Rattling the Cage: Towards Legal Rights for Animals.* London: Profile Books.

Wober, M. (1974) Towards an understanding of the Kiganda concept of intelligence. In J.W. Berry and P.R. Dasen (eds) *Culture and Cognition.* London: Methuen.

World Health Organization (1973) *Report of the International Pilot Study of Schizophrenia*, Vol. 1. Geneva: WHO.

World Health Organization (1979) *Schizophrenia: An International Follow-up Study.* London: Wiley.

Wright, L.K., Hickey, J.V., Buckwalter, K.C. and Clipp, E.C. (1995) Human development in the context of ageing and chronic illness: the role of attachment in Alzheimer's disease and stroke. *International Journal of Ageing and Human Development, 41*, 133–50.

Wundt, W. (1974 [1874]) *Grundzuge der physiologischen Psychologie.* Leipzig: Engelmann.

Yan, W. and Gaier, E.L. (1994) Causal attributions for college success and failure: an Asian-American comparison. *Journal of Cross-Cultural Psychology, 25*(1), 146–58.

Zebrowitz, L.A. (1990) *Social Perception.* Milton Keynes: Open University Press.

Zeldow, P.B. (1995) Psychodynamic formulations of human behaviour. In D. Wedding (ed.) *Behaviour and Medicine* (2nd edn). St Louis, MO: Mosby Year Book.

Zimbardo, P. (1973) On the ethics of intervention in human psychological research with special reference to the 'Stanford Prison Experiment'. *Cognition, 2*(2, Pt 1), 243–55.

Zimbardo, P. (1992) *Psychology and Life* (13th edn). New York: HarperCollins.

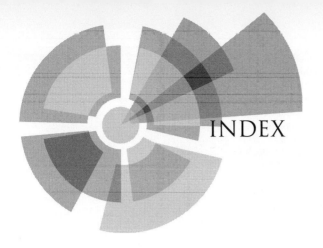

INDEX

abnormal behaviour 62, 72
   criteria 119-23, 127-30, 137, 138
   in religion 134
   of women viewed by men 96
   see also behaviour; mental disorders
absolute phenomena 131, 138
absolutism 143, 162
abuse, of patient by therapist 207, 209
acceptable behaviour 118, 137
accessibility, consciousness levels 274, 292
accidents 255, 265, 297
achievement motivation 29-30
actor observer effect (AOE) 23, 28, 39, 65
Adler, A. 321
adolescence, detachment from parents 180, 184
adoption studies 84, 93
adrenaline experiment 25, 39
aggregated observations 68, 73
aggression 75, 106
agoraphobia 180-1, 184
Ainsworth, M. D. S. 166, 167, 168, 169, 172
Allen, A. 67-8
allocentrism 35
Allport, G. W. 49-50, 54-5
altered states of consciousness (ASC) 299-302, 310
alternative therapy 307
Alzheimer's disease 179-80, 183
analysis of variance (ANOVA) 22, 23, 65, 66
androcentrism 96, 98, 99-100, 114, 115, 211
   see also masculinist bias; men, dominance
androids, behaviour 270, 292
anger 335
Anglocentric bias 146, 162
animals 278-9
   behaviourist view 223
   consciousness 271
   rights 203
   studies 339
   use in research 200-3, 208, 317-18
Animals (Scientific Procedures) Act 1986 201

anomalistic psychology (AP) 295, 298-9, 310
ANOVA 22, 23, 65, 66
Antaki, C. 4
anthropomorphism 271
anti-essentialism 331, 342
anti-psychiatry movement 121
anxious-ambivalence 172, 173, 174, 182
anxious-avoidance 166, 172, 173, 174, 182, 183
applied behaviour analysis (ABA) 206-7, 209
Archer, D. 336
Armstrong, D. M. 287
Aronson, E. 197
artificial intelligence (AI) 281, 293
Asch, S.E. 7
Association for Women in Psychology (AWP) 98
attachment 166-8, 170, 182
   religion 177-9
   to objects 165, 182
   see also death; grief; loss; love
attachment theory 163-85
attention 275
attitudes 151
   see also bias; masculinist bias; stereotyping
attribution theory 4, 17-23, 39, 65, 114
   application 19, 21, 39, 297, 310
attributional style 29-36, 40
automata 249, 280
   see also machines
automatic processing 250, 275, 292
avoidance patterns 173, 174, 175

baby X experiment 84
back-translation 155, 163
Bannister, D. 57
Bartholomew, K. 175-6
battered woman's syndrome 110
Beaman, A. 196-7
Bee, H. 170, 176
behaviour
   of androids/humanoids 270
   conscious, illusion 277

behaviour *continued*
  consistency 62, 64
  evil 259
  in evolutionary psychology 337
  and free will 246-7, 246-64
  interactionism 64, 65-6
  interpersonal 121
  normative 117-18
  plasticity 339
  predictability 61, 64, 122
  principle study of psychology 225
  religious 177-9
  self-derogating 30
  socialization 142
  unexpected 22-3, 122
  in weak and strong situations 62-4
  see also abnormal behaviour; attachment;
    causality; mental disorders
behaviour modification 206-7, 317, 341
behaviour therapy 204, 209, 317, 341
behavioural control 205-6, 209
behavioural genetics 87-9, 93, 94
behavioural neuroscience 317, 341
behavioural pharmacology 317, 341
behaviourism 76, 85, 222-5, 238, 242-3, 256-7,
    288-9, 313-19
belief systems 3, 5, 158, 177-9, 183, 296-8, 310
Bem, D. J. 27, 39, 67-8, 109-10, 115
Bentall, R. P. 71
bereavement *see* death; grief
Berkowitz, L. 37-8
Berry, J. W. 154, 155
Bhugra, D. 131
Bhui, K. 131
bias 65, 211, 215
  in cross-cultural psychology 145-6
  experimenter 229-30, 231-2
  masculine 95-6, 97, 105-6
  in science 100, 228
  and values 100-1, 192-3
  see also gender, bias; masculinist bias; self-
    serving bias (SSB); stereotyping
Big Five personality constructs 70-1, 73
biogenetic law 220
biological adaptation 13, 15
biological determinism 261-2, 266
biological essentialism 110, 115
biomedical model 306-7, 311
Blackmore, S. 277-8, 279
Blakemore, C. 285-6
blindsight 276, 292, 325
Bond, M. H. 35, 147, 155
bonding 167-8, 170, 182
Bowlby, J. 166
Bradley, J. M. 179
brain 220, 268-9, 281-2, 283, 284, 290, 291, 293,
    308, 311, 328
  see also mind-brain

Brehm, S. S. 31, 32, 195-6
Brislin, R. 132, 149, 154-5
British Psychological Society 186-8, 192-3, 199, 200
Broadbent, D. 290
Bronfenbrenner, U. 142, 162
Broverman, I. 104
Burgner, D. 28, 30
Burr, V. 332-3
Burt, Cyril 267
Buss, D. M. 338, 342
Byrne, W. 92-3
bystander intervention 37

Cafferty, T. P. 179
Caldwell, R. 279
Calkins, Mary 97
Campbell, A. 336
Cannon, W.B. 23-4
Cannon-Bard theory 24
Caplan, P. 103
cardinal traits 49, 58
caregiving 169, 179-80, 183
Carlsmith, J.M. 26-7
Cartesian automaton 248
Carver, C. S. 65, 72
case studies, as method 43, 54, 55
causal schemata 22, 39
causality
  attribution 17-18, 32
  common-sense psychology 3-4
  covariation 22
  determinism 241, 252, 253-5, 262
  external 4, 14, 17, 22, 30, 34, 39, 40
  internal 4, 14, 17, 22, 30, 34, 39, 109
  mind-body relationship 286
  perception of 37-8
  versus behaviourism 256-8
central state identity theory 289-90, 294
central traits 49, 58
centralist materialism 289-90, 293, 294
centre for consciousness 279, 292
Child, A.L. 142
children
  attachment 166-8, 179-80
  effect of experiences on personality 320
  exploration, of environment 170, 176
  foetal influences 83
  fundamental attribution error 158
  gay parenting 112
  gender differences 30, 40
  infanticide 340
  infantile sexuality theory 320
  intergroup conflict 160-2
  niche building 86-7
  Oedipus complex 159
  raising in different cultures 152, 154
  relationship with parents 166-8, 179-80
  theory of mind 14, 15

Children of the Garden Island 87
chimpanzees, use in research 202
choice 246, 249, 260, 265
Chomsky, N. 76, 93, 271, 338-9
chromosomes 78-81, 92
Cicirelli, V. G. 180
clairvoyance 296, 310
Claridge, G. 89, 90, 129
Clarke, V. 112
client-centred therapy 258, 265
Clift, S.M. 4
clinical psychologists 186-7
co-investigators 57, 59
co-operative enquiry 235, 238
codes of conduct 186-8, 193, 195, 198-9, 200, 206-7
coding, in cognitive psychology 328, 341
cognitive attribution theory of achievement motivation 29
cognitive behaviour therapy 327, 341
cognitive dissonance theory 26-7, 39-40, 160
cognitive labelling theory 19, 24, 26, 39
cognitive psychology 327-30, 342
collaborative/participative research 57, 59, 235, 239
collectivism 33, 40, 133, 148-9, 150-2, 158-9, 162, 163
Collins, N. L. 176
common-sense psychology 2-3, 4, 14, 17, 19, 39, 61, 241-2, 277, 292
  see also everyday psychology
comparative psychiatry 131
comparative psychology 220
compensation model of religious behaviour 178, 183
complementary and alternative medicine (CAM) 307
compulsive behaviour 243
computational theory of mind (CTM) 281
computers, comparison with humans 330, 342
conceptual equivalence 156, 163
confessing 36-7, 40
consciousness 13, 267-91, 292, 293, 299-302
  machines 280-1, 283
consensus/distinctiveness/consistency 22, 39
consent, participants' in research 189-91, 208
consistency 64, 66, 68, 71, 72, 73, 122
conspiratorial model of schizophrenia 121, 137
constitutional factors, in childhood resilience 87
construct theory 5-6, 10-12, 57, 69, 70-1, 85, 217, 288
contact, in cultures 152, 163
contraception, research bias 106
control see behavioural control
controllability, in causality 19-20, 38, 40
correlations, in study of psi 303-4, 311
correspondence hypothesis 178, 183
correspondence theory 331
correspondent inference theory 21-2, 39

counselling psychologists 186-7
covariation model 22, 39
Craik, K. 327
Craikian automaton 248-9
Crick, Francis 289
crime, and mental abnormality 243
critical psychology (CP) 333, 342
cross-cultural psychology 141-64, 212
cross-cultural studies 144-6, 162, 163
  culture specific research 155, 163, 331-2
  in mental disorders 131-4
  Oedipus complex 159
  see also cultural differences; culture
cues, in experimental psychology 230
cultural complexity 150, 163
cultural differences 33-4, 126, 133-4, 137, 138
  dimensions 148-53
  homogeneity v. heterogeneity 152
  nature-nurture debate 141-3, 162
  see also cross-cultural studies; culture
cultural feminism 113, 115
cultural psychiatry 131
cultural psychology 145
cultural relativity 131, 133, 138, 143
cultural specificity 155, 163, 331-2
cultural syndromes 150-3, 163
culture
  and common-sense psychology 3-4
  definition 141-2, 146-7, 162
  in evolutionary psychology 336
  features 149
  influence on experiments 231
  and psychiatric disorders 131-4, 136
  see also cross-cultural studies; cultural differences
culture-bound syndromes (CBS) 133-4, 138
culture-fair tests 157

Danziger, K. 162, 216-17, 225, 231-2
Darley, J. M. 196
data analysis, and bias 106, 114
Davis, C. 89, 90, 129
Davis, K. E. 21-2, 39
Davison, G. C. 29, 122, 205
Dawkins, R. 262, 266
death 168-9, 179, 183, 184
debriefing, in experiments 190, 208
deception, in experiments 11-12, 189-91, 196-9, 208
decision making 277
Deese, J. 8
deliberate control 250
demand characteristics 11, 15, 230, 231-2, 238, 305
dementia 179-80
Denmark, F. 104
Dennett, D. 263, 266, 269, 271, 279, 292
depression, attributional style 28, 33, 40

Descartes, René 76, 212-13, 244, 288
desirable behaviour 118, 137
determinism 163, 226, 241, 247, 252-6, 256-7,
    259, 263, 264, 265, 266
deviance *see* abnormal behaviour
deviation from mean/norm 120, 125-6,
    137, 138
Di Blasi, Z. 309, 309-10
Diab, L. N. 161
diagnosis, of mental disorders 136
Diagnostic and Statistical Manuals *see* DSM
differences
    absolute and relative 85
    sex differences 104, 105, 106, 107, 113, 338
    see also cultural differences
Diller, A. 270
Dilthey, W. 45-7
dimensions
    of cultural difference 148-53
    of personality 127
diminished responsibility 244, 264
discourse analysis (DA) 235-6, 238
discrimination
    against women psychologists 97-8, 98-9
    groups 35-6
    see also bias; masculinist bias; prejudice; racism;
        sexism
discursive psychology (DP) 239, 333, 342
dispositional causes 4, 14, 17, 30, 34, 39
dispositions 49, 64, 65, 68, 72, 84
    see also personality traits
distress 120, 124, 137, 198, 208
distress maintaining patterns 31
divorce 169, 181
DNA 78-80
doctors, and placebo effect 307-8, 311
double binds 121
drugs
    development through animal research 208
    effect on brain 317
    and placebo effect 309, 312
DSM classification 119, 128, 135
dualism 213, 237, 244, 264, 288, 291

eastern psychology 225, 238
Edelman, G. 272-3
ego 274-5
ego psychology 320-1, 341
ego-dystonic homosexuality (EDH) 135
Eiser, J. R. 282, 283
elderly, attachment theory 179-80
Ellis, A. 329
emic-etic distinction 153-5, 163
emotions 5, 335
    control vs expressiveness 152, 163
    and ethics in psychology 185
    theories 23-4
empathy 48

empiricism 8, 76-7, 93, 215, 237, 238
    see also experiments
enculturated lens theory 110-11, 115
enculturation 142, 162
endophenotypes 90, 94
endorphins, and placebo effect 309
environment
    in adverse childhood 87
    in behaviourism 314-16
    and collectivism 151
    facilitative 86
    and individualism 151
    macro environments 86
    micro environments 86
    in nature/nurture debate 75-7, 81-9, 93, 94
    shared/non-shared 84-5
    urban/rural 152
Environment of Evolutionary Adaptation 339, 342
environmental causes 4, 14, 17, 30, 34, 39
environmental enrichment studies 317, 341
epiphenomenon 263, 264, 288, 293
Epstein, S. 68
equivalence 155-7, 163
Erikson, E. H. 107, 321, 341
ESP 296, 297, 304, 310
essentialism 111-12, 331
ethical codes 186-8, 193, 195, 198-9, 200, 206-7,
    209
    see also legislation
ethical issues 38, 101, 185-210
    cost benefit analysis 197-8
    eugenics 91
ethnicity 30, 33
ethnocentrism 133, 138, 146, 162, 212
    see also western culture
ethogenics 234
etic approach, research 154, 163
eugenics 91, 94
Eurocentric bias 146, 162
everyday psychology 1-10, 17
    see also common-sense psychology
evolution 13-14, 15, 77-8, 93, 152, 219, 220, 238,
    283-5, 316
evolutionary continuity 200, 208
evolutionary psychology (EP) 336-40, 342
excuse giving 36-7, 40
exosystems 142, 162
experiential equivalence 157
experimental psychology 219-22, 227-32
experimental situation 11-12
experimental techniques, parapsychology 298-302
experimenter bias 229-30, 231-2, 238, 302
experimenter psi 306
experimenter/participant effects 305, 311
experiments
    adrenaline 25
    animals 200-3
    baby X 84

bias 212
chimpanzees and sign language 202
cognitive dissonance 26-7
consciousness 278
ethical principles 188-95
Ganzfeld study of ESP 299-301
laboratory situation 228
as method of study 43
open, in psi research 305-6
phenomenology 247
prison simulation 63, 72
Pygmalian 230
Robber's Cave field 160, 161, 163
social situations 231
see also empiricism
explicit theories 9
external causality 4, 14, 17, 22, 30, 34, 39, 40
external validity 228, 238
extra-sensory perception (ESP) 296, 297, 304, 310
Eysenck, H. J. 50, 51, 59, 127, 189

facilitative environments 86
factor analysis (FA) 44, 58, 70
falsification 9, 15, 321
family
    gay parenting 101-2, 112
    interaction model of schizophrenia 121
    in nature-nurture debate 80-1, 84-5
family integrity, in cultural syndromes 151
family resemblance 84-5
fatalism 163, 226, 241, 247, 252-6, 256-7, 259,
    263, 264, 265, 266
Fechner, G. 219
femininity, and masculinity dimension 148, 152, 162,
    163
feminism 95, 98, 114, 188-9
    feminist critique 99-100, 114, 115
    feminist psychology 95-6, 113, 114
    feminist research 98, 108, 115, 188-9
    see also women
Ferguson, K.E. 315, 316, 318
Fernando, S. 133-4, 136
Festinger, L. 26-7, 39-40, 160
Fisher, S. 324
Fiske, S. 18-19, 26
focal attention 275, 292
foetal alcohol syndrome 83
folk psychology *see* common-sense psychology
forensic psychiatry 243
formal and informal psychology 6-10
Fransella, F. 57
free association 253
free will 226, 242, 244-6, 246-7, 246-64, 264, 278
freedom 254, 258-61, 263, 266
French, C. 298, 299, 307
Freud, S. 4, 159, 253-6, 265, 274-5, 290, 292,
    319-26, 341
Fromm, E. 259-60, 266

fully automatic processing 250
functional disorders 130, 138
functional relationship, environment and behaviour
    314
functionalism 222, 238, 291
fundamental attribution error (FAE) 23, 28, 39, 65,
    158

Gahagan, J. 2, 6-7, 10, 22-3
Galton, Francis 77, 220
The Ganzfeld, study of ESP 299-302, 310
Garonzik, R. 191
gatekeepers 99, 114
Geisteswissenschaften 45-6, 58, 211
gender
    attributional style 29-30
    bias 84, 104, 105-6, 114
    in evolutionary psychology 337
    and expectations of behaviour 111
    experiments 84
    interpretation of difference 113
    male dominance 96
    see also men; sex differences; women
gender identity 110-11
gender polarization 110, 115
gene-environment correlations 84, 88, 94
gene-environment interactions 86, 88, 94
generalization 51, 53-4, 106
genes 78-80, 93, 161-2
genetics 77-82, 93
Gergen, K. J. 330-1
Gesell, Arnold 76, 93
Gestalt psychology 76, 93
Gilligan, Carol 101, 107
Glick, J. A. 157
Golombok, S. 102
GPs, and placebo effect 307-8, 311
Graham, H. 219, 225-6
Gray, J. 201
Great Ape Project (GAP) 202-3, 209
Greenberg, R. P. 324
grief 168, 168-9, 170
Groome, D. 295
group averages/norms 44, 58, 108, 115
groups
    in attribution theory 34
    discrimination 35-6
    separation from in-groups 151

Hamer, D. S. 93
Haney, C. 63
hard determinism 256-7, 263, 264, 266
Harnett, O. 100
Harré, R. 10, 189, 234, 290
Hayslip, B. 169
Hazan, C. 170, 171, 172-5, 176-7, 181
Heider, Fritz 2-4, 19, 39
Heisenberg, W. 237

helping behaviour 37-8
heredity 75-84, 87-93
Herrnstein, R.J. 195
Hewstone, M. 28, 30
hierarchies of decisions 249-50
higher order consciousness 280, 292
Hofstede, G. 33-4, 148-9, 162
Holmes, J. 203-4
Holt, R.R. 46-8, 50, 58
Homicide Act 1957 264
homo psychologicus 12-14, 15
homosexuality 91-3, 94, 96, 99, 118, 123-5, 135, 137, 138
Honorton, C. 299-300
Horgan, J. 337
horizontal relationships 151
hormones 102
Horowitz, F. D. 86
humanistic psychology 226-7, 238
humanoids, behaviour 270
Humphrey, N. 12-13, 273, 280, 283-5
hunter-gatherer societies 13, 339-40, 342

ICD 130
id 275, 321
identity 290, 294
idiocentrism 35
idiographic approach 44-6, 49, 52-8, 58, 59, 67, 115, 127, 211
illusion, of conscious behaviour 292
implicit personality theories 7-8
implicit theories 8-9, 15
imposed etic 154-5, 163
impression management 36, 40
in-groups, separation from 151
individual differences 44, 58, 75, 78, 93, 162, 222, 329, 337
individual norms 44, 58, 117-18
individualism 33, 40, 132, 148, 150-2, 158-9, 162, 163, 341
individuals
    distress over abnormality 120
    personality traits 49-51, 58
    protection in research 192
    study of see idiographic approach
industrialized cultures 150
infanticide, evolutionary psychologist view 340
infantile sexuality, theory 320, 341
informal and formal psychology 6-10
information processing operations, human beings and computers 282, 327, 328, 330, 342
informed consent 189-91, 203-4, 208, 209
inner working models (IWM) 173, 174, 178, 179, 181, 183
intelligence 119-20, 195
    and emic-etic approach 154, 156
intentionality 5, 22, 39
inter-individual consistency 62-3

interactionism 64-5, 93, 288, 293, 332
interdependence 151
internal causality 4, 14, 17, 22, 30, 34, 39, 109
internal validity 228, 238
interpersonal behaviour 121
intra-individual consistency 62, 72, 122
introspection 13, 15, 221, 222, 238, 267, 291, 292
intuition 48
intuitive theories 7, 15
IQ 119-20, 195

Jackson, G. 97
Jacobson, L. 230
Jahoda G. 147
James, W. 23-4, 222, 238, 251-3, 265
James-Lange theory 23-4
Jensen, A. R. 195
Johnson-Laird, P. N. 248-50, 265, 277, 292
Jones, E. E. 21-2, 39
Jones, S. 88
Jung, C. 321

Kelley, H. H. 22, 23, 39
Kelly, G. 10-11, 56, 57, 260-1, 266
Kelman, H. C. 190
Kirkpatrick, L. A. 177-9
Kitzinger, Celia 99
Klein, Melanie 321
Koestler, A. 250-1, 265
Kohlberg, L. 107
Kraepelin, Emil 129, 138
Krahé, B. 50-1, 54, 61, 70-1
Krupat, E. 191

labelling 234
laboratory research 185-6, 194
LAD 75, 76, 93, 338-9
Laing, R. D. 121, 137
Lalljee, M. 22-3, 236
language
    acquisition 75
    for concepts in cross-cultural research 155
    evolutionary psychologist view 338-9
    for mind and brain 291
    of psychology 234, 236
    social constructionist view 331, 332
Language Acquisition Device (LAD) 75, 76, 93, 338-9
Latané, B. 196
law of parsimony 316
lay people see everyday psychology
leadership, gender stereotypes 105
learned helplessness 28, 40
legislation 201, 264
    see also ethical codes
lesbianism 99, 114
    and parenthood 101-2, 112
    see also homosexuality

Leslie, J. C. 206, 315, 317, 318
LeVay, S. 92-3
Libet, B. 277-8
life changes, and mental illness 180-1, 184
life stories 112, 115
lifespan development theory 107
limits, and predictability 61, 72
Liotti, G. 181
Lipsedge, M. 130, 133-4
Littlewood, R. 130, 133-4
Locke, J. 76, 217-18
Lodge, David 271, 286
logical behaviourism 288-9
loneliness 172, 174
long-term consistency 68
loose cultures 152, 163
loss 181-2
    see also attachment; death; grief
love 169, 171-2
    see also attachment
lying 36-7

McGhee, P. 128-9, 197-8, 281
McGinn, C. 273
McGurk, H. 81
machines
    consciousness 280-1, 283
    see also automata
McNaughton Rules (diminished responsibility) 244
macrosystems 142, 162
male standard 102-4, 114
marital relationships, attributional style 30-3
masculinist bias 95-6, 97, 101-4, 108, 114, 188-9
    see also androcentrism; feminism; gender; men;
        sex differences; women
masculinity-femininity dimension 148, 152, 162,
    163
Maslow, A. H. 227, 238
Masson, J. 207, 209
materialism 213, 288-9, 294
maturation 93
May, Rollo 227
Maybin, J. 69
mechanism 213, 237
media, spread of behaviourism 224
medical model of mental disorder 129, 138
medicine, historical use of placebos 307, 311
meiosis 80-1, 93
men
    dominance 95-6
    view of problems 103
    see also androcentrism; feminism; gender;
        masculinist bias; sex differences; women
mental disorders 117, 127-33, 137
    and change in psychiatric view 135
    cross cultural study 131-4
    and free will 243, 264
    see also schizophrenia

mental processes 221, 238
mentalism 5, 6, 15, 288, 293
Merleau-Ponty, M. 282-3, 293
mesosystems 142, 162
methodological behaviourism 242, 264, 313-14,
    317, 341
methodology 43-7, 194, 208, 305
metric equivalence 156-7, 163
micro environments 86
microsystems 142, 162
Milgram, S. 190, 197, 199, 208
Miller, G. A. 48
mind, concept of 13, 15, 244, 254, 268-9, 274,
    291, 292, 337, 342
mind-body problem 268-73, 282-3, 286
mind-brain relationship 286, 287, 291, 293, 311
    identity theory 289-90, 294
    see also brain
mis-attribution effect 26, 39, 180
Mischel, W. 64, 72
mitosis 79, 81, 93
moderator variables 68, 73
Moghaddam, F. M. 34, 145, 146, 147, 160-1
molecular genetics 89-90, 94
Mollon, P. 324-5
monism 288, 293
moral development theory 107
moral responsibility 107, 245, 255, 257, 262, 265
moral sciences (Geisteswissenschaften) 45-6, 58,
    211
Morelli, G. 157-8
Moscovici, S. 334

nAch 29, 30
naïve scientists 3, 10, 14, 23, 39, 234-5
national cultures 147, 162
nativism 76-7, 93
natural sciences (Naturwissenschaften) 45, 58, 211
nature-nurture debate 75-8, 80-93, 93, 141-3
Naturwissenschaften 45, 58, 211
Neale, J. M. 29, 122, 205
need for achievement (nAch) 29, 30
negative feedback loop 327
neo-Darwinism see evolutionary psychology
neurological disorders 128
neuropsychoanalysis 325
neuroses 130, 138
new paradigm research (NPR) 234-5, 239
Newton, I. 214
niche building 86-7, 94
Nicolson, P. 100
Nietzsche, F. 215
Nisbett, R. E. 26, 67, 277, 292
nocebo effects 309
noise-reduction techniques, in ESP 300
nomothetic approach 44, 45-6, 50, 58, 59, 67, 127,
    211
Norman, D. 250, 265

normative behaviour 117
norms 44-5, 151
Nye, D. 323

object relations theory 323, 341
objectivity 212, 213, 238, 272, 303-4, 311
    in behaviourism 223
    in causality 18-19
    in research 192
obligatory behaviour 118, 137
observation, in culture specific research 155
Occam's razor (law of parsimony) 316
Ochert, A. 128
O'Donohue, W. 315, 316, 318
Oedipus complex 159, 320
old age, attachment theory 179
ontogenesis 14
operant conditioning 52-3, 59, 257, 315, 316, 317-18, 341
ordinary people see everyday psychology
organic disorders 129, 130, 138
origin myths 216-17, 219-22, 238
Orne, M. T. 11, 15, 230
out-of-body experiences (OBE) 304
overdetermination 255

Paludi, M. A. 97, 108
Panek, P. E. 169
paradox of reward 248
paranormal phenomena (psi) 295, 310
    scientific study 303-6
parapsychology (PP) 295-310
parent fixation, in dementia 179-80, 183
parents
    bonding with children 167-8
    lesbian parents 101-2, 112
    lifelong relationship with 167-8, 179-80, 183
    loss 168-9, 181-2
Parkin, A.J. 328
partially automatic processing 250
participative research 57, 59, 235, 239
Penfield, W. 247
perceived causes 17-18, 37-8, 40
perceivers 23, 69, 73, 122
peripheral attention 275, 292
peripheralist materialism 288-9, 293, 294
permissiblepre behaviour 118, 137
person perception 1, 10, 14, 84
personal construct theory (PCT) 10-12, 15, 260-1, 266, 288
personal distress, over abnormality 120, 124, 137
personality theories 71-2
    Big Five constructs 70-1, 73
    consistency 64, 71, 73
    implicit 7
personality traits 5, 49, 61, 64, 65, 66-9, 73, 127
personology 46-51, 56, 58
phenomenology 121, 227, 238

phenotypes 89, 90, 94
phenylketonuria (PKU) 80
philosophers 215
philosophical behaviourism 242, 264, 288-9
philosophical dualism 213, 237, 293
philosophy, influence on psychology 217-18
phobias 123, 125
phrenology 218
phylogenesis 12-14
physiology, influence on psychology 218
Piliavin, I. M. 37
pineal body 244-5
Pinker, S. 338
PKU 80
placebo effect (PE) 306-10, 310, 311
plasticity, of behaviour 339
Plomin, R. 78, 84, 88, 89
political systems 152
positivism 8, 15, 211-13, 213, 237, 238, 272, 331
    in science 100, 114, 189
Potter, J. 333, 334, 335
power
    over patient 205-6, 207, 209
    relationship with gender 111, 115
    of researcher 108, 186, 188-9, 208
power distance 148, 162
pre-menstrual syndrome (PMS) 102
precognition 296, 310
predictability, and behaviour 61, 64, 122
prejudice 36, 215, 228
    in psychological research 192
    reinforced by psychology 108
preoccupied model of self 175, 183
presumptive consent 199, 208
primary consciousness 278-9, 292
primates
    consciousness 271, 279
    studies of sexuality 339
    use in experiments 202, 209
Prince, J. 100
prior general consent 199, 208
prison simulation experiment 63, 72
process oriented research 302, 311
processing capacity 250
processing operations 281-2, 293
programming, applied to human behaviour 327-8
proof-oriented research 302, 311
protective factors, in child development 87
protein synthesis 80, 93
proxemic rules 152-3
proximity maintenance 166, 177, 182
psi see paranormal phenomena
psychedelic model, of schizophrenia 121
psychic determinism 253-6, 265
psychoanalysis
    and consciousness 274
    theory 14, 320-6, 341
psychodynamic approach 319-26, 341

psychokinesis 296, 310
psychological disorders 128
psychological reactance 247, 265
psychological situations 66, 73
psychologists
    need for ethics 185
    ordinary people as 1-10
    as people 1
    as practitioners 106-7
    as scientists 11, 186
psychology
    anomalistic 298-9
    common-sense 2-3, 4, 14, 17, 19, 61, 241-2
    cross cultural 141-64, 212
    discipline of 215-17, 219, 232-4
    eastern and western 225
    experimental 219-22
    feminist 95-6, 113
    formal and informal 6-10
    Gestalt 76, 93
    history 216-25, 237, 267, 296, 311, 321, 326,
        327-8
    humanistic 226-7
    as a science 2, 10, 211, 219-25, 237, 242, 258
    social 62
psychology of being/becoming 227
psychometric tests 44
psychopathology 131-2, 138
psychophysical parallelists 288, 293
psychoses 130, 138
psychosocial theory 321, 341
psychosomatic relationship 126
psychotherapists 187, 203-5, 207, 209
punishment, in behaviour modification 206-7
Pygmalian experiment 230

Q-sort 55-6, 59
qualia 272, 292
questions
    nurture-nature debate 75, 93
    for research 105-6, 114

racism 70, 92, 136, 195
radical behaviourism 242-3, 256-7, 264, 265, 314-
    15, 341
randomized control trials (RCT) 307
rational emotive behaviour therapy (REBT) 329, 342
RCT 307
reaction formation 323
Read, S. J. 176
Reason, P. 234-5
reductionism 213, 214, 237, 289-90, 294
reflexivity 232-3, 239
regulator genes 80, 93
reinforcement, in behaviour modification 206-7
relationship enhancing patterns 31
relationships
    attachment 166

attributional style 30-3, 40
    in individualist/collectivist cultures 151
    interactionism 66
    intimate, research of 194
    marital 30-3
    patterns 31
relativism 143, 162, 237, 335, 341
religion
    and attachment theory 177-9, 183
    and psychological abnormality 134, 138
    role 259
    and sexual mores 126
repertory grid technique (rep-grid) 56, 59
replication problem, in psi research 305, 311
repression 320, 341
required/obligatory behaviour 118, 137
research
    collaborative 235
    cross-cultural 153-60
    ethical principles 188-95
    male-centred 95
    methodology 106, 114, 194
    necessity for 195-6, 208
    participative 235
    sexism 104-8
    single studies 52-4, 59
    value laden 101
residual rules 118, 126, 137, 138
resilience, in adverse childhood 87
responsibility 243-4, 245-6
    attribution 32, 40
Rhine, J. B. 296
Rhine, Louisa 296
Richards, G. 218-19, 221, 234, 318-19, 327-8, 330
Robber's Cave field experiment 160, 161, 163
Roberts, R. 295, 303-5
Rogers, Carl 55-6, 227, 238, 258-9, 265
Rogoff, B. 157-8
romantic love 169, 171-2
Rose, S. 89-90, 261-2, 266, 277, 290, 337, 339-40
Rosenthal, D. 229-30
Ross, L. 67
Rowan, J. 234
Rutter, M. 84, 89
Ryle, G. 289

Sacco, W. P. 33
safe haven see secure base
SC 5-6, 15, 69-70, 73, 111, 233, 288, 330-6, 342
Scarr, S. 85
Schachter, S. 24-6, 39
Scheier, M.F. 65, 72
schematic processing 7, 15
schizophrenia 57, 90, 94, 117, 118, 121, 137, 138
    causes 132
    and cultural universality 131-2, 153
    organic origin 129
schizotypy 128

Schutz 7-8
Schweder, R.A. 144
science
    androcentric view 99-100
    history 212-15
    and psychology 2, 211, 219-25, 242, 258
scientific method 8, 9, 15
scientific realism 302-3, 311
Searle, J. R. 281, 283, 293
secondary traits 49, 58
Secord, P. F. 234
secure attachments 166, 170, 172, 173, 174, 183
secure base 166, 170, 171, 182
secure model of self 175, 183
Segall, M. H. 141-2, 143-4
self 68-70, 151
self-actualization 227, 238, 258
self-attribution 20, 27, 30, 39-40
self-awareness 250
    in therapists 137
self-concept 165, 182, 258
self-consciousness 280, 292
self-defeating personality disorder 103
self-derogating behaviour 30, 40
self-determination 248, 265
self-fulfilling prophecies 111, 115, 229-30, 238
self-image, discriminated groups 36
self-monitoring 68, 73
self-perception theory 19, 27-8, 39
self-reflective automata 249, 265, 280, 292
    see also machines
self-reliance 151
self-reports, in study of psi 303-4, 311
self-serving bias (SSB) 28, 39
    and ethnicity 33-4, 40
    and prejudice 36
    see also bias
self-understanding 48, 58
Seligman, M. E. P. 28-9
semantics, in understanding causality 255-6, 265
sensory experience 215
sentience 185, 207, 280
separation, and freedom 259
separation protest 166, 170, 171, 179, 182
sex differences 30, 40, 104, 105, 106, 107, 113, 114-15, 338
sexism, in psychology 95-6, 96-9, 104-8, 114
sexual dimorphism 337, 339, 342
sexual mores 126
sexual pair bond 167, 169, 170, 182, 338
Shallice, T. 250, 265
Shannon, C. E. 327
shared/non-shared environment 84-5
Shaver, P. R. 170, 172-5, 176-7, 181
Sherif, M. 160, 163
Singer, J. E. 25
single-subject studies 52-4, 59
situationism, and behaviour 62-4, 65, 66, 72

Skinner, B. F. 52-3, 205-6, 242, 256-8, 264, 265, 314-15, 341
sleep paralysis 298
Smith, P. B. 35, 147, 155
social cognition 328
social constructionism (SC) 5-6, 15, 69-70, 73, 111, 233, 288, 330-6, 342
social desirability scales 69
social deviance 119, 137
social evolution 12-14
social perception 19
social phenomenology 121
social psychology 5-6, 15, 62, 145-7, 160, 331, 333-4
    ethical issues 196, 197-8
social representation theory (SRT) 334-5, 342
social situations, in experiments 231
social systems 147
socialization 142, 162
socio-economic status (SES) 84
sociobiology 261-2, 266
sociology, of science 231-2
soft determinism 247, 252-3, 259, 265
species, nature-nurture debate 75, 76, 78, 93, 141, 162
speciesism 201
specificity 150, 155, 163, 331-2
Spencer, C. 161
stability 19, 38
Stanford-Binet intelligence test 100
Steele, H. 182
stereotyping 7, 15, 84, 96, 105, 106, 115
sterilization 100
Strange Situation (infant attachment) 166, 172, 182
stress
    cause of schizophrenia 132
    evolutionary psychology view 338
Stricklund, Bonnie 98
strong situations 62-4, 66, 72
structural genes 80, 93
studies
    bystander intervention 196
    Children of the Garden Island 87
    cultural difference 148-9
    lesbian and gay parenting 112
    primates 339
    psychiatrist's view of healthy men/women 104
    romantic love 172
    Strange Situation (infant attachment) 166, 172
    of twins 90
stuttering 57, 59
subjective awareness 268, 281
subjects (people) 11-12, 108, 189
substance abuse 123
superego 274
supernatural 295
Sutcliffe, Peter (Yorkshire Ripper) 243
systematic desensitization (SD) 205

Tasker, F. 112
Tavris, C. 102-4, 105, 111
Taylor, S. 18-19, 26
Taylor, R. 241
technological cultures 150
Teichman, J. 283
telepathy 296, 310
theories
    attachment 165-83
    attribution 4, 17-23, 39, 65, 114, 297, 310
    Cannon-Bard 24
    central state identity 289-90, 294
    child's theory of mind 14
    cognitive attribution theory of achievement
        motivation 29
    cognitive dissonance 26-7
    cognitive labelling 19
    computational theory of mind (CTM) 281
    consciousness 13
    construct 5-6, 57, 69, 70-1, 85, 217, 260-1, 288
    correspondence 331
    correspondent inference 21-2, 39
    enculturated lens 110-11
    everyday psychology 8-9
    identity 289-90, 294
    implicit and explicit 7-10
    James-Lange 23-4
    life-span development 107
    mind-body relationship 287
    moral development 107
    object relations 323
    personal construct theory 10-12
    personality 7, 64, 70-1, 71-2
    psychoanalysis 14, 320
    self perception 19, 27-8
    social representation 334-5, 342
    use in everyday psychology 7
theory, psychosocial 321, 341
therapists 187, 203-5, 207, 209
thinking 5, 185, 207, 318
Thomas, K. 4-5
Thorngate 52
tight cultures 152, 163
time, cultural understanding of 150
token economy 205-6, 209
token identity 290, 294
tolerable behaviour 118, 137
Tolman, E. C. 327, 341
traits see personality traits
transcultural psychiatry 131
transcultural psychology 144-6, 331, 342
translation equivalence 155, 163
Triandis, H. C. 35, 150-3, 155, 163
twins, studies 90, 93
Tyerman, A. 161
type identity 200, 204

ultimate attribution error (UAE) 36, 40

unacceptable behaviour 117, 118, 137
uncertainty avoidance 148, 162
Uncertainty Principle 237
unconscious 270, 275, 324, 341
Unger, R. K. 108
uniqueness 50, 59
universality
    cross-cultural psychology 144, 145
    in mental disorders 131, 138

Valins, S. 26
values 118, 134, 138, 196, 208
    and bias 96, 100-1, 106, 114, 136, 192-3
variables, measuring by cross-cultural research
    159
vertical relationships 151
visual processing 276
voluntary behaviour 247

Wachtel, P. 204-5
Washburn, Margaret 97-8
Watson, J. B. 76, 83, 91, 222-4, 238, 264, 288-9,
    313-14, 341
Watt, C. 295, 302
weak situations 62-4, 66, 72
Weiner, B. 29-30, 36-8, 39
Weiskrantz 276
Weiss, R. S. 168, 170
Weisstein, N. 108, 111
Wellman H. M. 5-6, 8-9
western culture
    dominance in research 153
    influence 33, 40, 134, 138, 145-7
    see also ethnocentrism
western psychology 153, 163, 225, 238
Wetherell, M. 69
Widdicombe, S. 236
Wilkinson, S. 98
Wilson, E. O. 262, 266, 277, 292
Windelband, W. 45-7, 211
Wise, R. 269, 279
women
    influence on animal studies 339
    discrimination in psychology 97-8, 98-9, 114
    history in psychology 98, 114
    masculine view of 101-4
    oppression 96, 110
    psychologists 97-8
    self-derogation 30, 40
    view of problems 103
    see also androcentrism; feminism; gender;
        masculinist bias; men; sex differences
work 170, 176-7, 183
Wundt, W. 219-22, 238

Zeifman, D. 170
Zeldow, P. B. 323
Zimbardo, P. 63